A JOURNAL

OF THE

LIFE, TRAVELS, SUFFERINGS, CHRISTIAN EXPERIENCES, AND LABOUR OF LOVE,

OF

GEORGE FOX.

JOURNAL

OF

GEORGE FOX;

BEING AN

HISTORICAL ACCOUNT

OF THE

LIFE, TRAVELS, SUFFERINGS, CHRISTIAN EXPERIENCES, AND LABOUR OF LOVE, IN THE WORK OF THE MINISTRY, OF THAT EMINENT AND FAITHFUL SERVANT OF JESUS CHRIST, WHO DEPARTED THIS LIFE, IN GREAT PEACE WITH THE LORD, THE 13TH OF THE 11TH MONTH, 1690.

SEVENTH EDITION.—IN TWO VOLUMES.

WITH NOTES—BIOGRAPHICAL AND HISTORICAL, ETC.

BY

WILSON ARMISTEAD.

VOL. II.

"They that turn many to righteousness, shall shine as the stars for ever and ever," Dan. xii. 3.
"Many shall run to and fro; and knowledge shall be increased," Dan. xii. 4.
"If we suffer, we shall also reign with him" (*i. e.* with Christ), 2 Tim. ii. 12.

LONDON:
W. AND F. G. CASH (LATE GILPIN), BISHOPSGATE STREET;
AND JOSEPH SMITH, OXFORD STREET, WHITECHAPEL.
DUBLIN: J. B. GILPIN; CARLISLE: HUDSON SCOTT;
MANCHESTER: JOHN HARRISON AND SON, NEW MARKET CHAMBERS;
LIVERPOOL: PAUL SMITH, FRIENDS' MEETING-HOUSE, HUNTER ST.
YORK: JAMES HUNTON; BIRMINGHAM: WHITE & PIKE.
GLASGOW: W. & R. SMEAL, GALLOWGATE.
AND MAY BE HAD OF ALL BOOKSELLERS.

MDCCCLII.

GLASGOW:
W. G. BLACKIE AND CO., PRINTERS,
VILLAFIELD.

CONTENTS OF VOL. II.

JOURNAL OF GEORGE FOX.

CHAPTER I.

1663–1666.—George Fox visits London—taken up at Tenterden and examined by the magistrates, but liberated—precious meetings in Wales—at Derwentwater meets with an old woman whose husband was aged 122 years—apprehended and taken before the magistrates at Holker Hall, but liberated on his parole to appear at the sessions—appears accordingly, and is committed to Lancaster jail—many poor Friends imprisoned there at the same time, whose families become chargeable in consequence—one of them (Oliver Atherton) dies in jail, where he was immured by the Countess of Derby for tithes—George Fox has the oath tendered him at the assizes, and is re-committed—Margaret Fell is also imprisoned there—the prisoners in Lancaster jail to Justice Fleming—a brief warning to the same by George Fox—George Fox disputes with Major Wiggan (who was also a prisoner), and confutes him—writes to the judges against giving nicknames—writes a warning to all high professors—also a warning against the spirit of John Perrot—at the assizes he points out many fatal errors in his indictment, and it is quashed in consequence, but the judge ensnares him with the oath, and he is again remanded to prison—suffers much from the badness of the prison—at the next assizes he again points out fatal errors in his indictment, and is immediately hurried away to jail, and sentence is passed on him in his absence—a testimony against tithes—he is removed to Scarbro' Castle—has several conferences and disputes with divers persons there—writes to the king respecting his imprisonment, and is set at liberty—copy of his discharge and passport—the day after George Fox's liberation the great fire broke out in London, a vision of which he had in Lancaster Castle—the hand of the Lord turned against persecutors.

HAVING passed through NORFOLK, SUFFOLK, ESSEX, and HERTFORDSHIRE, we came to LONDON again; where I stayed a while, visiting Friends in their meetings, which were very large, and the Lord's power was over all. After some time I left the city again, and travelled into KENT, having Thomas Briggs with me. We went to ASHFORD, where we had a quiet, and a very blessed meeting; and on First-day we had a very good and peaceable one at CRANBROOK. Then we went to TENTERDEN, and had one there, to which many Friends came from several parts, and many other people came in, and were reached by the truth. When the meeting was over, I walked with Thomas Briggs into a field, while our horses were got ready; and turning my head, I espied a captain coming, and a great company of soldiers with lighted matches and muskets. Some of them came to us, and said, "we must go to their captain." When they had brought us before him, he asked, "where is George Fox? which is he?" I said,

"I am the man." Then he came to me and was somewhat struck, and said, "I will secure you among the soldiers." So he called for them to take me. He took Thomas Briggs, and the man of the house, with many more; but the power of the Lord was mightily over them all. Then he came to me again, and said, "I must go along with him to the town;" and he carried himself pretty civilly, bidding the soldiers bring the rest after. As we walked, I asked him, "why they did thus;" for I had not seen so much to do a great while, and I bid him be civil to his peaceable neighbours. When we were come to the town, they had us to an inn that was the jailer's house; and after a while the mayor of the town, and this captain, and the lieutenant, who were justices, came together and examined me, "why I came thither to make a disturbance?" I told them, I did not come to make a disturbance, neither had I made any since I came. They said, "there was a law against the Quakers' meetings, made only against them. I told them, I knew no such law. Then they brought forth the act that was made against Quakers and others; I told them, that was against such as were a terror to the king's subjects, and were enemies, and held principles dangerous to the government, and therefore that was not against us, for we held truth; and our principles were not dangerous to the government, and our meetings were peaceable, as they knew, who knew their neighbours were a peaceable people. They told me, "I was an enemy to the king." I answered, We loved all people and were enemies to none; that I, for my own part, had been cast into Derby dungeon, about the time of Worcester fight, because I would not take up arms against him, and that I was afterwards brought by Colonel Hacker to London, as a plotter to bring in King Charles, and was kept prisoner there till set at liberty by Oliver. They asked me, "whether I was imprisoned in the time of the insurrection?" I said, yes; I had been imprisoned then, and since that also, and had been set at liberty by the king's own command. I opened the act to them, and showed them the king's late declaration; gave them the examples of other justices, and told them also what the House of Lords had said of it. I spoke also to them concerning their own conditions, exhorting them to live in the fear of God, to be tender towards their neighbours that feared Him, and to mind God's wisdom, by which all things were made and created, that they might come to receive it, be ordered by it, and by it order all things to God's glory. They demanded bond of us for our appearance at the sessions; but we, pleading our innocency, refused to give bond. Then they would have us promise to come no more there; but we kept clear of that also. When they saw they could not bring us to their terms, they told us, "we should see they were civil to us, for it was the mayor's pleasure we should all be set at liberty." I told them their civility was noble, and so we parted.

Then leaving Tenterden we went to NEWICK in SUSSEX, where we visited some Friends. Thence we passed through the country, visiting Friends, and having great meetings; all quiet and free from disturbance, except by some jangling Baptists, till we came into HAMPSHIRE. After a good meeting at SOUTHAMPTON, we went to PULNER, in the parish of Ringwood, where was a monthly meeting next day, to which many Friends came from Southampton, Poole, and other places; and the weather being very hot, some of them came pretty early in the morning. I took a friend and walked out with him into the orchard, inquiring of him how the affairs of truth stood amongst them; (for many of them had been convinced by me, before I was a prisoner in Cornwall.) While we were conversing, a young man came and told us the trained bands were raising, and he heard they would come and break up the meeting. It was not yet meeting-time for about three hours, and there being other Friends walking in the orchard, the Friend that I was discoursing with before, desired me to walk into a corn-field adjoining it, which we did. After a while the young man that spoke of the trained bands left us, and when he was gone some distance, he stood and waved his hat. Whereupon I spoke to the other young man that was with me, to go and see what he meant. He went, but did not return; for the soldiers were come into the orchard. And as I kept walking I could see the soldiers, and some of them, as I heard afterwards, saw me, but had no mind to meddle. Coming so long before the meeting-time, they did not tarry; but took what Friends they found at the house, and some whom they met in the lane coming, and led them away. After they were gone, it drew towards eleven, Friends began to come in apace, and a large and glorious meeting we had; for the everlasting Seed of God was set over all, and the people were settled in the new covenant of life, upon the foundation, Christ Jesus. Towards the latter part of the meeting, there came a man in gay apparel, and looked in while I was declaring, and went away again presently. This man came with an evil intent; for he went forthwith to Ringwood, and told the magistrates "they had taken two or three men at Pulner, and had left George Fox there preaching to two or three hundred people." Upon this the magistrates sent the officers and soldiers again; but the meeting being nearly ended when the man looked in, and he having about a mile and a half to go, with his information, to fetch the soldiers, and they as far to come, after they had received their orders, before they came our meeting was over; ending about three o'clock peaceably and orderly. After the meeting I spoke to the Friends of the house where it was held (the hostess lying then dead in the house), and then some Friends conducted me to another Friend's at a little distance; where, after we had refreshed ourselves, I took horse, having about twenty miles to ride that afternoon to one —— Frye's house in WILTSHIRE, where a meeting was appointed for the next day.

After we were gone, the officers and soldiers came in a great heat, and when they found they were too late, and had missed their prey, they were much enraged; and the officers were offended with the soldiers, because they had not seized my horse in the stable the first time they came. But the Lord, by his good providence, delivered me, and prevented their mischievous design. For the officers were envious men, and had an evil mind against Friends; but the Lord brought his judgments upon them, so that it was taken notice of by their neighbours. For "whereas before they were wealthy men, after this their estates wasted away; and John Line, the constable, who was not only very forward in putting on the soldiers to take Friends, but also carried those that were taken to prison, and took a false oath against them at the assize, upon which they were fined and continued prisoners, was a sad spectacle to behold. For his flesh rotting away while he lived, he died in a very miserable condition, wishing he had never meddled with the Quakers, and confessing that he had never prospered since he had had a hand in persecuting them; and that he thought the hand of the Lord was against him for it."

At —— Frye's, in Wiltshire, we had a very blessed meeting, and quiet, though the officers had purposed to break it up, and were on their way in order thereunto. But before they got to it, word was brought them, that there was a house just broken up by thieves, and they were required to go back again with speed, to search after and pursue them; by which means our meeting escaped disturbance, and we were preserved out of their hands.

We passed through Wiltshire into DORSETSHIRE, having large and good meetings. The Lord's everlasting power was with us, and carried us over all; in which we sounded forth his saving truth and word of life, which many gladly received. Thus we visited Friends, till we came to TOPSHAM in DEVONSHIRE, travelling some weeks eight or nine score miles a week, and had meetings every day. At Topsham we met with Margaret Fell and two of her daughters, Sarah and Mary, and with Leonard Fell and Thomas Salthouse.* Thence we passed to TOTNESS, where we visited some Friends, then to KINGSBRIDGE, and to Henry Pollexfen's, who had been an ancient justice of peace. There we had a large meeting. This old justice accompanied us to PLYMOUTH, and into CORNWALL to Justice Porter's, and thence to Thomas Mount's, where we had another large meeting. After which we went to Humphrey Lower's, where also we had a large meeting, and thence to Loveday Hambley's, where we had a general meeting for the whole country; and all was quiet.

A little before this, Joseph Hellen and G. Bewley, had been at Loo

* Thomas Salthouse of Lancashire, but who afterwards resided in the south of England, was born about 1630, and convinced when George Fox first came to Swarthmore. He became an eminent minister of the gospel, for which he suffered much. In 1655 he, and Miles Halhead, being pressed in spirit to visit the Friends imprisoned at Plymouth, they were taken up on suspicion of having a hand in an insurrection which broke out a little before; and though the high sheriff confessed he did not believe them concerned in it, he caused them to be kept close prisoners at Exeter fourteen days, and then sent them from officer to officer towards home. In going towards Bridgewater, the officer who conducted them fell down, and lay grovelling on the ground in the sight of many people, and was able to go no further. So they returned to the justice to tell him what had befallen the officer, and to know what further he would do with them. But he declined to interfere with them again; set them at liberty, and desired the Lord to be with them.

For further particulars of Thomas Salthouse, the reader is referred to Whiting's *Memoirs*, p. 452–460. Whiting concludes his account by saying, "He was a pleasant man in conversation, which rendered him acceptable to many others as well as Friends, had a large capacity, and an excellent gift in the ministry. He wrote some notable books, and excellent epistles to Friends, though never collected as they deserve. He died, at his own house in Cornwall in 1690, about sixty years of age, in peace with the Lord; and is no doubt at rest with him from all his labours and sufferings, and his works follow him."

to visit Blanch Pope, a Ranting woman, under pretence to convince and convert her; but before they left her, she had so darkened them with her principles, that they seemed to be like her disciples, especially Joseph Hellen; for she had asked them, "who made the devil; did not God?" This idle question so puzzled them, that they could not answer her. They afterwards asked me that question. I told them, no; for all that God made was good and was blessed; so was not the devil. He was called a serpent before he was called a devil and an adversary, and then he had the title of devil given to him. Afterwards he was called a dragon, because he was a destroyer. The devil abode not in the truth, and by departing from the truth, he became a devil. So the Jews, when they went out of the truth, were said to be of the devil, and were called serpents. Now there is no promise of God to the devil, that ever he shall return to truth again; but to man and woman, who have been deceived by him, the promise of God is, that "the Seed of the woman shall bruise the serpent's head,"—shall break his power and strength to pieces. Now when these things were opened more at large to the satisfaction of Friends, those two who had let up the spirit of that ranting woman, were judged by the truth; and one of them, Joseph Hellen, ran quite out, and was disowned by Friends; but George Bewley was recovered, and afterwards became serviceable.

We passed from Loveday Hambley's to Francis Hodges's, near FALMOUTH and PENRYN, where we had a large meeting. Thence we went to HELSTONE that night, where some Friends came to visit us; and next day passed to Thomas Teage's, where we had another large meeting, at which many were convinced. I was led to open "the state of the church in the primitive times, the state of the church in the wilderness, and the state of the false church that was got up since, and to show that now the everlasting gospel was preached again over the head of the whore, beast, false prophets, and antichrists, which had got up since the apostles' days; and now the everlasting gospel was received and receiving, which brought life and immortality to light, that they might see over the devil that had darkened them." The people received the gospel and the word of life gladly, and a glorious blessed meeting we had for the exalting of the Lord's everlasting truth and his name. After the meeting was over I walked out, and as I was coming in again I heard a noise in the court, and coming nearer, I found the man of the house speaking to the tinners and others, and telling them, "it was the everlasting truth that had been declared there that day;" and the people generally confessed to it.

From thence we passed to the LAND'S-END, to John Ellis's, where we had a precious meeting. Here was a fisherman, one Nicholas Jose, that was convinced. He spoke in meetings, and declared the truth amongst the people, and the Lord's power was over all. I was glad that the Lord had raised up his standard in those dark parts of the nation, where there is since a fine meeting of honest-hearted Friends; many are come to sit under Christ's teaching; and a great people the Lord will have in that country.

Thence we returned to REDRUTH, and next day to TRURO, where we had a meeting. Next morning, some of the chief of the town desired to speak with me, amongst whom was Colonel Rouse. I went and had much discourse with them concerning the things of God. In their reasoning, they said, "the gospel was the four books of Matthew, Mark, Luke, and John;" and they called it natural. I told them, "the gospel was the power of God, which was preached before Matthew, Mark, Luke, and John, or any of them were printed or written; and it was preached to every creature (of which a great part might never see or hear of those four books), so that every creature was to obey the power of God; for Christ, the spiritual man, would judge the world according to the gospel, that is, according to his invisible power. When they heard this, they could not gainsay; for the truth came over them. I directed them to their Teacher, the Grace of God, and showed them the sufficiency of it, which would teach them how to live, and what to deny; and being obeyed, would bring them salvation. So to that grace I recommended them, and left them.

Then we returned through the country, visiting Friends, and had meetings at Humphrey Lower's again, and at Thomas Mount's. Afterwards at George Hawkins's, at STOKE, we had a large meeting, to which Friends came from Launceston and several other places. A living, precious meeting it was, in which the Lord's presence and power was richly manifested amongst us; and I left Friends there under the Lord Jesus Christ's teaching.

In Cornwall I was informed there was one Colonel Robinson, a very wicked man, who, after the king came in, was made a justice of peace, and became a cruel persecutor of Friends, of whom he sent many to prison. Hearing that they had some little liberty, through the favour of the jailer, to come home sometimes to visit their wives and children, he made great complaint thereof to the judge at the assize against the jailer; whereupon the jailer was fined a hundred marks, and Friends were kept very strictly up for a while. After he was come home from the assize, he sent to a neighbouring justice, to desire him to go a fanatic-hunting with him. On the day that he intended, and was prepared to go, he sent his man about with his horses, and walked himself on foot from his dwelling-house to a tenement, where his cows and dairy were kept, and where his servants were then milking. When he came there he asked for his bull. The maid-servants said, they had shut him into the field, because he was unruly amongst the kine, and hindered their milking. Then he went into the field to the bull, and having formerly accustomed himself to play with him, he began to fence at him with his staff. But the bull snuffed at him, and passed a little back; then turning upon him again, ran fiercely at him and struck his horn into his thigh, and heaving him upon his horn, threw him over his back, and tore up his thigh to his belly. When he came to the ground again he gored him with his horns, run them into the ground in his rage and violence, roared, and licked up his master's blood. The maid-servant, hearing her master cry out, ran into the field, and took the bull by the horns to pull him off from her master. The bull, without hurting her, put her gently by with his horns, but still fell to goring him and licking up his blood. Then she ran and got some men, that were at work not far off, to come and rescue her master; but they could not at all beat off the bull, till they brought mastiff dogs to set on him; and then he fled in great rage and fury. Upon hearing of it his sister came, and said to him, "Alack! brother, what a heavy judgment is this that has befallen you!" He answered, "Ah! sister, it is a heavy judgment indeed. Pray let the bull be killed, and the flesh given to the poor," said he. They carried him home, but he died soon after. The bull was grown so fierce that they were forced to shoot him; for no man durst come near to kill him. Thus does the Lord sometimes make some examples of his just judgment upon the persecutors of his people, that others may fear, and learn to beware.

After I had cleared myself of Cornwall, and Thomas Lower had brought us over Horsebridge into DEVONSHIRE again, we took our leave of him. Thomas Briggs, Robert Widders, and I, came to TIVERTON; and it being their fair, and many Friends there, we had a meeting amongst them. The magistrates gathered in the street, but the Lord's power stopped them. I saw them in the street over against the door, but they had not power to come in to meddle with us, though they had will enough to do it.

After the meeting we passed to COLLUMPTON and WELLINGTON, for we had appointed a meeting five miles off, where we had a large one at a butcher's house, and a blessed meeting it was. The people were directed to their Teacher, the Grace of God, which would bring them salvation, and many were settled under its teaching. The Lord's presence was amongst us, and we were refreshed in him, in whom we laboured and travailed; and the meeting was quiet. There had been very great persecution in that country and town a little before, insomuch that some Friends questioned the peaceableness of our meeting; but the Lord's power chained all, and his glory shone over all. Friends told us how they had broken up their meetings by warrants from the justices, and how by their warrants they were required to carry Friends before the justices; and Friends bid them "carry them then." The officers told Friends, "they must go:" but Friends said, nay; that was not according to their warrants, which required them to carry them. Then they were forced to hire carts, and waggons, and horses, and to lift Friends into their waggons and carts, to carry them before a justice. When they came to a justice's house, sometimes he happened to be from home, and if he were a moderate man, he would get out of the way, and then they were obliged to carry them before another, so that they were many days carting and carrying Friends up and down from place to place. And when afterwards the officers came to lay their charges for this upon the town, the town's-people would not pay it, but made them bear it themselves; which broke the neck of their persecution there for that time. The like was done in several other places, till the officers had shamed and tired themselves, and then they were glad to give over.

At one place they warned Friends to come to the steeple-house. Friends met to consider of it, and finding freedom to go to the steeple-house, they met together there. Accordingly when they came thither, they sat down to wait upon the Lord in his power and Spirit, and minded the Lord Jesus Christ, their Teacher and Saviour; but did not mind the priest.

When the officers saw that, they came to them to put them out of the steeple-house again; but the Friends told them, it was not time for them to break up their meeting yet. A while after, when the priest had done, they came to the Friends again, and would have had them go home to dinner; but the Friends told them, they did not choose to go to dinner, they were feeding upon the bread of life. So there they sat, waiting upon the Lord, and enjoying his power and presence, till they found freedom in themselves to depart. Thus the priest's people were offended, because they could not get them to the steeple-house: and when there, they were offended, because they could not get them out again.

From the meeting near Collumpton we went to TAUNTON, where we had a large meeting. The next day we came to a general meeting in Somersetshire, which was very large; and the Lord's everlasting word of life and truth was largely declared. The people were refreshed thereby, and settled upon Christ, their Rock and Foundation, and brought to sit under his teaching; the meeting was peaceable. But about the second hour of the night there came a company of men who knocked at the door, and bid us open it, or they would break it open; for they wanted a man that they came to search the house for. I heard the noise, and got up, and at the window saw a man at the door with his sword by his side. When they had let him in, he came into the chamber where I was, and looked on me, and said, "You are not the man I look for:" and went his way.

We came thence to STREET, and to William Beaton's, at PUDDIMOOR, where we had a very large general meeting, wherein the Lord's everlasting truth was declared, the people refreshed, and all quiet. Thence we went to John Dandy's, where we had another large and very precious meeting; and then passed on to BRISTOL, where we had good service for the Lord, and all quiet. Here we met with Margaret Fell and her daughters again. After some time we went to SLATTENFORD in WILTSHIRE, where was a very large meeting in a great barn. Good service we had there; for the truth, as it is in Jesus, was published amongst them, and many were gathered by it into the name of the Lord.

After this I passed into GLOUCESTERSHIRE and HEREFORDSHIRE, having large meetings in each. In HEREFORD I had a meeting in the inn. When I was gone, the magistrates, hearing there had been a meeting, came to search the inn for me, and were vexed that they had missed me. But the Lord so ordered it, that I escaped their hands; and Friends were established upon Christ, their Foundation, the Rock of Ages.

Then I went into RADNORSHIRE, in WALES, and had several precious meetings there. The Lord's name and standard was set up, and many were gathered to it, and settled under the teaching of Christ Jesus, their Saviour, who bought them.

After I was clear of Wales, I came to a market-town between England and Wales, where there was a great fair that day; and several Friends being at the fair, we went to an inn, and they came to us. After we had had a fine opportunity with Friends, we parted from them, and went on our way. The officers of the town took notice, it seems, of our being there, and of Friends gathering to us. They began also to meet together to consult among themselves how to ensnare us, though it was the fair time; but before they could do anything we were gone on our journey, and so escaped them.

Thence we came into SHROPSHIRE, where we had a large and precious meeting. After many meetings in those parts we came into WARWICKSHIRE, and visited Friends there, and so into DERBYSHIRE and STAFFORDSHIRE, visiting Friends' meetings as we went. At WHITEHAUGH we had a large, blessed meeting, and quiet; after which we rode about twenty miles that night to Captain Lingard's. We heard afterwards that when we were gone, the officers came to seize us, and were much disturbed that they missed us; but the Lord disappointed them, and Friends were joyful in the Lord that we escaped them.

At Captain Lingard's we had a blessed meeting, the Lord's presence being wonderfully amongst us. After this we passed through the PEAK-COUNTRY in DERBYSHIRE, and went to SYNDERHILL-GREEN, where we had a large meeting. Here John Whitehead * and several other Friends came to me. Then I passed through the country, visiting Friends, till I came to the farther end of HOLDERNESS, and so passed by SCARBRO', WHITBY, and MALTON, to YORK, having many meetings in the way; and the Lord's everlasting power was over all.

We went from York to BOROUGHBRIDGE, where I had a glorious meeting. Thence we passed into Durham to one Richmond's, where there was a general meeting; and the Lord's power was over all, though people were grown exceedingly rude about this time. After the meeting we went to Henry Draper's, where we stayed all night. Next morning a Friend came to me, as I was passing away, and told me, "if the priests and justices (for many priests were made justices in that country at that time) could find me, they would destroy me."

Being clear of Durham, I went over STAINMORE into YORKSHIRE, and to SEDBERGH, where having visited Friends, I went into WESTMORLAND, visiting Friends there also. Thence I passed into LANCASHIRE and came to SWARTHMORE. Here I stayed but a little while before I went over the Sands to ARNSIDE, where I had a general meeting. After it was ended, there came some men to break it up; but understanding before they arrived that the meeting was over, they turned back. I went to Robert Widders's, and thence to UNDERBARROW, where I had a glorious meeting, and the Lord's power was over all. Thence I passed to GRAYRIGG, and having visited Friends there, I went to Ann Audland's, where they would have had me to stay their meeting next day; but I felt a stop in my spirit. It

* John Whitehead was a very eminent minister amongst the early Friends, valiant for the truth, and a great sufferer for it. His life and writings have recently been published, to which the reader is referred. He wrote a very beautiful and encouraging epistle to Friends, dated Aylesbury prison, 12th month, 1660, which is inserted in *Letters &c., of Early Friends*, 382–387. William Penn, in his Preface to *Whitehead's Works*, says, "He was among the most eminent for his sound mind and capacity, great zeal and boldness, and as great humility, patience, and labour in word, doctrine, and charity."

was upon me to go to John Blakelin's in SEDBERGH, and to be next day at the meeting there; which is large, and a precious people there is. We had a very good meeting next day at Sedbergh; but the constables went to Ann Audland's meeting to look for me. Thus by the good hand and disposing Providence of the Lord, I escaped their snare.

I went from John Blakelin's with Leonard Fell to STRICKLAND-HEAD, where on First-day we had a very precious meeting on the common. That night we stayed amongst Friends there, and next day passed into NORTHUMBERLAND. After the justices had heard of this meeting at Strickland-Head, they made search for me; but by the good hand of the Lord, I escaped them again, though there were some very wicked justices. We went to Hugh Hutchinson's house in NORTHUMBERLAND, a Friend in the ministry, whence we visited Friends thereabouts, and then went to DERWENTWATER, where we had a very glorious meeting. There came an ancient woman to me, and told me her husband remembered his love to me; she said, I might call him to mind by this token, that I used to call him "the Tall White Old Man." She said, he was six score and two years old, and that he would have come to the meeting, but his horses were all employed upon some urgent occasion. I heard he lived some years after.

When I had visited Friends in those parts, and they were settled upon Christ, their Foundation, I passed through NORTHUMBERLAND, and came to old Thomas Bewley's in CUMBERLAND. Friends came about me, and asked, "would I come there to go into prison?" For there was great persecution in that country at that time; yet I had a general meeting at Thomas Bewley's, which was large and precious, and the Lord's power was over all.

One Musgrave was at that time deputy-governor of Carlisle. Passing along the country, I came to a man's house that had been convinced, whose name was Fletcher; and he told me, "if Musgrave knew I was there, he would be sure to send me to prison, he was such a severe man." But I stayed not there, only calling on the way to see this man; and then I went to William Pearson's, near WIGTON, where the meeting was, which was very large and precious. Some Friends were then prisoners at Carlisle, whom I visited by a letter, which Leonard Fell carried. From William Pearson's I visited Friends, till I came to PARDSHAW-CRAG, where we had a general meeting, which was large; all was quiet and peaceable, and the glorious, powerful presence of the everlasting God was with us.

So eager were the magistrates about this time to stir up persecution in those parts, that some offered five shillings, and some a noble a day, to any that could apprehend the speakers amongst the Quakers; but it being now the time of the quarter sessions in that county, the men who were so hired were gone to the sessions to get their wages, and so all our meetings were at that time quiet.

From Pardshaw-Crag we went into WESTMORLAND, calling on the way upon Hugh Tickell,* near KESWICK, and upon Thomas Laythes, where

* Hugh Tickell was born in Cumberland about the year 1610. Being convinced

Friends came to visit us; and we had a fine opportunity to be refreshed together. We went that night to Francis Benson's, in Westmorland, near Justice Fleming's house. This Justice Fleming was at that time in a great rage against Friends, and me in particular; insomuch that in the open sessions at Kendal just before, he had bid five pounds to any man that should take me, as Francis Benson told me. And it seems, as I went to this Friend's house, I met one man coming from the sessions that had this five pounds offered him to take me, and he knew me; for as I passed by him, he said to his companion, that is George Fox; yet he had not power to touch me, for the Lord's power preserved me over them all. The justices being so eager to have me, and I being so often near them, and yet they missing me, tormented them the more.

I went thence to James Taylor's at CARTMEL, where I stayed First-day, and had a precious meeting; and after it I came over the Sands to SWARTHMORE.

When I came there, they told me, Colonel Kirby had sent his lieutenant thither to take me, and that he had searched trunks and chests for me. That night as I was in bed, I was moved of the Lord to go next day to KIRBY-HALL, which was Colonel Kirby's house, about five miles off, to speak with him, and I did so. When I came thither, I found the Flemings, and several others of the gentry (so called) of the country, come to take their leave of Colonel Kirby, he being about to go up to London to the parliament. I was shown into the parlour amongst them; but Colonel Kirby was not then within, being gone out; so they said little to me, nor I much to them. But presently he came in, and I told him, that understanding he was desirous to see me, "I came to visit him, to know what he had to say to me, and whether he had any thing against me." He said, before all the company, "As he was a gentleman, he had nothing against me. But," said he, "Mistress Fell must not keep great meetings at her house, for they meet contrary to the act." I told him, "that act did not take hold on us, but on such as met to plot and contrive, and to

by George Fox when he first visited Cumberland in 1653, he gave up his house for meetings, and entertained the Lord's messengers. He became a faithful and eminent minister, travelling up and down in the service of the Gospel, suffering much for it, both in the spoiling of his goods and in imprisonments. In 1664 he was cast into Carlisle jail, with four other Friends, by priest Marshall of Crosthwaite, and though he kept him in prison three years, yet he took tithe of his land. But afterwards this priest fell down stairs and broke his skull, upon which he died. Hugh Tickell was again imprisoned in Carlisle jail, when about sixty-eight years old, by Richard Lowry, another priest of Crosthwaite, because he could not pay him tithes, who kept him prisoner about nine months, part of it in a cold winter, and in a damp nasty place not fit for men to lie in. This priest Lowry was suddenly stricken, and had the use of one side of his tongue, and his understanding much taken from him, and so continued a long time—a remarkable judgment.

Hugh Tickell patiently bore all his sufferings, and willingly endured them for the testimony of Jesus and a good conscience. But in his last imprisonment he contracted a distemper of body, which, increasing upon him after he came home, he grew weak, but continued in great patience; and being sensible his end drew nigh, set his house in order, and, taking leave of friends and neighbours, he sweetly departed in great peace in 1680, being above seventy years of age.

raise insurrections against the king, whereas we were no such people; for he knew that they that met at Margaret Fell's house, were his neighbours, and a peaceable people." After many words had passed, he shook me by the hand, and said again, "he had nothing against me;" and others of them said, I was a deserving man. So we parted, and I returned to SWARTHMORE.

Shortly after, when Colonel Kirby was gone to London, there was a private meeting of the justices and deputy-lieutenants at Holker-Hall, where Justice Preston lived; and there they granted a warrant to apprehend me. I heard over-night both of their meeting and of the warrant, and so could have escaped out of their reach if I would; for I had not appointed any meeting at that time, and I had cleared myself of the north, and the Lord's power was over all. But I considered, there being a noise of a plot in the north, if I should go away, they might fall upon Friends; but if I gave up myself to be taken, it might stop them, and the Friends should escape the better. So I gave up to be taken, and prepared myself against they came. Next day an officer came with sword and pistols to take me. I told him, "I knew his errand before, and had given up myself to be taken; for if I would have escaped their imprisonment, I could have gone forty miles off before he came; but I was an innocent man, and so cared not what they could do to me." He asked me "how I heard of it, seeing the order was made privately in a parlour." I said it was no matter, it was sufficient that I heard of it. I asked him to let me see his order; whereupon he laid his hand on his sword, and said, "I must go with him before the lieutenants, to answer such questions as they should propose to me." I told him it was but civil and reasonable for him to let me see his order; but he would not. Then said I, I am ready. So I went along with him, and Margaret Fell accompanied us to HOLKER-HALL. When we came thither, there was one Rawlinson, a justice, and one called Sir George Middleton, and many more that I did not know, besides old Justice Preston who lived there. They brought Thomas Atkinson, a Friend of Cartmel, as a witness against me, for some words which he had told to one Knipe, who had informed them; which words were, "that I had written against the plotters, and had knocked them down." These words they could not make much of, for I told them I had heard of a plot, and had written against it. Old Preston asked me, whether I had a hand in that script? I asked him what he meant? He said, in the Battledore. I answered, Yes. Then he asked me, whether I understood languages. I said, sufficient for myself; and that I knew no law that was transgressed by it. I told them also, that "to understand outward languages, was no matter of salvation; for the many tongues began but at the confusion of Babel; and if I did understand anything of them, I judged and knocked them down again for any matter of salvation that was in them. Thereupon he turned away, and said, "George Fox knocks down all the languages: come," said he, "we will examine you of higher matters."

Then said George Middleton, "You deny God, and the church, and the faith." I replied, "Nay, I own God and the true church, and the true faith. But what church dost thou own?" said I, (for I understood he was a Papist). Then he turned again and said, "you are a rebel and a traitor." I asked him to whom he spoke, or whom did he call rebel: he was so full of envy that for a while he could not speak, but at last he said, "he spoke it to me." With that I struck my hand on the table, and told him, "I had suffered more than twenty such as he, or than any that was there; for I had been cast into Derby dungeon for six months together, and had suffered much because I would not take up arms against this king before Worcester fight. I had been sent up prisoner out of my own country by Colonel Hacker to Oliver Cromwell, as a plotter to bring in King Charles in the year 1654; and I had nothing but love and good-will to the king, and desired the eternal good and welfare of him and all his subjects." "Did you ever hear the like," said Middleton. "Nay," said I, "ye may hear it again if ye will. For ye talk of the king, a company of you, but where were ye in Oliver's days, and what did ye do then for him? But I have more love to the king for his eternal good and welfare than any of you have."

Then they asked me, "whether I had heard of the plot?" and I said, "yes, I had heard of it." They asked me, how I had heard of it, and whom I knew in it? I told them, I had heard of it through the high-sheriff of Yorkshire, who had told Dr. Hodgson that there was a plot in the north; that was the way I heard of it; but I never heard of any such thing in the south, nor till I came into the north. And as for knowing any in the plot, I was as a child in that, for I knew none of them. Then said they, "why would you write against it, if you did not know some that were in it." I said, "my reason was, because you are so forward to mash the innocent and guilty together, therefore I wrote against it to clear the truth from such things, and to stop all forward, foolish spirits from running into such things. I sent copies of it into Westmorland, Cumberland, Durham, and Yorkshire, and to you here. I sent another copy of it to the king and his council, and it is likely it may be in print by this time. One of them said, "O, this man hath great power!" I said, "yes, I had power to write against plotters." Then said one of them, "you are against the laws of the land." I answered, "nay, for I and my Friends direct all people to the Spirit of God in them, to mortify the deeds of the flesh. This brings them into well-doing, and from that which the magistrate's sword is against, which eases the magistrates, who are for the punishment of evil-doers. So people being turned to the Spirit of God, which brings them to mortify the deeds of the flesh,—this brings them from under the occasion of the magistrate's sword; and this must needs be one with magistracy, and one with the law, which was added because of transgression, and is for the praise of them that do well. In this we establish the law, are an ease to the magistrates, and are not against, but stand for, all good government."

Then George Middleton cried, "Bring the book and put the oaths of allegiance and supremacy to him." Now he himself being a Papist, I asked him, "whether he had taken the oath of supremacy, who was a swearer? As for us, we could not swear at all, because Christ and the apostle had forbidden it." Some of them would not have had the oath put to me, but have set me at liberty. But the rest would not agree to that; for this was their last snare, and they had no other way to get me into prison, as all other things had been cleared to them. This was like the Papist's sacrament of the altar, by which they ensnared the martyrs. So they tendered me the oath, which I could not take; whereupon they were about to make my mittimus to send me to Lancaster jail; but considering of it, they only engaged me to appear at the sessions, and so for that time dismissed me. I went back with Margaret Fell to Swarthmore; and soon after Colonel West came to see me, who was at that time a justice of peace. He told us, "he acquainted some of the rest of the justices, that he would come over to see me and Margaret Fell; but it may be," said he, "some of you will take offence at it." I asked him, "What he thought they would do with me at the sessions;" and he said "they would tender the oath to me again."

Whilst I was at Swarthmore, William Kirby came into Swarthmore meeting, and brought the constables with him. I was sitting with Friends in the meeting, and he said to me, "How now, Mr. Fox! you have a fine company here." "Yes," said I, "we meet to wait upon the Lord." So he began to take the names of Friends, and them that did not readily tell him their names, he committed to the constables' hands, and sent some to prison. The constables were unwilling to take them without a warrant, whereupon he threatened to set them by the heels; but one of the constables told him, "he could keep them in his presence, but after he was gone, he could not keep them without a warrant."

The sessions coming on, I went to LANCASTER, and appeared according to my engagement. There was upon the bench Justice Fleming, who had bid five pounds in Westmorland to any man that would apprehend me; for he was a justice both in Westmorland and Lancashire. There were also Justice Spencer, Colonel West, and old Justice Rawlinson the lawyer, who gave the charge, and was very sharp against truth and Friends; but the Lord's power stopped them. The session was large, and the concourse of people great; and way being made for me, I came up to the bar and stood there with my hat on, they looking earnestly upon me, and I upon them for a pretty space. Proclamation being made for all to keep silence upon pain of imprisonment, and all being quiet, I said twice, "Peace be among you." The chairman asked, "if I knew where I was;" I said, "yes, I do, but it may be," said I, "my hat offends you; that is a low thing, that is not the honour that I give to magistrates, for the true honour is from above; which I have received, and I hope it is not the hat which ye look upon to be the honour." The chairman said, "they looked for the hat too," and asked, "wherein I showed my respect to magistrates, if I did not put off my hat?" I replied, "in coming when they called me." Then they bid one, "take off my hat." After which it was some time before they spoke to me, and I felt the power of the Lord to arise. After some pause, old Justice Rawlinson, the chairman, asked me, "if I knew of the plot?" I told him, "I had heard of it in Yorkshire by a Friend, that had it from the high-sheriff." Then they asked me, "whether I had declared it to the magistrates." I said, "I had sent papers abroad against plots and plotters, and also to you, as soon as I came into the country, to take all jealousies out of your minds concerning me and my friends; for it was and is our principle to declare against such things." They asked me then, "if I knew not of an act against meetings." I said, "I knew there was an act that took hold of such as met to the terrifying of the king's subjects, and were enemies to the king, and held dangerous principles; but I hoped, they did not look upon us to be such men, for our meetings were not to terrify the king's subjects, neither are we enemies to him or any man." Then they tendered me the oaths of allegiance and supremacy. I told them, "I could not take any oath at all, because Christ and his apostle had forbid it; and they had had sufficient experience of swearers, first one way, then another; but I had never taken any oath in my life." Then Rawlinson asked me, "whether I held it was unlawful to swear?" This question he put on purpose to ensnare me; for by an act that was made, such were liable to banishment or a great fine, that should say, it was "unlawful to swear." But I seeing the snare, avoided it, and told him, "that in the time of the law amongst the Jews, before Christ came, the law commanded them to swear; but Christ, who doth fulfil the law in his gospel-time, commands, 'not to swear at all;' and the apostle James forbids swearing, even to them that were Jews, and had the law of God." After much discourse, they called for the jailer, and committed me to prison.

I had about me the paper which I had written as a testimony against plots, which I desired they would read, or suffer to be read, in open court; but they would not. So being committed for refusing to swear, "I bid them and all the people take notice, that I suffered for the doctrine of Christ, and for my obedience to his command." Afterwards I understood the justices said, they had private instructions from Colonel Kirby to prosecute me, notwithstanding his fair carriage and seeming kindness to me before, when he declared before many of them "that he had nothing against me." Several other Friends were committed to prison, some for meeting to worship God, and some for not swearing; so that the prison was very full. Many of them being poor men, that had nothing to maintain their families by but their labour, which now they were taken from, several of their wives went to the justices who had committed their husbands, and told them, "if they kept their husbands in jail for nothing but the truth of Christ, and for good conscience' sake, they would bring their children to them to be maintained." A mighty power of the Lord rose in Friends, and gave them great boldness, so that they spoke much to the justices. Friends also that were prisoners wrote to the justices, laying the weight of their sufferings upon them, and showing them both their injustice and want of compassion towards their poor neighbours, whom they knew to be honest, conscientious, peaceable people, that in tenderness of conscience could not take any oath; yet they sent them to prison for refusing to take the oath of allegiance. Several who were imprisoned on that account were known to be men that had served the king in his wars, and had hazarded their lives in the field in his cause, and had suffered great hardships, with the loss of much blood for him, and had always stood faithful to him from first to last, and had never received any pay for their service. To be thus requited for all their faithful services and sufferings, and that by them that pretended to be the king's friends, was hard, unkind, and ungrateful dealing. At length the justices being continually attended with complaints of grievances, released some of the Friends, but kept divers of them still in prison.

Amongst those that were then in prison, there were four Friends for tithes, who had been sent at the suit of the Countess of Derby, and had lain near two years and a half. One of these, Oliver Atherton, a man of a weakly constitution, was, through his long and hard imprisonment in a cold, raw, unwholesome place, brought so low and weak in his body, that there appeared no hope of his life, unless he might be removed. Wherefore a letter was written on his behalf to the Countess, and sent by his son Godfrey Atherton, wherein were laid before her "the reasons why he and the rest could not pay tithes; because, if they did, they should deny Christ come in the flesh, who by his coming had put an end to tithes, and to the priesthood to which they had been given, and to the commandment by which they had been paid under the law. His weak condition of body was also laid before her, and the apparent likelihood of his death if she continued to hold him there; that she might be moved to pity and compassion, and also warned not to draw the guilt of his innocent blood upon herself." When his son went to her with his father's letter, a servant of her's abused him, plucked off his cap, and threw it away, and put him out of the gate. Nevertheless the letter was delivered into her own hand, but she shut out all pity and tenderness, and continued him in prison till death. When his son returned to his father in prison, and told him, as he lay on his dying bed, that the Countess denied his liberty, he only said, "She hath been the cause of shedding much blood, but this will be the heaviest blood that ever she spilt;" and soon after he died. Friends having his body delivered to them to bury, as they carried it from the prison to Ormskirk, the parish wherein he had lived, they stuck up papers upon the crosses at Garstang, Preston, and other towns, through which they passed, with this inscription:—"*This is Oliver Atherton, of Ormskirk parish, persecuted to death by the Countess of Derby for good conscience' sake towards God and Christ, because he could not give her tithes,*" &c.; setting forth at large the reasons of his refusing to pay tithes, the length of his imprisonment, the hardships he had undergone, her hard-heartedness towards him, and the manner of his death.

After his death, Richard Cubban, another of her prisoners for tithes, wrote a large letter to her, on behalf of himself and his fellow-prisoners at her suit, laying their innocency before her; and "that it was not out of wilfulness, stubbornness, or covetousness, that they refused to pay her tithes, but purely in good conscience towards God and Christ; and letting her know that, if she should be suffered to keep them there till they every one died, as she had done their fellow-sufferer Oliver Atherton, they could not yield to pay her. And therefore desired her to consider their case in a Christian spirit, and not bring their blood upon herself also." But she would not show any pity or compassion towards them, who had now suffered hard imprisonment about two years and a half under her. Instead thereof she sent to Garstang, and threatened to complain to the king and council, and bring them into trouble, for suffering the paper concerning Oliver Atherton's death to be stuck upon their cross. The rage that she expressed made the people take the more notice of it, and some of them said, "the Quakers had given her a bone to pick." But she, that regarded not the life of an innocent sufferer for Christ, lived not long after herself; for that day three weeks that Oliver Atherton's body was carried through Ormskirk to be buried, she died; and her body was carried that day seven weeks through the same town to her burying-place. Thus the Lord pursued the hard-hearted persecutor.

I was kept till the assize; and Judge Turner and Judge Twisden coming that circuit, I was brought before Judge Twisden on the 14th day of the month called March, in the year 1663. When I was set to the bar, I said, "Peace be amongst you all." The judge looked upon me, and said, "What! do you come into the court with your hat on?" Upon which, the jailer taking it off, I said, "The hat is not the honour that comes from God." Then said the judge to me, "Will you take the oath of allegiance, George Fox?" I said, "I never took any oath in my life, nor any covenant or engagement." "Well," said he, "will you swear or not?" I answered, "I am a Christian, and Christ commands me 'not to swear,' and so does the apostle James, and whether I should obey God or man, do thou judge." "I ask you again," said he, "whether you will swear or not?" I answered again, "I am neither Turk, Jew, nor heathen, but a Christian, and should show forth Christianity." And I asked him, "if he did not know that Christians in the primitive times, under the ten persecutions, and some also of the martyrs in Queen Mary's days, refused swearing, because Christ and the apostle had forbidden it?" I told him also, "they had had experience enough, how many men had first sworn for the king and then against him. But as for me, I had never taken an oath in my life; and my allegiance did not lie in swearing, but in truth and faithfulness; for I honour all men, much more the king. But Christ, who is the great Prophet, and King of kings, who is the Saviour of the world, and the great Judge of all the earth, saith, 'I must not swear.' Now, whether must I obey Christ or thee? For it is in tenderness of conscience, and in obedience to the commands of Christ that I do not swear; and we have the word of a king for tender consciences." Then I asked the judge, "if he owned the king?" "Yes," said he, "I do own the king." "Why then," said I, "dost thou not observe his declaration from Breda, and his promises made since he came into England, 'that no man should be called in question for matters of religion, so long as he lived peaceably?' If thou ownest the king," said I, "why dost thou call me into question, and put me upon taking an oath, which is a matter of religion, seeing neither thou nor any else can charge me with unpeaceable living?" Upon this he was moved, and looking angrily at me, said, "Sirrah, will you swear?" I told him, "I was none of his sirrahs, I was a Christian; and for him, an old man and a judge, to sit there and give nick-names to prisoners, it did not become either his gray hairs or his office." "Well," said he, "I am a Christian too." "Then do Christian works," said I. "Sirrah!" said he, "thou thinkest to frighten me with thy words." Then catching himself, and looking aside, he said, "Hark! I am using the word [sirrah] again;" and so checked himself. I said, "I spoke to thee in love; for that language did not become thee, a judge. Thou oughtest to instruct a prisoner in the law, if he were ignorant and out of the way." "And I speak in love to thee too," said he. "But," said I, "love gives no nick-names." Then he roused himself up, and said, "I will not be afraid of thee, George Fox; thou speakest so loud, thy voice drowns mine and the court's; I must call for three or four criers to drown thy voice: thou hast good lungs." "I am a prisoner here," said I, "for the Lord Jesus Christ's sake; for his sake do I suffer, for him do I stand this day; and if my voice were five times louder, I should lift it up, and sound it for Christ's sake, for whose cause I stand this day before your judgment-seat, in obedience to Christ, who commands not to swear; before whose judgment-seat you must all be brought and must give an account." "Well," said the judge, "George Fox, say, whether thou wilt take the oath, yea or nay?" I replied, "I say, as I said before, whether ought I to obey God or man, judge thou? If I could take any oath at all, I should take this; for I do not deny some oaths only, or on some occasions, but all oaths, according to Christ's doctrine, who hath commanded his followers not to swear at all. Now if thou or any of you, or your ministers or priests here, will prove that ever Christ or his apostles, after they had forbid all swearing, commanded Christians to swear, then I will swear." I saw several priests there, but not one of them offered to speak. "Then," said the judge, "I am a servant to the king, and the king sent me not to dispute with you, but to put the laws in execution; therefore tender him the oath of allegiance." "If thou love the king," said I, "why dost thou break his word, and not keep his declarations and speeches, wherein he promised liberty to tender consciences? I am a man of a tender conscience, and, in obedience to Christ's command, I cannot swear." "Then you will not swear," said the judge; "take him away, jailer." I said, "It is for Christ's sake that I cannot swear, and for obedience to his command I suffer, and so the Lord forgive you all." So the jailer took me away; but I felt the mighty power of the Lord was over them all.

The sixteenth day of the same month I was brought before Judge Twisden again: he was somewhat offended at my hat; but it being the last morning of the assize before he was to leave town, and not many people there, he made the less of it. He asked me, "whether I would traverse, stand mute, or submit." But he spoke so fast that it was hard to know what he said. However, I told him, "I desired I might have liberty to traverse the indictment, and try it." Then said he, "Take him away, I will have nothing to do with him, take him away." I said, "Well, live in the fear of God, and do justice." "Why," said he, "have not I done you justice?" I replied, "That which thou hast done has been against the command of Christ." So I was taken to the jail again, and kept prisoner till the next assizes.

Some time before this assize, Margaret Fell was sent prisoner to Lancaster jail by Fleming Kirby, and Preston, justices; and at the assize the oath was tendered to her also, and she was again committed to prison, to lie till the next assize.

Now Justice Fleming being one of the fiercest and most violent justices in persecuting Friends, and sending his honest neighbours to prison for religion's sake, and many Friends being at this time in Lancaster jail committed by him, and some having died in prison, we that were then prisoners had it upon us to write to him, as follows:—

"O Justice Fleming!

"Mercy, compassion, love, and kindness adorn and grace men and magistrates. O! dost thou not hear the cry of the widows, and the cry of the fatherless, who were made so through persecution! Were they not driven, like sheep, from constable to constable, as though they had been the greatest transgressors or malefactors in the land? Which grieved and tendered the hearts of many sober people, to see how their innocent neighbours and countrymen, who were of a peaceable carriage, and honest in their lives and conversations amongst men, were used and served! One more is dead whom thou sent to prison, having left five children, both fatherless and motherless. How canst thou do otherwise than take care of these fatherless infants, and also of the other's wife and family? Is it not thy place? Consider Job (c. xxix). He was a father to the poor, he delivered the poor that cried, and the fatherless that had none to help. He broke the jaws of the wicked, and plucked the spoil out of his teeth. But oh! measure thy life and his, and take heed of the day of God's eternal judgment, which will come, and the sentence and decree from Christ, when every man must give an account, and receive a reward according to his deeds. Then it will be said, 'O, where are the months that are past!' Again, Justice Fleming, consider, when John Stubbs was brought before thee, having a wife and four small children, and little to live on, but what they honestly got by their own diligence, as soon as he appeared thou criedst out, 'Put the oath to that man.' And when he confessed that he was but a poor man, thou hadst no regard; but cast away pity, not hearing what he would say. And now he is kept in prison, because he could not swear, and break the command of Christ and the apostle; it is to be hoped thou wilt take care for his family, that his children do not starve; and see that they do not want bread. Can this be allegiance to the king, to do that which Christ and his apostle say is evil, and brings into condemnation? Would not you have cast Christ and the apostle into prison, who commanded 'not to swear,' if they had been in your days?

"Consider also thy poor neighbour, William Wilson,* who was known

* Of the William Wilson here alluded to, the following particulars have been gathered:—He was a man of an innocent life, and though he had little outward learning, God was pleased to teach him himself, and called him to bear a testimony to his name, which he did faithfully, not only in many parts of England, but in Germany and Scotland, which he visited several times. He was of a lowly and meek spirit, upright and just among his neighbours, which caused them often to submit their differences to his arbitration, in which he was careful to find out the real truth, and would never countenance deceit. In this service he was successful, seldom missing his desired end, viz., to restore peace. He was faithful in his testimony for the truth, and a sufferer for the same in prison at Kendal, in 1666, and several times afterwards, as well as by distress on his goods. Besides which he suffered cruel mockings, stoning, blows, and wounds, both from priests and people, particularly at Eskdale,

to all the parish and neighbours to be an industrious man, and careful to maintain his wife and children; yet had little, but what he got with his hands in diligence and travels to supply himself. How should his wife maintain her children, when thou hast cast her husband into prison, and thereby made him incapable of working for them? Therefore it may be expected, thou wilt have a care of his wife and children, and see they do not want; for how should they live, having no other way to be sustained, but by the little that he got? Surely the noise of this is in the very markets, the death of thy two neighbours; and the cry of the widows and fatherless is heard. All those fatherless and widows are made so for righteousness' sake. For might not John Stubbs and William Wilson have had their liberty still, if they would have sworn, though they had been such as go after mountebanks and stage-plays, or run a hunting? O! consider, for the Lord's mind is otherwise; he is tender. And the king hath declared his mind to be, that there should be no cruelty inflicted upon his peaceable subjects. Besides, several poor, honest people were fined, who had need to have something given them; and it had been more honourable to have given them something, than to fine them and send them to prison; some of whom live upon the charity of other people. What honour or grace can it be to thee, to cast thy poor neighbours into prison who are peaceable, seeing thou knowest these people cannot do that which thou requirest of them, if it were to save their lives, or all that they have? Because in tenderness they cannot take any oath, thou makest that a snare to them. What, thinkest thou, do the people say concerning this? 'We

where he exhorted the people "to mind that of God in their consciences, and turn to that holy light and law which he had put into their inward parts, that by the same they might come to know the will of God, and do it." Because of these and like words, one Parker, a priest, beat and wounded him, and with one of his crutches broke his head, causing the blood to run down his shoulders. The priest being lame, and not able as he would to effect his cruel purpose, caused his horse to be brought, on which he mounted, and in the sight of the people broke his staff in three pieces upon William Wilson's bare head, which made them cry out against such merciless behaviour. Before the priest got home, he was overtaken with sickness, and never came more to the steeple-house. During the time of his sickness he was very loathsome, and so died.

A few weeks after, William Wilson went to the same place at Eskdale, and for speaking to the people, one Fogo, a priest, took him by the hair of the head, pulled him to the ground, and drew him out. In rage and cruelty he also abused his brother Michael Wilson; but a few months after, this same Fogo, riding over some sands, accompanied by several people, fell into a quicksand, and was immediately smothered.

William Wilson left behind him a widow and two daughters, to whom he was a true husband and a tender father, instructing his children "to keep in the fear of the Lord, and to walk in the way of truth, which he walked in himself;" often saying to them, "it would be the best portion that they could enjoy." His last illness was short. Having recently returned from a long journey, wherein his body was much spent and weak, he said, "I have not served the Lord unfruitfully; I have no trouble upon me; and I am very sensible that all is well with me." Again he said, "He was content, whatsoever way the Lord pleased; he felt as a dove, harmless; and as a lamb, innocent." A few hours before he died, at which time he walked several times over the room, he said, as he had often before, "My peace far exceeds my pain;" and standing upon his feet between two Friends, he said, "O that every one would mind the Lord, that they might keep life." He then sat down, and drew breath no more.

He died at his own house at Langdale, the 10th of the 5th month, 1682.

know,' say they, 'the Quakers' principle, that keep to Yea and Nay; but we see others swear and forswear.' For many of you have sworn first one way and then another. So we leave it to the Spirit of God in thy conscience, Justice Fleming, who wast so eager for the taking of George Fox, and so offended with them that had not taken him, and now hast fallen upon thy poor neighbours. But, oh! where is thy pity for their poor, fatherless children, and motherless infants? O, take heed of Herod's hard-heartedness, and casting away all pity! Esau did so, not Jacob.

"Here is also Thomas Walters, of Bolton, cast into prison, and the oath imposed on him through thee; and for denying to swear at all, in obedience to Christ's command, he is continued in prison; having five small children, and his wife near confinement. Surely thou shouldst take care for them also, and see that his wife and small children do not want; who are as fatherless, and she as a widow, through thee. Dost thou not hear in thy ears the cry of the fatherless, and the cry of the widows, and the blood of the innocent speak, who through thee have been persecuted to prison, and are now dead? O! heavy sentence at the day of judgment! How wilt thou answer, when thou and thy works come to be judged,—when thou shalt be brought before the judgment-seat of the Almighty, who in thy prosperity hast made widows and fatherless for righteousness' sake, and for tenderness of conscience towards God? The Lord knows and sees it! O man! consider in thy life-time, how thou hast stained thyself with the blood of the innocent! When thou hadst power, and might have done good amongst thy peaceable neighbours, and would not, but used thy power not to a good intent, but contrary to the Lord's mind and to the king's. The king's favour, his mercy, and clemency to sober people, and to tender consciences, have been manifested by declarations and proclamations, which thou hast abused and slighted by persecuting his peaceable subjects. For at London, and in other parts, the Quakers' meetings are peaceable; and if thou look but as far as Yorkshire, where the plot hath been, Friends' innocency hath cleared itself in the hearts of sober justices; and for you here to fall upon your peaceable neighbours and people, and to be rigorous and violent against them that are tender, godly, and righteous, it is no honour to you. How many drunkards and swearers, fighters, and such as are subject to vice, have you caused to be brought before your courts? It were more honourable for you to look after such; for the law was not made for the righteous, but for sinners and transgressors. Therefore, consider, and be humbled for these things; for the Lord may do to thee as thou hast done to others; and thou dost not know how soon there may be a cry in thy own family, as the cry is amongst thy neighbours, of the fatherless and widows that are made so through thee. But the Quakers can and do say, 'the Lord forgive thee, and lay not these things to thy charge, if it be his will.'" *

* We cannot be surprised at the hard language sometimes used by the early Friends in protesting against the unchristian conduct of their persecutors. The rapacity of their enemies in the early periods of the Society carried their plunder to so great an excess, as not only to involve many in total ruin, but subjected them to long and cruel imprisonments, which, in many cases of particular hardship, terminated in death.

Besides this, which went in the name of many, I sent him also a line subscribed by myself only, and directed—

"*To Daniel Fleming.*

"FRIEND,

"Thou hast imprisoned the servants of the Lord, without the breach of any law; therefore take heed what thou doest, for in the light of the Lord God thou art seen, lest the hand of the Lord be turned against thee!"

G. F.

It was not long after this ere Fleming's wife died, and left him thirteen or fourteen motherless children.

When I was prisoner at Lancaster, there was prisoner also one Major Wiggan, a Baptist preacher. He boasted much beforehand what he would say at the assize, if the oath should be put to him; and that he would refuse to swear. But when the assize came, and the oath was tendered him, he desired time to consider of it; and that being granted him till the next assize, he got leave to go to London before the assize came again, and stayed there till the plague broke forth, and there both he and his wife were cut off. He was a very wicked man, and the judgments of God came upon him; for he had published a book against Friends, full of lies and blasphemies; the occasion of which was this. Whilst he was in Lancaster castle he challenged Friends to a dispute. Whereupon I got leave of the jailer to go up to them; and entering into discourse with him, he affirmed, "that some men never had the Spirit of God, and that the true light, which enlighteneth every man that cometh into the world, is natural." For proof of his assertion he instanced Balaam, affirming, that "Balaam had not the Spirit of God." I affirmed and proved, "that Balaam had the Spirit of God, and that wicked men have the Spirit of God; else how could they quench it, and vex it, and grieve it, and resist the Holy Ghost, like the stiff-necked Jews?" To his second affirmation I answered, "that the true light, which enlighteneth every man that cometh into the world, was the life in the Word, and that was divine and eternal, and not natural; and he might as well say that the Word was natural, as that the life in the Word was natural. And wicked men were enlightened by this light, else how could they hate it? Now it is expressly said, that they did hate it; and the reason given why they hated it was, because 'their deeds were evil;' and they would not come to it, because it reproved them; and that must needs be in them, that reproved them. Besides, that light could not be the Scriptures of the New Testament, for it was testified of before any part of the New Testament was written; so it must be the divine light, which is the life in Christ, the Word, before the Scriptures were. And the grace

It has already been stated that at one time there were 4500 Quakers in prison in England and Wales at one time. In 1622, twenty died in different prisons in London, and seven more after their liberation, from ill treatment. In 1664, twenty-five died, and in 1665, fifty-two more. The number which perished in this way, throughout the whole kingdom, amounted to 369. But for fuller particulars of the cruelties practised against the early Quakers, the reader is referred to the two closely printed folio volumes, entitled *Besse's Sufferings.*

of God, which brought salvation, had appeared unto all men, and taught the saints; but they that turned it into wantonness, and walked despitefully against the Spirit of grace, were the wicked. Again, the Spirit of Truth, the Holy Ghost, the Comforter, which leads the disciples of Christ into all truth, the same should reprove the world of sin, of righteousness, of judgment, and of their unbelief. So the wicked world had it to reprove them; and the true disciples and learners of Christ, that believed in the light as Christ commands, had it to lead them. But the world that did not believe in the light, though they were lighted; but hated the light which they should have believed in, and loved the darkness rather than it, —this world had a righteousness and a judgment, which the Holy Ghost reproved them for, as well as for their unbelief." Having proved that the good and the bad were enlightened, that the grace of God had appeared unto all, and that all had the Spirit of God, else they could not vex and grieve it, I told Major Wiggan, the least babe there might see him; and presently one Richard Cubham stood up, and proved him an antichrist and a deceiver by Scripture. Then the jailer had me away to my prison again. Afterwards Wiggan wrote a book of this dispute, and put in abundance of abominable lies; but it was soon answered in print, and himself not long after was cut off, as aforesaid.

This Wiggan was poor, and while he was a prisoner at Lancaster, he sent into the country, and got money gathered for relief of the poor people of God in prison; and many people gave freely, thinking it had been for us, when indeed it was for himself. But when we heard of it, we laid it upon him, and wrote also into the country, that Friends might let the people know the truth of the matter, that it was not our manner to have collections made for us; and that those collections were only for Wiggan and another, a drunken preacher of his society.

After this it came upon me to write to the judges, and other magistrates, concerning their "giving evil words and nicknames to such as were brought before them;" which was after this manner:—

"*To all judges, or other officers whatsoever, in the whole world, who profess yourselves to be Christians.*

"FRIENDS,

"Herein and by reading the Scriptures, ye may see both your own words and behaviour, and the words and practice of both Jews and Heathens, and of the King of kings, the great Lawgiver and Judge of the whole world. First, for the words and carriage of the Jews, when such as were worthy of death were brought before the rulers amongst them. When Achan had taken the Babylonish garment, and the two hundred shekels of silver, and the wedge of gold of fifty shekels weight, and Joshua, who was then judge of Israel, had by the lot found him out, he did not say unto him, Sirrah,* nor, you rascal, knave, rogue, as some, that are called Christian magistrates,

* The word Sirrah must not be confounded with Sir. It was no doubt made use of strictly in the sense of the only meaning Walker gives to it in his *Dictionary*, viz., "A compellation of reproach and insult."

are too apt to do. But Joshua said unto Achan, 'My son' (mark his clean language, his savoury expression and gracious words), 'My son,' said he, 'give, I pray thee, glory to the Lord God of Israel, and make confession unto him, and tell me now what thou hast done; hide it not from me.' Then Achan confessed, that he had sinned against the Lord God of Israel, and thus and thus he had done. Then Joshua the judge said, 'Why hast thou troubled Israel? The Lord shall trouble thee this day.' And they stoned him and his with stones, and burnt his goods with fire. But there was no unsavoury word given to him that we read of, though he was worthy of death. Josh. vii.

So when the man that gathered sticks upon the Sabbath-day was taken and brought before Moses, the judge of Israel, and put in ward until the mind of the Lord was known concerning him, we read not of any reviling language given him, but the Lord said to Moses, and Moses to the people, 'The man shall surely be put to death,' Numb. xv. 35.

"Likewise in the rebellion of Korah, Dathan, and Abiram, where Moses called them to trial, he did not sirrah them or miscall them, but said to Korah and the rest, 'Hear, I pray you, ye sons of Levi,' Numb. xvi. 8. And when he gave the sentence against them, he said, 'If these men die the common death of all men,' &c. He did not say, If these rascals or knaves, as many that profess themselves Christians now do.

"When Elihu spoke to Job, who was a judge, and to his friends, and said, 'Let me not, I pray you, accept any man's person, neither let me give flattering titles unto man, for I know not to give flattering titles: in so doing my Maker would soon take me away,' Job xxxii. Job did not say, 'Sirrah, hold thy tongue,' nor give him any unsavoury expression. Then for the words of David and Solomon, and other kings and officers, see in the books of the Kings and Chronicles the savoury language that they gave to them that were brought before them; nay, though Shimei cursed David the king, yet neither did David then, or afterwards, nor Solomon, when he caused him to be put to death, give him any reproachful language, or so much as call him sirrah; 2 Sam. xvi. and 1 Kings ii.

"Read the prophecies of Isaiah and Micah, Jeremiah, Ezekiel, and the rest of the prophets, who prophesied to several people, and against rulers, kings, and magistrates; yet where can it be found, that they had any bad language given them, as sirrah, or the like, by any ruler either of the Jews or heathens? Nay, though Jeremiah was cast into prison, and into the dungeon, yet there was no such word as sirrah, or knave given to him. Jer. xxxvii.

"Then for the words and carriage of the heathens: when Abraham was brought before Abimelech, who was a king, he gave Abraham no unsavoury expressions, Gen. xx. And when Isaac came before Abimelech, he gave him no taunting language either, Gen. xxvi. When Joseph was cast into prison, and that in Egypt, we do not read that he had any railing language given him, Gen. xxxix. Neither did Pharaoh, when Moses and Aaron appeared before him, give them bad language, as sirrah, knave, or the like.

"When Nebuchadnezzar sentenced the three children to the fiery furnace, there was no such language given them as sirrah, knave, rascal;

but he called them by the names they were known by, Dan. iii. And when Daniel was brought before Darius, and sentenced to be cast into the lions' den, he had no such names given him, as many give now, who call those rulers heathens, but themselves Christians.

"If ye look into the New Testament, in the parable of the wedding supper, the king, that came to view his guests, did not say unto him that was found without a wedding-garment, 'Sirrah, how camest thou in hither?' But, 'Friend, how camest thou in hither?' &c., though he was one that was to be bound hand and foot, and cast into outer darkness, Matt. xxii. Nay, when Judas had betrayed his master, Christ Jesus, the Lord of life, and had sold him to the priests, Christ did not call him sirrah, when he came to apprehend him, but friend: Matt. xxvi. 50. Stephen in his examination, sentence, and death, had no such reproachful word given him as sirrah, or knave, Acts vi. and vii. When the apostles Peter and John were brought before the high-priest and rulers of the Jews, and commanded not to preach in the name of Jesus, Acts iv., they were not called sirrah, or knaves, nor had they any such ill names given them. And when Paul and Silas were cast into prison by the magistrates, there was no such word given them in their examination, nor in their sentence, Acts xvi. They called them men, not rogues, sirrahs, or knaves. And when the magistrates had done contrary to law, they feared. So ye may see how short of this example many are, that call themselves Christian rulers, who are not afraid to cast innocent people into prison, and give them ill names besides, below both Jews and Heathens.

"When the uproar was at Ephesus about Diana's shrine, Demetrius, who bore great sway among the craftsmen, did not call Paul sirrah, but Paul, Acts xix. And when Paul was brought prisoner before the high-priest Ananias, and the council of the Jews, and told them, he had lived in all good conscience towards God until that day, though they, who professed the Scriptures but lived out of the life of them, could not bear to hear of living in a good conscience, as professors of the Scriptures now, that live not in the life, cannot bear to hear of living in a good conscience now-a-days: but Ananias caused Paul to be smitten on the mouth; yet he did not call him knave nor sirrah, Acts xxiii. The apostate Jews indeed, who, though they professed Scripture, were out of the life thereof, and had rejected Christ, in accusing Paul before the Roman magistrates, did once call him a 'pestilent fellow,' Acts xxiv., as the accusing professors, who live out of the life, will sometimes call us now. But Felix gave Paul no such language; neither did Festus nor King Agrippa, in all their examinations of him, give him any such words as sirrah, rascal, knave, or the like, but heard him patiently. So now Christians may see through all the Scriptures, that when any persons were brought before rulers, kings, or magistrates, whether Jews or Heathens, they did not use to call them evil names, as sirrah, rascal, knave, and the like; they had no such foul-mouthed language in their courts, nor did they use to say to them, 'Sirrah, put off your hat.' Now, ye that profess Christianity, and say the Scripture is your rule, may see, that more corrupt words proceed out of your mouths, than either out of the Jews or Heathens, if ye will try your practice by the Scriptures. And doth not the apostle tell you, that no corrupt communication should proceed out of your mouths, and that your words should be gracious? Now I query, where and whence ye, that call yourselves Christians, have got all these bad words and names, seeing neither God, nor Christ, nor the prophets, nor the judges, nor kings, nor rulers, ever gave any such names, so far as appears by Scripture, either amongst Heathens, Jews, or Christians?" G. F.

Before the next assizes, there was a quarter-sessions held at Lancaster by the justices; to which though we were not brought, I put Friends upon drawing up an account of their sufferings, and laying them before the justices in their open sessions. For Friends had suffered deeply by fines and distresses, the bailiffs and officers making great havock and spoil of their goods; but no redress was afforded.

And because some evil-minded magistrates would tell us sometimes of the late plot in the North, we gave forth the following paper to stop their mouths, and to clear truth and Friends therefrom.

"*A Testimony from the people of God, whom the world calls Quakers, to all magistrates and officers of what sort soever, from the highest to the lowest.*

"We are peaceable, and seek the peace, good, and welfare of all, as in our lives and peaceable conduct is manifested; and we desire the eternal good and welfare of all, and their souls' everlasting peace. We are become heirs of the blessing before the curse was, and of the power of God before the devil was, and before the fall of man. We are heirs of the gospel of peace, which is the power of God; and we are heirs of Christ, who have inherited him and his everlasting kingdom, and do possess the power of an endless life. Knowing this our portion and inheritance, this is to remove all jealousies out of your minds, and out of the minds of all people concerning us, that all plots and conspiracies, plotters and conspirators against the king, and all aiders and assisters thereunto, we always did and do utterly deny to be of us, or to be of the fellowship of the gospel of Christ's kingdom, or his servants. For Christ said, 'his kingdom was not of this world; if it were, his servants would fight.' And therefore he bid Peter 'put up his sword, for,' said he, 'he that taketh the sword, shall perish by the sword.' Here is the faith and patience of the saints, to bear and suffer all things, knowing that vengeance is the Lord's, and he will repay it to them that hurt his people, and wrong the innocent. Therefore we cannot avenge, but suffer for his name's sake. We know that the Lord will judge the world in righteousness, according to their deeds, and that, when every one shall give an account to him of the 'deeds done in the body,' then will the Lord give every man according to his works, whether they be good or evil. Christ said, he came not to 'destroy men's lives;' and when his disciples would have had 'fire to come down from heaven,' to consume them that did not receive him, he told them, 'they knew not what spirit they were of,' that would have men's lives destroyed, and therefore he rebuked them and told them, 'that he came not to destroy men's lives, but to save them.' We are of Christ's mind, who is the great Prophet, whom all ought to hear in all things, who saith to his, 'if they strike thee on one cheek, turn the other; and render to no one evil for evil.' This doctrine of his we have learned, and not only confess him in words, but follow his doctrine; therefore we suffer all manner of reproaches, scandals, slanders, spoiling of goods, buffetings, whippings, stripes, and imprisonments, for these many years; and can say, 'the Lord forgive them that have thus served us, and lay not these things to their charge.' And we know that the Jews' outward sword, by which they cut down the Heathen outwardly, was a type of the inward sword of the Spirit, which cuts down the inward Heathen, the raging nature in people. The blood of bulls, lambs, rams, and other offerings, and that priesthood which offered them, together with other things in the law, were types of Christ, the one offering, and of his blood, who is the everlasting priest and covenant, our life and way to God, the great prophet and shepherd, the head of his church, and the great bishop of our souls, whom we witness come; and he doth oversee and keep his flock. For in Adam, in the fall, we know the striving, quarrelling, unpeaceable spirits are in the enmity one with another, and not in peace; but in Christ Jesus, the second Adam, that never fell, is peace, rest, and life. The doctrine of Christ, who never sinned, is, to 'love one another;' and they who are in this doctrine, hurt no man, in which we are, in Christ, who is our life. Therefore it is well for you to distinguish between the precious and the vile, between them that fear God and serve him, and them that do not; and to make a difference between the innocent and the guilty, between him that is holy and pure, and the ungodly and profane; for they that do not so, bring troubles, burthens, and sorrows upon themselves. This we write in love to your souls, that ye may consider these things; for we cannot say that they who hate enemies and one another, are of God, or in Christ's doctrine, but are opposers of it. And such as wrestle with flesh and blood, with carnal weapons, are gone into the flesh, out of the Spirit. They are not in our fellowship in the Spirit, in which is the bond of peace; neither are they of us, nor have we unity with them in their fleshly state, and with their carnal weapons. For our unity and fellowship stand in the gospel, which is the power of God, before the devil was, the liar, and the murderer, the man-slayer, and the envious. Christ's mind and his doctrine being to save men's lives, we, who are of Christ's mind, are out of, and above these things. And our desire is, that in the fear of the Lord, ye may all live, and receive God's wisdom, by which all things were created, that by it all may be ordered to His glory.

"This is from them that love all your souls, and seek your eternal good."

Being now a prisoner in Lancaster castle, a deep sense came upon me of a day of sore trial and exercise that was come and coming upon all who had been in high profession of religion; and I was moved to give forth the following paper as a warning to such:—

"Now is the day that every one's faith and love to God and Christ will be tried; they who are redeemed out of the earth, and they who are in the earth, will be manifested; and who is the master they serve, and whether they will run to the mountains to cover them. Now will it appear who are the stony ground, who are the thorny ground, and who are the highway ground, in whom the fowls of the air take away the seed, and the thorns and cares of the world choke, and the heat of persecution scorches and burns up your green blade; for the day trieth all things. Therefore let not such as forsake truth, for saving the earth, say that your brother priest only 'serveth not the Lord Jesus Christ, but his own belly, and mindeth earthly things,' for such themselves also do the same, and hug and embrace self, and not the Lord. Now it will be made manifest, who is every one's God, Christ, and Saviour, and their love will be manifest, whether it be of the world, or of God; for if it be the love of the world, it is enmity, and the enmity will manifest itself what it is; and the day will try every spirit and his fruits. Therefore, my dear friends, in the everlasting Seed of God live, that is over all the house of Adam and his works in the fall; and so dwelling in the Seed, Christ, that never fell, in him you all have virtue, life, and peace, and through him ye will overcome all that is in the fall." G. F.

I wrote also another epistle to Friends, to warn them to keep out of the spirit, that wrought in John Perrot and his company against the truth:—

"Dear Friends,

"Dwell in the love of God, and in his righteousness; that will preserve you above all changeable spirits, that dwell not in the truth, but in quarrels. Avoid such, and keep your habitations in the truth. Dwell in the truth, and in the Word of God, by which ye are reconciled to him. Keep your meetings in the name of Jesus Christ, who never fell; then ye will see over all the gatherings of Adam's sons and daughters, you being met in the life over them all, in which are your unity, peace, and fellowship with God, and one with another, in the life, in which ye may enjoy God's presence among you. So remember me to all Friends in the everlasting Seed of God. The fellowship of all those that are got into fellowship in outward things, will corrupt and wither away. Therefore live in the gospel, the power of God, which was before the devil was. This fellowship in the gospel, the power of God, is a mystery to all the fellowships of the world. So look over all outward sufferings, and look at the Lord, and the Lamb, who is the First and the Last, the Amen; in whom farewell." G. F.

In the sixth month, the assizes were held again at Lancaster, and the same judges, Twisden and Turner, came that circuit again; but Judge Turner then sat on the crown bench, and so I was brought before him. Before I was called to the bar, I was put among the murderers and felons for about two hours, the people, the justices, and the judge also gazing upon me. After they had tried several others, they called me to the bar, and empannelled a jury. Then the judge asked the justices, "whether they had tendered me the oath at the sessions." They said, "they had." Then he bid, "give them the book, that they might swear they had tendered me the oath at the sessions." They said, "they had." Then he bid, "give them the book, that they might swear they had tendered me the oath according to the indictment." Some of the justices refused to be sworn; but the judge said, he would have it done, to take away all occasion of exception. When the jury were sworn, and the justices had sworn that "they had tendered me the oath according to the indictment," the judge asked me, "whether I had not refused the oath at the last assizes?" I said, "I never took an oath in my life, and Christ, the Saviour and Judge of the world, said, 'Swear not at all.'" The judge seemed not to take notice of my answer, but asked me, "whether or not I had refused to take the oath at the last assizes?" I said, "the words that I then spoke to them were, that if they could prove, either judge, justices, priest, or teacher, that after Christ and the apostle had forbidden swearing, they commanded that Christians should swear, I would swear." The judge said he was not at that time to dispute, whether it was lawful to swear, but to inquire whether I had refused to take the oath or not. I told him, "those things mentioned in the oath, as plotting against the king, and owning the Pope's, or any other foreign power, I utterly deny." "Well," said he, "you say well in that, but did you deny to take the oath? what say you?" "What wouldst thou have me to say?" said I; "for I have told thee before what I did say." Then he asked me, "if I would have these men to swear, that I had taken the oath?" I asked him, "if he would have those men to swear, that I had refused the oath?" at which the court burst out into laughter. I was grieved to see so much lightness in a court, where such solemn matters are handled, and thereupon asked them, "if this court was a play-house? where is gravity and sobriety," said I, "for this behaviour doth not become you." Then the clerk read the indictment, and I told the judge, "I had something to speak to it;" for I had informed myself of the errors that were in it. He told me, "he would hear afterwards any reasons that I could allege, why he should not give judgment." Then I spoke to the jury, and told them, "that they could not bring me in guilty according to that indictment, for the indictment was wrong laid, and had many gross errors in it." The judge said, "I must not speak to the jury, but he would speak to them," and he told them, I had denied to take the oath at the last assizes; and, said he, "I can tender the oath to any man now, and premunire him for not taking it;" and he said, they must bring me in guilty, seeing I refused to take the oath. Then said I, "What do ye do with a form? ye may throw away your form then." And I told the jury, "it lay upon their consciences, as they would answer it to the Lord God before his judgment-seat." Then the judge spoke again to the jury, and I called to him to "do me justice." The jury brought me in guilty. Whereupon I told them, that "both the justices and they had forsworn themselves, and therefore they had small cause to laugh, as they did a little before." O! the envy, rage, and malice that appeared against me, and the lightness; but the Lord confounded them, and they were wonderfully stopped. So they set me aside, and called up Margaret Fell, who had much good service among them; and then the court broke up near the second hour.

In the afternoon we were brought again to have sentence passed upon us. Margaret Fell desired, that sentence might be deferred till the next morning. I desired nothing but law and justice at his hands, for thieves had mercy; only I requested the judge to send some one to see my prison, which was so bad, they would put no creature they had in it; and I told him, that Colonel Kirby, who was then on the bench, said, "I should be locked up, and no flesh alive should come to me." The judge shook his head, and said, "when the sentence was given, he would leave me to the favour of the jailer." Most of the gentry of the country were gathered together, expecting to hear the sentence; and the noise among the people was, "that I should be transported." But they were all crossed at that time; for the sentence being deferred till next morning, I was sent to prison again. Upon my complaining of the badness of my prison, some of the justices, with Colonel Kirby, went up to see it; but when they came, they durst hardly go in, the floor was so bad and dangerous, and the place so open to wind and rain. Some that came up said, "sure it was a jakes-house." When Colonel Kirby saw it, and heard what others said of it, he excused the matter as well as he could, saying, "I should be removed ere long to some more convenient place."

Next day, towards eleven, we were called again to hear the sentence; and Margaret Fell being called first to the bar, had counsel to plead, who found many errors in her indictment; whereupon, after the judge had acknowledged them, she was set by. Then the judge asked, "what they could say to mine?" I was not willing to let any man plead for me, but to speak to it myself; and indeed, though Margaret had some that pleaded for her, yet she spoke as much herself as she would. But before I came to the bar, I was moved in my spirit to pray, that God would confound their wickedness and envy, set his truth over all, and exalt his Seed. The Lord heard and answered, and confounded them in their proceedings against me; and though they had most envy against me, yet the most gross errors were found in my indictment.

Now, I having put by others from pleading for me, the judge asked me, "what I had to say, why he should not pass sentence upon me?" I told him, "I was no lawyer, but I had much to say, if he would have patience to hear." At that he laughed, and others laughed also, and said, "Come, what have you to say? he can say nothing." "Yes," said I, "I have much to say, have but the patience to hear me." Then I asked him, "whether the oath was to be tendered to the king's subjects, or to the subjects of foreign princes?" He said, "to the subjects of this realm." "Then," said I, "look at the indictment, and ye may see that ye have left out the word, subject; so not having named me in the indictment as a subject, ye cannot premunire me for not taking the oath." Then they looked over the statute and the indictment, and saw that it was as I said; and the judge confessed it was an error. I told him, "I had something else to stop his judgment;" and I desired him to look what day the indictment said the oath was tendered to me at the sessions there. They looked, and said, "it was the eleventh day of January." "What day of the week were the sessions held on?" said I. "On a Tuesday," said they. "Then," said I, "look at your almanacs, and see whether there were any sessions held at

Lancaster on the eleventh day of January, so called?" So they looked, and found that the eleventh day was the day called Monday, and that the sessions were on the day called Tuesday, which was the twelfth day of that month. "Look now," said I, "ye have indicted me for refusing the oath in the quarter sessions held at Lancaster on the eleventh day of January last, and the justices have sworn that they tendered me the oath in open sessions here that day, and the jury upon their oaths have found me guilty thereupon; and yet ye see there were no sessions held in Lancaster that day." Then the judge, to cover the matter, asked, "whether the sessions did not begin on the eleventh?" But some in the court answered, "no; the sessions held but one day, and that was the twelfth." Then the judge said, "this was a great mistake, and an error." Some of the justices were in a great rage at this, and were ready to quit the bench; they stamped and said, "who hath done this? somebody hath done it on purpose;" and a great heat was amongst them. "Then," said I, "are not the justices here, that have sworn to this indictment, forsworn men in the face of the country? But this is not all," said I, "I have more yet to offer why sentence should not be given against me." Then I asked, "in what year of the king the last assize here was holden, which was in the month called March last?" The judge said, "it was in the sixteenth year of the king." "But," said I, "the indictment says it was in the fifteenth year." They looked, and found it so. This also was acknowledged to be another error. Then they were all in a fret again, and could not tell what to say; for the judge had sworn the officers of the court, that the oath was tendered to me at the assize mentioned in the indictment. "Now," said I, "is not the court here forsworn also, who have sworn that the oath was tendered to me at the assize holden here in the fifteenth year of the king, when it was in his sixteenth year, and so they have sworn a year false?" The judge bid them look whether Margaret Fell's indictment was so or not. They looked, and found it was not so. I told the judge, "I had more yet to offer to stop sentence;" and asked him, "whether all the oath ought to be put into the indictment or not?" "Yes," said he, "it ought to be all put in." "Then," said I, "compare the indictment with the oath, and there thou mayest see these words, viz. [or by any authority derived, or pretended to be derived from him, or his see] left out of the indictment, which is a principal part of the oath, and in another place the words [heirs and successors] are left out." The judge acknowledged these also to be great errors. "But," said I, "I have something further to allege." "Nay," said the judge, "I have enough, you need say no more." "If," said I, "thou hast enough, I desire nothing but law and justice at thy hands, for I don't look for mercy." "You must have justice," said he, "and you shall have law." Then I asked, "Am I at liberty and free from all that hath ever been done against me in this matter?" "Yes," said the judge, "you are free from all that hath been done against you. But then," starting up in a rage, he said, "I can put the oath to any man here, and I will tender you the oath again." I told him, "he had examples enough yesterday of swearing and false-swearing, both in the justices and the jury; for I saw before thine eyes, that both justices and jury had forsworn themselves." The judge asked me, "if I would take the oath?" "I bid him do me justice for my false imprisonment all this while; for what had I been imprisoned so long for? and I told him I ought to be set at liberty." "You are at liberty," said he, "but I will put the oath to you again." Then I turned me about and said, "All people, take notice, this is a snare, for I ought to be set free from the jailer and from this court." But the judge cried, "Give him the book;" and the sheriff and the justices cried, "Give him the book." Then the power of darkness rose up in them, like a mountain, and a clerk lifted up a book to me. I stood still and said, "if it be a Bible, give it me into my hand." "Yes, yes," said the judge and justices, "give it him into his hand." So I took it and looked into it, and said, "I see it is a Bible, I am glad of it." Now he had caused the jury to be called, and they stood by; for after they had brought in their former verdict, he would not dismiss them, though they desired it; but told them, "he could not dismiss them yet, for he should have business for them, and therefore they must attend and be ready when they were called." When he said so, I felt his intent, that if I was freed, he would come on again. So I looked him in the face, and the witness of God started up in him, and made him blush when he looked at me again, for he saw that I saw him. Nevertheless, hardening himself, he caused the oath to be read to me, the jury standing by; and when it was read, he asked me, "whether I would take the oath or not?" Then said I, "ye have given me a book here to kiss and to swear on, and this book which ye have given me to kiss, says, 'Kiss the Son;' and the Son says in this book, 'Swear not at all;' and so says also the apostle James. Now, I say as the book says, and yet ye imprison me; how chance ye do not imprison the book for saying so? How comes it that the book is at liberty amongst you, which bids me not swear, and yet ye imprison me for doing as the book bids me? Why don't ye imprison the book?" As I was speaking this to them, and held up the Bible open in my hand, to show them the place in the book, where Christ forbids swearing, they plucked the book out of my hand again; and the judge said, "Nay, but we will imprison George Fox." Yet this got abroad over all the country as a by-word, "that they gave me a book to swear on, that commanded me 'not to swear at all;' and that the Bible was at liberty, and I in prison for doing as the Bible said." Now when the judge still urged me to swear, I told him, "I never took oath, covenant, or engagement in my life, but my yea or nay was more binding to me than an oath was to many others; for had they not had experience how little men regarded an oath; and how they had sworn one way and then another; and how the justices and court had forsworn themselves now?" I told him, "I was a man of a tender conscience, and if they had any sense of a tender conscience, they would consider, that it was in obedience to Christ's command that I could not swear. But," said I, "if any of you can convince me, that after Christ and the apostle had commanded not to swear, they altered that command and commanded Christians to swear; then ye shall see I will swear." There being many priests by, I said, "if ye cannot do it, let your priests stand up and do it." But not one of the priests made any answer. "O," said the judge, "all the world cannot convince you."

"No," said I, "how is it like the world should convince me; for 'the whole world lies in wickedness;' but bring out your spiritual men, as ye call them, to convince me." Then both the sheriff and the judge said, "the angel swore in the Revelations." I replied, "when God bringeth in his first-begotten Son into the world, he saith, 'Let all the angels of God worship Him;' and He saith, 'swear not at all.'" "Nay," said the judge, "I will not dispute." Then I spoke to the jury, telling them, "it was for Christ's sake that I could not swear, and therefore I warned them not to act contrary to that of God in their consciences, for before his judgment-seat they must all be brought.'" And I told them, "that as for plots and persecution for religion and Popery, I do deny them in my heart; for I am a Christian, and shall show forth Christianity amongst you this day. It is for Christ's doctrine I stand." More words I had both with the judge and jury before the jailer took me away.

In the afternoon I was brought up again, and put among the thieves some time, where I stood with my hat on till the jailer took it off. Then the jury having found this new indictment against me "for not taking the oath," I was called to the bar; and the judge asked me, "what I would say for myself:" I bid them read the indictment, for I would not answer to that which I did not hear. The clerk read it, and as he read the judge said, "take heed it be not false again;" but he read it in such a manner that I could hardly understand what he read. When he had done, the judge asked me, "what I said to the indictment?" I told him, "at once hearing so large a writing read, and at such a distance that I could not distinctly hear all the parts of it, I could not well tell what to say to it; but if he would let me have a copy, and give me time to consider it, I would answer it." This put them to a little stand; but after a while the judge asked me "what time I would have?" I said, "till the next assize." "But," said he, "what plea will you now make? are you guilty or not guilty?" I said, "I am not guilty at all of denying swearing obstinately and wilfully; and as for those things mentioned in the oath, as jesuitical plots and foreign powers, I utterly deny them in my heart; and if I could take any oath, I should take that; but I never took any oath in my life." The judge said, "I said well; but," said he, "the king is sworn, the parliament is sworn, I am sworn, the justices are sworn, and the law is preserved by oaths." I told him, "they had had sufficient experience of men's swearing, and he had seen how the justices and jury had sworn wrong the other day; and if he had read in the *Book of Martyrs* how many of the martyrs had refused to swear, both within the time of the ten persecutions and in Bishop Bonner's days, he might see, that to deny swearing in obedience to Christ's command was no new thing." He said, "he wished the laws were otherwise." I said, "Our Yea is yea, and our Nay is nay; and if we transgress our yea and our nay, let us suffer as they do, or should do, that swear falsely." This, I told him, we had offered to the king; and the king said, "it was reasonable."

After some further discourse, they committed me to prison again, there to lie till the next assize; and Colonel Kirby gave order to the jailer, "to keep me close, and suffer no flesh alive to come at me, for I was not fit," he said, "to be discoursed with by men." Then I was put into a tower, where the smoke of the other prisoners came up so thick, that it stood as dew upon the walls, and sometimes it was so thick that I could hardly see the candle when it burned; and I being locked under three locks, the under-jailer, when the smoke was great, would hardly be persuaded to come up to unlock one of the uppermost doors, for fear of the smoke, so that I was almost smothered. Besides, it rained in upon my bed, and many times, when I went to stop out the rain in the cold winter season, my shirt was wet through with the rain that came in upon me, while I was labouring to stop it out. And the place being high and open to the wind, sometimes as fast as I stopped it, the wind blew it out again. In this manner did I lie, all that long cold winter, till the next assize; in which time I was so starved with cold and rain, that my body was greatly swelled, and my limbs much benumbed.

The assize began on the 16th day of the month called March, 1664–5. The same Judges, Twisden and Turner, coming that circuit again, Judge Twisden sat this time on the crown-bench, and before him I was brought. I had informed myself of the errors in this indictment also. For though at the assize before, Judge Turner had said to the officers in court, "Pray see that all the oath be in the indictment, and that the word, subject, be in, and that the day of the month and the year of the king be put in right; for it is a shame that so many errors should be seen and found in the face of the country;" yet there were many errors, and those great ones, in this indictment, as well as in the former. Surely the hand of the Lord was in it, to confound their mischievous work against me, and to blind them therein; insomuch, that although after the indictment was drawn at the former assize, the judge examined it himself and tried it with the clerks, yet the word, subject, was left out of this indictment also, the day of the month was put in wrong, and several material words of the oath were left out; yet they went on confidently against me, thinking all was safe and well. When I was set to the bar, and the jury called over to be sworn, the clerk asked me, first, "whether I had any objection to make against any of the jury?" I told him, "I knew none of them." Then, having sworn the jury, they swore three of the officers of the court to prove "that the oath was tendered to me at the last assizes, according to the indictment." "Come, come," said the judge, "it was not done in a corner." Then he asked me, "what I had said to it, or whether I had taken the oath at the last assize?" I told him, what I had said, viz., "that the book they gave me to swear on, says, 'swear not at all;'" and I repeated more of what I had formerly said to them, as it now came to my remembrance. Whereupon the judge said, "I will not dispute with you, but in point of law." "Then," said I, "I have something to speak to the jury concerning the indictment." He told me, I must not speak to the jury, but if I had anything to say, I must speak to him. Then I asked him, "whether the oath was to be tendered to the king's subjects only, or to the subjects of foreign princes?" He replied, "to the subjects of this realm; for I will speak nothing to you," said he, "but in point of law." "Then," said I, "look in the indictment, and thou mayest see that the word, subject, is left out of this indictment also. And therefore seeing the oath is not to be tendered to any but the subjects of this realm, and ye have not put me in as a subject, the court is to take no notice of this indictment." I had no sooner spoken than the judge cried, "Take him away, jailer, take him away." So I was presently hurried away. The jailer and people looked when I should be called for again; but I was never brought to the court any more, though I had many other great errors to assign in the indictment. After I was gone, the judge asked the jury, "if they were agreed?" They said, "yes," and found for the king against me, as I was told. But I was never called to hear sentence given, nor was any given against me, that I could hear of. I understood that when they had looked more narrowly into the indictment, they saw it was not good; and the judge having sworn the officers of the court, that the oath was tendered me at the assize before, such a day, according as was set in the indictment, and that being the wrong day, I should have proved the officers of the court forsworn men again, if the judge would have suffered me to plead to the indictment; which was thought to be the reason why he hurried me away so soon. The judge had passed sentence of premunire upon Margaret Fell, before I was brought in; and it seems, when I was hurried away, they recorded me as a premunired person, though I was never brought to hear the sentence, or knew of it; which was very illegal. For they ought not only to have had me present to hear the sentence given, but also to have asked me first, "what I could say why sentence should not be given against me?" But they knew I had so much to say, that they could not give sentence, if they heard it.

While I was prisoner in Lancaster castle, there was a great noise and talk of the Turks overspreading Christendom, and great fears entered many. But one day, as I was walking in my prison chamber, "I saw the Lord's power turn against him, and that he was turning back again." And I declared to some what the Lord had let me see, when there were such fears of his over-running Christendom; and within a month after the news came, that they had given him a defeat.

Another time, as I was walking in my chamber, with my eye to the Lord, "I saw the angel of the Lord with a glittering drawn sword stretched southward, as though the court had been all on fire." Not long after the wars broke out with Holland, the sickness broke forth, and afterwards the fire of London; so the Lord's sword was drawn indeed.

By reason of my long and close imprisonment in so bad a place, I was become very weak in body; but the Lord's power was over all, supported me through all, and enabled me to do service for him, and for his truth and people, as the place would admit. For while I was in Lancaster prison, I answered several books, as the *Mass*, the *Common-Prayer*, the *Directory*, and the *Church-Faith;* which are the four chief religions that are got up since the apostles' days. And there being several Friends in prison at Lancaster and other prisons for not paying tithes, I was moved to give forth the following lines concerning tithes:—

"In the time of the law, they that did not bring their tithes into the store-house, robbed God; then there was not meat in their house;

therefore the Lord commanded 'to bring them into his house, that there might be meat in the store-house, which was to fill the fatherless, stranger, and widow.' But these priests, who are counterfeits, who take people's tithes now by a law, are from the beast; and if any will not pay them, they imprison them, or make them pay treble. These rob the poor, rob the fatherless; and the stranger and the widow are not filled; so their cry is gone up to heaven against these. Many are made almost beggars by these oppressing priests, their cattle and corn being taken away, and they cast into prison. Others are sued at law by them, and have treble damage taken from them; yet such priests are cried up to be ministers of the gospel. Though when the unchangeable priest was come, the priesthood that was changeable, was denied, as we now deny these. But if any be moved now to cry against them, they are stocked, beat, or imprisoned. Many are now in prison at Lancaster, and in other places, by a national law; the like whereof was never done by the law of God, which was delivered to Moses. For we do not read, that under Moses's law any suffered imprisonment, or spoiling of their goods for not paying tithes, or had to pay treble damage. Surely, surely, the cry for vengeance will be heard, which arises from the oppressed souls that lie under the altar. There are many prisoners at Kendal, because they cannot pay tithes, as Captain Ward, Thomas Robertson,* and the widow Garland, who has many small children; these suffer because they cannot pay tithes. Others are in Kendal prison, who were moved of the Lord to speak to the priests, one to go in sackcloth, and with ashes upon her head. Others have been moved to go in sackcloth, as a lamentation for the miserable estate of this nation, seeing so much crying up of the preaching of the gospel, and yet so much strife, debate, and oaths, and dissension among people. But where the gospel is received indeed, strife and contention are ended, and oppression is taken off. O! the land mourns, because of the oppression of those called ministers! And though the cry of the oppressed hath not entered into the ears of the magistrates; yet is the cry of the poor, oppressed people of God, entered into the ears of the Lord of Sabaoth, who now will be avenged of all his adversaries. You unjust lawgivers, and unjust judges, to that in all your consciences I speak, to be cleared, when ye are judged by the just Judge of heaven and earth; whose terror is gone forth against all the ungodly, and all the oppressors of God's people whatsoever, whether ye will hear or forbear." G. F.

After the assize, Colonel Kirby and some other justices were very uneasy with my being at Lancaster; for I had galled them sore at my trials there, and they laboured much to get me removed to some remote place. Colonel Kirby threatened I should be sent far enough, and sometimes said,

* Of Thomas Robertson not much is known, but he appears to have been a faithful labourer in his day. Ambrose Rigge, in the *Account of his Life*, states, "A fellow-labourer was prepared for me, which was Thomas Robertson of Westmorland; who was made willing to leave his dear wife and tender babes, to go with me into the Lord's harvest." In *Letters, &c., of Early Friends*, p. 226, is a letter from Thomas Robertson to Margaret Fell, under date 1655.

I should be sent beyond sea. About six weeks after the assizes, they got an order from the king and council to remove me from Lancaster; and with it they brought a letter from the Earl of Anglesea, wherein was written, "that if those things were found true against me, which I was charged withal, I deserved no clemency or mercy;" yet the greatest matter they had against me was, because I could not disobey the command of Christ, and swear.

When they had prepared for my removal, the under-sheriff and the head-sheriff's man, with some bailiffs, came and fetched me out of the castle, when I was so weak with lying in that cold, wet, and smoky prison, that I could hardly go or stand. They had me into the jailer's house, where were William Kirby, a justice, and several others, and they called for wine to give me. I told them, "I would have none of their wine." Then they cried, "Bring out the horses." I desired them first to show me their order, or a copy of it, if they intended to remove me; but they would show me none but their swords. I told them, "there was no sentence passed upon me, nor was I premunired, that I knew of; and therefore I was not made the king's prisoner, but was the sheriff's; for they and all the country knew, that I was not fully heard at the last assize, nor suffered to show the errors that were in the indictment, which were sufficient to quash it, though they had kept me from one assize to another, to the end they might try me. But they all knew, there was no sentence of premunire passed upon me; and therefore not being the king's prisoner but the sheriff's, I desired to see their order." Instead of showing me their order, they haled me out, and lifted me upon one of the sheriff's horses. When I was on horseback in the street, the town's-people being gathered to gaze upon me, I told the officers, I had received neither Christianity, civility, nor humanity, from them. They hurried me away about fourteen miles to BENTHAM, though I was so very weak, I was hardly able to sit on horseback; and my clothes smelt so of smoke, that they were loathsome to myself. The wicked jailer, one Hunter, a young fellow, would come behind, and give the horse a lash with his whip, and make him skip and leap; so that I, being weak, had difficulty to sit him; and then he would come and look me in the face, and say, "How do you, Mr. Fox?" I told him, "it was not civil in him to do so." The Lord cut him off soon after.

When we were come to Bentham, there met us many troopers, and a marshal; and many of the gentry of the country were come in, and abundance of people to stare at me. I being very weak and weary, desired them to let me lie down on a bed, which the soldiers permitted me; for they that brought me thither, gave their order to the marshal, and he set a guard of his soldiers upon me. When they had stayed a while, they pressed horses, and raised the bailiff of the hundred, and the constables, and others, and had me to GIGGLESWICK that night; but exceedingly weak I was. There they raised the constables with their clog-shoes, who sat drinking all the night in the room by me, so that I could not get much rest. Next day we came to a market-town, where several Friends called to see me; and Robert Widders and divers Friends came to me on the road. The next night I asked the soldiers, "whither they intended to carry me, and whither

I was to be sent?" Some of them said, "beyond sea;" others said, "to Tynemouth Castle." A great fear there was amongst them, lest some one should rescue me out of their hands; but that fear was needless. Next night we came to YORK, where the marshal put me into a great chamber, where most part of two troops came to see me. One of these troopers, an envious man, hearing that I was premunired, asked me, "what estate I had, and whether it was copyhold or free land?" I took no notice of his question, but was moved to declare the word of life to the soldiers, and many of them were very loving. At night the Lord Frecheville (so called), who commanded these horse, came to me, and was very civil and loving. I gave him an account of my imprisonment, and declared many things to him relating to truth. They kept me at York two days, and then the marshal and four or five soldiers were sent to convey me to SCARBRO' CASTLE. Indeed these were very civil men, and carried themselves civilly and lovingly to me. On the way we baited at MALTON, and they permitted Friends to come and visit me. When we were come to SCARBRO', they had me to an inn, and gave notice to the governor, who sent six soldiers to be my guard that night. Next day they conducted me into the castle, put me into a room, and set a sentry on me. Being very weak and subject to fainting, they let me go out sometimes into the air with the sentry. They soon removed me out of this room, and put me into an open one, where the rain came in; and smoked exceedingly, which was very offensive to me. One day the governor, Sir John Crossland, came to see me, and brought with him Sir Francis Cobb. I desired the governor to go into my room, and see what a place I had. I had got a little fire made in it, and it was so filled with smoke, that when they were in, they could hardly find their way out again; and he being a Papist, I told him, that was his Purgatory which they had put me into. I was forced to lay out about fifty shillings to stop out the rain, and keep the room from smoking so much. When I had been at that charge, and made it somewhat tolerable, they removed me into a worse room, where I had neither chimney nor fire-hearth. This being to the sea-side and lying much open, the wind drove in the rain forcibly, so that the water came over my bed, and ran about the room, that I was fain to skim it up with a platter. And when my clothes were wet, I had no fire to dry them; so that my body was benumbed with cold, and my fingers swelled, that one was grown as big as two. Though I was at some charge in this room also, I could not keep out the wind and rain. Besides they would suffer few Friends to come to me, and many times not any, no, not so much as to bring me a little food; but I was forced for the first quarter to hire one of another society to bring me necessaries. Sometimes the soldiers would take it from her, and she would scuffle with them for it. Afterwards I hired a soldier to fetch me water and bread, and something to make a fire of, when I was in a room where a fire could be made. Commonly a threepenny loaf served me three weeks, and sometimes longer, and most of my drink was water with wormwood steeped or bruised in it. One time when the weather was very sharp, and I had taken great cold, I got a little elecampane beer, and I heard one of the soldiers say to the other, that they would play me a trick, for they would send for me up to the deputy-governor, and in the meantime drink my strong beer out; and so they did. When I came back, one of the soldiers came to me in a jeer, and asked me for some strong beer. I told him they had played their pretty trick; and so I took no further notice of it. But inasmuch as they kept me so very strait, not giving liberty for Friends to come to me, I spoke to the keepers of the castle to this effect: "I did not know till I was removed from Lancaster castle, and brought prisoner to this castle of Scarbro', that I was convicted of a premunire; for the judge did not give sentence upon me at the assizes in open court. But seeing I am now a prisoner here, if I may not have my liberty, let my friends and acquaintance have their liberty to come and visit me, as Paul's friends had among the Romans, who were not Christians but Heathens. For Paul's friends had their liberty; all that would, might come to him, and he had his liberty to preach to them in his hired house; but I cannot have liberty to go into the town, nor for my friends to come to me here. So you that go under the name of Christians, are worse in this respect than those Heathens were."

But though they would not let Friends come to me, they would often bring others, either to gaze upon me, or to contend with me. One time a great company of Papists came to discourse with me; they affirmed, "the Pope was infallible, and had stood infallible ever since Peter's time." But I showed them the contrary by history; for one of the bishops of Rome, (Marcellinus by name), denied the faith and sacrificed to idols; therefore he was not infallible. I told them, If they were in the infallible spirit, they need not have jails, swords, and staves, racks and tortures, fires and faggots, whips and gallows, to hold up their religion, and to destroy men's lives about it; for if they were in the infallible spirit they would preserve men's lives, and use none but spiritual weapons about religion. I told them also what one that had been of their society told me. A woman who lived in Kent, had not only been a Papist herself, but had brought over several to that religion; but coming to be convinced of God's truth, and turned by it to Christ her Saviour, she exhorted the Papists to the same. One of them, a tailor, being at work at her house, while she opened to him the falseness of the Popish religion, and endeavoured to draw him from it to the truth, drew his knife, and got between her and the door; but she spoke boldly to him, and bid him put up his knife, for she knew his principle. I asked the woman, "what she thought he would have done with his knife?" She said, "he would have stabbed her." "Stabbed thee," said I, "what would he have stabbed thee for? thy religion?" "Yes," said she, "it is the principle of the Papists, if any turn from their religion, to kill them if they can." This story I told those Papists, and that I had it from a person that had been one of them, but had forsaken their principles and discovered their practices. They did not deny this to be their principle; but said, "What! would I declare this abroad?" I told them, "yes, such things ought to be declared abroad; that it might be known how contrary their religion was to true Christianity." Whereupon they went away in a great rage.

Another Papist came to discourse with me, who said all the patriarchs were in hell, from the creation till Christ came, and that when Christ suffered he went into hell, and the Devil said to him, "What comest thou hither for, to break open our strongholds?" And Christ said, "to fetch them all out." So he said, "Christ was three nights and three days in hell, to bring them out." I told him that was false, for Christ said to the thief, "This day thou shalt be with me in paradise." And Enoch and Elijah were translated into heaven. And Abraham was in heaven, for the Scripture saith, Lazarus was in his bosom; and Moses and Elias were with Christ upon the Mount before he suffered. These instances stopped the Papist's mouth, and put him to a stand.

Another time came Dr. Witty, who was esteemed a great doctor of physic, with Lord Falconbridge; with these came also the governor of Tynemouth castle, and several knights. Being called to them, Witty undertook to discourse with me, and asked me, "what I was in prison for?" I told him, "because I would not disobey the command of Christ, and swear." He said, "I ought to swear my allegiance to the king." He being a great Presbyterian, I asked him, "whether he had not sworn against the King, and House of Lords, and taken the Scotch covenant? and had he not since sworn to the king? and what then was his swearing good for? But my allegiance," I told him, "did not consist in swearing, but in truth and faithfulness." After some further discourse, I was sent away to my prison again. And afterwards this Dr. Witty boasted in the town amongst his patients, that he had conquered me. When I heard of his boasting, I told the governor, "it was a small boast in him to say he had conquered a bondman." I desired to bid him visit me again, when he came to the castle. He came again a while after, with sixteen or seventeen great persons; and ran himself worse on ground than before. For he affirmed before them all, "that Christ hath not enlightened every man that cometh into the world; and that the grace of God, that bringeth salvation, hath not appeared unto all men; and that Christ died not for all men." I asked him, "what sort of men those were whom Christ had not enlightened? and to whom his grace had not appeared? and for whom he had not died?" He said, "Christ did not die for adulterers, and idolaters, and wicked men." I asked him, "whether adulterers and wicked men were not sinners?" He said, "Yes." "And did not Christ die for sinners?" said I. "Did he not come to call sinners to repentance?" "Yes," said he. "Then," said I, "thou hast stopped thy own mouth." So I proved that the grace of God hath appeared unto all men, though some turn it into wantonness, and walk despitefully against it; and that Christ hath enlightened all men, though some hate the light. Several of the people that were present, confessed it was true; but he went away in a great rage, and came no more to me.

Another time the governor brought a priest, but his mouth was soon stopped. Not long after he brought two or three parliament-men, who asked me, "whether I owned ministers and bishops?" I told them, "yes, such as Christ sent, such as had freely received, and would freely give, such as were qualified, and were in the same power and Spirit that the apostles were in. But such bishops and teachers as theirs were, that would go no farther than a great benefice, I did not own; for they were not like the apostles. Christ saith to his ministers, 'Go ye into all nations, and preach the gospel;' but ye parliament-men, who keep your priests and bishops in such great fat benefices, have spoiled them all. For do ye think they will go into all nations to preach; or any farther than a great fat benefice? Judge yourselves whether they will or not."

There came another time the widow of old Lord Fairfax, and with her a great company; one of whom was a priest. I was moved to declare the truth to them, and the priest asked me, "why we said, Thou and Thee to people? for he counted us but fools and idiots for speaking so." I asked him, "whether they that translated the Scriptures, and that made the grammar and accidence, were fools and idiots, seeing they translated the Scriptures so, and made the grammar so, Thou to one, and You to more than one, and left it so to us. If they were fools and idiots, why had not he, and such as he, that looked upon themselves as wise men, and that could not bear Thou and Thee to a singular, altered the grammar, accidence, and Bible, and put the plural instead of the singular. But if they were wise men that had so translated the Bible, and had made the grammar and accidence so, I wished him to consider whether they were not fools and idiots themselves, that did not speak as their grammars and Bibles taught them; but were offended with us, and called us fools and idiots for speaking so?" Thus the priest's mouth was stopped, and many of the company acknowledged the truth, and were pretty loving and tender. Some of them would have given me money, but I would not receive it.

After this came Dr. Cradock, with three priests more, and the governor and his lady (so called), and another that was called a lady, and a great company with them. Dr. Cradock asked me, "what I was in prison for?" I told him, "for obeying the command of Christ and the apostle, in not swearing. But if he, being both a doctor and a justice of peace, could convince me, that after Christ and the apostle had forbidden swearing, they commanded Christians to swear, then I would swear. Here was the Bible," I told him, "he might, if he could, show me any such command." He said, "it is written, 'Ye shall swear in truth and righteousness.'" "Ay," said I, "it was written so in Jeremiah's time; but that was many ages before Christ commanded 'not to swear at all;' but where is it written so, since Christ forbade all swearing? I could bring as many instances out of the Old Testament for swearing as thou, and it may be more; but of what force are they to prove swearing lawful in the New Testament, since Christ and the apostle forbade it? Besides," said I, "in that text where it is written, ye shall swear, what ye was this? Was it ye Gentiles, or ye Jews?" To this he would not answer. But one of the priests that were with him answered, "it was to the Jews that this was spoken." Then Dr. Cradock confessed, it was so. "Very well," said I, "but where did God ever give a command to the Gentiles to swear? For thou knowest that we are Gentiles by nature." "Indeed," said he, "in the gospel-times everything was to be established out of the mouths of two or three witnesses; but there was to be no swearing then."

"Why then," said I, "dost thou force oaths upon Christians, contrary to thy own knowledge, in the gospel-times. And why dost thou excommunicate my friends?" (for he had excommunicated abundance, both in Yorkshire and Lancashire). He said, "for not coming to church." "Why," said I, "ye left us above twenty years ago, when we were but young lads and lasses, to the Presbyterians, Independents, and Baptists, many of whom made spoil of our goods, and persecuted us, because we would not follow them. Now we being but young, knew little then of your principles; and if ye had intended to keep the old men that did know them, to you, and your principles alive, that we might have known them, ye should either not have fled from us as ye did, or ye should have sent us your epistles, collects, homilies, and evening-songs; for Paul wrote epistles to the saints, though he was in prison. But they and we might have turned Turks or Jews for any collects, homilies, or epistles, we had from you all this while. And now thou hast excommunicated us, both young and old, and so have others of you done: that is, ye have put us out of your church before ye have got us into it, and before ye have brought us to know your principles. Is not this madness in you, to put us out before we were brought in? Indeed, if ye had brought us into your church, and when we had been in, if we had done some bad thing, that had been something like a ground for excommunication or putting out again. But," said I, "what dost thou call the church?" "Why," said he, "that which you call the steeple-house." Then I asked him, "whether Christ shed his blood for the steeple-house; and purchased and sanctified the steeple-house with his blood? And seeing the church is Christ's bride and wife, and that he is the head of the church, dost thou think the steeple-house is Christ's wife and bride, and that he is the head of that old house, or of his people?" "No," said he, "Christ is the head of the people, and they are the church." "Then," said I, "but you have given the title, church, which belongs to the people, to an old house, and you have taught people to believe so." I asked him also, "why he persecuted Friends for not paying tithes? And whether God ever gave a command to the Gentiles, that they should pay tithes? And whether Christ had not ended tithes, when he ended the Levitical priesthood that took tithes? And whether Christ, when he sent forth his disciples to preach, had not commanded them to preach freely, as he had given them freely? And whether all the ministers of Christ are not bound to observe this command of Christ?" He said, "he would not dispute that;" neither did I find he was willing to stay on that subject, for he presently turned to another matter, and said, "you marry, but I know not how." I replied, "It may be so; but why dost thou not come and see?" Then he threatened that he would use his power against us, as he had done. "I bid him take heed; for he was an old man." I asked him also, "where he read from Genesis to the Revelations, that ever any priest did marry any?" And I wished him to show me some instance thereof, if he would have us come to them to be married; "for," said I, "thou hast excommunicated one of my friends two years after he was dead, about his marriage. And why dost thou not excommunicate Isaac, and Jacob, and Boaz, and Ruth? Why dost thou not use thy power against these; for we do not read that they were ever married by the priests; but they took one another in the assemblies of the righteous, in the presence of God and his people; and so do we. So that we have all the holy men and women, that the Scripture speaks of in this practice, on our side." Much discourse we had, but when he found he could get no advantage over me, he went away with his company.

With such people I was much exercised while I was there; for most that came to the castle would desire to speak with me, and great disputes I had with them. But, as to Friends, I was as a man buried alive; for though many came far to see me, yet few were suffered to come to me; and when any Friend came into the castle about business, if he looked towards me they would rage at him. At last the governor came under some trouble himself; for he having sent out a privateer to sea, they took some ships that were not enemies' ships, but their friends'; whereupon he was brought into trouble; after which he grew somewhat more friendly to me. For before I had a marshal set over me, on purpose to get money out of me; but I was not free to give him a farthing; and when they found they could get nothing off me, he was taken away again. The officers often threatened that I should be hanged over the wall. Nay, the deputy-governor told me once that the king, knowing I had great interest in the people, had sent me thither, that if there should be any stirring in the nation, they should hang me over the wall to keep the people down. There being, a while after, a marriage at a Baptist's house, upon which occasion a great many of them were met together, they talked much then of hanging me. But I told them, "if that was what they desired, and it was permitted them, I was ready; for I never feared death nor sufferings in my life, but I was known to be an innocent, peaceable man, free from all stirrings and plottings, and one that sought the good of all men." Afterwards, the governor growing kinder, I spoke to him when he was going to London to the Parliament, and desired him to speak to Esquire Marsh, Sir Francis Cobb, and some others; and let them know how long I had lain in prison, and for what; and he did so. When he came down again, he told me, that Esquire Marsh * said he would go a hundred miles barefoot for my liberty, he knew me so well; and several others, he said, spoke well of me. From which time the governor was very loving to me.

There were, amongst the prisoners, two very bad men, that often sat drinking with the officers and soldiers; and because I would not sit and drink with them too, it made them the worse against me. One time when these two prisoners were drunk, one of them (whose name was William Wilkinson, a Presbyterian, who had been a captain), came to me and challenged me to fight with him. Seeing what condition he was in, I got out of his way; and next morning, when he was more sober, showed him, "how

* The person whom George Fox here and elsewhere styles Esquire Marsh, was a gentleman attached to the court of Charles II. He always remained attached to George Fox, and ever retained a most friendly interest for the Society in general. From his station at court and office as a magistrate, he had frequent opportunities of interposing his authority to protect the early Friends from the unjust oppression of their persecutors.

unmanly a thing it was in him to challenge a man to fight, whose principle, he knew, it was not to strike; but if he was stricken on one ear to turn the other. I told him, if he had a mind to fight, he should have challenged some of the soldiers, that could have answered him in his own way. But however, seeing he had challenged me, I was now come to answer him with my hands in my pockets; and (reaching my head towards him) 'here,' said I, 'here is my hair, here are my cheeks, here is my back.'" With that he skipped away from me, and went into another room; at which the soldiers fell a laughing; and one of the officers said, "you are a happy man, that can bear such things." Thus he was conquered without a blow. After a while he took the oath, gave bond, and got out of prison; and not long after the Lord cut him off.

There were great imprisoments in this, and the former year, while I was prisoner at Lancaster and Scarbro'. At London many Friends were crowded into Newgate, and other prisons, where the sickness was; and many died in prison.* Many also were banished, and several sent on shipboard by the king's order. Some masters of ships would not carry them, but set them on shore again; yet some were sent to Barbadoes, to Jamaica, and to Nevis, and the Lord blessed them there. One master of a ship was very wicked and cruel to Friends that were put on board his vessel; for he kept them down under decks, though the sickness was amongst them; so that many died of it. But the Lord visited him for his wickedness; for he lost most of his seamen by the plague, and lay several months crossed with contrary winds, though other ships went out and made their voyages.

* The sickness here alluded to was the "Plague," which visited London in 1665. The state of the city during this dreadful visitation seems to have been most deplorable. The following striking description is from *Ellis's Original Letters in the British Museum.* The letter is one addressed to Dr. Sancroft from J. Tillison, dated Sept. 14, 1665 :—

"The desolation of the city is very great. That heart is either of steel or stone, that will not lament this sad visitation, and will not bleed for those unutterable woes! What eye would not weep to see so many habitations uninhabited—the poor sick not visited—the hungry not fed—the grave not satisfied! Death stares us continually in the face in every infected person that passes by us, in every coffin which is daily and hourly carried along the streets. The custom was in the beginning to bury the dead in the night only; but now both night and day will hardly be time enough to do it. The Quakers (as we are informed) have buried, in their piece of ground, a thousand for some weeks together past."

George Whitehead relates the satisfaction and comfort many innocent Friends expressed on their deathbeds, both in Newgate and other noisome places during the plague. Death was truly gain to these; "it being through death," says Whitehead, "that the Lord had appointed the final deliverance of many from the cruelties and rod of their oppressors, and from the miseries and evil to come."—"Whilst the plague was raging in the city," he adds, "our persecutors took fifty-five of our Friends (men and women) out of Newgate, where the distemper also prevailed, and forced them on board a ship for banishment, which lay for some time in the river. They were so crowded on board, and the distemper breaking out amongst them, most of them were infected, and twenty-seven of them soon died. I visited them, and had a meeting with them on board, and the Lord my God preserved me, both from the distemper and also from banishment, wherein I did humbly confess his power and special providence to his own praise and glory."

At last he came before Plymouth, and there the governor and magistrates would not suffer him, or any of his men, to land, though he wanted many necessaries for his voyage; but Thomas Lower, Arthur Cotton, John Light, and other Friends, went to the ship's side and carried necessaries for the Friends that were prisoners on board. The master being thus crossed and vexed, cursed them that put upon him this freight, and said, "he hoped he should not go far before he was taken." And the vessel was but just out of sight of Plymouth before she was taken by a Dutch man-of-war, and carried into Holland. When they came there, the States sent the banished Friends back to England, with a passport, and a certificate, "that they had not made an escape, but were sent back by them." In time the Lord's power wrought over this storm, and many of our persecutors were confounded and put to shame.*

After I had lain prisoner above a year in Scarbro' Castle, I sent a letter to the king, in which I gave him "an account of my imprisonment, and the bad usage I had received in prison; and also that I was informed, no man could deliver me but he." After this, John Whitehead being at London, and being acquainted with Esquire Marsh, went to visit him, and spoke to him about me; and he undertook, if John Whitehead would get the state of my case drawn up, to deliver it to the master of requests, Sir John Birkenhead, and endeavour to get a release for me. So John Whitehead and Ellis Hookes † drew up a relation of my imprisonment and sufferings, and carried it to Marsh; and he went with it to the master of requests, who procured an order from the king for my release. The substance of the order was, "that the king being certainly informed, that I was a man principled against plotting and fighting, and had been ready at all times to discover plots, rather than to make any, &c., therefore his royal pleasure was, that I should be discharged from my imprisonment," &c. As soon as this order was obtained, John Whitehead came to Scarbro' with it, and delivered it to the governor; who, upon receipt thereof, gathered the officers together, and without requiring bonds or sureties for my peaceable living, being satisfied that I was a man of a peaceable life, he discharged me freely, and gave me the following passport:—

"Permit the bearer hereof, George Fox, late a prisoner here, and now

* See extraordinary occurrences in an attempt to banish a number of Friends recorded in a note in *Letters, &c., of Early Friends*, p. 142–145.

† Ellis Hookes was employed in London as a recording clerk to the Society of Friends. It was he who commenced the *Record of Sufferings* (mentioned to George Fox in a letter bearing date 1660, inserted in *Letters, &c., of Early Friends*, p. 86, 87), which were written out into large folio volumes, still preserved among the Society's records in London. These are continued down to the present day in forty or more of these large volumes. The clear and excellent writing of Ellis Hookes extends over a large portion of the first of these bulky folios. To the narratives of sufferings and persecutions, were added accounts of what were regarded as judgments upon persecutors; which were, doubtless in that day, ordered to be recorded, under a sense of the fear of God, and in testimony unto his overruling power.

Ellis Hookes died in 1681. In the London *Register of Burials*, he is described "of Horslydown in Southwark, scrivenor;" and "died the 12th of the 9th month, 1681, of a consumption (having been clerk to Friends in London about twenty-four years)—he was buried in Checker Alley."

discharged by His Majesty's order, quietly to pass about his lawful occasions, without any molestation. Given under my hand at Scarbro' Castle, this first day of September, 1666." JORDAN CROSLANDS,

Governor of Scarbro' Castle.

After I was released, I would have made the governor a present for the civility and kindness he had of late showed me; but he would not receive anything; saying, "whatever good he could do for me and my friends he would do it, and never do them any hurt." And afterwards, if at any time the mayor of the town sent to him for soldiers to break up Friends' meetings, if he sent any down he would privately give them a charge "not to meddle." He continued loving to his dying day. The officers also and the soldiers were mightily changed, and became very respectful to me, and when they had occasion to speak of me, they would say, "he is as stiff as a tree, and as pure as a bell; for we could never bow him."

The very next day after my release, the fire broke out in London, and the report of it came quickly down into the country.* Then I saw the Lord God was true and just in his word, which he had showed me before in Lancaster jail, when I saw the angel of the Lord with a glittering sword drawn southward, as before expressed. The people of London were forewarned of this fire; yet few laid it to heart, or believed it; but rather grew more wicked, and higher in pride. For a Friend was moved to come out of Huntingdonshire a little before the fire, to scatter his money, and turn his horse loose on the streets, to untie the knees of his trowsers, let his stockings fall down, and to unbutton his doublet, and tell the people, "so should they run up and down, scattering their money and their goods, half undressed, like mad people, as he was a sign to them;" and so they did, when the city was burning. Thus hath the Lord exercised his prophets and servants by his power, showed them signs of his judgments, and sent

* The great fire of London occurred towards the latter end of 1660. The narratives given in the Diaries of Evelyn and Pepys, who were eye-witnesses of it, are sad indeed. Evelyn writes—"Sept. 8. The fire continued all this night (if I may call that night, which was light as day for ten miles about), after a dreadful manner—when conspiring with a fierce eastern wind, in a very dry season. I went on foot to the Bankside in Southwark, and saw the whole south part of the city burning from Cheapside to the Thames, and all along Cornhill, Tower Street, Gracious Street, and so along to Bainard's Castle, and was now taking hold of St. Paul's Church. The conflagration was so universal, and the people so astonished, that from the beginning (I know not by what despondency or fate) they hardly stirred to quench it; so that there was nothing heard or seen but crying out and lamentation, and running about like distracted creatures. O! the miserable and calamitous spectacle! such as happily the world had not seen the like since the foundation of it, nor to be outdone till the universal conflagration. All the sky was of a fiery aspect, like the top of a burning oven, the light [being] seen above forty miles round about for many nights. The poor inhabitants were dispersed about St. George's Fields and Moorfields, as far as Highgate, and several miles in circle—some under tents, some under miserable huts and hovels, many without a rag or necessary utensils, bed or board; who, from delicateness, riches, or easy accommodations in stately and well-furnished houses, were now reduced to extremest misery and poverty," &c., vol. i. p. 372–374.

them to forewarn the people; but, instead of repenting, they have beaten and cruelly entreated some, and some they have imprisoned, both in the former power's days and since. But the Lord is just, and happy are they that obey his word. Some have been moved to go naked in their streets, in the other power's days, and since, as signs of their nakedness; and have declared amongst them "that God would strip them of their hypocritical professions, and make them as bare and naked as they were." But instead of considering it, they have many times whipped, or otherwise abused them, and sometimes imprisoned them. Others have been moved to go in sackcloth, and to denounce the woes and vengeance of God against the pride and haughtiness of the people; but few regarded it. And in the other power's days, the wicked, envious, and professing priests, put up several petitions both to Oliver and Richard, called protectors, and to the parliaments, judges, and justices, against us, full of lies, vilifying words and slanders; but we got copies of them, and, through the Lord's assistance, answered them all, and cleared the Lord's truth and ourselves of them. But O! the body of darkness that rose against the truth in them that made lies their refuge. But the Lord swept them away; and in and with his power, truth, light, and life, hedged his lambs about, and preserved them as on eagles' wings. Therefore we all had, and have great encouragement to trust the Lord, who, we saw by his power and Spirit, overturned and brought to naught all the confederacies and counsels that were hatched in darkness against his truth and people; and by the same truth gave his people dominion, that therein they might serve him.

Indeed I could not but take notice, how the hand of the Lord turned against the persecutors, who had been the cause of my imprisonment, or had been abusive or cruel to me in it. The officer that fetched me to Holker-Hall wasted his estate, and soon after fled into Ireland. And most of the justices that were upon the bench at the sessions when I was sent to prison, died in a while after; as old Thomas Preston, Rawlinson, Porter, and Matthew West, of Borwick. And Justice Fleming's wife died, and left him thirteen or fourteen motherless children, who had imprisoned two Friends to death, and thereby made several children fatherless. Colonel Kirby never prospered after. The chief constable, Richard Dodgson, died soon after, and Mount, the petty constable, and the wife of the other petty constable John Ashburnham, who railed at me in her house, died soon after. William Knipe, the witness they brought against me, died soon after also. Hunter, the jailer of Lancaster, who was very wicked to me while I was his prisoner, was cut off in his young days: and the under-sheriff that carried me from Lancaster prison towards Scarbro', lived not long after. And Joblin, the jailer of Durham, who was prisoner with me in Scarbro' castle, and had often incensed the governor and soldiers against me, though he got out of prison, yet the Lord cut him off in his wickedness soon after. When I came into that country again, most of those that dwelt in Lancashire were dead, and others ruined in their estates; so that, though I did not seek revenge upon them, for their actings against me contrary to the law, yet the Lord had executed his judgments upon many of them.

CHAPTER II.

1666–1669.—George Fox visits a man above one hundred years old, who had been convinced—refutes a slander that Friends love none but themselves—has a meeting at Captain Taylor's [at Brighouse], where a neighbouring knight threatens again to imprison him—comes to London, and finds the city in ruins as he had seen it in a vision some years before—is moved to recommend the setting up of monthly meetings to take care of God's glory, and to admonish and exhort such as walk disorderly—travels through the nation for this purpose—meets with opposition in Huntingdonshire and Bedfordshire—when at Shrewsbury it was rumoured that "the great Quaker of England was come to town"—the hypocrisy of the Presbyterians detected—they and the Independents persecute when in power, but flinch in time of persecution by other powers—George Fox recommends certain regulations to be observed relative to Friends' marriages—he also recommends the establishment of a school at Waltham for boys, and one at Shacklewell for girls—the meetings for discipline are the means of a great reformation among the people—George Fox discovers a cheat, writes a prophetic warning to Friends—monthly meetings settled throughout the nation—the order and good results thereof—George Fox disputes with a Papist—confers with Esquire Marsh (Justice), and shows him how to distinguish between Friends and other dissenters who refused the oath—Justice Marsh is afterwards very serviceable to Friends in screening them from suffering, and recommends the king to grant liberty of conscience—fourteen monthly meetings are settled in Yorkshire—Isaac Lindley to George Fox—when at Scarbro' the governor presses George Fox to accept his hospitality—large and precious meetings.

Being now freed from my imprisonment in Scarbro' castle, I went about three miles to a large general meeting at a Friend's house, that had been a chief constable; and all was quiet and well. On the fourth day after, I returned to Scarbro', and had a meeting in the town at Peter Hodgson's house. To this came one called a lady, and several other great persons, also a young man, son to the bailiff of the town, who had been convinced, while I was there in prison. That lady (so called) came to me, and said, "I spoke against the ministers." I told her, "such as the prophets and Christ declared against formerly, I declared against now."

From hence I went to Whitby; and, having visited Friends there, passed to Burlington, where I had another meeting. Thence to Oram, where I had another meeting: and thence to Marmaduke Storr's, and had a large meeting at a constable's house, on whom the Lord had wrought a great miracle.

Next day, two Friends being to take each other in marriage, there was a very great meeting, which I attended. I was moved to open to the people the state of our marriages, declaring how the people of God took one another in the assemblies of the elders, and that it was God who joined man and woman together before the fall. And though men had taken upon them to join in the fall, yet in the restoration it was God's joining, that was the right and honourable marriage: but never any priest did marry any, that we read of in the Scriptures, from Genesis to the Revelations. Then

I showed them the duty of man and wife, how they should serve God, being heirs of life and grace together.

I passed thence to Grace Barwick's, where I had a general meeting, which was very large. I came next to Richard Shipton's, where I had another meeting; and so to a priest's house, whose wife was convinced, and himself grown very loving, and glad to see me. This was that priest, who, in the year 1651, threatened, "if ever he met me again, he would have my life, or I should have his;" and said, "he would lose his head, if I were not knocked down in a month." But now he was partly convinced, and become very kind. I went from his house towards the sea, where several Friends came to visit me; and amongst others, Philip Scafe, who had formerly been a priest, but, having received the truth, was now become a preacher of Christ freely, and continued so. Passing on, I called to see an ancient man, who was convinced of truth, and was above a hundred years old. Then I came to a Friend's house, where I had a great meeting, and quiet. I had a great meeting near MALTON; and another large one near HULL; from which I went to HOWDEN-DYKE. As we went into the town, the watchmen questioned me and those that were with me; but not having any warrant to stay us, we passed by them, who in a rage threatened they would search us out. I went to the house of one called the Lady Montague, where I lodged that night; and several friends came to visit me. Next morning, being up early, I walked into the orchard, and saw a man about sunrise go into the house in a great cloak. He stayed not long; but came soon out again, and went away, not seeing me. I felt something strike at my life; and went into the house, where I found the maid-servant affrighted and trembling. She told me, "that man had a naked rapier under his cloak." By which I perceived he came with an intent to do mischief, but the Lord prevented him.

I then visited Friends till I came to YORK, where we had a large meeting. After which I went to visit Justice Robinson, an ancient justice of the peace, who had been very loving to me and Friends from the beginning. There was a priest with him, who told me, "it was said of us, that we loved none but ourselves." I told him, "we loved all mankind, as they were God's creation, and as they were children of Adam and Eve by generation; and we loved the brotherhood in the Holy Ghost." This stopped him. After some other discourse, we parted friendly, and passed away.

About this time I wrote a book, entitled, *Fear God, and Honour the King;* in which I showed, "that none could rightly fear God, and honour the king, but they that departed from sin and evil." This book affected the soldiers much, and most people.

Having visited Friends at YORK, we passed to a market town, where we had a meeting at George Watkinson's, formerly a justice. A glorious, blessed meeting it was, and very large, and the Seed of life was set over all. We should have been troubled to get into this town, had not Providence made way for us; for the watchmen stood ready to stop us. But a man riding just before us, the watchmen questioned him first; and perceiving he was a justice of peace, they let him pass; and we riding close after him, by that means escaped.

From this place we passed to Thomas Taylor's, formerly a captain, where we had a precious meeting. Hard by Thomas Taylor's lived a knight, who was much displeased when he heard I was likely to be released out of prison; and threatened that, "if the king set me at liberty, he would send me to prison again the next day." But though I had this meeting so near him, yet the Lord's power stopped him from meddling, and the meeting was quiet. Colonel Kirby also, who had been the chief means of my imprisonment at Lancaster and Scarbro' castles, when he heard I was set at liberty, got another order for taking me up; and said, "he would ride his horse forty miles to take me, and would give forty pounds to have me taken." A while after I came so near as to have a meeting within two miles of him; he was then struck with the gout, and kept his bed, so that it was thought he would have died.

From Thomas Taylor's I visited Friends till I came to SYNDERHILL-GREEN, where I had a large, and general meeting. The priest of the place hearing of it, sent the constable to the justices for a warrant, and they rode their horses so hard, that they almost spoiled them; but the notice they had being short, and the way long, the meeting was ended before they came. I did not hear of them till I was going out of the house, after meeting was over, and then a Friend came and told me, "they were searching another house for me, the one I was then going to." As I went along the fields towards it, I met the constables, wardens, and the justice's clerk. I passed through them, they looking at me, and went to the house they had been searching. Thus they lost their design; for the Lord's power bound them, and preserved me over them; and Friends parted, and all escaped them. The officers went away as they came; for the Lord had frustrated their design; praised be his name for ever.

After this I went into DERBYSHIRE, where I had a large meeting. Some Friends were apprehensive of the constables coming; for they had great persecution in those parts; but our meeting was quiet. A justice of peace in that county had taken away much of Friends' goods; whereupon Ellen Fretwell had made her appeal to the sessions; and the rest of the justices granted her her goods again, and spoke to the persecuting justice, that he should not do so any more. She was moved to speak and warn him; whereupon he bid her, "come and sit down on the bench." "Ay," said she, "if I may persuade you to do justice to the country, I will sit down with you." "No," said he, "then you shall not; get out of the court." As she was going out, she was moved of the Lord to turn again, and say, "she should be there, when he should not." After the sessions were ended, he went home, and drove away her brother's oxen, for going to meetings. Then Susan Frith, a Friend of Chesterfield, was moved of the Lord to tell him, that "if he continued in persecuting the innocent, the Lord would execute his plagues upon him." Soon after which he fell distracted, and died. This relation I had from Ellen Fretwell herself.

I travelled into NOTTINGHAMSHIRE, and had a large meeting at SKEGBY; from thence I went to MANSFIELD, where also I had a meeting; thence to another town, where there was a fair, at which I met with many Friends. Then passing through the forest in a very thundering and rainy day, I came to NOTTINGHAM. So great was the tempest many trees were torn up by the roots, and some people killed; but the Lord preserved us. On First-day following I had a large meeting in Nottingham, very quiet; Friends were come to sit under their teacher, the Grace of God, which brought them salvation, and were established upon the rock and foundation, Christ Jesus. After the meeting I went to visit the Friend who had been sheriff about the year 1649, whose prisoner I then was.

From Nottingham I passed into LEICESTERSHIRE and came to SILEBY, where we had a large, blessed meeting. After which I went to LEICESTER to visit the prisoners there, and then to John Penford's, where we had a general meeting, large and precious. From thence I passed, visiting Friends and my relations, till I came to WARWICK, where having visited the prisoners, I passed to BADGLEY, and had a precious meeting there. Then I travelled through NORTHAMPTONSHIRE, BEDFORDSHIRE, BUCKINGHAMSHIRE, and OXFORDSHIRE, visiting Friends in each county. In Oxfordshire the devil had laid a snare for me, but the Lord broke it; his power came over all, his blessed truth spread, and Friends were increased therein. Thus after I had passed through many counties, visiting Friends, and had many large and precious meetings amongst them, I came to LONDON. But I was weak with lying almost three years in cruel and hard imprisonments; my joints and my body were so stiff and benumbed, that I could hardly get on my horse or bend my joints; nor could I well bear to be near the fire or to eat warm meat, I had been kept so long from it. Being come to London, I walked a little among the ruins, and took good notice of them. I saw the city lying, according as the word of the Lord came to me concerning it several years before.

After I had been a time in London, and visited Friends' meetings through the city, I went into the country again, and had large meetings at KINGSTON, READING, and in WILTSHIRE, till I came to BRISTOL, where also I had many large meetings. Thomas Lower came thither out of Cornwall to meet me: and Friends were there from several parts of the nation, it being then the fair time. After I was clear of Bristol, I left that city and went to Nathaniel Crisps's; and so through the country to LONDON again, having large meetings in the way, and all quiet, blessed be the Lord. Thus, though I was very weak, yet I travelled up and down in the service of the Lord, who enabled me to go through in it.

About this time some, that had run out from truth and clashed against Friends, were reached unto by the power of the Lord, which came wonderfully over, and made them "condemn and tear their papers of controversies to pieces." Several meetings we had with them, and the Lord's everlasting power was over all, and set judgment on the head of that which had run out. In these meetings, which lasted whole days, several who had run out with John Perrot and others, came in again, and condemned that spirit which led them to "keep on their hats, when Friends prayed, and when they themselves prayed." Some of them said, "that Friends were more righteous than they," and that, "if Friends had not stood, they had been gone, and had fallen into perdition." Thus the Lord's power was wonderfully manifested, and came over all.

Then I was moved of the Lord to recommend the setting up of five monthly meetings of men and women in the city of London (besides the women's meetings and the quarterly meetings), to take care of God's glory, and to admonish and exhort such as walked disorderly or carelessly, and not according to truth. For whereas Friends had had only quarterly meetings, now truth was spread, and Friends were grown more numerous, I was moved to recommend the setting up of monthly meetings throughout the nation.* And the Lord opened to me what I must do, and how the men's and women's monthly and quarterly meetings should be ordered and established in this and in other nations; and that I should write to those where I did not come, to do the same. After things were well settled at London, and the Lord's truth, power, seed, and life reigned and shone over all in the city, I went into ESSEX. After the monthly meetings were settled in that county, I went into SUFFOLK and NORFOLK, Thomas Dry being with me. When we had visited Friends in those parts, and the monthly meetings were settled, we went into HUNTINGDONSHIRE, where we had very large and blessed gatherings; and though we met with some opposition, the Lord's power came over all, and the monthly meetings were established there also. When we came into BEDFORDSHIRE, we had great opposition; but the Lord's power came over it all. Afterwards we went into NOTTINGHAMSHIRE, where we had many precious gatherings, and the monthly meetings were settled there. Then passing into LINCOLNSHIRE we had a meeting of some men Friends of all the meetings in the county, at his house who had formerly been sheriff of Lincoln, and all was quiet. After this we passed over Trent into NOTTINGHAMSHIRE again, the ex-sheriff of Lincoln being with me, where we had some of all the meetings in that county together. Our meeting was glorious and peaceable; and many precious meetings we had in that county.

At that time William Smith was very weak and sick, and the constables and others had seized all his goods, to the very bed he lay upon, for truth's sake. These officers threatened to break up our meeting; but the Lord's power chained them, so that they had not power to meddle with us, blessed be his name. After it, I went to visit William Smith, and there were constables and others watching his corn and beasts, that none of them might be removed.†

* For some very interesting particulars respecting the setting up of Monthly and other disciplinary Meetings and their object, see *Letters of Early Friends*, p. 288–292.

† The William Smith mentioned here was originally pastor of an Independent congregation, living after the strictest manner of that people. He was convinced about the year 1658, and became a faithful labourer in the gospel. Many were turned to God by him, for he proved himself a minister of Jesus Christ, in labours, in travails, in watchings, necessities, and distresses, suffering much loss of goods and long and tedious imprisonments. For not paying tithes he was imprisoned twenty-one weeks among felons in Nottingham jail; and another time had the value of £42 taken from him, whilst he was in prison, for £7 demanded by the priest of Elton.

In the times of his frequent imprisonments, William Smith wrote several books, which were printed together in a folio volume in 1675, entitled *Balm from Gilead, &c.* When at liberty he travelled abroad strengthening the brethren, and though often visited by sickness, he was kept in patience and content, much of the power and presence of God appearing in him many times when he was in great weakness of

Thence we passed into LEICESTERSHIRE and WARWICKSHIRE, where we had many blessed meetings. The order of the gospel was set up, and the men's monthly meetings established in all those counties. Then we went into DERBYSHIRE, where we had several large and blessed meetings. In many places we were threatened by the officers, but, through the power of the Lord we escaped their hands. Leaving things well settled in Derbyshire, we travelled over the Peak hills, which were very cold (for it was then frost and snow), and came into STAFFORDSHIRE. At Thomas Hammersley's we had a general men's meeting; where things were well settled in the gospel order, and the monthly meetings established also. But I was so exceedingly weak, I was hardly able to get on or off my horse's back; but my spirit being earnestly engaged in the work the Lord had concerned me in, and sent me forth about, I travelled on therein, notwithstanding the weakness of my body, having confidence in the Lord, that he would carry me through, as he did, by his power. We came into CHESHIRE, where we had several blessed gatherings, and a general men's meeting, wherein all the monthly meetings for that county were settled, according to the gospel order, in and by the power of God. After the meeting I passed away. But when the justices heard of it, they were very much troubled, that they had not come and broken it up, and taken me; but the Lord prevented them. After I had cleared myself there in the Lord's service, I passed into LANCASHIRE, to William Barnes's, near WARRINGTON, where met some of most of the meetings in that county; and there all the monthly meetings were established in gospel order. From thence I sent papers into WESTMORLAND by Leonard Fell and Robert Widders, and also into DURHAM, CLEVELAND, NORTHUMBERLAND, CUMBERLAND, and SCOTLAND, to exhort Friends to settle the monthly meetings in the Lord's power in those places; which they did. So the Lord's power came over all, and the heirs of it came to inherit it. For the authority of our meetings, is the power of God, the gospel, which brings life and immortality to light; that all may see over the devil that hath darkened them, and that all the heirs of the gospel may walk according to the gospel, and glorify God with their bodies, souls, and spirits, which are the Lord's; for the order of the glorious gospel is not of man, nor by man. To this meeting in Lancashire, Margaret Fell, being a prisoner, got liberty to come, and went with me to Jane Milner's in CHESHIRE, where we parted. I passed into SHROPSHIRE, and from thence into WALES, and had a large general men's meeting at Charles Lloyd's, where some opposers came in, but the Lord's power brought them down.

Having gone through DENBIGHSHIRE and MONTGOMERYSHIRE we passed

body, to the admiration of beholders. During his last sickness, one evening, many Friends being in the room sitting in silence, he turned in his bed towards them, and plentifully declared of the love of God, by which they were much refreshed and tendered. He also testified of a large portion which he had in life eternal. Then he spoke to Friends "to be mindful of truth, and of their service therein, more than of their daily food; and so committed them to the grace of God." The day before he died he called his children (six or seven), and tenderly exhorted them "to keep in the fear of God, and to love the truth, and God would be a father and portion to them."

into MERIONETHSHIRE, where we had several blessed meetings; and then went to the sea-side, where we had a precious meeting. And Friends in these parts, being established on Christ, their foundation, and the monthly meetings settled in the power of God, we left Wales, and returned into Shropshire, where the Friends of the country gathering together, the monthly meetings were established there also. Then coming into WORCESTERSHIRE, after many meetings amongst Friends in that county, we had a general men's meeting at Henry Gibb's house, at PASHUR, where also the monthly meetings were settled in gospel order.

The sessions were held that day in the town, and some Friends were concerned lest they should send officers to break up our meeting; but the Lord's power restrained them, so that it was quiet; through which power we had dominion. I had several meetings amongst Friends in that county till I came to WORCESTER; and it being the fair time, we had a precious meeting there. There was then in Worcester one Major Wild, a persecuting man; and after I was gone out of town, some of his soldiers inquired after me; but having left Friends there settled in good order, we passed to DROITWICH, and thence to SHREWSBURY, where also we had a very precious meeting. The mayor hearing that I was in town, got the rest of the officers together, to consult what to do against me; for they said, "the great Quaker of England was come to town." But when they were come together, the Lord confounded their councils, so that, when some were for imprisoning me, others opposed it; and so being divided among themselves, I escaped their hands.

We went also into RADNORSHIRE, where we had many precious gatherings, and the monthly meetings were settled in the Lord's power. As we came out of that county, staying a little at a market-town, a justice's clerk and other rude fellows combined together to do us mischief on the road. They followed us out of town, and soon overtook us; but there being many market-people on the way, they were somewhat hindered from doing what they intended. Yet observing two of our company ride at some distance behind, they set upon them; and one of them drew his sword, and cut one of those two Friends, whose name was Richard Moor, Surgeon, of Shrewsbury. Meanwhile another of these rude fellows came galloping after me and the other Friend that was with me; and having to pass over a narrow bridge, in his eagerness to get before us he rode into the brook, and plunged his horse into a deep hole in the water. I saw the design, and stopped, desiring Friends to be patient, and give them no occasion. By this time Richard Moor came up to us, with the other Friend that was with him, who knew the men and their names. Then we rode on, and a little further met another man on foot much in liquor, with a naked sword in his hand. And not far beyond him we met two men and women, one of whom had his thumb cut off by the drunken man; for he, being in drink, attempted rudeness to one of the women; and this man withstanding him, and rescuing her, he drew his sword and cut off his thumb. Now this drunken man had a horse, which, being loose, followed him some way behind. I rode after it, and having caught it, brought it to the man that had his thumb cut off; and bid him take the horse to the next justice of peace, by which means they might find out, and pursue the man that had wounded him.

On this occasion I wrote to the justices, and to the judge of the assize which was then at hand; and employed some Friends to carry it to the justices first. The justice to whom the clerk belonged, rebuked his clerk and the others also, for abusing us on the highway; so that they were glad to come and entreat Friends not to appear against them at the assize; which, on their submission and acknowledgment of their fault, was granted. This was of good service in the country, for it stopped many rude people, who before had been forward to abuse Friends.

We passed into HEREFORDSHIRE, where we had several blessed gatherings; and we had a general men's meeting also, where all the monthly meetings were settled. There was about this time a proclamation against meetings; and as we came through Herefordshire, we were told of a great meeting there of the Presbyterians, who had engaged themselves to stand and give up all, rather than forsake their meetings. When they heard of this proclamation, the people came, but the priest was gone, and left them at a loss. Then they met in Leominster privately, and provided bread, cheese, and drink in readiness, that if the officers should come, they might put up their Bibles and fall to eating. The bailiff found them out, and came in among them, and said, "their bread and cheese should not cover them, he would have their speakers." They cried, "what then would become of their wives and children?" But he took their speakers and kept them a while. This the bailiff told Peter Young, and said, "they were the veriest hypocrites that ever made a profession of religion."

The like contrivance they had in other places. For there was one Pocock at London, that married Abigail Darcy, who was called a lady; and she being convinced of truth, I went to his house to see her. This Pocock had been one of the triers of the priests; and, being a high Presbyterian, and envious against us, he used to call our Friends house-creepers. He being present, she said to me, "I have something to speak to thee against my husband." "Nay," said I, "thou must not speak against thy husband." "Yes," said she, "but I must in this case. Last First-day," said she, "he and his priests and people, the Presbyterians, met; they had candles and tobacco-pipes, bread, cheese, and cold meat on the table; and they agreed beforehand, that if the officers should come in upon them, then they would leave their preaching and praying, and fall to their cold meat." "O," said I to him, "is not this a shame to you, who persecuted and imprisoned us, and spoiled our goods, because we would not join you in your religion, and called us house-creepers, that now ye do not stand to your own religion yourselves? Did ye ever find our meetings stuffed with bread and cheese and tobacco-pipes? Or did you ever read in the Scriptures of any such practice among the saints?" "Why," said the old man, "We must be as wise as serpents." I replied, "this is the serpent's wisdom indeed. But who would have thought that you Presbyterians and Independents, who persecuted and imprisoned others, spoiled their goods, and whipped such as would not follow your religion, should now flinch yourselves, and not dare to stand to your own religion, but cover it with tobacco-pipes, flagons of drink, cold meat, and bread and cheese!" But this, and such-like deceitful practices, I understood afterwards, were too common amongst them in times of persecution.

After we had travelled through Herefordshire, and meetings were well settled there, we passed into MONMOUTHSHIRE, where I had several blessed meetings; and at Walter Jenkins's, who had been a justice of the peace, we had a large gathering, where some were convinced; this meeting was quiet. But to one before this, came the bailiff of the hundred, almost drunk, pretending he was to take up the speakers. There was a mighty power of God in the meeting, so that, although he raged, the power of the Lord limited him, that he could not break it up. When it was over, I stayed a while, and he stayed also. After some time I spoke to him, and so passed quietly away. At night some rude people came, and shot off a musket against the house, but did not hurt anybody. Thus the Lord's power came over all, and chained down the unruly spirits, so that we escaped them. We came to Ross that night, and had a meeting at James Merrick's.

After this we came into GLOUCESTERSHIRE and had a general men's meeting at Nathaniel Crips's house, where all the monthly meetings were settled in the Lord's everlasting power; and the heirs of salvation were exhorted to take their possessions in the gospel, the power of God, which was and is the authority of their meetings. Many blessed gatherings we had up and down in that county, before we came to BRISTOL. And after several powerful seasons, the men's and women's meetings were settled there also.

As I was in bed at Bristol, the word of the Lord came to me, that I must go back to London. Next morning Alexander Parker and several others came to me: I asked them, "what they felt?" They in like manner asked me, "what was upon me?" I told them, "I felt I must return to London." They said, "the same was upon them." So we gave up to return to London; for whatever way the Lord moved and led us, thither we went in his power. Leaving Bristol, we passed into WILTSHIRE, and established the men's monthly meetings in the Lord's power there; and visited Friends till we came to LONDON.

After we had visited Friends in the city, I was moved to exhort them to bring all their marriages to the men's and women's meetings, that they might lay them before the faithful; that care might be taken to prevent those disorders that had been committed by some. For many had married contrary to their relations' minds; and some young, raw people that came amongst us, had mixed with the world. Widows had married without making provision for their children by their former husbands, before their second marriage. Yet I had given forth a paper concerning marriages about the year 1653, when truth was but little spread over the nation; advising Friends who might be concerned in that case, "that they might lay it before the faithful in time, before anything was concluded, and afterwards publish it in the end of a meeting, or in a market, as they were moved thereto. And when all things were found clear, they being free from all others and their relations satisfied, they might appoint a meeting on purpose for the taking of each other, in the presence of at least twelve faithful witnesses." Yet these directions not being observed, and truth being now more spread over the nation, it was therefore ordered, by the same power and Spirit of God, "that marriages should be laid before the men's monthly and quarterly meetings, or as the meetings were then established; that Friends might see that the relations of those that proceeded to marriage, were satisfied; that the parties were clear from all others; and that widows had made provision for their first husbands' children, before they married again; and what else was needful to be inquired into; that all things might be kept clean and pure, and be done in righteousness to the glory of God." Afterwards it was ordered, in the wisdom of God, "that if either of the parties, that intended to marry, came out of another nation, county, or monthly meeting, they should bring a certificate from the monthly meeting to which they belonged; for the satisfaction of the monthly meeting before which they came to lay their intentions of marriage."*

These things, with many other services for God, being set in order, and settled in the churches in the city, I passed out of London, in the leadings of the Lord's power, into HERTFORDSHIRE. After I had visited Friends, and the men's monthly meetings were settled there, I had a great meeting at BALDOCK, of many sorts of people. Then returning towards London by WALTHAM, I advised the setting up of a school there for teaching boys; and also a girls' school at SHACKLEWELL for instructing them in whatsoever things were civil and useful.†

* Some interesting documents, exhibiting the early care of the Society with regard to marriages, may be referred to in *Letters, &c., of Early Friends*, p. 259, 279, 283, &c. So early as 1659, at a meeting of Friends from four counties, an *Epistle of Counsel and Advice* was issued on this, and other subjects; recommending "that no marriage take place hastily or rashly; but in the fear of the Lord, and in presence of many witnesses, according to Scripture example; that so no scandal or blemish may be laid upon the truth, but that all may be brought to the light; that a record in writing of the day, place, and year, be kept within the meeting where a marriage occurs, of which one or both are members; under which the witnesses may set their names."

† In the establishment of the schools at Waltham and at Shacklewell, at the suggestion of George Fox, we have evidence of his desire that a useful education should be imparted to youth. It is an error to suppose the early Friends depreciated human learning, and they must be exonerated from any such charge. They exhibited in their own persons the practicability of the union of knowledge and virtue. While they were, many of them, eminent for their learning, they were distinguished for the piety of their lives. They were indeed the friends of both, but did not patronize the one to the prejudice and expulsion of the other. They always maintained (as Friends continue to do) that learning is not necessary to make a gospel minister, and here it is that many have mistaken their meaning.

Barclay, in his celebrated *Apology*, nowhere condemns the propriety, or usefulness of human learning, or denies it to be promotive of the temporal comforts of man. He says the knowledge of Latin, Greek, and Hebrew, or of Logic and Philosophy, of Ethics or of Physics and Metaphysics, is not necessary. But mark his meaning. Not necessary to make a minister of the gospel. But where does he say that knowledge, which he himself possessed to such a considerable extent, was not necessary; or that it did not contribute to the innocent pleasures of life? What would have been the character of his own book, or what would have been its comparative value and usefulness, had he not been able to quote so many authors to his purpose in their

After I had had several precious meetings in the country, I came to LONDON again, where I stayed a while in the work and service of the Lord; and then went into BUCKINGHAMSHIRE, where I had many precious meetings. At John Brown's, of WESTON near Aylesbury, some of the men Friends of each meeting being gathered together, the men's monthly meetings for that county were established, in the order of the gospel, the power of God; and the power of the Lord confirmed it in all that felt it, and they came thereby to see and feel, that the power of God was the authority of their meetings. Then after the monthly meeting was settled there in the order of the gospel, and upon the foundation of Christ Jesus, I went to Nathaniel Ball's, at NORTH NEWTON near BANBURY, in Oxfordshire, who was a Friend in the ministry. And there being a general meeting, where some from all the meetings were present, the monthly meetings for that county were then settled in the power of God; and Friends were very glad of them; for they came into their services in the church, to take care for God's glory. After this meeting, we passed into GLOUCESTERSHIRE, visiting Friends till we came into MONMOUTHSHIRE, to Richard Hambery's; where meeting with some from all the meetings of that county, the monthly meetings were settled there also in the Lord's power, that all might take care of God's glory, and admonish and exhort such as did not walk as became the gospel. And indeed these meetings made a great reforma-

original texts, or to have detected so many classical errors, introduced such apposite history, or to have drawn up his propositions with so much logical and mathematical clearness and precision; or if he had not been among the first literary characters of his day?

William Penn was equally celebrated with Barclay as a scholar. His works afford abundant proof of his erudition, and of the high cultivation of his mind. Like the rest of his associates, he was no advocate for learning as a qualification for a minister of the gospel; but he was yet a friend to it, on the principle that it enlarged the understanding, and that it added to the innocent pleasures of the mind. He entreated his wife, in the beautiful letter he left her before he embarked on his first voyage to America, "not to be sparing of expense in procuring learning for his children; for that by such parsimony all was lost that was saved." And he recommended also, in the same letter, a mathematical and philosophical education.

Penn's Secretary, James Logan, was also a patron of learning among the early Friends. He was a correspondent of Sir Hans Sloane and other literati of Europe, a contributor to the Philosophical Transactions, and bequeathed his library, of 3000 vols. on arts and sciences in various languages, to the city of Philadelphia, with an endowment to preserve it for public use.

Thomas Ellwood, the companion of Milton, was so sensible of the disadvantages arising from a want of knowledge, that he revived his learning with great industry after he had become a Friend. "I mentioned before," says he in his Journal, "that when I was a boy I made some progress in learning, and that I lost it all again before I came to be a man. Nor was I rightly sensible of my loss therein, till I came amongst Friends. But there I both saw my loss and lamented it, and applied myself with the utmost diligence at all leisure times to recover it. So false I found that charge to be, which in those times was cast as a reproach on the Society, that they despised and decried all human learning, because they denied it to be essentially necessary to a gospel ministry, which was one of the controversies of those times." Ellwood's friend, Isaac Pennington, assisted him in this matter, and through his influence with Dr. Paget. procured him the means of improvement in becoming a reader to Milton.

tion amongst people, insomuch that the justices took notice of their usefulness.

Richard Hambery and his wife accompanied us a day's journey visiting Friends, till we came to a widow's house, where we staid that night. Thence we passed over the hills next day, visiting Friends and declaring truth to the people, till we came to another widow's, where we had a meeting. She could not speak English, yet she praised the Lord for sending us to visit them.

We travelled till we came to SWANSEA, where on the First-day we had a large and precious meeting, the Lord's presence being eminently amongst us. On a week day afterwards we had a general meeting beyond Swansea, of men Friends from Swansea, Tenby, Haverfordwest, and other places; and there the monthly meetings were settled in gospel order, and received by Friends in the power of the Lord; and the Lord's truth was over all.

From hence we endeavoured to go by water into Cornwall, and returned through Swansea to MUMBLES, thinking to get passage there, but the captain deceived us; for though he had promised to carry us, yet when we came he would not. We went to another place where there was a passage-boat, into which we got our horses; but some rude men in the boat (though called gentlemen) threatened to pistol the master, if he took us in, who, being afraid of them, turned our horses out again; which put us out of hopes of getting over that way. Wherefore turning back into the country, we stayed up all night, and about two in the morning took horse, and travelled till we came near CARDIFF, where we stayed one night. The next day we came to NEWPORT; and it being market-day there, several Friends came to us, with whom we sat a while; and after a refreshing season together, we parted from them, and went on our way.

Beyond this market-town we overtook a man, who lingered on the way, as if he stayed for somebody; but when we came up to him, he rode along with us, and asked us many questions. At length meeting with two others, who seemed to be pages to some great persons, he made acquaintance with them, and I heard him tell them he would stop us, and take us up. We rode on; being in our way; and when he came to us, and would have stopped us, I told him, "none ought to stop us on the king's highway, for it was as free for us as for them; and I was moved to exhort him to fear the Lord. Then he galloped away before us; and I perceived his intent was to stop us at SHIPTON in Wales, which was a garrison town, through which we were to pass. When we were come to Shipton, John-ap-John being with me, we walked down the hill into the town, leading our horses. It being the market-day there, several Friends met us, and would have had us to an inn. But we were not to go into any inn; so we walked directly through the town over the bridge, and then we were out of the limits of that town. Thus the Lord's everlasting arm and power preserved us, and carried us on in his work and service.

The next First-day we had a large meeting in the FOREST OF DEAN; and all was quiet. Next day we passed over the water to OLDSTONE; where, after we had visited Friends, we came again to William Yeoman's house, at IRB'S COURT in Somersetshire. From thence we went to a meeting at

PORTSHEAD, whither several Friends from Bristol came to us. After this we went further up into the country, and had several large meetings; and the Lord's living presence was with us, supporting and refreshing us in our labour and travel in his service.

We came to a place near MINEHEAD, where we had a general meeting of the men Friends in Somersetshire. There came also a cheat, whom some friendly people would have had me to take along with me. I saw he was a cheat; and therefore bid them bring him to me, and see whether he could look me in the face. Some were ready to think I was too hard towards him, because I would not let him go along with me; but when they brought him to me, he was not able to look me in the face, but looked hither and thither; for he was indeed a cheat, and had cheated a priest by pretending to be a minister; he had got the priest's suit and went away with it.

After the meeting we passed to MINEHEAD, where we tarried. In the night I had an exercise upon me, from a sense of a dark spirit, working and striving to get up to disturb the church of Christ. Next morning I was moved to write a few lines to Friends as a warning thereof, as follows:—

"DEAR FRIENDS,

"Live in the power of the Lord God, in his Seed that is set over all, and is over all trials that you may have with the dark spirit, which would be owned in its actings, and thrust itself amongst you; which is not come as yet: but in the power of the Lord God, and his Seed, keep over it, and bring it to condemnation. For I felt a kind of dark spirit thrusting itself up towards you, and heaving up last night; but you may keep it down with the power of God, that the witness may arise to condemn its actings, so far as it hath spread its dark works, before it have any admittance. So no more, but my love in the Seed of God, which changeth not." G. F.

Minehead in Somersetshire, 22d of 4th Month, 1668.

Next day several Friends of Minehead accompanied us as far as BARNSTAPLE and APPLEDON in DEVONSHIRE, where we had a meeting. Barnstaple had been a bloody, persecuting town. There were two men Friends of that place, who had been a great while at sea; and coming home to visit their relations, one of them having a wife and children, the mayor of the town sent for them, under pretence to converse with them; and he put the oaths of allegiance and supremacy to them. Because they could not swear, he sent them to Exeter jail, where Judge Archer premunired them, and kept them till one of them died in prison. When I heard of this, I was moved to write a letter to Judge Archer, and another to the mayor of Barnstaple, laying their wicked and unchristian actions upon their heads, and letting them know, "that the blood of that man would be required at their hands."

After a precious meeting at Appledon among some faithful Friends there, we passed to STRATTON, and stayed at an inn all night. Next day we rode to Humphrey Lower's, where we had a very precious meeting; and next day to TRURO; visiting Friends till we came to the LAND'S-END. Then coming up by the south part of that county, we visited Friends till we came to TREGANGEEVES, where at Loveday Hambley's we had a general meeting for all the county; in which the monthly meetings were settled in the Lord's power, and in the blessed order of the gospel; that all who were faithful might admonish and exhort such as walked not according to the gospel; that so the house of God might be kept clean, and righteousness might run down, and all unrighteousness be swept away. Several that had run out, were brought to condemn what they had done amiss; and through repentance came in again.

Being clear of the county of CORNWALL, we came into DEVONSHIRE, and had a meeting amongst Friends at PLYMOUTH. Whence passing to Richard Brown's, we came to the widow Phillips's, where we had some men Friends from all the meetings together; and there the men's monthly meetings were settled in the heavenly order of the gospel, the power of God; which answered the witness of God in all. There was a great noise of a troop of horse coming to disturb our meeting; but the Lord's power prevented it, and preserved us in peace and safety.

After things were well settled, and the meeting over, we came to KING'S-BRIDGE, and visited Friends there. Then leaving Friends in those parts well settled in the power of God, we passed to TOPSHAM, and MEMBURY, visiting Friends, and having many meetings in the way, till we came to ILCHESTER in SOMERSETSHIRE. Here we had a general men's meeting, and therein settled the men's monthly meetings for that county in the Lord's everlasting power; and Friends being refreshed and comforted in the Lord's power, and established upon Christ, their rock and foundation, we passed to PUDDIMOOR; where, at William Beaton's, we had a blessed meeting, and all was quiet; though the constables had threatened before.

When we had visited most of the meetings in Somersetshire, we passed into DORSETSHIRE to George Harris's house, where we had a large men's meeting. There all the men's monthly meetings for that county were settled in the glorious order of the gospel, that all in the power of God might "seek that which was lost, and bring again that which was driven away; cherish the good, and reprove the evil."

Then we came to SOUTHAMPTON, where we had a large meeting on First-day. Thence we went to Captain Reeves's, where the general men's meeting for Hampshire was appointed; to which some of all the county came, and a blessed time we had. There the men's monthly meetings for that county were settled in the order of the gospel, which had brought life and immortality to light in them. But there came a rude company of Ranters, who had opposed and disturbed our meetings much. One of the women had lain with a man, who declared it at the market-cross, and gloried in his wickedness. A company of these lewd people lived together at a house hard by the place where our meeting was. I went to it, and told them of their wickedness. The man of the house said, "Why! did I make so strange of that?" Another of them said, "It was to stumble me." I told them, "their wickedness should not stumble me, for I was above it." And I was moved of the Lord to tell them, "that the plagues and judgments of God would overtake them, and come upon them." Afterwards they went up and down the country, till at last they were cast into Winchester jail, where the man that had lain with the woman stabbed the jailer, but not mortally. And after they were let out of jail, this fellow that had stabbed the jailer hung himself; the woman also had like to have cut a child's throat, as we were informed. These people had formerly lived about London; and when the city was fired, they prophesied, "that all the rest of London should be burnt within fourteen days," and hastened out of town. Though they were Ranters, great opposers of Friends, and disturbers of our meetings, yet in the country where they came, some people that did not know them, would be apt to say they were Quakers. Wherefore I was moved of the Lord to write a paper, to be dispersed among the magistrates and people of Hampshire, to clear Friends and truth of these lewd people and their wicked actions.

After the men's monthly meetings in those parts were settled, and the Lord's blessed power was over all, we went to a town where we had a meeting with Friends. Thence we came to FARNHAM, where we met many Friends, it being the market-day. We had many precious meetings up and down that country. Friends in those parts had formerly been plundered, and their goods much spoiled, both for tithes, and for going to meetings; but the Lord's power at this time preserved both them and us from falling into the persecutor's hands.

We passed thence, and had a general men's meeting at a Friend's house in SURREY, who had been plundered so extremely, that he had scarcely a cow, horse, or swine, left. The constables threatened to come and break up our meeting, but the Lord restrained them. At this meeting the men's monthly meetings were settled in the authority of the heavenly power. After we had visited Friends in that county, and had many large and precious gatherings, we passed to a Friend's house in SUSSEX, where the general meeting for the men Friends of that county was appointed to be held; and thither came several Friends from London to visit us. We had a blessed meeting; and the men's monthly meetings for that county were then settled in the Lord's eternal power. There were at that time great threatenings of disturbance; but the meeting was quiet. We had several large meetings in that county, though Friends were then in great sufferings there, and many in prison. I was sent for to visit a Friend that was sick, and went to see those that were prisoners. There was danger of my being apprehended; but I went in the faith of God's power, and thereby the Lord preserved me in safety.

Having visited Friends through the country, we passed into KENT, where, after we had been at several meetings, we had a general meeting for the men Friends of that county. There also the men's monthly meetings for that county were settled in the power of God, and established in the order of the gospel, for all the heirs of it to enter into their services, and care in the church for the glory of God. Friends rejoiced in the order of the gospel, and were glad of the settlement thereof, which is not of man nor by man. After this I visited Friends in their meetings in KENT; and when I had cleared myself of the Lord's service in that county, I came up to LONDON.

Thus were the men's monthly meetings settled through the nation; for I had been in Berkshire before, where most of the ancient Friends of that county were in prison; and when I had informed them of the service of these monthly meetings, they were settled amongst them also. The quarterly meetings were generally settled before. I wrote also into Ireland by faithful Friends, and into Scotland, Holland, Barbadoes, and several parts of America, advising Friends to settle their men's monthly meetings in those countries. For they had their general quarterly meetings before; but now that truth was increased amongst them, they should settle those men's monthly meetings in the power and Spirit of God, that first convinced them. Since these meetings have been settled, and all the faithful in the power of God, who are heirs of the gospel, have met together in the power of God, which is the authority of them, to perform service to the Lord therein, many mouths have been opened in thanksgivings and praise, and many have blessed the Lord God, that ever he sent me forth in this service; yea, with tears have many praised the Lord. For now all coming to have a concern and care for God's honour and glory, that his name be not blasphemed, which they profess; and to see that all who profess the truth, walk in the truth, in righteousness, and in holiness, which becomes the house of God, and that all order their conversation aright, that they may see the salvation of God; all having this care upon them for God's glory, and being exercised in his holy Power and Spirit, in the order of the heavenly life and gospel of Jesus, they may all see and know, possess and partake of, the government of Christ, of the increase of which there is to be no end. Thus the Lord's everlasting renown and praise are set up in every one's heart that is faithful; so that we can say, the gospel order established amongst us, is not of man, nor by man, but of and by Jesus Christ, in and through the Holy Ghost. This order of the gospel, which is not of man, nor by man, but from Christ, the heavenly man, is above all the orders of men in the fall, whether Jews, Gentiles, or apostatized Christians, and will remain when they are gone. For the power of God, which is the everlasting gospel, was before the devil was, and will be and remain for ever. And as the everlasting gospel was preached in the apostles' days to all nations, that all nations might come into the order of it, through the divine power, which brings life and immortality to light, that they who are heirs of it, might inherit the power and authority of it; so now, since all nations have drunk the whore's cup, and all the world hath worshipped the beast (but they whose names are written in the book of life from the foundation of the world, who have worshipped God in spirit and in truth, as Christ commanded), the everlasting gospel is to be, and is, preached again, as John the divine foresaw it should, to all nations, kindreds, tongues, and people. This everlasting gospel torments the whore, and makes her and the beast to rage, even the beast that hath power over the tongues, which are called the original, to order them, by which they make divines, as they call them. But all that receive the gospel, the power of God, which brings life and immortality to light, come to see over the beast, devil, whore, and false prophet, that darkened them and all their worships and orders, and come to be heirs of the gospel, the power of God, which was before the beast, whore, false prophet, and devil were, and will be, when they are all gone and cast into the lake of fire. And they that are heirs of this power and of this gospel, inherit the power which is the authority of this order, and of our meetings. These come to possess the joyful order of the joyful gospel, the comfortable order of the comfortable gospel, the glorious order of the glorious gospel, and the everlasting order of the everlasting gospel, the power of God, which will last for ever, and will out-last all the orders of the devil, and that which is of men or by men. These shall see the government of Christ, who hath all power in heaven and earth given to him; and of the increase of his glorious, righteous, holy, just government, there is no end; but his government and his order will remain; for he who is the author of it, is the first and the last, the beginning and ending, the foundation of God, which over all stands sure, Christ Jesus, the Amen.

Being returned to LONDON, I stayed some time there, visiting Friends' meetings in and about the city. While I was in London, I went one day to visit Esquire Marsh, who had showed much kindness both to me and to Friends; I happened to go when he was at dinner. He no sooner heard my name, than he sent for me up, and would have had me sit down with him to dinner; but I had not freedom to do so. Several great persons were at dinner with him; and he said to one of them who was a great Papist, "Here is a Quaker, whom you have not seen before." The Papist asked me, "whether I owned the christening of children?" I told him, "there was no Scripture for any such practice." "What," said he, "not for christening children?" I said, "nay." I told him, "the one baptism by the one Spirit into one body we owned; but to throw a little water on a child's face, and say that was baptizing and christening it, there was no Scripture for that." Then he asked me, "whether I owned the Catholic faith?" I said, "yes," but added, that "neither the Pope nor the Papists were in that Catholic faith; for the true faith works by love, and purifies the heart, and if they were in that faith that gives victory, by which they might have access to God, they would not tell the people of a purgatory after they were dead." So I undertook to prove that "neither Pope nor Papists that held a purgatory hereafter, were in the true faith; for the true, precious, divine faith, which Christ is the author of, gives victory over the devil and sin, that had separated man and woman from God. And if they, the Papists, were in the true faith, they would never use racks, prisons, and fines, to persecute and force others to their religion, that were not of their faith. This was not the practice of the apostles and primitive Christians, who witnessed and enjoyed the true faith of Christ; but it was the practice of the faithless Jews and Heathens so to do. But," said I, "seeing thou art a great and leading man among the Papists, and hast been taught and bred up under the Pope, and seeing thou sayest, 'there is no salvation but in your church,' I desire to know of thee, what it is that doth bring salvation in your church?" He answered, "a good life." "And nothing else," said I. "Yes," he said, "good works." "And is this it that brings salvation in your church, a good life and good works? Is this your doctrine and principle?" said I. "Yes," said he. "Then," said I, "neither thou, nor the Pope, nor any of the Papists know what it is that brings salvation." Then he asked me, what brought salvation in our church? I told him, "that which brought salvation to the church in the apostles' days, the same brought salvation to us, and not another; namely, 'the Grace of God, which, the Scripture says, brings salvation, and hath appeared to all men, which taught the saints then, and teaches us now. This Grace which brings salvation, teaches to deny ungodliness and worldly lusts, and to live soberly, righteously, and godly. So it is not the good works nor the good life that brings salvation, but the Grace?" "What!" said the Papist, "doth this Grace that brings salvation, appear unto all men?" "Yes," said I. "Then," said he, "I deny that." I replied, "all that deny that, are sect-makers, and are not in the universal faith, grace, and truth, which the apostles were in."

Then he spoke to me about the mother-church. I told him, "the several sects in Christendom had accused us, and said, 'we forsook our mother-church.' The Papists charged us with forsaking their church, saying, 'Rome was the only mother-church.' The Episcopalians taxed us with forsaking the old Protestant religion, alleging, 'theirs was the reformed mother-church.' The Presbyterians and Independents blamed us for leaving them, each of them pretending, 'theirs was the right reformed church.'" But, I said, "if we could own any outward city or place to be the mother-church, we should own Jerusalem, where the gospel was first preached by Christ himself and his apostles, where Christ suffered, where the great conversion to Christianity by Peter was, where the types, figures, and shadows, which Christ ended, and where Christ commanded his disciples to 'wait until they were endued with power from on high.' If any outward place deserved to be called the mother, that was the place where the first great conversion to Christianity was. But the apostle saith, Gal. iv. 25–27, 'Jerusalem, which now is, is in bondage with her children; but Jerusalem which is above, is free, which is the mother of us all. For it is written, Rejoice, thou barren, that bearest not; break forth and cry, thou that travailest not; for the desolate hath many more children than she which hath an husband.' The apostle does not say, outward Jerusalem was the mother, though the first and great conversion to Christianity was there. And there is less reason for the title [mother] to be given to Rome, or to any other outward place or city, by the children of Jerusalem, that is above and free; neither are they Jerusalem's children that is above and free, who give the title of mother either to outward Jerusalem, to Rome, or to any other place or sect of people. And though this title [mother] hath been given to places and sects amongst and by the degenerate Christians, yet still we say, as the apostle said of old, 'Jerusalem that is above, is the mother of us all.' And we can own no other, neither outward Jerusalem nor Rome, nor any sect of people for our mother, but Jerusalem which is above, which is free, the mother of all that are born again, and are become true believers in the light, grafted in Christ, the heavenly Vine. For all who are born again of the immortal Seed, by the Word of God, which lives and abides for ever, feed upon the milk of the Word, the breast of life, and grow by it in life, and cannot acknowledge any other to be their mother but Jerusalem which is above." "O," said Esquire Marsh to the Papist, "You do not know this man, if he would but come to church now and then, he would be a brave man."

After some other discourse, I went aside with Justice Marsh into another room, to speak with him concerning Friends; for he was a justice of peace for Middlesex, and being a courtier, the other justices put much of the management of affairs upon him. He told me "he was in a strait how to act between us and some other Dissenters. For," said he, "you cannot swear, and the Independents, Baptists, and Fifth-monarchy people say also they cannot swear; therefore," said he, "how shall I know how to distinguish betwixt you and them, seeing they and you all say it is for conscience' sake that you cannot swear?" I answered, "I will show thee how to distinguish. They, or most of them, thou speakest of, can and do swear in some cases, but we cannot swear in any case. If a man should steal their cows or horses, and thou shouldst ask them whether they would swear they were theirs; many of them would readily do it. But if thou try our Friends, they cannot swear for their own goods. Therefore, when thou puttest the oath of allegiance to any of them, ask them, 'whether they can swear in any other case, as for their cow or horse; which, if they be really of us, they cannot do, though they can bear witness to the truth.'" Hereupon I gave him a relation of a trial in Berkshire, which was thus: A thief stole two beasts from a Friend of ours, the thief was taken and cast into prison, and the Friend appeared against him at the assizes. But somebody having informed the judge, that the prosecutor was a Quaker, and could not swear, the judge, before he heard what the Friend could say, said, "Is he a Quaker? and will he not swear? Then tender him the oaths of allegiance and supremacy." So he cast the Friend into prison, and premunired him, and set the thief at liberty that had stolen his goods. Justice Marsh, said, "that judge was a wicked man." "But," said I, "if we could swear in any case, we would take the oath of allegiance to the king, who is to preserve the laws that are to support every man in his estate. Whereas others, that can swear in some cases to preserve a part of their estates, if they be robbed, will not take this oath to the king, who is to preserve them in their whole estates and bodies also. So that thou mayest easily distinguish, and put a difference between us and those people. Justice Marsh was afterwards very serviceable to Friends in this and other cases; for he kept several, both Friends and others, from being premunired. When Friends were brought before him in time of persecution, he set many of them at liberty; and when he could not avoid sending to prison, he sent some for a few hours, or for a night. At length he went to the king, and told him, "he had sent some of us to prison contrary to his conscience, and he could not do so any more." Wherefore he removed his family from Limehouse, where he lived, and took lodgings near St. James's Park. He told the king that "if he would be pleased to give liberty of conscience, that would quiet and settle all; for then none could have any pretence to be uneasy." And indeed he was a very serviceable man to truth and Friends in his day.

We had great service at London this year; the Lord's truth came over all, and many that had gone out from truth came in again, confessing and condemning their outgoings. After I had stayed some time in London, I visited Friends in SURREY and SUSSEX, and in other places that way, and afterwards travelled northward, having Leonard Fell with me. We visited Friends till we came to WARWICK, where many were in prison; and we had a meeting in the town. I passed thence to BIRMINGHAM and BADGLEY. At BADGLEY I had a large meeting; after which I came to NOTTINGHAM, where on First-day we had a precious meeting, but not without danger of being apprehended, the constables having threatened to take up Friends.

I passed thence, visiting Friends, till I came to BALBY, and so to YORK, to the quarterly meeting; and a blessed time we had. Friends in Yorkshire had seven monthly meetings before; and they were so sensible of the service of them, that they desired to have seven more added to them, for truth was much spread in that county. So they were established; and now they have fourteen monthly meetings in that county.*

It being the assizes at York, I met with Justice Hotham, a well-wisher to Friends, who had been tender, and very kind to me from the first.

After I had finished my service for the Lord in York, I passed into the country. As I went a great burthen fell upon me, but I did not presently know the reason of it. I came to a meeting on First-day at Richard Shipton's, which was very large, but there being one the same day at another place also, the priest of that place, being misinformed that I was to be there, got a warrant, and made great disturbance at that meeting; of which Isaac Lindley, who was there, gave me an account in the following letter:—

"G. F.

"When thou went from York, the First-day after thou wast at Richard Shipton's, that day I had appointed a meeting ten miles from York, where there had not been one before. But the priest and the constable got a warrant on the seventh day, and put thy name only in the warrant, for they had heard that thou wast to be there. They came with weapons and staves, and cried, 'Where is Mr. Fox?' over and over; many Friends being there, they concluded thou wast among them. But those raveners, being disappointed, plucked me down and abused me, and beat some Friends, and then took me before a magistrate, but he set me at liberty."

ISAAC LINDLEY.

Then I visited Friends at WHITBY and SCARBRO'. When at Scarbro', the governor hearing I was come, sent to invite me to his house, saying, "surely I would not be so unkind as not to come and see him and his

* The fourteen monthly meetings mentioned above as settled in Yorkshire so early as 1669, were York, Balby, Pontefract, Brighouse, Knaresbro', Settle, Malton, Thirsk, Richmond, Gisbro', Scarbro', Kelke, Oustwick, and Elloughton.

wife." After the meeting I went up to visit him, and he received me very courteously and lovingly.

Having visited most of the meetings in Yorkshire, the Wolds, and Holderness, I came to Henry Jackson's, where I had a great meeting. Thence to Thomas Taylor's, and so to John Moor's at Eldreth, where we had a very large meeting; the Lord's power and presence were eminently amongst us. Not far from this place lay Colonel Kirby, lame of the gout, who had threatened that "if ever I came near, he would send me to prison again; and had bid forty pounds to any man that could take me;" as I was credibly informed.

After this I came into Staffordshire, and Cheshire, where we had many large and precious meetings. I had a very large one at William Barnes's house, about two miles from Warrington; and though Colonel Kirby was out again, as violent in breaking up meetings as before, and was then at Warrington, the Lord did not suffer him to come to this meeting; and so we were preserved out of his hands.

CHAPTER III.

1669-1671.—George Fox sails for Ireland in company with several other Friends—he there sends a challenge to the Popish priests to try their God, which is not accepted—he contrasts them with Baal's priests—the authorities of Cork threaten him, and issue warrants for his apprehension—he rides publicly through the city, and is seen by the mayor but not molested—writes to Friends in the ministry there—discourses with professors on election and reprobation—returns to England—a report is spread that George Fox is turned Presbyterian, through a trick to obtain a congregation for John Fox, the Presbyterian, which however turns to the advantage of Friends—George Fox is married to Margaret Fell at Bristol—writes to the quarterly meetings about putting children apprentices—Margaret Fox is cast into prison—two of her daughters go to the king, and obtain a promise of their mother's liberty—on the passing of the Conventicle Act, George Fox writes a declaration against seditious conventicles—writes to Friends to strengthen them in their trials—is apprehended at a meeting at Gracechurch Street—taken before the mayor, who discourses with him and sets him at liberty—visits Friends in Reading jail—undergoes great travail of spirit, loses his sight and hearing, and becomes as a sign—persecution becoming hot, some meeting-houses are pulled down, and Friends are much abused—George Fox endures great mental conflict—the faithfulness of Friends is said by some professors to have preserved the nation from debauchery—George Fox writes an encouraging letter to Friends—as persecution abates he recovers—writes a warning to the rulers of the nation—recommends certain regulations respecting marriage—writes a prayer.

Now was I moved of the Lord to go over into IRELAND, to visit the seed of God in that nation. There went with me Robert Lodge, James Lancaster, Thomas Briggs, and John Stubbs. We waited near Liverpool for shipping and wind. After waiting some days, we sent James Lancaster to take passage, which he did, and brought word the ship was ready, and would take us in at Black Rock. We went thither on foot; and it being some distance, and the weather very hot, I was much spent with walking. When we arrived, the ship was not there; so we were obliged to go to the town, and take shipping. When we were on board, I said to the rest of my company, "Come, ye will triumph in the Lord, for we shall have fair wind and weather." Many passengers in the ship were sick, but not one of our company. The captain and many of the passengers were very loving; and we being at sea on the first day of the week, I was moved to declare truth among them; whereupon the captain said to the passengers, "Here are things that you never heard in your lives." When we came before DUBLIN, we took boat and went ashore; and the earth and air smelt, methought, of the corruption of the nation, so that it yielded another smell to me than England did; which I imputed to the Popish massacres that had been committed, and the blood that had been spilt in it, from which a foulness ascended. We passed through among the officers of the custom four times, yet they did not search us; for they perceived what we were: some of them were so envious they did not care to look at us. We did not soon find Friends; but went to an inn, and sent out to inquire for some; who when they came to us were exceedingly glad of our coming, and received us with great joy. We stayed there the weekly meeting, which was a large one, and the power and life of God appeared greatly in it. Afterwards we passed to a province meeting, which lasted two days, there being one about the poor, and another meeting more general; in which a mighty power of the Lord appeared. Truth was livingly declared, and Friends were much refreshed therein.

Passing thence about four and twenty miles, we came to another place, where we had a very good refreshing meeting; but after it, some Papists that were there were angry, and raged very much. When I heard of it, I sent for one of them, who was a schoolmaster; but he would not come. Whereupon I sent a challenge to him, with all the friars and monks, priests and Jesuits, to come forth, and "try their God and their Christ, which they had made of bread and wine," but no answer could I get from them. Wherefore I told them, "they were worse than the priests of Baal; for Baal's priests tried their wooden god, but these durst not try their god of bread and wine; and Baal's priests and people did not eat their god as these did, and then make another."

We went to New Garden, where there was a great meeting. Thence we travelled on among Friends, till we came to Bandon Bridge and the Land's End, having many meetings as we went, in which the mighty power of the Lord was manifested, Friends were well refreshed, and many people were affected with the truth. At Bandon, the mayor's wife being herself convinced, desired her husband to come to the meeting; but he bid her, for her life, not to make known that I was at a meeting there.

He that was then mayor of Cork was very envious against truth and Friends, and had many Friends in prison; and knowing that I was in the country, he had issued four warrants to take me; wherefore Friends were desirous that I might not ride through Cork. But being at Bandon, there appeared to me, in a vision, "a very ugly visaged man, of a black and dark look: my spirit struck at him in the power of God; and it seemed to me, that I rode over him with my horse, and my horse set his foot on the side of his face." When I came down in the morning, I told a friend that was with me, that the command of the Lord was to me to ride through Cork; but bid him tell no man. So we took horse, many Friends being with me; and when we came near the town, they would have showed me a way on the backside of the town; but I told them, my way was through the streets. Wherefore taking one of them along with me, whose name was Paul Morrice, to guide me through the town, I rode on; and as we rode through the market-place, and by the mayor's door, he seeing me ride by, said, "there goes George Fox;" but he had not power to stop me. When we had passed through the sentinels, and were come over the bridge, we went to a Friend's house and alighted. There the Friends told me what a rage was in the town, and how many warrants were granted to take me. While I was sitting there with Friends, I felt the evil spirit at work in the town, stirring up mischief against me; and I felt the power of the Lord strike at that evil spirit. By and by some other Friends coming in, told me, that it was over the town, and amongst the magistrates, that I was in the town. I said, "let the devil do his worst." After a while, that Friends were refreshed one in another, and we travellers had refreshed ourselves, I called for my horse, and having a Friend to guide me, we went on our way. But great was the rage, that the mayor and others of Cork were in, that they had missed me; and great pains they afterwards took to take me, having their scouts abroad upon the roads, as I understood, to observe which way I went. Afterwards there was scarcely a public meeting I came to, but spies came to watch if I were there. And the envious magistrates and priests sent informations one to another concerning me, describing me by my hair, hat, clothes, and horse, so that when I was near a hundred miles from Cork, they had an account concerning me, and description of me, before I came amongst them. One very envious magistrate, who was both a priest and a justice, got a warrant from the judge of the assize to apprehend me; which warrant was to go over all his circuit, which reached near a hundred miles. Yet the Lord disappointed all their counsels, and defeated all their designs against me; by his good hand of Providence preserved me out of all their snares, and gave us many sweet and blessed opportunities to visit Friends, and spread truth through that nation. For meetings were very large, Friends coming to them far and near; and other people flocking in. The powerful presence of the Lord was preciously felt with and amongst us; whereby many of the world were reached, convinced, and gathered to the truth; the Lord's flock was increased, and Friends were greatly refreshed and comforted in feeling the love of God. O, the brokenness that was amongst them in the flowings of life! So that, in the power and Spirit of the Lord, many together broke out into singing, even with audible voices, making melody in their hearts.

At which time I was moved to declare to Friends in the ministry, as follows:—

"SOUND, sound abroad, ye faithful servants of the Lord, and witnesses in his name, ye prophets of the Highest, and angels of the Lord! Sound ye all abroad in the world, to the awakening and raising of the dead, that they may be awakened, and raised up out of the grave, to hear the voice that is living. For the dead have long heard the dead, the blind have long wandered among the blind, and the deaf amongst the deaf. Therefore sound, ye servants, prophets, and angels of the Lord, ye trumpets of the Lord, that you may awaken the dead, and them that are asleep in their graves of sin, death and hell, sea and earth, and who lie in the tombs. Sound abroad, ye trumpets, and raise up the dead, that they may hear the voice of the Son of God, of the second Adam that never fell; the voice of the Light and of the Life; the voice of the Power, and the voice of the Truth; the voice of the Righteous, and of the Just. Sound ye the trumpets, the melodious sound abroad, that all the deaf ears may be opened to hear the pleasant sound of the trumpet to judgment and life, to condemnation and light. Sound your trumpets all abroad, ye angels of the Lord, sons and daughters, prophets of the Highest, that all who are dead and asleep in the graves—who have been long dreaming and slumbering, may be awakened, and hear the voice of the Lamb;—that all who have long heard the voice of the beast, may now hear the voice of the Bridegroom and of the Bride;—that they may now hear the voice of the great Prophet and King—the Shepherd and Bishop of their souls. Sound, sound it all abroad, ye trumpets, among the dead in Adam; for Christ is come, the second Adam, that they might have life, yea have it abundantly. Awaken the dead, awaken the slumberers, the dreamers, them that are asleep, awaken them out of their graves, out of their tombs, out of their sepulchres, out of the seas! Sound abroad, ye trumpets that awaken the dead, that they may all hear the sound of it in the graves, and they that hear may live, and come to the Life, that is, the Son of God. He is risen from the dead; the grave could not hold nor contain him, neither could all the watchers of the earth, with all their guards, keep him therein. Sound, ye trumpets of the Lord, to all the seekers of the living among the dead, that he is risen from the dead; to all the seekers of the living among the dead, and in the graves that the watchers keep; he is not in the grave, he is risen; there is that under the grave of the watchers of the outward grave, which must be awakened and come to hear His voice, who is risen from the dead, that they may come to live. Therefore sound abroad, ye trumpets of the Lord, that the grave may give up her dead, and hell and the sea give up their dead; that all may come forth to judgment, to the judgment of the Lord before his throne, and have their sentence and reward according to their works." G. F.

To James Hutchinson's in Ireland came many great persons, desiring to discourse with me about election and reprobation. I told them, "though they judged our principle foolish, it was too high for them, they could not with their wisdom comprehend it; therefore I would discourse with them according to their capacities. You say (said I), that God hath ordained the greatest part of men for hell, and that they were ordained so before the world began; for which your proof is in Jude. You say Esau was reprobated, and the Egyptians, and the stock of Ham. But Christ saith to his disciples, 'Go, teach *all* nations,' and 'go into all nations and preach the gospel of life and salvation.' Now, if they were to go to *all* nations, were they not to go to Ham's stock and Esau's stock? Did not Christ die for *all?* then for the stock of Ham, of Esau, and the Egyptians. Doth not the Scripture say, 'God would have *all* men to be saved?' Mark, *all* men, then the stock of Esau and of Ham also. Doth not God say, 'Egypt, my people?' and that he would have an altar in Egypt? Isa. xix. Were there not many Christians formerly in Egypt? And doth not history say, that the Bishop of Alexandria would formerly have been Pope? And had not God a church in Babylon? I confess, 'the word came to Jacob, and the statutes to Israel; the like was not to other nations.' For the law of God was given to Israel; but the gospel was to be preached to *all* nations, and is to be preached. The gospel of peace and glad tidings to all nations, 'he that believes, is saved; but he that doth not believe, is condemned already;' so the condemnation comes through unbelief. And whereas Jude speaks of some, that were of old ordained (or written of before) to condemnation, he doth not say, before the world began; but, 'written of old,' which may be referred to Moses's writings, who wrote of those whom Jude mentions, namely, Cain, Korah, Balaam, and the angels that kept not their first estate. And such Christians as followed them in their way, and apostatized from the first state of Christianity, were and are ordained for condemnation by the light and truth, which they are gone from. And though the apostle speaks of God's loving Jacob and hating Esau; yet he tells the believers, 'we all were by nature children of wrath as well as others.' This includes the stock of Jacob, of which the apostle himself and all believing Jews were. Thus both Jews and Gentiles were *all* concluded under sin, and so under condemnation, that God might have mercy upon all, through Jesus Christ. The election and choice stands in Christ; and 'he that believes, is saved; and he that believes not, is condemned already.' Jacob typifies the second birth, which God loved; and both Jews and Gentiles must be born again, before they can enter the kingdom of God. When you are born again, ye will know election and reprobation; for the election stands in Christ, the Seed, before the world began; but the reprobation lies in the evil seed, since the world began." After this manner, but somewhat more largely, I discoursed with those great persons on this matter, and they confessed they had never heard so much before.

After I had travelled over Ireland, and had visited Friends in their meetings, as well for business as for worship, and had answered several papers and writings from monks, friars, and Protestant priests (for they all were in a rage against us, and endeavoured to stop the work of the Lord; and some Jesuits swore in the hearing of some of us, that we came to spread our principles in that nation, but we should not do it), I returned to DUBLIN to take passage for England. When I had stayed the First-day meeting there (which was very large and precious), a ship being ready and the wind serving, we took our leave of Friends, parting in much tenderness and brokenness, in the sense of the heavenly life and power, manifested amongst us. So having put our horses and necessaries on board in the morning, we went ourselves in the afternoon, many Friends accompanying us to the ship; and divers, both Friends and friendly people, came after us in boats when we were near a league at sea, their love drawing them, though not without danger. A good, weighty, and true people there is in that nation, sensible of the power of the Lord God and tender of his truth; and very good order they have in their meetings, for they stand up for righteousness and holiness, which dams up the way of wickedness. A precious visitation they had, and there is an excellent spirit in them, worthy to be visited. Many things more I could write of that nation, and of my travels in it, which would be large to mention particularly; but this I have thought good to signify, that the righteous may rejoice in the prosperity of truth.

James Lancaster, Robert Lodge, and Thomas Briggs came back with me; John Stubbs having further service there, stayed behind. We were two nights at sea; in one of which a mighty storm arose, that put the vessel in great danger. But I saw the power of God went over the winds and storms; he had them in his hand, and his power bound them. And the same power of the Lord God which carried us over, brought us back again; and in his life gave us dominion over all the evil spirits that opposed us there.

We landed at LIVERPOOL, and went to Richard Johnson's. Whence departing the next day, we passed to William Barnes's house, and so to William Gandy's, visiting Friends, and having many precious meetings in LANCASHIRE and CHESHIRE. When we came into GLOUCESTERSHIRE, we met with a report at NAILSWORTH, which was spread about that country, "that George Fox was turned Presbyterian; that they had prepared a pulpit for him, and set it in a yard, and that there would be a thousand people there the next day to hear him." I thought it strange that such a report should be raised of me; yet as we went further, from one Friend's house to another, we met with the same. We passed by the yard where the pulpit was, and saw it, and went on to the place where Friends' meeting was to be next day, and there we stayed that night. Next day, being First-day, we had a very large meeting, and the Lord's power and presence were amongst us.

The occasion of this strange report (as I was informed) was this. There was one John Fox, a Presbyterian priest, who used to go about preaching; and some changing his name (as was reported) from John to George, gave out that George Fox had changed his religion, and was turned from a Quaker to be a Presbyterian, and would preach at such a place such a day. This begot so great a curiosity in the people, that many went thither to hear this Quaker turned Presbyterian, who would not have gone to hear John Fox himself. By this means, it was reported, they had got together above a thousand people. But when they came there, and perceived they had a trick put upon them, and that he was but a counterfeit George Fox, and understood that the real George Fox was hard by, several hundreds of them came to our meeting, and were sober and attentive. I directed them to the grace of God in themselves, which would teach them, and bring them salvation. When the meeting was over, some of the people said, "they liked George Fox the Quaker's preaching better than George Fox the Presbyterian's." Thus, by my providential coming into those parts at that time, was this false report discovered; and shame came over the contrivers of it.

Not long after this, John Fox was complained of in the House of Commons, for "having a tumultuous meeting, in which treasonable words were spoken;" which (according to the best information I could get of it) was thus:—He had formerly been priest of Mansfield in Wiltshire; and being put out of that place, was afterwards permitted by a Common-Prayer priest to preach sometimes in his steeple-house. At length this Presbyterian priest, presuming too far upon the parish priest's former grant, began to be more bold than welcome, and attempted to preach there, whether the parish priest would or not. This caused a great bustle and contest in the steeple-house between the two priests, and their hearers, on each side; in which contest the Common-Prayer-Book was cut to pieces, and some treasonable words were spoken by some of the followers of John Fox. This was quickly put in the news: and some malicious Presbyterians caused it to be worded as if it had proceeded from George Fox the Quaker, when I was above two hundred miles from the place where this bustle happened. When I heard of it, I soon procured certificates from some of the members of the House of Commons, who knew this John Fox, and gave it under their hands, that it was John Fox, who had formerly been parson of Mansfield in Wiltshire, that was complained of to the House of Commons, to be the chief ringleader in that unlawful assembly.

And indeed this John Fox discovered himself to be an ill man; for when some, who had been his followers, came to be convinced of truth, and thereupon left him, he came to some of their houses to talk with them about it, and they telling him, "he was in the steps of the false prophets, preaching for hire and filthy lucre, like them whom Christ cried woe against, and the apostles declared against, such as served not the Lord Jesus Christ, but their own bellies; and telling him also, Christ said, 'freely ye have received, freely give;' and therefore he should not take money of people for preaching, especially now times were so hard;" he replied, "God bless preaching, for that brings in money, let times go how they will. Fill my belly with good victuals; and then call me false prophet, or what you will, and kick me about the house when ye have done, if ye will." This relation I had from a man and his wife, who had been formerly his hearers, and whom this John Fox, with others, caused deeply to suffer. For he and some other Presbyterian priests, using to resort to a widow-woman's house, who had the impropriation, and took the tithes of the parish, she told them, there was a Quaker in that parish that would not pay her tithes, and asked what she should do with him. They advised her "to send workmen to cut down and carry away his corn;" which she did, and thereby impoverished the man. But to proceed—

After this meeting in Gloucestershire was over, we travelled till we came to BRISTOL; where I met with Margaret Fell, who was come to visit her daughter Yeomans. I had seen from the Lord a considerable time before, that I should take Margaret Fell to be my wife. And when I first mentioned it to her, she felt the answer of Life from God thereunto. But though the Lord had opened this thing to me, yet I had not received a command from the Lord for the accomplishing of it then. Wherefore I let the thing rest, and went on in the work and service of the Lord as before, according as he led me; travelling up and down in this nation, and through Ireland. But now being at Bristol, and finding Margaret Fell there, it opened in me from the Lord, that the thing should be accomplished. After we had discoursed the matter together, I told her, "if she also was satisfied with the accomplishing of it now, she should first send for her children;" which she did. When the rest of her daughters were come, I asked both them and her sons-in-law, "if they had anything against it, or for it;" and they all severally expressed their satisfaction therein. Then I asked Margaret, "if she had fulfilled and performed her husband's will to her children." She replied, "the children knew that." Whereupon I asked them, "whether, if their mother married, they should not lose by it?" And I asked Margaret, "whether she had done anything in lieu of it, which might answer it to the children?" The children said, "she had answered it to them, and desired me to speak no more of it. I told them, "I was plain, and would have all things done plainly; for I sought not any outward advantage to myself." So after I had thus acquainted the children with it, our intention of marriage was laid before Friends, both privately and publicly, to their full satisfaction, many of whom gave testimony thereunto that it was of God. Afterwards, a meeting being appointed for the accomplishing thereof, in the meeting-house at Broad-Mead in Bristol, we took each other, the Lord joining us together in the honourable marriage, in the everlasting covenant and immortal Seed of life. In the sense whereof, living and weighty testimonies were borne thereunto by Friends, in the movings of the heavenly power which united us together. Then was a certificate, relating both the proceedings and the marriage, openly read, and signed by the relations, and by most of the ancient Friends of that city, besides many others from divers parts of the nation.*

We stayed about a week in Bristol, and then went together to OLDSTONE; where taking leave of each other in the Lord, we parted, betaking ourselves to our several services, Margaret returning homewards to the north, and I passing on in the work of the Lord, as before. I travelled through WILTSHIRE, BERKSHIRE, OXFORDSHIRE, and BUCKINGHAMSHIRE, and so to LONDON, visiting Friends; in all which counties I had many large and precious meetings.

Being in LONDON, it came upon me to write to Friends throughout the nation, about "putting out poor children to trades." Wherefore I sent the following epistle to the quarterly meetings of Friends in all counties:—

"MY DEAR FRIENDS,

"Let every quarterly meeting make inquiry through all the monthly and other meetings, to know all Friends that are widows, or others, that have children fit to put out to apprenticeships; so that once a quarter you may set forth an apprentice from your quarterly meeting; and so you may set forth four in a year in each county, or more, if there be occasion. This

* The date of the marriage of George Fox and Margaret Fell, in the Bristol Register of Friends, is 27th of 8th Month, 1669.

Margaret Fell, it will be remembered, was the widow of Judge Fell of Swarthmore Hall. It is remarkable with what high esteem and Christian love this devoted woman appears to have been regarded by our early and most eminent Friends. She seems to have been generally acknowledged as a faithful nursing-mother of the flock; and she often addressed them, when in bonds or otherwise, with letters of consolation and encouragement. (See numerous letters to and from her in *Barclay's Letters, &c., of Early Friends*). It is also probable she contributed largely from her means to the relief of their outward necessities. Having faithfully fulfilled her allotted labours, she died much beloved and lamented, at her own house at Swarthmore, in 1702, being near the eighty-eighth year of her age, and having survived George Fox about twelve years.

Some remarkable expressions of assured happiness fell from her lips during her last illness, if that could be called an illness, which was the decay of nature. At one time, under the meltings of heavenly love, she said, "Oh my sweet Lord! into thy holy bosom do I commit myself freely; not desiring to live in this troublesome, painful world—it is all nothing to me—for my Maker is my husband." A little before her departure she called her daughter Rachel to her, saying, "Take me in thy arms" —after which she said, "I am in peace!"

apprentice, when out of his time, may help his father or mother, and support the family that is decayed; and in so doing, all may come to live comfortably. This being done in your quarterly meetings, ye will have knowledge through the county in the monthly and particular meetings, of masters fit for them, and of such trades as their parents or you desire, or the children are most inclinable to. Thus being placed out with Friends, they may be trained up in truth; and by this means in the wisdom of God, you may preserve Friends' children in the truth, and enable them to be a strength and help to their families, and nursers and preservers of their relations in their ancient days. Thus also things being ordered in the wisdom of God, you will take off a continual maintenance, and free yourselves from much cumber. For in the country, ye know, ye may set forth an apprentice for a little to several trades, as bricklayers, masons, carpenters, wheelrights, ploughwrights, tailors, tanners, curriers, blacksmiths, shoemakers, nailers, butchers, weavers of linen and woollen, stuffs and serges, &c. And you may do well to have a stock in your quarterly meetings for that purpose. All that is given by any Friends at their decease (except it be given to some particular use, person, or meeting), may be brought to the public stock for that purpose. This will be a way for the preserving of many that are poor among you, and it will be a way of making up poor families. In several counties it is practised already. Some quarterly meetings set forth two apprentices; and sometimes the children of others that are laid on the parish. You may bind them for fewer or more years, according to their capacities. In all these things the wisdom of God will teach you, by which ye may come to help the children of poor Friends, that they may come to support their families, and preserve them in the fear of God. So no more, but my love in the everlasting Seed, by which ye will have wisdom to order all things to the glory of God." G. F.

London, 1st of 11th Month, 1669.

I stayed not long in LONDON; but having visited Friends, and finding things there quiet and well, the Lord's power being over all, I passed into ESSEX, and HERTFORDSHIRE, where I had many precious meetings. Intending to go as far as LEICESTERSHIRE, I wrote a letter to my wife, before I left London, to acquaint her therewith, that if she found it convenient to her she might meet me there. From Hertfordshire I turned into CAMBRIDGESHIRE, thence into HUNTINGDONSHIRE, and so into LEICESTERSHIRE; where, instead of meeting with my wife, I heard that she was haled out of her house to Lancaster prison again, by an order obtained from the king and council, to fetch her back to prison upon the old premunire; though she had been discharged from that imprisonment by their order the year before. Wherefore, having visited Friends as far as Leicestershire, I returned by DERBYSHIRE into WARWICKSHIRE, and so to LONDON, having had many large and blessed meetings in the several counties I passed through, and been sweetly refreshed amongst Friends in my travels.

As soon as I reached LONDON, I hastened Mary Lower and Sarah Fell (two of my wife's daughters) to the king, to acquaint him how their mother was dealt with, and see if they could obtain a full discharge for her, that she might enjoy her estate and liberty without molestation. This was somewhat difficult, but by diligent attendance they at length obtained it; the king giving command to Sir John Otway, to signify his pleasure therein by letter to the sheriff, and others concerned therein in the country. Which letter Sarah Fell going down with her brother and sister Rous, carried with her to Lancaster; and by them I wrote to my wife, as follows:—

"MY DEAR HEART IN THE TRUTH AND LIFE, THAT CHANGETH NOT,

"IT was upon me that Mary Lower and Sarah should go to the king concerning thy imprisonment, and to Kirby, that the power of the Lord might appear over them all in thy deliverance. They went, and then they thought to come down; but it was upon me to stay them a little longer, that they might follow the business till it was effected; which it now is, and is here sent. The late declaration of mine hath been very serviceable, people being generally satisfied with it. So no more, but my love in the holy Seed." G. F.

The declaration here mentioned was a printed sheet, written upon occasion of a new persecution stirred up. For by the time I was returned out of Leicestershire to London, a fresh storm was risen, occasioned (it was thought) by that tumultuous meeting in a steeple-house in Wiltshire or Gloucestershire, mentioned a little before; from which, it was said, some members of parliament took advantage to get an act passed against seditious conventicles;* which soon after came forth and was turned against us, who of all people were free from sedition and tumult. Whereupon I

* The "Conventicle Act" so called, first passed in 1664, was renewed at the above time (1670), with increased rigour. The penalties were £5, or three months to the house of correction, for the first offence of attending a conventicle, if above sixteen years of age; £10, or six months, for the second; *transportation* for seven years for the third, with sequestration of estate, or distraint for the charges; and *five years'* SLAVERY IN THE COLONIES, by contract between the sheriff and a purchaser, on being sent abroad, in defect of property to distrain upon; *or out of which to pay £100 as a liberating fine.* This fine to be repeated, and £100 added as oft as he should offend afterwards, or *transportation*, &c. (with *death* for returning), and the forfeiture of his *life-interest in his estate.*

Conventicles to be broken up by an armed force, under the direction of lieutenants of counties, sheriffs, &c. Even a *femme covert* could not escape; but must be redeemed by her husband, at the price of £40; or go to prison, or be transported with him. Nor could a *peer of the realm:* he must be fined £10 for the first offence, £20 for the second, and for the third, be tried by his peers. The fines to be levied by distress, by warrant of any two justices, or a chief magistrate.

The force of this Act was directed against the *Quakers*, by inserting, in the latter part of it, three sections, which brought *their refusal to take an oath* under its full penalties; and they suffered dreadfully through it! In the streets, or where they met to assert their religious rights, they were dragooned; in court they had oaths tendered, and were convicted under this Act upon their refusal.

"This Act," says Besse, "was forthwith put into a rigorous execution, and many hungry informers [for the sake of their *third* of the penalties] *made it their business* to live upon the spoil and ruin of conscientious people." Friends were great sufferers thereby, of the nature of which the reader may have some idea by reference to "Sufferings under the Conventicle Act;" *Select Miscellanies*, vol. iii., pp. 220–245.

wrote a declaration, showing from the preamble and terms of the act, that we were not such a people, nor our meeting such as were described in that act. I wrote also another short paper on the occasion of that act against meetings, opening our case to the magistrates, as follows:—

"O FRIENDS, consider this act, which limits us to five. Is this doing as ye would be done by? Would ye be so served yourselves? We own Christ Jesus as well as you, his coming, death, and resurrection; and if we be contrary-minded to you in some things, is not this the apostle's exhortation, 'to wait till God hath revealed it?' Doth not he say, 'what is not of faith, is sin?' Seeing we have not faith in things, which ye would have us to do, would it not be sin in us, if we should act contrary to our faith? Why should any man have power over another man's faith, seeing Christ is the author of it? When the apostles preached in the name of Jesus, and great multitudes heard them, and the rulers forbade them to speak any more in that name, did not they bid them judge whether it were better to obey God or man? Would not this act have taken hold of the twelve apostles and seventy disciples; for they met often together? If there had been a law made then, that not above five should have met with Christ, would not that have been a hindering of him from meeting with his disciples? Do ye think that He, who is the wisdom of God, or his disciples, would have obeyed it? If such a law had been made in the apostles' days, that not above five might meet together, who had been different-minded from either the Jews or the Gentiles, do ye think the churches of Christ at Corinth, Philippi, Ephesus, Thessalonica, or the rest of the gathered churches, would have obeyed it? O therefore consider! for we are Christians, and partake of the nature and life of Christ. Strive not to limit the Holy One; for God's power cannot be limited, and is not to be quenched. Do unto all men as ye would have them do unto you; for that is the law and the prophets."

"This is from those who wish you all well, and desire your everlasting good and prosperity, called Quakers; who seek the peace and good of all people, though they afflict us, and cause us to suffer."

G. F.

As I had endeavoured to soften the magistrates, and to take off the sharpness of their edge in the execution of the act, so it was upon me to write a few lines to Friends "to strengthen and encourage them to stand fast in their testimony, and bear, with Christian patience and content, the suffering that was coming upon them." This I did in the following epistle:—

"MY dear Friends, Keep in the faith of God above all outward things, and in his power, that hath given you dominion over all. The same power of God is still with you to deliver you as formerly; for God and his power is the same; his Seed is over all, and before all; and will be, when that which makes to suffer, is gone. Be of good faith in that which changeth not; for whatsoever any do against the truth, it will come upon themselves, and fall as a millstone on their heads. If the Lord suffer you to be tried, let all be given up; and look at the Lord and his power, which is over the whole world, and will remain when the world is gone. In the Lord's power and truth rejoice over that which makes to suffer, in the Seed, which was before it was; for the life, truth, and power of God is over all. All keep in that; and if ye suffer in that, it is to the Lord.

"Friends, the Lord hath blessed you in outward things; and now the Lord may try you, whether your minds be in outward things, or with the Lord that gave you them? Therefore keep in the Seed, by which all outward things were made, and which is over them all. What! shall not I pray, and speak to God, with my face towards heavenly Jerusalem, according to my wonted time? Let not any one's Delilah shave his head, lest he lose his strength; neither rest in its lap, lest the Philistines be upon you. For your rest is in Christ Jesus; therefore rest not in anything else." G. F.

London, 12th of 2nd Month, 1670.

On the First-day after the act came in force, I went to the meeting at GRACECHURCH-STREET, where I expected the storm was most likely to begin. When I came there, I found the street full of people, and a guard set to keep Friends out of their meeting-house. I went to the other passage out of Lombard Street, where also I found a guard; but the court was full of people, and a Friend was speaking amongst them; but he did not speak long. When he had done, I stood up, and was moved to say, "Saul, Saul, why persecutest thou me? it is hard for thee to kick against that which pricks thee. Then I showed that it is Saul's nature that persecutes still, and that they who persecute Christ in his members now, where he is made manifest, kick against that which pricks them. That it was the birth of the flesh that persecuted the birth born of the Spirit; and that it was the nature of dogs to tear and devour the sheep, but that we suffered as sheep that bite not again; for we were a peaceable people, and loved them that persecuted us." After I had spoken a while to this effect, the constable came with an informer and soldiers; and as they pulled me down, I said, "Blessed are the peacemakers." The commander of the soldiers put me among the soldiers, and bid them secure me, saying to me, "You are the man I looked for." They took also John Burnyeat and another Friend, and led us away first to the Exchange, and afterwards towards Moorfields. As we went along the streets the people were very moderate; some of them laughed at the constable, and told him, "we would not run away." The informer went with us unknown, till falling into discourse with one of the company, he said, "It would never be a good world till all people came to the good old religion that was two hundred years ago." Whereupon I asked him, "Art thou a Papist? What! a Papist informer; for two hundred years ago there was no other religion but that of the Papists." He saw he had ensnared himself, and was vexed at it; for as he went along the streets, I spoke often to him, and manifested what he was. When we were come to the mayor's house, and were in the court-yard, several of the people that stood about, asked me, "how and for what I was taken?" I desired them to ask the informer, and also know what his name was; but he refused to tell his name. Whereupon one of the mayor's officers looking out at a window, told him, "he should tell his name before he went away; for the lord mayor would know by what authority he intruded himself with soldiers into the execution of those laws which belonged to the civil magistrate to execute, and not to the military." After this, he was eager to be gone; and went to the porter to be let out. One of the officers called to him, saying, "Have you brought people here to inform against, and now will you go away before my lord mayor comes?" Some called to the porter not to let him out; whereupon he forcibly pulled open the door, and slipped out. No sooner was he come into the street, than the people gave a shout, that made the street ring again, crying out, "a Papist informer! a Papist informer!" We desired the constable and soldiers to go and rescue him out of the people's hands, fearing lest they should do him a mischief. They went, and brought him into the mayor's entry, where they stayed a while; but when he went out again, the people received him with another shout. The soldiers were fain to go and rescue him once more, and they led him into a house in an alley, where they persuaded him to change his periwig, and so he got away unknown.

When the mayor came, we were brought into the room where he was, and some of his officers would have taken off our hats, which he perceiving, called to them, and bid them, "let us alone, and not meddle with our hats; for," said he, "they are not yet brought before me in judicature." So we stood by while he examined some Presbyterian and Baptist teachers; with whom he was somewhat sharp, and convicted them. After he had done with them, I was brought up to the table where he sat; and then the officers took off my hat; and the mayor said mildly to me, "Mr. Fox, you are an eminent man amongst those of your profession; pray, will you be instrumental to dissuade them from meeting in such great numbers? for, seeing Christ hath promised that where two or three are met in his name, he will be in the midst of them, and the king and parliament are graciously pleased to allow of four to meet together to worship God; why will not you be content to partake both of Christ's promise to two or three, and the king's indulgence to four?" I answered to this purpose: "Christ's promise was not to discourage many from meeting together in his name, but to encourage the few, that the fewest might not forbear to meet, because of their fewness. But if Christ hath promised to manifest his presence in the midst of so small an assembly, where but two or three were gathered in his name, how much more would his presence abound where two or three hundred are gathered in his name? I wished him to consider, whether this act would not have taken hold of Christ, with his twelve apostles and seventy disciples, if it had been in their time, who used to meet often together, and that with great numbers? However, I told him this act did not concern us; for it was made against seditious meetings, of such as met, under colour and pretence of religion, 'to contrive insurrections, as (the act says) late experience had shown;' but we had been sufficiently tried and proved, and always found peaceable, and therefore he should do well to put a difference between the innocent and the guilty." He said, "the act was made against meetings, and a worship not according to the liturgy." I told him, "according to" was not the very same thing: and I asked him, "whether the liturgy was according to the Scriptures? and whether we might not read Scriptures, and speak Scriptures?" He said "Yes." I told him, "this act took hold only of such, as met to plot and contrive insurrections, as late experience had shown; but they had never experienced that by us. Because thieves are sometimes on the road, must not honest men travel? And because plotters and contrivers have met to do mischief, must not an honest, peaceable people meet to do good? If we had been a people that met to plot and contrive insurrections, &c., we might have drawn ourselves into fours; for four might do more mischief in plotting than if there were four hundred, because four might speak out their minds more freely one to another than four hundred could. Therefore, we being innocent, and not the people this act concerns, we keep our meetings as we used to do: and, I said, I believed that he knew in his conscience we were innocent." After some more discourse, he took our names and the places where we lodged, and at length, as the informer was gone, set us at liberty.

Being set at liberty, the Friends with me asked me "whither I would go?" I told them, "to Gracechurch Street meeting again, if it were not over." When we came there, the people were generally gone; only some few stood at the gate. We went into Gerrard Roberts's house; and from thence I sent out to know how the other meetings in the city were. I understood that at some of the meeting-places Friends were kept out; at others they were taken, but set at liberty again a few days after. A glorious time it was, for the Lord's power came over all, and his everlasting truth got renown. For as fast as some that were speaking were taken down, others were moved of the Lord to stand up and speak, to the admiration of the people; and the more, because many Baptists and other sectaries left their public meetings, and came to see how the Quakers would stand. As for the informer aforesaid, he was so frightened, that there durst hardly any informer appear publicly again in London for some time after. But the mayor, whose name was Samuel Starling, though he carried himself smoothly towards us, proved afterwards a very great persecutor of our Friends, many of whom he cast into prison, as may be seen in the trials of W. Penn, W. Mead, and others, at the Old Bailey this year.*

* The celebrated trial of Penn and Mead at the Old Bailey, above alluded to, may be seen at full length in Clarkson's *Life of Penn*—"a trial which, for the good it has done to posterity, ought to be engraved on tablets of the most durable marble." It was certainly one of those events which, in conjunction with others of a similar sort, by showing the inadequacy of punishment for religion to its supposed end, not only corrected and improved the notions of succeeding ages in this respect, but, by so doing, lessened the ravages of persecution, and the enmity between man and man. Nor ought posterity to be less grateful for it as a monument of the ferocity and corrupt usages of former times; for, contrasting these with the notions and customs of our own age, we see the improvement of our social and moral condition. Newgate is no longer the receptacle of innocent individuals suffering for conscience' sake. In our courts of law we see an order, a decorum, and an administration of justice, unknown at the period of this memorable trial. Nor will the prospect be less grateful, if we quit the present for a moment, and direct our eyes to the future. We have

After some time the heat of persecution in London began to abate, and meetings were quieter there. Being now clear of the city, I went to visit Friends in the country; and attended several meetings in MIDDLESEX, BUCKINGHAMSHIRE, and OXFORDSHIRE, which were quiet, though in some places there was much threatening. At READING most of the Friends were in prison, and I went to visit them. When I had been a while with them, the Friends that were prisoners gathered together, and several other persons came in; so that I had a fine opportunity amongst them, and "declared the Word of Life, encouraging them in the truth; and they were refreshed in feeling the presence and power of the Lord amongst them." When the meeting was ended, the jailer understanding that I was there, the Friends were concerned how to get me out safe again; for they feared lest he should stop me. But after I had stayed a while, and eaten with them, I went down stairs, and the jailer being at the door, I put my hand in my pocket, which he had such an eye to, hoping to get something off me, that he asked me no question. So I gave him something, and bade him "be kind and civil to my Friends in prison, whom I came to visit;" and he let me pass out without interruption. But soon after Isaac Pennington coming to visit them, he stopped him, and caused him to be made a prisoner.*

the best reason to hope, on contemplating the signs of the times, that the day is rapidly approaching when the Christian religion, which is capable of cementing men in the strongest possible union, and for the noblest purposes, will be stripped of its mischievous appendages—restored to its primitive purity, and made a blessing to all the dwellers upon the earth.

* Isaac Pennington has been mentioned before, but only cursorily, in the whole of this Journal. Little is known of his history, beyond what is to be gathered from testimonies given forth concerning him at his death, and a few other incidental notices of him. He was well descended as to his worldly parentage, being the eldest son of Alderman Pennington, who was two years successively Mayor of London, and a noted member of the Long Parliament. Born about the year 1617, he received a liberal education, having, according to Penn, "all the advantages the schools and universities of his own country could give, joined with the conversation of some of the most learned and considerable men of that time."

From childhood, Isaac Pennington was religiously inclined, and, in a paper written by himself, and found after his death amongst his writings, we have such a living portrait of a deeply-exercised mind, as demonstrates that godliness with him was indeed the "one thing needful." "In the sense of my lost estate," he writes, "I sought after the Lord; I read the Scriptures; I watched over mine own heart; and whatever I read in the Scriptures, as the way of God, to my understanding, I gave myself to the faithful practice of. He became fully convinced of the principles of Friends, and joined that despised people—becoming a faithful sufferer for the cause of Christ."

"Early believers in the light of Truth
Dwelt not at ease in Zion. They endured
Conflicts and trials, and imprisonments.
Even the humble Pennington, whose mind
Seemed purged and purified from dross
Of human nature—who appeared as meek
And harmless as an infant—was compelled
To dwell in loathsome prisons."

He was six times in jail, some of his imprisonments being long, yet borne with great quietness and constancy of mind. His first imprisonment was in Aylesbury jail

Next morning I rode about fourteen miles to a meeting at BAGHURST in HAMPSHIRE, Thomas Briggs being with me. When we came into the parish, some sober people told us, that "the priest of the town was an envious man, and threatened us." We went on to the meeting, which was large; and after some time Thomas Briggs stood up and spoke. It seems the priest had got a warrant, and sent the constables and other officers with it. They came to the house, stayed a while, and then went away again, without coming into the meeting; so we in the meeting did not know of their being there. After Thomas Briggs had done speaking, I was moved of the Lord to stand up, and declare the Word of Life to the people; and a precious meeting we had. When it was ended and risen, I heard a great clatter in the yard; and when we came out, the man of the house told us, "that the officers had been in the house before, but did not come into the meeting, going away without doing anything; and that now the priest in a great rage had sent them again, and his own servant with them." But the meeting being ended before they came, they could do nothing. Thus the good providence of the Lord preserved us from the wicked design of the envious priest.

Thence we went to a Friend's house on the edge of BERKSHIRE, where several Friends came to visit us. Afterwards we passed into SURREY, and had many precious meetings, till we came to Stephen Smith's, near GUILDFORD, where great persecution had been, and very much property taken away from Friends for their meetings; and under great threatenings they were at that time; yet we had several blessed meetings thereabouts, and the Lord's power was over all, in and by which we were preserved.

We went into SUSSEX, by Richard Baxe's, where we had a large, precious, quiet meeting, though the constables had given out threatenings before. I had many more meetings in that county; and though there were some threatenings, they were peaceable; and Friends were refreshed, and established upon the foundation of God, that stands sure. When I had thoroughly visited SUSSEX, I went into KENT, and had many glorious and precious meetings in several parts of that county. I went to a meeting near DEAL, which was very large; and returning from thence to CANTERBURY, visited Friends there. I then passed into the ISLE OF SHEPPY, where I stayed two or three days; and thither came Alexander Parker, George Whitehead, and John Rous to me.

Next day, finding my service for the Lord finished there, we passed towards ROCHESTER. On the way, as I was walking down a hill, a great weight and oppression fell upon my spirit; I got on my horse again, but the weight remained so that I was hardly able to ride. At length we came to Rochester, but I was much spent, being so extremely laden and burthened with the world's spirits, that my life was oppressed under them.

in 1661 and 1662, being committed there for worshipping God in his own house. He was kept there seventeen weeks, great part of it in winter—in a cold and very incommodious room without a chimney, from which usage he contracted so severe an indisposition, that for several weeks after he was unable to turn himself in his bed.

In the sixty-third year of his age "he died as he lived, in the faith that overcomes the world."

I got with difficulty to GRAVESEND, and lay at an inn there; but could hardly either eat or sleep. The next day John Rous and Alexander Parker went for London; and John Stubbs being come to me, we went over the ferry into ESSEX. We came to HORNCHURCH, where was a meeting on First-day. After it I rode with great uneasiness to STRATFORD, to a Friend's house, whose name was Williams, and who had formerly been a captain. Here I lay exceedingly weak, and at last lost both hearing and sight. Several Friends came to me from London: and I told them, that "I should be as a sign to such as would not see, and such as would not hear the truth." In this condition I continued some time. Several came about me; and though I could not see their persons, I felt and discerned their spirits, who were honest-hearted, and who were not. Divers Friends who practised physic, came to see me, and would have given me medicines, but I was not to meddle with any; for I was sensible I had a travail to go through; and therefore desired none but solid, weighty Friends might be about me. Under great sufferings and travails, sorrows and oppressions, I lay for several weeks, whereby I was brought so low and weak in body, that few thought I could live. Some that were with me went away, saying "they would not see me die;" and it was reported both in London and in the country, that I was deceased; but I felt the Lord's power inwardly supporting me. When they that were about me had given me up to die, I spoke to them to get a coach to carry me to Gerrard Roberts's, about twelve miles off; for I found it was my place to go thither. I had now recovered a little glimmering sight, so that I could discern the people and fields as I went, and that was all. When I came to Gerrard's, he was very weak; and I was moved to speak to him, and encourage him. After I had stayed about three weeks there, it was with me to go to Enfield. Friends were afraid of my removing; but I told them I might safely go. When I had taken my leave of Gerrard, and was come to ENFIELD, I went first to visit Amor Stoddart, who lay very weak, and almost speechless. I was moved to tell him, "he had been faithful as a man, and faithful to God; and that the immortal Seed of life was his crown." Many more words I was moved to speak to him, though I was then so weak, I was hardly able to stand; and within a few days after, Amor died. I went to the widow Dry's at Enfield, where I lay all that winter, warring in spirit with the evil spirits of the world, that warred against truth and Friends. For there were great persecutions at this time; some meeting-houses were pulled down, and many were broken up by soldiers. Sometimes a troop of horse, or a company of foot came; and some broke their swords, carbines, muskets, and pikes, with beating Friends; and many they wounded, so that their blood lay in the streets. Amongst others that were active in this cruel persecution at London, my old adversary Colonel Kirby was one; who, with a company of foot, went to break up several meetings; and he would often inquire for me at the meetings he broke up. One time as he went over the water to Horsleydown, there happening some scuffle between some of his soldiers and some of the watermen, he bid his men "fire at them." They did so, and killed some.

I was under great sufferings at this time, beyond what I have words to declare. For I was brought into the deep, and saw all the religions of the world, and people that lived in them, and the priests that held them up, who were as a company of men-eaters, eating up the people like bread, and gnawing the flesh from off their bones. But as for true religion and worship, and ministers of God, alack! I saw there were none amongst those of the world that pretended to it. For they that pretended to be the church, were but a company of men-eaters, men of cruel visages, and of long teeth; and, though they had cried against the men-eaters in America, I saw they were in the same nature. And as the great professing Jews did "eat up God's people like bread," and the false prophets and priests then preached peace to people, so long as they "put into their mouths and fed them;" but if they fed them not, they prepared war against them, "they ate their flesh off their bones, and chopped them for the caldron;" so these that profess themselves Christians now (both priests and professors), and are not in the same power and Spirit that Christ and the holy prophets and apostles were in, are in the same nature that the old professing Jews were in, and are men-eaters as well as they. These stirred up persecution and set the wicked informers to work; so that a Friend could hardly speak a few words in a private family, before they sat down to eat meat, but some were ready to inform against them. A particular instance of which I have heard as follows:—

At Droitwich John Cartwright came to a Friend's house, and being moved of the Lord to speak a few words before he sat down to supper, there came an informer, and stood hearkening under the window. When he had heard the Friend speak, hoping to get some gain to himself, he went and informed, and got a warrant to distrain his goods, under pretence that there was a meeting at his house; whereas there were none in the house at that time, but the Friend, the man of the house, his wife, and their maid-servant. But this evil-minded man, as he came back with his warrant in the night, fell off his horse, and broke his neck. So there was a wretched end of a wicked informer, who hoped to enrich himself by spoiling Friends; but the Lord prevented him, and cut him off in his wickedness.

Now, though it was a cruel, bloody, persecuting time, yet the Lord's power went over all, and his everlasting Seed prevailed; and Friends were made to stand firm and faithful in the Lord's power. Some sober people of other professions would say, "if Friends did not stand, the nation would run into debauchery."

Though by reason of my weakness, I could not travel amongst Friends as I used to do, yet in the motion of life, I sent the following lines as an encouraging testimony to them:—

"My Dear Friends,

"The Seed is above all. In it walk; in which ye all have life. Be not amazed at the weather; for always the just suffered by the unjust, but the just had the dominion. All along ye may see, by faith the mountains were subdued; and the rage of the wicked, and his fiery darts, were quenched. Though the waves and storms are high, yet your faith will keep you so as to swim above them; for they are but for a time, and the truth is without time. Therefore keep on the mountain of holiness, ye who are led to it by the light, where nothing shall hurt. Do not think that anything will outlast the truth, which standeth sure; and is over that which is out of the truth; for the good will overcome the evil; the light, darkness; the life, death; virtue, vice; and righteousness, unrighteousness. The false prophet cannot overcome the true; but the true prophet, Christ, will overcome all the false. So be faithful, and live in that which doth not think the time long." G. F.

After some time it pleased the Lord to allay the heat of this violent persecution; and I felt in spirit an overcoming of the spirits of those men-eaters, that had stirred it up, and carried it on to that height of cruelty, though I was outwardly very weak. And I plainly felt, and those Friends that were with me, and that came to visit me, took notice, that as the persecution ceased, I came from under the travails and sufferings, that had lain with such weight upon me; so that towards the spring I began to recover, and to walk up and down, beyond the expectation of many, who did not think I could ever have gone abroad again.

Whilst I was under this spiritual suffering, the state of the New Jerusalem, which comes down out of heaven, was opened to me; which some carnal-minded people had looked upon to be like an outward city dropped out of the elements. I saw the beauty and glory of it, the length, the breadth, and the height thereof, all in complete proportion. I saw, that all who are within the light of Christ, and in his faith, which he is the author of; and in the Spirit, the Holy Ghost, which Christ and the holy prophets and apostles were in; and within the grace, and truth, and power of God, which are the walls of the city;—such are within the city, are members of it, and have right to eat of the tree of life, which yields her fruit every month, and whose leaves are for the healing of the nations. But they that are out of the grace, truth, light, Spirit, and power of God; they who resist the Holy Ghost, quench, vex, and grieve the Spirit of God; who hate the light, turn the grace of God into wantonness, and do despite to the Spirit of Grace; they who have erred from the faith, and made shipwreck of it and of a good conscience, who abuse the power of God, and despise prophesying, revelation, and inspiration;—these are the dogs and unbelievers that are without the city. These make up the great city Babylon, confusion, and her cage, the power of darkness; and the evil spirit of error surrounds and covers them over. In this great city Babylon are the false prophets, in the false power and false spirit; the beast, in the dragon's power, and the whore that is gone a whoring from the Spirit of God, and from Christ her husband. But the Lord's power is over all this power of darkness, false prophets, and their worshippers, who are for the lake which burns with fire. Many things more did I see concerning the heavenly city, the New Jerusalem, which are hard to be uttered, and would be hard to be received. But, in short, this holy city is within the light, and all that are within the light, are within the city; the gates whereof stand open all the day (for there is no night there), that all may come in. Christ's blood being shed for every man, he tasted death for every man, and enlighteneth every man that cometh into the world; and his grace that brings salvation having appeared to all men, there is no place or language where his voice may not be heard. The Christians in the primitive times were called by Christ, "a city set upon a hill;" they were also called "the light of the world," and "the salt of the earth;" but when Christians lost the light, and salt, and power of God, then they came to be trodden under foot, like unsavoury salt. Even as the Jews, who while they kept the law of God, were preserved above all nations; but when they turned their backs on God and his law, they were trodden under foot of other nations. Adam and Eve, while they obeyed God, were kept in his image and in the paradise of God, in dominion over all the works of his hands; but when they disobeyed God, they lost his image, the righteousness and the holiness in which they were made; they lost their dominion, were driven out of paradise; and so fell under the dark power of Satan, and came under the chains of darkness. But the promise of God was, "that the Seed of the woman, Christ Jesus, should bruise the serpent's head,"—should break his power and authority, which had led into captivity, and had held man therein. So Christ, who is the first and the last, sets man free, and is the resurrection of the just and unjust, the judge of the quick and dead; and they that are in him are invested with everlasting rest and peace, out of all the labours, and travails, and miseries of Adam in the fall. So he is sufficient and of ability to restore man into the state he was in before he fell; and not into that state only, but into that also that never fell, even to himself.

I had also in this time a great exercise and travail of spirit upon me, concerning the powers and rulers of these nations, from the sense I had of the many tender visitations and faithful warnings, that had been given them, and of their great abuse thereof, who had refused to hear, and rejected the counsel of the Lord. And though I knew Friends would be clear of their blood, yet I could not but mourn over them, and gave forth these few lines following concerning them:—

"We have given them a visitation, have faithfully warned them, have declared to them our innocency and uprightness, and that we never did any hurt to the king, nor to any of his people. We have nothing in our hearts but love and good-will to him and his people, and desire their eternal welfare. But if they will not hear, the day of judgment and of sorrow, of torment, misery, and sudden destruction, will come from the Lord upon them, that have been the cause of the sufferings of many thousands of simple, innocent, harmless people that have done them no hurt, nor have had any ill-will towards him or them; but have desired their eternal good for the eternal truth's sake. Destruction will come upon them that turn the sword backward. Therefore do not blind your eyes, the Lord will bring swift destruction and misery upon you; surely he will do it, and will relieve his innocent people, who have groaned for deliverance from under your oppression, and have also groaned for your deliverance out of wickedness. Blessed be the Lord God, that he hath a people in this nation, that seek the good of all men upon the face of the earth; for we have the mind of the Lord Jesus Christ, that desires not the death of a sinner, but the salvation and good of all. Blessed be the name of the Lord our God for ever." G. F.

While I continued at Enfield, a sense came upon me of a hurt that sometimes happened, by persons under the profession of truth coming out of one country into another, to take a husband or wife amongst Friends, where they were strangers, and it was not known whether they were clear and orderly, or not. And it opened in me to recommend the following method unto Friends for preventing such inconveniences:—

"All Friends that marry, whether they be men or women, if they come out of another nation, island, or county, let them bring a certificate from the men's meeting of that county, nation, or island from which they came, to the men's meeting where they propose their intention of marriage. For the men's meeting being made up of the faithful, this will stop all wrong spirits from roving up and down. When any come with a certificate, or letter of recommendation from one men's meeting to another, one is refreshed by another, and can set their hands and hearts to the thing. This will prevent a great deal of trouble. And then what ye have to say to them in the power of God, in admonishing and instructing them, ye are left to the power and Spirit of God to do it, and to let them know the duty of marriage, and what it is; that there may be unity and concord in the Spirit, and power, and light, and wisdom of God, throughout all the men's meetings in the whole world, in one, in the life.

"Let copies of this be sent to every county, and nation, and island where Friends are, that so all things may be kept holy, and pure, and righteous, in unity and peace; and God over all may be glorified among you, his lot, his people and inheritance, who are his adopted sons and daughters, and heirs of his life. So no more, but my love in that which changeth not." G. F.

14th of 1st Month, 1670-1.

When I had recovered, so that I could walk a little, I went from Enfield to Gerrard Roberts's again, and thence to the women's school at Shacklewell, and so to the meeting at Gracechurch Street, London; where, though I was yet but weak, the Lord's power upheld and enabled me to declare his eternal Word of life.

About this time I was moved to pray to the Lord as follows:—

"O Lord God Almighty! Prosper truth, and preserve justice and equity in the land! Bring down all injustice and iniquity, oppression and falsehood, cruelty and unmercifulness in the land; that mercy and righteousness may flourish!

"O Lord God! Set up and establish verity, and preserve it in the land! Bring down in the land all debauchery and vice, whoredoms and fornication, and this raping spirit, which causeth people to have no esteem of thee, O God! nor of their own souls or bodies; nor of Christianity, modesty, or humanity.

"O Lord! Put it in the magistrates' hearts to bring down all this ungodliness, violence, and cruelty, profaneness, cursing, and swearing; and to put down all those lewd houses and play-houses, which corrupt youth and people, and lead them from thy kingdom, where no unclean thing can enter, neither shall come! Such works lead people to hell! Lord! In mercy bring down all these things in the nation, to stop thy wrath, O God! from coming on the land." G. F.

This Prayer was written at night, the 17th
of the 2d Month, 1671.

CHAPTER IV.

1671–1672.—His wife being still detained a prisoner, George Fox puts two women Friends upon going to the king to procure her discharge, which he granted under the broad seal, to clear her person and estate after being a prisoner under premunire ten years—he sails for the plantations in America with several other Friends—chased by a Sallee man-of-war—the master in a strait asks advice of George Fox, who seeks counsel of the Lord, and is assured of their preservation—the event verifies the prediction—they land at Barbadoes after a seven weeks' passage—a man in the island, who was greatly incensed against George Fox without just cause, and who had threatened his life, died a few days before his landing—is laid up for some weeks—writes to Friends in England—exhorts Friends to care and watchfulness in regard to marriages, keeping registers and records, providing burial grounds, &c.—to deal mildly with their negroes, and, after certain years of servitude, to set them free—writes a further exhortation to Friends in England—visits the governor, who is very kind—has many large meetings, and there is a great convincement; Colonel Lyne testifies how much Friends exalt Christ in all his offices beyond what he had ever heard—the priests rage, and try in vain to stir up persecution—there is much clamour and cavilling against Friends, and many slanders and false reports are issued, which George Fox answers in a paper addressed to the governor—the governor visits him—writes to his wife—sails for Jamaica, where he has many meetings, and many are convinced—Elizabeth Hooton dies there.

I MENTIONED before, that, upon the notice I received of my wife's being imprisoned again, I sent two of her daughters to the king, and they procured his order to the sheriff of Lancashire, for her discharge. But though I expected she would be set at liberty thereby, this violent storm of persecution coming suddenly on, the persecutors there found means to hold her still in prison. But now the persecution a little ceasing, I was moved to speak to Martha Fisher and another woman Friend, to go to the king about her liberty. They went in faith, and in the Lord's power, who gave them favour with the king, so that he granted a discharge under the broad-seal, to clear both her and her estate, after she had been ten years a prisoner, and premunired; the like whereof was scarcely to be heard of in England. I sent down the discharge forthwith by a Friend; by whom also I wrote to her, informing her how to get it delivered to the justices, and acquainting her that it was upon me from the Lord to go beyond the seas to visit America; and therefore desired her to hasten to London, as soon as she could conveniently, after she had obtained her liberty, because the ship was then fitting for the voyage. In the meantime I got to Kingston, and stayed at John Rous's till my wife came up, and then I began to prepare for the voyage. But the Yearly Meeting being near at hand, I stayed till that was over. Many Friends came up to it from all parts of the nation, and a very large and precious meeting it was; for the Lord's power was over all, and his glorious everlastingly-renowned Seed of life was exalted above all.

After this meeting was over, and I had finished my services for the Lord in England, the ship and the Friends that intended to go with me being ready, I went to GRAVESEND on the 12th of 6th month, my wife and several Friends accompanying me to the Downs. We went from Wapping in a barge to the ship, which lay a little below Gravesend, and there we found the Friends that were bound for the voyage with me, who had gone down to the ship the night before. Their names were Thomas Briggs, William Edmundson, John Rous, John Stubbs, Solomon Eccles, James Lancaster, John Cartwright, Robert Widders, George Pattison, John Hull, Elizabeth Hooton, and Elizabeth Miers. The vessel was a yacht, called the *Industry;* the captain's name Thomas Forster, and the number of passengers about fifty. I lay that night on board, but most of the Friends at Gravesend. Early next morning the passengers, and those Friends that intended to accompany us to the Downs, being come on board, we took our leave in great tenderness of those that came with us to Gravesend only, and set sail about six in the morning for the DOWNS. Having a fair wind, we out-sailed all the ships that were outward-bound, and got thither by evening. Some of us went ashore that night, and lodged at DEAL; where, we understood, an officer had orders from the governor to take our names in writing; which he did next morning, though we told him they had been taken at Gravesend. In the afternoon, the wind serving, I took leave of my wife and other Friends, and went on board. Before we could sail, there being two of the king's frigates riding in the DOWNS, the captain of one of them sent his press-master on board us, who took three of our seamen. This would certainly have delayed, if not wholly prevented, our voyage, had not the captain of the other frigate, being informed of the leakiness of our vessel, and the length of our voyage, in compassion and much civility, spared us two of his own men. Before this was over, a custom-house officer came on board to peruse packets and get fees; so that we were kept from sailing till about sunset; during which delay a very considerable number of merchantmen, outward-bound, were got several leagues before us. Being clear, we set sail in the evening, and next morning overtook part of that fleet about the height of Dover. We soon reached the rest, and in a little time left them all behind; for our yacht was counted a very swift sailer. But she was very leaky, so that the seamen and some of the passengers did, for the most part, pump day and night. One day they observed, that in two hours' time she sucked in sixteen inches of water in the well.

When we had been about three weeks at sea, one afternoon we spied a vessel about four leagues astern of us. Our master said it was a Sallee man-of-war, that seemed to give us chase. Our master said, "Come, let us go to supper, and when it grows dark we shall lose him." This he spoke to please and pacify the passengers, some of whom began to be very apprehensive of the danger. But Friends were well satisfied in themselves, having faith in God, and no fear upon their spirits. When the sun was gone down, I saw the ship out of my cabin making towards us. When it grew dark, we altered our course to miss her; but she altered also, and gained upon us. At night the master and others came into my cabin, and asked me, "what they should do?" I told them, "I was no mariner;" and I asked them, "what they thought was best to do?" They said, "There were but two ways, either to outrun him, or tack about, and hold the same course we were going before." I told them, "if he were a thief, they might be sure he would tack about too; and as for outrunning him, it was to no purpose to talk of that, for they saw he sailed faster than we." They asked me again, "what they should do? for," they said, "if the mariners had taken Paul's counsel, they had not come to the damage they did." I answered, "it was a trial of faith, and therefore the Lord was to be waited on for counsel." So retiring in spirit, the Lord showed me, "that his life and power was placed between us and the ship that pursued us." I told this to the master and the rest, and that the best way was to tack about and steer our right course. I desired them also to put out all their candles, but the one they steered by, and to speak to all the passengers to be still and quiet. About eleven at night the watch called and said, "they were just upon us." That disquieted some of the passengers; whereupon I sat up in my cabin, and looking through the port-hole, the moon being not quite down, I saw them very near us. I was getting up to go out of the cabin; but remembering the word of the Lord, "that his life and power was placed between us and them," I lay down again. The master and some of the seamen came again, and asked me, "if they might not steer such a point?" I told them, "they might do as they would." By this time the moon was quite down, a fresh gale arose, and the Lord hid us from them; and we sailed briskly on and saw them no more. The next day, being the first day of the week, we had a public meeting in the ship, as we usually had on that day throughout the voyage, and the Lord's presence was greatly among us. And I desired the people "to mind the mercies of the Lord, who had delivered them; for they might have been all in the Turks' hands by that time, had not the Lord's hand saved them." About a week after, the master and some of the seamen endeavoured to persuade the passengers, that it was not a Turkish pirate that chased us, but a merchantman going to the Canaries. When I heard of it, I asked them, "Why then did they speak so to me? why did they trouble the passengers? and why did they tack about from him and alter their course?" I told them "they should take heed of slighting the mercies of God."

Afterwards, while we were at Barbadoes, there came in a merchant from Sallee, and told the people, "that one of the Sallee men-of-war saw a monstrous yacht at sea, the greatest that ever he saw, and had her in chase, and was just upon her, but that there was a spirit in her that he could not take." This confirmed us in the belief that it was a Sallee-man we saw make after us, and that it was the Lord that delivered us out of his hands.

I was not sea-sick during the voyage, as many of the Friends and other passengers were; but the many hurts and bruises I had formerly received, and the infirmities I had contracted in England by extreme cold and hardships, that I had undergone in many long and sore imprisonments, returned upon me at sea; so that I was very ill in my stomach, and full of violent pains in my bones and limbs. This was after I had been at sea about a month; for about three weeks after I came first to sea, I perspired abundantly, chiefly my head, and my body broke out in pimples, and my legs and feet swelled extremely, so that my stockings and slippers could not be drawn on without difficulty and great pain. Suddenly the sweating ceased, so that when I came into the hot climate, where others perspired most freely, I could not perspire at all; but my flesh was hot, dry, and burning; and that which before broke out in pimples, struck in again to my stomach and heart, so that I was very ill, and weak beyond expression. Thus I continued during the rest of the voyage, which was about a month; for we were above seven weeks at sea.

On the third of the eighth month, early in the morning, we discovered the island of BARBADOES, but it was between nine and ten at night ere we came to anchor in CARLISLE-BAY. We got on shore as soon as we could, and I, with some others, walked to a Friend's house, a merchant, whose name was Richard Forstall, above a quarter of a mile from the bridge. But being very ill and weak, I was so tired with that little walk, that I was in a manner spent by the time I got thither. There I abode very ill for several days, and though they several times gave me things to make me perspire, they could not effect it. But what they gave me did rather parch and dry up my body, and made me probably worse than otherwise I might have been. Thus I continued about three weeks after I landed, having much pain in my bones, joints, and whole body, so that I could hardly get any rest; yet I was pretty cheerful, and my spirit kept above it all. Neither did my illness take me off from the service of truth, but both while I was at sea, and after I came to Barbadoes, before I was able to travel about, I gave forth several papers (having a Friend to write for me), some of which I sent by the first conveyance for England to be printed.

After I had rested three or four days at Richard Forstall's, where many Friends came to visit me, John Rous* having borrowed a coach of Colonel Chamberlain, came to fetch me to his father, Thomas Rous's house.* But it was late ere we could get thither, and little or no rest could I take that night. A few days after, Colonel Chamberlain, who had so kindly lent his coach, paid me a visit, and was very courteous towards me.

Soon after I came into the island, I was informed of a remarkable

* Thomas Rous was a wealthy sugar-planter of Barbadoes. John Rous was his son, and son-in-law to George Fox, having married his wife's eldest daughter. John Rous visited New England as a gospel minister when a young man, and suffered whipping and imprisonment there. After his release from Boston jail in 1658, except a visit which he paid to the island of Nevis towards the close of that year, we lose all trace of him until his marriage with Margaret, eldest daughter of Judge Fell, at Swarthmore Hall, in 1662. After his marriage he settled in London, in which, and in its vicinity, he appears to have resided during the remainder of his life. But few particulars respecting him are preserved, except a visit to the county of Kent in 1670, accompanied by Alexander Parker and George Whitehead; and to Barbadoes the following year with George Fox, as related in this Journal. Besides this, and a visit to the counties of York and Durham in 1689, we know nothing of his gospel labours after he settled in England. In his will, dated from Kingston in Surrey in 1692, he describes himself as a merchant, and his property, which, it appears was considerable, lay chiefly in Barbadoes. It is singular no record of his death has been found, but as his will was proved in 1695, it probably took place in that year.

passage,* wherein the justice of God did eminently appear; it was thus: There was a young man of Barbadoes, whose name was John Drakes (a person of some note in the world's account, but a common swearer and wicked man), who, when in London, had a mind to marry a Friend's daughter, left by her mother very young, and with a considerable portion, to the care and government of several Friends, whereof I was one. He made application to me, that he might have my consent to marry this young maid. I told him, "I was one of her overseers appointed by her mother, who was a widow, to take care of her; that if her mother had intended her for a match to any man of another profession, she would have disposed of her accordingly; but she committed her to us, that she might be trained up in the fear of the Lord, and therefore I should betray the trust reposed in me, if I should consent that he who was out of the fear of God, should marry her; which I would not do." When he saw that he could not obtain his desire, he returned to Barbadoes with great offence of mind against me, but without just cause. Afterwards, when he heard I was coming to Barbadoes, he swore desperately, and threatened, that "if he could possibly procure it, he would have me burned to death when I came there." Which a Friend hearing, asked him, "what I had done to him, that he was so violent against me?" He would not answer, but said again, "I'll have him burned." Whereupon the Friend replied, "Do not march on too furiously, lest thou come too soon to thy journey's end." About ten days after, he was struck with a violent burning fever, of which he died; and by which his body was so scorched, that the people said, "it was as black as a coal." Three days before I landed, his body was laid in the dust. This was taken notice of as a sad example.

While I continued so weak, that I could not go abroad to meetings, the other Friends that came over with me, bestirred themselves in the Lord's work. The day but one after we landed, they had a great meeting at the bridge, and after that several others in different parts of the island; which alarmed the people of all sorts, so that many came to our meetings, and some of the chief rank. For they had got my name, understanding I was come upon the island, and expected to see me at those meetings, not knowing that I was unable to go abroad. And indeed, my weakness continued the longer on me, by reason that my spirit was much pressed down at first with the filth and dirt and unrighteousness of the people, which lay as a heavy weight and load upon me. But after I had been above a month upon the island, my spirit became somewhat easier, and I began to recover in some measure my health and strength, and to get abroad among Friends. In the meantime, having opportunity to send to England, I wrote to Friends there, to let them know how it was with me, as follows:—

"Dear Friends,

"I have been very weak these seven weeks past, and not able to write myself. My desire is to you and for you all, that ye may live in the fear

* The words "passage" and "passages" occur frequently in the journals and other writings of the early Friends. In this instance it signifies a remarkable occurrence, but is generally applied to gospel services, travels, &c.

of God, and in love one unto another, and be subject one to another in the fear of God. I have been weaker in my body than ever I was in my life that I remember, yea, my pains have been such as I cannot express; yet my heart and spirit is strong. I have hardly perspired these seven weeks past, though I am come into a very hot climate, where hardly any but are well nigh continually perspiring; but as for me, my old bruises, colds, numbness, and pains, struck inwardly, even to my very heart. So that I have taken little rest, and the chief things that were comfortable to my stomach, were a little water and powdered ginger; but now I begin to drink a little beer as well as water, and sometimes a little wine and water mixed. Great pains and travails I have felt, and in measure am under; but it is well, my life is over all. This island was to me as all on a fire ere I came to it, but now it is somewhat quenched and abated. I came in weakness amongst those that are strong, and have so continued; but now I am got a little cheery, and over it. Many Friends, and some considerable persons of the world, have been with me. I tired out my body much when amongst you in England; it is the Lord's power that helps me; therefore I desire you all to prize the power of the Lord and his truth. I was but weak in body when I left you, after I had been in my great travail amongst you; but after that, it struck all back again into my body, which was not well settled after so sore travails in England. Then I was so tired at sea, that I could not rest, and have had little or no stomach a long time. Since I came into this island, my life hath been very much burthened; but I hope, if the Lord give me strength to manage his work, I shall work thoroughly, and bring things that have been out of course, into better order. So, dear Friends, live all in the peaceable truth, and in the love of it, serving the Lord in newness of life; for glorious things and precious truths have been manifested among you plentifully, and to you the riches of the kingdom have been handed. I have been almost a month in this island, but have not been able to go abroad or ride out; only very lately I rode out twice, a quarter of a mile at a time, which wearied me much. My love in the truth is to you all." G. F.

Because I was not well able to travel, the Friends of the island concluded to have their men's and women's meeting for the service of the church at Thomas Rous's, where I lay; by which means I was present at each of their meetings, and had very good service for the Lord in both. For they had need of information in many things, divers disorders having crept in for want of care and watchfulness. I exhorted them, more especially at the men's meeting, "to be watchful and careful with respect to marriages, to prevent Friends marrying in near kindreds, and also to prevent over-hasty proceedings towards second marriages, after the death of a former husband or wife; advising that a decent regard might be had in such cases to the memory of the deceased husband or wife. As to Friends' children marrying too young, as at thirteen or fourteen years of age, I showed them the unfitness thereof, and the inconveniences and hurts that attend such childish marriages. I admonished them to purge the floor thoroughly, to sweep their houses very clean, that nothing might remain that would defile, and to take care that nothing be spoken, out of their meetings, to the blemishing or defaming one of another. Concerning the registering of marriages, births, and burials, I advised them to keep exact records of each in distinct books for that only use; and also to record in a book for that purpose, the condemnations of such as went out from truth into disorderly practices, and the repentance and restoration of such of them as returned again. I recommended to their care the providing of convenient burying-places for Friends, which in some parts were yet wanting. Some directions also I gave them concerning wills, and the ordering of legacies left by Friends for public uses, and other things relating to the affairs of the church. Then as to their blacks or negroes, I desired them to endeavour to train them up in the fear of God, those that were bought, and those born in their families, that all might come to the knowledge of the Lord; that so, with Joshua, every master of a family might say, 'As for me and my house, we will serve the Lord.' I desired them also that they would cause their overseers to deal mildly and gently with their negroes, and not use cruelty towards them, as the manner of some hath been and is; and that after certain years of servitude, they would make them free."* Many sweet and precious things were opened in these meetings by the Spirit, and in the power of the Lord, to the edifying, confirming, and building up of Friends, both in the faith and holy order of the gospel.

After these meetings, the vessel bound for England not being gone, I was moved to write another epistle to Friends there, as follows:—

"DEAR Friends and brethren, to whom is my love in that which

* The interest of Friends in behalf of the Negro may be dated from the rise of the Society, at least from the time of their acquaintance with them at the above date. In proportion as intercourse was more frequently maintained with the distant colonies, and the abominations of Slavery were more generally known, Friends were more decided in their opposition to it. In 1727 the whole Society, at their Yearly Meeting in London, passed a general resolution: "That the importing of Negroes from their native country is not a commendable or allowable practice, and is therefore censured by this meeting." At several subsequent meetings, through a series of years, minutes were passed to the same effect, but gradually increasing in strength. In 1758, the practice was declared to be in direct violation of the gospel rule, and Friends were warned carefully to avoid being in any way concerned in reaping the unrighteous profits arising from so iniquitous a practice. In 1761 all were disowned who persisted in a practice so repugnant to Christianity, and so reproachful to a Christian profession.

Clarkson, in alluding to this subject, observes, "I must beg leave to stop here for a moment, just to pay the Quakers a due tribute of respect for the proper estimation in which they have uniformly held these miserable outcasts of society. What a contrast does it afford to the sentiments of many others concerning them! How have we been compelled to prove, by a long chain of evidence, that Negroes have the same feelings and capacities as ourselves! How many, professing themselves enlightened, even now view them as of a different species. But by the Friends we have seen them uniformly represented, as persons 'ransomed by one and the same Saviour,' 'as visited by one and the same light for salvation,' and 'as made equally for immortality as others.' These practical views of mankind, as they are highly honourable to the members of this Society, so they afford a proof both of the reality and of the consistency of their religion."

See Clarkson's *History of the Abolition of the Slave Trade*, and Copley's *History of Slavery*.

never changeth, but remains in glory, which is over all, the top and corner-stone. In this all have peace and life, as ye dwell in the blessed Seed, wherein all is blessed over that which brought the curse; where all shortness and narrowness of spirit, brittleness and peevishness are. Therefore keep the holy order of the gospel. Keep in this blessed Seed, where all may be preserved in temperance, patience, love, meekness, righteousness, holiness, and peace, in which the Lord may be seen amongst you, and no ways dishonoured, but glorified by you all. In all your meetings, in cities, towns, and countries, let righteousness flow among you, and the holy truth be uppermost; the pure Spirit your guide and leader, and the holy wisdom from above your orderer, which is gentle, and easy to be entreated. Keep in the religion that preserves from the spots of the world, which is pure and undefiled in God's sight. Keep in the pure and holy worship, in which the pure and holy God is worshipped, to wit, in the Spirit and in the truth, which the devil is out of, who is the author of all unholiness and of that which dishonours God Be tender of God's glory, of his honour, and of his blessed and holy name, in which ye are gathered. All who profess the truth, see that ye walk in it, in righteousness, godliness, and holiness; for 'holiness becomes the house of God, the household of faith.' And that which becomes God's house, God loves; for he loves righteousness—the ornament which becomes his house, and all his family. Therefore see that righteousness run down in all your assemblies, that it flow, to drive away all unrighteousness. This preserves your peace with God; for in righteousness, ye have all peace with the righteous God of Peace, and one with another.

"Every one that bears the name of the Anointed, that high title of being a Christian, named after the Heavenly Man, see that ye be in the divine nature, made conformable unto his image, even the image of the Heavenly Divine Man, who was before that image which Adam and Eve got from Satan in the fall; so that in none of you that fallen image may appear, but his image, and you made conformable unto him. Here translation is showed forth in life and conversation, not in words only; yea, and conversion and repentance, which is a change of the nature of the mind and of the heart, of the spirit and affections, which have been below, and come to be set above; and so receive the things that are from above, and have your conversation in heaven, not that conversation which is according to the power of the prince of the air, that now rules in the disobedient. So be faithful; this is the word of the Lord God unto you all. See that godliness and holiness, righteousness and truth, virtue, and the fruits of the good Spirit, flow over the bad and its fruits, that ye may answer that which is of God in all; for your heavenly Father is glorified in that you bring forth much fruit. Therefore ye, who are plants of his planting, and his trees of righteousness, see that every tree be full of fruit. Keep in true humility, and in the true love of God, which doth edify his body; that the true nourishment from the head, the refreshings, and springs, and rivers of water, and bread of life, may be plenteously known and felt amongst you; that so praises may ascend unto God. Be faithful to the Lord God, and just and true in all your dealings and doings with men.

Be not negligent in your men's meetings to admonish, to exhort, and reprove in the spirit of love and of meekness; to seek that which is lost, and to bring back again that which hath been driven away. So let all minds and spirits, souls and hearts, be bended down under the yoke of Christ Jesus, the power of God.

"Much I could write, but am weak, and have been mostly since I left you. Burthens and travails I have been under, and gone through many ways; but it is well. The Lord Almighty knows my work, which he hath sent me forth to do by his everlasting arm and power; which is from everlasting to everlasting. Blessed be his holy name, which I am in, and in which my love is to you all." G. F.

After I was able to go about, and had been a little amongst Friends, I went to visit the governor; Lewis Morice, Thomas Rous, and some other Friends being with me. He received us very civilly, and treated us very kindly, making us dine with him; and keeping us most part of the day before he let us go away.

The same week I went to BRIDGE-TOWN. There was to be a general meeting of Friends that week; and the visit I had made to the governor, and the kind reception I had with him, being generally known to the officers, civil and military, many came to this meeting from most parts of the island, and those not of the meanest rank; several being judges or justices, colonels or captains; so that a very great meeting we had, both of Friends and others. The Lord's blessed power was plentifully with us; and although I was somewhat straightened for time, three other Friends having spoken before me, yet the Lord opened things through me to the general and great satisfaction of them that were present. Colonel Lewis Morice came to this meeting, and with him a neighbour of his, a judge in the country, whose name was Ralph Fretwell; who was very well satisfied, and received the truth.

Paul Gwin, a jangling Baptist, came into the meeting, and asked me, "How I spelt Cain? and whether I had the same spirit as the apostles had?" I told him, "Yes." And he bade the judge take notice of it. I told him, "He that had not a measure of the same Holy Ghost as the apostles had, was possessed with an unclean spirit." And then he went his way.

I went home with Lewis Morice that night, being about nine or ten miles, going part of the way by boat, the rest on horseback. The place where his plantation was, I thought to be in the finest air of the island. The next day Thomas Briggs and William Edmundson came to see me, intending to leave the island the day following, to go on the Lord's service to Antigua and Nevis. Lewis Morice went with them; at Antigua they had several good meetings, to which there was a great resort of people; and many were convinced. But when they went to Nevis, the governor, an old persecutor, sent soldiers on board the vessel, to stop them, and would not suffer them to land. Wherefore, after Friends of the place had been on board the vessel with them, and they had been sweetly refreshed together, feeling the Lord's power and presence amongst them, they returned to Antigua; where having stayed a while longer, they came back again to Bardadoes, Thomas Briggs being weak and ill.

Of the other Friends that came over with me from England, James Lancaster, John Cartwright, and George Pattison, were gone some time before to Jamaica, and others to other places, so that few remained in Barbadoes with me. We had many great and precious meetings, both for worship and for the affairs of the church; to the former of which many of other societies came. At one of these meetings Colonel Lyne, a sober person, was so well satisfied with what I declared, that he said, "Now I can gainsay such as I have heard speak evil of you; who say, you do not own Christ, nor that he died; whereas I perceive you exalt Christ in all his offices beyond what I have ever heard before."* This man, observing a person take in writing the heads of what I delivered, desired to have a copy of it; and stayed another day with us; so great a love was raised in him to the truth. Indeed a very great convincement there was in most parts of the island; which made the priests and professors rage. Our meetings were very large, and free from disturbance from the government, though the envious priests and some professors endeavoured to stir up the magistrates against us. When they found they could not prevail that way, some Baptists came to the meeting at the town, which was full of people of several ranks and qualities. A great company came with them; and they brought a slanderous paper, written by John Pennyman, with which they made a great noise. But the Lord gave me wisdom and utterance to answer their cavils; so that the auditory generally received satisfaction, and those quarrelsome professors lost ground. When they had wearied themselves with clamour, they went away; but the people staying, the meeting was continued; the things they cavilled about were further opened and cleared; and the life and power of God came over all. But the rage and envy in our adversaries did not cease; they endeavoured to defame Friends with many false and scandalous reports, which they spread abroad through the island. Whereupon we drew up a paper, to go forth in the

* The faith of the early Friends in the divinity and offices of our Saviour being called in question by some, they boldly resented such an inference. From a work published by Samuel Crisp, in 1704, take the following extracts:—

"Our faith is, and always has been in that Christ, the Son of God, who, according to the flesh, was crucified without the gates of Jerusalem: He is the object of our faith, to the merit of whose death and passion, with the work of his Spirit in our hearts, we trust only for life and salvation; with his stripes we are healed."

"As to what he (a libeller) says of our forcing ourselves to speak with a seeming reverence and respect of the outward Christ, his death and sufferings, I would hope that he knows better in his own conscience than thus to represent us. We bear a true reverence and respect to Jesus Christ, his death and sufferings, and can never be sufficiently thankful to him who was pleased to humble himself to death, even the death of the cross; that all that believe in him might, through the cross, be made heirs of life and immortality."

For further elucidation of the soundness of the early Friends in their belief as to the divinity and offices of Christ, see Evans' *Exposition of the Faith of the Society of Friends*, especially John Banks' "Testimony concerning his faith in Christ," and an "Essay drawn up by John Burnyeat and John Watson in 1688," contained in the above-mentioned work.

name of the people called Quakers, for the clearing of truth and Friends from those false reports. It was directed thus:—

"*For the Governor of Barbadoes, with his Council and Assembly, and all others in power, both civil and military, in this Island; from the people called Quakers.*

"WHEREAS many scandalous lies and slanders have been cast upon us, to render us odious; as that 'We deny God, and Christ Jesus, and the Scriptures of truth,' &c. This is to inform you, that all our books and declarations, which for these many years have been published to the world, clearly testify the contrary. Yet, for your satisfaction, we now plainly and sincerely declare, 'that we do own and believe in the only wise, omnipotent, and everlasting God, the Creator of all things both in heaven and in earth, and the preserver of all that he hath made; who is God over all, blessed for ever; to whom be all honour and glory, dominion, praise, and thanksgiving, both now and for evermore!'

"And we own and believe in Jesus Christ, his beloved and only begotten Son, in whom he is well pleased; who was conceived by the Holy Ghost, and born of the Virgin Mary; in whom we have redemption through his blood, even the forgiveness of sins; who is the express image of the Invisible God, the first-born of every creature, by whom were all things created that are in heaven, and in earth, visible and invisible, whether they be thrones, or dominions, principalities, or powers, all things were created by him. And we own and believe that He was made a sacrifice for sin, who knew no sin, neither was guile found in his mouth; that he was crucified for us in the flesh, without the gates of Jerusalem; and that he was buried, and rose again the third day by the power of his Father, for our justification; and that he ascended up into heaven, and now sitteth at the right hand of God. This Jesus, who was the foundation of the holy prophets and apostles, is our foundation; and we believe that there is no other foundation to be laid than that which is laid, even Christ Jesus; who tasted death for every man, shed his blood for all men, and is the propitiation for our sins, and not for ours only, but also for the sins of the whole world; according as John the Baptist testified of him, when he said, 'Behold the Lamb of God, that taketh away the sins of the world.' Jn. i. 29. We believe that he alone is our Redeemer and Saviour, even the Captain of our Salvation, who saves us from sin, as well as from hell, and the wrath to come, and destroys the devil and his works; he is the Seed of the woman, that bruises the serpent's head, to wit, Christ Jesus, the Alpha and Omega, the First and the Last. He is (as the Scriptures of truth say of him) our wisdom and righteousness, justification and redemption; neither is there salvation in any other, for there is no other name under heaven given among men whereby we may be saved. He alone is the Shepherd and Bishop of our souls; He is our Prophet, whom Moses long since testified of, saying, 'A prophet shall the Lord your God raise up unto you of your brethren, like unto me; Him shall ye hear in all things, whatsoever he shall say unto you; and it shall come to pass, that every soul that will not hear that prophet, shall be destroyed from among the people.' Acts iii. 22, 23.

"He it is that is now come in the Spirit, and hath given us an understanding that we may know him that is true. He rules in our hearts by his law of love and of life, and makes us free from the law of sin and death. We have no life but by him; for he is the quickening Spirit, the second Adam, the Lord from heaven, by whose blood we are cleansed, and our consciences sprinkled from dead works to serve the living God. He is our Mediator, that makes peace and reconciliation between God offended and us offending, He being the oath of God, the new covenant of light, life, grace, and peace; the author and finisher of our faith. This Lord Jesus Christ, the heavenly Man, the Emmanuel, God with us, we all own and believe in; him whom the high-priest raged against, and said, he had spoken blasphemy; whom the priests and the elders of the Jews took counsel together against, and put to death; the same whom Judas betrayed for thirty pieces of silver, which the priests gave him as a reward for his treason, who also gave large money to the soldiers to breach a horrible lie, namely, 'that his disciples came and stole him away by night, whilst they slept.' After he was risen from the dead, the history of the Acts of the Apostles sets forth, how the chief priests and elders persecuted the disciples of this Jesus, for preaching Christ and his resurrection. This, we say, is that Lord Jesus Christ, whom we own to be our life and salvation.

"Concerning the Holy Scriptures, we do believe that they were given forth by the Holy Spirit of God, through the holy men of God, who (as the Scripture itself declares, 2 Pe. i. 21.) 'spake as they were moved by the Holy Ghost.' We believe they are to be read, believed, and fulfilled (he that fulfils them, is Christ); and they are 'profitable for doctrine, for reproof, for correction, and for instruction in righteousness, that the man of God may be perfect, throughly furnished unto all good works,' 2 Ti. iii. 16, and are 'able to make wise unto salvation, through faith in Christ Jesus.' We believe that the Holy Scriptures are the words of God; for it is said, Ex. xx. 1, 'God spake all these words, saying,' &c., meaning the ten commandments given forth upon Mount Sinai. And in Rev. xxii. 18, saith John, 'I testify to every man that heareth the words of the prophecy of this book: if any man addeth unto these, and if any man shall take away from the words of the book of this prophecy' (not the word), &c. So in Lu. i. 20, 'Because thou believest not my words.' And in John v. 47; xv. 7; xiv. 23; and xii. 47. So that we call the Holy Scriptures, as Christ and the apostles called them, and holy men of God called them, viz., the words of God.

"Another slander which they have cast upon us is, 'that we teach the negroes to rebel;' a thing we utterly abhor in our hearts; the Lord knows it, who is the searcher of all hearts, and knows all things, and can testify for us, that this is a most abominable untruth. For that which we have spoken to them is, 'to exhort and admonish them to be sober, and to fear God; to love their masters and mistresses, and to be faithful and diligent in their masters' service and business; and then their masters and overseers would love them, and deal kindly and gently with them; also, that they should not beat their wives, nor the wives their husbands, neither should the men have many wives; that they should not steal, or be drunk, —should not commit adultery, or fornication,—should not curse, swear, lie, or give bad words to one another, or to any one else: for there is something in them that tells them, they should not practise these or any other evils. But if, notwithstanding, they should do them, then we let them know there are but two ways, the one that leads to heaven, where the righteous go; and the other that leads to hell, where the wicked and debauched, whoremongers and adulterers, murderers and liars go. To the one the Lord will say, 'Come, ye blessed of my Father, inherit the kingdom prepared for you from the foundation of the world;' but to the other he will say, 'Depart, ye cursed, into everlasting fire, prepared for the devil and his angels:' so 'the wicked go into everlasting punishment, but the righteous into life eternal.' Matt. xxv.

"Consider, Friends, it is no transgression for a master of a family to instruct his family himself, or for some others to do it in his behalf; but rather it is a very great duty incumbent upon them. Abraham and Joshua did so: of the first the Lord said, Gen. xviii. 19, 'I know that Abraham will command his children and his household after him; and they shall keep the way of the Lord, to do justice and judgment, that the Lord may bring upon Abraham the things that he hath spoken of him.' And the latter said, Josh. xxiv. 15, 'Choose ye this day whom ye will serve; but as for me and my house, we will serve the Lord.' We declare that we esteem it a duty incumbent on us to pray with and for those in and belonging to our families, and to teach, instruct, and admonish them; this being a command of the Lord, disobedience whereunto will provoke his displeasure; as may be seen, Jer. x. 25, 'Pour out thy fury upon the heathen that know thee not, and upon the families that call not upon thy name.' Now Negroes, Tawnies, Indians, make up a very great part of the families in this island; for whom an account will be required by him who comes to judge both quick and dead, at the great day of judgment, when every one shall be 'rewarded according to the deeds done in the body, whether they be good or whether they be evil:' at that day, we say, of the resurrection both of the good and of the bad, of the just and of the unjust, when 'the Lord Jesus shall be revealed from heaven with his mighty angels, in flaming fire, taking vengeance on them that know not God, and obey not the gospel of our Lord Jesus Christ, who shall be punished with everlasting destruction from the presence of the Lord, and from the glory of his power, when he shall come to be glorified in his saints, and admired in all them that believe in that day.' 2 Thess. i. 8, &c. See also 2 Pet. iii. 3, &c."

This wicked slander (of our endeavouring to make the negroes rebel) our adversaries took occasion to raise, from our having had some meetings with and amongst the negroes; for both I and other Friends had several meetings with them in several plantations, wherein we exhorted them to justice, sobriety, temperance, chastity, and piety, and to be subject to their masters and governors; which was altogether contrary to what our envious adversaries maliciously suggested against us.

As I had been to visit the governor as soon as I was well able, after I came thither; so, when I was at Thomas Rous's, the governor came to see me, carrying himself very courteously.

Having been three months or more in Barbadoes, and having visited Friends, thoroughly settled meetings, and despatched the service for which the Lord brought me thither, I felt my spirit clear of that island, and found drawings to Jamaica. When I had communicated this to Friends, I acquainted the governor also, and divers of his council, that I intended shortly to leave the island, and go to Jamaica. This I did, that as my coming thither was open and public, so my departure also might be. Before I left the island, I wrote the following letter to my wife; that she might understand both how it was with me, and how I proceeded in my travels:—

"My dear Heart,

"To whom is my love, and to all the children in the Seed of Life that changeth not, but is over all; blessed be the Lord for ever. I have undergone great sufferings in my body and spirit, beyond words; but the God of heaven be praised, his truth is over all. I am now well; and, if the Lord permit, within a few days I pass from Barbadoes towards Jamaica; and I think to stay but little there. I desire that ye may be all kept free in the Seed of Life, out of all cumbrances. Friends are generally well. Remember me to Friends that inquire after me. So no more, but my love in the Seed and Life that changeth not." G. F.

Barbadoes, 6th of 11th Month, 1671.

I set sail from Barbadoes to Jamaica on the 8th of the 11th month, 1671; Robert Widders, William Edmundson, Solomon Eccles, and Elizabeth Hooton, going with me. Thomas Briggs and John Stubbs remained in Barbadoes; with whom were John Rous and William Bailey. We had a quick and easy passage to Jamaica, where we met with our Friends James Lancaster, John Cartwright, and George Pattison again, who had been labouring there in the service of truth; into which we forthwith entered with them, travelling up and down through the island, which is large; and a brave country it is, though the people are, many of them, debauched and wicked. We had much service. There was a great convincement, and many received the truth; some of whom were people of account in the world. We had many meetings there, which were large, and very quiet. The people were civil to us, so that not a mouth was opened against us. I was twice with the governor, and some other magistrates, who all carried themselves kindly towards me.

About a week after we landed in Jamaica, Elizabeth Hooton, a woman of great age, who had travelled much in truth's service, and suffered much for it, departed this life. She was well the day before she died; and departed in peace, like a lamb, bearing testimony to truth at her departure.

When we had been about seven weeks in Jamaica, had brought Friends into pretty good order, and settled several meetings amongst them, we left Solomon Eccles there; the rest of us embarked for Maryland, leaving Friends and truth prosperous in Jamaica, the Lord's power being over all, and his blessed Seed reigning.

Before I left Jamaica, I wrote another letter to my wife, as follows:—

"My dear Heart,

"To whom is my love, and to the children, in that which changeth not, but is over all; and to all Friends in those parts. I have been in Jamaica about five weeks. Friends here are generally well; and there is a convincement: but things would be too large to write of. Sufferings in every place attend me; but the blessed Seed is over all: the great Lord be praised, who is Lord of sea and land, and of all things therein. We intend to pass from hence about the beginning of next month, towards Maryland, if the Lord please. Dwell all of you in the Seed of God; in his truth I rest in love to you all." G. F.

Jamaica, 23rd of 12th Month, 1671.

CHAPTER V.

1672–1673.—George Fox embarks for Maryland, where he arrives after a seven weeks' voyage, and having experienced some remarkable deliverances—attends a General Meeting for Maryland, which held four days—several meetings for discipline established—has meetings with the Indian kings—travels towards New England—attends the half year's meeting on Long Island, which continued four days—has a meeting with some opposers—visits Rhode Island, where the Yearly Meeting for New England is held, which continued six days—attends a marriage there, and has a meeting with some Ranters—also one with some Indians on Shelter Island—one of his companions thrown from his horse and lays apparently dead, but soon recovers in an unexpected manner—they reach Maryland after nine days' travel overland between three and four hundred miles—visits a judge who is ill, but recovers—attends the General Meeting for Maryland, which held five days—sails for Virginia, and arrives in three days, a distance of 200 miles—thence proceeds towards Carolina—visits the Indians, and shows them that God made but one woman for one man—returns to Virginia—sails for Maryland—endures great extremes of heat and cold within a very short period—speaks to a woman who had been many years in trouble, and entreats the Lord for her, and she is thereupon restored—attends the General Meeting for Maryland, to the edification and comfort of Friends—sails for England, and arrives safe, after a six weeks' passage.

We went on board on the 8th of 1st Month, 1671–2; and having contrary winds, were a full week sailing forwards and backwards, before we could get out of sight of Jamaica. A difficult voyage this proved, and dangerous, especially in passing through the Gulf of Florida, where we met with many trials by winds and storms. But the great God, who is Lord of the sea and land, and who rideth upon the wings of the wind, did by his power preserve us through many and great dangers, when by extreme stress of weather our vessel was many times likely to be upset, and much of her tackling broken. And indeed we were sensible that the Lord was a God at hand, and that his ear was open to the supplications of his people. For when the winds were so strong and boisterous, and the storms and tempests so great, that the sailors knew not what to do, but let the ship go which way she would; then did we pray unto the Lord, who graciously heard us, calmed the winds and the seas, gave us seasonable weather, and made us to rejoice in his salvation; blessed and praised be the holy name of the Lord, whose power hath dominion over all, whom the winds and the seas obey.

We were between six and seven weeks in this passage from Jamaica to Maryland. Some days before we came to land, after we had entered the bay of Patuxent River, a great storm arose, which cast a boat upon us for shelter, in which were several people of account in the world. We took them in; but the boat was lost, with five hundred pounds' worth of goods in it, as they said. They continued on board us several days, not having any means to get off; and we had a very good meeting with them in the ship. But provisions grew short, for they brought none in with them; and ours, by reason of the length of our voyage, were well nigh spent when they came to us; so that with their living with us too, we had now little or none left. Whereupon George Pattison took a boat, and ventured his life to get to shore; the hazard was so great, that all but Friends concluded he would be cast away. Yet it pleased the Lord to bring him safe to land; and in a short time after, the Friends of the place came to fetch us to land also, in a seasonable time, for our provisions were quite spent.

We partook also of another great deliverance in this voyage, through the good providence of the Lord, which we came to understand afterwards. For when we were determined to come from Jamaica, we had our choice of two vessels, that were both bound for the same coast. One of these was a frigate, the other a yacht. The master of the frigate, we thought, asked unreasonably for our passage; which made us agree with the master of the yacht, who offered to carry us ten shillings a-piece cheaper than the other. We went on board the yacht, and the frigate came out together with us, intending to be consorts during the voyage; and for several days we sailed together; but what with calms and contrary winds, we were in a while separated. After that, the frigate, losing her way, fell among the Spaniards; by whom she was taken and plundered, and the master and mate made prisoners; afterwards, being retaken by the English, she was sent home to her owners in Virginia. Which when we came to understand, we saw and admired the providence of God, who preserved us out of our enemies' hands; and he that was covetous fell among the covetous.

Here we found John Burnyeat * intending shortly to sail for England; but on our arrival he altered his purpose, and joined us in the Lord's service. He had appointed a general meeting for all the Friends in the province of Maryland, that he might see them together, and take his leave of them, before he departed out of the country; and it was so ordered by the good providence of God, that we landed just in time to reach that meeting; by which means we had a very seasonable opportunity of taking the Friends of the province together. A very large meeting this was, and held four days; to which, besides Friends, came many other people, many of whom were of considerable quality in the world's account; for there were amongst

* John Burnyeat, a fellow-labourer in the gospel with George Fox, and who is several times named in this Journal, was born in Cumberland about the year 1631. He was well educated, and religiously inclined from his youth, and convinced by George Fox when he first came into Cumberland in 1653. He became an unwearied traveller in the gospel, both in this country and in America, boldly proclaiming the glad tidings of salvation, for which he fell in for his share of abuse and imprisonments. Once at Ripon, when visiting twenty-four of his friends imprisoned there for the testimony of Jesus, speaking a few words to them he was haled away before the mayor, and several times knocked off his knees when at prayer, being sent to prison to his friends, and kept there fourteen weeks.

He married and settled in Ireland, where his service mostly lay in his latter days. In 1683 he was imprisoned in the Marshalsea in Dublin two months, for meeting and preaching. His wife died in 1688; and he, having finished his course, and kept the faith, departed in peace in 1690. His works, and testimonies concerning him, with an account of his convincement, and journal of his travels, was published in a 4to volume, to which the reader is referred. Also, *Piety Promoted*, vol. i. p. 179; and Whiting's *Memoirs*, p. 416–430.

them five or six justices of the peace, a speaker of their parliament or assembly, one of the council, and divers others of note; who seemed well satisfied with the meeting. After the public meetings were over, the men's and women's meetings began; wherein I opened to Friends the service thereof to their great satisfaction. After this we went to a place called the CLIFFS, where another general meeting was appointed. We went some part of the way by land, the rest by water; and a storm arising, our boat was run on ground, in danger to be beaten to pieces; and the water came in upon us. I perspired much, having come very hot out of a meeting before, and was now wet with the water beside; yet having faith in the divine power, I was preserved from taking hurt; blessed be the Lord. To this meeting also many people came, and received the truth with reverence. We had also a men's meeting and a women's meeting, at which most of the backsliders came in again; and several of those meetings were established for taking care of the affairs of the church.

After these two general meetings, we parted company, dividing ourselves unto several coasts, for the service of truth. James Lancaster and John Cartwright went by sea for New England; William Edmundson and three other Friends sailed for Virginia, where things were much out of order; John Burnyeat, Robert Widders, George Pattison, and I, with several Friends of the province, went over by boat to the eastern shore, and had a meeting there on the First-day; where many people received the truth with gladness, and Friends were greatly refreshed. A very large and heavenly meeting it was; and several persons of quality in that country were at it, two of whom were justices of the peace. It was upon me from the Lord, to send to the Indian emperor and his kings to come to that meeting; the emperor came and was at it; but his kings, lying further off, could not reach in time; yet they came after with their cockarooses. I had in the evening two good opportunities with them; they heard the word of the Lord willingly, and confessed to it. What I spoke to them, I desired them to speak to their people; and let them know, that "God was raising up his tabernacle of witness in their wilderness country, and was setting up his standard and glorious ensign of righteousness." They carried themselves very courteously and lovingly, and inquired "where the next meeting would be, and they would come to it;" yet they said, "they had had a great debate with their council about their coming, before they came now."

Next day we began our journey by land to New England; a tedious journey through the woods and wilderness, over bogs and great rivers. We took horse at the head of TREDHAVEN CREEK, and travelled through the woods, till we came a little above the head of MILES RIVER; by which we passed, and rode to the head of WYE RIVER, and so to the head of CHESTER RIVER; where, making a fire, we took up our lodging in the woods. Next morning we travelled through the woods till we came to SAXIFRAX RIVER, which we went over in canoes (or Indian boats), causing our horses to swim by. Then we rode to BOHEMIA RIVER; where in like manner swimming our horses, we ourselves went over in canoes. We rested a little while at a plantation by the way, but not long, for we had thirty miles to ride that afternoon, if we would reach a town; which we were desirous to do, and therefore rode hard for it. I with some others, whose horses were strong, got to the town that night, exceedingly tired, and wet to the skin; but George Pattison and Robert Widders being weaker-horsed, were obliged to lie in the woods that night also. The town we went to, was a Dutch town, called NEWCASTLE, whither Robert Widders and George Pattison came to us next morning. We departed thence and got over the River Delaware, not without great danger of some of our lives. When we were over, we were troubled to procure guides; who were hard to get and very chargeable. Then had we that wilderness country to pass through, since called WEST JERSEY, not then inhabited by English; so that we have travelled a whole day together, without seeing man or woman, house or dwelling-place. Sometimes we lay in the woods by a fire, and sometimes in the Indians' wigwams or houses. We came one night to an Indian town, and lay at the king's house, who was a very worthy man. Both he and his wife received us very lovingly, and his attendants (such as they were) were very respectful to us. They laid us mats to lie on; but provision was very short with them, having caught but little that day.* At another Indian town where we stayed, the king came to us, and he could speak some English. I spoke to him much, and also to his people, and they were very loving to us. At length we came to MIDDLETOWN, an English plantation in EAST JERSEY, where there were some Friends, but we could not stay to have a meeting there at that time, being earnestly pressed in our spirits, to get to the half-year's meeting of Friends at

* The instances of heathen kindness and hospitality, experienced by George Fox and others who have visited the Indians in a friendly manner, contrast very favourably in comparison with the many acts of bigoted intolerance and cruelty recorded in these volumes on the part of those professedly civilized and Christian.

Many incidents might be related in proof of Indian kindness when unprovoked to opposite conduct. When the Quakers were under a cruel persecution by the magistrates of Boston, in New England, Nicholas Upshal, "a man of an unblameable conversation," and a church member of their communion, showed the sufferers kindness, by giving five shillings a week to the jailer to let those confined in prison have the sustenance necessary for life—*the magistrates having caused the jail window to be boarded up, that none might communicate with, or help them.* He proceeded afterwards to reason with the magistrates, and warn them not to be found fighting against God, for which he was fined £20, imprisoned, and then banished; though a weakly old man, and the season the depth of winter. In his banishment in the wilderness, he met an Indian, who, having understood how he had been dealt with, took compassion on him, and very kindly told him, *if he would live with him he would make him a warm house;* and further said, "What a God have these English, who deal so with one another about their God!"

See here the Red Indian's kindly care
Though he the name of *savage* bear.
Christian, more savage thou than he,
Blush for thy cruel deeds of infamy:
The Indian's unasked cup of charity
Is larger than as mixed by thee.
The white man ag'd, through frost and snows
A banish'd exile to his country goes,
Full many a welcome does he say,
To his warm house whate'er the day.
More Christian he who thus does prove
By practice kindred with a God of love.
More Christian he than they who thus pollute
Their faith, and for their God a brother persecute.

Oyster-Bay in Long Island, which was very near at hand. We went with a Friend, Richard Hartshorn, brother to Hugh Hartshorn, the upholsterer, in London, who received us gladly at his house, where we refreshed ourselves, and then he carried us and our horses in his own boat over a great water, which occupied most part of the day getting over, and set us upon LONG ISLAND. We got that evening to Friends at GRAVESAND, with whom we tarried that night, and next day got to FLUSHING, and the day following reached OYSTER-BAY; several Friends of Gravesand and Flushing accompanying us. The half-year's meeting began next day, which was the first day of the week, and lasted four days. The first and second days we had public meetings for worship, to which people of all sorts came; on the third day were the men's and women's meetings, wherein the affairs of the church were taken care of. Here we met with some bad spirits, who had run out from truth into prejudice, contention, and opposition to the order of truth, and to Friends therein. These had been very troublesome to Friends in their meetings there and thereabouts formerly, and likely would have been so now; but I would not suffer the service of our men's and women's meetings to be interrupted and hindered by their cavils. I let them know, that "if they had anything to object against the order of truth which we were in, we would give them a meeting another day on purpose." And indeed I laboured the more, and travelled the harder to get to this meeting, where it was expected many of these contentious people would be; because I understood they had reflected much upon me, when I was far from them. The men's and women's meetings being over, on the fourth day we had a meeting with these discontented people, to which as many of them as chose came, and as many Friends as desired were present also; and the Lord's power broke forth gloriously to the confounding of the gainsayers. Then some of those that had been chief in the mischievous work of contention and opposition against the truth, began to fawn upon me, and to cast the blame upon others; but the deceitful spirit was judged down and condemned, and the glorious truth of God was exalted and set over all; and they were all brought down and bowed under. Which was of great service to truth, and to the satisfaction and comfort of Friends; glory to the Lord for ever!

After Friends were gone to their several habitations, we stayed some days upon the island; had meetings in several parts thereof, and good service for the Lord. When we were clear of the island, we returned to Oyster-Bay, waiting for a wind to carry us to RHODE ISLAND, which was computed to be about two hundred miles. As soon as the wind served we set sail, and arrived there on the thirtieth day of the third month; and were gladly received by Friends. We went to Nicholas Easton's house, who at that time was governor of the island; where we rested, being very weary with travelling. On First-day following we had a large meeting, to which the deputy-governor and several justices came, who were mightily affected with the truth. The week following, the Yearly Meeting for all the Friends of New England and the other colonies adjacent, was held in this island; to which, besides very many Friends who lived in those parts, came John Stubbs from Barbadoes, and James Lancaster and John Cartwright from another way. This meeting lasted six days, the first four days being general public meetings for worship, to which abundance of other people came; for they having no priest in the island, and so no restriction to any particular way of worship; and both the governor and deputy-governor, with several justices of the peace daily frequenting the meetings; this so encouraged the people that they flocked in from all parts of the island. Very good service we had amongst them, and truth had a good reception. I have rarely observed people, in the state wherein they stood, hear with more attention, diligence, and affection, than generally they did, during the four days together; which also was taken notice of by other Friends. After these public meetings were over, the men's meeting began, which was large, precious, and weighty; and the day following was the women's meeting, which also was large and very solemn. These two meetings being for ordering the affairs of the church, many weighty things were opened and communicated to them, by way of advice, information, and instruction in the services relating thereunto; that all might be kept clean, sweet, and savoury amongst them. In these two meetings, several men's and women's meetings for other parts, were agreed and settled, to take care of the poor, and other affairs of the church; and to see, that all who profess truth, walk according to the glorious gospel of God. When this great general meeting in Rhode Island was ended, it was somewhat hard for Friends to part; for the glorious power of the Lord, which was over all, and his blessed truth and life flowing amongst them, had so knit and united them together, that they spent two days in taking leave one of another, and of the Friends of the island; and then, being mightily filled with the presence and power of the Lord, they went away with joyful hearts to their various habitations, in the several colonies where they lived.*

When Friends had taken their leave one of another, we, who travelled amongst them, dispersed ourselves into our several services, as the Lord ordered us. John Burnyeat, John Cartwright, and George Pattison, went into the eastern parts of New England, in company with the Friends that came from thence, to visit the particular meetings there; whom John Stubbs and James Lancaster intended to follow a while after, in the same service; but they were not yet clear of this island. Robert Widders and I stayed some time longer also upon this island; finding service still here for the Lord, through the great openness of the people, and the daily coming in of fresh people from other colonies, for some time after the general meeting; so that we had many large and serviceable meetings among them.

During this time a marriage took place amongst Friends in this island; and we were present. It was at a Friend's house, who had formerly been governor of the island; three justices of the peace, and many others not in profession with us, were there; and both they and Friends said, they never saw so solemn an assembly on such an occasion, so weighty a marriage and so comely an order. Thus truth was set over all. This might serve for an example to others, for there were some present from many other places.

* See Bowden's *History of Friends in America*, vol. i., p. 280–284.

After this I had a great travail in spirit concerning the Ranters in those parts, who had been rude at a meeting which I was not at. Wherefore I appointed a meeting amongst them, believing the Lord would give me power over them; which he did to his praise and glory; blessed be his name for ever. There were at this meeting many Friends, and other people; some of whom were justices of the peace, and other officers, who were generally well affected. One of the justices, who had been one twenty years, was convinced, and spoke highly of the truth; and more highly of me, than is fit for me to mention or take notice of.

Then we had a meeting at PROVIDENCE, which was very large, consisting of many sorts of people; I had a great travail upon my spirit, that it might be preserved quiet, and that truth might be brought over the people, might gain entrance, and have a place in them; for they were generally above the priests, in high notions; and some of them came on purpose to dispute. But the Lord, whom we waited upon, was with us, and his power went over them all; and his blessed Seed was exalted and set above all. The disputers were silent, and the meeting was quiet, and ended well; praised be the Lord! The people went away mightily satisfied, much desiring another meeting. This place (called Providence) was about thirty miles from Rhode Island; and we went to it by water. The governor of Rhode Island, and many others, went with me thither; and we had the meeting in a great barn, which was thronged with people, so that I was exceedingly hot, and perspired much; but all was well; the glorious power of the Lord shone over all; glory to the great God for ever!

After this we went to NARRAGANSET, about twenty miles from Rhode Island; and the governor went with us. We had a meeting at a justice's house, where Friends had never had any before. It was very large, for the country generally came in; and people came also from Connecticut, and other parts round about, amongst whom were four justices of the peace. Most of these people had never heard Friends before; but they were mightily affected with the meeting, and a great desire there is after the truth amongst them; so that our meeting was of very good service, blessed be the Lord for ever! The justice at whose house the meeting was, and another justice of that country, invited me to come again; but I was then clear of those parts, and going towards Shelter Island. But John Burnyeat and John Cartwright, being come out of New England into Rhode Island, before I was gone, I laid this place before them; and they felt drawings thither, and went to visit them. At another place, I heard some of the magistrates said among themselves, "if they had money enough, they would hire me to be their minister." This was, where they did not well understand us, and our principles; but when I heard of it, I said, "it was time for me to be gone; for if their eye was so much to me, or any of us, they would not come to their own teacher." For this thing (hiring ministers) had spoiled many, by hindering them from improving their own talents; whereas our labour is to bring every one to his own teacher *in* himself.

I went from hence towards Shelter Island, having with me Robert Widders, James Lancaster, George Pattison, and John Jay, a planter of Barbadoes. We went in a sloop; and passing by POINT JUDA and

BLOCK ISLAND, we came to FISHER'S ISLAND, where at night we went on shore; but were not able to stay for the mosquitoes which abound there, and are very troublesome. Wherefore we went into our sloop again, put off from the shore, and cast anchor; and so lay in our sloop that night. Next day we went into the SOUND, but finding our sloop was not able to live in that water, we returned again, and came to anchor before Fisher's Island, where we lay in our sloop that night also. There fell abundance of rain, and our sloop being open, we were exceedingly wet. Next day we passed over the waters called the TWO HORSE RACES, and then by GARNER'S ISLAND; after which we passed by the GULL'S ISLAND, and so got at length to SHELTER ISLAND; which, though it was but about twenty-seven leagues from Rhode Island, yet through the difficulty of passage we were three days in reaching. The day after, being First-day, we had a meeting there. In the same week, I had another among the Indians; at which were their king, his council, and about a hundred Indians more. They sat down like Friends, and heard very attentively, while I spoke to them by an interpreter, an Indian that could speak English well. After the meeting they appeared very loving, and confessed that what was said to them was truth. Next First-day we had a great meeting on the island, to which came many people who had never heard Friends before. They were very well satisfied with it, and would not go away when it was over, till they had spoken with me; wherefore I went amongst them, and found they were much taken with the truth; good desires were raised in them, and great love. Blessed be the Lord, his name spreads, and will be great among the nations, and dreadful among the heathen.

While we were in Shelter Island, William Edmundson came to us, who had been labouring in the work of the Lord in Virginia. From whence he travelled through the desert-country, through difficulties and many trials, till he came to ROAN-OAK, where he met with a tender people. After seven weeks' service in those parts, sailing over to Maryland and so to New York, he came to Long Island, and so to Shelter Island; where we met with him, and were very glad to hear from him the good service he had had for the Lord, in the several places where he had travelled since he parted from us.

We stayed not long in Shelter Island, but entering our sloop again put to sea for Long Island. We had a very rough passage, for the tide ran so strong for several hours, that I have not seen the like; and being against us, we could hardly get forwards, though we had a gale. We were upon the water all that day and the night following; but found ourselves next day driven back near to Fisher's Island. For there was a great fog, and towards day it was very dark, so that we could not see what way we made. Besides, it rained much in the night, which in our open sloop made us very wet. Next day a great storm arose, so that we were fain to go over the Sound, and got over with much difficulty. When we left Fisher's Island, we passed by Faulcon Island, and came to the Main, where we cast anchor till the storm was over. Then we crossed the Sound, being all very wet; and much difficulty we had to get to land, the wind being strong against us. But blessed be the Lord God of heaven and earth, and of the seas and waters, all was well. We got safe to OYSTER-BAY in Long Island, on the seventh of sixth month, very early in the morning, which is about two hundred miles from Rhode Island. At Oyster-Bay we had a very large meeting. The same day James Lancaster and Christopher Holder * went over the Bay to Rye, on the continent, in Governor Winthrop's government, and had a meeting there. From Oyster-Bay we passed about thirty miles to FLUSHING, where we had a very large meeting; many hundreds of people being there, some of whom came about thirty miles to it. A glorious and heavenly meeting it was (praised be the Lord God!) and the people were much satisfied. Meanwhile Christopher Holder and some other Friends went to a town in Long Island, called Jamaica, and had a meeting there. We passed from Flushing to GRAVESAND, about twenty miles, and there had three precious meetings; to which many would have come from New York, but the weather hindered them. Being clear of this place, we hired a sloop; and the wind serving, set out for the New Country, now called JERSEY. Passing down the Bay by Conny Island, Natton Island, and Stratton Island, we came to Richard Hartshorn's, at MIDDLETOWN-HARBOUR, about break of day, the 27th of sixth Month. Next day we rode about thirty miles into the country through the woods and over very bad bogs, one worse than all the rest; the descent into which was so steep, that we were fain to slide down with our horses, and then let them lie and breathe, before they could go on. This place the people of the country called Purgatory. We got at length to SHREWSBURY in EAST JERSEY, and on First-day had a precious meeting there, to which Friends and other people came from far; and the blessed presence of the Lord was with us. The same week we had a men's and women's meeting out of most parts of New Jersey. They are building a meeting-place in the midst of them, and there is a monthly

* This is the only mention of Christopher Holder in these volumes. He was a great sufferer in the New England persecution. In 1657 he and another Friend being at Salem, went to the Puritan place of worship there, and after the priest had concluded, Christopher Holder addressing the assembly, was not allowed to proceed; one of the commissioners, with much fury, "seizing him by the hair of his head," and violently thrusting a glove and handkerchief into his mouth. These two Friends were subsequently sentenced, under "the law against Quakers," to receive thirty lashes. The brutal manner in which this sentence was carried out, was in accordance with the spirit that prompted the rulers to pass the cruel law. A three-corded knotted whip was used on the occasion; and the executioner, to make more sure of his blows, "measured his ground," and then "fetched his strokes with all his might." Thirty strokes thus inflicted, as will be readily imagined, left the sufferers miserably torn and lacerated; and in this state they were conveyed to their prison cell. Here, without any bedding, or even straw to lie on, the inhuman jailer kept them for three days without food or drink; and, in this dismal abode, often exposed to damp and cold, were these faithful men confined for the space of nine weeks. We may wonder that, under such aggravated cruelties, their lives were spared; but He, for whose holy cause they thus suffered, was near to support and console them. His ancient promise was fulfilled in their experience, and they rejoiced in the comforting presence of his living power.—Bowden's *History of Friends in America*.

Previous to this, Christopher Holder and his companion had been banished from Rhode Island. The governor having hired an Indian to convey them off the island, ordered the Friends to pay for the passage themselves. But not being willing to

and general meeting set up; which will be of great service in those parts, in "keeping up the gospel order and government of Christ Jesus (of the increase of which there is no end), that they who are faithful, may see that all who profess the holy truth live in the pure religion, and walk as becometh the gospel."

While we were at Shrewsbury an accident befell, which, for the time, was a great exercise to us. John Jay, a Friend of Barbadoes, who came with us from Rhode Island, and intended to accompany us through the woods to Maryland, being to try a horse, got upon his back; and the horse fell a-running, and cast him down upon his head, and broke his neck, as the people said. They that were near him took him up as dead, carried him a good way, and laid him on a tree. I got to him as soon as I could; and feeling him, concluded he was dead. As I stood by him, pitying him and his family, I took hold of his hair, and his head turned any way, his neck was so limber. Whereupon I took his head in both my hands, and setting my knees against the tree, I raised his head, and perceived there was nothing out or broken that way. Then I put one hand under his chin, and the other behind his head, and raised his head two or three times with all my strength, and brought it in. I soon perceived his neck began to grow stiff again, and then he began to rattle in the throat, and quickly after to breathe. The people were amazed; but I bid them have a good heart, be of good faith, and carry him into the house. They did so, and set him by the fire. I bid them get him something warm to drink, and put him to bed. After he had been in the house a while he began to speak; but did not know where he had been. The next day we passed away (and he with us, pretty well) about sixteen miles to a meeting at MIDDLETOWN, through woods and bogs, and over a river; where we swam our horses, and got over ourselves upon a hollow tree. Many hundred miles did he travel with us after this.

To this meeting came most of the people of the town. A glorious meeting we had, and the truth was over all; blessed be the great Lord God for ever! After the meeting we went to MIDDLETOWN-HARBOUR, about five miles, in order to take our long journey next morning, through the

facilitate their own banishment, and not feeling that it was their Divine Master's will for them to leave the island, they declined to go, or to pay the Indian who was hired to take them. The governor directed the constable forcibly to obtain the requisite sum from the strangers, and gave peremptory orders to the natives to take them away in their canoes. The Algonquins, however, not being in any great haste to execute the bidding of the governor, contrary to the will of the Friends, and at a time too when the weather was stormy, entertained them for three days with marked kindness and hospitality. A change in the weather then taking place, and the banished ones feeling that it was no longer required of them to stay on the island, the Indians, at their own request, prepared to take them across. Before leaving the island, the Friends offered to remunerate the natives for their kindness, but these poor people, from the generous impulses of their hearts, acting more in unison with the spirit of Christianity than those who were wont to be their teachers, declined to receive any reward. "You are strangers," they replied, "and Jehovah hath taught us to love strangers." Such simple and feeling language from the lips of North American Indians, was a striking rebuke to the bigotry and intolerance which marked the conduct of their highly professing teachers.—Bowden's *History of Friends in America.*

woods towards Maryland; having hired Indians for our guides. I determined to pass through the woods on the other side of Delaware-Bay, that we might head the creeks and rivers as much as possible. On the 9th of the 7th month we set forwards, and passed through many Indian towns, and over some rivers and bogs; and when we had rode about forty miles, we made a fire at night, and laid by it. As we came among the Indians, we declared the day of the Lord to them. Next day we travelled fifty miles, as we computed; and at night, finding an old house, which the Indians had forced the people to leave, we made a fire and stayed there, at the head of Delaware-Bay. Next day we swam our horses over a river about a mile, at twice, first to an island called UPPER DINIDOCK, and then to the mainland; having hired Indians to help us over in their canoes. This day we could reach but about thirty miles, and came at night to a Swede's house, where we got a little straw, and stayed that night. Next day, having hired another guide, we travelled about forty miles through the woods, and made a fire at night, by which we lay, and dried ourselves; for we were often wet in our travels. The next day we passed over a desperate river, which had in it many rocks and broad stones, very hazardous to us and our horses. Thence we came to CHRISTIAN RIVER, where we swam over our horses, and went over ourselves in canoes; but the sides of this river were so bad and miry, that some of the horses had like to have been laid up. Thence we came to NEWCASTLE, heretofore called NEW AMSTERDAM; and being very weary, and inquiring in the town where we could buy some corn for our horses, the governor came and invited me to his house; and afterwards desired me to lodge there, saying he had a bed for me, and I should be welcome. So I stayed there, the other Friends being taken care of also. This was on the seventh day of the week; and he offering his house for a meeting, we had the next day a pretty large one; for most of the town were at it. There had never been a meeting here before, nor any within a great way of it; but this was a very precious one, many of the people were tender, and confessed to the truth; and some received it: blessed be the Lord for ever!

On the 16th of the 7th month we set forward again, and travelled, as near as we could compute, about fifty miles, through woods and over bogs, heading BOHEMIA and SAXIFRAX RIVERS. At night we made a fire in the woods, and lay there all night; and it being rainy weather, we got under some thick trees for shelter, and afterwards dried ourselves again by the fire. Next day we waded through CHESTER RIVER, a very broad water, and after passing through many bad bogs, lay that night also in the woods by a fire; not having gone above thirty miles that day. The day following we travelled hard; and though we had some troublesome bogs in our way, we rode about fifty miles; and got safe that night, but very weary, to Robert Harwood's, at MILES RIVER in MARYLAND. This was the eighteenth of the month; and though we were very weary, and much dirted with getting through the bogs in our journey, yet hearing of a meeting next day, we went to it, and then to John Edmundson's; from whence we went three or four miles by water to a meeting the First-day following. Here was a judge's wife, who had never been at any of our meetings before; who was reached, and said after, "she had rather hear us once than the priests a thousand times." Many others also were very well satisfied; for the power of the Lord was eminently with us; blessed for ever be his holy name! We passed thence about twenty-two miles, and had a meeting upon the KENTISH shore, to which one of the judges came; and a good meeting it was. Then, after another meeting hard by, at Henry Wilcock's house, where also we had good service for the Lord, we went by water about twenty miles to a very large meeting, where were some hundreds of people, four justices of the peace, the high-sheriff of Delaware, an Indian emperor or governor, and two chiefs. With these Indians I had a good opportunity the night before. I spoke to them by an interpreter; they heard the truth attentively, and were very loving. A blessed meeting this was, and of great service, both for convincing and establishing in the truth them that were convinced of it. Blessed be the Lord, who causeth his blessed truth to spread! After the meeting a woman came to me, whose husband was one of the judges of that part of the country, and a member of the assembly, and told me, "her husband was sick, not likely to live; and desired me to go home with her to see him." It was three miles to her house; and being just come hot out of the meeting, it was hard for me then to go; yet considering the service, I got a horse, went with her, visited her husband, and spoke what the Lord gave me to him. The man was much refreshed, and finally raised up by the power of the Lord; and he afterwards came to our meetings. I went back again to the Friends that night; and next day we departed thence about twenty miles to TREDHAVEN-CREEK, to John Edmundson's again; whence, on the 3d of the 8th month, we went to the general meeting for all Maryland Friends.

This held five days; the first three meetings for public worship, to which people of all sorts came; the other two men's and women's meetings. To the public meetings came many Protestants of divers sorts, and some Papists; amongst these were several magistrates and their wives, and other persons of chief account in the country. There were so many, besides Friends, that it was thought there were sometimes a thousand people at one of these meetings. So that, though they had not long before enlarged their meeting-place, and made it as large again as it was before, it could not contain the people. I went by boat every day four or five miles to it, and there were so many boats at that time passing upon the river, that it was almost like the Thames. The people said, "there were never so many boats seen there together before." And one of the justices said, "he never saw so many people together in that country before." It was a very heavenly meeting, wherein the presence of the Lord was gloriously manifested, and Friends were sweetly refreshed, the people generally satisfied, and many convinced; for the blessed power of the Lord was over all; everlasting praises to his holy name for ever! After the public meetings were over, the men's and women's meetings began, and were held the other two days; for I had something to impart to them which concerned the glory of God, the order of the gospel, and the government of Christ Jesus. When these meetings were over, we took our leave of Friends in those parts, whom we left well established in the truth.

On the 10th of the 8th Month we went thence about thirty miles by water, passing by CRANES ISLAND, SWAN ISLAND, and KENT ISLAND, in very foul weather and much rain; whereby (our boat being open) we were not only very much wet, but in great danger of being overset; insomuch that some thought we could not escape being cast away, till they saw us come to shore next morning. But blessed be God, we were very well. Having got to a little house, dried our clothes by the fire, and refreshed ourselves a little, we took to our boat again; and put off from land, sometimes sailing and sometimes rowing; but having very foul weather that day too, we could not get above twelve miles forward. At night we got to land, and made a fire; some lay by that, and some by a fire at a house a little way off. Next morning we passed over the GREAT-BAY, and sailed about forty miles that day. Making to shore at night, we lay there, some in the boat, and some at an ale-house. Next morning, being First-day, we went six or seven miles to a Friend's house, who was a justice of the peace; where we had a meeting: this was a little above the head of the Great-Bay. We were almost four days on the water, weary with rowing, yet all was very well: blessed and praised be the Lord. We went next day to another Friend's house, near the head of HATTON'S ISLAND, where we had good service amongst Friends and others; as we had also the day following at George Wilson's,* a Friend that lived about three miles further; where we had a very precious meeting, there being great tenderness amongst the people.

After this meeting we sailed about ten miles to James Frizby's, a justice of the peace, where, on the 16th, we had a very large meeting, at which, besides Friends, were some hundreds of people it was supposed; amongst whom were several justices, captains, and the sheriff, with other persons of note. A blessed, heavenly meeting this was; a powerful,

* This George Wilson, at whose house George Fox was entertained, is not mentioned elsewhere in the Journal. He was originally from Great Britain, and a great sufferer for the truth during the New England persecution. In 1661, it appears he was amongst twenty-seven other Friends in prison in Boston, who were liberated that year by an order from the home government. But these faithful messengers of the Lord, who were thus unexpectedly released from bondage, were concerned, almost immediately on leaving the jail, to preach to the inhabitants those truths for which they had suffered. The magistrates, already at their wits'-end, in fruitlessly endeavouring to arrest the spread of Quaker principles, being impatient at this fresh manifestation of devotedness, ordered a guard of soldiers to drive all the Friends out of their territory into the wilderness; an order which was speedily executed. George Wilson was among those who were thus forcibly expelled; but, undismayed by the new law for the application of the whip, they returned at once to their homes. There they were quickly apprehended, and were sentenced to undergo a flogging through three towns, and to be put out of the limits of the colony. The executioner, desirous of lending his ingenuity to increase the severity of the sentence, provided himself with a singularly constructed whip, or as it is called, a "cruel instrument," with which he "miserably tore" the bodies of the sufferers. Such was the new and barbarous character of the weapon used on this occasion, that Friends endeavoured, though unsuccessfully, to obtain it to send to England, as another proof of the malignant cruelty which actuated the rulers of Massachusetts towards the new Society. At the conclusion of this whipping at Boston, George Wilson, in the midst of his persecutors, knelt in solemn supplication to the Most High.

Being on a gospel mission in Virginia, George Wilson became a victim to the

thundering testimony for truth was borne therein; a great sense there was upon the people, and much brokenness and tenderness amongst them. We stayed after meeting till about eleven at night, that the tide turned for us; then taking boat, we passed that night and next day about fifty miles, to another Friend's house. The two next days we made short journeys, visiting Friends, and on the twentieth we had a great meeting at a place called SEVERN, where there was a meeting-house, but not large enough to hold the people. Divers chief magistrates were at it, and many other considerable people, and it gave them generally great satisfaction. Two days after we had a meeting with some that walked disorderly, and had good service. Then spending a day or two in visiting Friends, we passed to the WESTERN-SHORE; and on the twenty-fifth had a large and precious meeting at William Coale's,* where the speaker of their assembly, his wife, a justice, and several other people of quality were present. Next day we had a meeting six or seven miles further, at Abraham Birkhead's, where many of the magistrates and upper sort of people were, and the speaker of the assembly for that country was convinced: a blessed meeting it was, praised be the Lord! We travelled next day; and the day following, the 28th, had a large and very precious meeting at Peter Sharp's, on the CLIFFS, between thirty and forty miles distant from the former. Many of the magistrates and people of upper rank were at this meeting, and a heavenly meeting it was. The wife of one of the governor's council was convinced, and her husband was very loving to Friends. A justice from Virginia was convinced, and had a meeting afterwards at his house. Some Papists were at this meeting, and one of them threatened before he came, that he would dispute with

reigning intolerance, and was incarcerated in the dungeon at James' Town. The circumstances of his case evinced great barbarity on the part of his persecutors. The place of his imprisonment was an extremely loathsome one, without light or ventilation. Here, after being cruelly scourged and heavily ironed for a long period, he had to feel the heartlessness of a persecuting and dominant hierarchy; until, at last, his flesh actually rotted from his bones, and, within the cold damp walls of the miserable dungeon of James' Town, he laid down his life a faithful martyr for the testimony of Jesus.

The patience and resignation with which George Wilson bore his aggravated sufferings, and his faithfulness unto death, form a striking instance of the inflexible adherence to conscientious conviction, which so remarkably characterized the early Friends. Living near to Him who is the fountain and fulness of love, his enemies also became the objects of his solicitude; and, whilst lingering in the wretched dungeon, his heart was lifted up in prayer for his persecutors. "For all their cruelty," he writes, "I can truly say, Father, forgive them, for they know not what they do."—Bowden's *History of Friends in America*.

* William Coale, a Friend of Maryland, was convinced about the year 1657. He was a man of an innocent and tender spirit; and a living and weighty minister of the gospel of Christ. He visited Friends in Virginia with George Wilson, and was very serviceable, some being turned to the Lord through his ministry, and many established in the truth. He suffered cruel imprisonment for the gospel, which injured him so much that he never recovered it. In the time of his last illness he was cheerful, freely given up to die, saying, "The living presence of the Lord is with me;" with many more words of the great satisfaction he had from the Lord concerning his peace; adding, "I bless the Lord, I have finished my course, and I have nothing to do but to wait on the Lord and die." He departed very peaceably and quietly about the year 1678.

me; but he was reached, and could not oppose. Blessed be the Lord, the truth reached into the hearts of people beyond words, and it is of a good savour amongst them! After the meeting we went about eighteen miles, to James Preston's, a Friend that lived on Patuxent river; and thither came to us an Indian king, with his brother, to whom I spoke, and found they understood what I spoke of. Having finished our service in Maryland, and intending for Virginia, we had a meeting at PATUXENT on the 4th of the 9th Month, to take our leave of Friends. Many people of all sorts were at it, and a powerful meeting it was.

On the 5th we set sail for VIRGINIA, and in three days came to a place called NANCEMUM, about two hundred miles from Maryland. In this voyage we met with foul weather, storms, and rain, and lay in the woods by a fire in the night. At Nancemum lived a Friend, called the widow Wright. Next day we had a great meeting there, of Friends and others. There came to it Colonel Dewes, with several other officers and magistrates, who were much taken with the truth declared. After this, we hastened towards Carolina; yet had several meetings by the way, wherein we had good service for the Lord; one about four miles from Nancemum Water, which was very precious; and there was a men's and women's meeting settled, for taking care of the affairs of the church. Another very good one also we had at William Yarrow's, at PAGAN CREEK, which was so large, that we were fain to be abroad, the house not being large enough to contain the people. A great openness there was, the sound of truth spread abroad, and had a good savour in the hearts of people: the Lord have the glory for ever!

After this our way to Carolina grew worse, being much of it plashy, and pretty full of great bogs and swamps; so that we were commonly wet to the knees, and lay abroad at nights in the woods by a fire; saving one night we got to a poor house, at SOMMERTOWN, and lay by the fire. The woman of the house had a sense of God upon her. The report of our travel had reached thither, and drawn some that lived beyond Sommertown, to that house, in expectation to see and hear us (so acceptable was the sound of truth in that wilderness country:) but they missed us. The next day, the 21st of the 9th Month, having travelled hard through the woods, and over many bogs and swamps, we reached BONNER'S CREEK; and there we lay that night by the fireside, the woman lending us a mat to lie on.

This was the first house we came to in CAROLINA; here we left our horses, over-wearied with travel. From hence we went down the creek in a canoe, to Macocomocock River; and came to Hugh Smith's house, where the people of other professions came to see us (for there were no Friends in that part of the country), and many of them received us gladly. Amongst others came Nathaniel Batts, who had been governor of Roan-Oak; he went by the name of Captain Batts, and had been a rude, desperate man. He asked me about a woman in Cumberland, who, he said, he was told, had been healed by our prayers, and laying on of hands, after she had been long sick, and given over by the physicians; and he desired to know the certainty of it. I told him we did not glory in such things, but many such things had been done by the power of Christ.

Not far from hence we had a meeting among the people, and they were taken with the truth: blessed be the Lord! Then passing down the river MARATICK in a canoe, we went down the bay CONNIE-OAK, and came to a captain's house, who was very loving, and lent us his boat, for we were much wet in the canoe, the water splashing in upon us. With this boat we went to the governor's house; but the water in some places was so shallow that the boat being laden, could not swim; so that we were fain to put off our shoes and stockings, and wade through the water some distance. The governor, with his wife, received us lovingly; but a doctor there would needs dispute with us. And truly his opposing us was of good service, giving occasion for the opening of many things to the people, concerning the light and Spirit of God, which he denied to be in every one; and affirmed that it was not in the Indians. Whereupon I called an Indian to us, and asked him, "Whether or not, when he lied, or did wrong to any one, there was not something in him that reproved him for it?" he said, "There was such a thing in him, that did so reprove him; and he was ashamed when he had done wrong, or spoken wrong." So we shamed the doctor before the governor and the people; insomuch that the poor man ran out so far, that at length he would not own the Scriptures. We tarried at the governor's that night; and next morning he very courteously walked with us himself about two miles through the woods, to a place whither he had sent our boat about to meet us. Taking leave of him, we entered our boat, and went that day about thirty miles to Joseph Scott's, one of the representatives of the country. There we had a sound, precious meeting; the people were tender, and much desired after meetings. Wherefore at a house about four miles further, we had another meeting, to which the governor's secretary came, who was chief secretary of the province, and had been formerly convinced.

I went from this place among the Indians, and spoke unto them by an interpreter; showing them, "that God made all things in six days, and made but one woman for one man; and that God drowned the old world, because of their wickedness. Afterwards I spoke to them concerning Christ, showing them, that he died for all men, for their sins, as well as for others; and had enlightened them as well as others; and that if they did that which was evil, he would burn them, but if they did well, they should not be burned." There was among them their young king; and others of their chief men, who seemed to receive kindly what I said to them.

Having visited the north part of Carolina, and made a little entrance for truth upon the people there, we began to return towards Virginia, having several meetings in our way, wherein we had very good service for the Lord, the people being generally tender and open; blessed be the Lord. We lay one night at the secretary's house, to which we had much to do to get; for the water being shallow, we could not bring our boat to shore; but the secretary's wife seeing our strait, came herself in a canoe (her husband being from home) and brought us to land. Next morning our boat was sunk; but we got her up, mended her, and went away in her that day about twenty-four miles, the water being rough, and the winds high; but the great power of God was seen, in carrying us safe in that rotten boat. In our return we had a very precious meeting at Hugh Smith's; praised be the Lord for ever! The people were very tender, and very good service we had amongst them. There was at this meeting an Indian captain who was very loving, and acknowledged it to be truth that was spoken. There was also one of the Indian priests, whom they call a Pawaw, who sat soberly among the people. On the 9th of the 10th Month we got back to BONNER'S CREEK, where we had left our horses; having spent about eighteen days in North Carolina.

Our horses having rested, we set forward for VIRGINIA again, travelling through the woods and bogs, as far as we could well reach that day; and at night lay by a fire in the woods. Next day we had a tedious journey through bogs and swamps, and were exceedingly wet and dirty all the day, but dried ourselves at night by a fire. We got that night to SOMMERTOWN. When we came near the house, the woman of the house seeing us, spoke to her son to fasten up their dogs (for both in Virginia and Carolina they generally keep great dogs to guard their houses, living lonely in the woods); but the son said, "he need not, for the dogs did not use to meddle with these people." Whereupon, when we were come into the house, she told us, "we were like the children of Israel, whom the dogs did not move their tongues against." Here we lay in our clothes by the fire, as we had done many a night before. Next day, before we went away, we had a meeting; for the people having heard of us, had a great desire to hear us; and a very good meeting we had among them, where we never had one before; praised be the Lord for ever! After the meeting we hasted away. When we had rode about twenty miles, calling at a house to inquire the way, the people desired us to tarry all night with them, which we did. Next day we came among Friends, after we had travelled about a hundred miles from Carolina into Virginia; in which time we observed a great variety of climates, having passed in a few days from a very cold, to a warm and spring-like country. But the power of the Lord is the same in all, is over all, and doth reach the good in all; praised be the Lord for ever!

We spent about three weeks in travelling through Virginia, mostly among Friends, having many large and precious meetings in several parts of the country; as at the widow Wright's, where a great many magistrates, officers, and other high people came. A most heavenly meeting we had, wherein the power of the Lord was so great, that it struck a dread upon the assembly and chained all down, and brought a reverence upon the people's minds. Among the officers was a major, kinsman to the priest; he told me, "the priest threatened to come and oppose us." But the Lord's power was too strong for him, and stopped him; we were quiet and peaceable, and the people were wonderfully affected with the testimony of truth; blessed be the Lord for ever! Another very good meeting we had at CRICKATROUGH, at which many considerable people were, many of whom had never heard a Friend before; and they were greatly satisfied with the meeting, praised be the Lord! We had also a very good and serviceable meeting at John Porter's, which consisted mostly of other people; in which the power of the Lord was gloriously seen and felt, and it brought the truth over all evil walkers and talkers; blessed be the Lord! Divers other meetings we had, and many opportunities of doing service for the Lord amongst the people where we came. The last week we stayed, we spent some time and pains among Friends, sweeping away that which was to be swept out, and working down a bad spirit that was got up in some; blessed for ever be the name of the Lord! he it is that gives victory over all.

Having finished what service lay upon us in Virginia, on the 30th we set sail in an open sloop for MARYLAND. But having a great storm, and being much wet, we were glad to get to shore before night; and, walking to a house at WILLOUGHBY POINT, we got lodging there that night. The woman of the house was a widow, and a very tender person; she had never received Friends before; but she received us very kindly, and with tears in her eyes. We returned to our boat in the morning, and hoisted up our sail, getting forward as fast as we could; but towards evening a storm rising, we had much to do to get to shore; and our boat being open the water splashed often in, and sometimes over us, so that we were completely wet. Being got to land, we made a fire in the woods, to warm and dry us, and there we lay all night, the wolves howling about us. On the 1st of the 11th Month we sailed again, but the wind being against us, we made but little way, and were fain to get to shore at POINT COMFORT, where yet we found but small comfort; for the weather was so cold, that though we made a good fire in the woods to lie by, our water, that we had got for our use, was frozen near the fireside. We made to sea again next day; but the wind being strong and against us, we advanced but little, but were glad to get to land again, and travel about to find some house, where we might buy some provisions, for our store was spent. That night also we lay in the woods; and so extremely cold was the weather, the wind blowing high, and the frost and snow being great, that it was hard for some to abide it. On the 3d, the wind setting pretty fair, we fetched it up by sailing and rowing, and got that night to MILFORD-HAVEN, where we lay at Richard Long's, near Quince's Island. Next day we passed by Rappahannock River, where dwell much people; and Friends had a meeting there-aways at a justice's house, who had formerly been at a meeting where I was. We passed over Potomac River also, the winds being high, the water very rough, our sloop open, and the weather extremely cold; and having a meeting there-aways also, some people were convinced; and when we parted thence, some of our company went amongst them. We steered our course for Patuxent River, I sat at the helm most part of the day, and some of the night. About the first hour in the morning we reached James Preston's house, on Patuxent River, which is about two hundred miles from Nancemum in Virginia. We were very weary; yet the next day, being the first of the week, we went to the meeting not far from thence. The same week we went to an Indian king's cabin, where several of the Indians were, with whom we had a good opportunity to discourse; and they carried themselves very lovingly. We went also that week to a general meeting; then about eighteen miles further to John Geary's, where we had a very precious meeting; praised be the Lord God for ever! After this the cold grew so exceedingly sharp, the frost and snow so extreme, beyond what was usual in that country, that we could hardly endure it. Neither was it easy or safe to stir out; yet we got, with some difficulty, six miles through the snow to John Mayor's, where we met with some Friends come from New England, whom we had left there when we came away; and glad we were to see each other, after so long and tedious travels. By these Friends we understood, that William Edmundson, having been at Rhode Island and New England, was returned to Ireland; that Solomon Eccles, coming from Jamaica and landing at Boston in New England, was taken at a meeting there, and banished to Barbadoes; that John Stubbs and another Friend were gone into New Jersey, and several other Friends to Barbadoes, Jamaica, and the Leeward Islands. It was matter of joy to us, to understand that the work of the Lord went on and prospered, and that Friends were unwearied and diligent in the service.

On the 27th we had a very precious meeting in a tobacco-house; and next day returned to James Preston's, about eighteen miles distant. When we came there, we found his house was burnt to the ground the night before, through the carelessness of a servant; so we lay three nights on the ground by the fire, the weather being very cold. We made an observation, which was somewhat strange, but certainly true; that one day in the midst of this cold weather, the wind turning into the South, it grew so hot that we could hardly bear it; and the next day and night, the wind changing back into the North, we could hardly endure the cold.

The 2nd of 12th month we had a glorious meeting at Patuxent; and after it went to John Geary's again, where we waited for a boat to carry us to the monthly meeting at the CLIFFS, and a living one it was; praised be the Lord! This was on the 6th: another meeting we had on the 9th, wherein the glory of the Lord shone over all; blessed and magnified be his holy name for ever!

On the 12th month we set forward in our boat; and, travelling by night, ran aground in a creek near MANACO RIVER. There we were fain to stay till morning, when the tide came and lifted her off. In the meantime sitting in an open boat, and the weather being bitter cold, some of us had like to have lost the use of our hands, they were so frozen and benumbed with cold. In the morning, when the tide had set us afloat again, we got to land, and made a good fire, at which we warmed ourselves well. Then returning to our boat, we passed on about ten miles further to a Friend's house; where next day we had a very precious meeting, at which some of the chief of the place were. I went after it to a Friend's house, about four miles off, at the head of ANAMESSY RIVER, where, on the day following, the judge of the country and the justice with him came to me, and were very loving, and much satisfied with Friends' order. The next day we had a large meeting in the justice's barn, for his house could not hold the company. There were several of the great folks of that country, and among the rest an opposer; but all was preserved quiet and well; a precious meeting it was, and the people were much affected with the truth; blessed be the Lord! We went next day to see Captain Colburn, who was also a justice, and there we had some service; then returning again, we had a very glorious meeting at the same justice's, where we met before; to which came many people of account in the world, magistrates, officers, and others. It was large, and the power of the Lord was much felt, so that the people were generally well satisfied, and taken with the truth; and there being several merchants and masters of ships from New England, the truth was spread abroad; blessed be the Lord!

A day or two after, we travelled about sixteen miles through the woods and bogs, heading ANAMESSY RIVER and AMOROCA RIVER, part of which last we went over in a canoe, and came to MANAOKE, to a friendly woman's house; where, on the 24th, we had a large meeting in a barn. The Lord's living presence was with us, and among the people; blessed be his holy name for evermore! Friends had never had a meeting in those parts before. After this we passed over the River Wicocomaco, through many bad and watery swamps and marshy ways, and came to James Jones's, a Friend, and a justice of the peace; where we had a large and very glorious meeting; praised be the Lord God! Then passing over the water in a boat, we took horse and travelled about twenty-four miles through woods and troublesome swamps, and came to another justice's house, where we had a very large meeting, much people, and many of considerable account being present; and the living presence of the Lord was amongst us, praised for ever be his holy name! This was on the 3d of the 1st month, 1672-3;* and on the 5th we had another living and heavenly meeting, at which divers of the justices, with their wives, and many other people, were; amongst whom we had very good service for the Lord; blessed be his holy name! At this meeting was a woman that lived at Anamessy, who had been many years in trouble of mind, and sometimes would sit moping near two months together, and hardly speak or mind anything. When I heard of her, I was moved of the Lord to go to her, and tell her, "that salvation was come to her house." After I had spoken the word of life to her, and entreated the Lord for her, she mended, went up and down with us to meetings, and is since well, blessed be the Lord!

Being now clear of these parts, we left Anamessy on the 7th, and passing by water about fifty miles, came to a friendly woman's house at HUNGER RIVER. We had very rough weather in our passage to this place, and were in great danger, for the boat had nearly been turned over; but through the good providence of God we got safe thither; praised be his name! At this place we had a meeting; and amongst the people were two Papists, a man and a woman; he was very tender, and she confessed to the truth. This meeting was not so large as it would have been, if many, who had intended, could have got to it; but the weather was so foul, and the water, by reason of high winds, so rough, that it was not safe

* The difference implied here and elsewhere in the date is between the old style and the new. The above may be read either, the 3d of the 11th month, 1672; or the 3d of the 1st month, 1673. It would appear that an alteration in the mode of reckoning did not take place generally till made by Act of Parliament in 1752, when the Friends also adopted a change in the mode of reckoning the months, which is explained at large in the *Book of Discipline*, p. 73.

to pass over it. I had no Friend now with me but Robert Widders, the rest having dispersed themselves into several parts of the country in the service of truth.

As soon as the wind would permit, we passed hence about forty miles by water, rowing most part of the way, and came to the head of LITTLE CHOPTANK RIVER, to Dr. Winsmore's, who was a justice, lately convinced. Here we met with some Friends, with whom we stayed a while; and then went on by land and water, and had a large meeting out of doors, for the house we were at could not receive the people. Divers of the magistrates and their wives were present, and a good meeting it was; blessed be the Lord, who is making his name known in that wilderness country! We returned thence to a Friend's house, named William Stephens, where we met the Friends that had been travelling in other parts; and were much refreshed in the Lord together, imparting to each other the good success we had had in the Lord's work, and the prosperity and spreading of truth in the places where we travelled. John Cartwright and another Friend had been in Virginia, where there were great desires in people after truth; and being now returned, they stayed a little with us here, and then set forward for Barbadoes. Before we left this place we had a very glorious meeting, at which were very many people; amongst others, the judge of that country, three justices, and the high-sheriff, with their wives. Of the Indians was one called their emperor, an Indian king and their speaker, who all sat very attentive, and carried themselves very lovingly. An establishing, settling meeting it was. This was on the 23d of 1st month.

On the 24th we went by water ten miles to the Indian town where this emperor dwelt, whom I had acquainted before of my coming, and desired him to get their kings and councils together. In the morning the emperor came himself, and had me to the town; and they were generally come together, and had their speaker and other officers with them, and the old empress sat among them. They sat very grave and sober, and were all very attentive, beyond many called Christians. I had some with me that could interpret to them, and we had a very good meeting with them, and of very great service it was; for it gave them a good esteem for truth and Friends; blessed be the Lord.

After this we had many meetings in several parts of that country, one at William Stephens's, which was a general meeting once a month; others at Tredhaven Creek, Wye, Reconow Creek, and at Thomas Taylor's in the Island of Kent. Most of these were large, there being many people at them, divers of them of the most considerable account. The Lord's power and living presence were with us, and plenteously manifested amongst the people; by which their hearts were tendered and opened to receive the truth, which had a good savour amongst them; blessed be the Lord God over all for ever. Being clear of that side, we passed over the bay about fourteen miles to a Friend's house, where we met with several Friends. I sent for Thomas Thurston thither, and had a meeting with him, to bring the truth over his bad actions.

Having travelled through most parts of that country, and visited most of the plantations, having sounded the alarm to all people where we came, and proclaimed the day of God's salvation amongst them, we found our spirits began to be clear of these parts of the world, and draw towards Old England again. Yet we were desirous, and felt freedom from the Lord, to stay over the general meeting for the province of Maryland (which drew nigh) that we might see Friends generally together before we departed. Wherefore spending our time, in the interim, in visiting Friends and friendly people, in attending meetings about the Cliffs and Patuxent, and in writing answers to cavilling objections, which some of truth's adversaries had raised and spread abroad, to hinder people from receiving the truth, we were not idle, but laboured in the work of the Lord, until that general provincial meeting came on, which began on the 17th of the 3rd month, and lasted four days. On the first of these, the men and women had their meetings for business, wherein the affairs of the church were taken care of, and many things relating thereto were opened unto them, to their edification and comfort. The other three days were spent in public meetings for the worship of God, at which divers of considerable account in the government, and many others, were present, who were generally satisfied, and many of them reached; for it was a wonderful, glorious meeting, and the mighty presence of the Lord was seen and felt over all; blessed and praised be his holy name for ever, who over all giveth dominion!

After this meeting we took our leave of Friends, parting in great tenderness, in the sense of the heavenly life and virtuous power of the Lord, that was livingly felt amongst us; and went by water to the place where we were to take shipping, many Friends accompanying us thither and tarrying with us that night. Next day, the 21st of the 3rd month, 1673, we set sail for England; the same day Richard Covell came on board our ship, having had his own taken from him by the Dutch. We had foul weather and contrary winds, which caused us to cast anchor often, so that we were till the 31st ere we could get past the capes of Virginia and come out into the main sea. But after this we made good speed, and on the 28th of the 4th month cast anchor at King's Road, which is the harbour for BRISTOL. We had on our passage very high winds and tempestuous weather, which made the sea exceedingly rough, the waves rising like mountains; so that the masters and sailors wondered at it, and said they never saw the like before. But though the wind was strong, it set for the most part with us, so that we sailed before it; and the great God who commands the winds, who is Lord of heaven, of earth, and the seas, and whose wonders are seen in the deep, steered our course and preserved us from many imminent dangers. The same good hand of Providence that went with us, and carried us safely over, watched over us in our return, and brought us safely back again; thanksgiving and praises be to his holy name for ever! Many sweet and precious meetings we had on board the ship during this voyage (commonly two a week), wherein the blessed presence of the Lord did greatly refresh us, and often break in upon and tender the company.

CHAPTER VI.

1673–1675.—George Fox writes to his wife from Bristol—has a glorious powerful meeting there, in which he declares of three estates and three teachers—at Slattenford meets with much opposition to the settlement of women's meetings—the chief opposer, struck by the Lord's power, condemns his error—at Armscott is arrested by Justice Parker, and sent to Worcester jail with Thomas Lower—writes to his wife—he and T. Lower write to Lord Windsor and other magistrates, with a statement of their case—they are examined at the sessions, but George Fox is ensnared with the oath, and re-committed for refusing to take it—Thomas Lower is discharged, and afterwards visits Justice Parker, and gives the priest of the parish (who instigated their imprisonment) a severe rebuke in his presence, though unknown—George Fox disputes with Dr. Crowder on swearing—he is removed to London by Habeas Corpus—but ultimately remanded to Worcester—is examined at the assizes by Judge Turner, but the case is referred to the sessions—disputes with a priest on perfection—brought up at the sessions and re-committed, but has liberty till the next sessions—is again removed by Habeas Corpus, and tenders in court a declaration instead of the oath—attends the Yearly Meeting in London—appears again at the sessions of Worcester, and points out the flaws in his indictment—yet he is brought in guilty and premunired—writes to the king respecting the principle of Friends—is seized with illness, and his life almost despaired of—Justice Parker writes to the jailer to relax the rigour of his imprisonment—his wife intercedes with the king for his release, which he is willing to grant by a pardon—this George Fox could not accept, as it implied guilt—he is once more removed by Habeas Corpus—the under-sheriff quarrels with him for calling their ministers priests—he is brought before the judges, and Counsellor Corbet starts a new plea, that the Court cannot imprison on a premunire—The indictment is quashed for error, and he is freed by proclamation after nearly fourteen months' imprisonment—he writes many papers and pamphlets in Worcester jail.

WHEN we came into Bristol Harbour, there lay a man-of-war, and the press-master came on board us to press our men. We had a meeting at that time in the ship with the seamen before we went to shore, and the press-master sat down with us and stayed the meeting, and was very well satisfied with it. I spoke to him to leave two of the men he had pressed in our ship (for he had pressed four), one of whom was a lame man; and he said, "at my request, he would."

We went on shore that afternoon, and got to SHIREHAMPTON, where we obtained horses, and rode to BRISTOL that night, where Friends received us with great joy. In the evening I wrote a letter to my wife, to give her notice of my landing; as follows:—

"DEAR HEART,

"This day we came into Bristol near night, from the sea; glory to the Lord God over all for ever, who was our convoy, and steered our course! the God of the whole earth, of the seas and winds, who made the clouds his chariot, beyond all words, blessed be his name for ever! He is over all in his great power and wisdom, Amen. Robert Widders and James

Lancaster* are with me, and we are well; glory to the Lord for ever, who hath carried us through many perils, perils by water, and in storms, perils by pirates and robbers, perils in the wilderness and amongst false professors! praises to him whose glory is over all for ever, Amen! Therefore mind the fresh life, and live all to God in it. I intend (if the Lord will) to stay a while this away; it may be till the fair. So no more, but my love to all Friends." G. F.

Bristol, 28th of 4th Month, 1673.

Between this and the fair, my wife came out of the North to Bristol to me, and her son-in-law Thomas Lower, with two of her daughters† came with her. Her other son-in-law John Rous, W. Penn and his wife, and Gerrard Roberts, came from London, and many Friends from several parts of the nation, to the fair; and glorious, powerful meetings we had at that time, for the Lord's infinite power and life was over all. In the fresh openings whereof, I was moved to declare of

THREE ESTATES, AND THREE TEACHERS,

Viz: "God was the first teacher of man and woman in Paradise; and as long as they kept to and under his teaching, they kept in the image of God, in his likeness, in righteousness and holiness, and in dominion over all that he had made; in the blessed state, in the paradise of God. But when they hearkened to the serpent's false teaching (who was out of truth), disobeyed God and obeyed the serpent, in feeding upon that which God forbade them, they lost the image of God, the righteousness and holiness, came under the power of Satan, and were turned out of Paradise, out of the blessed into the cursed state. Then the promise of God was, 'that the Seed of the woman should bruise the serpent's head,' break his power that man and woman were under, and destroy his works. So here were 'three states and three teachers.' God was the first teacher in Paradise; and whilst man kept under his teaching, he was happy. The serpent was the second teacher; and when man followed his teaching, he fell into misery, into the fall from the image of God, from righteousness and holiness, and from the power that he had over all that God had made; and came under the serpent, whom he had power over before. Christ Jesus was the third

* This is nearly the last mention of James Lancaster, whose name occurs so often in these volumes. Perhaps there was no one who associated so much in gospel labours with George Fox as he; not only accompanying him throughout his visit to the western hemisphere, but was also with him during his visit to Scotland in 1657, and to Ireland in 1669, and on these occasions it appears that he frequently acted as his amanuensis. James Lancaster's residence was on the island of Walney, in Lancashire, and he was convinced by George Fox during his first visit to that county in 1652. In the following year he came forth as a minister, and in 1654, went on a gospel mission to Scotland with Miles Halhead. In 1665, he visited many of the midland counties of England.

† When George Fox married the widow of Judge Fell, she had one son; and seven daughters; viz., Margaret, who married John Rous; Bridgett, married to John Draper; Isabel; Sarah, married to William Mead; Mary, married to Thomas Lower; Susanna, married to —— Ingram; and Rachel, married to Daniel Abraham.

teacher; of whom God saith, 'This is my beloved Son, in whom I am well pleased, hear ye *him;*' and who himself saith, 'Learn of *me.*' This is the true gospel-teacher, who bruises the head of the serpent, the false teacher, and the head of all false teachers, and of all false religions, false ways, false worships, and false churches. Now Christ, who said, 'Learn of *me,*' and of whom the Father said, 'Hear ye *him,*' said, 'I am the Way to God, I am the Truth, I am the Life, and the true Light.' So as man and woman come to God, and are renewed up into his image, righteousness, and holiness by Christ, thereby they come into the Paradise of God, the state which man was in before he fell; and into a higher state than that, to sit down in Christ that never fell. Therefore the Son of God is to be heard in all things, who is the Saviour and the Redeemer; who laid down his life, and bought his sheep with his precious blood. We can challenge all the world. Who hath anything to say against our way? our Saviour? our Redeemer? our Prophet, whom God hath raised up that we may hear, and whom we *must* hear in all things? Who hath anything against our Shepherd, Christ Jesus, who leads and feeds us, and we know his heavenly voice? Who hath anything against our Bishop, in whose mouth was never guile found, who doth oversee us in his pasture of life, that we do not go astray from God, and out of his fold? Who hath anything against our Priest, Christ Jesus, made higher than the heavens, who gives us freely, and commands us to give freely? Who hath anything to say against our Leader and Counsellor, Christ Jesus, who never sinned; but is holy, harmless, and separate from sinners? God hath commanded us to hear Him; and He saith, 'Learn of *me;*' and if we should disobey God's and Christ's command, we should be like our father Adam and mother Eve, who disobeyed God's command, and hearkened to the serpent's teaching. Man commands, and would force us to hear the hirelings, who plead for sin and the body of death to the grave; which doctrine savours of the devil's teaching, not of Christ's; but we resolve to hear the Son, as both he and the Father command, and in hearing the Son we hear the Father also, as the Scripture testifies. For the author to the Hebrews says, 'God, who at sundry times, and in divers manners, spake in time past unto the fathers by the prophets, hath in these last days spoken unto us by his Son;' mark that, God hath spoken unto us (his apostles, disciples, church), by his Son. And whereas some have objected, that although Christ did speak both to his disciples and to the Jews, in the days of his flesh, yet since his resurrection and ascension he doth not speak now. The answer is, that 'as God did then speak by his Son in the days of his flesh, so the Son, Christ Jesus, doth now speak by his Spirit.' Wherefore John saith in the Revelations, 'He that hath an ear let him hear, what the Spirit saith to the churches,' Rev. ii. And Christ is said to 'speak from heaven,' Heb. xii. 25. 'See that ye refuse not him that speaketh; for if they escaped not who refused him that spake on earth, much more shall not we escape, if we turn away from Him that speaketh from heaven.' They that resisted Moses' law, who spake on earth, died for it without mercy, which was a natural death; but they that refuse Him that speaks from heaven, neglect and slight their own salvation, and so die a spiritual death through unbelief and hardness of heart. Therefore was the exhortation given of old, 'To-day, if ye will hear his voice, harden not your hearts, as in the provocation,' &c. Heb. iii. 15, &c. So that they who neglect or refuse to hear the voice of Christ, now speaking from heaven in this his gospel-day, harden their hearts. Let all therefore mark well these three estates and teachers; the God of Truth was the first teacher, while man was in Paradise and in innocency. The serpent was the second teacher, the false teacher, who by his false teaching came to be the god of the world, which lies in wickedness. Christ Jesus, that bruises the serpent's head, is the third teacher, who saith, 'Learn of *me*,' and of whom God saith, 'This is my beloved Son, in whom I am well pleased, hear ye *him*;' and of whom the testimony of the saints of old was, 'That God hath in these last days spoken unto us by his Son.' Thus they that come to be renewed up again into the divine, heavenly image, in which man was at first made, will know the same God, that was the first teacher of Adam and Eve in Paradise, to speak to them now by his Son, who changes not; glory be to his name for ever!"

Many deep and precious things were opened in those meetings by the Eternal Spirit, which searcheth and revealeth the deep things of God. After I had finished my service for the Lord in that city, I departed thence into GLOUCESTERSHIRE, where we had many large and precious meetings; and the Lord's everlasting power flowed over all. From Gloucestershire I passed into WILTSHIRE, where also we had many blessed meetings. At SLATTENFORD, in Wiltshire, we had a very good meeting, though we met there with much opposition from some who had set themselves against WOMEN'S MEETINGS; which I was moved of the Lord to recommend to Friends, for the benefit and advantage of the church of Christ. "That faithful women, who were called to the belief of the truth, being made partakers of the same precious faith, and heirs of the same everlasting gospel of life and salvation that men are, might in like manner come into the possession and practice of the gospel order, and therein be meet-helps unto the men in the restoration, in the service of truth, in the affairs of the church, as they are outwardly in civil, or temporal things. That so all the family of God, women as well as men, might know, possess, perform, and discharge their offices and services in the house of God, whereby the poor might be better taken care of, the younger instructed, informed, and taught in the way of God; the loose and disorderly reproved and admonished in the fear of the Lord; the clearness of persons proposing marriage more closely and strictly inquired into in the wisdom of God; and all the members of the spiritual body, the church, might watch over and be helpful to each other in love." But after these opposers had run into much contention and wrangling, the power of the Lord struck down one of the chief of them, so that his spirit sunk, and he came to be sensible of the evil he had done in opposing God's heavenly power, and confessed his error before Friends; and afterwards gave forth a paper of condemnation, wherein he declared, "that he did wilfully oppose (although I often warned him to take heed), until the fire of the Lord did burn within him; and he saw the angel of the Lord with his sword drawn in his hand, ready to cut him off," &c.

Notwithstanding the opposition at the meeting at Slattenford, yet a very good and serviceable one it was; for occasion was thereby administered to answer their objections and cavils, and to open the services of women in and for the church. At this the women's meetings, for that county, were established in the blessed power of God.

After this I went to MARLBOROUGH and had a meeting there, to which some of the magistrates came, and were civil and moderate. Then passing to Bartholomew Maylin's, I had a very precious meeting there; and then went a little beyond ORE, where we had a blessed meeting, and very large, as we had also soon after upon the border of HAMPSHIRE. Then turning into OXFORDSHIRE, we visited Friends there; and then went to READING, where we had a large meeting. Thence passing into BUCKINGHAMSHIRE, we had many precious meetings in that county. After which we visited Friends till we came to KINGSTON-UPON-THAMES, where my wife and her daughter Rachel met me.

I made no long stay at Kingston, but went to LONDON, where I found the Baptists and Socinians, with some old apostates, grown very rude, having printed many books against us; so that I had a great travail in the Lord's power, before I could get clear of that city. But blessed be the Lord, his power came over them, and all their lying, wicked, scandalous books were answered. I made a short journey into some parts of ESSEX and MIDDLESEX, visiting Friends at their meetings, and their children at their schools, and returned soon to LONDON. After some service there among Friends, I went to KINGSTON, and thence to Stephen Smith's in SURREY, where was a very large meeting, many hundreds of people attending it. I stayed in those parts till I had cleared myself of the service the Lord had given me to do there, and then returned by KINGSTON to LONDON, whither I felt my spirit drawn; having heard that many Friends were taken before the magistrates, and divers imprisoned in London and other towns, for opening their shop-windows on holidays and fast-days (as they were called), and for bearing testimony against all such observations of days. Which Friends could not but do, knowing that the true Christians did not observe the Jews' holidays in the apostles' times, neither could we observe the Heathens' and Papists' holidays (so called) which have been set up amongst those called Christians, since the apostles' days. For we were redeemed out of days by Christ Jesus, and brought into the day which hath sprung from on high, and are come into Him who is Lord of the Jewish Sabbath, and the substance of the Jews' signs.

After I had stayed some time in London, labouring for some relief and ease to Friends in this case, I took leave of Friends there, and went into the country with my wife, and her daughter Rachel, to HENDON, in MIDDLESEX, and thence to William Penn's at RICKMANSWORTH, in HERTFORDSHIRE, whither Thomas Lower, who married another of my wife's daughters, came next day to accompany us in our journey northward. After we had visited Friends thereabouts, we passed to a Friend's house near AYLESBURY, and thence to Bray Doily's at ADDERBURY, in OXFORDSHIRE, where, on First-day, we had a large and precious meeting. Truth being well spread, and Friends in those parts much increased in number, two or three new meetings were then set up.

At night, as I was sitting at supper, I felt I was taken; yet I said nothing then to any one of it. But getting out next morning, we travelled into WORCESTERSHIRE, and went to John Halford's, at ARMSCOTT, where we had a very large and precious meeting in his barn, the Lord's powerful presence being eminently with and amongst us. After the meeting, Friends being most of them gone, as I was sitting in the parlour, discoursing with some Friends, Henry Parker, a justice, came to the house, and with him one Rowland Hains, a priest of HUNNITON, in WARWICKSHIRE. This justice heard of the meeting by means of a woman Friend, who being nurse to a child of his, asked leave of her mistress to go to the meeting to see me; and she speaking of it to her husband, he and the priest plotted together to come and break it up and apprehend me. But from their sitting long at dinner, it being the day on which his child was sprinkled, they did not come till the meeting was over, and Friends mostly gone. But though there was no meeting when they came, yet I being in the house, who was the person they aimed at, Henry Parker took me, and Thomas Lower for company with me; and though he had nothing to lay to our charge, sent us both to Worcester jail, by a strange sort of mittimus; a copy of which here follows:—

"*To the constables of Tredington, in the said county of Worcester, and to all constables and tithing-men of the several townships and villages within the said parish of Tredington, and to the keeper of the jail for the county of Worcester.*

"COMPLAINT being made to me, being one of His Majesty's justices of the peace for the said county of Worcester, that within the said parish of Tredington in the same county, there has of late been several meetings of divers persons, to the number of four hundred persons and upwards at a time, upon pretence of exercise of religion, otherwise than what is established by the laws of England. And many of the said persons, some of them were teachers, and came from the North, and others from the remote parts of the kingdom; which tends to the prejudice of the reformed and established religion, and may prove prejudicial to the public peace. And it appearing to me that there was, this present day, such a meeting as aforesaid, to the number of two hundred or thereabouts, at Armscott, in the said parish of Tredington, and that George Fox of London, and Thomas Lower of the parish of Creed, in the county of Cornwall, were present at the said meeting, and the said George Fox was teacher or speaker of the said meeting; and no satisfactory account of their settlement or place of habitation appearing to me, and forasmuch as the said George Fox and Thomas Lower refused to give sureties to appear at the next sessions of the peace to be holden for the said county, to answer the breach of the common laws of England, and what other matters should be objected against them; these are, therefore, in His Majesty's name, to will and require you, or either of you, forthwith to convey the bodies of the said George Fox and Thomas Lower to the county jail of Worcester aforesaid, and there safely to be kept, until they shall be from thence delivered by due course of law; for which this shall be your sufficient warrant in that behalf. Dated the 17th day of December, in the 25th year of His Majesty's reign over England, &c." HENRY PARKER.

Being thus made prisoners, without any probable appearance of being released before the quarter sessions at soonest, we got some Friends to accompany my wife and her daughter into the North, and we were conveyed to WORCESTER jail. From whence, by that time I thought my wife could be got home, I wrote her the following letter:—

"DEAR HEART,

"Thou seemedst to be a little grieved when I was speaking of prisons, and when I was taken; be content with the will of the Lord God. For when I was at John Rous's at Kingston, I had a sight of my being taken prisoner, and when I was at Bray Doily's in Oxfordshire, as I sat at supper, I saw I was taken; and I saw I had a suffering to undergo. But the Lord's power is over all; blessed be his holy name for ever!" G. F.

When we had been some time in the jail, we thought fit to lay our case before the Lord Windsor, who was lord-lieutenant of Worcestershire, and before the deputy-lieutenants and other magistrates: which we did by the following letter:—

"THESE are to inform you, the lord-lieutenant (so called), and the deputy-lieutenants, and the justices of the county of Worcestershire, how unchristianly and inhumanly we have been dealt withal by Henry Parker, a justice (so called), in our journey towards the North. We coming to our Friend, John Halford's house, on the 17th of the 10th month, 1673, and some Friends bringing us on the way, and others coming to visit us there, towards night there came the aforesaid justice, and a priest, called Rowland Hains, of Hunniton, in Warwickshire, and demanded our names and places of abode. And though we were not in any meeting, but were discoursing together when they came in, yet he made a mittimus to send us to Worcester jail. Now, whereas he says in his mittimus, 'that complaint had been made to him of several by-past meetings of many hundreds at a time,' we know nothing of that, nor do we think that concerns us. And whereas he says further, 'that no satisfactory account of our settlement, or place of habitation appeared unto him.' This he contradicts in his own mittimus, mentioning therein the places of our abode and habitation, the account of which we satisfactorily and fully gave him. And one of us (Thomas Lower) told him, that he was going down with his mother-in-law (who is George Fox's wife), and with his sister, to fetch up his own wife and child out of the North into his own country. And the other of us (George Fox) told him, that he was bringing forward his wife on her journey towards the North (who had been at London, to visit one of her daughters that had lately lain in). And having received a message from his mother, an ancient woman in Leicestershire, that she earnestly desired to see him before she died, he intended, as soon as he had brought his wife on her journey as far as Causal, in Warwickshire, to turn into

Leicestershire, to visit his mother and relations there, and then to return to London again. But by his interrupting us on our journey, taking the husband from his wife, and the son from his mother and sister, and stopping him from visiting his wife and child so remote, we were forced to get strangers, or whom we could, to help them on their journey, to our great damage and their hinderance. We asked the priest, 'whether this was his gospel, and their way of entertaining strangers?' And we desired the justice to consider, 'whether this was doing as he would be done by?' But he said, 'he had said it, and he would do it.' And whereas he says, 'we refused to give sureties;' he asked only George Fox for sureties; who replied, 'he was an innocent man, and knew no law he had broken;' but he did not ask Thomas Lower for any, as if it had been crime and cause enough for his commitment, that he came out of Cornwall. If we were at a meeting, as he says in his mittimus, he might have proceeded otherwise than by sending us to jail, to answer the breach of the common laws; though he showed us no breach of any; as may be seen in the mittimus. We thought fit to lay before you the substance of his proceedings against us, hoping there will more moderation and justice appear in you towards us, that we may prosecute our intended journey."

GEORGE FOX.
THOMAS LOWER.

But no enlargement did we receive by our application to the Lord Windsor (so called). And although Thomas Lower received several letters from his brother, Dr. Lower, who was one of the king's physicians, concerning his liberty, and one, by his procurement, from Henry Savile, who was of the king's bed-chamber, to his brother, called the Lord Windsor, to the same effect; yet seeing it related only to his enlargement, not mine, so great was his love and regard to me that he would not seek his own liberty singly, but kept the letter by him unsent. So we were continued prisoners till the next general quarter sessions; at which time divers Friends from several places being in town, spoke to the justices concerning us, who answered fair, and said we should be discharged. For many of the justices seemed to dislike the severity of Parker's proceedings against us, and declared an averseness to ensnare us by the tender of the oaths. Some Friends also had spoken with Lord Windsor, who likewise answered them fair, so that it was the general discourse that we should be discharged. We heard also that Dr. Lower had procured a letter from Colonel Sands at London, to some of the justices in favour of us. Some of the justices also spoke to some Friends to acquaint us, that they would have us speak but little in the court, lest we should provoke any of the bench; and they would warrant we should be discharged.

We were not called till the last day of the sessions, which was the 21st of the 11th month, 1673. When we came in, they were stricken with paleness in their faces, and it was some time before anything was spoken; insomuch that a butcher in the hall said, "What, are they afraid? Dare not the justices speak to them?" At length, before they spoke to us, Justice Parker made a long speech on the bench, much to the same effect as was contained in the mittimus; often mentioning the common laws, but not instancing any that we had broken; adding, "that he thought it a milder course to send us two to jail, than to put his neighbours to the loss of two hundred pounds, which they must have suffered, had he put the law in execution against conventicles." But in this he was either very ignorant or very deceitful, for there being no meeting when he came, nor any to inform, he had no evidence to convict us, or his neighbours by.

When Parker had ended his speech the justices spoke to us, and began with Thomas Lower, whom they examined as to the cause of his coming into that country; of which he gave them a full and plain account. Sometimes I put in a word while they were examining him, and then they told me, "they were upon his examination, but that when it came to my turn, I should have free liberty to speak, for they would not hinder me; but I should have full time, and they would not ensnare us." When they had done with him, they asked me an account of my travel, which I gave them, as is mentioned before, but more largely. And whereas Justice Parker, to aggravate the case, had made a great noise of "there being some from London, some from the North, some from Cornwall, and some from Bristol, at the house when I was taken;" I told them, that "this was in a manner all but one family, for there was none from London, but myself; none from the North, but my wife and her daughter; none from Cornwall, but my son-in-law, Thomas Lower; nor any from Bristol but one Friend, a merchant there; who met us, as it were, providentially, to assist my wife and her daughter in their journey homewards, when by our imprisonment they were deprived of our company and help." When I had spoken, the chairman, whose name was Simpson, an old Presbyterian, said, "Your relation or account, is very innocent." Then he and Parker whispered a while together, and after that the chairman stood up and said, "You, Mr. Fox, are a famous man, and all this may be true which you have said; but, that we may be the better satisfied, will you take the oaths of allegiance and supremacy?" I told them, "they had said they would not ensnare us; but this was a plain snare; for they knew we could not take any oath." However, they caused the oath to be read; and when they had done, I told them, "I never took an oath in my life, but I had always been true to the government; that I was cast into the dungeon at Derby, and kept a prisoner six months there, because I would not take up arms against King Charles at Worcester fight; and for going to meetings was carried up out of Leicestershire, and brought before Oliver Cromwell, as a plotter to bring in King Charles. And ye know," said I, "in your own consciences, that we, the people called Quakers, cannot take an oath, or swear in any case, because Christ hath forbidden it. But as to the matter or substance contained in the oaths, this I can and do say, that I do own and acknowledge the king of England to be the lawful heir and successor to the realm of England; and do abhor all plots and plotters, and contrivances against him; and I have nothing in my heart but love and good-will to him and all men, and desire his and their prosperity; the Lord knows it, before whom I stand, an innocent man. And as to the oath of supremacy, I deny the Pope, and his power, and his religion, and abhor it with my heart." While I was speaking, they cried, "give him the book;" and I said, "the book saith, 'Swear not at all.'" Then they cried, "take him away, jailer;" and I still speaking on, they were urgent upon the jailer, crying, "take him away, we shall have a meeting here; why do you not take him away? that fellow (meaning the jailer) loves to hear him preach." Then the jailer drew me away, and as I was turning from them, I stretched out my arm, and said, "the Lord forgive you, who cast me into prison for obeying the doctrine of Christ." Thus they apparently broke their promise in the face of the country; for they promised I should have free liberty to speak, but now they would not give it me; and they promised they would not ensnare us, yet now they tendered me the oaths on purpose to ensnare me.

After I was had away Thomas Lower was stayed behind in the court, and they told him, "he was at liberty." Then he would have reasoned with them, asking them, "why I might not be set at liberty as well as he, seeing we were both taken together, and our case was alike?" But they told him, "they would not hear him," saying, "you may be gone about your business, for we have nothing more to say to you, seeing you are discharged." And this was all he could get from them. Wherefore after the court was risen, he went to speak with them at their chamber, desiring to know, "what cause they had to detain his father, seeing they had discharged him;" and wishing them to consider whether this was not partiality, and would be a blemish to them. Whereupon Simpson threatened him, saying, "if you be not content, we will tender you the oaths also, and send you to your father." To which he replied, "they might do that, if they thought fit; but whether they sent him or not, he intended to go, and to wait upon his father in prison, for that was now his business in that country." Then said Justice Parker to him, "Do you think, Mr. Lower, that I had not cause to send your father and you to prison, when you had so great a meeting, that the parson of the parish complained to me, that he has lost the greatest part of his parishioners; so that when he comes among them, he has scarcely any auditors left?" "I have heard," replied Thomas Lower, "that the priest of that parish comes so seldom to visit his flock (but once, it may be, or twice in a year, to gather up his tithes), that it was but charity in my father to visit so forlorn and forsaken a flock; and therefore thou hadst no cause to send my father to prison for visiting them, or for teaching, instructing, and directing them to Christ, their true teacher, who had so little comfort or benefit from their pretended pastor, who comes amongst them only to seek for his 'gain from his quarter.'" Upon this the justice fell a laughing, for it seems Dr. Crowder (who was the priest they spoke of) was then in the room, sitting among them, though Thomas Lower did not know him; and he had the wit to hold his tongue, and not undertake to vindicate himself in a matter so notoriously known to be true. But when Thomas Lower was come from them, the justices did so play upon Dr. Crowder, that he was pitifully ashamed, and so nettled with it that he threatened to sue Thomas Lower in the bishop's court, upon an action of defamation. Which when Thomas Lower heard, he sent him word, that he would answer his suit, let him begin it when he would; and would bring his whole parish in evidence against him. This cooled the doctor. Yet some time after, he came to the prison, pretending that he had a mind to dispute with me, and to talk with Thomas Lower about that business; and he brought another with him, he himself being then a prebendary at Worcester.

When he came in, he asked me, "What I was in prison for?" "Dost thou not know that?" said I. "Wast not thou upon the bench when Justice Simpson and Parker tendered the oath to me? And hadst not thou a hand in it?" Then he said, "It is lawful to swear; and Christ did not forbid swearing before a magistrate; but swearing by the sun, and the like." I bid him prove that by the Scriptures, but he could not. Then he brought that saying of Paul's, "All things are lawful unto me," 1 Cor. vi. 12. "And if," said he, "all things were lawful unto him, then swearing was lawful unto him." "By this argument," said I, "thou mayest also affirm, that drunkenness, adultery, and all manner of sin and wickedness is lawful also, as well as swearing." "Why," said Dr. Crowder, "do you hold that adultery is unlawful?" "Yes," said I, "that I do." "Why then," said he, "this contradicts the saying of St. Paul." Thereupon I called to the prisoners and the jailer, to hear what doctrine Dr. Crowder had laid down as orthodox, viz., "that drunkenness, swearing, adultery, and such like things, were lawful." Then he said, "he would give it under his hand;" and took a pen, but wrote another thing than that which he had spoken. Then, turning to Thomas Lower, he asked him, "whether he would answer what he had there written?" who undertook it. Whereupon, when he had threatened Thomas Lower to sue him in the bishop's court, for speaking so abusively (as he called it) of him before the justices, and Thomas had bid him begin when he pleased, for he would answer him, and bring his parishioners in evidence against him, he went away in a great fret, grumbling to himself as he went. A few days after Thomas Lower sent him an answer to the paper he had written and left with him; which answer a Friend of Worcester carried to him; and he read it and said, "he would reply to it;" but never did, though he often sent him word he would do it.

Soon after the sessions, the term coming on, an habeas corpus was sent down to Worcester for the sheriff to bring me up to the King's Bench bar. Whereupon, the under-sheriff, having made Thomas Lower his deputy to convey me to London, we set out the 29th of the 11th Month, 1673, and came to LONDON the 2d of the 12th; the ways being very deep, and the waters out. Next day, notice being given that I was brought up, the sheriff was ordered to bring me into court. I went accordingly, and appeared before Judge Wild; and both he and the lawyers were pretty fair, so that I had time to speak, to clear my innocency, and show my wrong imprisonment. After the return of the writ was entered, I was ordered to be brought into court again next day, the order of court being as follows:—

"WORCESTER. The King against George Fox.	Thursday, next after the morrow of the Purification of the Blessed Virgin Mary, in the 26th Year of King Charles the Second.

THE defendant being brought here into court, upon a writ of habeas corpus ad subjiciend, &c., under the custody of the sheriff of the county aforesaid; it is ordered, That the Return unto the habeas corpus be filed, and the defendant is committed unto the marshal of this court, to be safely kept until, &c. "By motion of Mr. G. STROUDE.

"By the Court."

In the morning, I walked in the hall, till the sheriff came to me (for he trusted me to go whither I would), and it being early, we went into the court of the King's Bench, and sat there among the lawyers almost an hour, till the judges came in. When they came in, the sheriff took off my hat; and after a while I was called. The Lord's presence was with me, and his power I felt was over all. I stood and heard the king's attorney, whose name was Jones, who indeed spoke notably on my behalf, as did also another counsellor after him; and the judges, who were three, were all very moderate, not casting any reflecting words at me. I stood still in the power and Spirit of the Lord, seeing how he was at work. When they had done, I applied to the chief justice to speak; and he said, I might. Then I related the cause of our journey, the manner of our being taken and committed, and the time of our imprisonment until the sessions; with a brief account of our trial there, and what I had offered to the justices then, as a declaration, that I could make or sign, instead of the oaths of allegiance and supremacy. When I had done, the chief justice said, "I was to be turned over to the King's Bench, and the sheriff of Worcester to be discharged of me." He said also "they would consider further of it; and if they found any error in the record, or in the justice's proceedings, I should be set at liberty." So a tipstaff was called to take me into custody, and he delivered me to the keeper of the King's Bench, who let me go to a Friend's house, where I lodged, and appointed to meet me at Edward Man's in Bishopsgate-Street, next day. But after this, Justice Parker, or some other of my adversaries, moved the court that I might be sent back to Worcester. Whereupon another day was appointed for another hearing, and they had four counsellors that pleaded against me. George Stroude, a counsellor, pleaded for me, and was pleading before I was brought into court; but they bore him down, and prevailed with the judges to give judgment, that "I should be sent down to Worcester sessions." Only they told me, I might put in bail to appear at the sessions, and to be of good behaviour in the meantime. I told them, "I never was of ill behaviour in my life; and that they, the four judges, might as well put the oath to me there, as send me to Worcester to be ensnared by the justices, in their putting the oath to me, and then premuniring me, who never took oath in my life." But I told them, "if I broke my Yea and Nay, I was content to suffer the same penalty that they should who break their oaths." This alteration of the judges' minds in my case, proceeded, as was thought, from some false informations, that my adversary, Justice Parker, had given against me; for between the times of my former appearance and this, he had spread abroad a very false and malicious story, viz., "that there were many substantial men with me, out of several parts of the nation, when he took me; and that we had a design or plot in hand; and that Thomas

Lower stayed with me in prison, long after he was set at liberty, to carry on our design." This was spoken in the parliament house, insomuch, that if I had not been brought up to London when I was, I should have been stopped at Worcester, and Thomas would have been recommitted with me. But although these lies were easily disproved, and laid open to Parker's shame, yet would not the judges alter their last sentence, but remanded me to Worcester jail; only this favour was granted, that I might go down my own way, and at my own leisure; provided I would be without fail there by the assize, which was to begin on the 2d of the 2d month following.

I stayed in and about London till toward the latter end of the 1st Month, 1674, and then went down leisurely (for I was not able to bear hasty and hard travelling), and came into WORCESTER on the last day of the 1st Month, 1674, being the day before the judges came to town. On the 2d of the 2d Month, I was brought from the jail to an inn near the hall, that I might be in readiness if I should be called. But not being called that day, the jailer came to me at night, and told me, "I might go home" (meaning to the jail). Whereupon Gerrard Roberts of London being with me, he and I walked down together to the jail without any keeper. Next day being brought up again, they set a little boy of about eleven years old, to be my keeper. I came to understand that Justice Parker and the clerk of the peace had given order, that I should not be put into the calendar, that so I might not be brought before the judge; wherefore I got the judge's son to move in court, that "I might be called;" and thereupon I was called, and brought up to the bar before Judge Turner, my old adversary, who had tendered me the oaths and premunired me once before at Lancaster. After silence made, he asked me, "what I desired?" I answered, "My liberty, according to justice." He said, "I lay upon the oath;" and asked, "if I would take it." I desired he would hear the manner of my being taken and committed, and he being silent, I gave him an account thereof at large, as is before set down, letting him also know, that "since my imprisonment I had understood that my mother, who was an ancient, tender woman, and had desired to see me before she died, hearing that I was stopped and imprisoned in my journey, so that I was not likely to come to see her, was so struck by it, that she died soon after: which was a very hard thing to me." When I had done speaking, he again asked me "to take the oaths;" I told him I could not take any oath for conscience' sake, and that I believed he and they all knew in their consciences, that it was for conscience' sake I could not swear at all. I declared amongst them what I could say, and what I could sign, in owning the king's right to the government, and in denying the Pope and his pretended powers, and all plotters, plots, and conspiracies against the government. Some thought the judge had a mind to set me at liberty, for he saw they had nothing justly against me; but Parker, who committed me, endeavoured to incense him against me, telling him, "that I was a ringleader; that many of the nation followed me, and he knew not what it might come to;" with many more envious words, which some that stood near took notice of; who also observed that the judge gave him no answer to it. However, the judge, willing to ease himself, referred me and my case to the sessions again, bidding the justices make an end of it there, and not trouble the assizes any more with me. So I was continued prisoner chiefly (as it seemed) through the means of Justice Parker, who, in this case, was as false as envious; for he had promised Richard Cannon, of London, who had acquaintance with him, that he would endeavour to have me set at liberty; yet he was the worst enemy I had in court, as some of the court observed and reported. Other justices were very loving, and promised that I should have the liberty of the town, and to lodge at a Friend's house till the sessions; which accordingly I had, and the people were very civil and respectful to me.

Between this time and the sessions, I had some service for the Lord, with several people that came to visit me. At one time three nonconformist priests and two lawyers came to discourse with me; and one of the priests undertook to prove, "that the Scriptures are the only rule of life." Whereupon, after I had plunged him about his proof, I had a fit opportunity to open unto them "the right and proper use, service, and excellency of the Scriptures; and also to show, that the Spirit of God, which was given to every one to profit withal—the grace of God, which bringeth salvation, and which hath appeared unto all men, and teacheth them that obey it to deny ungodliness and worldly lusts, and to live soberly, righteously, and godly in this present world; that this, I say, is the most fit, proper, and universal rule, which God hath given to all mankind to rule, direct, govern, and order their lives by."

Another time came a Common-Prayer priest, and some people with him. He asked me, "if I was grown up to perfection?" I told him, "what I was, I was by the grace of God." He replied, "it was a modest and civil answer." Then he urged the words of John, "If we say that we have no sin, we deceive ourselves, and the truth is not in us." And he asked, "what did I say to that?" I said, with the same apostle, "If we say that we have not sinned, we make Him a liar, and His word is not in us;" who came to destroy sin, and to take away sin. So there is a time for people to see that they have sinned, and there is a time for them to see that they have sin; and there is a time for them to confess their sin, and to forsake it, and to know "the blood of Christ to cleanse from all sin." Then the priest was asked, "whether Adam was not perfect before he fell? and whether all God's works were not perfect?" The priest said, "there might be a perfection, as Adam had, and a falling from it." But I told him, "there is a perfection in Christ, above Adam, and beyond falling; and that it was the work of the ministers of Christ, to present every man perfect in Christ; and for the perfecting of whom they had their gifts from Christ; therefore, they that denied perfection, denied the work of the ministry, and the gifts which Christ gave for the perfecting of the saints." The priest said, "we must always be striving." But I told him, "it was a sad and comfortless sort of st[illegible], to strive with a belief that we should never overcome." I told him also, "that Paul, who cried out of the body of death, did also 'thank God, who gave him the victory, through our Lord Jesus Christ.' So there was a time of crying out for want of victory, and a time of praising God for the victory. And

Paul said, 'there is no condemnation to them that are in Christ Jesus.'" The priest said, "Job was not perfect." I told him, "God said, Job was a perfect man, and that he did shun evil: and the Devil was forced to confess that 'God had set a hedge about him,' which was not an outward hedge, but the invisible heavenly power." The priest said, "Job said, 'He chargeth his angels with folly, and the heavens are not clean in his sight.'" I told him, "that was his mistake; for it was not Job who said so, but Eliphaz, who contended against Job." "Well but," said the priest, "what say you to that Scripture, 'The justest man that is sinneth seven times a day.'" "Why truly," said I, "I say, there is no such Scripture;" and with that the priest's mouth was stopped. Many other services I had with several sorts of people between the assizes and the sessions.

The next quarter sessions began the 29th of the 2nd month, and I was called before the justices. The chairman's name was —— Street, who was a judge in the Welsh circuit; and he misrepresented me and my case to the country, telling them, "that we had a meeting at Tredington, from all parts of the nation, to the terrifying of the king's subjects, for which we had been committed to prison: that for the trial of my fidelity the oaths were put to me; and having had time to consider of it, he asked me, 'if I would now take the oaths?'" I desired liberty to speak for myself; and having obtained that, began first to clear myself from those falsehoods he had charged on me and Friends, declaring "that we had not any such meeting from all parts of the nation, as he had represented it; but that (except the Friend from whose house we came, and who came with us to guide us thither, and one Friend of Bristol, who came accidentally, or rather providentially, to assist my wife homewards after we were taken) they that were with me were part of my own family, being my wife, her daughter, and her son-in-law. And we did not meet in any way that would occasion terror to any of the king's subjects, for we met peaceably and quietly, without arms; and I did not believe there could any one be produced, that could truly say he was terrified with our meeting. Besides, I told them, we were but in our journey, the occasion whereof I now related as before. Then as to the oaths, I showed why I could not take them (seeing Christ hath forbidden all swearing), and what I could say or sign in lieu of them, as I had done before." Yet they caused the oaths to be read to me again, and afterwards read an indictment also, which they had drawn up in readiness, having a jury ready also. When the indictment was read, the judge asked me, "if I was guilty?" I said, "Nay, for it was a great bundle of lies, which I showed and proved to the judge in several particulars, which I instanced; asking him, if he did not know in his conscience that they were lies?" He said, "it was their form." I said, "it was not a true form." He asked me again, "whether I was guilty?" I told him "nay, I was not guilty of the matter, nor of the form; for I was against the Pope and Popery, and did acknowledge and should set my hand to that." Then the judge told the jury what they should say, and what they should do, and what they should write on the backside of the indictment; and as he said, they did. But before they gave in their verdict, I told them, "that it was for Christ's sake, and in obedience to his and the apostle's command, that I could not swear; and therefore, said I, take heed what ye do, for before his judgment-seat ye shall all be brought." The judge said, "this is canting." I said, "If to confess our Lord and Saviour, and to obey his command, be called 'canting' by a judge of a court, it is to little purpose for me to say more among you: yet ye shall see that I am a Christian, and shall show forth Christianity, and my innocency shall be manifest." So the jailer led me out of the court; and the people were generally tender, as if they had been in a meeting. Soon after I was brought in again, and the jury found the bill against me, which I traversed; and then I was asked to put in bail till the next sessions, and the jailer's son offered to be bound for me. But I stopped him, and warned Friends not to meddle; for I told them, "there was a snare in that:" yet I told the justices, that I could promise to appear, if the Lord gave health and strength, and I were at liberty. Some of the justices were loving, and would have hindered the rest from indicting me, or putting the oath to me; but Justice Street, who was the chairman, said, "he must go according to law." So I was sent to prison again; yet within two hours after, through the moderation of some of the justices, I had liberty given me to go at large till next quarter-sessions. These moderate justices, it was said, desired Justice Parker to write to the king for my liberty, or for a Noli prosequi, because they were satisfied I was not such a dangerous person as I had been represented. This, it was said, he promised them to do; but he did it not.

After I had got a copy of the indictment, I went to LONDON, visiting Friends as I went. When I came there, some that were earnest to get me out of the hands of those envious justices, that sought to premunire me at Worcester, would needs be tampering again, to bring me before the judges of the King's Bench; whereupon I was brought again by a habeas corpus before them. I tendered them a paper, in which was contained what I could say instead of the oaths of allegiance and supremacy, as follows:—

"THIS I do in the truth, and in the presence of God declare, that King Charles the Second is lawful king of this realm, and of all other his dominions; that he was brought in, and set up king over this realm by the power of God: and I have nothing but love and good will to him and all his subjects, and desire his prosperity and eternal good. I do utterly abhor and deny the Pope's power and supremacy, and all his superstitions and idolatrous inventions; and do affirm, that he hath no power to absolve sin. I do abhor and detest his murdering of princes or other people, by plots or contrivances. And likewise I do deny all plots and contrivances, and plotters and contrivers against the king and his subjects; knowing them to be the works of darkness, the fruits of an evil spirit, against the peace of the kingdom, and not from the Spirit of God, the fruit of which is love. I dare not take an oath, because it is forbidden by Christ and the apostle; but if I break my Yea or Nay, let me suffer the same penalty as they that break their oaths." GEORGE FOX.

But the business being so far proceeded in at Worcester, they would not meddle in it, but left me to appear again before the justices, at the next general quarter-sessions at Worcester.

Meanwhile the YEARLY MEETING of Friends came on, at which (through the liberty granted me till the sessions) I was present, and exceedingly glorious the meetings were beyond expression; blessed be the Lord.

After the Yearly Meeting I set forward for Worcester, the sessions drawing on, which were held in the 5th month. When I was called to the bar, and the indictment read, some scruple arising among the jury concerning it, the judge of the court, Justice Street, caused the oaths to be read and tendered to me again. I told him, "I came now to try the traverse of my indictment, and that his tendering me the oaths anew, was a new snare." I desired him to answer me a question or two; and asked him, "whether the oaths were to be tendered to the king's subjects, or to the subjects of foreign princes?" He said, "to the subjects of this realm." "Then," said I, "you have not named me a subject in the indictment, and therefore have not brought me within the statute." The judge cried, "read the oath to him:" I said, "I require justice." Again I asked him, "Whether the sessions ought not to have been held for the king and the body of the county?" He said, "Yes." "Then," said I, "you have there left the king out of the indictment; how then can you proceed upon this indictment to a trial between the king and me, seeing the king is left out?" He said, "the king was in before." But I told him, "the king's name being left out, here was a great error in the indictment, and sufficient, as I was informed, to quash it. Besides," I told him, "that I was committed by the name of George Fox, of London; but now I was indicted by the name of George Fox, of Tredington, in the county of Worcester: and I wished the jury to consider, how they could find me guilty upon that indictment, seeing I was not of the place the indictment mentioned?" The judge did not deny that there were errors in the indictment; but said, "I might take my remedy in the proper place." I answered, "ye know we are a people that suffer all things, and bear all things; and therefore ye thus use us, because we cannot revenge ourselves; but we leave our cause to the Lord." The judge said, "the oath has been tendered to you several times, and we will have some satisfaction from you concerning the oath." I offered them the same declaration instead of the oath, which I had offered to the judges above; but it would not be accepted. Then I desired to know, seeing they put the oath anew to me, whether the indictment was quashed or not? Instead of answering me, the judge told the jury, "they might go out." Some of the jury were not satisfied; whereupon the judge told them, "they had heard a man swear that the oath was tendered to me the last sessions:" and then he told them what they should do. I told him, "he should leave the jury to their own consciences." However, the jury, being put on by him, went forth, and soon came in again, and found me guilty. I asked the jury "how they could satisfy themselves to find me guilty upon that indictment, which was laid so false, and had so many errors in it?" They could make but little answer; yet one, who seemed to be the worst of them, would have taken me by the hand; but I put him by, saying, "How now Judas, hast thou betrayed me, and dost thou now come with a kiss?" So I bid him and them repent. Then the judge began to tell me, "how favourable the court had been to me." I asked him, "how he could say so? Was ever any man worse dealt by than I had been in this case, who was stopped in my journey, when travelling upon my lawful occasions, and imprisoned without cause; and now had the oaths put to me only for a snare?" And I desired him to "answer me in the presence of the Lord, in whose presence we all were, whether this oath was not tendered me in envy?" He would not answer that, but said, "Would you had never come here to trouble us and the country." I told him, "I came not thither of myself, but was brought, being stopped in my journey. I did not trouble them, but they had brought trouble upon themselves." Then the judge told me, "what a sad sentence he had to tell me." I asked him, "Whether what he was going to speak was by way of passing sentence, or of information? For," I told him, "I had many things to say, and more errors to assign in the indictment, besides those I had already mentioned, to stop him from giving sentence against me upon that indictment." He said, "He was going to show me the danger of a premunire, which was the loss of my liberty, and of all my goods and chattels, and to endure imprisonment during life." But he said, "he did not deliver this as the sentence of the court upon me, but as an admonition to me." Then he bid the jailer take me away. I expected to be called again to hear the sentence; but when I was gone, the clerk of the peace (whose name was Twittey) asked him, as I was informed, "whether that which he had spoken to me should stand for sentence?" And he, consulting with some of the justices, told him, "Yes, that was the sentence, and should stand." This was done behind my back, to save himself from shame in the face of the country. Many of the justices, and the generality of the people, were moderate and civil; and John Ashley, a lawyer, was very friendly, both the time before and now, speaking on my behalf, and pleading the errors of the indictment for me; but Justice Street, who was the judge of the court, would not regard, but overruled all. This Justice Street said to some Friends in the morning before my trial, "that if he had been upon the bench the first sessions, he would not have tendered me the oath; but if I had been convicted of being at a conventicle, he would have proceeded against me according to that law; and that he was sorry that ever I came before him;" and yet he maliciously tendered the oath to me in the court again, when I was to have tried my traverse upon the indictment. But the Lord pleaded my cause, and met with both him and Justice Simpson, who first ensnared me with the oath at the first sessions; for Simpson's son was arraigned not long after, at the same bar, for murder. And Street, who, as he came down from London, after the judges had returned me back from the King's Bench to Worcester, said, "Now I was returned to them, I should lie in prison and rot," had his daughter, whom he so doted on that she was called his idol, brought dead from London in a hearse, to the same inn where he spoke those words, and brought to Worcester to be buried within a few days after. People took notice of the hand of God, how sudden it was upon him; but it rather hardened than tendered him, as his conduct afterwards showed.

After I was returned to prison, several came to see me; and amongst others, the Earl of Salisbury's son, who was very loving, and troubled that they had dealt so wickedly by me. He stayed about two hours with me, and took a copy of the errors in the indictment in writing.

The sessions being now over, and I fixed in prison by a premunire, my wife came out of the North to be with me; and the assizes coming on, in the 6th month, the state of my case being drawn up in writing, she and Thomas Lower delivered it to Judge Wild. In it were set forth the occasion of my journey; the manner of my being taken and imprisoned; the proceedings of the several sessions against me; and the errors in the indictment by which I was premunired. When the judge had read it, he shook his head, and said, "We might try the validity or invalidity of the errors, if we would;" and that was all they could get from him.

While I lay in prison, it came upon me to state our principle to the king; not with particular relation to my own sufferings, but for his better information concerning our principle, and us as a people.

"*To the King.*

"The principle of the Quakers is the Spirit of Christ, who died for us, and is risen for our justification; by which we know that we are his. He dwelleth in us by his Spirit; and by the Spirit of Christ we are led out of unrighteousness and ungodliness. It brings us to deny all plottings and contrivings against the king, or any man. The Spirit of Christ brings us to deny all manner of ungodliness, as lying, theft, murder, adultery, fornication, and all uncleanness, debauchery, malice, hatred, deceit, cozening, and cheating whatsoever, and the Devil and his works. The Spirit of Christ brings us to seek the peace and good of all men, and to live peaceably; and leads us from such evil works and actions as the magistrates' sword takes hold upon. Our desire and labour are, that all, who profess themselves Christians, may walk in the Spirit of Christ; that they, through the Spirit, may mortify the deeds of the flesh, and by the sword of the Spirit cut down sin and evil in themselves. Then the judges and other magistrates would not have so much work in punishing sin in the kingdom; neither then need kings or princes fear any of their subjects; if they all walked in the Spirit of Christ; for the fruits of the Spirit are love, righteousness, goodness, temperance, &c. If all, that profess themselves Christians, walked in the Spirit of Christ, and by it did mortify sin and evil, it would be a great ease to the magistrates and rulers, and would free them from much trouble; for it would lead all "to do unto others, as they would have others to do unto them;" and so the royal law of liberty would be fulfilled. For if all, that are called Christians, did walk in the Spirit of Christ, by it to have the evil spirits and its fruits mortified and cut down in them; then, not being led by the evil spirit, but by the good Spirit of Christ, the fruits of the good Spirit would appear in all. For as people are led by the good Spirit of Christ, it leads them out of sin and evil, which the magistrates' sword takes hold of, and so would be an ease to the magistrates. But as people err from this good Spirit of Christ, and follow the evil spirit, which leads them into sin and evil; that spirit brings the magistrate into much trouble, to execute the law upon the sinners and transgressors of the good Spirit. That Spirit which leads people from all manner of sin and evil, is one with the magistrates' power, and with the righteous law; for the law being added because of transgression, that Spirit that leads out of transgression, must needs be one with that law that is against transgressors. So that Spirit which leads out of transgression, is the good Spirit of Christ, and is one with the magistrates in the higher power, and owns it and them; but that spirit which leads into transgression, is the bad spirit, is against the law, against the magistrates, and makes them much troublesome work. Now the manifestation of the good Spirit is given to every man to profit withal; and no man can profit in the things of God, but by the Spirit of God, which brings to deny all sin and evil. It is said of Israel, Neh. ix., 'The Lord gave them his good Spirit to instruct them, yet they rebelled against it.' But if all people did mind this manifestation of the Spirit, which God hath given to instruct them, it would lead them to forsake all manner of sin and evil, enmity, hatred, malice, and all manner of unrighteousness and ungodliness, and to mortify it. And then in the Spirit of Christ they would have fellowship and unity, which is the bond of peace; then would love and peace, which are the fruits of the good Spirit, flow among all that are called Christians.

"We are a people, who, in tenderness of conscience to the command of Christ and his apostle, cannot swear; for we are commanded in Matt. v. and James v. to keep to Yea and Nay, and 'not to swear at all; neither by heaven, nor by the earth, nor by any other oath, lest we go into evil, and fall into condemnation.' The words of Christ are these, 'Ye have heard that it hath been said by (or to) them of old time, Thou shalt not forswear thyself, but shalt perform unto the Lord thine oaths.' These were true and solemn oaths, which they who made, ought to have performed in old time; but these Christ and his apostle forbid in the gospel times, as well as false and vain oaths. If we could take any oath at all, we could take the oath of allegiance, as knowing that King Charles was by the power of God brought into England, and set up king of England, &c., over the heads of our old persecutors; and as for the Pope's supremacy, we do utterly deny it. But Christ and the apostle having commanded us not to swear, but to keep to Yea and Nay, we dare not break their commands; and therefore many have put the oaths to us, as a snare, that they might make a prey of us. Our denying to swear is not in wilfulness, stubbornness, or contempt, but only in obedience to the command of Christ and his apostle; and we are content, if we break our Yea and Nay, to suffer the same penalty that they should who break their oaths. We desire, therefore, that the king would take this into consideration, and also how long we have suffered in this case. This is from one who desires the eternal good and prosperity of the king, and of all his subjects in the Lord Jesus Christ."

G. F.

About this time I had a fit of sickness, which brought me very low and weak in my body; and I continued so a pretty while, insomuch that some Friends began to doubt of my recovery. I seemed to myself to be amongst the graves and dead corpses; yet the invisible power did secretly support me, and conveyed refreshing strength into me, even when I was so weak, that I was almost speechless. One night, as I was lying awake upon my bed in the glory of the Lord, which was over all, it was said unto me, "that the Lord had a great deal more work for me to do for him, before he took me to himself."

Endeavours were used to get me released, at least for a time, till I was grown stronger; but the way of effecting it proved difficult and tedious; for the king was not willing to release me by any other way than a pardon, being told he could not legally do it; and I was not willing to be released by a pardon, which he would readily have given me, because I did not look upon that way as agreeable with the innocency of my cause. Edward Pitway, a Friend, having occasion to speak with Justice Parker, upon some other business, desired him to give order to the jailer, that, in regard of my weakness, I might have liberty to go out of the jail into the city. Whereupon Justice Parker wrote the following letter to the jailer, and sent it to the Friend to deliver.

"MR. HARRIS,

"I have been much importuned by some friends to George Fox to write to you. I am informed by them, that he is in a very weak condition, and very much indisposed; what lawful favour you can do for the benefit of the air for his health, pray show him. I suppose, the next term they will make application to the king.

"I am, Sir, your loving friend, HENRY PARKER."

Evesham, the 8th of October, 1674.

After this, my wife went to London, and spoke to the king, laying before him my long and unjust imprisonment, with the manner of my being taken, and the justices' proceedings against me, in tendering me the oath as a snare, whereby they had premunired me; so that I being now his prisoner, it was in his power, and at his pleasure, to release me, which she desired. The king spoke kindly to her, and referred her to the lord-keeper; to whom she went, but could not obtain what she desired; for he said, "the king could not release me otherwise than by a pardon;" and I was not free to receive a pardon, knowing I had not done evil. If I would have been freed by a pardon, I need not have lain so long, for the king was willing to give me pardon long before, and told Thomas Moore, "that I need not scruple being released by a pardon, for many a man, that was as innocent as a child, had had a pardon granted him;" yet I could not consent to have one. For I had rather have lain in prison all my days, than have come out in any way dishonourable to truth; wherefore I chose to have the validity of my indictment tried before the judges. And thereupon, having first had the opinion of a counsellor upon it (Thomas Corbet of London, whom Richard Davis of Welchpool was well acquainted with, and recommended to me), an habeas corpus was sent down to Worcester to bring me up once more to the King's Bench bar, for the trial of the errors in my indictment. The under-sheriff set forward with me the 4th of the 12th Month, there being with us in the coach the clerk of the peace and some others. The clerk had been my enemy all along, and now sought to ensnare me in discourse; but I saw, and shunned him. He asked me, "what I would do with the errors in the indictment?" I told him, "they should be tried, and every action should crown itself." He quarrelled with me for calling their ministers priests. I asked him, "if the law did not call them so?" Then he asked me, "what I thought of the church of England? were there no Christians among them?" I said, "they are called so, and there are many tender people amongst them." We came to LONDON on the 8th, and on the 11th I was brought before the four judges at the King's Bench, where Counsellor Corbet pleaded my cause. He started a new plea; for he told the judges, "that they could not imprison any man upon a premunire." Whereupon Chief Justice Hale said, "Mr. Corbet, you should have come sooner, at the beginning of the term, with this plea." He answered, "we could not get a copy of the return and the indictment." The judge replied, "you should have told us, and we would have forced them to make a return sooner." Then said Judge Wild, "Mr. Corbet, you go upon general terms; and if it be as you say, we have committed many errors at the Old Bailey, and in other courts." Corbet was positive that by law they could not imprison upon a premunire. The judge said, "there is summons in the statute." "Yes," said Corbet, "but summons is not imprisonment; for summons is in order to a trial." "Well," said the judge, "we must have time to look in our books and consult the statutes." So the hearing was put off till the next day.

The next day they chose rather to let this plea fall, and begin with the errors of the indictment; and when they came to be opened, they were so many and gross, that the judges were all of opinion that "the indictment was quashed and void, and that I ought to have my liberty." There were that day several great men, lords and others, who had the oaths of allegiance and supremacy tendered to them in open court, just before my trial came on; and some of my adversaries moved the judges, that the oaths might be tendered again to me, telling them, "I was a dangerous man to be at liberty." But Judge Hale said, "He had indeed heard some such reports, but he had also heard many more good reports of me;" and so he and the rest of the judges ordered me to be freed by proclamation. Thus after I had suffered imprisonment a year and almost two months for nothing, I was fairly set at liberty upon a trial of the errors in my indictment, without receiving any pardon, or coming under any obligation or engagement at all; and the Lord's everlasting power went over all, to his glory and praise. Counsellor Corbet, who pleaded for me, obtained great fame by it, for many of the lawyers came to him, and told him he had brought that to light which had not been known before, as to the not imprisoning upon a premunire; and after the trial a judge said to him, "You have attained a great deal of honour by pleading George Fox's cause so in court."

During the time of my imprisonment in Worcester, notwithstanding my illness and want of health, and my being so often hurried to and fro to London and back again, I wrote several books for the press; one of which was called, *A Warning to England.* Another was, *To the Jews, proving, by the Prophets, that the Messiah is come.* Another, *Concerning Inspiration,*

Revelation, and Prophecy. Another, *Against all Vain Disputes.* Another, *For all Bishops and Ministers to try themselves by the Scriptures.* Another, *To such as say, "We love none but ourselves."* Another entitled, *Our Testimony concerning Christ.* And another little book, *Concerning Swearing;* being the first of those two that were given to the parliament. Besides these, I wrote many papers and epistles to Friends to encourage and strengthen them in their services for God, which some, who had made profession of truth, but had given way to a seducing spirit, and were departed from the unity and fellowship of the gospel, in which Friends stand, endeavoured to discourage them from, especially in their diligent and watchful care for the well-ordering and managing of the affairs of the church of Christ.

CHAPTER VII.

1675–1677.—George Fox attends the Yearly Meeting, and afterwards sets forward towards the North—attends the Quarterly Meeting at Lancaster, and goes thence to Swarthmore—writes many books and papers for the Truth—the titles of several named—writes to Friends in Westmorland to keep in the power of God, and thereby avoid strife—writes an epistle to the Yearly Meeting—makes a collection and arrangement of his various papers and writings, and of the names of divers Friends engaged in particular service, or against the Truth—some meetings for discipline established in the North in 1653—recites his labours and travels for establishing meetings for discipline—a spirit of discord and separation appears in the church—the separatists are rebuked and reproved—the establishment of men's and women's meetings is much opposed—a narrative of the spreading of Truth, and of the opposition from the worldly powers—death of Priest Lampitt, a persecutor—George Fox travels again towards the South—writes to his wife from York—finds some slack in their testimony against Tithes—writes an epistle to Friends on the subject—attends the Yearly Meeting—with John Burnyeat, and other Friends, visits Wm. Penn at his house at Worminghurst, in Sussex—sets things in order for visiting Holland—precious meeting.

BEING now at liberty, I visited Friends in LONDON; and having been very weak, and not yet well recovered, I went to KINGSTON. I did not stay long, but having visited Friends there, I returned to LONDON, wrote a paper to the parliament, and sent several books to them. A great book against Swearing had been delivered to them a little before; the reasonableness whereof had so much influence upon many of them, that it was thought they would have done something towards our relief, if they had sat longer. I stayed in and near London till the Yearly Meeting, to which Friends came from most parts of the nation, and some from beyond the sea. A glorious meeting we had in the everlasting power of God.

This meeting being over, and the parliament also risen (who had done nothing for or against Friends), I was clear of my service for the Lord at London. And having taken my leave of Friends there, and had a glorious meeting with some of them at John Elson's in the morning, I set forward with my wife and her daughter Susan, by coach (for I was not able to travel on horseback) towards the North; many Friends accompanying us as far as HIGHGATE, and some to DUNSTABLE, where we lodged that night. We visited Friends, and were visited by them, at NEWPORT-PAGNEL, NORTHAMPTON, and COSSEL, where, amongst others, came a woman, and brought her daughter, for me to see how well she was; putting me in mind, "that when I was there before, she had brought her to me, much troubled with the disease called the king's evil, and had then desired me to pray for her;" which I did, and she grew well upon it, praised be the Lord! From Cossel we went on by John Simcock's and William Gandy's, to WARRINGTON and PRESTON, and so to LANCASTER.

I had not been at Lancaster since I was carried prisoner from thence by the under-sheriff and jailer, towards Scarbro' Castle. I found the town full of people; for it was both the fair time, and the trained bands were met upon a general muster. Many Friends were also in town from several parts of the county, because the Quarterly Meeting was to be there the next day. I stayed two nights and a day at Lancaster, and visited Friends both at their men's and women's meetings, which were very full, large, and peaceable; for the Lord's power was over all, and none meddled with us. Here met us Thomas Lower and his wife, Sarah Fell, James Lancaster, and Leonard Fell. Next day after the meeting, being the 25th of the 4th Month, we went over the Sands, with several other Friends, to SWARTHMORE.

After I had been a while at Swarthmore, several Friends from divers parts of the nation came to visit me, and some out of Scotland; by whom I understood that four young students of Aberdeen were convinced there this year, at a dispute held there by Robert Barclay, and George Keith, with some of the scholars of that university.*

Among others Colonel Kirby paid me a visit, who had been one of my great persecutors; but now, he said, he came to bid me welcome into the country; and carried himself in appearance very lovingly. Yet before I left Swarthmore, he sent for the constables of Ulverstone, and ordered them to tell me, "that we must have no more meetings at Swarthmore; for if we had, they were commanded by him to break them up; and they were to come the next First-day." That day we had a very precious meeting, the Lord's presence was wonderfully amongst us, and the constables did not come to disturb us. The meetings have been quiet since, and have increased.

The illness I got in my imprisonment at Worcester had so much weakened me, that it was long before I recovered my natural strength again. For which reason, and as many things lay upon me to write, both for public and private service, I did not stir much abroad during the time that I now stayed in the North; but when Friends were not with me, spent much time in writing for truth's service. While I was at Swarthmore, I gave several books to be printed. One, *Concerning Swearing.* Another, showing, "that none are successors to the Prophets and Apostles, but who succeed them in the same power and Holy Ghost that they were in." Another, "that Possession is above Profession, and how the professors now do persecute Christ in Spirit, as the professing Jews did persecute him outwardly in the days of his flesh." Also the eight following books, viz.:—*To the Magistrates of Dantzic; Cain against Abel;* or, *an Answer to the New Englandmen's Laws; To Friends at Nevis, concerning Watching;*† *A General Epistle to all Friends in America; Concerning Cæsar's due, and God's due,* &c.; *Concerning the Ordering of Families; The Spiritual Man judgeth all things; Concerning the Higher Power.*

Besides these, I wrote several epistles to Friends, both in England, and beyond the seas; and answers to divers papers concerning "the run-

* Some particulars of the controversy here alluded to, may be seen in Barclay's *Works;* also in Jaffray's *Diary*, p. 328–330. The students who were convinced issued a written declaration, stating the grounds of their change, which remains on record.

† See *Selections from the Epistles of George Fox,* by Samuel Tuke.

ning out of some, who had opposed the order of the gospel, and had stirred up much strife and contention in Westmorland." Wherefore I was moved to write a few lines, particularly to Friends there.

"This is for Friends in Westmorland.

"All live in the power of God, in his Light and Spirit, which first convinced you; that in it ye may keep in the ancient unity, in humility, in the fear of the Lord, and his gentle and peaceable wisdom, which is easy to be entreated; that in the same Power, Light, and Spirit of God, ye may all be serviceable in your men's and women's meetings, in the possession of the gospel-order; which gospel, the power of God, hath brought life and immortality to light; that in this ye may see over him that hath darkened you. In this power, the glorious gospel, no apostates can come; for the power of God was before apostates were, or the fall of man and woman was, or the devil either, and will be when he is gone. Therefore praise God in the eternal fellowship of the everlasting gospel of Jesus Christ, which is not of man, nor by man. And therefore, all Friends in Westmorland, keep in the power of God, which will and must preserve and cover you, if ye be preserved. Let your faith stand in the power of God, and not in the wisdom of men's words, lest ye fall. In God's power ye have peace, life, and unity; and for want of keeping in God's power, and in his righteousness and Holy Ghost, is all this strife come among you." G. F.

I also wrote the following general epistle to Friends at the Yearly Meeting in London:—

"My dear Friends and Brethren,

"Whom the Lord hath preserved by his eternal power to this day, over and through many troubles, storms, tempests, and prisons. Let, therefore, every one's faith stand in the power of God, which is over the Devil, and was before him. So your faith standing in the invisible power of God, stands in that which does not change; and the faith, that Christ Jesus, the power of God, is the author of, must stand in the power of God; so then it stands in that which is over all, in which they are established. To this the apostle brought the church, the true Christians; and so now the faith of all true Christians, which Christ is the author of, must stand in the power of God, in which the everlasting kingdom stands. As every one's faith stands in the power of God, it keeps all in the power of godliness.

"For as it was in the days of the apostles, when some were crying up Paul and Apollos, and so forth, he judged them as carnal; and exhorted and admonished them, that their faith should not stand in men, nor in the words of man's wisdom, but in the power of God. He said 'he would not know the speech of them, but the power amongst them; for the kingdom of God is not in word, but in power.' So it is to be now. Every one's faith must stand in the power of God, and not in men, nor in their speeches or good words. For we have seen by experience, when any begin to cry up men, and their faith stands in them, such men as would have people's faith stand in them, love popularity, and bring not people's faith to stand in the power of God. Such cannot exalt Christ; and when such fall, they draw a great company after them. Therefore the apostle would not know such after the flesh, but would know them that were in the power and Spirit; and struck down every one's faith that stood in the words of man's wisdom, that they might stand in the power of God. So it must be now. They whose faith doth not stand in the power of God, cannot exalt his kingdom that stands in power; therefore every one's faith must stand in the power of God.

"The apostle denied popularity, when he judged the Corinthians, for looking at Paul and Apollos, to be carnal; such are carnal still. Therefore all should know one another in the Spirit, life, and power, and look at Christ; this keeps all in humility. They, whose faith stands in men, will make sects; as in the days of J. N. and J. P. and others. The faith of such Christ is not the author of; and if he hath been, they have erred from it, and made shipwreck of it. All that are in the true faith, that stands in the power of God, will judge them as carnal, and judge down that carnal part in them, that cries up Paul or Apollos; that their faith may stand in the power of God, and that they may exalt Christ, the author of it. For every one's eye ought to be to Jesus; and every just man and woman may live by their faith, which Jesus Christ is the author and finisher of. By this faith every man and woman may see God, who is invisible; this faith gives the victory, and by it he hath access to God. So every one's faith and hope standing in the power of God, all therein have unity, victory, and access to God's throne of grace; in which faith they please God. By this faith they are saved;—by this faith they obtain the good report, and subdue all the mountains that have been betwixt them and God.

"This power hath preserved Friends over their persecutors, over the wrath of men, and above the spoilings of their goods, and imprisonments; as seeing God who 'created all—who gives the increase of all, and upholds all by his word and power.' Therefore let every one's faith be in his power. In this no schism or sect can come; for it is over them, before they were, and will be when they are gone. But perfect unity is in the truth, in the Spirit, that circumcises the body of death, that puts off the sins of the flesh, and plunges it down with the Spirit. In the Spirit of God, there is perfect fellowship; and Christ is the minister of this circumcision and baptism.

"This is upon me from the Lord, to write unto you, that every one of you, whose faith Jesus is the author of, may stand in the power of God. From the Lord I warn you, and all everywhere, of the same. For if a star should fall, which has been a light, either the earth or the sea does receive it; that is, the earthly mind, or the foaming, raging people; though neither the seed, light, power, nor truth ever fell, nor the faith itself, the gift of God; but men going from it, become unsavoury.

"Adam, whilst he kept in truth, and obeyed the command of God, was happy; but when he disobeyed the Lord, he fell under the power of Satan, and became unhappy, though he might talk after of his experiences in Paradise; but he lost his image, his power and dominion, in which God had created him.

"The Jews received the law of God, and as long as they kept the law, which was just, holy, good, and perfect, it kept them good, just, holy, and savoury; but when they turned their backs on the Lord, and forsook his law, then they came under the power of darkness, under the powers of the earth, and were trodden under as unsavoury.

"So the Christians were called 'a city set on a hill, the light of the world, and the salt of the earth;' but when they forsook the power of God, and their faith stood in words and men, and not in the power, then their walls fell down, though the power in itself stood; and they lost their hill, their saltness, and their shining. And as Christendom now does confess, they are not in the same power and spirit that the apostles were in; so not in the same salt, nor upon the same hill. So they came to be trodden under; and the beast, the whore, and the false prophet are uppermost, the unsavoury. Their dead faith is in men, and in words; therefore they are full of sects, and one against another.

"And now the everlasting gospel, the power of God, is preached again, which was before the devil was, that darkened man; and by this power of God, life and immortality are brought to light again. Therefore every one's faith is to stand in this power, that hath brought life and immortality to light in them, that so all may come to be heirs of the power of God, the gospel. Herein all have a right to the power of God, which is the authority of the men's and women's meetings, and of all other meetings set up thereby.

"Now, as the gospel is preached again, if your faith does not stand in the power, but in men, and in the wisdom of words, you will grow carnal; and such are for judgment, who cry up Paul or Apollos, and not Christ, the author of your faith. They who love to be popular, would have people's faith to stand in them; and such do not preach Christ, but themselves. But such as preach Christ and his gospel, would have every man and woman to be in the possession of it, and every man and woman's faith to stand in Christ, the author of it, and in the power of God. And as their faith stands in the power of God, nothing can get between them and God; for if any should fall amongst us, as too many have done, that [love of popularity] leads its followers either into the waters, or into the earth.

"If any should go from the spirit of prophecy, that did open to them, and from the power, they may speak their experiences, which the power opened to them formerly. So might Adam and Eve speak of what they saw and enjoyed in Paradise; so might Cain and Balaam of what they saw; and also the Jews, Korah and Dathan, who praised God on the banks, saw the victory over Pharaoh, ate of the manna, drank of the rock, came to Mount Sinai, and saw the glory of the Lord. So also might the false apostles speak of their experiences, and all those false Christians, that turned from the apostles and Christ. And so may those do now, that err from the Spirit, that are come out of Egypt (in spirit) and Sodom; and have known the raging of the Sodomites, as Lot did the outward; and the pursuit of the spiritual Egyptians, as the outward Jew did of the outward Egyptians; yet if they do not walk in the Spirit of God, in the light, and in the grace, which keeps their hearts established, and their words seasoned, and also their faith in the power of God, in which the kingdom stands; they may go forth like the false Christians, like the Jews, like Adam and Eve, Cain, Korah, and Balaam, and be wandering stars, trees without fruit, wells without water, and clouds without rain; and so come to be unsavoury and trodden down; as Adam who lost Paradise, and the Jews who lost the Holy Land, not walking in the law, and keeping the command of God; and as the Christians who lost the city, the hill, the salt, and the light since the apostle's days, and came to be unsavoury, and to be trodden under foot of men.

"Therefore, let every one's faith stand in the Lord's power, which is over all; through which they may be built upon the Rock, the Foundation of God, the Seed Christ Jesus. So all in Christ may be always fresh and green; for he is the green tree that never withers. All are fresh and green that are grafted into and abide in him, bringing forth heavenly fresh fruits to the praise of God. And though Adam and Eve fell from Paradise, the Jews fell from the law of God, and many of the Christians fell from their prophecies, and erred from the faith, the Spirit, and the grace; and the stars have fallen, as was spoken in the Revelations: yet the Spirit, grace, faith, and power of God remain.

"Many such states have I seen within these twenty-eight years; though there is a state that shall never fall, nor be deceived, in the Elect before the world began. These are come to the end of the prophecies, are in Him where they end, and renewed by Christ into the image of God which man was in before he fell,—in that power where he had dominion over all that God made: and not only so, but they 'attain to a perfect man, unto the measure of the stature of the fulness of Christ,' who never fell. In him is the sitting down in life eternal, where there feet stand sure and fast in the gospel, his power. Here their bread is sure; and he that eats this bread lives for ever.

"And all Friends and brethren, that declare God's eternal truth, and word of life, live in it; be seasoned with grace, and salted with the heavenly salt, that your lives and conversations may preach wherever you come;—that there be no rawness, no quenching of the Spirit, no despising of prophecy either in men or women. For all must meet in the faith that Jesus is the author of, and in the light that comes from Jesus, and be so grafted into the life, that your knowledge may be there one of another, in Christ; and that there may be none slothful, nor sitting down in earthly things, minding them, like Demas of old; lest you clothe yourselves with another clothing than you had at first; but all keep chaste; for the chaste follow the Lamb.

"And Friends, that are ministers, possess, as if ye did not; be married, as if ye were not; and be loose to the world in the Lord's power; for God's oil will be above all visible things, which makes his lamps burn, and give light afar off. Let none strive nor covet to be rich in this world, in these changeable things that will pass away; but let your faith stand in the Lord God, who changes not, who created all, and gives the increase of all.

"Now Friends, concerning faithful men's and women's meetings, which were set up in God's counsel; whoever oppose them, oppose the power of God, which is the authority of them. They are no ministers of the gospel, nor of Christ, that oppose his power, which all are to possess. The gospel is to be preached to all nations: as deceit is gone over all nations, and all nations have drunk the whore's cup, and she hath them in her cage, her unclean power from the beast and dragon, out of the power of God, and out of truth, and the Spirit of God the apostles were in; the power of God must come over all this again; and all the true ministers that preach the gospel, the power of God, must bring people into the possession of it again. I say, whosoever preaches the gospel of Christ and him to people or nations, those people and nations receiving the gospel, receive the power of God, that brings life and immortality to light in them; they see over the devil that hath darkened them, and over the beast, the whore, and her cage. So, by the power of God, life and immortality are brought to light in them; then these men and women, being heirs of this power, the gospel, are heirs of authority and power over the devil, beast, whore, and dragon.

"This is their possession and portion; and they are to labour in their possession and portion, and do God Almighty's business and service in the possession of the power of God, the gospel, which is a joyful, glorious, everlasting order. And here is the authority of our men's and women's meetings, and other meetings in the name of Jesus, the gospel of Christ, the power of God, which is not of man, nor by man. In this are all to meet and to worship God; by this are all to act; and in this all have fellowship, a joyful fellowship, a joyful and comfortable assembly. This is the day when, in the eternal light, all are to take their possession of the gospel and its order, that power of God, which they are heirs of. All faithful men and women in every country, city, and nation, whose faith stands in the power of God, the gospel of Christ, who have received, and are in the possession of, this gospel, the power of God, have all right to the power in these meetings; for they are heirs of the power, which is the authority of the men's and women's meetings.

"So here is God's choice (and not man's) by his power, of his heirs; and they have all freedom in this gospel, the power of God, to go to the meetings, the men to the men's, and the women to the women's; for they are heirs of the power, which is received in the Holy Ghost; and they see over enmity, and before it was, by the light, by the life, and immortality, which are brought to light in them.

"The devil, the author of enmity, cannot get into this authority, power, order, nor fellowship of the gospel; nor into this life, light, nor unity of the faith, which gives victory over him that hath separated man from God. Into the unity of this faith the serpent cannot come, nor into the worship of God in Spirit and truth can the devil come, or any enmity. And they that are in this, are in unity over him. Therefore, let every one's faith stand in the power of God, the glorious gospel; and let all walk as becomes the gospel, and the order of it. As every one hath received Christ Jesus, the Lord, so walk in him, and let him be their Lord and Orderer.

For the preaching of the gospel of Christ Jesus is to the intent that all may come to be heirs of the gospel, and into the possession of it; and to be heirs of Christ and of his government, of the increase of which there is no end; who is over all in his righteousness, and over all in his light, life, power, and dominion. Therefore know one another in his power, his gospel, which is the authority of your meetings; know one another in Christ Jesus, who is able to restore man out of the state of the fall, into the image of God, into that power and dominion that man had before he fell, and into Himself, that never fell, whence they shall go no more forth. Here is the rock and foundation of God that stands sure.

"And, Friends, be tender to the tender principle of God in all. Shun vain disputes and janglings, both amongst yourselves and others; for that many times is like a blustering wind, that hurts and bruises the tender buds and plants. For the world, though they have the words, are out of the life; and the apostle's disputing with them, was to bring them to the life. And those disputers, that were amongst the Christians, about genealogies, circumcision, and the law, meats, drinks, and days, came to be the worst sort of disputers, whom the apostles judged; for such destroyed people from the faith. Therefore the apostles exhorted the churches, that every one's faith should stand in the power of God, and to look at Jesus, the author of it. There every graft stands in Christ, the vine, quiet; where no blustering storms can hurt them; there is safety. There all are of one mind, one faith, one soul, one spirit, baptized into one body with the one Spirit, and made all to drink into one Spirit, one church, one head, that is heavenly and spiritual; one faith in this head, Christ, who is the author of it, and hath the glory of it; one Lord to order all, who is the baptizer into this one body. So Christ hath the glory of this faith out of every man and woman; and God through him hath his glory, the Creator of all in his power, the gospel that hath brought life and immortality to light in them; and their faith standing in it, they know the immortal God, serve and worship him, in his Spirit and in his truth; by which they are made God's free men and women, from him that is out of the truth.

"Now, Friends, you that have long been labourers, and have known the dealings of the Lord these twenty years (more or less), as I have often said to you, draw up what you can, of those passages and sufferings which the Lord hath carried you through by his power, and how by Him ye have been supported from the first; that the Lord may be exalted by his power now, and in ages to come, who hath been the only support, defence, and stay, of his people all along, over all to himself; to whom be all glory and praise for ever and ever, Amen. He deserves it in his church throughout all ages, from his living members, who return the praise to the living God, who lives and reigns over all, blessed for ever; who is the life, and strength, and health, and length of days of all his people. Therefore let there be no boasting, but in the Lord, and in his power and kingdom; this keeps all in humility.

"And, Friends, in the Lord's power and truth, what good you can do for Friends in prison, or sufferers, by informing or helping them, every one bend yourselves to the Lord's power and spirit, to do his will and his business; and in that all will have a fellow-feeling of one another's condition, in bonds, or in what trials and tribulations soever; you will have a fellow-feeling one of another, having one head, one Lord, and being one body in him. For God's heavenly flail hath brought out his seed, his heavenly plough hath turned up the fallow ground, and his heavenly seed is sown by the heavenly man, which brings forth fruits to the heavenly sower, in some fifty, sixty, and a hundred fold in this life; and such in the world without end will have life eternal. O, therefore, all keep within; let your lights shine, and your lamps burn, that you all may be wells full of the living water, and trees full of the living fruit of God's planting, whose fruit is unto holiness, and the end everlasting life.

"The Lord God of power preserve you all in his power. Let your faith stand therein, that you may have unity in the faith, and in the power; and by this faith and belief you may be all grafted into Christ, the sure root, where the eternal Sun of Righteousness shines, in the heavenly and eternal day, upon his plants and grafts. This sun never goes down; and the heavenly springs of life, and showers are known to water and nourish the grafts, and plants, and buds, that they may always be kept fresh and green, and never wither; bringing forth fresh and green, and living fruit, which is offered up to the living God, who is glorified in that you bear much fruit. The Lord God Almighty keep you, and preserve you all in his power, light, and life, over death and darkness; that therein you may spread his truth abroad, and be valiant for it upon the earth, answering that of God in all; that with it, the minds of people may be turned to him, so that with it they may come to know the Lord Christ Jesus in the new covenant, in which the knowledge of the Lord shall cover the earth as the waters do the sea. His life must go over death, and his light must go over darkness, and the power of God must go over the power of Satan.

"So, all ye that are in the light, life, and power, keep the heavenly fellowship in the heavenly power, the heavenly unity in the heavenly divine faith, and the unity of the Spirit, which is the bond of the heavenly Prince of princes' peace; who bruises the head of the enemy, the adversary, and reconciles man to God, and all things in heaven and in the earth: a blessed reconciliation! Let every one's faith stand in the power of God, which Jesus Christ is the author of; that all may know their crown of life. For all outward things without the substance, life, and power, are as the husk without the kernel, and do not nourish the immortal soul, nor the new-born babe; but that by which it is nourished, is the milk of the Word, whereby it groweth in the heavenly life, strength, and wisdom. The gospel is not of man, nor by man, but is the power of God, and answers the truth in all; all the possessors of it are to see that all walk according to it; which everlasting order is ordained of God already, and all the possessors of him possess their joy, their comfort, and salvation. My love unto you all, with him that reigns and is over all, from everlasting to everlasting.

"Dwell in the love of God, which passeth knowledge, and edifieth the living members of the body of Christ; which love of God come to be built up in, and in the holy faith. This love of God will bring you to bear all things, endure all things, and hope all things. From this love of God which you have in Christ Jesus, nothing will be able to separate you; neither powers nor principalities, heights nor depths, things present nor things to come, prisons nor spoiling of goods, neither death nor life. The love of God keeps above all that which would separate from God, and makes you more than conquerors in Christ Jesus. Therefore in this love of God dwell, that with the same love you may love one another, and all the workmanship of God—that you may glorify God with your bodies, souls, and spirits, which are the Lord's. Amen." G. F.

"All Friends sit low in the life, the Lord's power. Keep your place in it, till the Lord and Master of the feast bid you 'sit higher;' lest you take the highest place, and be put down with shame. He that hath an ear, let him hear." G. F.

"Friends, take heed of speaking the things of God in the words that men's wisdom hath taught; for those words will lift up the foolish, that have erred from the Spirit of God; which words and wisdom are for condemnation, and that which is lifted up by them, and they that thereby speak the things of God in them. So that old house, with its goods, must be thrown under the foot of the new birth.

"And, Friends, I desire that you may all keep the holy order, which is in the gospel, the glorious order in the power of God, which the devil is out of; which was before all his orders were, and before the world made any.

"This joyful order keeps all hearts pure to God, in everlasting peace, unity, and order; feel it, and keep the order of it, both men and women, and come to be heirs of the gospel, which brings life and immortality to light; and to see over that power of darkness, by Him who was before the power of death was. In this is the holy order of love and peace. So keep in this, that keeps you always pure; what men and women act in this, they act in that which will stand when the world is gone.

"There hath been some scruple about men's and women's meetings. Men and women in the gospel are heirs of the power, which was before the devil was; heirs of this, then enter into the possession of it, and do the Lord's business therein. Every one take care of God's honour, and keep all things in righteousness, in holiness which becomes God's house, and in that which honours the Lord God. It eased me, when those meetings were set up; for men and women, that are heirs of the gospel, have right to the gospel order; and it belongs to them. Then take your possessions, and practise in it; be not talkers only, but live and walk in the gospel, the power of God, which is the authority of your meetings." G. F.

Swarthmore, the 28th of the 2nd Month, 1676.

[Read at the Yearly Meeting in London, the 17th of the 3rd Month, 1676.]

During this time I collected together as many as I could, of the epistles I had written in former years to Friends. I made a collection of the several papers that I had written to O. Cromwell, and his son Richard, in the time of their protectorships; and to the parliaments and magistrates that were in their times. I collected also the papers I had written to King Charles II. since his return, and to his council and parliaments, and the justices or other magistrates under him. I made another collection of certificates, which I had received from divers governors of places, judges, justices, parliament-men, and others, for the clearing of me from many slanders, which the envious priests and professors, both here and beyond the seas, had cast upon me. This I did for the truth's sake, as knowing that their design in slandering me, was to defame the truth published by me, and hinder the spreading thereof amongst the people. Besides these, I made two books of collections; one was, a list or catalogue of the names of those Friends who went out of the North of England, when truth first broke forth there, to proclaim the day of the Lord through this nation. The other was of the names of those Friends that went first to preach the gospel in other nations, countries, and places, in what years, and to what parts they went.

I made another collection, in two books; one of epistles and letters from Friends and others, on several occasions, to me; the other of letters of mine to Friends and others.

I wrote also a book of the types and figures of Christ, with their significations; and many other things, which will be of service to truth and Friends in time to come.

I took notice also of those who had run out from truth, drawn others out after them, and turned against truth and Friends at several times since the first breaking forth of truth in this latter age, and what became of them; noting particularly the repentance and return of such of them as came back to truth again. Some ran quite out, and never returned, but were cut off in their gainsaying and rebellion: for the word and power of God hath blasted and is blasting them, and the holy seed hath ground, and is grinding them to pieces. I have observed, that they who have been convinced, and have not lived and walked in the truth, have been the worst enemies to the truth, and done most hurt amongst Friends in the truth, and to others. In these I have seen fulfilled what the Lord did long since show me, "that such should be greater deceivers than all the priests and professors." For such as came as far as Cain, Balaam, Korah, and Dathan, and could "preach Christ," and say, "they had preached in his name;" such as came to be apostles, and had tasted of the power of Christ, and then turned from it, could yet speak their old experiences, and have good words, like Korah and Balaam: but not keeping in the life and truth, they deceived the hearts of the simple. Such come to be of the devil, who abode not in the truth; as Cain, and all the Jews, that abode not in the truth, were. For though Cain did sacrifice to God, and did talk with God; and the Jews could talk of Abraham, Moses, and the prophets, yet Christ told them, "they were of their father, the devil." In like manner, though they who are called Christians, can talk of Christ, and use his and his apostles' and disciples' words, yet not abiding in the truth, and power, and Spirit, that the apostles were in, they are of the devil, out of truth, and do his work. So are all those that have been convinced of God's eternal truth since it sprang up in this nation, that have not abode in the light, and in the Spirit and power of Christ Jesus; but have turned against the power, and have opposed the work thereof; though they may retain their former experiences, and be able to speak many good words, yet not living in the life and power that gave them those experiences, they live in the power of darkness, which is of the devil: and by the light and truth both he and they are condemned; and must own their condemnation if ever they come to truth again. For to resist the heavenly power, and to oppose the workings and divine manifestations thereof through any, is not a light matter.

As I had been moved of the Lord to travel in his power round this nation, and in other parts, to preach the everlasting gospel, and to declare the Word of Life, which was in the beginning, through many imprisonments, hardships, sufferings, and trials; so I was afterwards moved to travel, in the same heavenly power, about the nation again (and to write to such places where I came not) to recommend to Friends the "setting up of the quarterly and monthly meetings in all counties, for looking after the poor, taking care for orderly proceedings in marriages; and other matters relating to the church of Christ;" though some meetings for this end were settled in the North of England, in the year 1653.

After this also, truth still spreading further over the nation, and Friends increasing in number, I was moved, by the same eternal power, to recommend the setting up of women's meetings also; that all, both male and female, who had received the gospel, the Word of eternal Life, might come into the order of the gospel, brought forth by the power of God, and might act for God in the power, and therein do business and service for him in his church. All the faithful must labour in God's vineyard, they being his hired servants, and he having given them the earnest of his Spirit. For a master that hires a servant, and gives him the earnest of his hire, expects he should do his work, after he knows his will, in the outward creation; so all God's people, that are of the new creation, and have received the earnest of his Spirit, ought to labour with, by, and in his Spirit, power, and grace, and faith, in the light, in God's vineyard, that they may have their wages when they have done God's work and business in his day, which is eternal life. But none can labour in his vineyard, and do his work and will, but as they walk in the heavenly divine light, grace, and Spirit of Christ; which it hath been, and is, my travail and labour in the Lord to turn all to.

Some that professed truth, and had made a great show therein, being gone from the simplicity of the gospel into jangling, division, and a spirit of separation, endeavoured to discourage Friends (especially the women), from their godly care and watchfulness in the church over one another in the truth; opposing their meetings, which, in the power of the Lord, were set up for that end and service. Wherefore I was moved of the Lord to write the following epistle, and send it among Friends, for the discovering of that spirit, by which those opposers acted, its work and way, by which it wrought, and to warn Friends of it, that they might not be betrayed by it:—

"All my dear Friends, Live in the seed of peace, Christ Jesus, in whom ye have life. That spirit that comes amongst you to raise up strife, is out of Christ; for it is the spirit that is not easy to be entreated, not gentle, so not of the wisdom of God, which is justified of her children. They that follow that spirit, are none of Wisdom's children. There is a spirit that hath made a separation, and has been against men's and women's meetings; yet those of this spirit have set up one of their own, to which they have given power, and allow none to sit amongst them but such as they give power to, looking upon others as usurpers of authority. This spirit and its work is not of God, though it has made a jumble amongst some; and the path it may travel in, is through the earthly affections, amongst the unestablished, or apostates. But all that are in the life, Spirit, and light, in the grace, truth, and power of God, bar it out; and such as sit under their own vine, Christ Jesus, and are grafted into him, have no need of their exhortation or counsel; for the true believers are entered into their rest. Therefore all keep in the gospel of peace; and you that are heirs of the kingdom, keep in your possession of it.

"Some of this spirit have said to me, 'they see no service in women's meetings.' My answer is, and hath been to such, if they be blind and without sight, they should not oppose others; for none impose anything upon them. God never received the blind for a sacrifice, neither can his people. But Christ has enlightened all; and to as many as receive him, he gives 'power to become the sons of God.' Such as are heirs of his power, and of his gospel, which brings life and immortality to light, can see over him that has darkened them; and all such keep the order of the gospel, the power of God, and their meetings therein, which preserves them in life and immortality. These see the great service of men's and women's meetings, in the order of the gospel, the power of God; for they are meet-helps in this power, which is the authority of their meetings. Now I say to all of you, that are against women's meetings or the men's, and say, 'you see no service for the women's meetings,' and oppose them, you are therein out of the power of God, and his Spirit you live not in. For God saw a service for the assemblies of the women in the time of the law, about those things that appertained to his worship and service, and to the holy things of his tabernacle; and so they in his Spirit see now their service in the gospel; many things in these meetings being more proper for the women than the men; and they in the power and wisdom of God may inform the men of such things as are not proper for them; and the men may inform the women of such things as are not proper for them, as meet-helps to each other. For in the time of the law, the women were to offer as well as the men; so in the time of the gospel much more are they to offer their spiritual sacrifices; for they are all called, both men and women, a royal priesthood; they are of the household of faith; they are the living stones that make up the spiritual building, which Christ is the head of; and are to be encouraged in their labour in the gospel; for all things that they do, both men and women, are to be done *in the power of God*. All such as see no service for these women's meetings, or the men's, but oppose them, and make strife amongst Friends, are in the spirit of the world, that is against, and forbids our other meetings;—are in the same spirit of the world, that hath been, and is against women's speaking in meetings, and say, 'they must be silent,' &c., though the same apostle commands, 'that men should keep silence as well as the women,' if there were not an interpreter. Therefore, you may see that the spirit of the world hath entered such opposers, though they come under another colour; for they would not have us to meet at all. And these are against the women's meetings, and some of them against the men's also, and say, 'they see no service for them;' then they may hold their tongues, and not oppose them that do see their service for God in these meetings.

"Therefore, all you that feel the power of God, and your service for God in them, both men and women, keep your meetings in the power of God, the authority of them, as they were settled in it; then ye will be preserved both over this spirit that opposes them, and over the spirit of the world that opposes your other meetings; for it is all one in the ground, and would bring you into bondage. Such are out of the peaceable gospel, who oppose its order; out of the faith that works by love; out of the wisdom that is gentle, easy, and peaceable, &c., and out of the kingdom that stands in peace and joy. Therefore, keep over that spirit that sows discord or dissension, and would draw you from your habitation and possession in the order of the gospel; for it is the same spirit that deceived Adam and Eve, by which they lost their habitation in righteousness and holiness, and their dominion; so that spirit got over them; and so it would get over you. One while it will tell you, 'it sees no service for your meetings,' and another time oppose you. But I say, this is the blind spirit, which is out of the power of God, and which the power of God is over. Therefore, keep in the power, that ye may stand up for your liberty in Christ Jesus, males and females, heirs of him and of his gospel, and his order. Stand up for your liberty in the gospel, and in the faith, which Christ Jesus hath been the author of; for if ye lose it, and let another spirit get over you, ye will not soon regain it. I knew the devil would bestir himself in his instruments, when men's and women's meetings came to be set up in the power, light, and truth, and the heirs of the gospel, to take their possession of it in every county and city, therein to walk, and to watch one over another, to take care of God's glory and honour, and his precious truth; and to see that all walk in the truth, and as becomes the gospel, and that nothing be lacking; and so to exhort all whatsoever is decent, modest, virtuous, lovely, comely, righteous, and of good report, to follow after; to admonish all that are not faithful, and to rebuke all that do evil. I knew this would give such a check to all loose speakers, talkers, and walkers, that there would be an opposition against such meetings. But never heed, truth will come over them all, and is over them all, and faith must have the victory; for the gospel and its order is everlasting; the Seed (Christ) is the beginning and the ending, and will outlast all; the Amen, in whom ye have peace. I say all that oppose the men's and women's meetings, or that marriages should be laid before them, or the recording of condemnations of sin and evil, or admonishing or exhorting such as walk not in the truth, are of a loose spirit, and their spirits tend to looseness.

Let those take them that will; truth will not have them, nor any of their sacrifice; for nothing is accepted of God, but what is done in truth, and in his Spirit, which is peaceable. The authority of our men's and women's meetings is the power of God; and all the heirs of the gospel are heirs of that authority and dignity; this is of God, and shall answer the witness of God in all. The greatest opposers of this practice and work, are such as have been convinced of God's truth, but have not lived in it. Such were the greatest troublers of the church in Moses' day, and in the days of the apostles; but mark their end, and read what became of them all. And therefore, all keep your habitation in the truth, and therein ye may see what has become of all the opposers of it for twenty years past; they are all gone, and the truth lives and reigns; the Seed is over all, and all are one in it, in rest, peace, and life everlasting; and therein they sit down together in the heavenly places in Christ Jesus, the Amen." G. F.

Swarthmore, the 5th of the 8th Month, 1676.

Narrative of the spreading of Truth, and of the opposition thereto.

"The truth sprang up first to us, so as to be a people to the Lord, in Leicestershire in 1644, in Warwickshire in 1645, in Nottinghamshire in 1646, in Derbyshire in 1647, and in the adjacent counties in 1648, 1649, and 1650; in Yorkshire in 1651, in Lancashire and Westmorland in 1652; in Cumberland, Durham, and Northumberland in 1653; in London, and most of the other parts of England, Scotland, and Ireland, in 1654.

"In 1655 many went beyond sea, where truth also sprang up, and in 1656 it broke forth in America and many other places.

"In the authority of this divine truth, Friends stood all the cruelties and sufferings that were inflicted upon them by the Long Parliament; to the spoiling of goods, imprisonment, and death, and over all reproaches, lies, and slanders; as well as those in Oliver Cromwell's time, and all the acts made by him and his parliament; his son Richard after him, and the Committee of Safety; and afterwards withstood and outlasted all the acts and proclamations since 1660, that the king came in.

"Friends never feared their acts, prisons, jails, houses of correction, banishment, nor spoiling of goods, nay, nor the loss of life itself; nor was there ever any persecution that came, but we saw in the event it would be productive of good; nor were there ever any prisons that I was in, or sufferings, but it was for the bringing multitudes out of prison; though they who imprisoned the truth, and quenched the Spirit in themselves, would imprison and quench it without them; so that there was a time when so many were in prison, that it became as a by-word, 'truth is scarce anywhere to be found but in jails.'

"And after the king came in, divers Friends suffered much, because they would not drink his health, and say, 'God bless the king;' so that many Friends were in danger of their lives from rude persons, who were ready to run them through with their swords for refusing it, until the king gave forth a proclamation against drinking healths; for we were and are against drinking any healths, and all excess, both before his coming in and after; and we desire the king's good, and that the blessing of God might come upon him and all his subjects, and all people upon the face of the earth; but we desired people not to drink the king's health, but let him have his health, and all people else; and to drink for their own health and necessity only; for that way of drinking healths, and to excess, was not for the king's health, nor their own, nor any others'; which excess often brought forth quarrelling and destroying one another; for they destroyed the creation and one another; and this was not for the king's wealth, nor health, nor honour, but might grieve him to have the creatures and his subjects destroyed; and so the Lord's power gave us dominion over that also, and all our other sufferings. But,

"O! the number of sufferers in the Commonwealth's and Oliver Cromwell's days, and since; especially those who were haled before the courts for not paying tithes, refusing to swear on their juries, not putting off their hats, and for going to meetings on the First-days; under pretence of breaking the Sabbath; and to meetings on other days of the week; who were abused both in meetings and on the highways.

"O! how great were the sufferings we then sustained upon these accounts! for sometimes they would drive Friends by droves into the prison-houses like penfolds, confine them on the First-days, and take their horses from them, and keep them for pretended breach of their Sabbath, though they would ride in their coaches and upon their fat horses to the steeple-houses themselves, and yet punish others. And many Friends were turned out of their copyholds and customary tenements, because, in obedience to the command of Christ and his apostle, they could not swear; and as they went to meetings, they have been stoned through the streets, and otherwise cruelly abused. Many were fined with great fines, and lay long in prison for not putting off their hats, which fines Friends could never pay, though they kept them in prison till they had satisfied their own wills, and at last turned them out, after keeping them a year or more in prison.

"Many books I gave forth against tithes, showing how the priesthood was changed that took them; and that Christ sent forth his twelve, and afterwards seventy disciples, saying unto them, 'Freely ye have received, freely give.' So all who do not obey the doctrine and command of Christ therein, we cannot receive them.

"I was also moved to give forth several books against swearing, and that our Yea and Nay might be taken instead of an oath, which, if we broke, let us suffer the same punishment as they who broke their oaths. And in Jamaica the governor and the assembly granted the thing; it is also granted in some other places; and several of the parliament-men in England have acknowledged the reasonableness thereof. The magistrates, after some time, when they saw our faithfulness in Yea and Nay, they who were moderate, both before and since the king came in, would put Friends into offices without an oath; but the cruel and envious would fine Friends to get money off them, though they could not pay them any.

"Thus the Lord's power hath carried us through all, and over all, to his everlasting glory and praise; for God's power hath been our hedge, our wall and our keeper (the preserver of his plants and vineyard), who have not had the magistrates' sword and staff to help us, nor ever trusted in the arm of flesh, but have gone without these, or Judas' bag, to preach the Word of life, which was in the beginning before they were; which reconciles to God. And thousands have received this Word of reconciliation, and are born again of the immortal Seed, by the Word of God; and are feeding upon the milk of the Word, which lives and abides for ever.

"Many have suffered death for their testimony, in England and beyond the seas, both before and since the king came in; which may be seen in an account given to the king and both houses of parliament; being 'A brief, plain, and true relation of the late and sad sufferings of the people of God in scorn called Quakers, for worshipping and exercising a good conscience towards God and man.'

"By reason whereof eighty-nine have suffered till death; thirty-two of whom died before the king came into England, and fifty-seven since, by hard imprisonment and cruel usage. Forty-three have died in the city of London and Southwark since the Act made against meetings, &c., about 1661, of which a more particular account was given, with the names of the sufferers, to the king and parliament, about 1663.

"And though divers laws were designed against us, yet never could any of them justly touch us, being wrested and misapplied in their execution by our adversaries, which some have been made to confess. All those laws that were made, and the oath which they imprisoned us for, because, in obedience to the command of Christ Jesus, we could not swear at all, were not originally intended against us; and yet we suffered by the several powers, and their laws, both spoiling of goods and imprisonment, even to death. And the governor of Dover castle, when the king asked him if he had dispersed all the sectaries' meetings? said, that 'he had; but the Quakers, the devil himself could not; for if he did imprison them, and break up their meetings, they would meet again; and if he should beat them or knock them down, or kill some of them, all was one, they would meet, and not resist again.' Thus the Lord's power supported and kept them over their persecutors, and made them to justify our patience and lamb-like nature. This was about 1671.

"Since the king came in, three acts have been made against us, besides the proclamations, by which many have suffered imprisonment and banishment, and many to death. And yet for all these acts and proclamations, persecutions, sufferings, banishments, faithful Friends are as fresh as ever in the Lord's power, and valiant for his name and truth.

"Some weak ones there were, when the king came in, who took the oath; but after they had so done, they were sore troubled for disobeying the command of Christ and the apostle, and went to the magistrates, condemned themselves, and offered to go to prison.

"Thus the Lord, in his everlasting power, hath been the support and stay of his people; and still his Seed reigns, his truth is over all, and exceedingly spreads unto this year 1676.

In 1676, while I was at Swarthmore, died William Lampitt, the old priest of Ulverstone (which parish Swarthmore is in). He was an old deceiver, a perverter of the right way of the Lord, and a persecutor of the people of God. Much contest I had with him, when I first came into those parts. He had been an old false prophet; for in 1652 he prophesied (and said he would wage his life upon it), "that the Quakers would all vanish, and come to nought within half a year:" but he came to nought himself. For he continued in his lying and false accusing of God's people, till a little before he died, and then he cried for a little rest. To one of his hearers that came to visit him before he died, he said, "I have been a preacher a long time, and thought I had lived well; but I did not think it had been so hard a thing to die."

After I had finished the services which lay upon me then to do, feeling my spirit drawn again towards the south (though I was yet but weakly, and not able to travel far in a day), I left Swarthmore the 26th of the 1st Month, 1677, and went to Thomas Pearson's at POOBANK, in WESTMORLAND, where I had a meeting the next day; and thence to Thomas Camm's,* at CAM'S-GILL, where Robert Widders with his wife, and several other Friends came to see me before I left the country, and to attend the meeting there next day, which was very large, and in which I was largely drawn forth in testimony to the truth. I had much discourse with some of that meeting, who were not in unity with the quarterly meeting they belonged to; but afterwards several of them that were somewhat tender, came to see their error, and gave forth condemnations against themselves. Next day John Blakelin came to Thomas Camm's, to bring me to his house at DRAWELL in SEDBERGH, whither I went with him, visiting Friends in the way. I stayed at Drawell two or three nights, having meetings there and thereabouts; for while I was there the men's and women's meetings were held there, which were very large and precious. The First-day following I had a meeting at BRIGFLATS, to which came most of the Friends from the several meetings round about, and a great concourse of others also; it was

* Thomas Camm, of Camsgill, in Westmorland, was born in 1641, and had a good education. He was from childhood inclined to be religious, was early convinced of Friends' principles, and after some time called to the work of the ministry. He counted nothing too near or dear to part with for truth's sake, but left all to follow the Lord, and, with his whole strength and substance, was given up to serve him. He was an able preacher, diligent and laborious in the work of the Lord, and instrumental to convince and establish many in the way of truth. His doctrine was sound, and his delivery in the demonstration of that Divine power which reached the witness of God in the hearts of his hearers.

Great and many were the sufferings he met with and went through, as, imprisonments, spoiling of goods, mockings and scoffings from those without, and suffering among false brethren; in all which, he stood firm and faithful, approving himself a true follower of Jesus Christ, suffering joyfully for his name's sake, who had counted him worthy not only to believe, but suffer for him. During an illness of some continuance, many were the weighty expressions that fell from him, often magnifying the Lord to the tendering of all hearts present. When grown very weak, being asked how he felt, he would say, "Weak of body, but strong in the Lord;" saying also, "In Abraham's bosom there is sweet repose." Seeming to be faint, a friend gave him a little wine, thinking it might refresh him, but his stomach could not bear it; then looking at him he said, "Thou seest these things will not do; but one cup of new wine in the heavenly kingdom, with my dear and blessed Lord and Saviour Jesus Christ, will make up all."—For further particulars, see *Piety Promoted*, vol. ii., p. 101–108.

thought there were five or six hundred people. A very good meeting it was, wherein truth was largely declared and preciously opened, to the comforting and refreshing of the faithful, and the drawing near of them that were afar off. I had another meeting at John Blakelin's, at which were many Friends that were going to the quarterly meeting at Kendal. With them my wife went back, who, with her daughter Rachel, had accompanied me thus far; and I, having Leonard Fell with me, passed on through SEDBERGH and GARSDALE, into WENSLEYDALE, visiting Friends as we went. At night I reached Richard Robinson's at COUNTERSIDE, where several Friends came to me that evening; some of whom went with me next day over the hills to the widow Tenant's at SCARHOUSE, in LANGSTROTH-DALE, which we had much difficulty to reach, the snow lay so deep, though it was a week in the 2d Month. Here, on First-day, we had a large meeting, Friends coming to it from several parts round about; and the Lord gave me a very seasonable testimony to bear amongst them, which I did for several hours, to their great satisfaction and comfort. Thence passing through BISHOPDALE, MIDDLEHAM, BARTON, and so by BEDALE and NORTHALLERTON, I came to George Robinson's at BURROWBY; where also Friends coming out of several parts, we had a very large and good meeting, and very peaceable. But not long after, an envious justice, who lived not far off, hearing that I had a great meeting there, troubled Friends about it, and made them appear at the sessions, where he asked them many ensnaring questions; for he knew not how to convict them, because he had no proof against them. When he saw his questions did not catch them, he told them, "he had heard that George Fox was at a large meeting with them, and they all sat silent, and none spoke in the meeting." This false story he cunningly feigned, thinking thereby to draw out some of the Friends to contradict him, and say, "that I had spoken in the meeting;" that so he might convict them upon their own confession, and fine them. But Friends standing in the wisdom of God, did not answer him according to his desire, and so escaped his snare. But two Friends that came out of Ireland, and were at this meeting, having another that evening about three miles off, this evil-minded justice got information thereof, and fined Friends, and plundered them very sorely for it.

I went from Burrowby to Isaac Lindley's, calling upon Friends as I went. Robert Lodge and other Friends being with me, we passed next day to YORK, and the day following, being First-day, I was at Friends' meeting there, which was large and peaceable. Second day also I stayed in York, and had two meetings with Friends at John Taylor's;* whence I wrote to my wife, as follows:—

"DEAR HEART,

"To whom is my love, and to thy daughters, and to all Friends that inquire after me. My desires are, that ye all may be preserved in the

* John Taylor was an able minister amongst the early Friends, but a very brief account is preserved of his religious labours. He was born in Huntingdonshire (?) about the year 1638. He embarked on a gospel mission to America in 1660, being then only in the twenty-second year of his age. How long he was occupied there is not stated, but his religious services were not confined to the English settlers.

Lord's everlasting Seed, in whom ye will have life and peace, dominion and settlement in the everlasting home or dwelling in the house built upon the foundation of God. In the power of the Lord I am brought to York, having had many meetings in the way. The road was many times deep and bad with snow, our horses sometimes were down, and we were not able to ride; and sometimes we had great storms and rain; but by the power of the Lord I went through all. At Scarhouse there was a very large meeting, and another at Burrowby, to which Friends came out of Cleveland and Durham; and many other meetings we have had. At York, yesterday, we had a very large meeting, exceedingly thronged, Friends being at it from many parts, and all quiet, and well satisfied: O! the glory of the Lord shone over all. This day we have had a large men's and women's meeting, many Friends, both men and women, being come out of the country, and all was quiet; and this evening we are to have the men's and women's meeting of the Friends of the city. John Whitehead is here, with Robert Lodge* and others; Friends are mighty glad, above measure. So I am in my holy element, and holy work in the Lord, glory to his name for ever! To-morrow I intend to go out of the city towards Tadcaster, though I cannot ride as in days past; yet praised be the Lord that I can travel as well as I do! So with my love in the fountain of life, in which as ye all abide,

Trusting to the never-failing arm of Divine guidance and protection, he travelled alone among the Indian tribes, and "had meetings in the woods and wilderness, to declare the truth to them," as he remarks, "and to turn them from darkness to the light of Christ Jesus in their own hearts." By these untutored sons of the forest the stripling preacher was "received with kindness," and in their wigwams he became a welcome guest. "They heard me soberly," he says, "and confessed to the truth I spoke, by an interpreter; and they were loving and kind afterwards to Friends."

On his return from America, John Taylor, being on gospel service in London, was taken from a meeting and committed to prison. He visited America a second time, and resided some time in Jamaica, also in Barbadoes, where he became a merchant, but finally returned to England, and settled at York as a sugar-refiner. After which, he was also largely engaged in the ministry in different parts of the nation, and died in 1708, aged about seventy, a minister about fifty years.

John Taylor is described by a contemporary as "an able minister of the New Testament; in the publishing of which, the Spirit of God and of glory rested upon him, to the comforting and true refreshment of the churches, where the Lord ordered him, or his lot was cast."

* Robert Lodge, mentioned before, was of Masham, in Yorkshire, born about the year 1636. He was religiously inclined from his youth, was convinced about 1658, and became a valiant gospel minister. He was very serviceable in gathering many out of the ways of the world, into the way of life, travelling up and down in the service of his Lord, enduring many trials, exercises, and imprisonments, for his sake. John Whiting says of him, "He was an excellent minister; he had a fine refreshing testimony, and an extraordinary gift in prayer. He was instrumental to turn many to righteousness, and to build them up in the most holy faith. His testimony reached to the witness of God in the consciences of many; and was a consolation to the watering and refreshing many weary souls. He kept his first love and habitation in the truth to the last; and, towards his latter end, laboured much with and for the young generation, that they might come up in the footsteps of those who were gone before. He was a man of a sweet disposition, and left a good savour behind him. Much might be said of him, but I refer to the *Several Living Testimonies given forth by divers Friends concerning him, and his Faithful Labours and Travels*, printed in 1691."

ye will have refreshment of life, that by it ye may grow and gather eternal strength to serve the Lord, and be satisfied. To the God of all power, who is all-sufficient to preserve you, I commit you all to his ordering."

York, the 16th of the 2nd Month, 1677. G. F.

Leaving York, I visited Friends at TADCASTER, KNOTTINGLEY, DONCASTER, and BALBY, having meetings as I went. At Balby I stayed the First-day meeting, and went next day to Thomas Stacy's at BALLOWFIELD, where in the evening I had a meeting, to compose a difference that had happened between some that professed truth, and they were reconciled. Next day I came to STAINSBY in DERBYSHIRE, in which county I had formerly lived about the first breaking forth of truth. Here I had a good meeting with Friends, and afterwards passed to SKEGBY in NOTTINGHAMSHIRE, and from thence to NOTTINGHAM, to John Reckless's. I had a meeting with Friends at his house that evening, and another next day in Friends' public meeting-house, which was peaceable and well.

I went the day following to John Fox's at WIMESWOULD in LEICESTERSHIRE, where I had a meeting that evening; and next day to William Smith's at SILEBY, where, it being First-day, we had a very large meeting; for besides Friends from several places, many of the town's-people hearing I was there, came to it, and heard the truth declared gladly. Next day I went to LEICESTER, where finding many Friends come out of the country, to be at the horse-fair next day, I had a very good meeting with them that night; and another next evening at William Wells's house at KNIGHTON, about a mile from Leicester. Next day I passed to SWANNINGTON, and had a meeting there; thence to Samuel Fretwell's at HARTSHORN in DERBYSHIRE, where I had a meeting also; then to Henry Sidon's, at BADGLEY in WARWICKSHIRE, and stayed the meeting there, which, it being First-day, was very large and peaceable, notwithstanding a justice had threatened to come and break it up. Having stayed a while with Friends, I went in the evening to Richard Baal's of WHITTINGTON, where several Friends came to visit me. Next day I went to Nathaniel Newton's at HARTSHILL, where several Friends met me, with whom I had good service. After this I passed on, visiting Friends in divers places, till I came to DINGLEY, where a meeting was appointed before, which was very large, and truth was largely opened to the people. It was peaceable and quiet, and the people generally sober; saving that while I was showing how Christendom (so called) was gone from the pure religion that is undefiled, &c., one man rushed out in a furious manner, and said, "I deny that." After this meeting I went with Thomas Charles to his house at ADINGWORTH, and next day to NORTHAMPTON, where I stayed the First-day meeting, which was very large and peaceable. I had much service among Friends besides. Next day Edward Cooper of Northampton, accompanied me to OLNEY in BUCKINGHAMSHIRE, where I stayed at James Brierlie's, several Friends coming to see me in the evening. Next day I went to a meeting at TURVEY in BEDFORDSHIRE, to which Friends came from several parts; so that it was very large. Here I met with William Dewsbury, who after the meeting took me to his son-in-law John Rush's of KEMPSTON, where I stayed with William that night and most of next day, passing thence towards evening through AMPTHILL, to Thomas Gamboll's of BULLOCK'S HILL. William Dewsbury went along with me, and several Friends came to visit us. Next day, passing through LUTON, I went to MARKET STREET, William Dewsbury accompanying me part of the way, and the day following Leonard Fell* and I had a meeting at KENSWORTH, which was pretty large and peaceable. After it we went to ALBAN'S, where we visited Friends; and next day passing through SOUTH MIMS and BARNET, where also we visited Friends, we came that night to widow Hayley's at GUTTERSHEDGE in HENDON, in MIDDLESEX. Next day, being First-day, we had a very large meeting there, several Friends coming from London. I stayed there Second-day, and on third went to William Mead's house at HIGHGATE, with whom next day I went to LONDON. It being Fourth-day, I went to the meeting at Gracechurch Street, where Friends and I were greatly refreshed in each other in the Lord, and the Lord's power and Seed were set over all, blessed be his name for ever!

Thus it pleased the Lord to bring me safe to London, though much wearied, for though I rode not very far in a day, yet through weakness of body, continual travelling was hard to me. Besides, I had not much rest at night to refresh nature; for I often sat up late with Friends, where I lodged, to inform and advise them in things wherein they were wanting; and when in bed, I was often hindered of sleep by great pains in my head and teeth, occasioned, as I thought, from cold taken by riding often in the

* The above is the last mention of Leonard Fell, whose name has frequently occurred in the progress of this Journal. Very little is known of him but that he was a faithful minister amongst the early Friends. I feel inclined to insert an anecdote respecting him, as an instance among others that might be adduced, of the carrying out of the non-resistant principle. The conduct of several "Friends" who, having "fallen among thieves," were, of course, precluded from retaliating violence, even in their own defence, affords an exemplification of this feature in the Christian character.

Leonard Fell, when travelling alone, was attacked by a highwayman, who demanded his money, which he gave him; then he desired to have his horse; Leonard dismounted and let him take it. Then feeling the power of truth rise in his mind, he turned to the robber, and, under its authority, solemnly warned him of the evil of his ways; but he flying into a passion, asked the Friend why he preached to him, and threatened to blow out his brains. But Leonard replying to this effect, "Though I would not give my life for my money or my horse, I would give it to save thy soul," so struck the astonished robber, that he declared, if he was such a man as that, he would take neither his money nor his horse from him; and, returning both to the faithful Friend, went his way, leaving Leonard to the enjoyment of that peace, attending the honest discharge of his conscience, to obtain which he had not counted his life dear.

The courage and presence of mind exhibited by the true soldier of Jesus Christ, when permitted, in the course of Divine Providence, to be cast into straits and trying situations, is often conspicuous. He not only knows the strength of that preserving arm, which rules or overrules all circumstances for the good of those that are faithful, he not only is furnished for all occasions, and "out of weakness is made strong," so as even to "stop the mouths of lions," and "quench the violence of fire" (Heb. xi.), but is abundantly furnished with resignation to submit unto the Lord in all things; and, with one who was "in perils of robbers," and "in deaths oft," he can say, "Whether we live or die, we are the Lord's." (Rom. xiv. 8).

rain. But the Lord's power was over all, and carried me through all, to his praise.

In my journey I observed a slackness and shortness in some that professed the truth, in keeping up the ancient testimony against tithes; for wherever that spirit got entrance, which wrought division in the church, and opposed the men's and women's meetings, it weakened those that received it in their testimony against tithes. Wherefore I was moved of the Lord to issue a short "Epistle to Friends," to stir up the pure mind, and to encourage and strengthen them in their Christian testimony against that antichristian yoke and oppression:—

"My Dear Friends,

"Be faithful to the Lord in your testimony for Jesus, who ended the Levitical priesthood of Aaron, that took tithes, and sent his ministers forth freely, to give freely that which they had received of him freely, without a bag or a staff. Christ's disciples could not join with those that made a trade of preaching. And as there was a testimony to be borne against those tithes which were commanded, in the law, for Levi and Aaron, so there is a testimony to be borne against these tithes, which have been set up by man, in the dark time of Popery, and not by God or Christ. Now to cry against the priests in words, and yet to give them means, and put into their mouths, that they may not prepare war against you, is a contradiction. Therefore take heed; for if the Lord bless you with outward creatures, and you bestow them upon Baal's priests, he may justly require the outward things from you again, which he hath given you: who saith, that his ministers should freely give, as they have freely received. So all the preachers for tithes and money, and the takers and payers of tithe, must be testified against in the Lord's power and Spirit; that all may stand up in their testimony for Jesus Christ, in his power and Spirit, against the tithe-mongers. Consider how many faithful servants and valiants of the Lord, have laid down their lives against them, in this day of the Lord; and in the days of the martyrs they did witness against them. Consider also what judgments have come upon those that spoiled Friends' goods, and cast them into prison for tithes and maintenance. Therefore in the power of the Lord, maintain the war against the beast, and do not put into his mouth, lest he cry peace to you; which peace you must not receive; but it must be broken, and thrown out by the Spirit of God. Then in the same Spirit, ye will receive from the Son of Peace, that peace which the beast, and the whore, and the world, with all their earthly teachers for the earth, made by man, cannot receive, nor bereave you of. Therefore keep your authority and dominion in the power, Spirit, and name of Jesus, in whom my love is to you.' G. F.

3d Month, 1677.

I came to London on the 23rd of the 3rd Month, ten or twelve days before the Yearly Meeting, in which time I fell in with Friends there in the service of truth, visiting them at the meetings. The parliament then sitting, we prepared something to lay before them, concerning the seizing of the third part of Friends' estates, as Popish recusants, which was a great suffering, and a grievance we complained of; but we obtained no redress.

To the Yearly Meeting many Friends came from most parts of the nation; and some out of Scotland, Holland, &c., and very glorious meetings we had, wherein the Lord's powerful presence was very largely felt; and the affairs of truth were sweetly carried on in the unity of the Spirit, to the satisfaction and comfort of the upright-hearted; blessed be the Lord for ever! After the Yearly Meeting, having stayed a week or two with Friends in London, I went down with William Penn* to his house in SUSSEX; John Burnyeat and some other Friends being with us. As we passed through SURREY, hearing the quarterly meeting was that day, William Penn, John Burnyeat, and I, went from the road to it; and after the meeting returning to our other company, went with them to William Penn's that night; which is forty miles from London. I stayed at WORMINGHURST about three weeks; in which time John Burnyeat and I answered a very envious and wicked book, which Roger Williams, a priest of New England (or some colony thereabouts) had written against truth and Friends. When we had finished that service, we went with Stephen Smith to his house at WARPLEDON in SURREY, where we had a large meeting. Friends thereaway had been exceedingly plundered about two months

* A close intimacy existed between William Penn and George Fox, which enabled the former to indite so admirable an introduction to these volumes. The name of William Penn occurs frequently in these pages. Scarcely any name is more generally known or respected by those of other religious persuasions than his; indeed, so familiar are most readers with his history, that it would be superfluous to enter into much relating to him.

It may suffice briefly to state that his birth and education were both good; he being the son of Admiral Penn, who was knighted by Charles II; and became a great favourite with the Duke of York, afterwards James II. William, his son, was born at London in 1644. He imbibed religious impressions as early as his twelfth year. In his fifteenth year he entered a student at Christ church, Oxford. On his return home he exhibited a religious seriousness and manner of deportment, which (as likely to stand in the way of his worldly preferment) was so displeasing to his father that he turned him out of doors.

Ultimately he joined the despised Quakers, a step which highly displeased his father the Admiral; but he became quite reconciled to him before his death. Penn continued to advance in religious growth, became a minister amongst the Quakers, and a considerable writer in defence of their principles, suffering persecution and imprisonment in consequence. It was whilst he was imprisoned in the Tower that he wrote that excellent work, *No Cross, No Crown.*

The persecution of Dissenters continuing to rage in England, notwithstanding their repeated applications to parliament for sufferance and protection, William Penn turned his thoughts towards a settlement in the New World, as a place where himself and his friends might enjoy their religious opinions without molestation, and where an example might be set to the nations of a just and righteous government. He therefore, in 1681, obtained a patent from Charles II., for a province in North America, in consideration of his father's services, and of a debt still due to him from the crown. He founded the colony of Pennsylvania, and watched it with a paternal eye till his death in 1718. Its prosperity is a lasting monument of his wisdom as a politician and a legislator. For further particulars, the reader is referred to Clarkson's *Life of William Penn,* a cheap edition of which has recently been published by Bradshaw and Blacklock, Manchester. It is a highly interesting work, well worthy of perusal.

before on the priest's account; for they took from Stephen Smith five kine (being all he had) for about fifty shillings' tithes. Thence we went to KINGSTON, and so to LONDON, where I stayed not long; for it was upon me from the Lord to go into Holland, to visit Friends and to preach the gospel there, and in some parts of Germany. Wherefore setting things in order for my journey as fast as I could, I took leave of Friends at London; and with several other Friends went down to COLCHESTER, in order to my passage for Holland. Next day, being First-day, I was at the public meeting of Friends there, which was very large and peaceable. In the evening I had another large one, but not so public, at John Furly's house, where I lodged. The day following I was at the women's meeting there, which also was very large. Thence next day we passed to HARWICH, where Robert Duncan, and several other Friends out of the country, came to see us; and some from London came to us there, that intended to go over with me. The packet in which we were to go not being ready, we went to the meeting in the town, and a precious opportunity we had together; for the Lord, according to his wonted goodness, by his overcoming, refreshing power, opened many mouths to declare his everlasting truth, and to praise and glorify him.

CHAPTER VIII.

1677.—George Fox sails for Holland, with several other Friends, and lands at Briel—attends the Quarterly Meeting at Amsterdam—writes an epistle to Friends against the spirit of separation—writes to the Princess Elizabeth—her answer—a Monthly Meeting is established at Frederickstadt—Friends are imprisoned and banished from Embden, and suffer greatly—a Monthly Meeting settled at Harlingen—a priest assents to the doctrine promulgated by George Fox—he is questioned for it by his hearers—George Fox writes an epistle to Friends respecting the seducing spirit—he writes an epistle of encouragement to Friends under suffering at Dantzic—and again to Friends respecting the spirit of separation—spends considerable time at Amsterdam in writing on Truth's account—a warning to the magistrates and people of Oldenburg—an epistle concerning fasts, prayers, honour, persecution, true liberty, and the observance of days and times—a warning to the magistrates, priests, and people of Hamburg—to the ambassadors met to effect a treaty of peace in the city of Nimeguen—completes his travels in Holland—writes a book addressed to the Jews.

After the meeting at Harwich we returned to John Vandewall's, where I had lodged; and when the boat was ready, taking leave of Friends, we that were bound for Holland, went on board about nine in the evening, on the 25th of the 5th Month, 1677.

The Friends that went over with me, were William Penn, Robert Barclay, George Keith and his wife, John Furly and his brother, William Tallcoat, George Watts, and Isabel Yeomans, one of my wife's daughters. About one in the morning we weighed anchor, having a fair brisk wind, which by next morning brought us within sight of Holland. But that day proving very clear and calm we got forward little, till about four in the afternoon, when a fresh gale arose, which carried us within a league of land. Then being becalmed again, we cast anchor for that night, it being between the hours of nine and ten in the evening: but William Penn and Robert Barclay, understanding that Benjamin Furly was come from Rotterdam to the Briel to meet us, got two of the boatmen to let down a small boat that belonged to the packet, and row them to shore; but before they could reach it the gates were shut; and there being no house without the gates, they lay in a fisherman's boat all night. As soon as the gates were opened in the morning, they went in, and found Benjamin Furly, with other Friends of Rotterdam, that were come thither to receive us; and they sent a boat, with three young men in it, that lived with Benjamin Furly, who brought us to the Briel, where the Friends received us with great gladness.

We stayed about two hours to refresh ourselves, and then took boat, with the Holland Friends, for Rotterdam, where we arrived about eleven that day, the 28th of the Month. I was very well this voyage, but some of the Friends were sea-sick. A fine passage we had, and all came safe and well to land; blessed and praised be the name of the Lord for ever!

Next day, being First-day, we had two meetings at Benjamin Furly's, where many of the town's-people and some officers came in, and all were civil. Benjamin Furly or John Claus, a Friend of Amsterdam, interpreted, when any Friend declared. I spent the next day in visiting Friends there. The day following, William Penn and I, with other Friends, went towards Amsterdam with some Friends of that city, who came to Rotterdam to conduct us thither. We took boat in the afternoon, and, passing by OVERKIRK, came to DELFT, through which we walked on foot; and then took boat again to LEYDEN, where we lodged that night at an inn. This is six Dutch miles from Rotterdam, which are eighteen English miles, and five hours' sail or travelling; for our boat was drawn by a horse that went on the shore. Next day taking boat again, we went to HAARLEM, fourteen miles from Leyden, where we had appointed a meeting, which proved very large; for many of the town's-people came in, and two of their preachers. The Lord gave us a blessed opportunity, not only with respect to Friends, but to other sober people, and the meeting ended peaceably and well. After it we passed to AMSTERDAM, accompanied by several Friends of that city and of Alkmaar.

Next day was the quarterly meeting at Amsterdam, to which came Friends from Haarlem and Rotterdam, and with them those of our company, whom we had left at Rotterdam, viz.: Robert Barclay, George Keith and his wife, &c. The meeting was at Gertrude Dirick Nieson's house. A very large and serviceable one it was; for both William Penn and I were drawn to open many things concerning the order of the gospel, and to show the benefit and service of yearly, quarterly, and monthly meetings of men and women. We had another meeting at Gertrude's the next day, more public, and very large, at which were professors of several sorts, unto whom the way of life and salvation was largely and livingly opened; which they hearkened very attentively to, none making any objection to what was declared. In the afternoon we had another meeting in the same place, but less, and more private. The day following we had a meeting of Friends only, wherein by joint agreement were settled several meetings; to wit, monthly, quarterly, and a yearly meeting, to be held at Amsterdam for Friends in all the United Provinces of Holland, and in Embden, the Palatinate, Hamburg, Frederickstadt, Dantzic, and other places in and about Germany; which Friends were glad of, and it has been of great service to truth.

Next day an exercise came upon me concerning that deceitful spirit, which wrought in some to make divisions in the church; and the care of the churches being upon me, I was moved to write a few lines to warn Friends of it, as follows:—

"ALL Friends, keep over that spirit of separation and division, in the peaceable truth, and in the Seed of life, which will wear it all out and outlast it. For the Lamb will have the victory over all the spirits of strife, as it hath had since the beginning; and they will wither, as others have done; but all that keep in the Seed, which is always green, shall never wither; as Friends have been to this day kept. And if any have backslidden, and thrown off the cross, are grown loose and full, and are gone into strife and contention with their earthly spirits, and therein plead for liberty, this spirit taketh with loose, earthly spirits, and cries imposition to such as admonish them to come to the life, light, Spirit, and power of God, that they may be alive, and may live again with the living. Upon this admonition, their spirits rise into contention, strife, and separation, turning against the living, in their loose, earthly spirits, which would have the name of truth, but are not in the nature of it, but are for eternal judgment of the living Seed. This is it which doth deceive; but it is judged by that which doth undeceive and save." G. F.

Amsterdam in Holland, the 5th of the 6th Month, 1677.

This being First-day, we had a very large meeting again, there coming to it a great concourse of people of different opinions, as Baptists, Seekers, Socinians, Brownists, and some of the collegians. Robert Barclay, George Keith, William Penn, and I, declared the everlasting truth among them; opening the state of man in the fall, and showing by what way man and woman may come into the restoration by Christ Jesus. Indeed, the mystery of iniquity, and the mystery of godliness, were very plainly laid open; and the meeting ended quietly and well.

The day following, George Keith, Robert Barclay, and William Penn, leaving me and some other Friends at AMSTERDAM, set forward towards GERMANY; where they travelled many hundred miles, and had good service for the Lord; Benjamin Farly going with them and interpreting.

That day and the next I stayed at AMSTERDAM, visiting Friends, and assisting them in some business concerning their meetings. Three Baptists came to discourse with me, to whom I opened things to their satisfaction, and they parted from me in kindness. I wrote a letter also to the Princess Elizabeth, which Isabel Yeomans delivered to her, when George Keith's wife and she went to visit her:—

"PRINCESS ELIZABETH,

"I HAVE heard of thy tenderness towards the Lord and his holy truth, by some Friends that have visited thee, and also by some of thy letters, which I have seen: it is indeed a great thing for a person of thy quality to have such a tender mind after the Lord and his precious truth; seeing so many are swallowed up with voluptuousness, and the pleasures of this world; yet all make an outward profession of God and Christ one way or other, but without any deep, inward sense and feeling of him. For it is not many mighty, nor wise of the world, that can become fools for Christ's sake, or can become low in the humility of Christ Jesus from their mighty state, through which they might receive a mightier estate, and a mightier kingdom through the inward Holy Spirit—the divine light and power of God; and a mightier wisdom which is from above, pure and peaceable. This wisdom is above that which is below; that is earthly, sensual, and devilish, by which men destroy one another, yea, about their religions, ways, worships, and churches; but this they have not from God nor Christ. The wisdom which is from above, by which all things were made and created, which the holy fear of God in the heart is the beginning of, keeps the heart clean: and by this wisdom are all God's children to be ordered, and with it to order all things to God's glory. This is the wisdom that is justified of her children. In this fear of God and this wisdom, my desire is, that thou mayest be preserved to God's glory. For the Lord is come to teach his people himself, and to set up his ensign, that the nations may flow unto it. There hath been an apostacy since the apostles' days, from the divine light of Christ, which should have given them 'the light of the knowledge of the glory of God, in the face of Christ Jesus;' and from the Holy Spirit, which would have led them into all truth; and therefore have people set up so many leaders without them, to give them knowledge; and also from the holy and precious faith, which Jesus Christ is the author and finisher of; which purifies the heart, and gives victory over that which separates from God; through which faith they have access to God, and in which they please God; the mystery of which is held in a pure conscience. And also from the gospel which was preached in the apostles' days (which gospel is the power of God), which brings life and immortality to light in man and woman, by which people should have seen over the devil that has darkened them; which gospel will preserve all them that receive it, in life and immortality. For the eyes of people have been after men, and not after the Lord, who writes his law in the hearts, and puts it into the minds, of all the children of the new covenant of light, life, and grace, through which they all come to know the Lord, from the least to the greatest; so that the knowledge of the Lord may cover the earth, as the waters do the sea. This work of the Lord is beginning again, as it was in the apostles' days; people shall come to receive an unction in them again from the Holy One, by which they shall know all things, and shall not need any man to teach them, but as the anointing doth teach them; and also to know, what the righteousness of faith speaks, the Word nigh in the heart and mouth, to obey it and to do it. This was the Word of faith the apostles preached; which is now received and preached again, and which it is the duty of all true Christians to receive. So now people are coming out of the apostasy to the light of Christ and his Spirit, and to receive faith from him, and not from men; to receive the gospel from him, their unction from him, the Word; and as they receive him, they declare him freely, as his command was to his disciples, and is still to the learners and receivers of him. For the Lord God, in his Son Jesus Christ, is come to teach his people, and to bring them from all the world's ways to Christ, the way, the truth, and the life, who is the way to the Father; and from all the world's teachers and speakers, to him the Speaker and Teacher, as Heb. i. 1; and from all the world's worshippers, to worship God in the Spirit and in the truth, which worship Christ set up above sixteen hundred years ago, when he put down the Jews' worship at the temple at Jerusalem, and the worship at the mountain where Jacob's well was; to bring people from all the world's religions, which they have made since the apostles' days, to the religion that was set up by Christ and his apostles, which is pure and undefiled before God, and keeps from the spots of the world; to bring them out of all the world's churches and fellowships, made and set up since the apostles' days, to the church that is in God, the Father of our Lord Jesus Christ; Thess. i. 1, and to bring to the unity and fellowship in the Holy Spirit, that doth mortify, circumcise, and baptize, to plunge down sin and corruption, that has got up in man and woman by transgression. In this Holy Spirit there is a holy fellowship and unity: yea, it is the bond of the Prince of princes, and King of kings, and Lord of lords' peace; which heavenly peace all true Christians are to maintain with spiritual weapons, not with carnal.

"And now, my friend, the holy men of God wrote the Scriptures as they were moved by the Holy Ghost; and all Christendom are on heaps about those Scriptures, because they are not led by the same Holy Ghost as those were that gave forth the Scriptures; which Holy Ghost they must come to in themselves, and be led by, if they come into all the truth of them, and to have the comfort of God, of Christ, and of them. For none can call Jesus Lord, but by the Holy Ghost; and all that call Christ Lord without the Holy Ghost, take his name in vain. Likewise all that name his name are to depart from iniquity; then they name his name with reverence, in truth and righteousness. O therefore, feel the grace and truth in thy heart, that is come by Jesus Christ, that will teach thee how to live, and what to deny. It will establish thy heart, season thy words, and bring thy salvation; it will be a teacher unto thee at all times. By it thou mayest receive Christ from whom it comes; and as many as receive him, to them he gives power, not only to stand against sin and evil, but to become the sons of God; if sons, then heirs of a life, a world, and kingdom, without end, and of the eternal riches and treasures thereof. So in haste, with my love in the Lord Jesus Christ, who tasted death for every man, and bruises the serpent's head, who is between man and God, that through Christ man may come to God again, and praise him through Jesus Christ, the Amen; who is the spiritual and heavenly rock and foundation for all God's people to build upon, to the praise and glory of God, who is over all, blessed for evermore." GEORGE FOX.

Amsterdam, the 7th of the 6th Month, 1677.

"*Postscript.*—The bearer hereof is a daughter-in-law of mine, that comes with Gertrude Dirick Nieson and George Keith's wife, to visit thee."

G. F.

The Princess Elizabeth's Answer.

"DEAR FRIEND,

"I cannot but have a tender love to those that love the Lord Jesus Christ, and to whom it is given, not only to believe in him, but also to suffer for him; therefore your letter and your friends' visit have been both very welcome to me. I shall follow their and your counsel as far as God will afford me light and unction; remaining still your loving friend,

Hertford, the 30th of August, 1677. "ELIZABETH."*

* Elizabeth, Princess of the Rhine, was the eldest daughter of Frederick V., Elector Palatine, and king of Bohemia—her mother being a daughter of king James I. of England. This excellent princess is spoken of as a woman of great amiability and religious character. She possessed only a small territory; but she governed with great judgment, and attention to the happiness of her subjects. She made it a rule to hear, one day in the week, all such causes as were brought before her. On these occasions, her wisdom, justice, and moderation were very conspicuous. She frequently remitted forfeitures, in cases where the parties were poor, or in any respect worthy

Next day John Claus and I took a boat and passed to BUYCKSLOTE, thence to PURMERENT, where having refreshed ourselves, we went by waggon to ALKMAAR, about thirty miles from Amsterdam. We went to a Friend's house there, whose name was Willem Willems, where I had a meeting that night. I had another next day, which was larger; for several professors came, and all was quiet and well. After the meeting, I visited some Friends; and then, taking boat, passed to HOORN, which is counted the chief city in North Holland. We lodged at an inn; and, taking waggon early next morning, passed to ENCKHUYSEN, where we took ship for FRIESLAND; and landing in the afternoon at WORKUM, took waggon and rode upon the high bank of the Friezen Seas, till we met two Friends coming with a waggon to meet us; with whom (discharging our waggon at Mackum, a village hard by) we went to HARLINGEN, the chief seaport town in Friesland. We went to Hessel Jacobs', whither several Friends came to visit us that night. Next day we visited the Friends of the place; and I wrote a paper, "To all them that persecute Friends for not observing their fast-day."

The day following being First-day, Friends had a meeting there, to which we went, and many professors came to it. I declared the everlasting gospel amongst them, John Claus interpreting. They were all very civil, and heard attentively; and when it was done, departed peaceably, without making any opposition. After meeting I went to Hessel Jacobs' again, whither after a while came a Calvinist to ask me some questions,

of favour. It was remarkable that she often introduced religious considerations, as motives to persuade the contending parties to harmony and peace. She was greatly beloved and respected by her subjects; and also by many persons of learning and virtue not resident in her dominions; for she patronised men of this character, whatever their country or their religious profession.

The respect in which this exemplary Christian held Friends and their principles, was unreservedly expressed in her letters to individuals connected with the English court; and her good offices were more than once exerted to preserve this persecuted people from the penalties of those laws which interdicted the exercise of public worship in conventicles, as all meeting-houses were then denominated. William Penn and Robert Barclay paid her two visits. She received them with great openness, and was much affected by the interview which, on the second visit, took place, as is related by William Penn. They went from Amsterdam to Herwerden, the residence of the Princess and of her intimate acquaintance, Anna Maria, Countess de Hornes, who dwelt much in her house, and was, as well as herself, a woman seeking after the best things, and a favourer of such (says Penn) as separate themselves from the world for the sake of righteousness.

The visitors were welcomed by the Princess and her friend the day after their arrival, and were invited to dine with them. They held a religious meeting together, which was so satisfactory that the Princess desired another might be appointed, at which several persons were present. William Penn thus speaks of it:—"The eternal word showed itself as a hammer this day; yea, sharper than a two-edged sword, dividing asunder between the soul and the spirit, between the joints and the marrow. Let my right hand forget its cunning, and my tongue cleave to the roof of my mouth, when I shall forget the loving-kindness of the Lord, and the sure mercies of our God, to us that day." The following day they paid two visits at this little court; and the day after, which was the first of the week, they held a meeting there, appointed by the direction of the Princess, which several others attended besides those of her household. Of this meeting Penn says: "The quickening power and life of Jesus

which I answered to his satisfaction; and he departed friendly. Soon after he was gone, a preacher of the collegians came to discourse with me, who seemed well satisfied also, and we parted lovingly. That evening I had another meeting with the Friends there, and next morning, when we had taken our leave of them, we passed to LEEUWARDEN, the chief city in FRIESLAND, and lodged that night at a Friend's house there, whose name was Sybrand Dowes.

Next morning early, taking boat, we passed to DOCKUM, and walking through the city, took boat again to STROBUS, which is the utmost part of Friesland. There we baited at a commissary's house; and then taking boat again, passed to GRONINGEN, the chief city of the province of Groningland. One of the magistrates of that city came with us from Leeuwarden, with whom I had some discourse on the way, and he was very loving. We walked nearly two miles through the city, and then took boat for Delfziel; and passing in the evening through a town called APPINGDALEM, where had been a great horse-fair that day; there came many officers rushing into the boat, and being somewhat in drink, they were very rude. I spoke to them, exhorting them to "fear the Lord, and beware of Solomon's vanities." They were boisterous fellows; yet somewhat more civil afterwards. We landed at DELFZIEL about ten at night, having travelled about fifty English miles that day. We went to an inn to lodge, and as we passed through the guards, they examined John Claus, whether I was not a militia soldier; and when he had told them I was not, they let us pass peaceably.

DELFZIEL stands on the river Embs, over which we passed next day to EMBDEN, a place where Friends had been cruelly persecuted, and from which they had been often banished. I went to an inn, where I dined with some men that understood English, with whom I had a fine time, and they were loving. Meanwhile John Claus went with his wife to her father's, in Embden; whither, after I had dined, I went also, understanding the old man was desirous to see me. In the afternoon John Claus and I walked through the city to the place where the waggon, which he had hired, was to meet us; and while we waited for it, the Friends that were in the city came to the house where we were, and we had a little meeting. When it was over, and the waggon came not, we sent to know the reason. The master of it sent us word, that he durst not let it go; for the bishop of Munster's soldiers were up in the country, and he was afraid they would

wrought and reached them; and virtue from him, in whom dwelleth the Godhead bodily, went forth." After this meeting, which was held late in the evening, the visitors took their leave, but not before they had been witnesses of the tender disposition of mind of the Princess; who, attempting to set forth her sense of the power and presence of God prevalent among them, could not proceed, but turned herself to the window, and said, "My heart is full, I cannot speak to you." Penn, on another occasion, says, "I cannot forget her last words when I took my leave of her: 'Let me desire you to remember me, though I live at so great a distance, and you should never see me more. I thank you for this good time. Be assured, though my condition subjects me to divers temptations, yet my soul has strong desires after the best things.'"

The Princess Elizabeth lived to the age of 60, departing this life in 1680, as much lamented, as she had been beloved, by her people.

take away his horses. So being disappointed of our passage, we returned to John Claus's father-in-law's house, where I left him, and went to my inn at night.

We took shipping next day, and passed about fifteen miles upon the river Embs, to a market-town in East-Friesland, called LEER, where lived a Friend that had been banished from Embden. When we had visited him, we hired a waggon in that town, and passed to a garrisoned town, called STRIKEHUYSEN, where the guards examined us; and then went on to DETEREN, where, hiring another waggon, we passed to another garrisoned town, where we were very strictly examined. Thence we passed to APRE, in Denmark, where we lodged that night. In our travelling this day, we met the Earl of Oldenburg, going to the treaty of peace at Lembachie.

Next day, we passed by waggon to OLDENBURG, lately a great and famous place, but then burnt down, and but few houses left standing in it. At this place we hired another waggon, and went to DELMENHURST; where, after we had been examined by the guards, we went to a burgher-master's to lodge, whose house was an inn. There being many people, I declared the way of truth to him and them, warning them of the day of the Lord that was coming upon all evil-doers.

We passed next day by waggon to BREMEN, a stately city in GERMANY; and thence, after a double examination, we went to a water called OVERDELAND, and there took boat to FISHERHOLDER; where, finding many people together, I declared the way of God to them, and exhorted them to fear the Lord. There we took waggon again, and travelled in the bishop of Munster's country, to CLOSTERSEVEN; and having no inclination to stay there, got fresh horses, intending to travel all night. We went a little way, but it quickly grew so dark, and rained so hard, that we thought it best to turn back again; for our waggon being open, we had no defence against the rain, and our clothes were already wet with what had fallen for several days before. So we went to an inn, and got a little fresh straw, upon which we lay till about break of day; and then set out and travelled to BUXTEHUDE.

The people in the bishop of Munster's country were very dark. As we passed amongst them, I preached truth to them, warning them of the great and notable day of the Lord; and exhorting them to soberness, and to mind the good Spirit of God *in* themselves.

It was on a First-day that we went through BUXTEHUDE; and without the walls there was a great fair of sheep and geese that day. We stayed a little to refresh ourselves, and went on as fast as we could to HAMBURG, partly by waggon, and partly by water.

We got to HAMBURG in time enough to get a meeting there that evening; and a good and glorious one it was. There were at it, amongst others, a Baptist teacher and his wife, and a great man of Sweden and his wife; and all was quiet, blessed be the Lord, whose power was exalted over all. Yet a dark, hard place this is, and the people are much shut up from truth.

At Hamburg was a woman that had spoken against me in John Perrot's time, though she had never seen me till now. She had been troubled for it ever since; and now was glad of an opportunity to acknowledge her fault; which she very readily did, and I as readily and freely forgave her.

We stayed that night at Hamburg, encouraging and strengthening the Friends there in their testimony to the truth; and betimes next morning set forward towards Frederickstadt, two long days' journey from Hamburg. We went the first day to Elmshoorn, where we baited; and then rode on through a garrison-town of the king of Denmark's; and passing by the monument of the Earl of Rantzow, came to the city of Itzeho, where we lodged that night. I had some service in the evening among the people in the inn, whom I exhorted to soberness, and to live in the fear of the Lord. Next morning we travelled to Hoghenhorn, where we dined at an inn with one of the council of Frederickstadt; to whom, and to the rest of the people present, I declared the truth, with which they seemed to be affected. Then travelling on, we came to a river called Eyder, where we took boat and so went to Frederickstadt, to William Paul's, where several Friends came to us, for there is a pretty company of Friends in that city. We had a fine refreshing meeting together that evening, which made us forget our weariness; for we were indeed very weary, having travelled hard two days, and being wet through our clothes, having had much rain in our open waggons. But the Lord made all easy and good to us; and we were well, and glad to see Friends; blessed be his holy name for ever!

This city is in the Duke of Holstein's country, who would have banished Friends out of the city and country, and sent to the magistrates of the city to do it; but they said, they would lay down their offices rather than do it; inasmuch as Friends came to that city to enjoy liberty of conscience. Friends still enjoy their liberty there, and truth and they are of good report amongst the people, both in city and country.

On First-day I had a meeting here, to which many people came, and some rough spirits; but the power of the Lord bound them down, and the Seed of life was set over all. While I was here I had a discourse with a Jew that was a Levite, concerning the coming of the Messiah, and he was much confounded in what he said; yet he carried himself lovingly, and invited me to his house. I went, and there I discoursed with another Jew, who showed me their Talmud and many other Jewish books; but they are very dark, and do not understand their own prophets.

There was at this city a Baptist teacher, who had reproached and belied Friends; wherefore John Claus went with two Friends of the town, to the house where he lodged, and cleared truth and Friends from his reproaches; and laid his lies and slanders upon his own head, to his shame.

Before we left this place I had another meeting with the Friends only, wherein I laid before them the usefulness and benefit of a monthly meeting, for looking after the poor, and taking care that marriages, and all other things relating to the church, were performed in an orderly manner. The thing answered the witness of God in their consciences, so that they readily agreed to have monthly meetings thenceforward among themselves, that both men and women might take care of the outward concerns of the church.

After this meeting, feeling my spirit clear of that place, we took leave of Friends there, whom we left in good order, and turned back again for Hamburg. When we had travelled one day's journey, and were come to an inn at night to lodge, I inquired whether there were any tender people in the town that feared God, or that had a mind to discourse of the things of God? The innkeeper told me there were few such in that town. Next night we got to HAMBURG; and having passed the guards, went to a Friend's house, being very weary; for we had been up those two mornings before three, and had travelled each day hard and late. Here we met with John Hill, an English Friend, who had been travelling in Germany, and being in a ship bound for Amsterdam, that waited for a wind, he had lain sick on board about two weeks. Hearing I was in the country, he left the ship and came hither to meet me, and go along with me.

The day after we came to Hamburg we had a very good meeting, and very peaceable. After it I had discourse with a Swede, an eminent man in his own country; who, having been banished thence on the account of his religion, was come to Hamburg, and was at the meeting I had there before. When I had done with him, I had another discourse with a Baptist concerning the sacraments, so called; in both which I had good service, having opportunity thereby to open truth unto them.

Being clear of Hamburg, we took leave of Friends there, whom we left well; and taking John Hill with us, passed by boat to a city in the Duke of LUNEBURG's country; where, after we were examined by the guards, we were had to the main-guard, and there examined more strictly; but after they found we were not soldiers, they were civil, and let us pass. In the afternoon we travelled by waggon, and the waters being much out, by reason of heavy rains, when it drew towards night, we hired a boy on the way to guide us through a great water we had to pass. When we came to it, the water was so deep before we could come at the bridge, that the waggoner had to wade, and I drove the waggon. When we were come on the bridge, the horses broke part of it down, and one of them fell into the water, the waggon standing upon that part of the bridge which remained unbroken; and it was the Lord's mercy to us that the waggon did not run into the brook. When they had got the horse out, he lay a while as if dead; but at length they got him up, put him to the waggon again, and laid the planks right; and then, through the goodness of the Lord to us, we got safe over.

After this we came to another water, which finding to be very deep, and it being in the night, we hired two men to help us through, who put cords to the waggon to hold it by, that the force of the water might not drive it from the way. But when we came into it, the stream was so strong, that it took one of the horses off his legs, and was carrying him down the stream. I called to the waggoner to pluck him to him by his reins, which he did, and the horse recovered his legs, and with much difficulty we got over the bridge, and went to BORMER-HAVEN, the town where the waggoner lived. It was the last day of the 6th month that we escaped these dangers; and it being about eleven at night when we came in here, we got some fresh straw and lay upon it, till about four in the morning. Then getting up, we set forward again towards Bremen, by waggon and boat. On the way I had good opportunities to publish truth among the people, especially at a market-town, where we stayed to change our passage; where I declared the truth to the people, warning them of the day of the Lord, that was coming upon all flesh; and exhorting them to righteousness, telling them, "that God was come to teach his people himself," and that they should turn to the Lord, and hearken to the teachings of his Spirit *in* their own hearts.

At Bremen, after we were examined, we went to an inn, and stayed till another waggon was provided to carry us further. Though I felt the Lord's power was over the city, and kept the wicked and unruly spirits down, yet my spirit suffered much in this place for the people's sake. When our waggon was ready, we left Bremen and travelled to Keby, where we lodged at an inn, and early next morning set out for Oldenburg. It was a lamentable sight to see so great and brave a city burnt down. We went to an inn, and though it was First-day, the soldiers were drinking, and playing at shovel-board; and at the few houses that were left, the shops were open, and the people trading one with another. I was moved to declare the truth among them, and warn them of the judgments of God; and though they heard me quietly, and were civil, yet I was burthened with their wickedness. Many times in mornings, noons, and nights, at the inns and on the ways as I travelled, I spoke to the people, preaching the truth to them, warning them of the day of the Lord, and exhorting them to turn to the light and Spirit of God *in* themselves, that thereby they might be led out of evil.

Next day, passing through many great waters, we came at night to Leer, and the day following to Embden, where John Claus's wife's father lived; at whose house, when we went into Germany, we left a young man sick, who travelled with me, and used to write for me; whom now we found pretty well recovered. John Claus went to his father-in-law's; John Hill and I to an inn, where we dined. After dinner we went also to John Claus's father's, and had a good meeting there in the evening.

The day following we took shipping at Embden, passed to Delfziel, and went to an inn, where a Friend came to us that then lived there, having been often banished from Embden; he was a goldsmith, and had a house and shop in Embden; and still as they banished him, he went again. Then they imprisoned him, and fed him with bread and water; and at length took his goods from him, and banished him, his wife, and children, leaving them neither place to come to, nor anything to subsist on. We comforted and encouraged him in the Lord, exhorting him to be faithful, and stand stedfast in the testimony committed to him. When we had taken leave of him, we took boat, and passed the same day to Groningen, where we met with Cornelius Andries, a Friend that had also suffered much by imprisonment and banishment at Embden. We went with him to his house, and next day had a good meeting in that city, to which several professors came, who were very peaceable and attentive. After meeting we passed by boat to STROBUS, and so to DOCKUM, where we lodged at an inn. Taking boat again next morning we passed to LEEUWARDEN, the chief city of Friesland, where I found my daughter Yeomans, who was come from Amsterdam to meet me. That day we had a precious meeting at Sybrand Dowes's house. After the meeting I had discourse with some that were at it, who had been formerly convinced of truth, but were not come into obedience to it. We stayed there that night; but John Hill left us, and went that day to Harlingen, and so to Amsterdam.

Next day we passed down the river to the lake of HEMPEN-SARMER, and thence by the lake LUGMER, and so to a town called ANDEBIGO; whence sailing through the lake WHISPOOL, we came to GARDICK within night. We lodged at an inn; and next day, being First-day, we were at Friends' meeting there, which was very large, many of the town's-people coming in; amongst whom I declared the truth, in the power of the Lord that was upon me, which tendered the people, and they were very sober. After it we stayed a little while to refresh ourselves, and then went to take boat again; but the people observing us, gathered together at a bridge, which we were to pass; and there I spoke unto them again, declaring the way of life and salvation; and they were very attentive and civil.

We went back that evening to LEEUWARDEN, twenty-seven miles; but before we could reach it, the gates were shut, and the bridges drawn up, so that we could not get into the city, but lay in the boat all night. Next morning, there having been a man killed in the city that night, it was late before the gates were opened. When we could get in, we went to a Friend's house, where we stayed a while; then taking boat again, we passed through FRANEKER to HARLINGEN, to Hessel Jacobs's, where we found several Dutch Friends, who were come to be at the meeting there next day. In the evening William Penn came to us from Amsterdam; who having returned two or three days before out of Germany, had been at a large meeting at Amsterdam on First-day; and after it, understanding I was at Harlingen, he came thither to me.

The next day was the monthly meeting for the men and women, to which we went; it was large and good. And there it was agreed, that "a meeting should be held there once a month, both for the men and for the women, to take care of the outward concerns of the church."

In the afternoon we had a public meeting, to which came people of several sorts, Socinians, Baptists, Lutherans, &c., amongst whom were a doctor of physic and a priest. After I had declared the truth pretty largely to the people, opening the happy state that man and woman were in, whilst they kept under God's teaching, and abode in the Paradise of God; and on the other hand, the woe and misery that came upon them when they went from God's teaching, hearkening to the Serpent's—when they transgressed God's command, and were driven out of Paradise; and then came to set forth the way, whereby man and woman might come into that happy state again; the priest, an ancient, grave man, stood up, just as I had done speaking, and putting off his hat, said, "I pray God to prosper and confirm that doctrine, for it is truth, and I have nothing against it." He would willingly have stayed till the meeting ended, but having to preach that evening, he could not stay longer, the time for his own worship being come. Wherefore when he had made confession to the truth, he hastened away, that he might come again; and did come, it seems, to the meeting-place, but the meeting was ended first. After meeting we went to Hessel Jacobs's, where I had a meeting with Friends, and the doctor of physic came thither to discourse with William Penn, who had a good opportunity to open truth to him. By this doctor the priest sent his love to me, wishing him to tell me, that he had left preaching that evening half an hour sooner than he used to do, that he might come to our meeting again, to hear more of that good doctrine. I heard afterwards that his hearers questioned him, for what he had said in our meeting; and that, he standing by his words, they had complained of him for it to the other priests of the city, who called him to account about it; but the result I could not learn.

Early next morning William Penn, taking John Claus with him, passed from Harlingen for Leeuwarden, where he had appointed a meeting; intending after that, to travel into some other parts of Germany, to visit a tender people there. I with those Friends that were with me, took ship the same day for AMSTERDAM, where we arrived a little after midnight, but the gates being shut, we lay on board till morning; then went to Gertrude Dirick Nieson's, where many Friends came to see us, being glad of our safe return. Next day, feeling a concern upon my mind, with relation to those seducing spirits that made division among Friends, and being sensible that they endeavoured to insinuate themselves into the affectionate part, I was moved to write a few lines to Friends concerning them, as follows:—

"ALL these that set up themselves in the affections of the people, set up themselves, and the affections of the people, and not Christ. But Friends, your peaceable habitation in the truth, which is everlasting, and changes not, will outlast all the habitations of those that are out of the truth, be they ever so full of words. So they that are so keen for J.S. and J.W. let them take them, and the separation; and you, that have given your testimony against that spirit, stand in your testimony, till they answer by condemnation. Do not strive, nor make bargains with that which is out of the truth; nor save that alive to be a sacrifice for God, which should be slain, lest you lose your kingdom." G. F.

Amsterdam, the 14th of the 7th Month, 1677.

On the First-day following, I was at Friends' meeting at Amsterdam, to which many people came, and were very civil and attentive, hearing truth declared several hours. John Roeloffs interpreted for me.

Before this time, several of the Friends that came over with me, were returned to England, as Robert Barclay,* George Keith's wife, and others;

* This being the last mention of Robert Barclay in these volumes, the following brief particulars may interest the reader who is not already acquainted with his history. He was the son of Colonel David Barclay, descended from the Barclays of Mathers, an ancient and honourable Scotch family, and of Katharine Gordon, from the Gordons of the house of the Duke of Gordon. He was born at Edinburgh in 1648, educated in France, and returned to Scotland in 1664. His father having joined the despised Quakers, Robert Barclay, though uninfluenced by him, soon

and now my daughter Yeomans went back also; so that I was left alone at Amsterdam. While I was there, it came upon me to visit my suffering Friends at Dantzic with a few lines, to encourage and strengthen them in their sufferings, as follows:—

"DEAR FRIENDS,

"To whom is my love in the Lord's truth, that is over all, and by which all God's people are made free men and women, being thereby set free from him that is out of the truth; that walking in the truth, they may answer the witness of God in all people; which truth all must come to, if they be made free. Therefore be faithful unto what the Lord makes known unto you. I am glad the Lord hath witnesses in that city, to stand for his glory and name, and for Christ Jesus, the great Prophet, whom God hath raised up, who is to be heard in all things; so that ye need none of the prophets, which men have raised up. Therefore, stand faithful to Christ Jesus, your Shepherd, that he may feed you; hear his voice, and follow him, who laid down his life for you: but follow none of the shepherds and hirelings, that are made by men, though they be angry, because ye will not follow them to their dry and barren mountains; who have been, and are, the thieves, persecutors, and robbers, that climb up another way, than by Christ. Set up Christ to be your Counsellor and Leader, and then, ye will have no need of any of the counsellors and leaders of the world; for Christ is sufficient, whom God has given you. Set up Christ Jesus to be your Bishop and Overseer, who is sufficient to oversee you, that ye go not astray from God; by which ye may see over all the hireling-overseers made by men, who keep the people, that they do not go astray from the rudiments and formalities, fashions and customs of the world; which hath been and is their work. I am glad ye are come to own Christ Jesus, your High-

followed his example, and came forth a zealous witness for the truth, receiving a gift in the ministry, in which he laboured to bring others to God. He was much exercised in controversy, from the many contradictions that fell upon truth, and upon him for its sake. He published several works in defence of the principles he had espoused, which he believed to be those of the New Testament, as promulgated by Christ and his apostles. His chief work was his *Apology for the True Christian Divinity*, which has gone through many editions, and remains uncontrovertible.

In common with the early Friends, Robert Barclay suffered imprisonments and ill usage, which he bore with exemplary patience. He travelled extensively to spread the gospel of Christ, for he loved the truth above all the world; not ashamed of it before men, but bold and able in maintaining it, sound in judgment, strong in argument, of a pleasant disposition, yet solid and exemplary in his conversation. He was a learned man, a good Christian, an able minister, a tender and careful father, and a good and kind neighbour and friend. His last illness was short. James Dickenson of Cumberland, in his journey in Scotland, visiting him when on his deathbed, as he sat by him, the Lord's power and presence bowed their hearts together, and Robert Barclay was sweetly melted in the sense of God's love, and, with tears, expressed his love to all faithful brethren in England; and adding a message of love to dear George Fox, he said, "God is good still, and though I am under great weight of sickness and weakness as to my body, yet my peace flows, and this I know, whatever exercises may be permitted to come upon me, it shall tend to God's glory and my salvation, and in that I rest."

He died at his own house, at Ury, in Scotland, in 1690, aged forty-two, leaving behind him four sons and three daughters.

Priest, who is holy, harmless, separate from sinners, and made higher than the heavens, as the church and the apostle owned him in their days, Heb. vii., who is the High-Priest over the household of faith; which faith Jesus Christ is the author and finisher of: and this do all the children of the new covenant witness, who walk in the new and living way. Therefore my desire is, that ye all may be steadfast, whether in bonds or out, in the faith of Christ Jesus, which is the gift of God; by which faith all the valiants overcame the devil and all their enemies; in which faith they had victory and access to God; and in that was their unity: which mystery of faith is held in a pure conscience, hidden from the world. I do believe, that your imprisonments and sufferings in that place will be for good in the end, as it hath been in other places, ye standing faithful to the Lord, who is all-sufficient. For your sufferings and trials will try their teachers and religions, churches and worships, and make manifest what birth they are of; even that which persecutes him that is born of the Spirit: for ye know, that there is no salvation by any other name under the whole heaven, than by the name of Jesus; therefore it is time to leave them, when there is no salvation by or in any of them.

"Now, Friends, I desire that you would take a list of the names of all those that belong to the king of Poland, and where they live, and how ye may send books or epistles to them, and keep a correspondence with them: also the name of the bishop or cardinal that I heard was with you; and, if ye can, get any of them that belong to the king to come and visit the prisoners, that they may inform the king of their cruel sufferings. Also I desire you to get as many books of mine as you can dispose of, that set forth your sufferings, and the cruelty of the magistrates of Dantzic; and give them to the king, his council, attendants, and bishops. And some of the women may speak to the queen, if they can, that she may signify to the king their cruel sufferings; and especially some of the sufferers' wives, if there be any of a capacity to do it. You may likewise give his attendants any other Friends' books; what books ye lack, send for to Amsterdam, where ye may be furnished with them, to answer every tender desirer, and inquiring mind after the Lord. So let all your minds be bended with the Lord's power, to spread his truth abroad; and where ye hear of any, or have any correspondence in outward trading with any sober people, far or near, send them books, that their understandings may be opened after the Lord. The Lord God Almighty preserve you! To his protection, in his eternal power, do I commend you all, in bonds or at liberty, with my love to you in the everlasting Seed of God, Christ Jesus, who bruises the head of the serpent, that makes you suffer. Christ is over him, and will be when he is gone; who is First and Last, over all, from everlasting to everlasting, in whom ye have life, knowledge, wisdom, and salvation; and through him live to the praise and glory of God, who is blessed for evermore. Amen." G. F.

Amsterdam, the 18th of the 7th Month, 1677, English style.

Next day, the fourth of the week and 19th of the month, I had a large meeting at Amsterdam, many professors being at it; and truth was largely opened to them, in the demonstration of the heavenly power. The day following I went by boat from Amsterdam, many Friends going with me, to LANDSMEER in Waterland (a town in which, they say, there are above a hundred bridges), where I had a very good meeting, to which several professors came. After it I returned with Friends to AMSTERDAM, where I stayed till the First-day following, and went to their meeting, which was large. Many professors of several sorts were at it, and heard the truth declared with great attention.

I tarried there next day, and in the night following had a great exercise upon my spirit concerning that loose spirit, that was run out into strife and contention among Friends, and had drawn some after it into division and separation; the way, work, and end whereof the Lord opened to me: wherefore feeling the motion of life upon me, I got up in the morning and wrote the following epistle to Friends:—

"MY DEAR FRIENDS,

"Keep your first love in the truth, power, and Seed of life in Christ Jesus; for this last night, as I was lying in my bed at Amsterdam, I had a great travail in the holy Seed of life and peace, and my spirit was troubled with that spirit of strife and separation. I saw it was a destroying spirit, and did seek not only to get over the Seed, but to destroy it, and to eat out the minds of the people from it by strife and contention; and, under pretence of standing for the ancient truth, its work is to root it out, and destroy the appearance of it, to set up itself. It is a creeping spirit, seeking whom it can get into; and what it cannot do itself it stirreth up others to do, and setteth their spirits afloat, with the dark wisdom to destroy the simple. This spirit is managed by the prince of the air, and leadeth some to do things which they would have been ashamed to have done as men, which doth unman them; and they would not have suffered them if they had kept to the tender principle of God, which leadeth to peace. It is a despising, backbiting, secret-whispering spirit, a sower of dissension, and a taker of advantage of all prejudiced spirits, that are disobedient to their first principle, and love of truth, and begetteth into hatred; so it begetteth all into that spirit, whose work is to destroy both the good within, and the good order without. Nay, it would, if it could, destroy the government of Christ, and the order of the gospel, to set up its own will and spirit, which is not of God; and, under pretence of crying down man, is setting up man, and gathering into a separation of disobedient men, who float above their conditions. This spirit, which neither liveth in the truth nor its order, but opposeth them that do, I cannot express it, as I see it and its work, whose end will be accordingly. Therefore, Friends, I am to warn you all, that have not lost your simplicity, not to touch it, nor to have any unity with it, lest you be defiled, and lose your eternal estate and everlasting portion; and that your inward man, which is after God, may be preserved, and Christ may reign in all your hearts. It will be very hard for those that are joined with them, ever to come down to truth in themselves, to see their own conditions, and to have that spirit of strife and contention (which eateth as a canker) brought down in them; which is carnal, and slayeth the tender babe, which was once begotten in themselves.

The Philistine is got up in them, that stoppeth the wells and springs, maketh a great bustle, and is crying up men, and pleading for them, instead of Christ. So, Friends, strive not with them, but let those take them that cry them up. Keep you to the Lord Jesus Christ with his light, that cometh from him, that he may be your Lord; and ye in him may be all in unity, in one light, life, power, and dominion, in Christ, your head. The God of peace and power preserve you all in Christ Jesus, your Saviour; and out of and from that mischievous spirit, which is idle and slothful as to the work of the power, and Spirit, and light of God and Christ. Its very act worketh strife and disturbance against the peace of the church of Christ. It thinks, in its wilfulness, stubbornness, and unruliness, to set up itself, and in that to have peace; but destruction will be the end of it, and it is sealed for the fire and eternal judgment. Therefore, let Christ, the Seed, be the head and crown of every one of you, that nothing may be between you and the Lord God. Be not deceived with vain, feigned, or rough words; for Satan is transforming himself, as an angel of light, to deceive; but God's foundation standeth sure, and God knoweth who are his, and will preserve them upon the rock and foundation of life, in his peaceable truth and habitation, that in the same they may grow. Keep out of strife and contention with it, after ye have borne your testimony in the Lord's power and truth against it, then keep in the truth; for it hath a life in scribbling, strife, and jangling, because it would enlarge itself, and bring others into its misery with the airy power, and would get power over the good, disjoin people from it, and so commit rapes upon the simplicity by its subtilty. But I do believe the Lord will defend his people, though he may try them and exercise them with this spirit for a time, as he hath done in days past, in other vessels it hath made use of, as it doth of these now; who have a more seeming fair outside, but foul, rough, and rugged enough within, against the Seed of Christ, as ever were the Pharisees to destroy it. They, under a pretence of preaching Christ, are destroyers and crucifiers of him, and killers of the just, not only in themselves, but are endeavouring, with all their might, to destroy it in others, where it is born. Pharaoh and Herod slay the young Jews in the Spirit, as the old did; I feel it worrying them. That is got up to be king which knew not suffering Joseph. But God will plague him, and the Seed will have more rest, and be better entertained in Egypt, than under Herod, into whom old Pharaoh's spirit is entered. He that hath an ear to hear, let him hear; and an eye to see, let him see, how this spirit hath transformed in all ages against the just and righteous; but mark, what hath been its end? The Seed reigneth; glory to the Lord God over all for ever! His truth spreadeth, and Friends here are in unity and peace, and of good report, answering the good, or that of God in people. My desires are, that all God's people may do the same in all places, that the Lord may be glorified in their bringing forth much fruit that is heavenly and spiritual. Amen."

Amsterdam, the 25th of the 7th Month, 1677. G. F.

After I had given forth the foregoing epistle, whereby my spirit was in some measure eased of the weight that lay upon it, I went in the afternoon to the monthly meeting of Friends at Amsterdam, where the Lord was present with us, and refreshed our spirits together in himself.

I had thought to go next day to Haarlem; but a fast being appointed to be kept that day, I was stopped in my spirit, and moved to stay at Friends' meeting that day at Amsterdam. We had a very large meeting, a great concourse of people coming to it, and amongst them many great persons. The Lord's power was over the meeting; and in the openings thereof I was moved to declare to the people, "that no man, by all his wit and study, nor by reading history in his own will, could declare or know the generation of Christ, who was not begotten by the will of man, but by the will of God." After I had largely opened this unto them, "I showed them the difference between the true fast and the false; manifesting, that the professed Christians, Jews, and Turks, were out of the true fast, and fasted for strife and debate, being under the band and fists of iniquity and oppression, wherewith they were smiting one another; but the pure hands were not lifted up to God. And though they did all appear to men to fast, and did hang down their heads for a day like a bulrush, yet that was not the fast which God did accept; but in that state all their bones were dry, and when they called upon the Lord, he did not answer them, neither did their health grow; for they kept their own fast and not the Lord's. I exhorted them to keep the Lord's fast, which was to fast from sin and iniquity, from strife and debate, from violence and oppression, and to abstain from every appearance of evil." These things were opened to the astonishment of the fasters; and the meeting ended peaceably and well.

I went to Haarlem the day following, having before appointed a meeting. Peter Hendricks and Gertrude Dirick Nieson went with me; and a blessed meeting we had. There were professors of several sorts, and a priest of the Lutherans, who sat very attentive for several hours, while I declared the truth amongst them, Gertrude interpreting. When the meeting was done, the priest said "he had heard nothing but what was according to the Word of God; and desired that the blessing of the Lord might rest upon us, and our assemblies." Others also confessed to the truth, saying, "they had never heard things so plainly opened to their understandings before."

We stayed that night at Haarlem at a Friend's house, whose name was Dirick Klassen; and, returning next day to Amsterdam, went to Gertrude's house; where we had not been long, before a priest of great note, who had formerly belonged to the Emperor of Germany, and with him another German priest came, desiring to have some conference with me. I took the opportunity to declare the way of truth unto them, opening unto them "how they might come to know God and Christ, and his law and gospel;" and showing them that "they could never know it by study, nor by philosophy, but by divine revelation through the Spirit of God, opening to them in the stillness of their minds." The men were tender, and went away well satisfied.

On the First-day following I was at Friends' meeting at Amsterdam; where, amongst several sorts of professors that were present, was a doctor from Poland, who for his religion was banished the place he lived in; and being affected with the testimony of truth in the meeting, he came afterwards to have some discourse with me; and after we had been some time together, and I had opened things further to him, he went away very tender and loving.

While I was at Amsterdam, I spent much of my time in writing books, papers, or epistles on truth's behalf. I wrote several epistles from Amsterdam to Friends in England and elsewhere, on several occasions, as the Lord moved me by his Spirit thereunto. I wrote also from thence, "A Warning to the Inhabitants of the City of Oldenburg, which was lately burnt down;" also, "A Warning to the Inhabitants of the City of Hamburg," both of which were as follows:—

"*A Warning to the Magistrates and People of the City of Oldenburg.*

"FRIENDS,

"Have you not seen and felt the judgments of God upon your city, the Lord sending lightning from heaven that destroyed and burnt it? As I passed through your city on a First-day of the week, which you call your Sabbath, I saw some drinking, and soldiers playing at shuffleboard, and others with their shops open and trading, when they should have been waiting upon God and worshipping him; and your people were light and vain, without any sense of God's judgments or repentance. O therefore repent, lest the all-seeing God, who sees all your actions and is over all, bring swift judgment upon you in his wrath, fury, and indignation. Repent, and lay aside all manner of evil and wickedness, ungodliness, and unrighteousness; for the day of the Lord will come upon all that do evil, all the workers of iniquity. This mighty day of the Lord will find them all out, and will burn as an oven, and burn up all the proud and wicked, and neither leave them root nor branch. Therefore, all ye magistrates, priests, and people, search in yourselves to find out the cause, and what evil you have committed, that has brought the wrath, vengeance, and judgment of God upon you and your city, in burning it. All return, and come to the light of Christ in your hearts, and to God's Spirit, and to the grace and truth in your hearts, that comes by Jesus Christ; that with it ye may search your hearts. Do not grieve, nor vex, nor quench God's good Spirit in your hearts, and walk not despitefully against the Spirit of grace, nor turn from it into wantonness; and yet make a profession of God and Christ in words, when your hearts are afar off, living in pleasures and wantonly upon the earth, sporting yourselves, killing the just, crucifying to yourselves Christ afresh, and putting him to open shame; and so dishonouring God, and Christ, and Christianity, and making a profession and a trade of the Scriptures, keeping people always learning, that they may be always paying.

"Cease from man, whose breath is in his nostrils, and look unto the Lord, all ye ends of the earth, and be saved; for the Lord God of heaven and earth is come, to teach his people himself by his light, Spirit, grace, and truth, and to bring them off all the world's teachers. God hath raised up Christ Jesus, his Prophet, whom people should hear; and saith, 'This is my beloved Son, hear ye Him;' and Christ saith, 'Learn of me, I am the way, the truth, and the life; and no man comes to the Father, but by me.' There is no salvation by any other name under the whole heaven than by the name of Jesus, who saith, 'I am the good Shepherd, and have laid down my life for my sheep; and my sheep hear my voice and follow me, and will not follow the hireling; for Christ feeds them in the pastures of life, that will never wither. God hath anointed Christ Jesus to preach, if you will hear him; and God hath given Christ for a Counsellor and a Leader, if you will be led and counselled by him; and God hath given Christ for a Bishop to oversee you, and a King to rule you, if you will be overseen and ruled by him. You that will not have Christ to rule over you, who never sinned, nor was guile found in his mouth, you may read his sentence in the New Testament upon such. Is not Christ a sufficient teacher, whose blood was shed for you, and who tasted death for every man? Doth not Christ say to his ministers, 'Freely ye have received, freely give?' . And the apostle saith, 'We covet no man's gold, silver, or apparel.' They laboured with their hands, and kept the gospel without charge. Have they that are called ministers amongst you done the same, and kept this command of Christ Jesus? Let them be examined and examine themselves. Have you not trimmed your outsides? but look within with the light and Spirit of Christ Jesus, and see if your insides be not black and foul. For Christ Jesus, who doth enlighten every man that cometh into the world, with the life in himself, saith, 'Believe in the light, that ye may become children of the light.' With the light ye may see all the evil and ungodly deeds that ye have committed; all your ungodly words you have spoken; and all your ungodly thoughts ye think; that ye may turn from them to Christ, from whom the light comes; who is your Saviour and Redeemer, who hath given you a light to see your sin, and that you are dead in Adam: that with the same light you may see Christ, the quickening Spirit, who makes you alive to God, and saves you from your sin. But if you hate the light, which is the life in Christ, the Prince of Life, and love the darkness and the prince of darkness more than the light or the life in Christ, because it will reprove you; Christ tells you, 'This light will be your condemnation,' John iii.

"Therefore be warned now in your day, and while you have time, turn to the Lord. Do not quench the Spirit of the Father, by which he draws to his Son; nor hate the light of Christ; for if you do, you hate the life in Christ, and so remain under condemnation from God and Christ with the light, who now speaks to his people by his Son, as he did in the apostles' days; the same God, that was the speaker by the prophets to the fathers, and speaker to Adam and Eve in Paradise; and happy had Adam and Eve, and the Jews, and all Christians been, if they had kept to this speaker, and not followed the serpent, that false speaker, and his instruments. And now God is the true speaker by his Son, who bruises the head of the serpent, the false teacher, who is the head of all false ways, false prophets, false churches, and false religions and worships. So God in Christ is bringing people to the pure and undefiled religion, that will keep them from the spots of the world, into the new and living way, Christ Jesus; and to the church in God, which Christ is the head of, as he was in the apostles' days; and to worship God in the Spirit and in truth, which worship Christ set up above sixteen hundred years since. Therefore must all people come to the grace and Spirit of truth in their own hearts, to know the God of truth, who is a Spirit; and in the Spirit and truth to worship, serve, honour, and glorify the living God, who is over all, and worthy of all, blessed for evermore. Amen.

"Ye magistrates and officers, read this in all your assemblies, and cause all your priests to read it in their churches; that they and you, and all people may hear and fear the God of heaven, as you will answer it at the great and terrible day of judgment, and vengeance of the Lord God Almighty. This is in love to your souls, and for your temporal and eternal good." G. F.

Amsterdam, the 19th of the 7th Month, 1677.

"*A Warning to the Magistrates, Priests, and People, of the City of Hamburg, to humble themselves before the Lord, and not be high-minded.*

"FRIENDS,

"You have painted and garnished the inside of your outward houses and high places; but look within your hearts with the light of Christ, which he hath enlightened you and every man that cometh into the world withal, and with it you may see how foul your hearts and insides are with sin and evil, which Christ tells you ye should make clean; who told the Pharisees how they 'painted the sepulchres of the righteous,' and they themselves were full of rottenness and corruption. Therefore look into yourselves, and your own hearts, what you are full of. To paint the sepulchres of the righteous apostles, and make a trade and a profession of their words, without the same Holy Ghost, and power, and light, and truth which they were in, will not stand the day of God's vengeance. Therefore repent while you have time, turn to the Lord with your whole hearts, and do not think yourselves secure, without his immediate, almighty protection. For not all your works, nor all your own strength, and power, and defence, can protect you; it is not for you to look at them, and think yourselves secure, to sit down in your security, and in it let your hearts be merry, and at rest and ease. But when the Lord brings a scourge upon you, that you are filled with terrors and fears, remember you were warned, that you were set down, but not in the true rest. Then all your own strength and force will stand you in no stead; and you will acknowledge that it must be God that must protect you. Therefore take warning; for your priests and people are too high, and are swallowed up too much in this world. The vanities of it carry your minds away from God, and your care is more for the world than for God, and more after the riches of this world, than after the riches of the world that has no end. Know you not, that all your heaps of outward treasure must have an end, and that you must leave them all behind you? Therefore I am to warn and advise you, both high and low, priests and people, to come to the grace, light, and truth, that comes by Jesus Christ; to the manifestation of the good Spirit of God, which is given to you to profit withal; that with this grace, and truth, light, and Spirit of Christ, you may turn to Christ Jesus, from whence it comes, who saith, 'Learn of me;' and God saith, 'This is my beloved Son, hear ye Him.' So all the children of the new covenant, that walk in the new and living way, hear Christ their Prophet, that God has raised up, and anointed to be their Teacher and Priest. So now, God doth speak to his people by his Son, as he did in the apostles' days. The Lord is come to teach his people himself by his grace, light, truth, and Spirit, and to bring them off all the world's teachers that are made by men since the apostles' days; who have kept people always learning, that they may be always paying them. He is come to bring them off all the world's religions, to the religion that he set up in the apostles' days, in the new covenant, which is pure and undefiled before God in his sight, and keeps from the spots of the world, &c. And the Lord is come to bring them off all the world's churches, to the church *in* God, which Christ the heavenly man is head of; and to bring them off all the world's worships, to worship God in Spirit and in truth, which Christ set up above sixteen hundred years since. So all men and women must come to the Spirit and truth in their hearts, by which they must know the God of truth, who is a Spirit; and then in the Spirit and in truth they will worship him, and know what and whom they worship. Also the Lord is come to bring his people off all the world's temples, that with the Spirit they may know their bodies to be the temples of the Holy Ghost. And the Lord is come to bring his people off all the world's crosses, pictures, images, and likenesses, to know that the power of God is the cross of Christ, which crucifies them to the world, and brings them up into the likeness and image of God, that man and woman were in before they fell; and so to Christ that never fell. This work must all know in their hearts, by the light of Christ Jesus, who 'is the true light, that lighteth every man that cometh into the world.' It is called the light in man and woman, and the life in Christ the Word: and Christ saith, 'Believe in the light, that ye may be the children of light.' And the light lets you see all your evil actions, that you have committed; your ungodly ways you have walked in; and your ungodly words and thoughts. If you hate this light, and love the darkness, and the prince of it, more than this light, which is the life in Christ, the Prince of Life, and will not come to it, because your deeds are evil, it will reprove you; Christ tells you, 'this light is your condemnation.' Then what is all your profession good for, when you remain under the condemnation of the true light, in which you should believe; and so become children of light, and out of condemnation? Therefore every one must believe in the light, if they receive Christ Jesus; and as many as receive him, he gives them 'power to become the sons of God.' He that hath the Son of God, hath life; and they that have not the Son of God, have not life: if then you have not life, what good doth all your profession of the Scriptures from Genesis to Revelations do you, any more than the Jews, Scribes, and Pharisees, that would not receive Christ the life, upon whom God brought his overflowing scourge. Therefore do you take heed, for your strength will be no better than theirs, if you have not God and Christ's supporting power, when God's scourge comes upon you, and you are filled with horrors and fears. My desires are, that you may all repent, even from the highest to the lowest, and not grieve, nor quench, nor vex, nor rebel against, God's good Spirit in you, nor 'walk despitefully against the Spirit of Grace,' which would teach you, and bring your salvation; nor turn from it unto wantonness. If you do, how can you escape the overflowing scourge of the Almighty, and the wrath of the Lamb? My desires are, that you may all obey God's good Spirit of truth, which will lead you out of all evil into all truth, and reprove you for your own righteousness, and for your own judgment and sin. It will bring you to cleave to that which is good, to forsake that which is evil, and to turn to the Lord, who will receive you in his mercy and kindness; by which means you may escape the overflowing scourge in the day of vengeance, which dreadful day is coming upon all evil-doers. This is a warning to you, both for your temporal and eternal good; to read in your assemblies, and your priests in their churches, that all people may hear and fear; as you will answer it at the terrible and dreadful day of judgment." G. F.

Amsterdam, the 19th of the 7th Month, 1677.

I wrote also an Epistle to the ambassadors that were treating about a peace at Nimeguen,* as follows:—

"*For the Ambassadors, that are met to treat for Peace at the City of Nimeguen, in the States' dominions.*

"Christ Jesus saith, 'Blessed are the peace-makers, for they shall be called the children of God,' Matt. v. 9, so all Christian men are to forsake evil, and do good, to seek peace and follow it, if they will 'love life, and see good days,' 1 Pet. iii. 11. God hath called all true Christians unto peace, 1 Cor. vii., and therefore all Christians ought to follow this peace, which God calls them to. They should let the peace of God rule in all their hearts; which is above the peace of this world, that is so soon broken. For the apostle commands the Christians to let the peace of God rule in their hearts, to which all Christians should be subject. The practice of this should be among all that profess Christianity; and this peace is above that, which Christ takes from the earth, Rev. vi., which is the peace of the wicked. And the apostle saith to the Christians, 'Be at peace among yourselves,' 1 Thess. v. Now all Christians should obey this command, and be at peace among themselves; not in wars and strife. And further, the apostle exhorts the Christians to 'keep the unity of the Spirit in the bond of peace.' So this unity, this bond of peace, should be kept (and not be broken) by all that bear that noble name, Christian. They should keep the unity of the Spirit of Christ in the bond of the Prince of princes, King

* These ambassadors were deputies from the King of France, the United Netherlands, and several other potentates of Europe, who met to consult the peace of Christendom. George Fox's *Epistle* to them was translated and printed in Latin. Robert Barclay also wrote a treatise in Latin, which was addressed and presented to each of the ambassadors, with a copy of his principal work, *An Apology for the True Christian Divinity*. In the former, Barclay strongly urged them to promote the good work for which they were assembled, pointing out the true causes of war, and its incompatibility with Christian principles. Before the year ended, a peace was concluded.

of kings, and Lord of lords' peace, which is the duty of all true Christians to keep. Herein they may honour Christ, in bringing forth the fruits of peace, which are love and charity. For the apostle tells you, 'The fruit of the good Spirit is love, joy, peace, long-suffering, gentleness, goodness,' &c. Gal. v.

"And the apostle exhorts the Christians, and saith, 'If it be possible, as much as lieth in you, live peaceably with all men:' this should be the endeavour of all Christians. For it is no honour to Christ, that Christians should war and destroy one another, that profess his name, who saith, 'He came to save men's lives, and not to destroy them.' Christians have enemies enough abroad without them, and therefore they should love one another, as Christ commands, who saith, 'By this ye shall be known to be my disciples, if ye love one another.' For Christians are commanded to love enemies; therefore much more, one another. And Christ saith, 'As the Father hath loved me, so I have loved you: continue ye in my love,' John xv. 8, and 'By this shall all men know that ye are my disciples, if ye love one another,' John xiii. 35. But if Christians war and destroy one another, this will make Jews, Turks, Tartars, and Heathens say, that you are not disciples of Christ. Therefore, as you love God, and Christ, and Christianity, and its peace, all make peace, as far as you have power, among Christians, that you may have the blessing. You read, that Christians were called the household of faith, the household of God, a holy nation, a peculiar people: and they are commanded to be 'zealous of good works,' not of bad: and Christians are also commanded not to bite and devour one another, lest they be consumed one of another.

"Is it not a sad thing for Christians to be biting and consuming one another in the sight of the Turks, Tartars, Jews, and Heathens, when they should 'love one another, and do unto all men, as they would have them do unto them?' Such devouring work as this, will open the mouths of Jews and Turks, Tartars and Heathens, to blaspheme the name of Christ, who is the King of kings, and Lord of lords, and cause them to speak evil of Christianity, for them to see how the unity of the Spirit is broken among such, as profess Christ and Christ's peace. Therefore all Christians are to mind God and Christ's teaching, who teacheth Christians to love one another, yea enemies; and persuade all kings and princes, to give liberty to all tender consciences in matters of religion and worship, they living peaceably under every government: so that for the time to come, there may be no more imprisonment and persecution among Christians, for tender consciences about matters of faith, worship, and religion, that the Jews, Turks, Tartars, and Heathens, may not see how Christians are persecuting one another for religion: seeing, from Christ and the apostles, Christians have no such command, but on the contrary, to love one another; and knowing, that Christ said to such as would have been plucking up tares, 'Let the tares and the wheat grow together till the harvest (which is the end of the world) lest they plucked up the wheat;' and at the end of the world Christ would send forth his angels, and they should sever the wheat from the tares. So Christ tells you, that it is the angels' work at the end of the world, and not men's work, before the harvest at the end of the world. Hath not all this persecution, banishing, and imprisoning, and putting to death, concerning religion, been the pretence of plucking up tares? and hath not all this been before the harvest, before the end of the world? And therefore, have not all these been actors against the express command of Christ, the King of Heaven? All kings and rulers, especially they that call themselves Christians, should obey their Lord and Saviour's command: 'Let the tares and the wheat grow together, till the harvest;' and the harvest is the end of the world. Christ also told some of his disciples, that in their zeal would have had fire to come down from heaven, to destroy such as would not receive him, 'That they did not know what spirit they were of:' and rebuked them, and said, 'He came not to destroy men's lives, but to save them.' And therefore all such as have destroyed men's lives concerning religion, and the worship of God, have they known what spirit they have been of? Have they not done that which they should not do? done that which Christ forbade, who saith, 'Lest ye should pluck up the wheat with the tares,' and saith, 'It is the angels' work at the end of the world?' And hath not God showed unto man what is good, and his duty, 'To love mercy, to do justly, and to walk humbly with his God?' which man is to mind.

"And the apostle exhorts Christians, 'To follow peace with all men, and holiness, without which no man shall see the Lord,' Heb. xii. 14. Why should Christians war and strive one with another, seeing they all own in words one King, Lord, and Saviour, Christ Jesus, whose command is, that they should 'love one another;' which is a mark that they shall be known by, to be Christ's disciples, as I said before. And Christ, who is the King of kings, and Lord of lords, saith, 'This is my commandment, that ye love one another, as I have loved you,' John xv. 12, and John xiii. And the apostle saith, Christians ought to 'be patient towards all men,' 1 Thess. v. 14.

"From him, who is a lover of truth, righteousness, and peace, who desires your temporal and eternal good; and that in the wisdom of God, that is from above, pure, gentle, and peaceable, you may be ordered, and order all things, that God hath committed to you, to his glory; and stop those things among Christians, so far as you have power, which dishonour God, Christ, and Christianity!" G. F.

Amsterdam, the 21st of the 7th Month, 1677.

To the magistrates and priests of Embden I wrote, showing them their unchristian practices in persecuting Friends.* And several other books I wrote, in answer to priests and others of Hamburg, Dantzic, and other places, to clear the truth and Friends from their charges and false slanders.

"*An Epistle concerning true Fasting, true Prayer, true Honour, and against Persecution, and for the true Liberty in Christ Jesus; that all may have a care, that the apostle hath not bestowed his labour in vain upon you in your*

* William Penn also addressed the Council and Senate of the city of Embden, relative to the sufferings of Friends there. Though these appeals did not procure any immediate relief, yet, in about ten years after, Friends enjoyed perfect liberty there. See Sewell's *History*, vol. ii., 420–425.

observing of Days, Months, Times, Feasts, and Years, and of coming under the beggarly elements and the yoke of bondage again, and of bringing and forcing people into them.

"WHERE did ever Christ or his apostles command any believers or Christians to observe holidays or feast-days? Let us see where it is written in the Scriptures of the New Testament, in the four Evangelists, or the Epistles, or the Revelation, that ever Christ or his apostles commanded Christians to observe the time called Christmas, or a day for Christ's birth? or to observe the time called Easter, or Whitsuntide, or Peter's or Paul's, Mark's, Luke's, or any other saint's day?

"You, that profess yourselves to be the reformed churches from the Papists, Jews, and Heathens, and the Scriptures to be your rule, and are professors of the new covenant, where do you prove out of the New Testament, that the apostles and the primitive church practised or forced any such thing, or that Christ and his apostles gave any such command to the churches that they should practise and observe any such days? Let us see where this command is written. Did not the apostle say unto the Galatians in the fourth chapter, 'But now, after that ye have known God, or rather ye are known of God, how turn ye again to the weak and beggarly elements, whereunto ye desire again to be in bondage? Ye observe days, and months, and times, and years; I am afraid of you, lest I have bestowed upon you labour in vain.' And in the third of Galatians it is said, 'O foolish Galatians, who hath bewitched you, that you should not obey the truth,' &c. And in Galatians the fifth, the apostle exhorts them to 'stand fast in the liberty wherewith Christ had made them free;' and moreover said, 'Be not entangled again with the yoke of bondage.'

"Now doth not this manifest, that there were some teachers, that were drawing the church of the Galatians into these beggarly elements, and bringing them again into bondage, in observing days, months, times, and years? It was the apostle's work to bring them out of those bondages and beggarly elements; and therefore, when they were going back again into observing days, months, times, and years, he was afraid that he had 'bestowed his labour upon them in vain;' and he exhorts them to 'stand fast in the liberty wherewith Christ Jesus hath made them free, and not to be entangled again with the yoke of bondage,' and again signifies, that 'they had been once entangled with that yoke of bondage and beggarly elements.' But O! how are people, called Christians, since the apostles' days, gone again under this yoke of bondage, and these beggarly elements, in observing days, months, times, and years, let their practice declare. Nay, do not both Papists and Protestants force people to observe days, months, and times? And therefore is not the apostle's labour and travail bestowed upon Christendom in vain, which was to bring people from under such beggarly elements, and that yoke of bondage (which the law did require), to 'stand fast in the liberty wherewith Christ hath made them free, and not to be entangled again with the yoke of bondage?' It was and is Christ, that hath made and doth make his people free from these beggarly elements; therefore, they that are redeemed, are to 'stand fast in that liberty wherewith Christ hath made them free.' This liberty all true

Christians are to stand fast in; they are made free by Christ and not by man; for man, without the Spirit and mind of Christ, seeks to force and compel Christ's followers, such as are made free from the yoke of bondage, to outward things that the law commanded, to the observing of days, months, times, feasts, and years. From such weak, beggarly elements, they that know God, or are known of God and Christ, are to stand fast in their liberty, and not come under, nor be entangled with the yoke of bondage to such things again, seeing he hath made them free. For they that are in such things, and would force others to them, are gone from that which gives the knowledge of God, and have not stood fast in the liberty wherewith Christ makes free.

"Concerning Prayer, we do not read that ever Christ or his apostles did seek by force to compel any to fast or pray with them. But Christ taught them how they should pray, and be distinct from the hypocrites. His words are as follows:—'When thou prayest, thou shalt not be as the hypocrites are; for they love to pray standing in the synagogues, and in the corners of the streets, that they may be seen of men,' &c. 'But thou, when thou prayest, enter into thy closet, and when thou hast shut thy door, pray to thy Father, which is in secret, and thy Father which seeth in secret, shall reward thee openly. But when ye pray, use not vain repetitions, as the heathen do; for they think they shall be heard for their much speaking. Be not ye therefore like unto them; for your Father knoweth what things ye have need of, before ye ask him,' &c. As the apostles and saints did, so do we; we pray in secret, and we pray in public, as the Spirit gives us utterance, which helps our infirmities, as it did the apostles and true Christians; after this manner we pray for ourselves, and for all men both high and low.

"Concerning Fasting, Christ saith, 'Moreover when ye fast, be not as the hypocrites, of a sad countenance; for they disfigure their faces, that they may appear unto men to fast. But when thou fastest, anoint thy head and wash thy face, that thou appear not unto men to fast, but unto thy Father which is in secret; and thy Father, which seeth in secret, shall reward thee openly.'

"You may see in Isaiah the lviiith, what the true fast is which the Lord requires; where it is said to the prophet, 'Cry aloud, and spare not, lift up thy voice like a trumpet, and show my people their transgression, and the house of Jacob their sins; yet they seek me daily, and delight to know my ways as a nation that did righteousness, and forsook not the ordinance of their God; they ask of me the ordinances of justice; they take delight in approaching to God. Wherefore have we fasted, say they, and thou seest not? wherefore have we afflicted our soul, and thou takest no knowledge? Behold, in the day of your fast ye find pleasure, and exact all your labours. Behold, ye fast for strife and debate, and to smite with the fist of wickedness, ye shall not fast, as ye do this day, to make your voice to be heard on high. Is it such a fast that I have chosen? A day for a man to afflict his soul? Is it to bow down his head as a bulrush, and to spread sackcloth and ashes under him? Wilt thou call this a fast, and an acceptable day to the Lord? Is not this the fast that I have chosen, saith the Lord; to loose the bands of wickedness, to undo the heavy burthens, and to let the oppressed go free, and that ye break every yoke?' So this fast that the Lord requires, is not to lay yokes, to oppress, and lay heavy burthens, and to make fast the bands of wickedness; but to loose and to break such things.

"And further, concerning the true fast the Lord requires, 'Is it not to deal thy bread to the hungry, and that thou bring the poor, that are cast out, to thy house? When thou seest the naked, that thou cover him, and that thou hide not thyself from thy own flesh? (Do you keep this true fast?) Then shall thy light break forth as the morning, and thine health shall spring forth speedily; and thy righteousness shall go before thee, the glory of the Lord shall be thy rere-ward. Then shalt thou call, and the Lord shall answer; thou shalt cry, and he shall say, Here I am; if thou take away from the midst of thee the yokes, the putting forth of the finger and speaking vanity; and if thou draw out thy soul to the hungry, and satisfy the afflicted soul, then shall thy light arise out of obscurity, and thy darkness be as the noon-day. And the Lord shall guide thee continually, and satisfy thy soul in drought, and make fat thy bones; and thou shalt be like a watered garden, and like a spring of water, whose waters fail not,' &c.

"Now here is the practice of the true fast the Lord requires of his people; and to them that observe this fast, the Lord saith, 'When they call, he will answer.' You may see what glorious and happy comforts they receive from the Lord, that keep this true fast; but such as fast for strife and debate, smite with the fists of wickedness, and make their voices to be heard on high; who afflict their souls for a day, bow down their head as a bulrush, and loose not the bands of wickedness; who do not undo every heavy burthen, break not off every yoke, nor let the oppressed go free; who do not deal their bread to the hungry, clothe not the naked, nor bring the poor to their house, but hide themselves from their own flesh:—such fasts and fasters the Lord doth not accept, neither hath he chosen them. But these appear to men with their disfigured faces, and hang down their heads as a bulrush for a day, like the hypocrites, to fast, as Christ speaks in Matt. vi.

"And is it not the command of Christ, that in their fast they should not appear unto men to fast? And now you that would force us to shut up our shops on fasting-days, or for a day, does not this fast appear to men? and is not this the fast that the Lord saith in Isaiah, he 'doth not accept?' for he saith, 'Is this the fast that I have chosen, a day for a man to afflict his soul, and bow down his head as a bulrush,' &c. 'Wilt thou call this a fast, and an acceptable day to the Lord?' Isa. lviii.

"Therefore all God's people are to keep the true fast of the Lord from debate and strife, and the fists of wickedness; that fast that breaks the bands of wickedness, and undoes every heavy burthen; breaks every yoke, and lets the oppressed go free; deals bread to the hungry, clothes the naked, and brings the poor that are cast out to his own house. Every one that keeps this true fast, their health shall grow, and when they call, the Lord will hear them; he will be their guide continually, satisfy their souls in drought, and make their bones fat; and they shall be like a watered garden, and like a spring of water, whose waters fail not. Now you, that keep not this true fast, when you call upon the Lord on your own fasting-days, does the Lord answer you, and say, 'Here I am?' Doth the Lord guide you continually? Are your bones made fat by him, and your souls satisfied in drought? Are you like a watered garden, and like a spring, whose waters fail not? But you that keep not this true fast, do you not want these waters, which fail not? so your souls are not satisfied in drought, but your bones are lean, and you hear not the voice of the Lord, who saith, 'Here I am;' so you lose the heritage of Jacob, and ride not upon the high places there; but come under. Therefore every man and woman, shut your hearts against all manner of evil whatsoever, and trade not with Babylon's merchants of confusion; but keep the supernatural day of Christ that is sprung from on high, that is kept by believing and walking in the light of Christ, and being grafted into him. This will bring you to the true fast, from feeding upon any evil, and to the true praying in the Spirit, as Christ and the apostles have taught. The fruit of the Spirit is love, &c. The birth of the Spirit is not a persecuting birth; but he that is born of the flesh, will persecute him that is born of the Spirit, because he will not follow the birth of the flesh, with its weak, beggarly elements, that entangles with its yoke of bondage, and its observing of days, months, times, fasts, feasts, and years; which the birth of the Spirit is to stand fast against in the liberty wherewith Christ hath made it free.

"Do you not know, that the Turks keep their Sabbath on the sixth day, the Jews upon the seventh day, and the Christians meet together on the First-day of the week? And that day which the Turks keep, the Jews' and Christians' shops are open; and that day the Jews keep, Christians' and Turks' shops are open; and the First-days that the Christians keep, both Jews' and Turks' shops are open? The Turk does not force the Jews nor the Christians to shut up their shops on their meeting-days, but lets them have their liberty in Turkey. And where do you read, that ever the Turks forced any Christians to observe any of their holidays, fasts, or feasts? If not, should not Christians be beyond the Turks in giving liberty to all tender consciences to serve God, seeing Christ and the apostles command not, nor force people to observe holidays, or times, or months, or years, but that they should pray always in the Spirit, and fast always from strife and debate, from all manner of sin and evil; and that will keep down the fist of wickedness, and the bond of iniquity, &c. Why should not people of a tender conscience have their liberty to exercise their consciences towards God, that they may have 'a good conscience always towards God and man,' to perform that which God requires, and to 'do unto all men, as they would have them to do unto them, and to love their neighbours as themselves;' seeing so many debauched, evil, and seared consciences, as with a hot iron, have liberty in their loose lives and conversations, and in their loose words, whose tongues are at liberty to swear and curse, and their spirits at liberty in drunkenness and uncleanness? Let the magistrates look and see, how this evil, seared conscience hath its liberty to be exercised in all manner of evil things all Christendom over;

which is a great shame and dishonour to God, and Christ, and Christianity, yea, and humanity. Therefore why should not God's people have their liberty to exercise their good and tender consciences towards God and man? For the mystery of faith, which Jesus Christ is the author and finisher of, is held in a pure conscience; and should not the work of the true Christian magistrate be to encourage the exercise of this pure conscience towards God and man, and to discourage the exercise of this evil, seared conscience, that dishonours both God and Christ, and true Christianity? If not, how are they a praise to them that do well, and a terror to evil-doers?

"Concerning the not putting off our hats to men. Many that go under the name of Christians, have taken offence at us, because we could not put off our hats, and bow down to them; for which we find no command from Christ or his apostles, but rather to the contrary. For Christ saith, 'I receive not honour of men' (mark, he did not receive honour of men); and further Christ saith, 'How can ye believe which receive honour one of another, and seek not the honour that comes from God only?' Now Christ declares it to be a mark of unbelievers, that seek 'honour one of another,' and seek not that 'honour that comes from God only;' and is not the putting off the hat, and bowing with it, an honour to men, which they seek one of another, and are offended if they have it not? Nay, have they not fined, persecuted, and imprisoned some, because they did not put off their hats to them? Nay, do not the very Turks mock at the Christians in their proverb, saying that 'the Christians spend much of their time in putting off their hats, and showing their bare head to one another?' But should not those be beyond the Turks, that bear the noble name of Christian, above seeking honour one of another, and persecuting them that will not give it, when all true believing Christians should seek the honour that comes from God only? which is the duty of all true believers in Christ Jesus, for he would not receive honour of men. And 'He that believeth on the Son of God, hath everlasting life; and he that believeth not the Son, shall not see life; but the wrath of God abideth on him,' John iii. 36. Is not the Turks' proverb a reproach to the Christians, who say 'that the Christians spend much of their time in putting off their hats, and showing their bare heads one to another?' Have you not fined and imprisoned many, because they would not put off their hats to you, and show you their bare heads? Nay, in many of your courts they shall not have right and justice, nor liberty and freedom in cities or states, though they have truly served their time, and are honest and civil men, unless they will put off their hats and show their bare heads? Have you not made a law against such, that they must forfeit two guilders if they do not? Do you not seek to compel and force them to do it, and fine such as do not, as at Lansmeer in Waterland? Is not this the honour that you seek one of another? Did not the Pharisees and Jews do the same?

"As for your saying, 'the apostle commands to honour all men; and such as rule well are worthy of double honour.' If this 'honouring all men,' were to put off their hats to all men, and show all men their bare heads, then this command you break yourselves; for you do not this to all men generally; and if they that rule well must have double hat-honour, then they must put off their hats twice; and show them their bare heads. If this hat-honour, and showing the bare head, be an invention of men, and not from God, and ye cannot prove it by Scripture, yet say, 'it is your rule;' then you act beside the rule, and compel people to act contrary to your rule. For where did ever the prophets, Christ, or the apostles command any such thing? Let us see a command, a practice, and an example for it. Nebuchadnezzar, who was a persecutor, and cast the three children of Israel into the fire with their hose, cloaks, and hats, we do not read that he was offended at them, because they did not put off their hats, and show him their bare heads; but because they would not bow to his image. And is it not said in the margin of the Bible, where it is said, 'honour all men,' 'have all men in esteem?' Then they that rule well are worthy of double esteem; and this esteem must be truly in the heart, without any envy, malice, or hatred. As all men are the workmanship of God, they are to be esteemed in the heart with the Spirit of God; and they that rule well, are worthy of double esteem; here is true honour from the heart, both to God, and man, his workmanship. For people may put off their hats, and show their bare heads one to another once or twice to the officers and magistrates, and yet be full of envy, and malice, and hatred, and murder in their hearts one against another; and give them that honour, as you call it, and yet speak or wish bad things to them, when they have turned their backs on them. The true honour or esteem in the heart to all men, as they are God's creation, is without any evil wish or thought in the heart to any men, and especially to them that rule well, who have the double esteem, whom God hath placed over people. There is no evil in the heart that gives this respect, esteem, or honour, and brings them to love their neighbours as themselves, and to 'do unto all men, as they would have them do unto them;' in that they esteem all men, and have a double esteem for them that rule well. This is beyond all the honour of putting off the hats once to all men, and twice to them that are worthy of the double honour, as you may call it. But we would ask Christians that practise this hat-honour, and show one another their bare heads, Who invented this single honour and double honour, seeing they cannot prove, that ever Christ or the apostles did command or practise any such thing, or Moses in the time of the law? Now, do not say or think, that we had this practice of not putting off our hats from the Turk; for we were moved by the Spirit of the Lord, before ever we heard of the Turks' proverb and practice, to leave the honour that is below, and seek the honour that comes from above, when we came to be true believers in Christ Jesus.

"Now concerning persecuting, imprisoning, and banishing God's people, in whom Christ is manifest, and dwells in their hearts; doth not Christ tell you, that in so doing you imprison him? Then do you not banish him, and persecute him out of your cities and corporations? And how can you enter into, and have a share in his kingdom, though you may profess him in words? Are not such to go into everlasting punishment, that do not visit Christ in prison? Then what will become of you that banish and imprison him, where he is manifest in his members, and suffer them not to meet together to enjoy him amongst them, according to his promise? Therefore you, that will not let Christ reign in his people, and have his liberty in them, in your cities and countries, to exercise his offices, you will not have your liberty in heaven. You that will not let Christ reign in your hearts, nor suffer him to reign in his people here upon the earth, in this world, in your kingdoms;—you will not reign with Christ in heaven in his kingdom, nor in the world without end.

"You, that banish the truth out of your cities or countries, or his people for its sake, banish the truth and Christ out of your hearts from ruling there; so you yourselves are not the temples of God. When you have banished Christ and his truth out of your own hearts, you banish such in whom he rules out of your estates and country: then see what judgments the Lord doth bring upon you, when you are left to yourselves; yea, fears and troubles, one judgment after another, come upon you; you are even filled with them. But the banished, the sufferers for truth and Christ's sake, have a peaceable habitation in the truth, which the devil is out of, and cannot get into; which habitation will outlast all the habitations of the wicked and persecutors, though they be ever so full of words without life and truth. The life and the truth will outlast all airy notions, and Christ, the Lamb and patient Seed, will overcome the devourer and the unpatient seed; and they that have the garment, the righteousness of Christ, which is the fine linen, will find it to outlast all the rags and inventions of men. For Christ saith to his learners, 'Be of good cheer, I have overcome the world,' the persecuting world. He said also to his disciples, 'If the world hate you, ye know that it hated me before it hated you.' Therefore let all that profess themselves Christians lay aside persecution about religion, churches, or worship, fasting or praying days; for you have no command from Christ and his apostles to persecute any. Christ, who is the King of kings and Lord of lords, when they called him a deceiver, and blasphemed him, and said, 'He had a devil,' did not persecute any of them for it, nor force or compel any to hear and believe him, nor the apostles after him; but he bade them, that would have been plucking up the tares, 'Let the tares and wheat grow together until the harvest.' So you have no command from Christ or his apostles to persecute, imprison, banish, or spoil the goods of any, for matter of pure conscience and religion, worship, faith, and church, in the gospel-times." G. F.

Harlingen in Friesland, the 11th of the 6th Month, 1677.

After some time George Keith and William Penn came back from Germany to Amsterdam, and had a dispute with one Galenus Abrahams (one of the most noted Baptists in Holland), at which many professors were present; but not having time to finish the dispute then, they met again two days after, and the Baptist was much confounded, and truth gained ground.* Between these two disputes we had a very great meeting at

* It appears that Galenus Abrahams asserted that nobody in the present day could be accepted as a messenger of God, unless he confirmed his doctrine by miracles. See Sewell's *History*, vol. ii., 366–368.

Friends' meeting-place, at which many hundreds of people were, and some of high rank in the world's account. An earl, a lord, and divers other eminent persons, were present, who all behaved themselves very civilly. But when the meeting was ended, some priests began to make opposition; which, when William Penn understood, he stood up again, and answered them to the great satisfaction of the people, who were much affected with the several testimonies they had heard declared. After the meeting several of them came to Gertrude's, where we were, with whom George Keith had much discourse in Latin.

Having now finished our service at Amsterdam, we took leave of the Friends there, and passed by waggon to LEYDEN, about twenty-five miles; where we stayed a day or two, seeking out and visiting some tender people we heard of there. We met with a German, who was partly convinced. He informed us of an eminent man that was inquiring after truth. Some sought him out, and visited him, and found him a serious man; I also spoke to him, and he owned the truth. William Penn and Benjamin Furly went to visit another great man, that lived a little out of Leyden, who, they said, had been general to the King of Denmark's forces. He and his wife were very loving to them, and heard the truth with joy.

From Leyden we went to the HAGUE, where the Prince of Orange kept his court; and we visited one of the judges of Holland, with whom we had pretty much discourse. He was a wise, tender man, and put many objections and queries to us; which, when we had answered, he was satisfied, and parted with us in much love. Leaving the Hague, we went to DELFT, and thence to ROTTERDAM that night, where we stayed some days, and had several meetings. While I was here I gave forth a book for the Jews; with whom, when I was at Amsterdam, I had a desire to have some discourse, but they would not. Here also I reviewed several other books and papers which I had given forth before, and which were now transcribed.

CHAPTER IX.

1677–1680.—George Fox, with other Friends, sails for England, and lands at Harwich, after a hazardous voyage of three days—has a large meeting at Colchester, and proceeds thence to London—writes to his wife—receives further accounts of persecution in New England—travels into Buckinghamshire, and meets with some false brethren, who are unruly and troublesome at meetings—Friends have a special meeting with them afterwards—at Reading meets with opposition to the settlement of a women's meeting—visits Bristol during the fair, where are many Friends from various parts—the separatists there are very rude and abusive—he aids Friends in drawing up a breviat of their sufferings, to present to the judges at Gloucester assizes—meets with some separatists at Finchcomb—is engaged with other Friends in soliciting Parliament to grant them relief from the statutes made against Popish recusants—attends the Yearly Meeting, which was a glorious and heavenly one—Friends greatly united in testifying against the spirit of separation—not one mouth opened on its behalf—the Truth prospers at home and abroad—George Fox writes to his wife—writes to the king of Poland to dissuade him from persecution—to Friends in Amsterdam—Friends again press their suit for relief from the statutes made against Popish recusants without success—are much exercised with the spirit of separation, which opposes the order and discipline of the church—George Fox writes a paper to open the understandings of the weak, and as a reproof to a censorious judging spirit—has conferences with some of the opposers at Hertford—writes again to Friends to warn them of this spirit of false liberty—visits Friends in prison at Leicester—advises Friends how to end their differences—writes an epistle to Friends in London—writes to Friends in prison to console them under suffering—writes an epistle to the Yearly Meeting—an encouragement to Friends to be valiant for the Truth—also a caution to Friends to keep in humility—travels again towards the South—visits prisoners in York Castle—recommends Friends to lay their sufferings before the judge at the assizes—attends the Yearly Meeting in London—writes to the Great Turk and to the Dey of Algiers—to the latter particularly respecting Friends who are captives there—at Hertford meets with John Story (the schismatic) and some of his party, but the Truth prevails—has a meeting with some of the opposers—solicits the Parliament to grant relief to Friends under suffering—writes a paper against plots and plotters.

FINDING our spirits clear of the service which the Lord had given us to do in Holland, we took leave of Friends of Rotterdam, and passed by boat to the BRIEL, in order to take passage that day for England; several Friends of Rotterdam accompanying us, and some of Amsterdam, who were come to see us again before we left Holland. But the packet not coming in till night, we lodged that night at the Briel; and next day, being the 21st of the 8th month, and the First-day of the week, we went on board, and set sail about ten, viz., William Penn, George Keith, and I, and Gertrude Dirick Nieson, with her children.

We were in all about sixty passengers, and had a long and hazardous passage; for the winds were contrary, and the weather stormy; the boat also was very leaky, insomuch that we had to have two pumps continually going, day and night; so that, it was thought, there was quite as much water pumped out as the vessel would have held. But the Lord, who is able to make the stormy winds to cease, and the raging waves of the sea calm, yea, to raise them and stop them at his pleasure, He alone did preserve us: praised be his name for ever! Though our passage was hard, yet we had a fine time, and good service for truth on board among the passengers, some of whom were great folks, and were very kind and loving. We arrived at HARWICH on the 23d, at night, having been two nights and almost three days at sea. Next morning William Penn and George Keith took horse for Colchester; but I stayed, and had a meeting at Harwich; and there being no Colchester coach there, and the post-master's wife being unreasonable in her demands for a coach, and deceiving us of it also after we had hired it, we went to a Friend's house about a mile and a half in the country, and hired his waggon, which we bedded well with straw, and rode in it to Colchester.

I stayed there till First-day, having a desire to be at Friends' meeting that day; and a very large and weighty one it was; for Friends, hearing of my return from Holland, flocked from several parts of the country, and many of the town's-people coming in also, it was thought there were about a thousand people at it; and all was peaceable. Having stayed a day or two longer at Colchester, I travelled through ESSEX, visiting Friends at HALSTEAD, BRAINTREE, FELSTEAD, and SALING, and having meetings with them. At CHELMSFORD I had a meeting in the evening; and there being many Friends prisoners, they got liberty and came to the meeting; and we were all refreshed together in the Lord. Next day, the 9th of the 9th month, I got to LONDON, where Friends received me with great joy; and on the First-day following went to Gracechurch Street meeting, where the Lord visited us with his refreshing presence, and the glory of the Lord surrounded the meeting: praised be the Lord.

After I had been a little while in London, I wrote the following letter to my wife:—

"DEAR HEART,

"To whom is my love, and to the children, and to all the rest of Friends, in the Lord's truth, power, and Seed, that is over all; glory to the Lord, and blessed be his name for ever beyond all words! who hath carried me through and over many trials and dangers, in his eternal power! I have been twice at Gracechurch Street meeting; and though the opposite spirits were there, yet all was quiet; the dew of heaven fell upon the people, and the glory of the Lord shone over all. Every day I am fain to be at meetings about business, and sufferings, which are great abroad; and now many Friends are concerned with many persons about them: so in haste, with my love to you all—" G. F.

London, the 24th of the 9th Month, 1677.

About this time I received letters from New England, which gave account of the magistrates' and rulers' cruel and unchristian-like proceedings against Friends there, whipping and abusing them very shamefully; for they whipped many women Friends. One woman they tied to a cart, and dragged her along the street, stripped above the waist. They whipped some masters of ships that were not Friends, only for bringing Friends thither. And at that very time, while they were persecuting Friends in this barbarous manner, the Indians slew threescore of their men, took one of their captains, and flayed the skin off his head while he was alive, and carried it away in triumph; so that the sober people said "the judgments of God came upon them for persecuting the Quakers;" but the blind dark priests said, "it was because they did not persecute them enough."* Great exercise I had in seeking relief here for our poor suffering Friends there, that they might not lie under the rod of the wicked.

Upon this and other services for truth, I stayed in London a month or five weeks, visiting meetings, and helping and encouraging Friends to labour for the deliverance of their suffering brethren in other parts. Afterwards I went down to KINGSTON, and visited Friends there and thereaway. Having stayed a little among Friends there, looking over a book I had then ready to go to press, I went into Buckinghamshire, visiting Friends, and having several meetings amongst them, as at AMERSHAM, HUNGER-HILL, JORDANS, HEDGERLY, WICKHAM, and TURVILLE-HEATH. In some of which, they that were gone out from the unity of Friends in truth into strife, opposition, and division, were very unruly and troublesome; particularly at the men's meeting at Thomas Ellwood's at HUNGER-HILL, where the chief of them came from Wickham, endeavouring to make disturbance, and to hinder Friends from proceeding in the business of the meeting. When I saw their design I admonished them to be sober and quiet, and not trouble the meeting by interrupting its service; but rather, if they were dissatisfied with Friends' proceedings, and had anything to object, let a meeting be appointed on purpose some other day. So Friends offered them to give them a meeting another day: and at length it was agreed to be at Thomas Ellwood's† the week following. Accordingly Friends met them there, and the meeting was in the barn; for there came so many, that the house could not receive them. After we had sat a while they began their jangling. Most of their arrows were shot at me; but the Lord was with me, and gave me strength in his power to cast back their darts of envy and falsehood upon themselves. Their objections were answered, and things were

* For full particulars of the great intolerance and spirit of persecution manifested by the Puritans of New England towards the Quakers, the reader is referred to Bowden's *History of Friends in America*, vol. v., from the commencement to p. 308.

† Thomas Ellwood is only mentioned twice incidentally in these volumes. It was he who, after the death of George Fox, transcribed this excellent work for the press. (See *Letters, &c., of Early Friends*, p. 213.) He was also the author of several works, including *A Life of David*, in verse; a work on tithes; a *Sacred History*, &c. Ellwood was born in 1639, at Crowell, in Oxfordshire, and joined Friends when about twenty years of age. Brought up in ease, luxury, and fashion, he had much to learn; much to unlearn, much to forsake, of the manners, the pride, and the will-worship of the world; and to follow after that plainness and purity of life unto which the spirit of truth leads. Nothing but religion could have enabled one, with a disposition naturally so high and resolute as his, to submit, as he did, to buffetings, beatings, cruel treatment, and persecution, with becoming meekness and patience.

In 1662, Ellwood became the companion of the poet Milton, and it was he who suggested to the latter the writing of *Paradise Regained*. He had a peculiar gift for government in the church, and was very serviceable therein; an ornament to the meeting he belonged to, and much missed when he died. According to his bio-

opened to the people; a good opportunity it was, and serviceable to the truth; for many that before were weak, were now strengthened and confirmed; some that were doubting and wavering, were satisfied and settled; and faithful Friends were refreshed and comforted in the springings of life amongst us. For the power arose, and life sprung, and in the arisings thereof many living testimonies were borne against that wicked, dividing, rending spirit, which those opposers were joined to, and acted by; and the meeting ended to the satisfaction of Friends. That night I lodged with other Friends, at Thomas Ellwood's; and the same week had a meeting again with the opposers at WICKHAM, where they again showed their envy, and were made manifest to the upright-hearted.

After I had visited Friends in that upper side of Buckinghamshire, I called upon Friends at HENLEY in OXFORDSHIRE, and afterwards went by CORSHAM to READING, where I was at meeting on First-day, and in the evening had a large meeting with Friends. Next day there being another meeting about settling a women's meeting, some of them that had let in the spirit of division, fell into jangling, and were disorderly for a while, till the weight of truth brought them down. After this I passed on, visiting Friends, and having meetings in several places, through BERKSHIRE and WILTSHIRE, till I came to BRISTOL, which was on the 24th of the 11th Month, just before the fair.

I stayed at Bristol all the time of the fair, and some time after. Many sweet and precious meetings we had; many Friends being there from several parts of the nation, some on account of trade, and some in the service of truth. Great was the love and unity of Friends that abode faithful in the truth, though some who were gone out of the holy unity, and were run into strife, division, and enmity, were rude and abusive, and behaved themselves in a very unchristian manner towards me. But the Lord's power was over all; by which being preserved in heavenly patience, which can bear injuries for his name's sake, I felt dominion therein over the rough, rude, and unruly spirits; and left them to the Lord, who knew my innocency, and would plead my cause. The more these laboured to reproach and vilify me, the more did the love of Friends, that were sincere and upright-hearted, abound towards me; and some that had been betrayed by the adversaries, seeing their envy and rude behaviour, broke off from them; who have cause to bless the Lord for their deliverance.

When I left Bristol, I went with Richard Snead to his house in the country, and thence to Hezekiah Coale's at WINTERBOURNE, in GLOUCESTERSHIRE, whither came several Friends that were under great sufferings for truth's sake, whom I had invited to meet me there. Stephen Smith,*

grapher, he was "a man of a comely aspect, of a free and generous disposition, of a courteous and affable temper, and pleasant conversation; a gentleman born and bred; a scholar, a true Christian, an eminent author, a good neighbour, a kind friend." He proved a very useful and acceptable elder in the church, devoting nearly the whole of his time and talents to its service. He died in 1713, and was buried at Jordans, leaving behind him a most interesting autobiography, to which the reader is referred for further particulars.

* This being the last mention of Stephen Smith, it may be added, that he was born in 1623, and being convinced in 1665, suffered both in person and estate by

Richard Snead, and I, drew up a breviat of their sufferings, setting forth the illegal proceedings against them, which was delivered to the judges at the assizes at Gloucester; and they promised to put a stop to those illegal proceedings. Next day we passed to SUDBURY, and had a large meeting in the meeting-house there, which at that time was of very good service. We went next day to Nathaniel Crips's at TEDBURY, and thence passed on to NAILSWORTH; where on First-day we had a brave meeting, and large. Thence we went to the quarterly meeting at FINCHCOMB, where were several of the opposite spirit, who, it was thought, intended to make some disturbance amongst Friends; but the Lord's power was over, and kept them down, and good service for the Lord we had at that meeting. We returned from Finchcomb to NAILSWORTH, and had another very precious meeting there, to which Friends came from the several meetings thereabouts; which made it very large also.

We went from Nailsworth the 1st of the 1st Month, 1678, and travelled through the country visiting Friends and having many meetings at CIRENCESTER, CROWN-ALLINS, CHELTENHAM, STOKE-ORCHARD, TEWKESBURY, &c., so went to WORCESTER, where I had formerly suffered imprisonment above a year for truth's sake; and Friends rejoiced greatly to see me there again. Here I stayed several days, and had many very precious meetings in the city, and much service amongst Friends. After which, I had meetings at PERSHORE and EVESHAM; and then struck to RAGLEY in WARWICKSHIRE, to visit the Lady Conway,* who I understood was very desirous to see me, and whom I found tender and loving, and willing to detain me longer than I had freedom to stay. About two miles hence I had two meetings at a Friend's house, whose name was John Stanley, whither William Dewsbury came, and stayed with me about half a day. Afterwards I visited Friends in their meetings, at STRATFORD, LAMCOAT, and ARMSCOTT (whence I was sent prisoner to Worcester in 1673), and thence passed into OXFORDSHIRE, visiting Friends, and having meetings at SIBFORD, NORTH-

imprisonment and spoiling of goods, for his testimony on behalf of Christ. He was a man of account in the world, who, in his younger years, travelled much abroad, having resided some time at Scanderoon, in Syria, as a merchant, and afterwards published a work called, *Wholesome Advice and Information,* wherein he shows how much some of the Turks exceeded some Christians in their dealings.

He was an honest upright man, one that feared God and was of good report, being a preacher of righteousness in his daily conduct, ever ready to do good. He became a valiant gospel minister, and spoke to the comfort and encouragement of those that heard him, travelling in many parts of England in gospel service. He died in peace at his own house, near Guildford, in Surrey, in 1678. He wrote many serviceable works, which were collected and published in an 8vo volume, entitled, *The True Light Discovered to all who Desire to Walk in the Day.*

* Lady Conway was a person of great piety, and a favourer of Friends. In a letter to the learned and excellent Dr. Henry More, who was her particular friend, she thus expresses herself concerning them:—

"Your conversation with them (the Friends) at London might be, as you express it, charitably intended, like that of a physician frequenting his patients for the increase or confirmation of their health; but *I* must confess, that *my* converse with them is, to receive health and refreshment from them."—See Appendix to Barclay's second edition of *Isaac Pennington's Letters,* p. 311.

NEWTON, BANBURY, ADDERBURY, &c. Then visiting Friends through BUCKINGHAMSHIRE, at LONG-CRENDON, ILMERE, MENDLE, WESTON, CHOLSBERRY, CHESHAM, &c., I came to Isaac Pennington's, where I stayed a few days; and then turning into HERTFORDSHIRE, visited Friends at CHARLEWOOD, WATFORD, HEMPSTEAD, and MARKET-STREET, at which places I had meetings with Friends. From Market-Street I went in the morning to LUTON in BEDFORDSHIRE, to see John Crook, with whom I spent good part of the day, and went towards evening to ALBAN'S, where I lay that night at an inn. And visiting Friends at SOUTH-MIMS, BARNET, and HENDON, where I had meetings, I came to LONDON the 8th of the 3rd Month. It being the fourth day of the week, I went to Gracechurch-Street meeting, which was peaceable and well; and many Friends, not knowing I was come to town, were very joyful to see me there; and the Lord was present with us, refreshing us with his living virtue; blessed be his holy name!

The parliament was sitting when I came to town, and Friends having laid their sufferings before them, were waiting on them for relief against the laws made against Popish recusants, which they knew we were not; though some malicious magistrates took advantages to prosecute us in several parts of the nation upon those statutes. Friends attending on that service when I came, I joined them therein; and there was some probability that something might be obtained towards Friends' ease and relief in that case, many of the parliament-men being tender and loving towards us, believing we were much misrepresented by our adversaries. But when I went down one morning with George Whitehead to the parliament house, to attend upon them on Friends' behalf, suddenly they were prorogued, though but for a short time.

About two weeks after I came to London, the Yearly Meeting began, to which Friends came up out of most parts of the nation, and a glorious heavenly meeting we had. O the glory, majesty, love, life, wisdom, and unity, that were amongst us! The power reigned over all, and many testimonies were borne therein against that ungodly spirit, which sought to make rents and divisions amongst the Lord's people; but not one mouth was opened amongst us in its defence, or on its behalf. Good and comfortable accounts also we had, for the most part, from Friends in other countries; of which I find a brief account in a letter, which soon after I wrote to my wife, the copy whereof here follows;—

"DEAR HEART,

"To whom is my love in the everlasting Seed of life that reigns over all. Great meetings here have been, and the Lord's power hath been stirring through all, the like hath not been. The Lord hath in his power knit Friends wonderfully together, and his glorious presence did appear among them. And now the meetings are over, blessed be the Lord! in quietness and peace. From Holland I hear things are well there: some Friends are gone that way, to be at their Yearly Meeting at Amsterdam. At Embden, Friends that were banished are got into the city again. At Dantzic, Friends are in prison, and the magistrates threatened them with harder imprisonment; but the next day the Lutherans rose, and plucked down (or defaced) the Popish monastery; so they have work enough among themselves. The King of Poland received my letter, and read it himself; and Friends have since printed it in High Dutch. By letters from the half-yearly meeting in Ireland, I hear that they are all in love there. At Barbadoes, Friends are in quietness, and their meetings settled in peace. At Antigua also and Nevis, truth prospers, and Friends have their meetings orderly and well. Likewise in New England and other places, things concerning truth and Friends are well; and in those places the men's and women's meetings are settled; blessed be the Lord! So keep in God's power and Seed, that is over all, in whom ye all have life and salvation; for the Lord reigns over all in his glory, and in his kingdom; glory to his name for ever, Amen. In haste, with my love to you all, and to all Friends."

G. F.

London, the 26th of the 3rd Month, 1678.

The letter to the King of Poland mentioned is as follows:—

"*To Johannes III. King of Poland, &c.*

"O King!

"We desire thy prosperity both in this life and that which is to come. And we desire that we may have our Christian liberty to serve and worship God under thy dominion; for our principle leads us not to do anything prejudicial to the king or his people. We are a people that exercise a good conscience towards God through his Holy Spirit, and by it do serve, worship, and honour him; and towards men in the things that are equal and just, doing to them as we would have them do unto us; looking unto Jesus, who is the author and finisher of our faith; which faith purifies our hearts, and bring us to have access to God; without which we cannot please him; by which faith all the just live, as the Scripture declares. That which we desire of thee, O king, is, that we may have liberty of conscience to serve and worship God, and to pray unto him in our meetings together in the name of Jesus, as he commands, with a promise that he will be in the midst of them. The king, we hope, cannot but say that this duty and service is due to God and Christ; and we give Cæsar his due, and pay our tribute and custom equal with our neighbour, according to our proportion. We never read in all the Scriptures of the New Testament, that Christ or his disciples banished or imprisoned any that were not of their faith or religion, and would not hear them, or gave them any such command; but, on the contrary, let the tares and the wheat grow together, till the harvest; and the harvest is the end of the world. Then Christ will send his angels to sever the wheat from the tares, &c. He rebuked such as would have had fire from heaven to consume those that would not receive Christ; and told them that they did not know what spirit they were of. He came not to destroy men's lives, but to save them.

"We desire the king to consider how much persecution there has been in Christendom, since the apostles' days, concerning religion. Christ said, they should go into everlasting punishment, that did not visit him in prison; then what will become of them that imprison him in his members, where he is manifest? None can say that the world is ended; and therefore how will Christendom answer the dreadful and terrible God at his day of judgment, that have persecuted one another about religion, before the end of the world, under pretence of plucking up tares; which is not their work, but the angels', at the end of the world? Christ commands men to love one another, and to love enemies, and by this they should be known to be his disciples. O! that all Christendom had lived in peace and unity, that they might, by their moderation, have judged both Turks and Jews; and let all have their liberty that do own God and Jesus, and walk as becomes the glorious gospel of the Lord Jesus Christ. Our desires are, that the Lord God of heaven may soften the king's heart to all tender consciences, that fear the Lord, and are afraid of disobeying him.

"We entreat the king to read some of the noble expressions of several kings and others, concerning liberty of conscience; and especially Stephanus, king of Poland's sayings, viz.: 'It belongeth not to me to reform the consciences; I have always gladly given that over to God, which belongeth to him; and so shall I do now, and also for the future. I will suffer the weeds to grow till the time of harvest, for I know that the number of believers is but small: therefore,' said he, when some were proceeding in persecution, 'I am king of the people, not of their consciences.' He also affirmed, that 'religion was not to be planted with fire and sword.' *Chron. Liberty of Religion*, part 2.

"Also a book written in French by W. M., anno 1576, hath this sentence, viz.: 'Those princes that have ruled by gentleness and clemency, added to justice, and have exercised moderation and meekness towards their subjects, always prospered and reigned long; but, on the contrary, those princes that have been cruel, unjust, prejudiced, and oppressors of their subjects, have soon fallen, they and their estates, into danger, or total ruin.'

"Veritus saith, 'Seeing Christ is a Lamb, whom you profess to be your head and captain, then it behoveth you to be sheep, and to use the same weapons that he made use of; for he will not be a shepherd of wolves and wild beasts, but only of sheep. Wherefore, if you lose the nature of sheep,' said he, 'and be changed into wolves and wild beasts, and use fleshly weapons, then will you exclude yourselves out of his calling, and forsake his banner; and then will he not be your captain,' &c.

"Also we find it asserted by King James, in his speech to the parliament, in the year 1609, 'That it is a pure rule in divinity, that God never planted his church with violence of blood.' And furthermore he said, 'it was usually the condition of Christians to be persecuted, but not to persecute.'

"King Charles, in his 'Εικὼν Βασιλική, page 61, said, in his prayer to God, 'Thou seest how much cruelty amongst Christians is acted under the colour of religion; as if we could not be Christians unless we crucified one another.'

"Page 28, 'Make them at length seriously to consider, that nothing violent nor injurious can be religious.'

"Page 70, 'Nor is it so proper to hew out religious reformation by the sword as to polish them by fair and equal disputations among those that are most concerned in the differences; whom not force, but reason, must convince.'

"Page 66, 'Take heed, that outward circumstances and formalities in religion devour not all.'

"Pages 91, 92, 'In point of true conscientious tenderness I have so often declared, how little I desire my laws and sceptre should entrench on God's sovereignty, who is the only King of conscience.'

"Page 123, 'Nor do I desire any man should be further subject unto me, than all of us may be subject unto God.'

"Page 200, 'O thou Sovereign of our souls, the only Commander of our consciences!'

"Page 346 (In his 'Meditations on Death'), 'It is indeed a sad state to have his enemies to be his accusers, parties, and judges.'

"The Prince of Orange testified, anno 1579, 'That it was impossible the land should be kept in peace, except there was a free toleration in the exercise of religion.'

"'Where hast thou read in thy day (said Menno) in the writings of the apostles, that Christ or the apostles ever cried out to the magistrates for their power against them that would not hear their doctrine, nor obey their words? I know certainly,' said he, 'that where a magistrate shall banish with the sword, there is not the right knowledge, spiritual word, nor church of Christ; it is, Invocare brachium seculare (to invoke the secular arm).'

"'It is not Christian-like, but tyrannical (said D. Philipson), to banish and persecute people about faith and religion; and they that so do are certainly of the Pharisaical generation, who resisted the Holy Ghost.'

"Erasmus said, 'That though they take our money and goods, they cannot therefore hurt our salvation; they afflict us much with prisons, but they do not thereby separate us from God.'—*In de Krydges wrede*, fol. 63.

"Lucernus said, 'He that commandeth anything, wherewith he bindeth the conscience, this is an antichrist.'—*In de Bemise Disp.* fol. 71.

"Irenæus affirmed, 'that all forcing of conscience, though it was but a forbidding of the exercise which is esteemed by one or another to be necessary to salvation, is in no wise right nor fitting.' He also affirmed, 'that through the diversity of religions the kingdom should not be brought into any disturbance.'

"Constantius, the emperor, said, 'That it was enough that he preserved the unity of the faith, that he might be excusable before the judgment-seat of God; and that he would leave every one to his own understanding, according to the account he will give before the judgment-seat of Christ. Hereto may we stir up people (said he), not compel them; beseech them to come into the unity of the Christians, but to do violence to them we will not in any wise.'—*Sebast. Frank, Chron.* fol. 127.

"Augustinus said, 'Some disturbed the peace of the church while they went about to root out the tares before their time; and through this error of blindness (said he) are they themselves separated so much the more from being united unto Christ.'

"Retnaldus testified, 'That he who, with imprisoning and persecuting, seeketh to spread the gospel, and greaseth his hands with blood, shall much rather be looked upon for a wild hunter, than a preacher, or a defender of the Christian religion.'

"'I have for a long season determined (said Henry IV., king of France, in his speech to the parliament, 1599), to reform the church, which, without peace, I cannot do: and it is impossible to reform or convert people by violence. I am king, as a shepherd, and will not shed the blood of my sheep, but will gather them through the mildness and goodness of a king, and not through the power of tyranny: and I will give them that are of the reformed religion right liberty to live and dwell free, without being examined, perplexed, molested, or compelled to anything contrary to their consciences; for they shall have the free exercise of their religion, &c.'—[*Vid. Chron. Van de Underg.* 2. deel, p. 1514.]

"Ennius said, 'Wisdom is driven out when the matter is acted by force. And therefore the best of men, and most glorious of princes, were always ready to give toleration.'

"Eusebius, in his second book of the life of Constantine, reports these words of the emperor: 'Let them which err, with joy receive the like fruition of peace and quietness with the faithful; sith the restoring of communication and society may bring them into the right way of truth: let none give molestation to any; let every one do as he determines in his mind. And indeed, there is great reason for princes to give toleration to disagreeing persons, whose opinions cannot by fair means be altered; for if the persons be confident, they will serve God according to their persuasions: and if they be publicly prohibited, they will privately convene: and then all those inconveniences and mischiefs, which are arguments against the permission of conventicles, are arguments for the public permission of differing religions, &c., they being restrained and made miserable, endears the discontented persons mutually, and makes more hearty and dangerous confederations.'

"The like counsel, in the divisions of Germany at the first reformation, was thought reasonable by the Emperor Ferdinand, and his excellent son Maximilian; for they had observed, 'that violence did exasperate, was unblessed, unsuccessful, and unreasonable; and therefore they made decrees of toleration.'

"The Duke of Savoy, repenting of his war undertaken for religion against the Piedmontese, promised them toleration; and was as good as his word.

"It is remarkable, that till the time of Justinian the emperor, Anno Domini 525, the Catholics and Novatians had churches indifferently permitted, even in Rome itself.

"And Paul preached the kingdom of God, teaching those things which concerned the Lord Jesus Christ, with all confidence; and no man forbade him: and this he did for the space of two years in his own hired house at Rome, and received all that came to him.

"Now, O king, seeing these noble testimonies concerning liberty of conscience from kings, emperors, and others, and the liberty that Paul had at Rome in the days of the heathen emperor, our desire is, that we may have the same liberty at Dantzic to meet together in our own hired houses; which cannot be any prejudice, either to the king or the city, for us to meet together to wait upon the Lord, and pray unto him, and to serve and worship him in Spirit and in truth in our own hired houses; seeing our principle leads us to hurt no man, but to love our enemies, and to pray for them: yea, them that persecute us. Therefore, O king, consider, and the city of Dantzic, would you not think it hard for others to force you from your religion to another, contrary to your consciences? And if it be so, that you would think it hard to you, then 'do you unto others as you would have them do unto you;' do not you that unto others, which you would not have them do unto you; for that is the royal law, which ought to be obeyed. And so in love to thy immortal soul, and for thy eternal good, this is written." G. F.

"*Postscript.*—'Blessed be the merciful, for they shall obtain mercy.' And remember, O king, Justin Martyr's two Apologies to the Roman emperors, in the defence of the persecuted Christians; and that notable Apology, which was written by Tertullian, upon the same subject; which are not only for the Christian religion, but against all persecution for religion."

"*Dear Peter Hendricks, John Claus, J. Rawlins, and all the rest of Friends in Amsterdam, Friesland, and Rotterdam, to whom is my love in the Seed of life, that is over all.*

"I RECEIVED your letter with one from Dantzic: I have written something directed to you, to the King of Poland, which you may translate into High Dutch, and send to Friends there to give to the king; or you may print it, after it be delivered in manuscript, which may be serviceable to other princes. So in haste, with my love. The Lord God Almighty over all give you dominion in his eternal power, and in it over all preserve you, and keep you to his glory, that you may answer that of God in all people. Amen." GEORGE FOX.

London, the 13th of the 9th Month, 1677.

I continued yet in and about London some weeks, the parliament sitting again, and Friends attending to get some redress of our sufferings, which about this time were very great, and heavy upon many Friends in divers parts of the nation; being very unduly prosecuted upon the statutes made against Popish recusants; though our persecutors could not but know that Friends were utterly against Popery; having borne testimony against it in word and writing, and suffered under it. But though many of the members of parliament in each house were kind to Friends, and willing to do something for their ease, yet having much business, they were hindered from doing the good they would, so that the sufferings of Friends continued.

But that which added much to the grief and exercise of Friends, was, that some who made a profession of the same truth with us, being gone from the simplicity of the gospel into a fleshly liberty, and labouring to draw others after them, opposed the order and discipline, which God by his power had set up and established in his church; and made a great noise and clamour against prescriptions; whereby they easily drew after them such as were loosely inclined, and desired a broader way than the path of truth to walk in. Some also that were more simple, but young in truth, or weak in judgment, were apt to be betrayed by them, not knowing the depths of Satan in these wiles; for whose sake I was moved to write the following paper, for undeceiving the deceived, and opening the understandings of the weak in this matter:—

"ALL you that deny prescriptions without distinction, may as well deny all the Scriptures, which were given forth by the power and Spirit of God. For do not they prescribe how men should walk towards God and man, both in the Old Testament and in the New? Yea, from the very first promise of Christ in Genesis, what people ought to believe and trust in, and all along, till ye come to the prophets? Did not the Lord prescribe to his people by the fathers, and then by his prophets? Did he not prescribe to the people how they should walk, though they turned against the prophets in the old covenant, for declaring or prescribing to them the way, how they might walk to please God, and keep in favour with him? In the days of Christ, did not he prescribe and teach, how people should walk and believe? And after him, did not the apostles prescribe to people how they might come to believe, and receive the gospel and the kingdom of God, directing to that which would give them the knowledge of God, and how they should walk in the new covenant in the days of the gospel, and by what way they should come to the holy city? And did not the apostles send forth their decrees by faithful chosen men, that had hazarded their lives for Christ's sake, to the churches, by which they were established? So you that deny prescriptions given forth by the power and Spirit of God, do thereby oppose the Spirit that gave them forth in all the holy men of God. Were there not some all along in the days of Moses, in the days of the prophets, in the days of Christ, and in the days of his apostles, who did withstand that which they gave forth from the Spirit of God? And hath there not been the like since the days of the apostles? How many have risen, since truth appeared, to oppose the order which stands in the power and Spirit of God? who are but in the same spirit which hath opposed the Spirit of God all along from the beginning. See, what names or titles the Spirit of God gave that opposing spirit in the old covenant, and also in the new; which is the same now; for after the Lord had given forth the old covenant, there were some among themselves that opposed; these were worse than public enemies. And likewise, in the days of the new covenant, in the gospel-times, you may see what sort opposed Christ and the apostles, after they came to some sight of the truth, and how they turned against Christ and his apostles? See what a liberty they pleaded for, and ran into, in the apostles' days, who could not abide the cross, the yoke of Jesus.

"We see the same rough and high spirit cries now for liberty, which the power and Spirit of Christ cannot give—cries, 'Imposition,' and yet is imposing;—cries, 'liberty of conscience,' and yet is opposing liberty of conscience; and cries against 'prescriptions,' and yet is prescribing both in words and writing. So with the everlasting power and Spirit of God this Spirit is fathomed; its rise, beginning, and end; and it is judged. This spirit cries, 'we must not judge conscience; we must not judge matters of faith; and we must not judge spirits, nor religions,' &c. Yes; they that are in the pure Spirit and power of God, which the apostles were in, judge of conscience, whether it be a seared conscience, or a tender conscience; they judge of faith, whether it be a dead one, or a living one; they judge of religion, whether it be vain, or pure and undefiled; they judge of spirits, and try them, whether they be of God or not; they judge of hope, whether it be that of hypocrites, or the true hope that purifies, even as God is pure; they judge of belief, whether it be that which is born of God, and overcometh the world, or that which runs into the spirit of the world, which lusts to envy, and doth not overcome the world; they judge of worships, whether they be will-worships, and the worship of the beast and dragon, or the worship of God in Spirit and in truth; they judge of angels, whether they be fallen, or those that keep their habitation; they judge the world, that grieves and quenches the Spirit, hates the light, turns the grace of God into wantonness, and resists the Holy Ghost; they judge of the hearts, ears, and lips, which are circumcised, and which are uncircumcised; they judge of ministers, and apostles, and messengers, whether they be of Satan or of Christ; they judge of differences in outward things, in the church or elsewhere; yea, the least member of the church hath power to judge of such things, having the one true measure, and true weight to weigh things, and measure things withal, without respect to persons. This judgment is given, and all these things are done, by the same power and Spirit the apostles were in. Such also can judge of election and reprobation; who keep their habitation, and who do not; who are Jews, and who are of the synagogue of Satan; who are in the doctrine of Christ, and who are in the doctrines of devils; who prescribes and declares things from the power and Spirit of God, and who prescribes and declares things from a loose spirit, to let all loose from under the yoke of Christ, the power of God, into looseness and liberty.

"These likewise can judge and discern, who brings people into the possession of the gospel of light and life, over death and darkness, and into the truth, where the devil cannot get in; and who brings them into the possession of death and darkness, out of the glorious liberty of the gospel, and of Jesus Christ, his faith, truth, Spirit, light, and grace. For there is no true liberty, but in that; and that liberty answers the grace, the truth, the light, the Spirit, the faith, the gospel of Christ in every man and woman, and is the yoke to the contrary in every man and woman. That makes it rage, and swell, and puff up; for it is restless, unruly, out of patience, and ready to curse his God, and that which reigns over him, because it hath not its will. It works with all subtilty and evasion with its restless spirit, to get in and defile the minds of the simple, and to make rapes upon the virgin minds. But as they receive the heavenly wisdom, by which all things were made (which wisdom is above that spirit), through this wisdom they will be preserved over that spirit.

"And Christ hath given judgment to his saints in his church, though he be judge of all; and the saints, in the power and Spirit of God, had and have power to judge of words and manners, of lives and conversations, of growths and states, from a child to a father in the truth; and to whom they are a savour of death, and to whom they are a savour of life; who serve the Lord Jesus Christ and preach him, and who preach themselves and serve themselves; and who talk of the light, of faith, of the gospel, of hope, and of grace, and preach such things; yet in their works and lives deny them all, and God and Christ, and preach up liberty from that in themselves to that in others, which should be under the yoke and cross of Christ, the power of God. So the saints, in the power and Spirit of Christ, can discern and distinguish, who serves God and Christ, and who serves him not; and can put a distinction between the profane and the holy. But such as have lost their eye-salve, and whose sight is grown dim, lose this judgment, discerning, and distinction in the church of Christ; and such come to be spewed out of Christ's mouth, except they repent; and if not, they come to corrupt the earth, and burden it, that it vomits them out of it.

"Therefore, all are exhorted to keep in the power and Spirit of Christ Jesus, in the word of life, and the wisdom of God (which is above that which is below), in which they may keep their heavenly understandings and discernings; and so set the heavenly, spiritual judgment over that which is for judgment, which dishonours God, and leads into loose and false liberty; out of the unity, which stands in the heavenly Spirit, which brings into conformity to the image of the Son of God, and his gospel, the power of God (which was before the devil was), and his truth (which the devil is out of), in which all are of one mind, heart, and soul, and come to drink into one Spirit, being baptized into one Spirit, and so into one body, of which Christ is the head; and so keep one fellowship and unity in the Spirit, which is the bond of peace, the Prince of princes' peace. And they that cry so much against judging, and are afraid of judgment, whether they be apostates, professors, or profane, are the most judging with their censorious, false spirits, and judgment; and yet they cannot bear the true judgment of the Spirit of God, nor stand in his judgment. This hath been manifest from the beginning, they having the false measures, and the false weights; for none have the true measure and true weight but they who keep in the light, power, and Spirit of Christ. And now there is a loose spirit, that cries for liberty, and against prescriptions, and yet is prescribing ways, both by words and writings. The same spirit cries against judging, and would not be judged, and yet is judging with a wrong spirit. This is given forth in reproof to that spirit." G. F.

London, the 9th of the 4th Month, 1678.

When I had finished what service I had for the Lord at this time here, I went towards Hertford; visiting Friends, and having several meetings in the way. At HERTFORD I stayed some days, having much service for the Lord there, both amongst Friends in their meetings, and in conferences with such as having let in evil surmisings and jealousies concerning Friends, stood in opposition to the order of truth: and in answering some books written against truth and Friends. While I was here, it came upon me to write a few lines, and send them abroad amongst Friends, as follows:—

"Dear Friends,

"Let the holy Seed of life reign over death and the unholy seed in you all; that in the holy Seed of the kingdom ye may all feel the everlasting holy peace with God, through Christ Jesus, your Saviour, and sit down in Him, your life and glorious rest, the holy rock and foundation, that standeth sure over all from everlasting to everlasting, in whom all the fulness of blessedness is; so that ye may glory in Him that liveth for evermore, Amen! who is your eternal joy, life, and happiness; through whom you have peace with God. This holy Seed bruiseth the head of the serpent, and will outlive all his wrath and rage, malice and envy; who was before he and it were, and remains when he and it are gone into the fire that burns with brimstone. The Seed, Christ, will reign; and so will ye, as ye do live and walk in Him, sit down in Him, and build up one another in the love of God." G. F.

Hertford, the 10th of the 5th Month, 1678.

Next day a fresh exercise came upon me, with respect to those unruly and disorderly spirits, that were gone out from us, and were labouring to draw others after them into a false liberty. In the sense I had of the hurt and mischief these might do, where they were given way to, I was moved to write a few lines to warn Friends of them, as follows:—

"All Friends,

"Keep in the tender life of the Lamb, over that unruly, puffed up, and swelling spirit, whose work is for strife, contention, and division, under a pretence of conscience, and drawing into looseness and false liberty, dangerous to the welfare of youth. They that do encourage them, will be guilty of their destruction, and set up a sturdy will, instead of conscience, in their rage and passion; which will quench the universal Spirit in themselves, and in every man and woman: and so, that spirit shall not have liberty in themselves, nor in others; thus they shut up the kingdom of heaven in themselves, and also in others. So a loose spirit getting up under a pretence of liberty of conscience; or a stubborn will, making a profession of the words of truth in a form without power, all looseness and vileness will be sheltered and covered under this pretence, which is for eternal judgment: for that doth dishonour God. Therefore, keep to the tender Spirit of God in all humility, that in it you may know that ye are all members of one another, and all have an office in the church of Christ. All these living members know one another in the Spirit, and not in the flesh. So here is no man ruling over the woman, as Adam did over Eve in the fall: but Christ, the spiritual man, among and over his spiritual members, which are edified in the heavenly love that is shed in their heart from God, where all strife ceases." G. F.

Hertford, the 11th of the 5th Month, 1678.

I went from Hertford to a meeting at Rabley-Heath, and thence to Edward Crouch's, of Stevenage. Next day to Baldock, where I had a meeting that evening; and after that had meetings at HITCHIN and ASHWELL. Then passing through part of BEDFORDSHIRE, where I had a meeting or two, I went to HUNTINGDON, in which county I stayed several days, having many meetings, and much service amongst Friends; labouring to convince gainsayers, and to confirm and strengthen Friends in the way and work of the Lord. At IVES, in Huntingdonshire, George Whitehead came to me, and travelled with me, in the work of the Lord, for five or six days in that county, and in some part of NORTHAMPTONSHIRE; and leaving me in GREAT BOWDEN in LEICESTERSHIRE, he went towards Westmorland. I stayed longer in Leicestershire, visiting Friends at SADDINGTON, WIGSTON, KNIGHTON, LEICESTER, SILEBY, SWANNINGTON, and divers other places; where I had very precious meetings, and good service amongst Friends and other people: for there was great openness, and many weighty and excellent truths did the Lord give me to deliver amongst them.

At LEICESTER I went to the jail to visit the Friends that were in prison there for the testimony of Jesus, with whom I spent some time; encouraging them in the Lord to persevere stedfastly and faithfully in their testimony, and not to be weary of suffering for his sake. And when I had taken my leave of them, I spoke with the jailer, desiring him to be kind to them, and let them have what liberty he could, to visit their families sometimes.

I had a meeting or two in WARWICKSHIRE, and then went into STAFFORDSHIRE, where I had several sweet and opening meetings, both for gathering into truth and establishing therein. While I was in Staffordshire, I was moved to give forth the following paper:—

"DEAR FRIENDS of the quarterly and monthly meetings everywhere: My desire is, that ye may all strive to be of one mind in the Lord's power and truth, which is peaceable, and into which strife and enmity cannot come; also in the wisdom of God, which is pure, peaceable, and easy to be entreated, which is above that which is below, that is earthly, devilish, and sensual; and that with, and in this heavenly wisdom, you may be all ordered, and do what ye do, to God's glory. And, dear Friends, if there should happen at any time anything that tends to strife, dispute, or contention in your monthly or quarterly meetings, let it be referred to half a dozen, or such a like number, to debate and end, out of your meetings, as it was at first, that all your monthly and quarterly meetings may be kept peaceable. And then they may inform the meeting what they have done; that the weak and youth amongst you may not be hurt, through hearing of strife or contention in your meetings, where no strife or contention ought to be; but all to go on, and determine things in one mind, in the power of God, the gospel order: in which gospel of peace ye will preserve the peace of all your meetings. If any man or woman have anything against any one, let them speak to one another, and end it between themselves; if they cannot so decide, let them take two or three to end it. In case these determine it not, let it be laid before the church; and let half a dozen, or such a number out of your monthly or quarterly meeting hear it, and finally end it, without respect of persons. Let all prejudice be laid aside and buried; also all shortness one towards another; and let love, which is not puffed up, envies not, seeks not her own, but bears all things, have the dominion in all your meetings; for that doth edify the body, which Christ is the head of; and this will rule over all sounding brass and tinkling cymbals. This love will suffer long, and is kind; it will keep down that which would vaunt itself, or be puffed up, or behave itself unseemly, or is easily provoked; it hath a sway over all such fruits, as are not of the Spirit, the fruit of which is love, &c. And that with this Holy Spirit ye may all be baptized into one body, and be made to drink into one Spirit; in which Spirit ye will have unity, in which is the bond of the King of kings', and Lord of lords' peace. They that dwell in love, dwell in God; for God is love: therefore let every one keep his habitation. My love to you in Christ Jesus, the everlasting Seed, which is over all." G. F.

Staffordshire, the 20th of the 6th Month, 1678.

Out of Staffordshire I went to visit John Gratton* at MONYASH in DERBYSHIRE, with whom I tarried one night; and went next day to William Shaw's of the Hill, in YORKSHIRE, where I appointed a meeting to be on First-day following. Many Friends out of Derbyshire, and from several meetings in Yorkshire, came, and a precious, comfortable meeting it was; wherein was opened the blessed state of man before he fell; the means by which he fell; the miserable condition into which he fell; and the right way of coming out of it, into a happy state, again by Christ, the promised Seed.

I spent about two weeks in Yorkshire, travelling from place to place amongst Friends in the Lord's service; and many heavenly meetings I had in that county. Then visiting Robert Widders, at KELLET, in LANCASHIRE, I passed to ARNSIDE, in WESTMORLAND, where I had a precious, living meeting in the Lord's blessed power, to the great satisfaction and comfort of Friends, who came from divers parts to it. Next day I went to SWARTHMORE; and it being the meeting-day there, I had a sweet opportunity with Friends, our hearts being opened in the love of God, and his blessed life flowing amongst us.

I had not been long at Swarthmore, ere a concern came upon me to

* John Gratton was born about the year 1641. He was first brought under religious conviction when he was a shepherd boy about eleven years old, but he remained in a halting state till he attained to manhood, after which he became more devoted in heart to the Lord. He was brought into great grief on observing the instability of some professed preachers of the gospel, in times of persecution. In 1670 he began to preach among the Baptists, but soon left this people because they also flinched in the day of trial, and becoming convinced of the soundness of the principles held by Friends, and seeing their constancy under suffering, he joined them in 1671. The third time he attended a Friends' meeting, he spoke under the constraining influence of the Divine Spirit; and he soon became an able minister of Christ. He often left his temporal concerns to make apostolic visits to various parts of Great Britain and Ireland. He also suffered imprisonment for about five years and a half for the gospel's sake. His residence was for many years at Monyash, in Derbyshire, but in 1708 he removed to Needham, and resided with a daughter, at whose house he died in 1711, aged 68—a minister about forty years.

visit the churches of Christ in London and elsewhere, by an epistle, as follows:—

"DEAR FRIENDS,

"To whom is my love in the heavenly Seed, in whom all nations are blessed. O, keep all in this Seed, in which ye are blessed, and in which Abraham and all the faithful were blessed, without the deeds of the law; for the promise was and is to, and with the Seed, and not with the law of the first covenant. In this Seed all nations, and ye, are blessed, which bruiseth the head of the seed that brought the curse, and separated man from God; this is the Seed which reconciles you to God, this is the Seed in which ye are blessed both in temporals and spirituals; through which ye have an inheritance among the sanctified, that cannot be defiled, neither can any defiled thing enter into its possession; for all defilements are out of this Seed. This is that which leavens into a new lump, and bruises the head of the wicked seed, which leavens into the old lump, upon which the Sun of Righteousness goes down and sets; but it never goes down and sets to them that walk in the Seed, in which all nations are blessed: by which Seed they are brought up to God, which puts down that Seed which separated them from God; so that there comes to be nothing between them and God. Now, all my dear Friends, my desires are, that ye may all be valiant in this heavenly Seed, for God and his truth upon the earth, and spread it abroad, answering that of God in all; that with it the minds of people may be turned towards the Lord, that he may come to be known, and served, and worshipped; and that ye may all be as the salt of the earth, to make the unseasoned savoury. And in the name of Jesus keep your meetings, who are gathered into it, in whose name ye have salvation; he being in the midst of you, whose name is above every name under the whole heaven. So ye have a Prophet, Bishop, Shepherd, Priest, and Counsellor (above all the counsellors and priests, bishops, prophets, and shepherds under the whole heaven) to exercise his offices among you, in your meetings, that are gathered in his name. For Christ's meeting and gathering is above all the meetings and gatherings under the whole heaven; and his body, his church, and he the head of it, is above all the bodies, churches, and heads under the whole heaven. And the faith that Christ is the author of, the worship that he hath set up, and his fellowship in the gospel, are above all historical faiths, and the faiths that men have made, together with their worships and fellowships under the whole heaven.

"And now, dear Friends, keep your men's and women's meetings in the power of God, the gospel, the authority of them, which brings life and immortality to light in you; and this gospel, the power of God, will preserve you in life, and in immortality, that ye may see over him that hath darkened, and kept from the knowledge of the things of God: for it is he and his instruments which have darkened you from life and immortality, that would throw down your men's and women's meetings, and would darken you again from this life and immortality, which the gospel hath brought to light, and will preserve you, as your faith stands in this power, in which every one sees his work and service for God. Every heir in the power of God, the gospel, hath right to this authority, which is not of man, nor by man; which power of God is everlasting, an everlasting order and fellowship; and in the gospel is everlasting joy, comfort, and peace, which will outlast all those joys, comforts, and peaces, that will have an end; and that spirit also, that opposes its order, and the glorious fellowship, peace, and comfort in it.

"And, dear Friends, my desire is, that ye may keep in the unity of the Spirit, that baptizes you all into one body, of which Christ is the heavenly and spiritual Head; so that ye may see and bear witness thereto, and all drink into the one Spirit; which all people upon the earth are not likely to do, while they grieve, quench, and rebel against it; nor to be baptized into one body, and to keep the unity of the Spirit, which is the bond of peace, yea, the King of kings' and Lord of lords' peace; which it is the duty of all true Christians to keep, who are inwardly united to Christ. My love to you all in the everlasting Seed." G. F.

Swarthmore, the 26th of the 7th Month, 1678.

There were about this time several Friends in prison for bearing testimony to the truth, to whom I was moved to write a few lines, to comfort, strengthen, and encourage them in their sufferings; having a true sense of their sufferings upon my spirit, sympathizing with them therein. That which I wrote was after this manner:—

"My dear Friends,

"Who are sufferers for the Lord Jesus' sake, and for the testimony of his truth; the Lord God Almighty with his power uphold and support you in all your trials and sufferings, and give you patience and content in his will, that ye may stand valiant for Christ and his truth upon the earth, over the persecuting and destroying spirit, which makes to suffer in Christ (who bruises his head), in whom ye have both election and salvation. For his elect's sake the Lord hath done much from the foundation of the world; as may be seen throughout the Scriptures of truth. They that touch them touch the apple of God's eye; they are so tender to him; and therefore it is good for all God's suffering children to trust in the Lord, and to wait upon him: for they shall be as Mount Sion, that cannot be removed from Christ, their rock and salvation, who is the foundation of all the elect of God, of the prophets and the apostles, and of God's people now, and to the end. Glory to the Lord and the Lamb over all! Remember my dear love to all Friends, and do not think the time long; for all time is in the Father's hand, his power. Therefore keep the word of patience, and exercise that gift; and the Lord strengthen you in your sufferings, in his Holy Spirit of Faith. Amen." G. F.

Swarthmore, the 5th of the 12th Month, 1678.

I abode in the North at this time above a year, having service for the Lord amongst Friends there, and being much taken up in writing in answer to books published by adversaries; and for opening the principles and doctrines of truth to the world, that they might come to have a right understanding thereof, and be gathered thereunto. Several epistles also to Friends I wrote in this time, on divers occasions; one was to the Yearly

Meeting of Friends held in London this year, 1679, a copy of which here follows:—

"MY DEAR FRIENDS AND BRETHREN,

"Who are assembled together in the name and power of the Lord Jesus Christ; grace, mercy, and peace from God the Father, and from the Lord Jesus Christ, fill all your hearts, and establish you in his grace, mercy, and peace upon Christ, the holy, living Rock and Foundation, who is the First and Last, and over all the rocks and foundations in the whole world; a Rock and Foundation of life for all the living to build upon, which stands sure in his heavenly, divine light, which is the life in Him, by whom all things were made: who is the precious stone laid in Zion (and not in the world), which all the wise master-builders rejected, who pretended to build people up to heaven with the words of the prophets, and the law from Mount Sinai, but out of the life of both. Such builders therefore could not receive the law of life from Christ, the precious Stone laid in Sion, nor the word from heavenly Jerusalem. But you, my dear Friends, that have received this law from heavenly Sion, and the word from heavenly Jerusalem, in the new covenant, where the life and substance is enjoyed, you see the end and abolishing of the Jews' law and ceremonies from Mount Sinai. And therefore, my desire is, that you all may keep in the law of life and love, which ye have in Christ Jesus, by which love the body is edified, knit, and united together to Christ Jesus, the Head. This love beareth all things, and fulfils the law; and it will preserve all in humility, to be of one mind, heart, and soul; so that all may come to drink into that one Spirit that doth baptize and circumcise them; plunging down and cutting off the body of the sins of the flesh, that is gotten up in man and woman by their transgressing of God's commands. So that in this holy, pure Spirit, all may serve and worship the pure God in Spirit and in truth, which is over all the worships that are out of God's Spirit and his truth. In this Spirit ye will all have a spiritual unity and fellowship, over all the fellowships of the unclean spirits which are out of truth in the world. By this holy Spirit all your hearts, minds, and souls, may be knit together to Christ, from whence it comes; and by the grace and truth which came by Jesus Christ, which all should be under the teachings of in the new covenant, and not under the law, as the outward Jews were in the old covenant—by this grace and truth in the new covenant, all may be made God's free men and women, to serve God in the new life, and in the new and living way; showing forth the fruits of the new heart and new spirit, in the new covenant, over death and darkness; glory be unto the Lord for ever!

"Now, Friends, in this grace and truth is your heavenly, gracious, and true liberty to every spiritual mind, that makes you free from him that is out of truth, where your bondage was; also your liberty in the holy, divine, and precious faith, which gives you victory over that which once separated you from God and Christ, and by which faith ye have access to God again, through Jesus Christ. So in this divine and holy faith, ye have divine, holy, and precious liberty, yea, and victory over him that separated you from God: and this faith is held in a pure conscience. So the liberty in the Spirit of God, is in that which baptizes and plunges down sin and iniquity, and puts off the body of death and of the sins of the flesh, that is gotten up by transgressing God's command. And also the liberty of the gospel, which is sent from heaven by the Holy Ghost, which is the power of God, which was, and is again to be, preached to all nations: in this gospel (the power of God, which is over the power of Satan) is the true liberty, and the gospel-fellowship and order. So that the evil spirit or conscience, or false, dead faith, and that which is ungracious and out of truth, and not in the Spirit of God, nor in his gospel, nor in the divine faith, its liberty is in the darkness: for all the true liberty is in the gospel, and in the truth that makes free; in the faith, in the grace, and in Christ Jesus, who destroys the devil and his works, that hath brought all mankind into bondage. So in this heavenly, peaceable Spirit, and truth, and faith, which works by love, and in the gospel of peace, and in Christ Jesus, is all the saints' peace, and pure, true, and holy liberty; in which they have salt, and sense, feeling, discerning, and savour, yea, unity and fellowship one with another, and with the Son and the Father, heavenly eternal fellowship. So all being subject to the grace, and truth, to the faith, and gospel (the power of God), and to his good Spirit; in this they distinguish all true, pure, and holy liberty, from that which is false. This will bring all to sit low: for patience runs the race, and the Lamb must have the victory; and not the rough, unruly, and vain talkers, unbaptized, uncircumcised, and unsanctified. Such travel not in the way of regeneration, but in the way of unregeneration; neither go they down into death with Christ by baptism; and therefore such are not like to reign with him in his resurrection, who are not buried with him in baptism. Therefore, all must go downward into the death of Christ, and be crucified with him, if they will arise, and follow him in the regeneration, before they come to reign with him.

"And, Friends, many may have precious openings; but I desire all may be comprehended in that thing which doth open to them; and that they may all keep in the daily cross; then they keep in the power, that kills and crucifies that, which would lead them amongst the beasts and goats, to leaven them into their rough, unruly spirit; that through the cross, the power of God, *that* may be crucified, and they in the power may follow the Lamb. For the power of God keeps all in order, subjection, and humility —in that which is lovely and virtuous, decent, comely, temperate, and moderate; so that their moderation appears to all men. My desire is, that all your lights may shine, as from a city set upon a hill, that cannot be hid; and that ye may be the salt of the earth, to salt and season it, and make it savoury to God, and you all seasoned with it. Then all your sacrifices will be a sweet savour to the Lord, and ye will be as the lilies and roses, and garden of God, which gives a sweet smell unto him; whose garden is preserved by his power, the hedge, that hedges out all the unruly and unsavoury, and the destroyers and hurters of the vines, buds, and plants, and God's tender blade, which springs up from his Seed of life; who waters it with his heavenly water, and word of life continually, that they may grow and be fruitful; that so he may have a pleasant and fruitful garden. Here all are kept fresh and green, being watered every moment with the everlasting, holy water of life, from the Lord, the fountain.

"My dear Friends, my desire is, that this heavenly Seed, that bruises the head of the serpent, both within and without, may be all your crown and life, and ye in him, one another's crown and joy, to the praise of the Lord God over all, blessed for evermore! This holy Seed will outlast and wear out all that which the evil seed, since the fall of man, has brought forth and set up. As every one hath received Christ Jesus the Lord, so walk in him in the humility which he teaches; and shun the occasions of strife, vain janglings, and disputings with men of corrupt minds, who are destitute of the truth: for the truth is peaceable, and the gospel is a peaceable habitation in the power of God; his wisdom is peaceable and gentle, and his kingdom stands in peace. O, his glory shines over all his works! and in Christ Jesus, who is not of the world, ye will have peace, yea, a peace that the world cannot take away: for the peace which ye have from him, was before the world was, and will be when it is gone. This keeps all in that, which is weighty and substantial, over all chaff. Glory to the Lord God over all for ever and ever! Amen.

"And now, my dear Friends, the Lord doth require more of you than he doth of other people; because he hath committed more to you. He requires the fruits of his Spirit, of the Light, of the Gospel, of the Grace, and of the Truth; for herein is he glorified (as Christ said) in your bringing forth much fruit—fruits of righteousness, holiness, godliness, virtue, truth, and purity; so that ye may answer that which is of God in all people. Be valiant for his everlasting, glorious gospel, in God's Holy Spirit and truth; keeping in unity, and in the Holy Spirit, Light, and Life, which is over death and darkness, and was before death and darkness were. In this Spirit ye have the bond of peace, which cannot be broken, except ye go from the Spirit; and then ye lose this unity and bond of peace, which ye have from the Prince of Peace.

"The world also expects more from Friends than from other people; because you profess more. Therefore you should be more just than others in your words and dealings, and more righteous, holy, and pure in your lives and conversations; so that your lives and conversations may preach. For the world's tongues and mouths have preached long enough; but their lives and conversations have denied what their tongues have professed and declared.

"And, dear Friends, strive to excel one another in virtue, that ye may grow in love, that excellent way which unites all to Christ and God. Stand up for God's glory, and mind that which concerns the Lord's honour, that in nowise his power may be abused, or his name evil spoken of, by any evil talkers or walkers: but that in all things God may be honoured, and ye may glorify him in your bodies, souls, and spirits, the little time ye have to live. My love to you all in the holy Seed of Life, that reigns over all, and is the First and Last; in whom ye all have life and salvation, and your election and peace with God, through Jesus Christ, who destroys him that hath been between you and God; so that nothing may be between you and the Lord, but Christ Jesus. Amen.

"My life and love is to you all, and amongst you all. The Lord God Almighty by his mighty power, by which he hath preserved all his people unto this day, preserve and keep you all in his power, and peaceable, holy truth, in unity and fellowship one with another, and with the Son and the Father. Amen." G. F.

The 24th of the 3rd Month, 1679.

Divers other epistles and papers I wrote to Friends, during my stay in the North; one was in a few lines, to encourage Friends to be bold and valiant for the Truth, which the Lord had called them to bear witness to; it was thus:—

"Dear Friends,

"All be valiant for the Lord's Truth upon the earth, which the serpent, Satan, and the devil is out of; and in the truth keep him out, in which you all have peace and life, and unity with God and his Son, and one with another. Let the love of God fill all your hearts, that in it ye may build up and edify one another in the light, life, Holy Spirit, and power of God, the glorious, comfortable gospel of Christ, the heavenly Man, your Lord and Saviour; who will fill all your vessels with his heavenly wine and water of life; clothe you with his heavenly clothing, his fine linen, that never waxeth old; and arm you with his heavenly weapons and armour, that ye may stand faithful witnesses for God and his Son, who is come, and hath given you an understanding to know Him, and ye are in him. So walk in Him, in whom ye all have life and salvation, and peace with God. My love to you all in the Lord Jesus Christ, in whom I have laboured; and God Almighty, in his eternal power and wisdom, preserve you all to his glory. Amen." G. F.

Swarthmore, the 29th of the 10th Month, 1679.

The next day, having a sense upon me that some who had received the Truth, and had openings thereof, for want of keeping low, had run out therefrom, I was moved to give forth the following epistle, as "a warning and exhortation to all to dwell in humility:"—

"My Dear Friends,

"Whom the Lord in his tender mercies, hath visited with the day-spring from on high, and hath opened you to confess and bow to his name; keep low in your minds, and learn of Christ, who teacheth you humility, to keep in it; so that in nowise, ye that are younger, be exalted, or puffed up, or conceited through your openings, and by that means lose your conditions, by being carried up into presumption; and then fall into despair, and so abuse the power of God. For it was the apostles' care, that none should abuse the power of the Lord God; but in all things their faith was to stand therein, that they all might be comprehended into the truth, which they spoke to others, that they might not be preachers to others, and themselves cast-aways. Therefore it doth concern you to be comprehended into that, which ye do preach to others, and to keep low in it; then the God of Truth will exalt the humble in his truth, light, grace, power, and Spirit, and in his wisdom to his glory. Here all are kept in their measures of grace, light, faith, and the Spirit of Christ, the heavenly and spiritual Man. So let none quench the Spirit, or its motions, grieve it, or err from it; but be led by it, which keeps all in their tents; which giveth an understanding, how to serve, worship, and please the holy, pure God, the Maker and Creator in Christ Jesus, and how to wait, speak, and answer the Spirit of God in his people; in which Holy Spirit is the holy unity and fellowship. The Holy Spirit teacheth the holy, gentle, meek, and quiet lowly mind to answer the seed, that Christ hath sown upon all grounds; and to answer the light, grace, and Spirit, and the gospel in every creature, though they are gone from the Spirit, grace, light, and gospel in the heart. So by holy walking all may come to do it, as well as by holy preaching, that God in all things may be glorified by you, and that ye may bring forth fruits to his praise. Amen." G. F.

Swarthmore, the 30th of the 10th Month, 1679.

About the latter end of this year I was moved of the Lord to travel into the South again. I set forward in the beginning of the first month, 1679–80; and passing through part of WESTMORLAND and LANCASHIRE, I visited Friends at several meetings, and came into YORKSHIRE. Divers large and weighty meetings I had in Yorkshire, before I came to YORK. When I came there it was the assize time; and there being many Friends in prison for truth's sake, I put those, that were at liberty, upon drawing up the sufferings of Friends in prison, to lay before the judges; and I assisted them therein. There were then in York many Friends from several parts of the county, for the quarterly meeting was at that time; so that I had a brave opportunity among them. Many weighty and serviceable things did the Lord open through me to the meeting, relating to the inward state of man, how man by faith in Christ comes to be grafted into him, and made a member of his spiritual body; and also to the outward state of the church, how each member ought to walk and act, according to his place in the body. I spent several days in York, having divers meetings; and all was peaceable and well. I went also to the castle, to visit Friends that were prisoners; with whom I spent some time, encouraging and strengthening them in their testimony.

Then leaving York, I travelled southward, having meetings in many places amongst Friends, till I came to BARTON in LINCOLNSHIRE; where, on First-day, I had a large and precious meeting. Then turning into NOTTINGHAMSHIRE, I travelled through good part of that county, in which I had several good meetings; and then passed into DERBYSHIRE, LEICESTERSHIRE, and WARWICKSHIRE, having meetings all along as I went, till I came to WARWICK; there William Dewsbury came to me, and several other Friends, and we had a little meeting in that town. Then passing through SOUTHAM and RADWAY, at each of which places I had a very good meeting, I came to Nathaniel Ball's of NORTH NEWTON in OXFORDSHIRE, and so to BANBURY to a monthly meeting there. And after I had visited Friends in the bordering parts of OXFORDSHIRE, GLOUCESTERSHIRE, and NORTHAMPTONSHIRE, I passed to Richard Baker's* of BIDDLESDON in

* Richard Baker is described as a man of circumspect life, and a pattern of good works. He suffered cheerfully for Christ both the spoiling of his goods and imprisonment of his body; and would often say, "If people did but know the pleasure of

BUCKINGHAMSHIRE; and next day, being First-day, I had a very large meeting in Biddlesdon, at an old abbey-house, which a Friend rented and dwelt in. Many Friends and people came to it out of Oxfordshire, Northamptonshire, and the parts adjacent; and of good service it was. After this, I visited Friends in those parts, having meetings at LILLINGSTONE, LOVEL, and BUGBROOKE. Then going to STONY-STRATFORD, I went from thence into some parts of BEDFORDSHIRE, till I came to Edward Chester's of DUNSTABLE. Passing on by MARKET STREET, I had a meeting at ALBAN'S; and calling on Friends at MIMS and BARNET, I came to the widow Hayley's, at GUTTERSHEDGE, in HENDON, Middlesex, on a Seventh-day night, and had a very large and good meeting there the day following.

I passed thence to LONDON on the Third-day following, and went directly to the Peel-meeting at John Elson's; and next morning to the meeting at Gracechurch Street, which was very large and quiet; and Friends rejoiced in the Lord to see me. The Yearly Meeting was the week following, to which many Friends came out of most parts of the nation; and a blessed opportunity the Lord gave us together; wherein the ancient love was sweetly felt, and the heavenly life flowed abundantly over all. After the Yearly Meeting, I continued a month or five weeks in and about London, labouring in the work of the Lord both in and out of meetings; for besides the public testimony which the Lord gave me to bear both to Friends and to the world in meetings, I had much service upon me, with respect to Friends' sufferings, in seeking to get ease and liberty for them in this and other nations. Much pains and time I spent, while in London, in writing letters to Friends in divers parts of England, and in Scotland, Holland, Barbadoes, and several parts of America.

After this I was moved of the Lord to visit Friends in some parts of Surrey and Sussex. I went to KINGSTON by water, and tarried certain days; for while I was there, the Lord laid it upon me to write both to the great Turk, and the Dey of Algiers severally, to warn them, and the people under them, to turn from their wickedness, fear the Lord, and do justly; lest the judgments of God should come upon them, and destroy them without remedy. To the Algerines I wrote more particularly, concerning the cruelty they exercised towards Friends and others, whom they held captives in Algiers.* When I had finished that service, and visited Friends in

godliness, they would not live in the earth as they did." He was a zealous labourer, a vigilant watchman, a sharp reprover of evil, an encourager of the good, and a faithful minister, endeavouring to bring those he ministered to into an inward exercise of spirit towards God, and to a greater acquaintance with, and subjection to, the power of God. Concerning this he wrote a treatise entitled, *A Testimony to the Power of God, being Greater than the Power of Satan.*

He died in 1697, having often said in his last sickness, "All is well," and testified that the power and strength of God was with him.

* There appear to have been at this time a number of Friends captured at Algiers. In the early times of the Society many of its members were seafaring men; and to such, of whatever religious profession, it was no uncommon thing to be taken at sea by the Algerines or other *corsairs*, who continually scoured the Mediterranean, and

their meetings at Kingston, I went further into the country, and had meetings amongst Friends at WORPLESDON, GUILDFORD, ESHER, CAPEL, PATCHGATE, WORMINGHURST, BLETCHINGTON, HORSHAM, IFIELD, REIGATE, GATTON, &c., and so came back to KINGSTON again; and thence to HAMMERSMITH. And having spent some days in the service of truth amongst Friends at Hammersmith, BATTERSEA, WANDSWORTH, and thereabouts, I crossed over, by KENSINGTON, to HENDON, where I had a very good meeting on a First-day; and went thence to LONDON.

When I had been about ten days in LONDON, I was drawn again to visit Friends in the country; and went to EDMONTON, to Christopher Taylor's, who kept a school for the educating of Friends' children. I had some service here amongst the youth; and then went towards Hertford, visiting several Friends on the way. At HERTFORD I met with John Story, and some others of his party;* but the testimony of truth went over them, and kept them down, so that the meeting was quiet. It was on a First-day; and the next day being the men's and women's meeting for business, I visited them also, and the rather, because some in that place had let in a disesteem of them. Wherefore I was moved to open the service of those meetings, and the usefulness and benefit thereof to the church of Christ, as the Lord opened the thing in me; and it was of good service to Friends. I had a meeting also with some of those, that were gone into strife and contention, to show them wherein they were wrong; and having cleared

ventured occasionally beyond its limits to make prize of merchant ships, and consign their crews to slavery.

Great care was exercised towards these captive Friends by the Society, and efforts made for their redemption. They are mentioned in the Yearly Meeting epistles of 1682–1687, and in most of the succeeding ones. In the epistle of 1698 it is stated, "Divers of our Friends who were captives at Mequinez, and suffered great hardships there, are dead; and there yet remain five, for whose ransom great endeavours have been used, but it is not yet effected." The epistle of the following year states, "Earnest endeavours have again lately been used for the liberty of our Friends, captives in Barbary, though not as yet obtained; and there being at this time some negotiations on foot, by the tenderness and care of the government, for the redemption of all the English there; and though the persons in Barbary, employed therein by Friends, do wait some time to see the effect of that, yet we shall continue our further endeavours for their discharge, and in the meantime take care to send them supplies for food, they having little allowance in that country, of anything to support their bodies, under the great severities of labour, and undeserved stripes, that captives often endure."

In the epistle of 1702 the conclusion of the Barbary captives is stated, namely, that five Friends, being all who remained alive in that long and sore captivity, *have been this year redeemed*, whose ransom (including a Friend's son from Pennsylvania) cost the Society upwards of £480. The redeemed tenderly and gratefully acknowledged Friends' love and care of them.

* A schism, of which Story and Wilkinson were at the head, is frequently referred to in the writings of some of the early Friends. It commenced and spread mostly in the north. There were, however, those in London, Bristol, and some southern counties, who, through ease and unwatchfulness, having lost their first love and the discerning spirit, were deceived by a specious bait, and became the cause of much exercise and trouble to their brethren.

The ground of difference was alleged by them to be, their objection to those meet-

myself of them, I left them to the Lord. Then, after another public meeting in the town, I returned towards London by WALTHAM ABBEY, where I had a public meeting on the First-day following; and another with Friends in the evening. Next day I went to Christopher Taylor's at EDMONTON, and stayed there a day or two, having some things upon me to write, which were for the service of truth. When I had finished that service, I went to LONDON by SHACKLEWELL, where was a school kept by Friends, for the bringing up of young women that were Friends' daughters.

I abode at LONDON most part of this winter, having much service for the Lord there, both in and out of meetings: for as it was a time of great suffering among Friends, I was drawn in spirit to visit Friends' meetings more frequently; to encourage and strengthen them both by exhortation and example. The parliament also was sitting, and Friends were diligent in waiting upon them, to lay their grievances before them. We received fresh accounts almost every day of the sad sufferings Friends underwent in many parts of the nation. In seeking relief for my suffering brethren I spent much time; together with other Friends, who were freely given up to that service, attending at the parliament-house for many days together, and watching all opportunities to speak with such members of either house, as would hear our just complaints. And indeed, some of these were very courteous to us, and appeared willing to help us if they could; but the parliament being then earnest in examining the Popish plot, and contriving ways to discover such as were Popishly affected, our adversaries took advantages against us (because they knew we could not swear nor fight) to expose us to those penalties that were made against Papists; though they knew in their consciences that we were no Papists, and had had experience of us, that we were no plotters. Wherefore, to clear our innocency, and to stop the mouths of our adversaries, I drew up a short paper, to be delivered to the parliament; as follows:—

"IT is our principle and testimony, to deny and renounce all plots and plotters against the king, or any of his subjects; for we have the Spirit of Christ, by which we have the mind of Christ, who came to save men's

ings for regulating the affairs of the church, exercising a salutary discipline over its members; and more especially against the establishment of women's meetings, which G. Fox and other Friends "were moved to set up." They stated, with a show of plausibility which gained some, chiefly the looser sort, to their ranks, "That such meetings were needless, some years having been passed in peace and unity without them; and that every individual ought to be guided by the Spirit, and left free to act; that meetings for discipline were a form, and the exercise of that discipline an infringement upon individual liberty." Great endeavours were made for their enlightenment and restoration. In 2d Month 1676, a meeting was held at Drawell, which lasted four days, in which "many Friends laboured much for their preservation, but they were too far gone in a separate spirit to be reclaimed." They, therefore, became out of unity with the body who, "walking by the same rule, minded the same thing." They fell to jangling, and, after a while, the best among them came to see how they had been deceived; and the rest, after having had separate meetings, are said to have "vanished as snow in the fields."—*See* Sewell's *History*, folio edition, pp. 583, 584.

lives, and not to destroy them. We desire the safety of the king and of all his subjects. Wherefore we declare, that we will endeavour, to our power, to save and defend him and them, by discovering all plots and plotters (which shall come to our knowledge) that would destroy the king or his subjects. This we do sincerely offer unto you. But as to swearing and fighting, which in tenderness of conscience we cannot do, ye know that we have suffered these many years for our conscientious refusal thereof. And now that the Lord hath brought you together, we desire you to relieve us, and free us from these sufferings; and that ye will not put upon us to do those things, which we have suffered so much and so long already for not doing; for if you do, you will make our sufferings and bonds stronger, instead of relieving us." G. F.

CHAPTER X.

1681–1683.—George Fox answers two envious books written abroad—writes to magistrates to persuade them to moderation—writes to the Quarterly Meetings—attends the judges at Chambers, respecting a tithe-suit against himself and his wife—George Fox had bound himself not to intermeddle with his wife's estate—this is shown to the judges in court, at which they wonder—his counsel thereon founds an argument in his favour—he again writes against the spirit of strife and division in the church—writes to the magistrates who had illegally condemned Friends upon *ex-parte* evidence—writes two papers respecting the choice of sheriffs—Friends are interrupted at Gracechurch Street Meeting by a civil and military force—George Fox writes divers books and papers in support and defence of the Truth—the Spirit of God directed to as the rule to distinguish between Truth and error, whereby the evil of persecution may be avoided—an epistle to encourage Friends under their sufferings, both from the outward powers, and from false brethren—the laws are now more strictly enforced against Dissenters—an epistle to Friends, commending them to the power of God in themselves—writes to Friends imprisoned at Denbigh, to console them in their sufferings, and exhorting them to faithfulness—Friends are kept out of their meeting-houses, and fined for speaking—a Friend is speedily restored from a sudden illness, in a remarkable manner, through the prayers of George Fox—persecution is now hot, and George Fox writes to Friends not to risk the loss of other people's goods through their sufferings.

About this time I received two very envious books, written against Truth and Friends; one of them by a doctor (so called) of Bremen, in Germany, the other by a priest of Dantzic. They were both full of gross falsehoods, and reproachful slanders. I found it upon me to answer them both; and that I might not be much interrupted therein by other business and company, I went to Kingston-upon-Thames, where I wrote an answer to each of them; and also to some other scandalous papers, which had been printed and scattered about to misrepresent Friends.

While I was there I wrote also the following paper, to persuade the magistrates to moderation towards Dissenters, and take off their edge to persecution. That it should have its full service, I directed it—

"*To all the Rulers, Magistrates, and Law-makers in England, Scotland, and Ireland, from the highest to the lowest; and to all other Magistrates everywhere, in that which is called Christendom; desiring their health, peace, tranquillity, life, and salvation in Christ Jesus, the Lord of Glory, and Lamb of God, who takes away the sins of the world, who is the King of kings, and Lord of lords, to whom all power in heaven and in earth is given; and who will reward every man according to his words and works.*

"You that bear the name of Christian magistrates, my desire is, that you may all be found in Christ; and not only have the name, but be made partakers of his divine nature; that ye may be not only sayers, but doers of the word; not only professors and talkers of Christ, but letting him rule in your hearts by faith, and be walkers in Christ. For as his great apostle saith, 'As every one hath received the Lord Jesus Christ, so let him walk in him; for in him there is peace.' If all that profess Christ, did walk in Christ, they would walk in peace, and be in unity; for the apostle exhorted the Christians in his day to keep the unity of the Spirit; which is the bond of peace, yea, of Christ the King of kings' peace. All Christians, who have the Scriptures, and are not in this Spirit of Christ, are not in unity one with another; and so have broken this bond of peace, which should knit and unite them together. Likewise all that profess the truth of Christ, should live in it; for it is peaceable, and the gospel is the gospel of peace; which, if all Christians lived in, they would be at peace one with another, and in the glorious fellowship of the gospel. And if all Christians kept in the fear of God, which is the beginning of the pure, heavenly, peaceable, and gentle wisdom, which is easy to be entreated (above that wisdom, which is earthly, sensual, devilish, and destroying), there would be no difference and destroying about matters of religion.

"I do declare the mighty day of the Lord is come and coming; and the Lord God is come to teach his people himself by his Son, Heb. i., who bruises the serpent's head, that false teacher, that led Adam and Eve from God their Teacher. God will teach his people by his Son, who was the Teacher of Adam and Eve in paradise, before they fell and disobeyed the Lord, forsook him, and followed the serpent; whose head Christ bruises, and renews man and woman up again into the image of God, which Adam and Eve were in before they fell: glory and honour be to God through Jesus Christ, who hath called us by his Son into his glorious image, to serve and worship him in Spirit and truth; which Holy Spirit and truth the devil is out of, and into which he cannot come.

"I desire all Christian magistrates to take heed of persecuting any, though they differ from you in matters of faith, worship, and religion. For Christ saith, 'Let the tares and the wheat grow together till the harvest;' and he forbade such as would be plucking up tares: the reason was, 'lest they should pluck up the wheat also;' for Christ said, it should be his angels' work, to separate the tares from the wheat. Moreover, Christ said, they should go into everlasting punishment that did not visit him in prison in his members: then what will become of them that cast him into prison, where he is made manifest in his members! O, lay these things to heart! A day of judgment will come, vengeance and recompense upon every one according to his works.

"To those disciples who would have had fire to come down from heaven to consume them that would not receive them, Christ turned him about, rebuked them, and told them, 'they knew not what spirit they were of; for he came not to destroy men's lives, but to save them.'

"Therefore, let all magistrates and priests in that which is called Christendom, consider who have destroyed men's lives since the apostles' days, because they could not receive the religions, ways, and worships which they have made and set up: have they known what spirit they have been of? Are they not all reproved by, and come under the judgment of Christ? Therefore let all persecution be laid aside concerning religion; let love bear the sway, to overcome evil and enemies; and let patience oversway passion in all, that all may retain the heavenly reason, and the pure understanding,—that your moderation in true Christianity may be known to all men. For have you not the Turks, Jews, Tartars, Indians, and atheists' eyes upon you, and upon Christendom. Therefore be in unity, and let not the name of God and Christ be blasphemed amongst them by means of any that bear the name of Christians. So God may be glorified by all and in all, through Jesus Christ, who is over all, who calls all to peace, and is blessed for ever.

"I would have you to be as noble as the Bereans, and search the Scriptures of Christ and the apostles. Where did he or they give any command to imprison, banish, persecute, or put to death, any that would not receive or conform to them, or that were contrary-minded to them in religion, or differed from them in matters of worship.

"Again, I desire all Christian magistrates to search both Scriptures and Chronicles, and see what was the end of all persecutors, and what judgments came upon them. What came to Cain, who was the first persecutor for matters of faith and sacrifice? Did not he become a vagabond and a fugitive in the earth? What became of the old world, that grieved God, and Noah, a preacher of righteousness? What became of Sodom, that vexed just Lot? What became of Pharaoh, that persecuted God's people in Egypt (though the more he persecuted them the more they grew)? What became of Ahab and Jezebel, that persecuted the Lord's prophets? And what became of Haman, that would have destroyed the Jews? What became of the Jews and Jerusalem, that persecuted Christ and the apostles? What was the end of all these? Are they not become vagabonds in the earth, and driven away from their native country? Therefore I beseech you in the love and fear of God, be so noble as to search both Scripture and history, and let not your divine understanding be clouded. What will become of the beast and whore spoken of in the Revelations, with their false prophets, that have drunk the blood of the saints, martyrs, and prophets of Jesus? Must they not all go with the devil, who is a murderer, destroyer, and adversary of mankind, into the lake of fire, that burns with brimstone? And ye may be sure that spirit that stirs you up to persecution, let it be in whomsoever it will, is not of Christ, and of his lamb-like nature; who takes away the sins of the world, not the lives of men.

"Paul was a persecutor, and a haler to prison, before he was converted to Christianity; but never after. And therefore, are not all in Saul's nature, let them be of what name or profession soever, that are persecutors, and unconverted into Paul's life of Christianity? He said, the life that he lived after he was converted, was 'by the faith of the Son of God;' and that he lived, yet not he, but 'Christ lived in him,' who came to save men's lives, and not to destroy them. This life should be the life of all Christians now, which Paul in his converted state lived in. And the apostle saith, 'The law is good if a man use it lawfully; knowing this, that the law is not made for a righteous man, but for the lawless and disobedient, for the ungodly, and for sinners, for unholy and profane, for murderers of fathers and murderers of mothers, for manslayers, for whoremongers, for them that defile themselves with mankind, for men-stealers, for liars, and for perjured persons,' 1 Tim. i. 8–10. So the law, in its place, is good against such. Again the apostle says, 'The law was added because of transgression,' Gal. iii. 19. Here all magistrates may see what the law in its place is good against; what it was made for and against; and what evils, the apostle says, it takes hold of. He does not say the law should be laid upon men that differed from them in their religion and judgment, nor upon righteous men. So you may see in what condition the law is good, and what it was made against; not against righteous men, against whom ye have nothing in their lives and conversations, only because they differ from you in matters of religion; letting manslayers, whoremongers, perjured persons, ungodly, profane persons, liars, &c., go unpunished; such do not use, nor execute the law lawfully, as the apostle says, 'The law is good, if a man use it lawfully.' Therefore it ought to be used lawfully; which law, the apostle says, 'is for the punishment of evildoers, and a praise for them that do well;' as may be seen, Rom. xiii. So, as the apostle said, 'We do not break the law, nor make it void; but we establish the law,' Rom. iii. 31.

"This is from him who desires the eternal good and salvation of you all in Christ Jesus. Amen." G. F.

Kingston-upon-Thames, the 4th of the 1st Month, 1680-1.

After I had finished these services I returned to LONDON, where I stayed about a month, labouring amongst Friends in the work of the Lord, both in public meetings for worship, and in those relating to the outward affairs of the church. Then feeling my spirit drawn to visit Friends about Enfield, I went to WALTHAM ABBEY, where I had a very precious meeting; and another at FLAMSTEAD HEATH. Having spent some time among Friends thereabouts, and had divers good meetings at EDMONTON, ENFIELD, WINCHMORE-HILL, and other places, I came back to LONDON a little before the Yearly Meeting, which was in the 3d month, 1681. It was a very precious time, in which the glorious presence and power of the Lord was eminently felt and enjoyed.

Some time after the Yearly Meeting it came upon me to write the following epistle:—

"*To the Men's and Women's Quarterly Meetings that are gathered in the name and power of Jesus.*

"CHRIST, the second Adam, who is both Head and Husband of his church, the Redeemer, Purchaser, Saviour, Sanctifier, and Reconciler of his sons and daughters (his church) to God, I say, his presence (to wit, Christ's) feel among you, to exercise his prophetical office, in opening you with his light, grace, truth, power, and Spirit; and to exercise his office, as he is a Bishop, to oversee you with his light, grace, power, and Spirit, that ye do not go astray from God. And as Christ is a Shepherd, feel, see, and hear him exercising that office, who laid down his life for his sheep, feeding them in his living pastures of life, and making them to drink of his living, eternal springs. Let Him rule and govern in your hearts, as he is

King, that his heavenly and spiritual government all may live under, as true subjects of his righteous, peaceable kingdom, which stands in righteousness, peace, joy in the Holy Ghost, over Satan and his power, and all unrighteousness. So all ye subjects to Christ's kingdom of peace, if ye want wisdom, or knowledge, life, or salvation, Christ is the treasure; feel Him the treasure among you. And all, as ye have received Christ, walk in him, in whom ye have peace; who bruises the head of the serpent, the author of all strife, distraction, and confusion: yea, you have peace with God, and one with another, though the trouble be from the world and the world's spirit. Therefore, my dear Friends, brethren and sisters, love one another with the love that is of God shed in your hearts; that ye may bear the marks of Christ's disciples, and it may appear that Christ is *in* you, and ye *in* Him; so that God Almighty may be glorified among you. Whatever ye do, let it be done in the name of Jesus, to the praise of God the Father, keeping in unity in the Holy Spirit of God, which was before the unholy spirit was: which Holy spirit is your bond of peace, yea, the Holy King of kings' and Lord of lords' peace. And in this holy, pure Spirit is your eternal unity and fellowship; in which ye serve and worship the God of Truth, who is over all, blessed for ever, Amen. So the Lord guide you all with his Word of patience, life, power, and wisdom, in all your actions, lives, conversations, and meetings, to God's glory. My love to you all in the Lord Jesus Christ, by whom all things were made, and who is over all, the First and the Last." G. F.

London, the 9th of the 4th Month, 1681.

About this time I had occasion to go to several of the judges' chambers upon a suit about tithes. For my wife and I and several other Friends, were sued in Cartmel-Wapentake Court in Lancashire, for small tithes, and we had demurred to the jurisdiction of that court. Whereupon the plaintiff prosecuted us in the Exchequer Court at Westminster, where they run us up to a writ of rebellion, for not answering the bill upon oath; and got an order of court to the sergeant, to take me and my wife into custody. This was a little before the Yearly Meeting, at which time it was thought they would have taken me up; and according to outward appearance, it was likely, and very easy for him to have done it, lodging at the places where I used to do, and being very public in meetings. But the Lord's power was over them, and restrained them; so that they did not take me. Yet understanding there was a warrant out against me, as soon as the Yearly Meeting was over, I took William Mead with me, and went to several of the judges' chambers to speak with them about it; and to let them understand both the state of the case, and the ground and reason of our refusing to pay tithes. The first I went to was Judge Gregory, to whom I tendered mine and my wife's answer to the plaintiff's bill; in which was set forth, that she had lived three and forty years at Swarthmore, and in all that time there had been no tithe paid or demanded: and an old man, who had long been a tithe-gatherer, had made affidavit, that he never gathered tithe at Swarthmore-Hall in Judge Fell's time, or since. There were many particulars in our answer, but it would not be accepted without an oath. I told the judge that both tithe and swearing among Christians came from the Pope, and it was matter of conscience to us not to pay tithes, nor to swear; for Christ bid his disciples, who had freely received, give freely; and he commanded them "not to swear at all." The judge said, there was tithe paid in England before Popery was: I asked him by what law or statute they were paid then; but he was silent. Then I told him, there were eight poor men brought up to London out of the North about two hundred miles for small tithes, and one of them had no family but himself and his wife, and kept no living creature but a cat. I asked him also, whether they could take a man and his wife, and imprison them both for small tithes, and so destroy a family; and if they could, I desired to know by what law: he did not answer me, but only said, "that was a hard case." When I found there was no help to be had there, we left him, and went to Judge Montague's chamber; and with him I had much discourse concerning tithes. Whereupon he sent for our adversary's attorney; and when he came I offered him our answer. He said, if we would pay the charges of the court, and be bound to stand trial, and abide the judgment of the court, we should not have the oath tendered to us. I told him that they had brought those charges upon us, by requiring us to put in our answer upon oath; which they knew before we could not do for conscience' sake; and as we could not pay any tithe nor swear, so neither should we pay any of their charges. Upon this he would not receive our answer. So we went from thence to Judge Atkyns's chamber, and he being busy, we gave our answers and our reasons against tithes and swearing to his clerk; but neither could we find any encouragement from him to expect redress there. Wherefore leaving him we went to one of the most noted counsellors, and showed him the state of our case and our answers: he was very civil to us, and said, "this way of proceeding against us was somewhat like an inquisition." A few days after, those eight poor Friends that were brought up so far out of the North, appeared before the judges; and the Lord was with them, and his power was over the court, so that the Friends were not committed to the Fleet. Our cause was put off till the next term (called Michaelmas), and then it was brought before the four judges again. Then William Mead told the judges that I had engaged not to meddle with my wife's estate. The judges could hardly believe that any man would do so: whereupon he showed them the writing under my hand and seal, at which they wondered. Then two of the judges and some of the lawyers stood up, and pleaded for me, that I was not liable to the tithes: but the other two judges and divers lawyers, pressed earnestly to have me sequestered; alleging that I was a public man. At length they prevailed with one of the other two judges to join with them; and then they granted a sequestration against me and my wife together. Thereupon, by advice of counsel, we moved for a limitation, which was granted, and that much defeated our adversary's design in suing out the sequestration; for this limited the plaintiff to take no more than was proved. One of the judges, Baron Weston, was very bitter, and broke forth in a great rage against me in the open court; but shortly after he died.

After the Yearly Meeting, I tarried about a month in London; and then went into SUSSEX, to visit Friends there, amongst whom I had many large and very precious meetings in divers parts of that county. Yet I spent not much time now in Sussex, but returned pretty soon to LONDON, whither I felt drawings in spirit; and had very good service for the Lord there, both in public meetings and amongst Friends. When I had tarried some time in London, I went to EDMONTON; thence into BUCKINGHAMSHIRE, where I visited Friends at several meetings in that county: and then went by HENLEY to READING, where I tarried several meetings. I went no farther westward at this time than to ORE, where I had a very large meeting; after which, striking through the edge of OXFORDSHIRE, I had a large and very precious meeting at WARBOROUGH, in which the glory of the Lord shone over all. Many Friends came to it out of Berkshire, Buckinghamshire, and Hampshire. Thence I passed to ILMORE in the vale of Buckinghamshire, where we had a glorious meeting; and the day following I returned to Mary Penington's, visiting the men's and women's monthly meetings at HUNGER-HILL, and some other meetings thereabouts; and then passed to WATFORD, where was a marriage of two Friends, at which I was present. A very large meeting we had on that occasion, and the Lord's power was over all. I went from Watford to LONGFORD in MIDDLESEX, visiting Friends at UXBRIDGE in the way. At Longford we had a large meeting on First-day, and the presence of the Lord was preciously felt amongst us; blessed be his name! I passed from Longford to KINGSTON, visiting Friends as I went, at STAINES and SUNBURY. At Kingston I abode with Friends two meetings, wherein we were sweetly refreshed together in the Lord. Passing thence towards London, I had a very precious meeting at WANDSWORTH: then crossing over to HAMMERSMITH, I had a good meeting there, which was larger on account of a burial; and there being openness in the people, I had a fine opportunity to open the way of truth amongst them.

After I was come to LONDON, I was moved to write the following paper, concerning that spirit which had led some, who professed truth, into strife and division, and to oppose the way and work of the Lord:—

"FRIENDS,

"You that keep your habitations in the truth, that is over all, see that it is the same spirit that leads the backsliders and apostates now, from the spiritual fellowship and unity of God's people, and the church of Christ, that led Adam and Eve from God, and the Jews from God and his law, to rebel against his Spirit. This spirit is the same that was in the world, which got into the Jews, when they were gone from the Spirit of God; and then they turned against God and his prophets, and against Christ and his apostles. This spirit led them to be as bad as Pilate, or worse. The enmity or adversary got within them against the truth, and them that walked in it, and the Spirit of the Lord; so that they killed and destroyed the Just. This was the spirit of the devil, the destroyer, who sought not only to destroy the truth, but the order of it, and them that walked in it, when true Christianity was planted among the possessors of the light, grace, and truth, and the holy gospel faith and Spirit, who enjoyed Christ in their hearts. But when some began to err from the Spirit and faith, to hate the light, disobey the gospel, turn the grace of God into wantonness, walk despitefully against the Spirit of Grace, turn from the truth, crucify to themselves Christ afresh, and put him to open shame; these were they, that let in the spirit of the world; who held the form of godliness, but denied the power thereof; and troubled the churches in the apostles' days. When the spirit of Satan had got into such, they were more troublesome to the church than the open persecutors that were without: these got into the assemblies to deceive the hearts of the simple, having the good words, fair speeches, and sheep's clothing. Paul, Peter, John, Jude, and James had much to do with such, to keep them from troubling the church of Christ; for they are out of the light, power, and Spirit; therefore the apostles of Christ exhorted the saints to keep to the Word of life within; to the anointing; to the grace, truth, and Holy Spirit *in* their hearts. This foul spirit will profess all the Scriptures in words; but by the Spirit of God, which is holy, this spirit is tried, and its fruits. So the apostates went from the power and Spirit of God, and turned against the prophets, and the martyrs of Jesus; and became the whore, whose cup all nations drank of. The dragon with his tail threw down many of the stars, and would have devoured the woman with his flood; but the woman, the true church, was preserved; for the gates of hell cannot prevail against her; and then the dragon made war with her seed. So the dragon, the whore, the beast, and false prophets, all made war against the Lamb and the saints; but the Lamb and the saints will overcome them all, and will have the victory. And now the everlasting gospel is preached again to all nations, tongues, and peoples; and many are gathered into the gospel, the power of God, are turned to the light, which is the life in Christ, are grafted into him, and are come to walk in the order of the new covenant of light and life, in the gospel of peace and salvation. The same spirit that opposed the apostles and the churches in their days, opposes now; yea, it is the same that opposed Christ, and disdained him, that disdaineth God's servants now. The same that opposed the prophets, and rebelled against Moses, opposes and rebels against God's servants and people now. It is the same dark, blind, disobedient, faithless, wilful, jealous spirit, that persecutes some with the hands, and others with the tongue. It is the same spirit of enmity, the adversary and destroyer, that tempted Adam and Eve to disobey God, and deceived them; which deceived the Jews and tempted them, and deceived all those that went from the church in the apostles' days. And it is the same spirit that is now going about sometimes like a roaring lion, sometimes like a twisting serpent to tempt, to deceive, and to devour, in those who have fair speeches, good words, and sheep's clothing, in a form of godliness, and under pretence of light and liberty, but who deny the power thereof, and inwardly are ravening wolves; and if it were possible, they would deceive the very elect. But the elect are in the covenant of light and life, and in the power of God over them, and in Christ, who will grind them to pieces; and will slay all his enemies with his spiritual sword, who will not have him to rule over, or in them. In Christ all his people have rest and peace, who is their sanctuary over all storms and tempests. In Christ, the sanctuary, no deceiver nor destroyer can come; for he is a place of sweet rest and safety. Hallelujah! praise the Lord for his sanctuary. Amen." G. F.

Sufferings continuing severe upon Friends at LONDON, I found my service lay mostly there; wherefore I went but little out of town, and not far; being frequent at the most public meetings, to encourage Friends, both by word and example, to stand fast in the testimony to which God had called them. At other times I went about from house to house, visiting Friends that had their goods taken away for their testimony to truth. And because the wicked informers were grown very audacious, by reason that they had too much countenance and encouragement from some justices, who, trusting wholly to their information, proceeded against Friends without hearing them; whereby many were made to suffer, not only contrary to right, but even contrary to law also; I advised with some Friends about it; and we drew up a paper, which was delivered to most of the magistrates in and about the city; which was as follows:—

"WHEREAS informers have obtained warrants of some justices of peace, who have convicted many of us without a hearing, or once summoning us to appear before them; by which proceedings many have had their goods seized and taken away, being generally fined ten pounds each for an unknown speaker: and some of those persons so fined, have not been at the meetings they were fined for; and the speaker notwithstanding has himself been fined for the same meeting, the same day the others were fined for the unknown speaker. By this the justices may see the wickedness of these informers, by whose false oaths we have been convicted for an unknown preacher, when the preacher has been both known and fined. Also in their swearing such persons to have been at such a meeting such a day, when indeed they, whom they have so sworn against, have not been at that meeting. By which proceedings several families of the king's peaceable subjects are likely to be ruined, if a speedy stop be not put thereunto. Therefore we hope and desire, that you, the king's justices, for the time to come, when any informers shall come to any of you with information against any of us, will summon such as are accused to appear before you, and hear us and our accusers face to face; that none for the time to come may suffer for that they are not guilty of. For Pilate the governor heard Christ and his accusers, face to face, before he condemned him, John xix. The council and chief priests heard Stephen and his accusers, with the witnesses that were brought against him, face to face, before they condemned him, Acts vii. The Roman captain heard Paul and his accusers face to face, Acts xxiii. Felix the governor heard Paul, and Ananias the high priest, and the elders that accused Paul, face to face, Acts xxiv. And when the high priests and chief of the Jews accused Paul to Festus, he heard Paul and his accusers, and them that witnessed against him, face to face, Acts xxv. Doth the law of God, or did the Roman law, or doth the law of the land judge any man, before he and his accusers, and they that witness against him, be heard face to face?"

This somewhat moderated the justices; and after this several Friends, that had been illegally prosecuted and fined, entered their appeals; and upon trial were acquitted, and the informers cast: which was a great discouragement to the informers, and some relief to Friends.

A little before the time for choosing new sheriffs for the city, they who put up to be chosen desiring our Friends to give their voices for them, I wrote a few lines, tending to discover what spirit they were of, and how they stood affected to true liberty; and it was by way of inquiry, thus:—

"Do any here in London, who stand to be chosen sheriffs, own that Christ, that was crucified without the gates of Jerusalem, to be the light of the world, that 'enlightens every man that cometh into the world,' who saith, 'Believe in the light, that ye may become children of light?' Are any of you against persecuting people for their religion and worship of God in Spirit and in truth, as Christ commandeth? For Christ said, 'I am not of this world, nor my kingdom;' therefore he doth not uphold his spiritual worship and pure religion with worldly and carnal weapons. Christ said, 'Swear not at all;' and his apostle James saith the same; but will not you force us to swear, and so to break Christ's and his apostle's commands, in putting oaths to us? Christ saith to his apostles, 'Freely ye have received, freely give.' Will not you force us to give tithes and maintenance to such teachers as we know God hath not sent? Shall we be free to serve and worship God, and keep his and his Son's commands, if we give our voices freely for you? For we are unwilling to give our voices for such as will imprison and persecute us, and spoil our goods."

But whatever they were that stood to be chosen, I observed heat and strife in the spirits of the people that were to choose; wherefore I wrote a few lines to be spread amongst them, directed thus:—

"To the People who are choosing Sheriffs in London.

"People,—All keep in the gentle and peaceable wisdom of God, which is above all that which is earthly, sensual, and devilish; and live in that love of God that is not puffed up, nor is unseemly; which envieth not, but beareth and endureth all things. In this love ye will seek the good and peace of all, and the hurt of no man. Keep out of all heats, and be not hot-headed; but be cool and gentle, that your Christian moderation may appear to all men; for the Lord is at hand, who beholds all men's words, thoughts, and actions, and will reward every one according to his works; and what every man soweth, that shall he reap."

Now I had some inclination to go into the country to a meeting, but hearing that there would be a bustle at our meetings, and feeling a great disquietness in people's spirits in the city about choosing sheriffs, it was upon me to stay in the city, and go to the meeting in Gracechurch Street upon the First-day of the week. William Penn went with me, and spoke; and while he was declaring the truth to the people, a constable came in with his great staff, and bid him give over, and come down; but he continued, declaring truth in the power of God. After a while the constable drew back, and when William Penn had done, I stood up, and declared to the people "the everlasting gospel, which was preached in the apostles' days, and to Abraham; and which the church in the apostles' days received, and came to be heirs of. This gospel, I declared, was sent from heaven by the Holy Ghost in the apostles' days, and is so now; and was not of man, neither by man; but by the revelation of the Holy Ghost. And now this gospel is preached again (as John saw, and said it should be) to all nations, tongues, and people; and all people now are to hear Christ the prophet, in this his gospel of the new covenant. For as Moses said, 'Like unto me will God raise up a prophet, and Him shall ye hear in all things;' so, said I, this prophet, Christ, is come, and all the Jews in spirit, the true believing Christians in the light, who have the law of God written in their hearts, and put into their minds, are to hear Christ in his gospel, new testament, and new covenant, which is the law of the spirit of life in Christ Jesus, who bruises the serpent's head (which is the head of enmity), and makes free from the law of sin and death. I showed, that all whom Christ quickens and makes alive, he makes to sit together in the heavenly places in himself. So that they do not wander up and down, like the fool's eye, in the corners of the earth; nor are their eyes abroad in the world, to sit down in the world's invented seats of religion; but they sit together in Him, as the saints did in the apostles' days. So Christ was and is their treasure of wisdom, life, knowledge, and salvation." As I was thus speaking, two constables came in with their great staves, and bid me give over speaking, and come down; but, feeling the power of the Lord with me, I spoke on therein, both to the constables and to the people. To the constables I declared, "that we were a peaceable people, who meet to wait upon God, and worship him in Spirit and in truth; and therefore they needed not to come with their staves amongst us, who were met in a peaceable manner, desiring and seeking the good and salvation of all people." Then turning my speech to the people again, I declared what further was upon me to them; and while I was speaking, the constables drew out towards the door; and the soldiers stood with their muskets in the yard. When I had done speaking, I kneeled down and prayed, desiring the Lord to open the eyes and hearts of all people, both high and low, that their minds might be turned to God by his Holy Spirit; that he might be glorified in all and over all. After prayer the meeting rose, and Friends passed away; the constables being come in again, but without the soldiers; and indeed, both they and the soldiers carried themselves civilly. William Penn and I went into a room hard by, as we used to do, and many Friends went with us; and lest the constables should think we would shun them, a Friend went down and told them, that if they would have anything with us, they might come where we were, if they pleased. One of them came to us soon after, but without his staff; which he chose to do, that he might not be observed; for he said, the people told him he busied himself more than he needed. We desired to see his warrant; and therein we found, that the informer was one Hilton, a North-countryman, who was reputed to be a Baptist. The constable was asked, whether he would arrest us by his warrant on that day; it being the First-day of the week, which in their law was called the Lord's day; he said, he thought he could not. He told us also, that he had charged the informer to come along with him to the meeting, but he had run away from him. We showed the constable that both he and we were clear; yet to free him from all fear of danger, we were free to go to the alderman that granted the warrant. Then a Friend that was present said, he would go with the constable to speak with the alderman; which they did, and came presently back again, the alderman being gone from home. Seeing the constable in a strait, and finding him to be a tender man, we bid him fix an hour to come to us again, or send for us, and we would come to him. So he appointed five in the afternoon; but neither came, nor sent for us; and a Friend meeting him afterwards in the evening, the constable told him, he thought it would come to nothing, and therefore did not look after us. So the Lord's power was over all; to him be the glory!

On the Fourth-day following, it was upon me to go to Gracechurch Street meeting again; for I had heard that they would come to break it up that day. The neighbours, it seems, were informed so; a justice had granted a warrant for that purpose, and the constable told a Friend, that Hilton the informer had been with him about it. The constable would have had the informer to go with him to the meeting, but he would not; but would have the constable to go without him; whether that put the constable by, I know not; but he did not come. I was in a travail of spirit in the power of God, and was moved in it to go to the meeting; and the Lord's power chained all down. Though they threatened to bring the red coats, none came, nor was there any disturbance; but a glorious, powerful meeting it was, and very peaceable. Glory, honour, and praises be to the Lord over all for ever. Amen!

During the time I thus abode at London, as I had leisure between meetings, and from other public services, I wrote divers books and papers, some of which were printed, and others spread about in manuscript. Of these, one was directed "To the bishops and others, that stirred up persecution; to show them from the Holy Scriptures that they did not walk therein according to the royal law, 'to love their neighbour as themselves, and to do to others as they would be done unto.'" Another was, "To all the several sorts of professed Christians, as well Protestants as Papists, whose religion and worship stand in outward observances and ceremonies; pressing them from those words of the apostle Paul to the Galatians, chap. v. ver. 2–4, 'Behold, I Paul say unto you, that if ye be circumcised, Christ shall profit you nothing. For I testify again to every man that is circumcised, that he is a debtor to the whole law. Christ is become of no effect unto you, whosoever of you are justified by the law; ye are fallen from grace,' to consider whether they, being gone back into legal observations and shadowy ceremonies (in upholding tithes, offerings, first-fruits, priests' garments, outward altars, temples, lamps, lights, &c., and in observing days, months, times, years, with many other things commanded by the law), were not gone into the same state that the Galatians were running into; and so were fallen from grace, and become debtors to do the whole law." Another was, "To direct and turn all people to the Spirit of God, that they might thereby receive a right understanding, and be able to distinguish between right and wrong, truth and error; that under pretence of punishing evil-doers, they might not themselves do evil in persecuting the righteous." That paper, being short, is here inserted:—

"THE Spirit of God, which he hath poured upon all, giveth an understanding to all that are led by it; and to those who do not quench the motions of it, it giveth knowledge and understanding to distinguish good from evil, light from darkness, Christ from antichrist, the old testament or covenant from the new, the old way from the new and living way; the sheep and lambs from the goats and wolves; the worship of God, which Christ set up above sixteen hundred years ago, from the dragon's and beast's worship; and all them that worship the works of men's hands, and the will-worshippers, from them that worship God in his Spirit and in his truth, in which God's people worship him; which worship is over all false worships and worshippers. They who believe in the light, which is the life in Christ, become the children of light, and are the lambs of Jesus. These lambs follow the Lamb of God, that taketh away the sins of the world; and they will not follow the hirelings, nor the strangers, to be led into strange ways, doctrines, religions, worships, and churches; for the lambs of Christ follow Christ, the Lamb of God, and know his heavenly voice. They know also, that they who are without Christ are dogs and wolves, adulterers, idolaters, liars, and unbelievers, who would devour the lambs; but these are in the hand of the Lord, which is his power, that is over all. Such do good in his power unto all; for they have the mind of Christ, who would have all to come to the knowledge of the truth, and be saved. They that do good to all, do hurt to none; for that spirit that doth hurt to any, is not of God; but that spirit which doth good to all, and especially to the household of faith, is of God. Christ came not to destroy men's lives, but to save them: it is the devil that is the destroyer of men's lives about religion, that corrupts men, and makes them deaf and blind to the things of God, and to halt out of God's way. They that obey the evil one and forsake the Lord, such the destroyer doth destroy; but Christ destroys that destroyer; and in Christ all have life." G. F.

I wrote another paper also concerning meditation, delight, exercise, and study; showing from the Scriptures of truth, what the true Christians ought to meditate upon, and to exercise their minds in; what they should take delight in, and what they should study to do. For in these things, not the profane and loose people only, but even the great professors of religion are very much mistaken; taking delight in earthly, fading, perishing things; whereas they ought to meditate on heavenly things, delight in the law of God after the inward man, and exercise themselves to have always "a conscience void of offence towards God, and towards men," as the apostle Paul did.

As sufferings continued very sore and heavy upon Friends, not only in the city but in most parts of the nation, I drew up a paper to be presented to the king; setting forth our grievances, and desiring redress from him in those particular cases which I understood were in his power. But not having relief from him, it came upon me to write an epistle to Friends, to encourage them in their sufferings, that they might bear with patience the many exercises that were brought upon them, both from the outward magistrates, and by false brethren and apostates, whose wicked books and filthy slanders grieved the upright-hearted. This epistle I wrote at DALSTON, whither I went to visit an ancient Friend that lay sick:—

"FRIENDS and brethren in Christ Jesus, whom the Lord hath called and gathered into himself, in him abide; for without him ye can do nothing, and through him ye can do all things. He is your strength and support in all your trials, temptations, imprisonments, and sufferings, who for Christ's sake are accounted as sheep for the slaughter: in all these things we are more than conquerors, through Christ who hath loved us. And therefore, Friends, though you suffer by the outward powers, ye know that the prophets, Christ, and the apostles, suffered by the unconverted. And though ye suffer by false brethren and false apostates for a time, and by their filthy books and tongues; whose tongues indeed are become no slander, let them speak, write, or print what they will; for the sober people even of the world hardly regard it: it is well they have manifested themselves to the world, that their folly may proceed no farther. Though, to the utmost of their power, they have showed their wicked intent, to stir up the magistrates, professors, and profane against us, and to speak evil of the way of truth, God's judgments will overtake them, and come upon them, as sure as they have come upon those that are gone before them. Let their pretence be ever so high, mark their end; for they will fall like untimely figs, and wither like the grass upon the top of the house. Though they may seem to flourish, and make a boast and a noise for a time, yet the Seed is on the head of such, and will grind them to powder; which Seed bruises the serpent's head. Therefore in this Seed, Christ, who is your sanctuary, rest, peace, and quiet habitation, who is the First and the Last, and over all, in Him walk; for the Lord taketh pleasure in his people that are faithful, that serve and worship him. Therefore let the saints be joyful in glory; and the God of peace, 'the God of all grace, who hath called us into his eternal glory by Jesus Christ, after that ye have suffered a while, make you perfect, stablish, strengthen, settle you.' Cast all your care upon the Lord, for he careth for you. And, dearly beloved, think it not strange concerning the fiery trial that is to try you, as though some strange thing had happened unto you; for it is better, if the will of God be so, that ye suffer for well-doing, than for evil-doing: and rejoice, inasmuch as ye are made partakers of Christ's sufferings. Wherefore let them that suffer according to the will of God, commit the keeping of their souls to him in well-doing, as unto a faithful Creator; for unto you is given, in the behalf of Christ, not only to believe in him, but also to suffer for his sake. So it is given, or is a gift from Christ, to suffer for his name; and therefore rejoice, inasmuch as ye are made partakers of Christ's sufferings. If ye be reproached, or evil spoken of for the name of Christ, happy are ye; for the spirit of glory and of God resteth upon you: on their part he is evil spoken of, but on your part he is glorified. Therefore, if any suffer as Christians, let them not be ashamed; but let them glorify God on this behalf, though now for a season ye are in sufferings, and trials, and temptations, that the trial of your faith, being much more precious than that of gold, which perishes, though it be tried with fire, may be found unto praise, honour, and glory, who are kept by the power of God, through faith, unto salvation. Therefore mind your Keeper, wherever ye are, or what sufferings soever ye be in; and mind the example of the apostle, how he suffered trouble as an evil-doer unto bonds. But the Word of God is not bound, which is everlasting and endures for ever; and they who are in that, which is not everlasting, and doth not endure for ever, cannot bind the Word. The apostle said, I endure all things for the elect's sake, that they may also obtain the salvation, which is in Christ Jesus, with eternal glory (mark, with eternal glory). And if we suffer with Christ, we shall reign with Christ, who abide faithful. Therefore strive not about words to no profit, but shun profane and vain babblings, for they will increase unto more ungodliness; that ye may be vessels of honour, sanctified and meet for Christ your Master's use, and prepared unto every good work. Follow after righteousness, godliness, faith, love, patience, and meekness. Fight the good fight of faith with your heavenly weapons; which faith is victory (or gives victory) by which ye lay hold on eternal life, and have access unto God, 'who will render to every man according to his deeds; to them who, by patient continuing in well-doing, seek for glory, and honour, and immortality, eternal life; but unto them that are contentious, and do not obey the truth, but obey unrighteousness, indignation and wrath, tribulation and anguish upon every soul of man that doeth evil; but glory, honour, and peace to every man that worketh good.' Christ said to his disciples, 'If the world hate you, ye know that it hated me before it hated you. If ye were of the world, the world would love its own; but because ye are not of the world, but I have chosen you out of the world, therefore the world hateth you.' And, 'If they have persecuted me, they will also persecute you.' And John, in his general epistle to the church, saith, 'Marvel not, my brethren, if the world hate you. We know that we have passed from death unto life, because we love the brethren.' And Christ, in his prayer to his Father, saith of his followers, 'As thou hast sent me into the world, even so have I also sent them into the world; and the glory which thou gavest me I have given them, that they may be one, even as we are one.' And, therefore, all ye that know God and Jesus Christ, whom to know is eternal life, and are partakers of his glory, keep the testimony of Jesus, and be valiant for his truth upon earth, that ye may be all settled upon Christ, the rock and foundation." G. F.

Dalston, the 3rd of the 8th Month, 1682.

I made but little stay at Dalston, but returned to London, where I continued most part of the winter, labouring in the service of truth amongst Friends; save that I was a little while at Kingston, in the 10th month of this year, where I wrote a book, setting forth "The state of the birth temporal, and the birth spiritual; and the duty and state of a child, youth, young men, aged men, and fathers in the truth," &c. But I stayed not long at Kingston, for the heat of persecution still continuing, I felt my service to be chiefly at London; where our meetings were for the most part disturbed and broken up, or Friends were forced to meet without doors, being kept out of their meeting-houses by the officers. Yet sometimes, beyond expectation, we got a quiet and peaceable meeting in the houses. One time I intended to go a mile or two out of town, to visit a Friend that was not well; but hearing that the king had sent to the mayor to put the laws in execution against Dissenters, and that the magistrates thereupon intended to nail up the meeting-house doors, I had not freedom to go out of town, but was moved to go to the meeting in Gracechurch Street; and notwithstanding all the threats, a great meeting it was, and very quiet; the glory of the Lord shone over all.

The same week I went to the meeting at the PEEL in John's Street; and the sessions were holden the same day at Hicks's-Hall. I went to the Peel in the morning; and William Mead being to appear at the sessions-house for not going to the steeple-house worship, came once or twice from Hicks's-Hall to me at the Peel; which some ill-minded people observing, went and informed the justices at the bench, that he was gone to a meeting at the Peel. Whereupon the justices sent a messenger, to see if there was a meeting; but this being in the forenoon, there was none; so the messenger, when he had looked about, went back and told them. Then others informed the justices that there would be one there in the afternoon; whereupon they sent for the chief constable, and asked him "why he suffered a meeting to be at the Peel, so near him?" He told them, "he did not know of any meeting there." They asked him, "how he could not know, and live so near it?" He said, "he was never there in his life, and did not know that there was a meeting there." They would have persuaded him that he must needs know of it; but he standing stedfast in the denial of it, they said, "they should take order to have it looked after in the afternoon." But a multitude of business coming before them at the sessions, when dinner time came, they hastened to it, without giving order, and when they came to the bench again after dinner, the Lord put it out of their minds, so that they sent no officer. The meeting was quiet, beginning and ending in peace; and a blessed one we had, the Lord's presence being preciously amongst us. Many Friends had a concern upon their minds, when they saw me come into the meeting, lest I should be taken; but I was freely given up to suffer, if it was the Lord's will, before I went to the meeting; and had nothing in my mind concerning it but the Lord's glory. I do believe the Lord put it out of their minds, that they should not send to break up our meeting that day. Yet the First-day after, three or four justices (as I heard) came to the Peel, and put Friends out of their meeting there, and kept them out; and inquired for William Mead,* but he was not there.

That day I was moved to go to GRACECHURCH STREET meeting; and it was expected that the officers would come to break it up, or keep Friends

* William Mead is often mentioned in these pages; and his trial, along with William Penn, is alluded to in a previous note. Of his life and ministry we have much less account than of most others of note in his day. George Fox sometimes calls him his son, he having married Sarah, a daughter of Judge Fell; George Fox's wife being her mother. Before his joining Friends, William Mead appears to have

out; and many hundreds of people came to see what would be done to us. But the officers came not; so we were in peace and quietness; and many of the people that came to look on, stayed all the time; and a glorious, precious meeting we had; for the Lord's presence was plentifully amongst us, and his power came over all; glory to his name for ever, who is over all!

I had seen the mayor's printed speech for putting the laws in execution against Dissenters; and it was much in my mind that we should draw up a paper to send to the mayor and aldermen, to clear ourselves from being such, as those laws were made against; and to set forth our peaceable behaviour both towards the king and the government. Accordingly a paper was drawn up and signed, and delivered to the mayor; copies of which were also delivered to the aldermen, and the bishop of London, who generally took it kindly, and were civil to the Friends that delivered it.

About this time I was moved to write the few lines following to Friends:—

"DEAR FRIENDS,

"Feel the power of God in you all, and over all, and by it let your hearts be united to one another, and to the Lord God, who hath gathered you to himself, by his power and Spirit, to be a people to serve and worship him. So you may all strive to excel one another in virtue, and in that love that beareth all things, and edifieth the body of Christ, the body of the second Adam. For the body of old Adam in the fall is full of malice, envy, and vice. Therefore you, that are called out of old Adam in the fall, and have put on Christ, the second Adam, that never fell, walk in Him, the treasure of life, wisdom, and knowledge, in whom ye have peace with God, who is the First and the Last, the Beginning and the Ending. So let all be gathered up to God, into Him who reconcileth all things in one, both things in heaven and things on earth; who is the faithful and true witness in male and female. In Him sit down, who is above the subtle foxes in their holes, and the fowls of the air in their nests; I say, sit down in Christ, who hath no place among them to lay his head; He is your rest. So in him is my love to you all." G. F.

London, the 20th of the 11th Month, 1682.

Not long after this, I received an account by letter, from some Friends, that were prisoners at Denbigh, in Wales, that many Friends there were under great sufferings for the testimony of a good conscience. In the tender sense whereof I was moved, in the love of God, to visit them with a few lines, as a word of consolation to them in their sufferings; and of exhortation, to stand fast in the testimony committed to them, after this manner:—

"DEAR suffering lambs for the name and command of Jesus; be valiant for his truth, and faithful, and ye will feel the presence of Christ

been a captain in the army. In his remarks in court on the term, *vi et armis*, during his trial, he observes, "Time was when I *had freedom to use a carnal weapon*, and then I thought I feared no man; but now I fear the living God, and dare not make use thereof, nor hurt any man." He died in 1713, aged eighty-six.

with you. Look at Him, who suffered for you, who hath bought you, and will feed you; who saith, 'Be of good comfort, I have overcome the world;' who destroys the devil and his works, and bruises the serpent's head. I say, look at Christ, your sanctuary, in whom ye have rest and peace. To you it is given not only to believe, but to suffer for his name's sake. They that will live godly in Christ Jesus, shall suffer persecution by the ungodly professors of Christ Jesus, who live out of him. Therefore be valiant for God's truth upon the earth, and look above that spirit that makes you suffer, up to Christ, who was before it was, and will be when it is gone. Consider all the prophets, Christ, and the apostles, who suffered, and were persecuted; but they were never persecuted as true men, but as deceivers, and yet true. Christ is the same to-day as he was yesterday; a rock and foundation for your age and generation, for you to build upon. I have written concerning you (since I heard your letter) to Friends in Cheshire to visit you, understanding that you belong to their quarterly meeting; and therefore I desire that some Friends of your county would go, and lay your suffering condition before the monthly or quarterly meeting in Cheshire. I have written likewise to Richard Davis,* that some of that side may go and visit you, and see how your condition is. My love is to you in the Lord, who is your alone support." G. F.

London, the 27th of the 11th Month, 1682.

Now because the magistrates were many of them unwilling to have fines laid upon meeting-houses, they kept Friends out in many places, setting officers and guards of soldiers at the doors and passages; yet sometimes Friends were fined for speaking or praying, though it was abroad. One First-day it was upon me to go to Devonshire-House meeting in the afternoon; and because I had heard Friends were kept out there that morning (as they were that day at most meetings about the city), I went sooner, and got into the yard before the soldiers came to guard the passages; but the constables were there before me, and stood in the door-way with their staves. I asked them to let me go in; they said, "they could not, nor durst not; for they were commanded the contrary, and were sorry for it." I told them I would not press upon them; so I stood by, and they were very civil. I stood till I was weary, and then one gave me a stool to sit down on; and after a while the power of the Lord began to spring up among Friends, and one began to speak. The constables soon forbade him, and said he should not speak; and he not stopping, they began to be wroth. But I gently laid my hand upon one of the constables, and wished him to let him alone; the constable did so, and was quiet; and the man did not speak long. After he had done, I was moved to stand up and speak; and in my declaration, I said, "they need not come against us

* Richard Davis—some account of whose life, written by himself, was published after his decease, and a third edition of the volume in 1771—was convinced of the truth about the year 1657. He resided in Montgomeryshire; and his life contains an interesting account of the first spreading of truth in Wales. Richard Davis was a faithful minister of the gospel, endued with spiritual gifts, and serviceable in the exercise thereof in the churches of Christ; sound in doctrine, and exemplary in conversation.

with swords and staves, for we were a peaceable people; and had nothing in our hearts but good-will to the king and magistrates, and to all people upon the earth. We did not meet, under pretence of religion, to plot and contrive against the government, or to raise insurrections; but to worship God in Spirit and in truth. We had Christ to be our Bishop, Priest, and Shepherd to feed us, and oversee us, and he ruled in our hearts; so we could all sit in silence, enjoying our teacher; so to Christ, their Bishop and Shepherd, I recommended them all." I then sat down; and after a while I was moved to pray, and the power of the Lord was over all; and the people, the constables, and soldiers, put off their hats. When the meeting was done, and Friends began to pass away, the constable put off his hat, and desired the Lord to bless us; for the power of the Lord was over him and the people, and kept them under.

After this I went up and down, visiting Friends at their houses, who had their goods taken from them for worshipping God. We took an account of what had been taken from them; and some Friends met together about it, and drew up the case of the sufferings of our Friends in writing, and gave it to the justices at their petty sessions. Whereupon they made an order, "that the officers should not sell the goods of Friends which they had in their hands, but keep them until the next sessions;" which gave some discouragement to the informers, and put a little stop to their proceedings.

Next First-day it was upon me to go to the meeting at the SAVOY; and by the time it was gathered the beadle came in; and after him the wild people, like a sea; but the Lord's power chained them all. The Spirit of the Lord went through and over all, and they were quiet, and we had a glorious, peaceable meeting; blessed be the Lord for his unspeakable goodness. This was in the 12th month, 1682.

In the 1st month, 1683, I went to KINGSTON-UPON-THAMES; and it being then a time of persecution, as I went to the meeting, I met the chief constable, who had been at the meeting-place, and had set watchmen there to keep us out; yet he was pretty civil, and the watchmen let Friends have a couple of forms out, to sit upon in the highway; so we met together there, and a very precious meeting we had; for the refreshing presence of the Lord was with us, in which we parted in peace.

Having visited and encouraged Friends there, I returned to LONDON, and went to the meeting at the Bull-and-Mouth, where the constables with their watchmen kept a guard, to keep Friends out of the house. So we met in the street; and when any Friend spoke, the officers and watchmen made a great bustle to pull him down, and take him into custody. After some other Friends had spoken, it was upon me to speak; and I said, "Heaven is God's throne, and earth is his footstool; and will ye not let us stand upon God's footstool to worship, and serve the living God?" While I spoke they were quiet; and after I had cleared myself, we broke up our meeting in peace. This was on the Sixth-day of the week.

On the First-day following I was moved to go to the meeting at GRACECHURCH STREET. When I came there, I found a guard set at the entrance in Lombard Street, and another at the gate in Gracechurch Street, to keep Friends out of the meeting-place; so we had to meet in the street. After some time I got a chair, stood up on it, and spoke largely to the people, "opening the principles of truth to them, and declaring many weighty truths concerning magistracy, and concerning the Lord's prayer." There were, besides Friends, a great multitude of people, and amongst them many professors; all was very quiet; for the Lord's power was over all, and in his time we broke up our meeting, and departed in peace.

The next day I went to GUILDFORD in SURREY; and having visited Friends there, passed to WORMINGHURST in SUSSEX, where I had a very blessed meeting among Friends, free from disturbance. While I was there, James Claypole, of London (who was there with his wife also), was suddenly taken ill with so violent a fit, that he could neither stand nor lie; but, through the extremity of pain, cried out. When I heard it, I was much exercised in spirit for him; and went to him. After I had spoken a few words to him, to turn his mind inward, I was moved to lay my hand upon him, and prayed the Lord to rebuke his infirmity. As I laid my hand on him, the Lord's power went through him; and through faith in that power he had speedy ease, so that he quickly fell into a sleep. When he awoke, he was so well, that next day he rode with me five-and-twenty miles in a coach; though he used formerly (as he said) to lie sometimes two weeks, sometimes a month, in one of those fits. But the Lord was entreated for him, and by his power soon gave him ease at this time; blessed and praised be his holy name therefore!

After I had had some meetings in Sussex and Surrey, and had visited Friends thereaway, I returned to London by KINGSTON, where I had a meeting on the 1st of the 2d month, being First-day. We were kept out of the meeting-house by a constable and watchmen, as before, and so were obliged to meet in the highway. But it being the monthly meeting day, and many people being there, the meeting was pretty large, and very quiet; and the Lord's blessed presence was amongst us; blessed be his name for ever!

Being come to LONDON, I went to the meeting at WHEELER STREET, near Spitalfields, which that day proved very large; and a glorious, blessed time it was; for the Lord's power and truth were over all, and many deep and weighty things were opened to the people, to their great satisfaction.

I tarried in and near London, visiting Friends' meetings, and labouring in the service of the gospel, till the Yearly Meeting came on, which began on the 28th of the 3d month. It was a time of great sufferings; and much concerned I was, lest Friends that came up out of the country on the church's service, should be taken and imprisoned at London. But the Lord was with us; his power preserved us, and gave us a sweet and blessed opportunity to wait upon him, to be refreshed together in him, and to perform his services for his truth and people for which we met. As it was a time of great persecution, and we understood that in most counties Friends were under great sufferings, either by imprisonments or spoiling of goods, or both, a concern was weightily upon me lest any Friends that were sufferers, especially such as were traders and dealers in the world, should hazard the losing of other men's goods or estates through their sufferings. Wherefore, as the thing opened in me, I drew up an epistle of caution to Friends in that case, which I communicated to the Yearly Meeting; and from thence it was sent forth among Friends throughout the nation; a copy of which here follows:—

"Dear Friends and brethren in the Lord Jesus Christ, who is your only sanctuary in this day of storm and persecution, spoiling of goods, and imprisonments! Let every one's eye be unto him, who has all power in heaven and in earth given unto him; so that none can touch a hair of your head, nor you, nor anything ye have, except it be permitted or suffered in this day, to try his people, whether their minds be with the Lord, or in outward things. Dear Friends, take care that all your offerings be free, and of your own, that has cost you something; so that ye may not offer of that which is another man's, or that which ye are entrusted withal and not your own, or fatherless' or widows' estates; but all such things settle and establish in their places. You may remember many years ago, in a time of great persecution, divers Friends, who were traders, shop-keepers, and others, had the concerns of widows and fatherless, and other people's estates in their hands. And when a great suffering, persecution, and spoiling of goods came upon Friends, especial care was taken that all might offer up to the Lord in their sufferings what was really their own, and not any other people's estates or goods which they had in their hands; and that they might not offer up another body's, but that which they had bought and paid for, or were able to pay for. Afterwards several letters came out of the country to the meeting at London, from Friends that had goods of the shopkeepers at London upon credit, which they had not paid for; who wrote to their creditors whom they had their goods of, entreating them to take their goods again. And some Friends came to London themselves, and treated with their creditors, letting them understand 'that they lay liable to have all that they had taken from them;' and told them, 'they would not have any man to suffer by them: neither would they by suffering offer up anything but what was really their own, or what they were able to pay for.' Upon which several took their goods again. This wrought a very good savour in the hearts of many people, when they saw such a righteous, just, and honest principle in Friends, that would not make any suffer for their testimony; but what they did suffer for the testimony of Jesus should be really and truly their own, not other people's. In this they owed nothing to any, but love. So in this every man and woman stands in the free offering, a free people, whether it be spiritual or temporal, which is their own; and in that they wrong no man, neither inwardly, nor outwardly. Ornan said unto David, 'I give thee the thrashing-floor, &c., and the oxen for burnt-offerings, and the thrashing instruments for wood, and the wheat for the meat-offering; I give it all.' But king David said unto Ornan, 'Nay, but I will verily buy it for the full price; for I will not take that which is thine for the Lord, nor offer burnt-offerings without cost,' 1 Chron. xxi. 22, &c. So it should be his own; and so should it be every man's that offers. You may see here that David would not accept of another man's gift for an offering to the Lord; he would not offer up that which cost him nothing; but what should be really his own, Psal. cxii. 5. 'A good man......will guide his affairs with discretion.'

"Let this be read in your monthly and quarterly men's and women's meetings." G. F.

London, the 2nd of the 4th Month, 1683.

CHAPTER XI.

1683–1685.—A salutation of love to Friends, designed to stir up the pure mind—an epistle to Friends commending them to Christ, the rock and sure foundation—an epistle of counsel to Friends—George Fox taken from a meeting and examined by a magistrate, but soon released—writes an epistle to the faithful to beware of a seducing spirit—after the Yearly Meeting sails for Holland, and lands at the Briel—attends the Yearly Meeting at Amsterdam—writes to Galenus Abrahams, a Mennonist or Baptist, who, seven years before, bid him "keep his eyes off him," for he said "they pierced him," but now he was become very loving and tender, as well as his family—George Fox returns to England—writes to the Duke of Holstein an able defence of women's preaching—writes an epistle of counsel to Friends—advises with, and assists them in, drawing up an account of sufferings, which is printed and spread amongst Parliament-men—writes a caution to Friends to keep out of the world's spirit, &c.—and a warning against pride and excess in apparel.

Some time after the Yearly Meeting I went down to Kingston-upon-Thames to visit Friends there; and while I was there it came upon me to write the following epistle to Friends in general, as a salutation of love, and to stir up the pure mind in them:—

"Dear Friends and Brethren,

"Who are turned from darkness to light, and from the power of Satan to God, who are believers in the light, which is the life in Christ, and are become children of the light and of the day;—who are grafted into Christ, the second Adam, the Lord from heaven, and are gathered in the name of Jesus, in whom ye have salvation, and not in any other name under the whole heaven. For Christ Jesus saith, 'Where two or three are gathered together in my name, there am I in the midst of them,' Matt. xviii. 20. So you being gathered in the name of Jesus, he is in the midst of you, a Saviour, a Mediator, a Prophet, a Shepherd, a Bishop, a Leader, a Counsellor, the Captain of your salvation, who bruises the serpent's head, and destroys the devil and his works. Therefore, brethren in Christ Jesus, exhort one another daily, while it is called to-day, lest any of you be hardened through the deceitfulness of sin. For you are made partakers of Christ, if ye hold fast the beginning of your confidence stedfast to the end, Heb. iii. 14. Therefore hear Christ's voice, for he is in the midst of you a teacher. Take heed, lest there be in any of you an evil heart of unbelief, in departing from the living God, as there is in too many in this day of provocation and temptation. While it is to-day hear his voice, and let us consider one another, to provoke unto love and to good works. Let us hold fast the profession of our faith without wavering (for he is faithful that hath promised and hath called you), not forsaking the assembling of ourselves together, as the manner of some is; (mark) as the manner of some is, that did and do forsake the assembling of themselves together: but exhorting one another, and so much the more as you see the day of light appearing. For if we sin wilfully, after we have received the knowledge of the truth, there remains no more sacrifice for sins; but a certain fearful looking for of judgment and fiery indignation, which shall devour the adversaries, Heb. x. And therefore it is good not to forsake the assembling of ourselves together, but exhort one another daily; for Christ is in the midst of his people a teacher and a prophet, who saith, 'Learn of me; the way, the truth, and the life.' We being many, are one body in Christ, gathered in his name, and every one members one of another. Having then gifts differing according to the grace that is given us, whether they be prophecy, let us prophesy according to the proportion of faith; and let those that minister, wait on their ministry; those that be teachers, on their teaching; and him that exhorteth, on exhortation; he that giveth, let him do it with simplicity; and he that ruleth, with diligence; and he that showeth mercy, is to do it with cheerfulness. Abhor that which is evil; cleave to that which is good. Be kindly affectioned one towards another, with brotherly love, in honour preferring one another. Rejoice in hope; be patient in tribulations; be not overcome with evil, but overcome evil with good; and, if it be possible, as much as lieth in you, live peaceably with all men, Rom. xii. This is and was the practice of the church of Christ. And now the God of hope fill you with all joy and peace in believing, that ye may abound in hope, through the power of the Holy Ghost. I myself also am persuaded of you, my brethren, that ye also are full of goodness, filled with all knowledge, and are able also to admonish one another, Rom. xv. 13, 14. Here the church of Christ, in which He was in the midst a teacher and the head of the church, were and are able through him to admonish one another. Let the peace of God rule in your hearts, to which ye are also called into one body, to wit, of Christ. Let the word of Christ dwell in you richly in all wisdom, teaching and admonishing one another, &c., Col. iii. Whatsoever ye do, in word or deed, do all in the name of the Lord Jesus Christ, giving thanks to God and the Father by him: and above all things put on charity, which is the bond of perfectness. The apostle said to Timothy, 'Be not thou ashamed of the testimony of our Lord, nor of me, his prisoner: but be thou partaker of the afflictions of the gospel, according to the power of God, who hath saved us, and called us with a holy calling; not according to our works, but according to his own purpose and grace, which was given us in Christ Jesus before the world began,' 2 Tim. i. 8, 9. It concerns every one not to be ashamed of the testimony of our Lord, who hath called them by his grace; and not to be ashamed of any of Christ's prisoners, and afflicted ones for Christ's and his gospel's sake, who abolishes death, and brings life and immortality to light through his gospel: you that believe in the light, know it. Peter saith, in his general epistle to the church of Christ, 'As every man' (mark, every man) 'hath received the gift, so minister the same one to another as good stewards of the manifold grace of God. If any man speak, let him speak as the oracles of God, not of men; if any man minister, let him do it as of the ability which God gives, not of the ability of men's arts and sciences, that God in all things may be glorified through Jesus Christ,' &c. For these gifts and grace come from Jesus into the hearts of the members of his church, whom he is in the midst of. And if any man suffer as a Christian, let him not be ashamed; but let him glorify God, &c. Every true Christian hath the presence of Christ, who hath all power in heaven and in earth given him, to support him with his power, light, and life. Christ saith to his believers, 'Beware of men, for they will deliver you up to the councils, and they will scourge you in the synagogues, and you shall be brought before governors and kings for my name's sake, for a testimony against them and the Gentiles. But when they deliver you up, take no thought how or what ye shall speak; for it shall be given you in the same hour what ye shall speak: for it is not you that speak, but the Spirit of your Father that speaketh in you. And ye shall be hated of all men for my name's sake: but he that endureth to the end, shall be saved. The disciple is not above his Master, nor the servant above his lord; it is enough for the disciple that he be as his Master, and the servant as his lord: for if they have called the master of the house Beelzebub, what will they do to his servant. Fear not them which kill the body, but are not able to kill the soul, &c. A sparrow shall not fall to the ground without your heavenly Father, &c. The hairs of your head are all numbered; ye are of more value than many sparrows. Whosoever therefore shall confess me before men, him will I confess also before my Father who is in heaven; but whosoever shall deny me before men, him will I also deny before my Father, who is in heaven. And whosoever shall be ashamed of me and of my words, of him shall the Son of Man be ashamed,' &c. Matt. x. And again Christ saith, 'Whosoever shall be ashamed of me and of my words in this adulterous and sinful generation, of him also shall the Son of Man be ashamed, when he comes in the glory of his Father with his holy angels.' Mark viii. 38. And Christ saith to his disciples, 'He that receiveth you receiveth me; and he that receiveth me, receiveth him that sent me: he that receiveth a prophet in the name of a prophet, shall receive a prophet's reward; and he that receiveth a righteous man in the name of a righteous man, shall receive a righteous man's reward. And whosoever shall give to drink unto one of these little ones a cup of cold water only, in the name of a disciple, verily I say unto you, he shall in no wise lose his reward.' Matt. x. 40–42. Here ye may see how Christ encourages his disciples, and them that receive them. And John saith, 'Among the chief rulers of the Jews many believed in Christ; but because of the Pharisees, they did not confess him, lest they should be put out of the synagogue,' John xii. 42. Too many such believers there are now-a-days, who dare not confess Christ, lest they should lose the favour of men. But Christ encouraged the faithful disciples, and told them they would put them out of their synagogues; yea, that the time should come, that whosoever killed them would think they did God service: And 'these things,' said he, 'will they do unto you, because they have not known the Father, nor me. But these things have I told you, that when the time shall come, ye may remember that I told you of them,' John xvi. 2—4. Here ye may see what Christ told his disciples should come to pass to them. And Saul, before he was converted, compelled the Christians to blaspheme, and made havock of the church of Christ, Acts viii. and chap. xxii. and xxvi. And did not the beast in the

Revelations compel both small and great to worship him and his image? And did not all worship it, but they who had their names written in the Lamb's book of life? Did not Nebuchadnezzar set up an image sixty cubits high, and six cubits broad? And did not he cause a herald to cry aloud, 'It is commanded that all people, nations, and languages fall down, and worship the golden image that Nebuchadnezzar hath set up: and whoso falleth not down, and worshippeth, shall the same hour be cast into the midst of the fiery furnace?' And were not Shadrach, Meshach, and Abednego, cast into the furnace? Dan. iii. But God delivered them. Therefore it is good to be faithful to God and his worship in Spirit and in truth. The Jews agreed, that if any man should confess Christ, he should be put out of their synagogue, John ix. 22. So it was for Christ's sake they were excommunicated out of their synagogues. But as it is written, 'Behold, I lay in Zion a stumbling-stone, and a rock of offence; and whoso believes on him, shall not be ashamed.' So Christ is a stumbling-stone and a rock of offence to all the unbelievers in the light, which is the life in Christ, whether they be Jews, Christians, or Gentiles. The Jews believed Christ was to come, from the Scriptures; and the Christians believe he is come, by the Scriptures; but do not believe in the light, as Christ commands, and so do not become children of light. Therefore ye that are believers in the light, and are become children of light, walk in Christ, your way, life, and salvation." G. F.

Kingston, the 5th Month, 1683.

Before I left Kingston, something further opened in me, which I was moved to write, and send amongst Friends; as follows:—

"Dear Friends,

"My love is to you all in the holy Seed, that reigns over all. And my desire is, that every one, both male and female, may feel the Seed Christ in you, which is heir of the promise of life eternal, that ye may all grow up in Christ Jesus your head, and be built upon Him, the rock and foundation that God hath laid, which stands sure over all rocks and foundations in the world;—that ye may eat and drink of this spiritual rock, the spiritual water and food; so that ye may truly and inwardly say, that your rock and foundation, your bread and water of life, is from heaven, and your bread and water is sure; and that ye know his voice that feeds you, and leads you into the pastures of life, which are always fresh and green. In this, your affections are set on things that are above, seeking that which comes down from above, where Christ sits at the right hand of God, making intercession for you; who is your Mediator, making peace between God and you; who is your heavenly Bishop to oversee you, that ye keep in his light, life, and power, and do not go astray from his heavenly fold and pasture, that He your Shepherd may feed you therein; who is your Prophet, to open to you the fulfilling of the promises and prophecies, himself being the substance; that ye may live in him, and he in you, yea, and reign in your hearts, there to exercise his offices, his prophetical, priestly, and kingly office, who is heavenly and spiritual;—that ye may know the three, that bear witness in the earth, the Spirit, the Water, and the Blood, which is the life of Christ, which cleanseth from all sin; the Water that washes and refreshes you; and the Spirit that baptizes and circumcises you, and leads you into all truth; that ye may come all to drink into one Spirit, and keep the unity of the Spirit, which is the bond of the heavenly peace. So being led by the Spirit of God, ye are his sons and daughters, and by his Spirit will come to know the three that bear witness in heaven, the Father, the Word, and the Holy Ghost. These are the three witnesses that are in heaven, that bear record of all things; for he is God in heaven, and God in the earth. Therefore I desire, that ye may all feel his love shed in your hearts, and in it live (above the love of the world, which is enmity), and in that you will keep in the excellent way. For love edifies the body of Christ, builds his church up, and keeps out of the enmity, for it is above it, and brings and keeps all in true humility, and in the true divinity; to be courteous, kind, and tender one towards another, and to show forth the nature of Christ, and true Christianity in all your lives and conversations; that the blessings of the Lord may rest upon you, as ye all live in the seed of the gospel, the seed of the kingdom of God, in which all nations are blessed. In that ye will all have a care of God's glory. There is the hill or mountain, where the light shines to the answering the witness of God in all; and the salt, that is a good savour to the witness of God in the hearts of all; and that savour being kept in, the salt doth not come under the feet of men. So my love to you all in Christ Jesus, whom God hath given to be a sanctuary for all his people, who is from above and not of this world, in whom you have life, peace, and salvation. In Him God Almighty keep and preserve you all to his glory. Amen. As you live in the peaceable truth of God, it keeps you under, and within, his protection; but they that make a profession of the Scriptures of truth, and yet live out of the truth, in the spirit of strife, unquietness, and discontent, in a contriving, plotting, ravenous, destroying spirit, which is of the devil, and not of God, that spirit is judged out of the truth, and to be of him, in whom there is no truth, whose portion is in the lake, and in the fire that burns." G. F.

Kingston, the 27th of the 5th Month, 1683.

Having visited Friends at and about Kingston, I returned to LONDON; for it being a suffering time with Friends there, I had not freedom to be long from the city. I went to the meeting at the PEEL, which but a little before the justices and constables had broken up, and had carried themselves very roughly; but that day it was in the house, and quiet; and a glorious one it was, blessed be the Lord.

On the First-day following I went to the meeting at GRACECHURCH STREET. When I came there, I found three constables in the meeting-house, who kept Friends out; so we met in the court. After I had been some time there, I stood up and spoke to the people, and continued speaking some time. Then one of the constables came, and took hold of my hand, and said, "I must come down." I desired him to be patient, and went on speaking to the people; but after a little time he pulled me down, and had me into the meeting-house. I asked them, if they were not weary of this work. One of them said, "indeed they were." They let me go into the widow Foster's house, which joined to the meeting-house, where I stayed, being hot. When the meeting was ended, for one prayed after I was taken away, the constables asked some Friends, "which of them would pass their words that I should appear, if they should be questioned about me; but the Friends telling them, they need not require that, for I was a man well known in the city, to be one that would neither fly nor shrink; they went away, and I heard no further of it. The same week I was at the meeting at the SAVOY, which used to be kept out and disturbed; but that day it was within doors and peaceable; and a precious time it was. The First-day after, it was upon me to go to the meeting at WESTMINSTER, where there used to be great disturbances; but there also the meeting was within doors that day, and very large. The Lord's power was over all, and kept all quiet and still; for though many loose spirits were there, yet they were bound down by the power and Spirit of the Lord, that they could not get up to make disturbance.

About this time I was moved to write the following epistle:—

"FRIENDS AND BRETHREN,

"Who have received the peaceable truth, let the fruits of its peaceableness and of your quiet spirit appear in all your meetings, and in all your words and actions; for he that inhabits eternity dwells with a humble heart, he gives grace to the humble, and resisteth the proud. Heaven is his throne, and the earth ye walk upon is his footstool; happy are ye, that see and know him, that is invisible. And now, Friends, let all things be done in your meetings, and otherwise, in love, without strife or vainglory. For love fulfils the law, love overcomes, and edifies the body of Christ. There is neither self nor envy in love, neither is it puffed up; but abides and bears all things. See that this love of God have the sway in you all and over you all. Christ saith, 'Blessed are the poor in spirit; for theirs is the kingdom of heaven. Blessed are they that mourn; for they shall be comforted. Blessed are the meek; for they shall inherit the earth. Blessed are they that do hunger and thirst after righteousness; for they shall be filled. Blessed are the merciful; for they shall obtain mercy. Blessed are the pure in heart; for they shall see God. Blessed are the peace-makers; for they shall be called the children of God. Blessed are they that are persecuted for righteousness' sake; for theirs is the kingdom of heaven. Blessed are ye, when men shall revile you, and persecute you, and shall say all manner of evil against you falsely for my sake. Rejoice and be exceeding glad; for great is your reward in heaven; for so persecuted they the prophets which were before you.'

"Now Friends, here is a great deal in these words; and all must be in these states and conditions, if they have these blessings. The children of God are peace-makers, and strive to make peace in the truth; and to live in peace with all men, if it be possible. So live in peace and good-will to all men; which good-will is both for their sanctification and salvation. And, Friends, consider, the wisdom of God, which is from above, is pure, peaceable, gentle, and easy to be entreated, full of mercy and good fruits, without partiality and without hypocrisy. Dear Friends, let this pure, peaceable, gentle wisdom, that is from above, that is easy to be entreated, and is full of mercy and good fruits, be exercised and practised in all the true churches of Christ, so that wisdom may be justified of her children. For the works of the flesh, or fleshly spirit, are hatred, variance, wrath, strife, envyings, drunkenness, revellings, adultery, fornication, lasciviousness, uncleanness, &c., and they which do such things shall not inherit the kingdom of God. But the fruits of the Spirit of God are love, joy, peace, long-suffering, gentleness, goodness, faith, meekness, temperance, &c. So, dear Friends and brethren, strive to exceed one another, and all people upon the earth, in humility, meekness, gentleness, temperance, love, patience, pureness, and in mercy; then ye will show forth the fruits of the Spirit of God, and of his heavenly wisdom that is from above. In this, wisdom will be justified of her children; ye will be the salt of the earth, the light of the world set on a hill, that cannot be hid; and your moderation will appear to all men. Be ye just and righteous, faithful and true in all your words, dealings, and conversations, so that ye may answer the truth in all people; for Christ saith, his Father is glorified by such as bring forth fruits, when men do see their good works; for he that doeth righteousness, is accepted with God. And he that dwells in love, dwells in God; for love is his habitation. Let that be the habitation of every one that hath received the truth; for if it be not, such do not dwell in God, let them profess what they will. Therefore my desire is, that all you who have received Christ, the Seed, which bruises the serpent's head, may walk in Him, your sanctuary, life, and salvation, your rest and peace. Amen." G. F.

London, the 14th of the 6th Month, 1683.

I continued yet at LONDON, labouring in the work and service of the Lord both in and out of meetings; sometimes visiting Friends in prison for the testimony of Jesus, encouraging them in their sufferings, and exhorting them to stand faithful and steadfast in the testimony, which the Lord had committed to them to bear; sometimes also visiting those that were sick and weak in body, or troubled in mind, helping to bear up their spirits from sinking under their infirmities. Sometimes our meetings were quiet and peaceable; sometimes they were disturbed and broken up by the officers. One First-day it was upon me to go to the meeting at the SAVOY, which was large; for many professors and sober people were there. The Lord opened many precious, weighty things in me to the people, which I declared amongst them, and "directed them to the Spirit of God *in* themselves, which the Lord had given them a measure of; that all by the Spirit might understand the Scripture, which were given forth from the Spirit of God; and that by the Spirit of God, they might know God, and Christ whom God hath sent; whom to know is eternal life; and that by the Spirit, they might all come into Christ, and know Him to be their sanctuary, who destroys the devil, the destroyer, and his works, and bruises the serpent's head. For Christ was a sanctuary to them, to whom he was a Saviour, whom he saved from the destroyer. And Christ did baptize them with the Holy Ghost and with fire, and did thoroughly purge his floor, and burn up their chaff with unquenchable fire; that is, sin and corruption, which is got into man by transgression; but Christ gathereth his wheat into his garner. So all that are baptized with Christ's baptism, their wheat is in God's garner; and no spoiler can get into God's garner to meddle with the wheat there, though they may be permitted to meddle with the outward goods," &c. As I was speaking in the power of the Lord, and the people were greatly affected therewith, suddenly the constables, with the rude people, came in like a sea. One of the constables said to me, "Come down;" and he laid hands on me. I asked him, "Art thou a Christian? We are Christians." He had hold of my hand, and was very fierce to pluck me down; but I stood still, and spoke a few words to the people; desiring of the Lord that the blessings of God might rest upon them all. The constable still called upon me to come down, and at length plucked me down, and bid another man with a staff take me, and carry me to prison. That man led me to another officer's house, who was more civil; and after a while they brought in four Friends more, whom they had taken. I was very weary and in a great perspiration; and several Friends hearing where I was, came to me in the constable's house; but I bid them all go their ways, lest the constables and informers should stop them. After a while the constables led us almost a mile to a justice, who was a fierce, passionate man; who, after he had asked me my name, and his clerk had taken it in writing, upon the constable's informing him that "I preached in the meeting," said in an angry manner, "Do not you know, that it is contrary to the king's laws to preach in such conventicles, contrary to the Liturgy of the Church of England?" There was present one —— Shad (a wicked informer, who was said to have broken jail at Coventry, and to have been burned in the hand at London), who hearing the justice speak so to me, stepped up to him, and told him, "that he had convicted them on the Act of the 22d of King Charles the Second." "What! you convict them?" said the justice; "Yes," said Shad, "I have convicted them, and you must convict them too upon that Act." With that the justice was angry with him, and said, "You teach me! what are you? I'll convict them of a riot." The informer hearing that, and seeing the justice angry, went away in a fret; so he was disappointed of his purpose. I thought he would have sworn somebody against me, whereupon I said, "Let no man swear against me, for it is my principle 'not to swear;' and therefore I would not have any man swear against me." The justice thereupon asked me, "If I did not preach in the meeting;" I told him, "I confessed what God and Christ had done for my soul, and praised God; and I thought I might have done that in the streets, and in all places, viz., praise God and confess Christ Jesus; and this I was not ashamed to confess. Neither was this contrary to the Liturgy of the Church of England." The justice said, "the laws were against such meetings as were contrary to the Liturgy of the Church of England." I said, "I knew no such laws against our meetings; but if he meant that Act that was made against such as met to plot, contrive, and raise insurrections against the king, we were no such people, but abhorred all such actions; and bore true love and good-will to the king, and to all men upon the earth." The justice then asked me, "if I had been in orders;" I told him, "No." Then he took his law-books and searched for laws against us; bidding his clerk take the names of the rest in the mean time: but when he could find no other law against us, the clerk swore the constable against us. Some of the Friends bid the constable "take heed what he swore, lest he were perjured; for he took them in the entry, and not in the meeting." Yet the constable, being an ill man, swore "that they were in the meeting." However, the justice said, "seeing there was but one witness, he would discharge the rest; but he would send me to Newgate, and I might preach there." I asked him, "If it stood with his conscience to send me to Newgate for praising God, and for confessing Christ Jesus?" He cried, "Conscience! conscience!" but I felt my words touched his conscience. He bid the constable take me away, and he would make a mittimus to send me to prison when he had dined. I told him, "I desired his peace, and the good of his family, and that they might be kept in the fear of the Lord;" so I passed away. And as we went the constable took some Friends' word, that I should come to his house the next morning by eight. Accordingly I went with those Friends; and then the constable told us, that he went to the justice for the mittimus after he had dined, and he bid him come again after the evening service; which he did; and then the justice told him he might let me go. "So," said the constable, "you are discharged." I blamed the constable for turning informer, and swearing against us; and he said he would do so no more. Next day the justice meeting with Gilbert Latey, asked him, "if he would pay twenty pounds for George Fox's fine." He said, "No." "Then," said the justice, "I am disappointed; for being but a lodger I cannot come by his fine, and he having been brought before me, and being of ability himself, I cannot lay his fine on any other."

After I was discharged, I went into the city. The same week the sessions coming on, where many Friends were concerned, some as prisoners, and some on trials of appeals upon the conventicle act, I went to a Friend's house not far off, that I might be in readiness to assist them with counsel, or otherwise, as occasion should offer; and I found service in it. But as my spirit was concerned on behalf of Friends, with respect to their outward sufferings by the persecutors without; so an exercise also came weightily upon me at this time, in the sense I had of the mischievous working of that adulterated spirit, which, being gone out from the heavenly unity, and having drawn out some that professed truth into enmity and opposition against Friends, endeavoured to trouble the church of Christ with their janglings and contention. And as a further discovery of the working of that seducing spirit, and a warning to all Friends to beware of it, I was moved to write the following epistle:—

"*To all the elect, faithful, called, and chosen of God, the flock and heritage of God, who have been acquainted with the dealings of the Lord, and have kept your habitations in his life, power, and truth, being built upon the holy, heavenly rock and foundation, Christ Jesus, who was the foundation of the prophets and apostles; which foundation stands sure.*

"MANY foundations have been laid since the apostles' days, by such as have gone from Christ, the true and sure Foundation; but their foundations have proved rotten, and come to nought; and they themselves have come to loss. Many, since the day of Christ and the truth hath appeared in this nation, have had some openings and sights, and come among us for a time; and then gone out from us again; these have been the comers and goers, like those in the apostles' days. Such had an outward profession of the truth, and have gone from the true foundation, Christ Jesus, and so from the heavenly society and unity of the saints in light. Then they set up foundations of their own; and having a form of godliness, but out of the power thereof, out of the order thereof, such have turned to janglings and vain disputings. This sort of spirit you have been acquainted with, who have kept your habitations in Christ Jesus, the First and the Last. And you are not insensible of the scurrilous and filthy books of lies and defamations, which have been spread abroad in this nation, and beyond the seas, against the faithful. It is very well that the Lord hath suffered them to publish their own shame in print, that truth's enemies may be discovered; that their fruits and spirits have appeared and manifested themselves both in print and otherwise. And I do believe, that the Lord will yet suffer this spirit so to publish its fruits, its shame and nakedness, to professor and profane, and to all sober, moderate, and innocent people, that its shame and nakedness shall more fully appear. Though for a time it hath been hid and covered with the fig-leaves of an outward profession, and sometimes with fawning and flattering words, as at other times, it hath discovered itself by rough, lying, and defaming words; yet the Lord God will blast all such vain talkers, that do not walk in the order of life, truth, and the gospel. Therefore, ye that are faithful, stand fast in the liberty wherewith Christ hath made you free in his government. It is upon his shoulders; he bears it up; of the increase of it, and of its peace, there is no end. For all quarrellers against his order and government are not in him, nor in his heavenly, spiritual government and peace. Therefore, ye faithful ones, who have stood the trial through many persecutions, imprisonments, spoilings of goods; you know that there is a crown of glory laid up for you. You that suffer with Christ, shall reign with him in his kingdom of glory; ye that die with Christ, shall live with him in eternal life, in the world that hath no end, who have gone through the sufferings without, and within, by false brethren, by comers and goers, that have caused the way of truth to be evil spoken of, and have been the persecutors of the faithful with their tongues; and by printing and publishing their lying, defaming books against the faithful, these have stirred up the magistrates and priests, who were willing to get any occasion to speak evil of the right way, and precious truth of Christ, by which his people are made free; it would have been better for such had they never been born. But God hath brought them to light, and their fruits and ravenous spirit are seen, savoured, and known; who are become Judases, and sons of perdition, to betray Christ now within (where he is made manifest) to the priests, magistrates, and profane, as Judas betrayed Christ without to the priests and Pilate; though some of the magistrates and sober people see their envy and folly, and that they have more malice than matter against the faithful. But the Lord will consume this Judas, or son of perdition. The Lord will consume him with the Spirit of his mouth, and destroy him with the brightness of his coming. So let all the faithful look unto the Lord. And let that wicked son of perdition know, though he may be got as high as Judas without (who was partaker of the ministry with the apostles), 'the Lord will consume him with the Spirit of his mouth, and destroy him with the brightness of his coming.' That is his portion. The brightness of the Lord will destroy him, and the Spirit of his mouth will consume him. And when he is destroyed and consumed, there will not be a son of perdition to betray Christ in his people, and his people that live and walk in Christ, who hath all power in heaven (mark, in heaven) and in earth given to him; and with his holy and glorious power he limits and orders; so that nothing shall be done against his people, but what is suffered for their trial and their good, neither by apostates, persecutors with the tongue, Judases, sons of perdition to betray, or the outward powers to imprison, or spoil goods; all these are limited by Christ's power, who hath all power in heaven and in earth given to him. Every one's faith is to stand in him and his power, and rejoice in his power, and see the increase of his righteous, holy, heavenly, spiritual, peaceable government, in which the glorious, holy order of life is lived and walked in, by all his sons and daughters. In his Spirit is the holy unity and bond of peace; though ye be absent in body one from another, yet all joying and rejoicing, being present in his Spirit, and beholding in the same Spirit your spiritual order, unity, and fellowship, and the steadfastness of your faith in Christ Jesus, who is steadfast for ever, the First and the Last, whose presence is among his people, and who is their head. Here is heavenly Sion known, and heavenly Jerusalem, and the innumerable company of angels (which are spirits) and the spirits of the just men made perfect. Here is the general assembly, and a general, heavenly, holy, and spiritual joy and rejoicing, lauding and praising the Lord God Almighty, and the Lamb, that lives for evermore. Amen." G. F.

London, the 14th of the 8th Month, 1683.

"Read this in your assemblies amongst the faithful."

I tarried a little in LONDON, visiting Friends and meetings, and labouring in the work of the Lord there. And being on a First-day at the Bull-and-Mouth, where the meeting had long been kept out, it was that day in the house, peaceable and large; the people were so affected with the truth, and refreshed with the powerful presence of the Lord, that when it was ended, they were loth to go away.

After some time, having several things upon me to write, I went to KINGSTON, that I might be free from interruptions. When I came there, I understood the officers had been very rude at the meeting, abusing Friends, and had driven them out of the meeting-place, and very abusive they continued to be for some time. Whilst I was there I wrote a little book (printed soon after), entitled, "The Saints' heavenly and spiritual worship, unity, and communion, &c., wherein is set forth what the true gospel worship is, and in what the true unity and communion of the saints stands; with a discovery of those that were gone from this holy unity and communion, and were turned against the saints, that abode therein."

When I had finished the services for which I went thither, and had visited the Friends, I returned to LONDON, and visited most of the meetings in and about the city. Afterwards I went to visit a Friend in ESSEX; and returning by DALSTON, made some stay at the widow Stot's, where I wrote an epistle to Friends, which may be read amongst my other printed books.

I came from Dalston to LONDON, and next day was sent for in haste to my son Rous's at KINGSTON, whose daughter, Margaret, lay very sick, and had a desire to see me. I tarried now at Kingston about a week, and then returned to LONDON; where I continued for the most part of the winter and the spring following, until the general meeting in 1684, save that I went once as far as Enfield, to visit Friends thereabouts. In this time I ceased not to labour in the work of the Lord, being frequent at meetings, and visiting Friends that were prisoners, or that were sick; and in writing books for the spreading of truth, and opening the understandings of the people to receive it.*

The Yearly meeting was in the 3d month. A blessed weighty one it was, wherein Friends were sweetly refreshed together; for the Lord was with us, and opened his heavenly treasures amongst us. And though it was a time of great difficulty and danger, by reason of informers and persecuting magistrates, yet the Lord was a defence and place of safety to his people.

Now had I drawings in Spirit to go into Holland, to visit the Seed of God there. And as soon as the Yearly Meeting was over I prepared for my journey. There went with me from London Alexander Parker, George Watts, and Nathaniel Brassey, who also had drawings into that country.

* Frequent mention being made by George Fox of his being engaged with his pen on behalf of the truth, it may be well to apprize the reader that these volumes contain only a very small portion of his writings. Many others of his works were collected and printed in 1706, forming a large volume, entitled, *Gospel Truth Demonstrated, in a collection of Doctrinal Books, given forth by that faithful minister of Jesus Christ, George Fox, &c.* This collection consists of above 1000 folio pages, comprising about 160 pieces, the dates from 1653–1689.

In addition to treatises in explanation or defence of the principles and doctrines taught by George Fox, this volume contains many others of a more extended character. There are three addressed to the Jews; and papers in behalf of the doctrine of the gospel, and against persecution, to be delivered to the following rulers:—The Great Turk, the magistrates of Malta, the Emperor of Austria, the Kings of France and Spain, the Pope, and the Emperor of China. And in 1688, Sultan Mahomet IV. having sent a defiance to the Emperor Leopold in his Christian character, threatening to ruin him, *and pursue his crucified God,* George Fox wrote a Reply to this public document; warning the Turk to fear the great God that made him and all things, and showing him, out of their own Koran, that the founder of their religion wrote more respectfully of Christ; whom he then proceeds to set forth to the notice of the Sultan by citations from the Scriptures.

In the books and treatises forming the above collection, the doctrine of our blessed Lord, and these matters essential to salvation and true Christianity, are plainly

We took coach the 31st of the 3d month, 1684, and got to COLCHESTER that night. Next day being First-day, we went to the meeting there; and though there was no notice given of my coming, yet our being there was presently spread over the town, and in several places in the country at seven and ten miles distance; so that abundance of Friends came in double-horsed, which made the meeting very large. I had a concern and travail in my mind, lest this great gathering should have stirred up the town, and been more than the magistrates could well bear; but it was very quiet and peaceable, and a glorious meeting we had, to the settling and stablishing of Friends both in town and country; for the Lord's power was over all; blessed be his name for ever! Truly the Lord's power and presence was beyond words; for I was but weak to go into a meeting, and my face (by reason of a cold I had taken) was sore; but God manifested his strength in us and with us, and all was well: the Lord have the glory for evermore for his supporting power. After the meeting, I think above a hundred Friends of the town and country came to see me at John Furley's, and very glad we were to see one another, and greatly refreshed together, being filled with the love and riches of the Lord; blessed be his name for ever!

We tarried at Colchester two days more; which we spent in visiting Friends, both at their meetings for business and at their houses. Then early in the morning of Fourth-day we took coach for Harwich, where we met William Bingley, and Samuel Waldenfield, who went over with us. About eight at night we went on board the packet, Richard Gray master; but by reason of contrary winds it was one in the morning before we sailed. We had a very good passage; and about five in the afternoon next day we landed at the BRIEL in HOLLAND, where we stayed that night. Early next morning we went to ROTTERDAM, where we abode some days. The day after we came to Rotterdam, one Wilbert Frouzen, a burgomaster, and kinsman of Aarent Sunneman's, hearing I was there, invited me to his country house, having a desire to speak with me about some business, relating to Aarent Sunneman's daughters. I took George Watts with me, and a brother of Aarent Sunneman's had us thither. The burgomaster received us very kindly, and was very glad to see me; and entering into discourse about his kinsman's daughters, I found he was apprehensive that,

asserted and fully demonstrated according to the Scriptures. For although he gave preference to the Holy Spirit (as all true spiritual Christians do), yet his true love to, and sincere esteem of, the Holy Scriptures (as being given by Divine inspiration), is clearly manifest: 1st, In his frequent advice to Friends to keep to Scripture language, terms, words, and doctrines, as taught by the Holy Ghost, in matters of faith, religion, controversy, and conversation; and not to be imposed upon and drawn into unscriptural terms, invented by men in their human wisdom. 2d, In his great industry in searching the Scriptures, and frequently quoting, reciting, aptly applying and opening the same in his writings, as appears in the above-named work. He truly testified, both in his ministry and writings, of Christ Jesus, his power, and coming, in the flesh and in the spirit. He was both for the sacred history and mystery of Christ revealed according to the Scripture testimonies of him, respecting his sufferings without, the work of his power within, and his kingdom and glory; and, under his guidance, he faithfully warred against the spirit of Antichrist and persecution—against the false church—the corruptions of the world, its deceit and hypocrisy, under all professions.

their father being dead, and having left them considerable portions, they might be stolen and married to their disadvantage. Wherefore I told him, "that it was our principle and practice, that none should marry amongst us unless they had a certificate of the consent of their relations or guardians; for it was our Christian care to watch over and look after all young people that came among us; especially those whose natural relations were dead. And as for his kinsman's daughters, we should take care that nothing should be offered to them but what should be agreeable to truth and righteousness, and that they might be preserved in the fear of God, according to their father's mind." This seemed to give him great satisfaction. While I was with him there came many great people to me, and "I exhorted them all to keep in the fear of God, and to mind his good Spirit in them, to keep their minds to the Lord." After I had stayed two or three hours, and had conversed with him on several things, I took my leave of him, and he very kindly sent me to Rotterdam in his chariot.

Next day being First-day, we were at the meeting at Rotterdam, which was pretty large, and declared to the people by an interpreter. The day following Alderman Gaul came to speak with me, with whom we had much discourse about religious matters; he seemed to be well satisfied, and was very tender. Several other persons of account had intended to come to speak with me that day, but being hindered by extraordinary business (as I understood), they came not.

We went next day to AMSTERDAM, where we had a large and very precious meeting. In the afternoon I was at another meeting with Friends there, about business.

There is a Yearly Meeting at Amsterdam for the Friends of Holland and Germany, &c., which begun now on the 8th of the 4th month, and ended on the 12th. Here we had a fine opportunity of seeing Friends from many parts, and of being refreshed together in the love of God. After this meeting, before those that came out of the several provinces were gone, we had a meeting with some particular Friends, about the places and countries into which we who came out of England in the work of the ministry were to travel; and to inquire who among them were suitable persons to go along with us for interpreters. When this was concluded on, William Bingley * and Samuel Waldenfield † took shipping for Friesland, with Jacob Claus, their interpreter.

* William Bingley became a minister among Friends while residing in Yorkshire, and visited Ireland in 1675 and in 1682. He settled in London as a stuff merchant when in the meridian of life; and in 1684 accompanied Samuel Waldenfield on an apostolic journey in Holland and the Netherlands. He was one of the Friends who preached at the funeral of George Fox, in 1690; and he appears to have paid religious visits to different parts of Great Britain at various periods. He died in London in 1714, aged sixty-four years.

† Samuel Waldenfield, born at Edmondsbury, in Suffolk, in 1652, was religiously inclined in his youth, and a hearer of the Independents. But becoming convinced of the principles of truth, as held by Friends, about the year 1670, he came forth a powerful preacher of the word of life; and, with the Lord's blessing on his labours, many were convinced of the truth, and turned from darkness to light, and from the power of Satan unto God, and were as the seals of his ministry. In 1684 he married, and settled in

Alexander Parker and George Watts remained with me. We tarried a few days longer at Amsterdam, where I had further service. Before I left I went to visit one Galenus Abrahams, a teacher of chief note among the Mennonites, or Baptists. I had been with him when I was in Holland about seven years before; and William Penn and George Keith had disputes with him. He was then very high and shy, so that he would not let me touch him, nor look upon him (by his good will), but bid me "Keep my eyes off him, for," he said, "they pierced him." But now he was very loving and tender, and confessed in some measure to truth; his wife also and daughter were tender and kind, and we parted from them very lovingly.

Feeling our spirits drawn towards Friesland, Alexander Parker, George Watts, and I, having John Claus of Amsterdam with us for our interpreter, took shipping, and having sailed nine or ten leagues, we left the ship and travelled through Friesland, sometimes by boat, sometimes by waggon, visiting Friends and tender people in the towns and villages where we came; having one or two meetings in a day. After we had been at LEUWARDEN, we passed by FRANEKER to HARLINGEN in West Friesland, which was the furthest place we went to that way. And having been six days from Amsterdam, and had very good service in that time, visiting Friends and publishing truth amongst the people, we took ship at Harlingen for Amsterdam on the 26th of 4th month, and arrived there that night. The First-day following we were at the meeting at AMSTERDAM, which was very large and precious. Many of the people were there, their teachers, and some great persons also. They seemed very attentive; and a good opportunity we all had, one after another, to declare the word of the Lord and open the way of truth amongst them, John Claus interpreting for us. I tarried next day at Amsterdam; but George Watts went to a burial at Haarlem, attended by many hundreds of people, amongst whom he had a good opportunity, and came back at night to us

The day following we went by boat to OSAN-OVERTON in WATERLAND, and thence, in another small boat, about a league over a small river, where we passed over and by a hundred bridges, and so went to LANSMEER to a Friend's house whose name was Timon Peters; where we had a very good meeting. We returned to AMSTERDAM that night, and were at the meeting there next day. Many were at this meeting besides Friends, and among the rest the great Baptist teacher, Galenus, who was very attentive to the testimony of the truth, and when it was over, came and got me by the hand very lovingly.

We went next day by boat to ALKMAAR, about eight leagues from Amsterdam, passing through SARDAM, the great town of ship-carpenters,

London, continuing faithful and diligent in the work he was called unto; and suffered for his testimony by imprisonment, &c. His travels on gospel service, to the year 1700, were near 40,000 miles, which were also, subsequently, very considerable. Samuel Waldenfield is spoken of as being very considerate of the poor, humble and merciful, and as an elder worthy of double honour. He was a bright ornament to our religion in his conversation, gaining great reputation to truth and Friends among rich and poor. He was ill about two months before his decease, during which time he uttered many expressions worthy of being noted. He died in great peace in 1715. —See *Piety Promoted*, vol. ii., pp. 248–252.

and several other towns in the way. At Alkmaar, which is a pretty city, we stayed, and had a meeting next day at William Williams's. There were, besides Friends, many very sober people at this meeting, who were very attentive to the testimonies of truth, that were borne both by Alexander Parker, George Watts, and myself, John Claus being our interpreter. This was on a sixth day, and on the seventh we returned to AMSTERDAM, being willing to be at the meeting at Amsterdam on First-day, because it was likely to be the last we should have there. Accordingly we were at it, and a very large and open meeting it was. Many great persons were at it, some earls, we were told, with their attendants, out of Germany, who were very grave and sober, and the everlasting gospel was preached unto them.

After this we took leave of the Friends of Amsterdam; and next morning departed thence to HAARLEM, where we had a meeting at a Friend's house, whose name is Abraham Frondenberg. Great numbers of people were at this meeting, and of great service it was. After it a watch-maker of Amsterdam, who, with his wife, attended it, desired to speak with me concerning religion. I had much discourse with him, and both he and his wife were very low and tender, received with gladness what I spoke to them, and seemed well satisfied when they went away.

We went next day to ROTTERDAM, where we tarried two meetings; and on the 16th of the 5th month went to the BRIEL, to take ship for England.

About four in the afternoon we went on board the packet, William Sherman master, and set sail from the Briel. But when we had gone over the Maese about a league, we cast anchor at a place called the PITT, because it is near to the sands, where we stayed till about four next morning; when, having a pretty fair wind, and the tide with us, we weighed anchor, and by four next day were within five leagues of Harwich, over against Aldborough Castle; but the wind falling short, and the tide being weak, it was one in the afternoon before we came so near to HARWICH that boats could come to receive the passengers and goods. There were on board about forty passengers in all; English, Scotch, Dutch, French, Spanish, Flemish, and some Jews.

I spent a day with Friends at Harwich, while Alexander Parker and George Watts went by water to visit Friends at Ipswich, and returned at night. Next morning early we all took coach for Colchester, and were at the meeting there, which was large and peaceable; after it, we travelled to WITHAM, and lodged there that night, Next day, William Mead meeting us on the way at HARE STREET, I went with him to his house, the other Friends going on for London.

Here, being weak with travel and continual exercise, I spent some time to rest myself, and recover my health; visiting in the mean time the Friends in that part of the country, as I was able to get abroad.* When

* After returning from his last visit to Holland, George Fox did not travel far from London, his usual residence during the latter part of his life. His health had been gradually declining for some years, i[illegible] consequence of his many and grievous imprisonments, and the great fatigue of bo[illegible] and mind, occasioned by his long travels for the promotion of the cause of truth, an[illegible] by his incessant labours in "defence of

I was a little recovered, I went to ENFIELD, visiting Friends there and thereabouts; and so to DALSTON to see the widow Stot; and thence to LONDON, some Friends being come over from New Jersey in America, about business, which I was desired to be present at.

It was the latter end of the summer when I came to LONDON, where I stayed the winter following; saving that once or twice, my wife being in town with me, I went with her to her son Rous's at Kingston. And though my body was very weak; yet I was in continual service, either in public meetings, when I was able to bear them, or in particular business amongst Friends, and visiting those that were sufferers for truth, either by imprisonment or loss of goods. Many things also in this time I wrote, some for the press, and some for particular service; as letters to the King of Denmark and Duke of Holstein, on behalf of Friends that were sufferers in their dominions; of the latter, the following is a copy:—

"*For the Duke of Holstein, whom I entreat, in the love of God, to read over this, which is sent in love to him.*

"I UNDERSTAND that formerly, by some evil-minded persons, it was reported to thee, when Elizabeth Hendricks came to Frederickstadt to visit the people called Quakers, that it was a scandal to the Christian religion, that a woman should be suffered to preach in a public assembly religiously gathered together, &c. Upon which thou gave forth an order to the rulers of Frederickstadt, 'to make the said people leave that place forthwith, or to send them away.' But the said rulers being Arminians, and they, or their fathers, having come to live there, as a persecuted people in Holland, not much above threescore years ago, made answer to the duke, 'they were not willing to persecute others for conscience' sake, who had looked upon persecution on that account in their own case as antichristian,' &c. But after that, the people of God, in scorn called Quakers, wrote unto thee, O duke, from Fredrickstadt; and since that time they have had their liberty, and their meetings peaceable, to serve and worship God almost these twenty years at Fredrickstadt, and thereabouts, freely without any molestation; which liberty they have acknowledged as a great favour and kindness from thee.

"And now, O duke, thou professing Christianity from the great and mighty name of Christ Jesus, who is King of kings and Lord of lords, and the Holy Scriptures of truth of the Old and New Testament, do not you use many women's words in your service and worship out of the Old and New Testament? The apostle saith, 'Let your women keep silence in the

the gospel" against the clamour and opposition of apostate brethren, and the unfounded imputations of others, decidedly hostile to the truth as it is in Jesus. His solicitude, however, to promote the welfare of the Society, and procure relief to his Friends under suffering, both at home and abroad, remained undiminished. In the course of his declining state, he wrote many epistles to his friends, some of sympathy and consolation, to encourage and strengthen them in their deep sufferings; others of counsel, exhortation, and reproof, "stirring up the pure mind by way of remembrance," and labouring to build them up in the most holy faith; and, on all occasions, seeking not his own honour, but the honour of God only, and the edification of his church and people.

churches;' and that, 'he did not permit a woman to speak, but to be under obedience; and if she will learn anything, to ask her husband at home; for it is a shame for a woman to speak in the church.' And 1 Tim. ii. 11, 12. 'Women are to learn in silence and not suffered to teach, nor to usurp authority over the man, but to be in silence.' 1 Cor. xiv. 34. Now, here the duke may see, what sort of women were to be in silence and in subjection, whom the law commands to be silent, and not to usurp authority over the man, nor to speak in the church; these were unruly women. In the same chapter, he commands women 'not to plait or broider their hair, nor to wear gold, pearls, or costly array.' These things were forbidden by the apostle; and such women, as wear such things, are to learn in silence and to be subject, and not to usurp authority over the men; for it is a shame for such to speak in the church. But do not such women as these, that wear gold and silver, and pearls and gaudy apparel, or costly array, and plait and broider their hair, speak in your church, when your priest sets them to sing psalms? Do not they speak when they sing psalms? Consider this, O duke! Yet you say, 'your women must keep silence in the church, and must not speak in the church;' but when they sing psalms in your churches, are they then silent? Though the apostle forbids such women before-mentioned to speak in the church, yet in another place the apostle encourages the good or holy women to be teachers of good things, as in Tit. ii. 3, 4. The apostle said, 'I entreat thee, true yoke-fellow, help those women which laboured with me in the gospel, and with other my fellow-labourers, whose names are written in the book of life.' Here he owns these holy women, and encourages them, which laboured with him in the gospel, and did not forbid them; Phil. iv. 2, 3. He likewise commends Phœbe unto the church of the Romans, calls her 'a servant unto the church of Cenchrea,' sends his epistle by her to the Romans from Corinth, and desires the church at Rome to 'receive her in the Lord as becometh saints:' and to 'assist her in whatsoever business she had need of; for she had been a succourer of many and of himself also.' And he said, 'Greet Priscilla and Aquila, my helpers in Christ Jesus, who have for my life laid down their own necks; unto whom not only I give thanks, but also all the churches of the Gentiles.' Now here the duke may see these were good, holy women, whom the apostle did not forbid speaking, Rom. xvi. 1—4, but commended them. And Priscilla and Aquila instructed and expounded unto Apollos the way of God more perfectly, Acts xviii. 26. So here Priscilla was an instructor as well as Aquila; which holy women the apostle doth not forbid. Neither did the apostle forbid Philip's four daughters, which were virgins, to prophesy. Women might pray and prophesy in the church, 1 Cor. xi. 5.

"The apostles showed to the Jews the fulfilling of Joel's prophecy: 'That in the last days God would pour of his Spirit upon all flesh, and their sons and daughters, servants and handmaids, should prophesy with the Spirit of God.' So the apostle encourages daughters and handmaids to prophesy as well as sons; and if they do prophesy, they must speak to the church or people, Joel ii. 28; Acts ii. 17, 18. Did not Miriam the prophetess sing unto the Lord, and all the women with her, when the Lord had delivered the children of Israel from Pharaoh? Did not she praise the Lord, and prophesy in the congregation of the children of Israel? and was not this in the church? Exod. xv. 21. Moses and Aaron did not forbid her prophesying or speaking; but Moses said, 'Would God all the Lord's people were prophets!' and the Lord's people are women as well as men. Deborah was a judge and a prophetess; and do not you make use of Deborah's and Miriam's words in your service and worship? See (Judg. v. 1—31) Deborah's large speech or song. Barak did not forbid her, nor any of the Jewish priests. Did not she make this speech or song in the congregation or church of Israel? In the book of Ruth there are good speeches of those good women, which were not forbidden. Hannah prayed in the temple before Eli, and the Lord answered her prayer. See what a speech Hannah makes, and a praising of God before Eli the high-priest, who did not forbid her, 1 Sam. ii. 1—10. Josiah the king sent his priest, with several others, to ask counsel of Huldah the prophetess, who dwelt at Jerusalem in the college, 2 Kings xxii. 14; 2 Chron. xxxiv. 22. So here the king and his priests did not despise the counsel of this prophetess; and she prophesied to the congregation of Israel, as may be seen in these chapters.

"And in Luke i. 41—55, see what a godly speech Elizabeth made to Mary, and what a large godly speech Mary made also. Mary said, 'that the Lord did regard the low estate of his handmaid,' &c. And do not you make use in your worship and service of Mary's and Elizabeth's words from Luke i. 41—55, in your churches, and yet forbid women's speaking in your churches? Yet all sorts of women speak in your churches, when they sing, and say Amen. In Luke ii. there was Anna the prophetess, a widow of about fourscore and four years; who departed not from the temple, but served God with fasting and prayer night and day. Did not she confess Christ Jesus in the temple, and give thanks to the Lord, and 'speak of Christ to all that looked for redemption in Jerusalem?' Luke ii. 36—38. So such holy women were not forbidden to speak in the church, neither in the law nor gospel. Was it not Mary Magdalene and other women that first preached Christ's resurrection to the apostles? The woman indeed (namely, Eve) was first in transgression; and so they were women that first preached the resurrection of Christ Jesus; for Christ said to Mary, &c., 'Go to my brethren, and say unto them, I ascend unto my Father and to your Father, and to my God and to your God,' John xx. 17. And Luke xxiv. 10, it was Mary Magdalene and Joanna, and Mary the mother of James, and other women that were with them, who told the apostles, 'that Christ was risen from the dead, and their words and these women's words, were as idle tales to the apostles, and they believed them not,' ibid. ver. 11. And ver. 22, 'Certain women also of our company made us astonished,' they said: so here it may be seen, that the women's preaching the resurrection of Christ did astonish the apostles. Christ sent these women to preach his resurrection; so it is no shame for such women to preach Christ Jesus; neither are they to be silent when Christ sends them. The apostle says, 'Every tongue shall confess to God,' Rom. xiv. 11; and 'Every tongue shall confess that Jesus Christ is Lord, to the glory of

God the Father,' Phil. ii. 11. So here it is clear, that women must confess Christ as well as men, if every tongue must confess. And the apostle saith, 'There is neither male nor female; for ye are all one in Christ Jesus.' Gal. iii. 28.

"And whereas it is said, 'Women must ask their husbands at home,' &c., the duke knows very well virgins have no husbands, nor widows; for Anna the prophetess was a widow; and if Christ be the husband, men must ask counsel of him at home as well as women, before they teach. And set the case, that a Turk's wife should be a Christian, or a Papist's wife should be a Lutheran, or a Calvinist, must they ask and learn of their husbands at home, before they confess Christ Jesus in the congregation of the Lord? Their counsel will be to them to turn Turks or Papists.

"I entreat the duke to consider these things. I entreat him to mind God's grace and truth in his heart that is come by Jesus; that by his Spirit of Grace and truth he may come to serve and worship God in his Spirit and truth; so that he may serve the living eternal God that made him, in his generation, and have his peace in Christ, that the world cannot take away. And I do desire his good, peace, and prosperity in this world, and his eternal comfort and happiness in the world that is everlasting. Amen." G. F.

London, 26th of the 8th Month, 1684.

Besides the foregoing, I wrote also epistles to Friends; of one of which the following is a copy:—

"Friends and Brethren in the Lord Jesus Christ, in whom you have all life, peace, and salvation; walk in Him, who is your heavenly Rock and Foundation, that stands sure, who hath all power in heaven and earth given unto him. So his power is over all. Let your faith stand in his power, which is over all from everlasting to everlasting, over the devil and his power; that in the holy, heavenly wisdom of God, ye may be preserved and kept to God's glory, out of all snares and temptations; so that God's wisdom may be justified of all his children in this day of his power, and they all may be faithful, serving and worshipping God in his Spirit and truth, and valiant for it upon the earth. For, as the apostle saith, 'They that believe are entered into their rest, and have ceased from their own works, as God did from his.' Now this rest is an eternal rest in Christ, the eternal Son of God, in whom every true believer hath everlasting life in Christ Jesus, their rest and everlasting day. For Christ the Rest bruiseth the serpent's head, and through death destroyeth death, and the devil, the power of death, and his works. He is the Eternal Rest, that giveth eternal life to his sheep. Christ fulfilleth the prophets, and all the figures, shadows, and ceremonies, as in the Old Testament; and all the promises are yea and amen in Christ, who was the Eternal Rest to all true believers in the apostles' days, and ever since, and is so now. Christ is the beginning and the ending, the first and the last, who is ascended above all principalities, powers, thrones, and dominions, that he might fill all things. For 'by Jesus Christ all things were made and created, whether they be things in heaven, or things in the earth;' and he is the Eternal Rest. They that believe are entered into Christ, their Eternal Rest, in whom they have eternal life and peace with God. Wherefore I say again, in Him who is your Rest, live and abide; for in Him ye are happy, and his blessings will rest upon you. God Almighty keep and preserve you all, his true believers, in Christ your Rest and Peace this day. Amen." G. F.

London, the 18th of the 12th Month, 1684–5.

About a month after I got a little out of London, visiting Friends, at SOUTH STREET, FORD GREEN, and ENFIELD, where I had meetings. Afterwards I went to WALTHAM ABBEY, and was at the meeting there on a First-day, which was very large and peaceable. Then returning through ENFIELD and EDMONTON SIDE, I came back to LONDON in the 3rd Month, to advise with and assist Friends, in laying their sufferings before the Parliament then sitting. We drew up a short account thereof, which we caused to be printed and spread among the Parliament-men.

The Yearly Meeting coming on, I was much concerned for the Friends that came up to it out of the country, lest they should meet with any trouble or disturbance in their passages up or down; and the rather, because about that time a great bustle arose in the nation on the Duke of Monmouth's landing in the West. But the Lord, according to his wonted goodness, was graciously pleased to preserve Friends in safety, gave us a blessed opportunity to meet together in peace and quietness, and accompanied our meeting with his living, refreshing presence; blessed for ever be his holy name!

Now, considering the hurries that were in the nation, it came upon me, at the close of this meeting, to write a few lines to Friends, "to caution all to keep out of the spirit of the world, in which the trouble is, and to dwell in the peaceable truth;" as follows:—

"DEAR FRIENDS AND BRETHREN,

"Whom the Lord hath called and chosen in Christ Jesus, your Life and Salvation, in whom ye have all rest and peace with God; the Lord God by his mighty power, which is over all, hath preserved and supported you to this day, to be a peculiar, holy people to himself, so that by his eternal Spirit and power ye might be all kept out of the world; for in the world is trouble. And now, in this great day of the Lord God Almighty, he is shaking the heavens and the earth of outward professions, their elements are in a heat, their sun and their moon are darkened, the stars falling, and the mountains and hills shaking and tottering, as it was among the Jews in the day of Christ's appearing. Therefore, dear Friends and brethren, dwell in the Seed, Christ Jesus, the Rock and Foundation, that cannot be shaken; that ye may see with the light and Spirit of Christ, that ye are as fixed stars in the firmament of God's power; and in this his power and light, you will see over all the wandering stars, the clouds without water, and trees without fruit. That which may be shaken, will be shaken; as will all they that are wandered from the firmament of God's power.

"Dear Friends and brethren, you that are redeemed from the death and fall of Adam, by Christ the second Adam, in Him ye have life, rest, and peace; for Christ saith, 'In me ye shall have peace; but in the world trouble.' And the apostle saith, 'They that believe, are entered into their Rest,' namely, Christ, who hath overcome the world, who bruiseth the serpent's head, destroys the devil and his works, and fulfils the types, figures, and shadows of the Old Testament and the prophets; in whom the promises are yea and amen; who is the first and the last, the beginning and the ending—the Eternal Rest. So keep and walk in Christ, your Rest, every one that have received him.

"And now, dear Friends and brethren, whatever bustlings and trouble, tumults and outrages, quarrels and strife, arise in the world, keep out of them all; concern not yourselves with them: but keep in the Lord's power and peaceable truth, that is over all such things; in which power ye seek the peace and good of all men. Live in the love which God hath shed abroad in your hearts through Christ Jesus; in which nothing is able to separate you from God and Christ, neither outward sufferings, persecutions, nor any outward thing, that is below and without; nor to hinder or break your heavenly fellowship in the light, gospel, and Spirit of Christ; nor your holy communion in the Holy Ghost, that proceeds from the Father and the Son, and which leads you into all truth. In this Holy Ghost, in which is your holy communion, that proceeds from the Father and the Son, you have fellowship with the Father and the Son, and one with another. This is it which links and joins Christ's church or body together, to Him the heavenly and spiritual head, and in unity in his Spirit, which is the bond of peace, to all his church and living members, in whom they have eternal rest and peace in Christ, and with God everlasting, who is to be blessed and praised for ever. Amen.

"Dear Friends, forsake not the assembling of yourselves together, who are gathered in the name of Jesus, who is your Prophet, whom God hath raised up in the New Testament, to be heard in all things; who opens to you, and no man can shut; and shuts, and no man can open; who is your Priest, made higher than the heavens by the power of an endless life, by whom you are made a royal priesthood, to offer up to God spiritual sacrifice; who is the Bishop of your souls, to oversee you, that ye do not go astray from God; who is the good Shepherd, that hath laid down his life for his sheep; and they hear his voice, and follow him, and he gives them eternal life.

"And now, dear Friends and brethren, abide in Christ, the vine, that ye may bring forth fruit to the glory of God. And as every one hath received Christ, walk in Him, who is not of the world, that lies in wickedness; so that ye may be preserved out of the vain fashions and customs of the world, which satisfy the lust of the eye, the lust of the flesh, and the pride of life, which are not of the Father, but of the world that passes away. Whoever joins to that which is not of the Father, or encourages it, draws the mind from God the Father, and the Lord Jesus Christ. Therefore let Christ rule in your hearts, that your minds, souls, and spirits may be kept out of the vanities of the world, in their words, ways, and actions, that ye may be a peculiar people, zealous of good works, serving the Lord through Jesus Christ, to the praise and glory of God; that by the Word of his grace your words may be gracious, and in your lives and conversations ye may show forth righteousness, holiness, and godliness; that so God Almighty may be glorified in you all, and through you all, who is above all, blessed and praised for ever. Amen." G. F.

London, the 11th of the 4th Month, 1685.

Several other letters also I wrote at this time to Friends in divers foreign countries, from whom I had received letters about the affairs of truth. Which when I had despatched, the Yearly Meeting being over, and country Friends for the most part being gone, I got a little way out of town; being much spent with the heat of the weather, throngs in meetings, and continual business. I went at first to SOUTH STREET, where I abode some days. And among other services I had there, a great sense entered me of the growth and increase of pride, vanity, and excess in apparel; and that not only amongst the people of the world, but too much also amongst some that came among us, and seemed to make profession of the truth. In the sense I had of the evil thereof, it came upon me to give forth the following, as a reproof and check thereunto:—*

"THE apostle Peter saith (in 1 Pet. iii.) of the women's adorning; 'Let it not be (mark, let it not be; this is a positive prohibition) that outward adorning of plaiting the hair, and of wearing of gold, or of putting on of apparel; but let it be the hidden man of the heart, in that which is not corruptible, even the ornament of a meek and quiet spirit, which is in the sight of God of great price; for after this manner in the old time the holy women also, who trusted in God, adorned themselves.'

"Here ye may see what is the ornament of the holy women, which was in the sight of God of great price, and which the holy women, who trusted in God, adorned themselves with. But the unholy women, that trust not in God, their ornament is not a meek and a quiet spirit; they

* Those Christians whose experience enters most deeply into the spiritual nature of the gospel dispensation, will find that it leads them into simplicity as regards their outward appearance. The practice in the primitive church, as regards "outward adorning," is thus spoken of by Coleman, in his *Antiquities of the Christian Church:*—

"Nothing may appear more purely a matter of indifference than the fashion and colour of dress; and yet, in the circumstances of the primitive Christians, articles of that nature did acquire such an importance that they gradually fell into a style of clothing peculiar to themselves. Not that they affected any singularities in their personal appearance, for their habiliments were made and worn in the ordinary fashion of the time and place; and Christians, whether found in the high, the middle, or the lower ranks, were accustomed to equip themselves in a manner suited to the decencies of the state or profession to which they belonged; but, looking to the moral influence of dress, and desirous of avoiding everything that might minister to vanity, or lead the wearer to forget, in attending to the outward man, the ornament of a 'meek and quiet spirit,' they studiously rejected all finery as unbecoming the humility of their character, and confined themselves to a suit of apparel, remarkable not so much for the plainness of the material as for the absence of all superfluous ornament. Everything gandy or sumptuous, that partook of the costly stuffs or the crimson dyes that suited the luxurious taste of the times, was discountenanced by the spiritually-minded followers of Christ. The same simplicity reigned throughout their domestic establishments; and even those of their number who were persons of rank and opulence, chose to content themselves with such things as were recommended by their utility rather

adorn themselves with plaiting the hair, putting on of apparel, and wearing of gold; which is forbidden by the apostle in his general epistle to the church of Christ, the true Christians.

"And the apostle saith (1 Tim. ii. 9, 10), 'In like manner also, that women adorn themselves in modest apparel, with shamefacedness and sobriety; not with broidered hair, or gold, or pearls, or costly array, but (which becometh women professing godliness) with good works.'

"Here ye may see what the women were not to adorn themselves with, who professed godliness; they were not to adorn themselves with broidered hair, nor gold, nor pearls, nor costly array; for this was not looked upon to be modest apparel for holy women, that professed godliness and good works. But this adorning or apparel is for the immodest, unshamefaced, unsober women, that profess not godliness, neither follow those good works that God commands. Therefore it doth not become men and women who profess true Christianity and godliness, to be adorned with gold, or chains, or pearls, or costly array; or with broidered hair; for these things are for the lust of the eye, the lust of the flesh, and the pride of life, which are not of the Father. All holy men and women are to mind that which is more precious than gold; who are 'redeemed not with corruptible things, as silver and gold, from your vain conversation; but with the precious blood of Christ, as of a Lamb without blemish and without spot. Therefore as obedient children to God, not fashioning yourselves according to your former lusts in your ignorance; but as he which hath called you is holy, so be ye holy in all manner of conversation,' 1 Pet. i. 14, 15.

"Christ saith, 'The life is more than meat, and the body is more than raiment,' Luke xii. 23.

"I read of a wise moral philosopher, who, meeting a woman with her neck and breast bare, laid his hand upon her, and said, 'Woman, wilt thou sell this flesh?' and she replying, No; 'Then pray,' said he, 'shut up thy shop;' (meaning her bare breasts and neck.) So they were looked upon as harlots, that went with their necks, breasts, and backs bare, and not modest people, even among the moral heathens. Therefore they that profess the knowledge of true Christianity, should be ashamed of such things. You may see a book written by the very Papists, and another by Richard Baxter the Presbyterian, against bare breasts and bare backs. They that were but in an outward profession, declared against such things; therefore they who are in the possession of truth and true Christianity, should be ashamed of such things. Read, I pray you, the third of Isaiah, and there

than their elegance, and calculated to answer the purposes of necessity and comfort, rather than to gratify 'the lust of the eye, and the pride of life.' And however refined or exquisite the taste, which, through education and the habits of society, any of them had acquired, they learned to subject it to the higher principle of denying themselves to everything that tended too much to captivate the senses, and increase their love to a world, the fashion whereof, they thought, was soon to pass away."

The remarks of John Wesley on simplicity in dress are excellent, but too long to be quoted here. He says that "following the fashions of the world is directly at war with the spirit of the gospel." See *Select Miscellanies*, vol. v., p. 288, for Wesley's views on this subject; also of T. A. Kempis, and others.

see how that holy prophet was grieved with the foolish women's vain attire, and how he was sent by the Lord to reprove them. Envious, persecuting Jezebel's attired head and bravery, like a painted harlot out of the truth, did not keep her from the judgments of God, when the Lord stirred up Jehu against her. Doth not pride go before a fall, and a haughty mind before destruction? God resisteth the proud, and giveth grace to the humble. Solomon saith, 'The Lord will destroy the house of the proud,' Prov. xv. 25. 'For the day of the Lord shall be upon every one that is proud and lofty, &c., and he shall be brought low,' Isa. ii. 12, and Mal. iv. Therefore take heed of calling the proud happy; for 'the Lord will scatter the proud in the imaginations of their own hearts, and exalt them of low degree.' And you may read in the Revelations (chap. xvii. 4, and xviii. 16), of the false church, how she was outwardly decked, but full of abomination, and came to a downfall at last. Therefore it is good for all that profess the truth, to use this world as not abusing it; for the fashion of this world passeth away; but the Word of the Lord endureth for ever. 'The Lord taketh pleasure in his people, he will beautify the meek with salvation,' Psa. cxlix. 4. All that know the truth as it is in Jesus, are to be beautified and clothed with this salvation, which salvation is a strong wall or a bulwark against that spirit, that would lead you further into the fall from God, into those things which the fallen man and woman delight in, and beautify or adorn themselves with. Therefore, all that profess the truth, be circumspect, sincere, and fervent, following the Lord Jesus Christ, who is not of this world; in whom ye have life and peace with God."

South-street, the 24th of the 4th Month, 1685. G. F.

CHAPTER XII.

1685–1686.—George Fox tarries in London, labouring in the service of Truth—removes to Epping on account of his health—writes an epistle to Friends—returns to London—writes a paper concerning order in the Church of God—and a warning to backsliders—assists in distributing money raised for sufferers by Friends in Ireland—writes an epistle to the king of Poland, on behalf of Friends of Dantzic, who suffer imprisonment for conscience' sake—a paper concerning judging—looks diligently after Friends' sufferings in London, and obtains a general release of prisoners—writes an epistle to Friends, many having been recently liberated from prison—another on a similar occasion—an epistle to Friends to keep in the unity in the Truth—another to remind them of the evidence and seal they had received of their meetings for discipline having been set up in the power and spirit of God—a paper concerning the state of the true Church—a paper respecting the "falling away" foretold by the apostle Paul, 2 Thess. ii. 3—a paper showing how the Lord, in all ages, called the righteous out from amongst the wicked, before he destroyed the latter.

After I had been some weeks at South Street and Enfield, in which time I had several meetings with Friends, I returned to London. Amongst other services I found there, one was to assist Friends in drawing up a testimony to clear our Friends from being concerned in the late rebellion in the West, and from all plots against the government: which was delivered to the chief justice, who was then going down into the West with commission to try prisoners.

I tarried some time in London, visiting meetings, and labouring among Friends in the service of truth. But finding my health much impaired for want of fresh air, I went to Charles Bathurst's country-house at Epping-Forest, where I stayed a few days. While I was there it came upon me to write the following epistle to Friends:—

"Dear Friends,

"Who are called, chosen, and faithful in this day of trial, temptations, and sufferings, whom the Lord by his right hand hath upholden in all your sufferings (and some to death) for the Lord and his truth's sake. Christ saith, 'Be of good cheer, I have overcome the world; in me ye have peace; but in the world ye have trouble.' The children of the Seed, who are heirs of the kingdom, know this is true. And though ye have trials by false brethren, Judases and sons of perdition, that are got into the temple of God, and exalted above all that is called God, whom the Lord will destroy with the breath of his mouth, and the brightness of his coming: and though ye be tried by powers or principalities, yet there is nothing able to separate you from the love of God, which ye have in Christ Jesus. In that love dwell, which bears all things and fulfils the law; in which edify one another, and be courteous, kind, and humble; for to such God giveth his grace plentifully, and such he teacheth. And pray in the Holy Ghost, which proceeds from the Father and the Son; in it keep your holy communion, and unity in the Spirit, the bond of peace, which is the King of kings' heavenly peace. In that you are all bound to good behaviour, to keep peace among yourselves, to seek the peace of all men; and to show forth the heavenly, gentle, and peaceable wisdom to all, in righteousness and truth, answering the good in all people in your lives and conversations (for the Lord is glorified in your bringing forth spiritual fruit), that ye may eye and behold the Lord in all your actions; that his blessings ye may all feel to rest upon you. Whether ye be the Lord's prisoners for his name and truth's sake, or at liberty, in all things labour to be content, for that is a continual feast; and let no trouble move you; then ye will be as Mount Sion, that cannot be removed. In all things exercise the word of patience, which word will sanctify all things to you. Study to be quiet, and do the Lord's business that he requires of you, and your own, in truth and righteousness: and whatsoever ye do, let it be done to the praise and glory of God in the name of Jesus Christ. All they that make God's people suffer, make the Seed suffer in their own particulars, and imprison the Just there. Such will not visit the Seed in themselves, but cast it into prison in others, and not visit it in prison. You may read that Christ saith, such must go into everlasting punishment. That is a sad punishment and prison. All such as become apostates and backsliders, that crucify to themselves Christ afresh, put him to open shame, and trample under feet the blood of the Son of God, by which they were cleansed, and come to be unclean; such grieve, vex, quench, and rebel against, the Spirit of God in themselves; and then rebel against them that walk in it. Such are unfaithful to God and man, and are enemies to every good work and service of God: but their end will be according to their works; who are like unto the earth, that hath often received rain, but brings forth briars and thorns, which are to be rejected, and are for the fire. Therefore, dear Friends, in all your sufferings feel the Lord's eternal arm and power, which hath supported you to this day, and will to the end, as your faith stands in it, and as you are settled upon the rock and foundation Christ Jesus, that cannot be removed; in whom ye have life and peace with God. The Lord God Almighty in him give you dominion, and preserve you all to his glory; that in all your sufferings ye may feel his presence: and that, when ye have finished your testimony, ye may receive the crown of glory, which God hath laid up for them that fear and serve him. Amen." G. F.

The 15th of the 7th Month, 1685.

Having spent about a week in the country, I returned to LONDON, where I continued about two months, visiting meetings, and labouring to get relief for Friends from their sufferings, which yet lay heavy upon them in many parts of the nation. Several papers also I wrote relating to the service of truth, one of which was concerning order in the church of God, which some that were gone out of the unity of Friends much opposed. It was as follows:—

"AMONG all societies, families, or nations of people in the world, there exists some sort of order. There was the order of Aaron in the Old Testament; and the order of Melchizedeck before that, after whose order Christ Jesus came; and he did not despise that order. God is a God of order in his whole creation, and in his church: and all believers in the light, the life in Christ, that pass from death to life, are in the order of the Holy Spirit, power, light, life, and government of Christ Jesus, of the increase whereof there is no end. This is a mystery to all those disorderly people, who have written and printed so much against the order which the Lord's power and Spirit hath brought forth among his people. And you that cry so much against order, is it not manifest that you are gone into a land of darkness, and of the shadow of death, into disorder, and where the light is as darkness? Is not this your condition seen by all them that live and walk in the truth, whose conversations are according to the gospel of life and salvation?

"The devil, Satan, dragon, the first and second beast, the whore and false prophets, and their worshippers and followers, are all out of the truth, abode not in it, nor in the order of it; and the truth is over them all. In Salem is God's tabernacle; and his tabernacle is in Shiloh; these are far beyond the tabernacles of Ham (Ps. lxxvi. and lxxviii.).

"All the figures and shadows were and are comprehended in time; but Christ the substance is the beginning and the ending. And all trials, troubles, persecutions, and temptations, came up in time; but the Lord's power which is everlasting, is over all such things; in which is safety.

"The black world of darkness lieth in wickedness, and by its wisdom knoweth not God, that made the world and all things therein; for the god of the world and prince of the air ruleth in the hearts of all that disobey the living God that made them. So the God of this wicked world hath blinded the eyes of the infidels or heathen; so that by their wisdom they know not the living God.

"In the Old Testament the Lord said, 'With all thy offerings thou shalt offer salt,' Lev. ii. 13. And Christ saith in his new covenant, 'Every one shall be salted with fire, and every sacrifice shall be salted with salt. Salt is good; but if the salt have lost its saltness, wherewith will you season it? Have salt in yourselves; and have peace one with another,' Mark ix. 49, 50.

"We have received the earnest of the Spirit, which is the earnest of the inheritance, that fadeth not away. For God poureth out of his Spirit upon all flesh. It is God's Spirit which is above our natural spirit, by which alone we do not know God; for it is by the Spirit of God that we know the things of God. And the Spirit of God doth witness to our souls and spirits, that this Spirit of God is the earnest of an eternal inheritance. 'God opens his people's ears to discipline, and commands that they turn from iniquity. If they obey and serve him, they shall spend their days in prosperity and their years in pleasure; but if they obey him not they shall perish by the sword, and they shall die without knowledge,' Job xxxvi. 10–12. So the disobedient that do not turn from their iniquity have not this prosperity and pleasure, but die without the knowledge of God; and their ears are shut to this discipline, which God opens to his people."

G. F.

When I had been about two months in London, I was sent for to my son Rous's at KINGSTON, to visit a daughter of his, who at that time lay very sick; but recovered. Whilst I stayed there I had several meetings with Friends; and returning by HAMMERSMITH, stayed the First-day meeting there, which was large and peaceable. Having visited Friends thereabouts, I came back to LONDON again, being very intent upon the business of getting redress for suffering Friends. In this and other services I continued at London, till the latter end of the 11th month; save that I went to visit an ancient Friend at BETHNAL-GREEN, with whom I tarried three or four days. While I was there, I was much exercised in the sense of the enemy's working, to draw from the holy way of truth into a false liberty, and so into the world's ways and worships again. And the example of the backsliding Jews coming before me, I was moved to write the following as a warning to all such:—

"YOU may see, when the Jews rebelled against the good Spirit of God, which he gave to instruct them, they forsook him and his law, way, and worship, and went a whoring after Balaam's ways, and became like the wild ass's colt, snuffing up the wind, as in Jer. ii. 24. And in Jer. iii., see how Judah played the harlot under every green tree, and upon every high mountain; and therefore the Lord divorced Judah, as he had divorced Israel, when she forsook his way and followed the ways of the heathen. Though the Lord had fed them to the full, yet they forsook him, 'they committed adultery, and assembled themselves together in harlots' houses.' Jer. v. 7. 'And with their whoredom they defiled the land, and committed adultery with stocks and stones.' Jer. iii. 9. Here you may see, when they forsook the living eternal God, they followed the religions and worships of other nations, whose gods were made of stocks and stones, which the Jews worshipped, and committed adultery withal. When they forsook the living God, and his way and worship, they forsook the worship at the temple at Jerusalem, and followed the heathen's worships in the mountains and fields; so it was called adultery and whoredom to join with other religions and forsake God; as in Jer. xiii. 27.

"And now, if the children of New Jerusalem that is above, should forsake the worship, that Christ in his New Testament set up (which is in Spirit and in truth) and follow the worships of nations, which men have set up, will not they that do so, commit adultery with them, in forsaking God's worship, and Christ, the new and living way?

"In Jer. xliv., ye may see how the children of Judah provoked the Lord against them, by worshipping the works of their own hands, and following the gods of the land of Egypt. In this they committed adultery, forsaking the living God, their husband, and his worship; and there ye may see God's judgments pronounced against them to their destruction. And what will become of those that forsake the worship in Spirit and in truth, which Christ set up, and worship the works of their own hands in spiritual Egypt, and follow spiritual Egypt's will-worship, which they invented? may not this be called whoredom in them that forsake Christ, the new and living way, and his pure religion, and his worship, that he hath set up? And they that forsake the Lord's way, and his worship that he set up, and follow the world's ways and worships that they set up, do not they, whose way they follow, become at last their enemies? as in Lam. i. See how the Jews forsook the Lord's way and worship, and doted on their lovers (the Assyrians, &c.), and with all their idols they were defiled; and how they did not leave the whoredoms brought from Egypt, and how they were polluted with the Babylonians' bed; as ye may read in Ezek. xxiii. When they forsook the Lord, his way and worship, and followed the way and worship of the heathen; then it was said they went a whoring after other lovers, and committed adultery with them.

"Ye may see in Ezek. xvi. the state of the Jews was likened unto that of their sister Sodom, and how they had played the harlot with the Assyrians, and committed fornication with the Egyptians, and had increased their whoredoms in following their abominable idols. And therefore the Lord carried away the two tribes that forsook him into Babylon; as you may see in Ezek. xvii. 20. And they that forsake Christ, the new and living Way, and the worship of God in Spirit and in truth, which Christ set up in his New Testament, go into captivity in spiritual Babylon.

"In Hosea ii., see how he discovers the whoredoms and idolatry of the Jews, who forsook the Lord, and compares them to a harlot. And in chap. viii., the destruction threatened against the Jews, for their impiety and idolatry. In chap. ix. also, the distress and captivity of the Jews is threatened for their sins and idolatry. And again they are reproved and threatened for their impiety and idolatry, Hos. x. This was for forsaking the Lord and his way, and following the ways of their own inventions, and the ways of the heathen.

"Doth not Isaiah say, 'That the Lord would visit Tyre, and that she should commit fornication with all the kingdoms of the world upon the face of the earth;' and therefore the Lord threatened destruction upon her, chap. xxiii. And in chap. lvii. see how the Lord reproved the Jews for their whorish idolatry, and said, 'Upon a high and lofty mountain hast thou set thy bed; even thither wentest thou up to offer sacrifices. Thou hast enlarged thy bed, and made a covenant with them; thou lovedst their bed, where thou sawest it.' This was a joining to the heathen's religions, altars, and sacrifices, and a forsaking of the Lord's altar and sacrifices, which he commanded in the law; and therefore that was committing whoredom with the heathen, and going into their beds from the living God that made them. And now in the New Testament God having 'poured his Spirit upon all flesh,' that by his Spirit all might come to be 'a royal priesthood, to offer up spiritual sacrifices to God by Jesus Christ;' all that err from the Spirit of God and rebel against it, are not like to offer spiritual sacrifices to God; the sacrifice of such God doth not accept, no more than he did that of the heathens, or of the Jews, who rebelled against his good Spirit, that he gave to instruct them.

"And ye may see in the xviith, xviiith, and xixth chapters of the Revelations, the punishment of the great whore, Babylon, the mother of harlots; and the victory of the Lamb, and how he calleth God's people out of Babylon; for 'in her was found the blood of the prophets, and of the saints, and of all that were slain upon the earth.' There ye may read her judgment and her downfall. This whore are they, that are whored from the Spirit of God, and so from God and from his holy worship in spirit and in truth, from the pure, undefiled religion, that keeps from the spots of the world, and from the new and living way, Christ Jesus; these are whored from the Spirit of God into false religions, ways, and worships, and so have corrupted the earth with her abominations. But her judgment and downfall are seen, over whom Christ hath the victory; and the marriage of the Lamb is come, glory to the Lord for ever! And God's pure religion, and pure worship in Spirit and in truth Christ hath set up, as it was in the apostles' days. Hallelujah!" G. F.

I soon returned to LONDON, but made no long stay there, my body not being able to bear the closeness of the city long together. While I was in town, besides the usual services of visiting Friends, and looking after their sufferings to get them eased, I assisted Friends of the city in distributing certain sums of money, which our Friends of Ireland had charitably and very liberally raised, and sent over for the relief of their brethren, who suffered for the testimony of a good conscience; which money was distributed amongst poor, suffering Friends in the several counties, in proportion as we understood their need.

Before I left the city, I heard of a great doctor lately come from Poland; whom I invited to my lodging, and had much discourse with him. After I had informed myself by him of such things as I had a desire to know, I wrote a letter to the King of Poland on behalf of Friends at Dantzic, who had long been under grievous sufferings. A copy whereof follows:—

"*To John the Third, King of Poland, great Duke of Lithuania, Russia, and Prussia, Defender of the city of Dantzic, &c. Concerning the innocent and afflicted people, in scorn called Quakers, who are now fed with bread and water in Bridewell of the aforesaid city, under close confinement, where their friends, wives, and children, are hardly suffered to come to see them.*

"O KING!

"The magistrates of the city of Dantzic say, that it is thy order and command, that these innocent and afflicted people should suffer such oppression. Now this punishment is inflicted upon them only because they come together in the name of Jesus Christ, their Redeemer and Saviour, who died for their sins, and is risen from the dead for their justification; who is their Prophet, whom God hath raised up like unto Moses; whom they ought to hear in all things in this day of the gospel and new covenant; who went astray like scattered sheep, but now are returned to the chief Shepherd and Bishop of their souls, 1 Pet. ii. 25. 'Who has given his life for his sheep, and they hear his voice and follow him;' who leads them into his 'pastures of life,' John x.

"Now, O King! I understand that thou openly professest Christianity, and the great and mighty name of Jesus Christ, who is King of kings, and Lord of lords, to whom is given all power in heaven and in earth, who rules all nations with a rod of iron. Therefore, O king, it seems hard to us, that any who openly confess Christ Jesus (yea, the magistrates of Dantzic do the same) should inflict those punishments upon an innocent and harmless people, by reason of their tender conscience, only because they come together to serve and worship the Eternal God, who made them, in Spirit and in truth; which worship Christ Jesus set up sixteen hundred years ago; as we read in John iv. 23, 24.

"I beseech the king, that he would consider, whether Christ in the New Testament, ever gave such a command to his apostles, that they should shut up any in prison, and feed them with bread and water, who were not conformable in every particular to their religion, faith, and worship? Where did the apostles exercise such things in the true church after Christ's ascension? Is not this the doctrine of Christ and the apostles, that his followers should 'love their enemies, and pray for them that hate them, and persecute and despitefully use them?' Matt. v.

"Is it not a shame to Christendom among the Turks and others, that one Christian should persecute another for the doctrine of faith, worship, and religion? They cannot prove that Christ ever gave them such a command, whom they profess to be their Lord and Master. For Christ says, that his believers and followers should 'love one another,' and by this they should be known to be his disciples. And did not Christ reprove those who would have 'fire to come down from heaven,' to destroy them who would not receive him? and did not he tell them, 'they did not know what spirit they were of?' Have all who have persecuted men, or taken away their lives, because they would not receive their religion, known what spirit they were or are of? Is it not good for all to know, by the Spirit of Christ, what spirit they are of? For the apostle says, Rom. viii. 9, 'If any man have not the Spirit of Christ, he is none of his.' And 2 Cor. x. 4, 'The weapons of our warfare are not carnal, but spiritual,' &c. And 'We wrestle not against flesh and blood, but against spiritual wickedness,' &c. Thus we see, that the fight of the first Christians, and their weapons in the days of the apostles, were spiritual.

"Now would not the king and the magistrates of Dantzic think it contrary to their consciences, if they should be forced by the Turk to his religion? Would it not in like manner seem hard to the magistrates of Dantzic, and contrary to their consciences, if they should be forced to the religion of the King of Poland? or to the King of Poland, if he should be compelled to the religion of the magistrates of Dantzic? And if they would not be subject thereunto, that then they should be banished from their wives and families, and out of their native country, or otherwise be fed with bread and water under strict confinement?

"Therefore we beseech the king with all Christian humility, and the magistrates, that they would order their proceedings in this matter according to the royal law of God, which is, 'to do unto others as they would have others do unto them,' and 'to love their neighbour as themselves.' For we have this charity, that we hope and believe, that the King of Poland and his people, with the magistrates of Dantzic, own the writings of the New Testament, as well as of the Old; and therefore we beseech the king and magistrates to take heed, that their work of imprisoning an innocent people, for nothing but their meeting together, in tenderness of conscience, to serve and worship God, their Creator, may not be contrary and opposite to the royal law of God, and to the glorious and everlasting gospel of truth.

"We desire the king, in Christian love, earnestly and weightily to consider these things, and to give order to set the innocent prisoners, our friends, called Quakers, at liberty from their strict confinement in Dantzic; that they may have freedom to serve and worship the Living God in Spirit and in truth, to go home to their habitations, and follow their trades and calling, to maintain their wives, children, and families. And we believe that the king, in doing such a noble, glorious, yea Christian work, will not go unrewarded from the Great God who made him, whom we serve and worship, who has the hearts of kings, and their lives and length of days in his hands.

"From him who desires that the king and all his ministers may be preserved in the fear of God, and receive his Word of wisdom, by which all things were made and created; that by it he may come to order all things to the glory of God, which God has put under his hand: that both he and they may enjoy the comforts and blessings of the Lord in this life, and in that which is to come, life eternal. Amen." G. F.

London, the 10th of the 3rd Month, commonly called May, 1684.

"*Postscript.*—The king may please to consider, that his and all men's consciences are the prerogative of God."

After this I went to ENFIELD, where, and in the country around, several Friends had country-houses, amongst whom I tarried some time, visiting and being visited by Friends, and having meetings with them. Several things I wrote in this time, relating to the service of truth; one was 'Concerning judging:' for some, who had departed from the truth, were so afraid of its judgment, that they made it much of their business to cry out against judging. Wherefore I wrote a paper, proving by the Scriptures of truth, that the church of Christ has power and ability to judge those that profess to be of it, not only with respect to outward things relating to this world, but with respect to religious matters also. A copy of which follows:—

"*Concerning Judging.*

"'THE natural man receiveth not the things of the Spirit of God, for they are foolishness to him, neither can he know them, because they are spiritually discerned; but he that is spiritual judgeth all things (mark) all things; yet he himself is judged of no man,' 1 Cor. ii. 14, 15. So the natural man cannot judge of those things he receives not, for they are foolishness to him; but he is comprehended by the spiritual man, and his foolishness, and is judged, though he cannot judge the spiritual man.

"'Do not ye judge them that are within?' saith the apostle (this power the church had, and hath), therefore put away from amongst yourselves that wicked person.' Did not this wicked person, think you, profess and plead for liberty for his wickedness, and his freedom, as he was a Christian, who was looked upon as a member of the church?

"The apostle saith, 'For I verily, as absent in body, yet present in spirit, have judged already, as though I were present, concerning him that hath done this wicked deed,' 1 Cor. v. 3, 12. Here the apostle judged, though afar off, and set up judgment in the church against false liberty, under what pretence soever it was.

"And the apostle saith, 'Dare any of you, having a matter against a brother, go to law before the unjust, and not before the saints?' Here the saints, the church, are to judge of things amongst themselves, and not for the unjust to judge of their matters. 'Do ye not know the saints shall judge the world?' So the saints are to judge the unjust, and not the unjust to judge their matters.

"And farther, the apostle saith, 'If the world shall be judged by you (to wit, the saints), are you unworthy to judge the smallest matters amongst you?'

"It is clear that the saints have a judgment given them of Christ, by his power and Spirit, light and wisdom, to judge the world, and not to carry their matters before the unjust, but to judge of them amongst themselves; and if they carry them before the unjust, they show their unworthiness of the saints' judgment.

"Again, 'Know ye not that we shall judge angels? (and angels are spirits) how much more things which pertain to this life?'

"'If ye then have judgment of things pertaining to this life, set them up to judge who are least esteemed in the church,' 1 Cor. vi. 4. Here it is clear the church of Christ has a judgment in the power and Spirit of God, not only to judge in things that pertain to this life, but are also to judge of things between brethren, without brother going to law with brother before unbelievers; which was a fault, and to be judged, if they did so.

"But also the saints have a judgment to judge angels that kept not their habitations, and the world. As in Jude, 'He judged the angels that kept not their habitations, their first state.' Did not he judge in divine matters here? He judged the state of Cain, and Balaam, and Core, and such Christians as were gotten into their steps, and were gone as far as they, though they professed themselves Christians? Here again he judged in divine matters; and of their states and beings, who stood in the divine principle, and who were fallen from it.

"The apostle saith, 'Try the spirits, and believe not every spirit,' 1 John iv. Here again was a judgment in divine matters; and he judged such as went out from them; these, whilst they were with them, had sight of things and openings; but when they went from them they went from the anointing; and therefore he exhorts the saints to keep to the anointing. Such as went from them that had the anointing, came to be the seducers and false prophets that went into the world.

"John had a judgment to try sacrifices, and distinguished Cain's from Abel's; and, by the Spirit of God, knew which God accepted, and which he did not accept, 1 John iii. 12. Paul judged and tried such messengers and apostles, and transformers of themselves like to the apostles of Christ; and would have the church to try such, and have the same judgment that he had, 2 Cor. xi.

"The apostle Peter judged Ananias and Sapphira, and the thoughts of Simon Magus, who would have been a worker of miracles for money. Was not all this judgment in divine matters? And the apostle Paul judged the preachers of circumcision, both in the Romans and Galatians. For it was the faith and liberty of those preachers to preach up circumcision, though it was a wrong faith. Did not the apostle here again judge in divine matters?

"James judged in matters of faith, and manifested the living faith from the dead one. He also judged in matters of religion, the vain from the pure religion, and distinguished them.

"Paul judged of the false brethren, that would spy out the liberty of the true; to whom he would give no place by subjection, no, not for an hour, that the truth of the gospel might continue with the saints; as in Gal. ii. Did not the apostle here judge in divine matters? And he judged concerning the matters of the gospel when some came to pervert them with another gospel, and said, 'The gospel which I received is not of man, neither was I taught it, but by the revelation of Jesus Christ,' Gal. i. 12. So here was a judgment to distinguish the gospel of Christ from all other gospels, which were accursed, which are after man, received and taught of man, and not by the revelation of Jesus Christ, Gal. i. And he had a judgment to know, 'who made the gospel chargeable, and who kept it without charge.'

"He set up a judgment in the church that the believers should not be unequally yoked; and to see when men had a communion in the light, and when they had it in the darkness; when with Christ, and when with Baal; with the believer and unbeliever; with the temple of God and with idols: as in 2 Cor. vi. Did he not set up a clear judgment here in divine matters in the church?

"And the apostle judged such libertines as through their knowledge could sit at meat in the idol's temple; who through their knowledge and liberty caused the weak brother to perish, for whom Christ died. These, it is like, did profess it was their faith and their liberty; yet they did not keep in the unity of the true faith, but went about to destroy it, 1 Cor. viii.

"Peter gives judgment upon the angels that sinned, and were cast down into hell; upon the state of the old world, and of Sodom, and the state of the false prophets then amongst them, that could speak great swelling words of vanity; and whilst they promised them liberty, they themselves were the servants of corruption. And had not Peter here a judgment in divine matters? These were such whose work was to bring into bondage, and these were like the dog and sow that were washed; which shows that they had been washed, but were turned into the mire again. The apostle Paul had a judgment upon such as, with their fair words and men's wisdom, deceived the hearts of the simple; and upon such as 'served not the Lord Jesus Christ, but their own bellies, and were enemies to the cross of Christ.' He had a judgment and discerning who lived in the cross of Christ, and who did not; and exhorted all to live in the cross of Christ, the righteous power of God, that slew all deceit, and the deeds of the old man, agreeably to Christ's words, 'He that will be my disciple, must take up his cross and follow me.' Was not here a judgment again in divine matters, of such as walked in the divine power, and such as did not?

"Christ sets up a judgment in his seven churches, and commends them that did keep in his judgment, and had tried them which said, 'they were apostles,' who might pretend they were sent of God and Christ, and were not; but the church of Christ had found them liars. Christ commended this judgment of the church of Ephesus, because they had 'not borne with them that were evil, but had tried those false apostles:' and Christ commends this church, for they had 'hated the deeds of the Nicolaitanes, which he also hated:' and had not these Nicolaitanes sprung from Nicolas, one of the deacons? and were not these become a sect of Christians? though they might talk and preach of Christ, yet Christ hated their doctrine.

"Christ saith to the church of Smyrna, 'I know the blasphemy of them which say they are Jews, and are not, but are of the synagogue of Satan.' So the church is to have a judgment upon these blasphemers, and to distinguish the Jews in the Spirit from such as are not, but of the synagogue of Satan.

"To the church in Pergamos Christ saith, 'I have a few things against thee, because thou hast there them that hold the doctrines of Balaam,' &c., and 'also them that hold the doctrine of the Nicolaitanes, which thing I hate.' Now, these that held the doctrine of Balaam, and the doctrine of the Nicolaitanes, were got into the church, and might look upon themselves to be high Christians, and take great liberty to go into Balaam's doctrine, and Nicolas's doctrine, which was hated by Christ; but the church was to keep a spiritual and divine judgment upon the heads of all these.

"To the church of Thyatira, saith Christ, 'I have a few things against thee, because thou sufferest the woman Jezebel to teach, which seduces my people,' &c. Here was a suffering, which should have been a judgment by Christ's Spirit, upon that Jezebel, which was erred from his Spirit, and so from Christ. Such as these were high preachers. And is not the church to beware of suffering such now, lest they come under the reproof of Christ, for not passing judgment against the false teacher and seducer?

"The church of Sardis 'had a name to live, but was dead, and her works were not found perfect before God.' There is a judgment to be set up in the church, to judge all imperfect works, and such as would have a name, but not the nature; a name to live, but are dead. All the members of Christ's church must be in Christ, living members, and live to his name. This church had a few names that had not defiled their garments, that did walk in white; but such as have a name to live, but are dead, whilst they are in the dead state, cannot walk in white, nor judge in divine matters. 'Behold,' saith Christ, 'I will make them of the synagogue of Satan, which say they are Jews, and are not, but do lie; behold, I will make them to come, and to worship before thy feet, and to know that I have loved thee,' Rev. iii. 9.

"And to the church of Laodicea, that was 'neither cold nor hot,' but lukewarm; 'I would thou wert cold or hot: I will spew thee out of my mouth, because thou saidst thou wast rich, and wanted nothing;' when thou wast 'wretched, miserable, poor, blind, and naked.' Now this was for want of living in the Power and Spirit of Christ. These could talk of high experiences, and great enjoyments, but were naked, miserable, and blind; so lived not in the power, and Spirit, the light, and righteousness of Christ, by which they might be clothed, and have the eternal riches. So the church of Christ had a spiritual judgment given to them that are faithful in his power, and Spirit, and light, to judge of temporal things, and the things of this life; and to judge of eternal and divine things and states; of angels and wicked men, and such as go from truth; and of the states of election and reprobation; yea, and of the devils who are out of truth; these being in Christ Jesus, who is the First and Last, from whom they have the eternal judgment, to judge eternal, spiritual, and divine things; and in this Word of power and wisdom, by which all things were made, and by which all things are upheld, to order all things to God's glory, and to judge of all things in righteousness.

"The apostle judged, and set up a judgment in the church, of gifts, of prophecies, of mysteries, of faith, and of giving the body to be burned, and of giving goods to the poor, and of speaking with tongues of men and angels; that yet, if they had not love, all this was nothing, but as a sounding brass and tinkling cymbal. Therefore they are to be tried by the fruits of the good Spirit, which is love. So here the apostle not only judged himself in divine things, but set up a judgment in the church in those spiritual and divine matters.

"The apostle James judges of fountains, and of fig-trees, of the wisdom from below, and of the wisdom from above, and of the fruits of both, James iii. And Paul judged in divine matters when he said, 'The Spirit spake expressly, that in the latter times some should depart from the faith,' 1 Tim. iv. And he judged in divine matters, when he judged all those teachers that were high-minded, and had got the form of godliness, but denied the power; and termed them like unto Jannes and Jambres, who withstood Moses, coming out of outward Egypt; as these with their form of godliness, oppose Christ and his power, that brings them out of spiritual Egypt now. Was not he a judge here in divine matters, who judged such as had gotten the form of godliness, but denied the divine power? 2 Tim. iii.

"When the apostle said, 'the priesthood of Aaron was changed, and the law was changed, and the commandment disannulled, that gave them their tithes, 'did not he judge here in divine and spiritual matters? and was not the law spiritual, which served till the Seed came?

"Did not the apostle judge in divine and spiritual matters, in the sixth of the Hebrews, where he saith, 'Let us go on to perfection, not laying again the foundation of repentance from dead works, and of faith towards God, and of the doctrine of baptisms, and of laying on of hands, and of the resurrection of the dead, and of eternal judgment: and this will we do, if God permit,' &c. And does not the apostle judge here, 'that it was impossible for those who were once enlightened, and tasted of the heavenly gift, and were partakers of the Holy Ghost, and had tasted of the good word of God, and of the power of the world to come, if they shall fall away, to renew them again unto repentance; seeing they crucify to themselves the Son of God afresh, and put him to open shame?' Heb. vi. Were not these spiritual, eternal, and divine matters and states, that the apostle judged of? and have not the saints the same judgment given unto them in the same Spirit? Have not the apostles and the church a spiritual judgment to judge of prophets, mysteries, faith, apostles, angels, the world, and the devil? And is not this judgment given them of God in divine matters, besides the judgment given them in matters pertaining unto this life?

"And had not they judgment to discern the true gospel from the false? and all such as had a profession of the form, and did not live in the power? and such as spoke the things of God, in the words that man's wisdom did teach? which things of God were not to be spoken in the words which man's wisdom taught, but in the words which the Holy Ghost taught. Therefore did not the apostle exhort to know the power, and that their faith might stand in the power of God? for the kingdom of God stands not in word, but in power.

"Had not all the prophets a divine judgment to judge in divine matters? as Jeremiah, when he judged the prophets. Ezekiel also judged all such as came with a pretence of the Word of the Lord, using their tongues, and saying, 'Thus saith the Lord, when the Lord never spoke unto them;' as in Jer. xxiii. Ezek. xiii., and many other places might be instanced. Did not he judge Hananiah, who prophesied falsely? and did not this Hananiah pretend to speak the Word of the Lord to the priests and people? as in Jer. xxviii.

"Did not Isaiah judge in divine matters, when he judged the watchmen and the shepherds? Isa. lvi. Did not Micah judge in divine and spiritual matters when he said 'he was full of the power by the Spirit of the Lord, and of judgment?' Did not he judge of priests, prophets, and judges, though they would lean upon the Lord, and say, 'Is not the Lord amongst us, and no evil can come unto us;' yet did not he let them see their states and conditions, and divide the precious from the vile? Mic. iii. And so the rest of the prophets. You may see they judged for God in his divine matters, 'who served him, and who served him not; and who lived in truth, and who not;' and likewise the apostles. And this divine, spiritual, and heavenly judgment was given of God to his holy men and women.

"They that judge in God's divine matters, must live in his divine Spirit, power, and light now, as they did then; which spiritual and divine judgment Christ has given to his church, the living stones, and living members, that make up his spiritual household; to try Jews, apostles, and prophets; to try faiths and religions, trees and fruits, shepherds and teachers; and to try spirits. So the living members have a living, divine judgment in the church of Christ, which he is the Head of, the Judge of all.

"Nay, the church has a power given them, which is farther than a judgment: for what they 'bind on earth, is bound in heaven by the power of God: and what they loose on earth, is loosed in heaven by the power of God.' This power has Christ given to his living members, the church."

The 20th of the 12th Month, 1685–6. G. F. to Friends.

I came back to LONDON in the 1st month, 1686, and set myself with all diligence to look after Friends' sufferings, from which we had now some hopes of getting relief. The sessions came on in the 2nd month at Hicks's-Hall, where many Friends had appeals to be tried; with whom I was from day to day, to advise and see that no opportunity were slipped, nor advantage lost; and they generally succeeded well. Soon after also the king was pleased, upon our often laying our sufferings before him, to give order for the "releasing of all prisoners for conscience' sake; that were in his power to discharge." Whereby the prison-doors were opened, and many hundreds of Friends, some of whom had been long in prison, were set at liberty. Some of them, who had for many years been restrained in bonds, came now up to the Yearly Meeting, which was in the 3rd month this year. This caused great joy to Friends, to see our ancient, faithful brethren, again at liberty in the Lord's work, after their long confinement. And indeed a precious meeting we had; the refreshing presence of the Lord appearing plentifully with us and amongst us. After the meeting I was moved to write a few lines, to be sent amongst Friends: the tenor whereof was thus:—

"DEAR FRIENDS,

"My love is to you all in the holy Seed, Christ Jesus, that bruises the serpent's head, and destroys the devil and his works; and who hath all power in heaven and in earth given him. Let every one's faith stand in Him, and in his power, who is the author and finisher of your faith. And now for you, who have been partakers of his power, and are sensible of it in this day of his power, that is over darkness and its power; by whose power the hearts of the king and rulers have been opened, and your outward prison-doors set open for your liberty, my desires are, that all may be preserved in humility and thankfulness, in the sense of the mercies of the Lord; and live in the peaceable truth, that is over all; that ye may answer God's grace, and his light and Spirit in all, in a righteous, godly life and conversation. Let none be lifted up by their outward liberty, neither let any be cast down by suffering for Christ's sake; but all live in the Seed (which is as wheat) which is not shaken, nor blown away by the winds and storms, as the chaff is. Which Seed of life none below can make higher or lower; for the children of the Seed are the children of the everlasting, unchangeable kingdom of Christ and God. In Christ Jesus, whom God hath given you for a sanctuary, God Almighty keep you, in whom ye have life everlasting, and wisdom from above, which is pure, peaceable, gentle, and easy to be entreated, full of mercy and good fruits;

that all now may be exercised in, and may practise this wisdom in holy lives and conversations; so that this wisdom may be justified of all her children, and they exercised and preserved in it in this day of the power of Christ, in which all his people are made a willing people, to serve and worship God in righteousness and holiness, in Spirit and in truth.

"Let none abuse the power of the Lord, nor grieve his Spirit, by which you are sealed, and kept to the day of salvation and redemption; but always exercise yourselves to have 'a good conscience, void of offence towards God and towards all men,' being exercised in holiness, godliness, and righteousness; and in the truth, and in the love of it. All study to be approved unto God in innocency, virtue, simplicity, and faithfulness, labouring and studying to be quiet in the will of God. 'And whatsoever ye do in word or deed, do all in the name of the Lord Jesus; giving thanks to God the Father by him;' that he who is over all, may have the praise for all his mercies and blessings, with which he hath refreshed his people, and by his eternal arm and power hath kept and preserved them to this day; glory to his name over all for ever. Amen! Christ hath called you by his grace into one body, to him the holy Head; therefore live in charity, and in the love of God, which is the bond of perfectness in his body. This love edifies the body of Christ; which body and all his members are knit together, and increased with the increase of God, from whom they receive nourishment. For by one Spirit we are all baptized into one body, and have been made all to drink into one Spirit, in which Spirit the body and all its members have fellowship with Christ, the Head, and one with another. The unity of this Holy Spirit is the bond of peace of all the living members of Christ Jesus, of which he is the spiritual Head, Rock, and Foundation. In the midst of his church of living members, Christ exercises his spiritual prophetical office, to open to them the mysteries of his kingdom. He is a spiritual Bishop to oversee them, that they do not go astray from the living God that made them; a Shepherd that feeds them with bread and water of life from heaven; and none is able to pluck his sheep out of his hands. He is a Priest that died for them, sanctifies them, and presents them to God; who ruleth in their hearts by the divine faith, which he is the author and finisher of. His living members praise God through Jesus Christ, in whom they have life and salvation, who reconciles them to God, that they can say they have 'peace with God through Jesus Christ;' and so praise God through him that was dead, and is alive again, who reigns over all, and liveth for evermore, blessed for ever; Hallelujah. Amen!

"Greet one another with a holy kiss of charity. Love or charity beareth all things, believeth all things, hopeth all things, endureth all things. It envieth not, vaunteth not itself, is not puffed up, nor doth it behave itself unseemly. It rejoices not in iniquity, but rejoices in the truth. Charity is not easily provoked, and thinks no evil, but suffereth long and is kind. Charity never faileth. I say, greet one another with this holy kiss of charity, and peace be with you all, that are in Christ Jesus, your life and salvation." G. F.

The 30th of the 3rd Month, 1686.

I remained most part of this year in LONDON, save that sometimes I got out to BETHNAL-GREEN for a night or two, or as far as ENFIELD and thereabouts amongst Friends, and once or twice to CHISWICK, where an ancient Friend had set up a school for the educating of Friends' children; in all which places I found service for the Lord. At LONDON, I spent my time amongst Friends, either in public meetings (as the Lord drew me) or visiting those that were not well, and in looking after the sufferings of Friends. For though many were released out of prisons, yet some remained prisoners still for tithes, &c., and sufferings of several sorts lay heavy on Friends in many places. Yet inasmuch as many Friends, that had been prisoners, were now set at liberty, I felt a concern upon me, that none might look too much at man, but might eye the Lord therein, from whom deliverance comes. Wherefore I wrote an epistle to them, as follows:—

"FRIENDS,

"The Lord, by his eternal power, hath opened the heart of the king to open the prison doors, by which about fifteen or sixteen hundred are set at liberty, and hath given a check to the informers; so that in many places our meetings are pretty quiet. My desires are, that both liberty and sufferings may be sanctified to his people, that Friends may prize the mercies of the Lord in all things, and to him be thankful, who stilleth the raging waves of the seas, allayeth the storms and tempests, and maketh a calm. Therefore it is good to trust in the Lord, and cast your care upon him, who careth for you. For when ye were in jails and prisons, the Lord did, by his eternal arm and power, uphold you, and sanctified them to you (and unto some he made them as a sanctuary), and tried his people as in a furnace of affliction, both in prisons and spoiling of goods. In all this the Lord was with his people, and taught them to know that 'the earth is the Lord's, and the fulness thereof;' and that He was in all places; 'who crowneth the year with his goodness,' Psal. lxv. Therefore let all God's people be diligent, and careful to keep the camp of God holy, pure, and clean, and to serve God and Christ, and one another in the glorious, peaceable gospel of life and salvation, which glory shines over God's camp; and his great Prophet, Bishop, and Shepherd is among, or in the midst of them, exercising his heavenly offices in them; so that you his people may rejoice in Christ Jesus, through whom you have peace with God. For he that destroyeth the devil and his work, and bruises the serpent's head, is all God's people's heavenly Foundation and Rock to build upon; which was the holy prophets' and apostles' Rock in days past, and is now the Rock of our age; which Rock and Foundation of God standeth sure. Upon this the Lord God establish all his people. Amen." G. F.

London, the 25th of the 7th Month, 1686.

Divers other epistles and papers I wrote this year; one of which was an exhortation "to Friends to keep in unity in the truth, in which there is no division nor separation;" it was thus:—

"DEAR FRIENDS AND BRETHREN IN THE LORD JESUS CHRIST,

"IN whom ye have all peace and life, and in whom there is no division, schism, rent, strife, nor separation; for Christ is not divided: there can be no separation in the truth, nor in the light, grace, faith, and Holy Ghost, but unity, fellowship, and communion. For the devil was the first that went out of the truth, separated from it, and tempted man and woman to disobey God, and to go from the truth into a false liberty, to do that which God forbade. So it is the serpent now that leads men and women into a false liberty, even the god of the world, from which man and woman must be separated by the truth; that Christ the Truth may make them free, and then they are free indeed. Then they are to stand fast in that liberty, in which Christ hath made them free, and in Him there is no division, schism, rent, or separation; but peace, life, and reconciliation to God, and to one another. So in Christ, male and female are all one; for whether they be male or female, Jew or Gentile, bond or free, they are all one in Christ. And there can be no schism, rent, or division in Him; nor in the worship of God in his Holy Spirit and truth; nor in the pure and undefiled religion, that keeps from the spots of the world; nor in the love of God that beareth and endureth all things; nor in the Word of God's grace, for it is pure and endureth for ever. Many, you see, have lost the Word of patience and the Word of wisdom, that is pure, and peaceable, and gentle, and easy to be entreated: then they run into the wisdom that is below, that is 'earthly, sensual, and devilish,' and very uneasy to be entreated. They go from the love of God that beareth all things, endureth all things, thinketh no evil, and doth not behave itself unseemly: then they cannot bear, but grow brittle, and are easily provoked, run into unseemly things, and are in that, that vaunteth itself, are puffed up, rash, heady, high-minded, and fierce, and become as sounding brass, or a tinkling cymbal; but this is contrary to the nature of the love of God. Therefore, dear Friends and brethren, dwell in the love of God; for they who dwell in love, dwell in God, and God in them. Keep in the Word of wisdom, that is gentle, pure, and peaceable, and in the Word of patience, that endureth and beareth all things; which Word of patience the devil, and the world, and all his instruments can never wear out; it will wear them all out; for it was before they were, and will be, when they are gone, the pure, holy Word of God, by which all God's children are borne again, feed on the milk thereof, and live and grow by it. My desires are, that ye may all be of one heart, mind, soul, and spirit in Christ Jesus. Amen." G. F.

Soon after this, finding those apostates, whom the enemy had drawn out into division and separation from Friends, continued their clamour and opposition against our monthly, quarterly, and yearly meetings, it came upon me to write another short epistle to Friends, to put them in mind of the "evidence and seal they had received in themselves by the Spirit of the Lord, that those meetings were of the Lord, and accepted by him," that so they might not be shaken by the adversaries. I wrote as follows:—

"My dear Friends in the Lord Jesus Christ!

"All you, that are gathered in his holy name, know, that your meetings for worship, your quarterly and other meetings are set up by the power and Spirit of the Lord God, and witnessed by his Spirit and power in your hearts; and by the Spirit and power of the Lord God they are established to you, and in the power and Spirit of the Lord God you are established in them. The Lord God hath with his Spirit sealed to you, that your meetings are of his ordering and gathering, and he hath owned them, by honouring you with his blessed presence in them; and you have had great experience of his furnishing you with his wisdom, life, and power, and heavenly riches from his treasure and fountain, by which many thanks and praises have been returned in your meetings to his holy, glorious name. He hath sealed your meetings by his Spirit to you, and that your gathering together hath been by the Lord, to Christ his Son, and in his name; and not by man. So the Lord hath the glory and praise of them and in them, who hath upheld you and them, by the arm of his power, against all opposers and backsliders, and their slanderous books and tongues. For the Lord's power and Seed doth reign over them all, in which he doth preserve his sons and daughters to his glory, by his eternal arm and power, in his work and service, as a willing people in the day of his power, without being weary or fainting, but strong in the Lord, and valiant for his glorious name and precious truth, and his pure religion; that ye may serve the Lord in Christ Jesus, your Rock and Foundation, in your age and generation. Amen." G. F.

London, the 3rd of 11th Month, 1686–7.

A little after it came upon me to write something concerning the state of the true church, and of the true members thereof, as follows:—

"*Concerning the Church of Christ being clothed with the Sun, and having the Moon under her feet.*

"They are living members, living stones, built up a spiritual household, children of the promise, and of the Seed and flesh of Christ; and as the apostle saith, 'Flesh of his flesh, and bone of his bone.' They are the good seed, the children of the everlasting kingdom written in heaven; and have put on the Lord Jesus Christ. They sit together in heavenly places in Christ, are clothed with the Sun of Righteousness, Christ Jesus, and have the moon under their feet, as Rev. xii. So all changeable things, that are in the world, all changeable religions, worships, ways, fellowships, churches, and teachers in the world, are as the moon; for the moon changes, but the sun doth not change. The Sun of Righteousness never changeth, nor goes down; but all the ways, religions, worships, fellowships of the world, and the teachers thereof, change like the moon. The true church, which Christ is the head of, which is in God, the Father, is called 'the pillar and ground of truth,' whose conversation is in heaven; this church is clothed with the Sun, Christ Jesus, her head, who doth not change, and hath all changeable things under her feet. These are the living members, born again of the immortal Seed, by the Word of God, who feed upon the immortal milk, and live and grow by it. Such are the new creatures in Christ Jesus, who makes all things new, and sees the old things pass away. His church and all his members, which are clothed with the Sun, their worship is in Spirit, and in truth, which doth not change; which truth the devil, the foul, unclean spirit, is out of, and cannot get into this worship in Spirit and in truth. Their religion is pure and undefiled before God, that keeps from the spots of the world, &c., and their way is the new and living way, Christ Jesus. So the church of Christ, that is clothed with the Sun, that hath the moon and all changeable religions and ways under her feet, hath an unchangeable worship, religion, and way, an unchangeable Rock and Foundation, Christ Jesus, and an unchangeable High Priest; and so are children of the New Testament, and in the everlasting Covenant of Light and Life.

"Now all, that profess the Scriptures both of the New and Old Testament, and are not in Christ Jesus, the apostle tells them, they are 'reprobates, if Christ be not *in* them.' Therefore these, that are not in Christ, cannot be clothed with Christ, the Sun of Righteousness, that never changes. They are under the changeable moon, in the world, in the changeable things, changeable religions, ways, worships, teachers, rocks, and foundations. But Christ, the Son of God, and Sun of Righteousness, doth not change; in whom his people are gathered, and sit together in heavenly places in him, clothed with Christ Jesus, the Sun, who is the mountain, that filleth the whole earth with his divine power and light. So all his people see him, and feel him both by sea and land. He is in all places of the earth, felt and seen of all his. And Christ Jesus saith to the outward professors, the Jews, 'I am from above,' ye are from below, 'ye are of this world.' So their religions, worships, ways, teachers, faiths, beliefs, and creeds are made by men, and are below, of this world that changeth like the moon. You may see their religions, ways, worships, and teachers, are all changeable, like the moon; but Christ, the Sun, with which the church is clothed, doth not change, nor his church; for they are spiritually minded, and their way, worship, and religion is spiritual, from Christ, who is from above, and not of this world. Christ hath redeemed his people from the world, and its changeable rudiments, elements, and old things, and from its changeable teachers, faiths, and beliefs. For Christ is the author and finisher of his church's faith, who is from above, and saith, 'Believe in the light, that ye may become children of light:' and it is given them not only to believe, but to suffer for his name. So this faith and belief is above all faiths and beliefs, which change, like the moon. God's people are a holy nation, a peculiar people, a spiritual household, and royal priesthood, offering up spiritual sacrifice to God, by Jesus Christ; and are zealous of righteous, godly, good works; and their zeal is for that which is of God, against the evil which is not of God.

"Christ took upon him the Seed of Abraham; he doth not say, the corrupt seed of the Gentiles: so, according to the flesh, he was of the holy seed of Abraham and of David; and his holy body and blood was an offering and a sacrifice for the sins of the whole world, as a lamb without blemish, whose flesh saw no corruption. By the one offering of himself in the New Testament or New Covenant, he has put an end to all the offerings and sacrifices amongst the Jews in the Old Testament. Christ, the holy Seed, was crucified, dead, and buried, according to the flesh, and raised again the third day; and his flesh saw no corruption. Though he was crucified in the flesh, yet he was quickened again by the Spirit, and is alive, and liveth for evermore; he hath all power in heaven and in earth given to him, and reigneth over all; and is the one Mediator between God and man, even the man Christ Jesus. Christ said, 'He gave his flesh for the life of the world:' and the apostle says, 'His flesh saw no corruption:' so that which saw no corruption he gave for the life of the corrupt world, to bring them out of corruption. Christ said again, 'He that eateth my flesh and drinketh my blood hath eternal life: for my flesh is meat indeed, and my blood is drink indeed. And he that eateth my flesh and drinketh my blood dwelleth in me, and I in him.' He that eats not his flesh and drinks not his blood, which is the life of the flesh, hath not eternal life. As the apostle saith, all died in Adam; then all are dead. Now all coming spiritually to eat the flesh of Christ, the second Adam, and drink his blood, his blood and flesh gives all the dead in Adam life, and quickens them out of their sins and trespasses, in which they were dead; so they come to sit together in heavenly places in Christ Jesus, living members of the church of Christ, that he is the head of; are clothed with the Sun of Righteousness, the Son of God, that never changes, and have the changeable moon under their feet, and all changeable, worldly things and inventions, and works of men's hands. These see the people, how they change from one worship to another, from one religion to another, from one way to another, and from one church to another; and yet their hearts are not changed. The letter of Scripture is read by the Christians like the Jews; but the mystery is hid: they have the sheep's clothing, the outside, but are inwardly ravened from the Spirit, which should bring them into the Lamb's and Sheep's nature. The Scripture saith, 'All the uncircumcised must go down into the pit:' and therefore all must be circumcised with the Spirit of God, which puts off the body of death, and sins of the flesh, that came into man and woman by their disobedience, and transgressing of God's commands. I say, all must be circumcised with the Spirit, which puts off the body of death and sins of the flesh, before they come up into Christ, their Rest, that never fell, and be clothed with Him, the Sun of Righteousness." G. F.

Towards the latter end of this year I went to KINGSTON to visit Friends there; and stayed some time at my son Rous's. I wrote there a paper concerning "the falling away" foretold by the apostle Paul, 2 Thess. ii. 3, as follows:—

"THE apostle saith that there must be 'a falling away' first, before the wicked one, that man of sin, the son of perdition, be revealed, which betrayeth Christ within, as the son of perdition betrayed Christ without; and they that betray Christ within, crucify to themselves Christ afresh, and put him to open shame. Before the apostles died, this man of sin, the son of perdition, was revealed: for they saw antichrist come, and false prophets, false apostles, and deceivers come, having a form of godliness, but denying the power thereof. They saw the wolves dressed in the sheep's clothing, and such as went in Cain's, Korah's, and Balaam's way, and Jezebel's; and the whore of Babylon, the whore of confusion, the mother of harlots, and such as were enemies to the cross of Christ, that served not the Lord Jesus Christ, but their own bellies. These Christ saw should come, and said, 'If it were possible, they should deceive the elect;' and commanded his followers not to go after them. The apostle said, 'Turn away from such;' and Christ and his apostles warned the church of Christ of such. And now, in this day of Christ and his gospel, after the long night of apostasy from the light, grace, truth, life, and Spirit of Christ Jesus, the son of perdition, the wicked one, the man of sin, is revealed again; and the inwardly ravening wolves in sheep's clothing, and the spirit of Cain, Korah, Balaam, Jezebel, the antichrists, false prophets, and false apostles, and such as are enemies to the cross of Christ, who serve not the Lord Jesus, but their own bellies; and crucify Christ to themselves, and put him to open shame. This Spirit have we seen in this gospel-day of Christ; but Christ will consume them with the Spirit of his mouth, and destroy them with the brightness of his coming. But God's people, whom he hath chosen unto salvation in Christ from the beginning, 'through sanctification of the Spirit and belief of the truth,' stand stedfast in Christ Jesus; and are thankful to God, by and through his Son, their rock and salvation, who is their happiness and eternal inheritance.

"The apostle saith, 'Ye were as sheep going astray; but are now returned to the Shepherd and Bishop of your souls.' So when people are returned to Christ, their Shepherd, they know his voice, and follow him; and are returned to the Bishop of their souls: then they believe in him, and receive wisdom and understanding from him, who is from above, heavenly and spiritual. Then they act like spiritual and holy men and women; and come to be members of the church of Christ. Then a spiritual care cometh upon the elders in Christ, that all the members walk in Christ, in his light, grace, Spirit, and truth, that they may adorn their profession of Christ; and see that all walk in the order of the Holy Spirit, and the everlasting gospel of peace, life, and salvation. This order keeps out of confusion; for the gospel of peace, the power of God, was before confusion was. And all the heirs of the gospel are heirs of its order, and are in this gospel, which brings life and immortality to light in them; by which all may see their work and service in it, to look after the poor, widows, and fatherless, and to see that nothing be lacking; and that all honour the Lord in their lives and conversations.

"When the whole house of Israel were in their graves and sepulchres, and were called 'the scattered dry bones,' yet they could speak, and say, 'their bones were dry, their hope was lost,' or they were without hope, 'and they were cut off.' They were alive outwardly, and could speak outwardly. So that which is called Christendom may very well be called 'the scattered dry bones,' and they may be said to be in their graves and sepulchres, dead from the heavenly breath of life, the Spirit and Word of life, that gathereth to God. Though they can speak, and are alive outwardly, yet they remain in the congregations or churches of the dead, that want the virtue of life. For the Jews, whom God poured his Spirit upon, and gave them his law, when they rebelled against the Spirit of God, and turned from God and his law, came to be dry scattered bones, and were turned into their graves and sepulchres. So Christendom, that is turned from the grace, truth, and light of Christ, and the Spirit, that God poureth upon all flesh, they are become the scattered dry bones, are in their graves and sepulchres, and are the congregations or churches of the dead, though they can speak, and are alive outwardly.

"Christ saith, 'I am come that they might have life, and that they might have it more abundantly.' He gave his flesh for the life of the world. And he saith, 'I am the resurrection and the life;' and, 'I am the way, the truth, and the life; no man cometh unto the Father but by me.' Christ is the quickening Spirit. All being dead in Adam, are to be quickened and made alive by Christ, the second Adam. And when they are quickened and made alive by him, they meet together in the name of Jesus Christ their Saviour, who died for their sins, and is risen for their justification; who was dead and is alive again, and liveth for evermore. All whom he hath quickened and made alive (even all the living) meet in the name of Jesus, who is alive, and He, their living Prophet, Shepherd, and Bishop, is in the midst of them; and is their living Rock and Foundation, and a living Mediator between them and the living God. So the living praise the living God through Jesus Christ, through whom they have peace with God. All the living have rest in Christ, their life. He is their sanctification, their righteousness, their treasure of wisdom, knowledge, and understanding, which is spiritual and heavenly. He is the spiritual tree and root, which all the believers in the light, the life in Christ, that pass from the death in Adam to the life in Christ, and overcome the world, and are born of God, are grafted into; even Christ, the heavenly tree, which beareth all the spiritual branches or grafts. These meet in his name, are gathered in him, and sit together in heavenly places in Christ Jesus, their life, who hath quickened and made them alive. So all the living worship the living God in his Holy Spirit and truth, in which they live and walk. Into this worship, the foul, unclean spirit, the devil, cannot get; for the Holy Spirit and truth is over him, and he is out of it. This is the standing worship, which Christ set up in his new covenant. And they that are quickened by Christ are the living stones, living members, and spiritual household and church, or congregation of Christ, who is the living head and husband. They that are made alive by Christ are a living church, have a living head, and are come from the congregations or churches of the dead in Adam, where death and destruction talk of God, and of his prophets and apostles, in their wisdom that is below, earthly and devilish; in the knowledge that is brutish, and in the understanding that comes to naught. For what they know is natural, by their natural tongues, arts, sciences; in which they corrupt themselves. This is the state of the dead in Adam: but the quickened, they that are made alive by Christ, discern between the living and the dead." G. F.

Kingston-upon-Thames, the 12th Month, 1686–7.

While I was at Kingston, I wrote also another paper, showing "that the Lord, in all ages, called the righteous out from amongst the wicked, before he destroyed them;" after this manner:—

"NOAH and his family were called into the ark, before the old world was destroyed with the flood. And all the faithful generation, that lived before, were taken away, and died in the faith, before that flood of destruction came upon the wicked old world.

"The Lord called Lot out of Sodom, before he destroyed and consumed it, and the wicked there.

"Christ said, 'It cannot be that a prophet perish out of Jerusalem:' and he said, 'O Jerusalem, Jerusalem, which killest the prophets, and stonest them that are sent unto thee, how often would I have gathered thy children together, as a hen gathereth her brood under her wings! and ye would not,' Luke xiii. 33, 34. And he said to the Jews, 'Therefore also said the wisdom of God, I will send them prophets and apostles, and some of them they shall slay and persecute; that the blood of all the prophets, which was shed from the foundation of the world, may be required of this generation; from the blood of Abel, unto the blood of Zacharias, which perished between the altar and the temple. Verily, I say unto you, it shall be required of this generation,' Luke xi. 49–51. And he said to the Jews, 'Behold your house is left unto you desolate,' Matt. xxiii. 34, &c. Christ told his disciples, that the temple at Jerusalem should be thrown down, and there should not be one stone left upon another, that should not be thrown down, Matt. xxiv. 2. Also, that he must go to Jerusalem, and 'suffer many things of the Jews, elders, and chief priests, and be killed, and raised again the third day,' Matt. xvi. 21. And Christ said, 'When ye shall see Jerusalem compassed with armies, then know the desolation thereof is nigh.' He foretold, that the Jews should fall by the edge of the sword, and should be led away 'captive into all nations; and Jerusalem should be trodden down of the Gentiles,' Luke xxi. 20, 24. Here you may see, how Jerusalem was often warned by Christ, and how often he would have 'gathered them, but they would not,' before they were scattered over or into all nations, their houses left desolate, and their temple and Jerusalem besieged with armies, destroyed, and thrown down. And though the disciples and apostles of Christ did meet, with the elders and church, at Jerusalem, after Christ was risen, yet Eusebius reports in his *Ecclesiastical History*, that the Christians at Jerusalem had a vision, or a revelation to depart out of Jerusalem. Being forewarned also by Christ, that when they should see Jerusalem compassed with armies, its desolation was nigh; and that the temple should be thrown down, and not one stone left upon another; it is said, that the Christians did depart out of bloody Jerusalem, before it and the temple were destroyed by Titus, the emperor, who besieged it with his armies. He was of the Gentiles, and destroyed the temple and Jerusalem, as Christ had fore-spoken to his disciples, because of the wickedness of the Jews, and the innocent blood that they had shed in it. So the Lord called his people out of bloody Jerusalem, before he destroyed it. And it is said, that Titus destroyed the temple and Jerusalem about forty-two years after Christ was crucified, and risen again; and that with so great a destruction, that the Jews never built the city again, nor the temple (as Sodom was never built again, nor the cities of the old world). But the Jews for above these thousand years have been, and are a scattered people in all nations to this day; and Christ (whom they crucified) and his doctrine, is preached, and set over them; and the Gentiles, whom they hated, have received, and do receive him and his doctrine, and praise God for it through Jesus Christ. Amen.

"God called his people out of Egypt, after he had poured out his ten plagues upon the Egyptians; when he had destroyed the first-born of Egypt, then the Lord brought his people out of Egypt. And after the Lord had clearly brought his people out, he destroyed Pharaoh, and all his hosts and chariots.

"John says, he heard a voice, saying, 'Come out of her, my people, (to wit, out of Babylon, the false church), that ye be not partakers of her sins, and that ye receive not of her plagues; for her sins have reached to heaven, and God hath remembered her iniquities,' Rev. xviii. 4, 5. Here ye may see that God called his people out of spiritual Babylon, before he destroyed her, and cast her down, to be utterly burnt with fire, ver. 8, 9, 21.

"Was not Nebuchadnezzar's empire thrown down and ended by Cyrus and Darius, who were of the seed of the Medes, before Cyrus and Darius gave forth their proclamation for all the Jews to go into their own land, out of Babylon's captivity? And was there not a prophecy of Cyrus, 'that he should subdue nations, and that the Lord would loose the loins of kings before him, and break in pieces the gates of brass, and cut in sunder the bars of iron, and open the two-leaved gates; and that the gates should not be shut?' And the Lord said, 'This is for Jacob, my servant's sake, and for Israel mine elect,' Isa. xlv. Was not this fulfilled in Cyrus's and Darius's time? For did not then the Jews go out of captivity into their own land,' Ezra i. 2–4; vi. 1, 12; Isa. xliv. 28; xlv. 13. Was not this prophecy of Isaiah fulfilled when the children of Israel came out of Babylon? Were not the Assyrians, that carried away the ten tribes, subdued? and the Babylonians, that carried away the two tribes, were they not subdued in the days of Cyrus and Darius, in whose days the 'loins of kings were loosed, and the two-leaved gates of brass and iron were opened?' and had not Israel and Jacob their liberty by them in their days, to go into their own land?

"And here in England, was it not observed, that most of the honest and sober people were turned out of the army, and their commissions, offices, and places taken from them, because they could not join with others in their cruelty and persecuting? And others laid down their commissions themselves, and came out from amongst those persecutors, before they were overthrown and brought to confusion. All that are wise, see these things, and learn by such examples and way-marks to shun such bogs. The righteous are safe, that keep *in* Christ, their everlasting sanctuary, that changes not; in whom they have rest and peace with God. Amen." G. F.

Kingston, the 29th of the 12th Month, 1686–7.

CHAPTER XIII.

1686–1687.—The first and the second Adam compared—the two seeds distinguished—George Fox is daily exercised in London in services relating to the church, visiting the sick or afflicted, and writing in defence of Truth, or refuting error—true prayer distinguished from the practice of the Papists—visits his son-in-law William Mead—a distinction between the true offering, and sacrifice, and the false, under the old and new covenant—a general toleration and liberty being now granted, George Fox writes a word of counsel and caution to Friends, to walk circumspectly in a time of liberty—how redemption by Christ is known and witnessed—repentance must precede the reception of the gospel, baptism, &c.—a paper showing wherein God's people are to be like him—the right way to Christ—the kingdom of God is to be measurably known in this life—George Fox is benefited by being three months in the country—has much service in London again—at Kingston writes a paper, showing how the Jews, by disobedience, lost the Holy City and the Holy Land, designed as a warning to Christians—everlasting life through, and in, Christ, to be received and witnessed in this life—the stone cut out of the mountain signifies the kingdom and power of Christ—a miscellaneous paper, being a collection of Scripture passages respecting regeneration, sanctification, &c.

While I was at Kingston, one day, as I was meditating on the things of God, some particular observations arose in my mind, concerning the first, and the second or last Adam. As that—

"The first man Adam was made on the sixth day of the week; and Christ, the second Adam, was crucified on the sixth day of the week.

"The first Adam was betrayed by the serpent in the garden of Eden; Christ our Saviour, the second Adam, was betrayed by Judas in a garden near Jerusalem.

"Christ arose from the dead on the First-day of the week; and they that believe on him are entered into Christ, their Rest; the Christians meet together to worship God on the First-day of the week; and on the First-day of the week it was that God said, 'Let there be light, and there was light.' The Jews' rest was on the seventh-day of the week, which was given to them as a sign of the eternal rest of the Lord, sanctifying them, after they came out of the land of Egypt; for before that time the Lord had not given to man and woman his outward Sabbath-day to keep, neither in the old world, nor after in Abraham's time, nor in Isaac's, nor in Jacob's time; until the Jews came out of Egypt to Mount Sinai in the wilderness. Then the Lord gave the law and his Sabbath, as a sign in the old covenant, of Christ the Eternal Rest in the new covenant; and they that believe do enter into Christ, their Rest.

"Adam, the first man, is the root from whence we all spring naturally; and Christ is called the last, or second Adam, because he is the beginning and root of all that are spiritual.

"The first Adam was made a living soul; and Christ, the last Adam, is a quickening spirit.

"Christ by the grace of God tasted death for every man, that they might all come into favour with God; and that every tongue should confess, that 'Jesus Christ is Lord, to the glory of God the Father.'"

I wrote also a paper there, concerning the two seeds, distinguishing the seed wherein the blessing is received, from the seed which the curse remains upon. Of which the following is a copy:—

"The Lord said to Abraham, 'In thy seed shall all the nations of the earth be blessed,' Gen. xxii. 18. 'And thy seed shall be as the stars of heaven, and as the sand, which is upon the sea-shore, and as the dust of the earth, that cannot be numbered,' chap. xiii. 16; xv. 5; xxii. 17. In this seed all nations and families of the earth are blessed; but not in the seed of evil-doers and of falsehood, nor in the seed of the adulterer and the whore, Isa. i. 4, and lvii. 3, 4; 'for the seed of the wicked shall be cut off,' saith the Lord, Psal. xxxvii. 28. The Lord said to David, 'That his seed should endure for ever,' Psal. lxxxix. 36. And again it is said, Psal. cii. 28, 'The children of thy servants shall continue, and their seed shall be established before thee.' Here is a distinction between the two seeds; for the seed of evil-doers, of the adulterer, and of the wicked, shall be cut off; and so it is not blessed. But Christ bruises the head of the serpent, and his seed which he soweth in them, that disobey and transgress God's command, and rebel against God's good Spirit. This wicked seed of the serpent is cursed, and is an enemy to the Seed in whom all are blessed; but Christ bruises the head of this cursed seed of enmity, and destroys the devil and his works; and in his seed are all blessed, and all are in unity in this seed. All the children of the seed are the children of the kingdom of God, and of Christ, and are blessed with faithful Abraham. Whoever are of the saving, divine, precious faith, are of Abraham, walk in the steps of the seed and faith of Abraham, and are blessed with him, yea, of all nations, and all the families of the earth.

"And the Lord said to Abraham, 'Thy seed shall be a stranger in a land that is not theirs, and shall serve them; and they shall afflict them four hundred years; and that nation whom they shall serve, will I judge; and afterwards shall they (to wit, God's seed) come out with great substance,' Gen. xv. 13, 14. Here ye may see, that which afflicts God's seed, he will judge, and did judge; for he destroyed the first-born of Pharaoh, and overthrew him and his host.

"A holy man said, 'Except the Lord of Sabaoth had left us a seed or remnant, we had been as Sodom,' &c., that is, destroyed. But in the Seed, which destroys the devil and his works, and bruises the head of the serpent and his seed, are all nations and families of the earth blessed.

"Christ, according to the flesh, was of Abraham and of David, for he took not on him the nature of angels, but the seed of Abraham, in which seed all nations and families of the earth are blessed. So they that are of his seed, are of the generation of Christ; are 'flesh of his flesh, and bone of his bone.' Now, all nations and families of the earth must be in this holy Seed, if they have the blessings and are blessed. And 'out of the mouth of this Seed's seed shall not God's word depart;' but shall remain and abide in the mouth of this Seed's seed, in which they are blessed, Isa. lix. 21. So it is not the first-birth's talking of the words of Christ, the Seed, in whose mouth the word of God doth not abide; that makes an outward profession, like the Jews who killed and persecuted the prophets, and crucified Christ, the Seed, and substance of the law and prophets, which the Jews professed in words, but they denied Christ, the Seed and Life. And all Christians (so called) that profess the Scriptures in words, and are not in the Seed, Christ, are in the confusion, and are like the Jews; and so, neither Jews nor Christians are blessed, except they be *in* Christ, the Seed of Life.

"But though Christ is said to be of the Seed of David, and of Abraham, as his generation is declared by Matthew and Luke; yet Christ was not born of the will of the flesh, nor of the will of man, but of God. For he was conceived by the Holy Ghost, born of the Virgin, and supposed to be son of Joseph, but was the Son of God. His name was called Jesus, because he should 'save his people from their sins;' and Emmanuel, God with us. Christ took not upon him the nature of angels, but the seed of Abraham (as I said before) and so 'was made of the seed of David according to the flesh; and declared to be the Son of God with power, according to the Spirit of holiness, by the resurrection from the dead,' Rom. i. 4. So the generation of Christ is a mystery. Christ saw his Seed or Word grow up in his disciples; and 'Christ *in* you, the hope of glory,' the apostle calls 'The mystery, which hath been hid from ages and generations; but now is made manifest to the saints,' or sanctified ones, Col. i. 26, 27. 'Whom we preach; warning every man, and teaching every man in all wisdom, that we may present every man perfect *in* Christ Jesus,' ver. 28. For *in* Christ, the second Adam, all are made perfect and complete; and in Adam in the fall, all are deformed and made imperfect; so out of Christ all mankind are imperfect and deformed: let them paint, and dress themselves with the sheep's clothing, and with the form of godliness, of the prophets', and Christ's, and his apostles' words ever so much; yet if Christ be not *in* them, they are incomplete, imperfect, deformed, reprobates. But the apostle tells the church of Christ, 'Ye are complete *in* Christ, which is the head of all principality and power,' Col. ii. 10 (for he hath all power in heaven and in earth given to him, Matt. xxviii. 18). So all the saints are made perfect and complete *in* Christ Jesus; blessed be the Lord God over all for ever, through Jesus Christ. Amen, Amen." G. F.

Kingston, the 15th of the 1st Month, 1686–7.

Quickly after this I returned to London, and continued there a month in the service of the Lord; being daily exercised either in public meetings, or more particular services relating to the church of Christ; as visiting such as were sick or afflicted, and writing books or papers for the spreading of truth, or refuting of error. As it was a time of general liberty, the Papists appeared more open in their worship than formerly: and many unsettled people going to view them at it, a great talk there was of their praying to saints, and by beads, &c., whereupon I wrote a short paper concerning prayer; as follows:—

"CHRIST JESUS, when he taught his disciples to pray, said unto them, 'When ye pray, say, Our Father, which art in heaven, hallowed be thy name,' &c. Christ doth not say, that they should pray to Mary, the mother of Christ; nor doth he say, that they should pray to angels, or to saints, that were dead. Christ did not teach them to pray to the dead, nor for the dead: neither did Christ or his apostles teach the believers to pray by beads, nor to sing by outward organs; but the apostle said he would sing and pray in the Spirit; 'for the Spirit itself maketh intercession; and the Lord, that searcheth the heart, knoweth the mind of the Spirit.'

"To take counsel of the dead, was forbidden by the law of God; they were to take counsel of the Lord. And he hath given Christ in the new covenant, in his gospel-day, to be a counsellor and a leader to all believers in his light. Men are not to run to the dead for the living; for the law and testimony of God forbids it. Those Jews that refused the running waters of Shiloh, the floods and waters of the Assyrians and Babylonians came over them, and carried them into captivity; and they that refuse the waters of Christ, are overflowed with the flood of the world, that lieth in wickedness. They that asked counsel of stocks and stones, were in the spirit of error and whoredom; they were gone a whoring from God. Hos. iv. 12. And they that joined themselves to Baal-Peor, and ate the sacrifices of the dead, provoked the Lord's anger, and brought the Lord's displeasure upon them, Psal. cvi. 28, 29. So here ye may see, the sacrifices of the dead were forbidden. The living know that they shall die, but the dead know not anything, neither have they any more a reward; for the memory of them is forgotten, Eccl. ix. 5. 'Woe to the rebellious children, saith the Lord, that take counsel, but not of me; and that cover with a covering, but not of my Spirit, that they may add sin to sin,'" Isa. xxx. 1. G. F.

When I had stayed about a month in London, I got out of town again; for by reason of the many hardships I had undergone in imprisonments, and other sufferings for truth's sake, my body was grown so infirm and weak, that I could not bear the closeness of the city long together; but was obliged to go a little into the country, for the benefit of the fresh air. At this time I went with my son-in-law William Mead, to his country-house called GOOSES in ESSEX, where I stayed about two weeks; and among other services I had there, I wrote the following paper:—

"*A Distinction between the True Offering and Sacrifice, and the False, in the Old and New Covenant.*

"THE Lord saith, 'He that sacrificeth to any God, save unto the Lord only, he shall be utterly destroyed.' Exod. xxii. 20. So no God is to be minded, nor sacrificed to, but the Lord God: it is death to sacrifice to any other God, save the Lord. The Lord saith also, 'Thou shalt not offer the blood of my sacrifice with leavened bread.' Exod. xxiii. 18. So that sour, heavy leaven, must not be offered with the Lord's sacrifice. Again the Lord saith, 'Thou shalt not build an altar of hewn stone: for if thou lift up thy tool upon it, thou hast polluted it,' Exod. xx. 25. Therefore have a care of polluting the altar with your own tools, you that profess to offer the spiritual sacrifice.

"Jonah said, 'he would sacrifice unto the Lord with the voice of thanksgiving,' when he was in the fish's belly; and there he prayed unto the Lord, Jonah ii. For Jonah in the whale's belly had no lambs, nor rams, nor outward sacrifices to offer.'

"The Lord forbids his people to sacrifice with harlots, Hos. iv. 14. And the Lord forbids his people to offer sacrifice of the blind, lame, sick, or that which was deformed, or had any blemish; as in Mal. i. and many other places. So they that offer spiritual sacrifice, must not offer the blind, lame, blemished, or deformed sacrifice to God."

"The scribe saith unto Christ, 'To love God with all the heart, and with all the understanding, and with all the soul, and with all the strength, and to love his neighbour as himself, is more than all whole burnt-offerings and sacrifices,' Mark xii. 33. And when Jesus saw that he answered discreetly, he said unto him, 'Thou art not far from the kingdom of God,' v. 34. To love God, and their neighbour as themselves, was more than whole burnt-offerings and sacrifices in the time of the law; therefore all offerings and sacrifices in the time of the gospel, if there be not love to God, and to their neighbour as themselves, avail nothing.

"David said, 'Let them sacrifice a sacrifice of thanksgiving, and declare his works with rejoicing,' Psal. cvii. 22. These are the sacrifices that the Lord requires of his people, more than outward sacrifices. David said, 'Let my prayer be set forth before thee, as incense; and the lifting up of my hands, as the evening sacrifice,' Psal. cxli. 2. Here David looks upon his prayer to the Lord, and the lifting up of his hands to him, to be accepted with the Lord, as much as the outward incense, and the outward evening sacrifice. Again David says, 'The sacrifices of God are a broken spirit; a broken and a contrite heart, O God, thou wilt not despise,' Psal. li. 17. (See also Isa. lvii. 15; lxvi. 2.) These are the sacrifices that David said God would accept, and not despise; which are beyond the unbroken spirit, and uncontrite heart, with outward offerings and sacrifices.

"The adversaries of the Jews would have joined with them towards the building of the temple, saying unto them, 'Let us build with you, for we seek your God, as ye do; and we do sacrifice unto him.' But the Jews refused them, and said, 'You have nothing to do with us, to build a house unto our God,' Ezra iv. 2, 3. Here ye may see that God's people refused their building with them, and their sacrifice. Solomon saith, 'The sacrifice of the wicked is an abomination to the Lord,' Prov. xv. 8. (See also Isa. i. 11; lxvi. 3.) Solomon also saith, 'Better is a dry morsel, and quietness therewith, than a house full of sacrifices with strife,' Prov. xvii. 1. Now let all people consider, what good your house full of sacrifices doth with strife, when a dry morsel and quietness therewith is better? Consider, all people, if ye live in wickedness, your sacrifice is an abomination to the Lord.

"Again, Solomon speaking of the sacrifice of fools, saith, 'They consider not that they do evil,' Eccl. v. 1. Fools are such as do not walk in the Spirit of God, or begin in the Spirit, and end in the flesh, like the foolish Galatians; for the Spirit of God is the Spirit of wisdom and understanding, and cannot join with the sacrifices of the dead, nor of the fools, nor of the wicked whose sacrifice is abominable; who grieve and quench the Spirit of God; by which the spiritual and righteous offer up spiritual sacrifices, acceptable to God by Jesus Christ.

"The apostle Paul said, he was the 'minister of Jesus Christ to the Gentiles, ministering the gospel of God, that the offering up of the Gentiles might be acceptable, being sanctified by the Holy Ghost,' Rom. xv. 16. So ye may see, that all the acceptable offerings and sacrifices to God must be sanctified by the Holy Ghost. The same apostle saith to the Corinthians, 'Ye are bought with a price; therefore glorify God in your body, and in your spirit, which are God's,' 1 Cor. vi. 20. And to the Romans, he saith, 'I beseech you, brethren, by the mercies of God, that you present your bodies a living sacrifice, holy, acceptable unto God, which is your reasonable service,' Rom. xii. 1. This is the duty of all true Christians.

"Peter also saith, in his general epistle to the church of Christ, 'Ye also, as lively stones, are built up a spiritual house, a holy priesthood, to offer up spiritual sacrifices, acceptable to God by Jesus Christ,' 1 Pet. ii. 5. So every man and woman must come to the Spirit of God *in* their own hearts, if they offer up spiritual sacrifices, acceptable to God by Jesus Christ. For as Christ saith, 'Every sacrifice shall be salted with salt,' Mark ix. 49. And in the Old Testament ye may see, all their outward offerings they were to season with salt, Lev. ii. 13, a type and figure of Christ, who gave himself for us, an offering and a sacrifice to God, for a sweet-smelling savour, Eph. v. 2. Therefore all his people must be baptized with the Holy Ghost and with fire, that they may be salted with fire, and every sacrifice salted with salt, with the Spirit of grace, that is poured upon all; so that they may offer up this spiritual sacrifice, acceptable to God by Jesus Christ.

"Samuel said to king Saul, 'Hath the Lord as great delight in burnt-offerings and sacrifices, as in obeying the voice of the Lord? behold, to obey is better than sacrifice; and to hearken, than the fat of rams,' 1 Sam. xv. 22. So ye may see, all offerings and sacrifices are nothing, if there be not a hearkening to the Lord in his Spirit, and an obeying of his voice. Christ told the Jews, that were outward sacrificers, that he would have mercy, and not sacrifice; and bid them 'Go and learn what that meaneth,'" Matt. ix. 13. G. F.

Gooses, the 28th of the 2nd Month, 1687.

The beginning of the 3d month I returned to LONDON, and continued there till after the Yearly Meeting, which began on the 16th of the same, and was very large, Friends having more freedom to come up out of the counties to it, by reason of the general toleration and liberty now granted. The meeting lasted several days; and at the close thereof it was upon me to write the following lines, to be dispersed amongst Friends everywhere, as—"A word of counsel and caution to them to walk circumspectly in this time of liberty:"—

"DEAR FRIENDS AND BRETHREN, IN THE LORD JESUS CHRIST,

"The Lord, by his eternal arm and power, having supported you in all your sufferings, and great spoiling of goods, and tedious imprisonments, only for serving and worshipping the living God that made you; who gave up wife and children, and goods, and suffered the spoil of them, and imprisonment for his truth and name's sake;—the Lord, by his infinite power and mercy, having been pleased to open the king's heart towards you, by which you are set at liberty from jails, and the spoilers of your goods are stopped, whereby ye may follow your callings, confess Christ Jesus, and call him Lord by the Holy Ghost, in your assemblies and meetings, without being cast into jails, or having your goods spoiled; a great concern lies upon me from the Lord to write unto you, dear brethren, that none may abuse this liberty, nor the mercies of the Lord, but prize them; for there is great danger in time of liberty, of getting up into ease, looseness, and false liberty. And now, seeing that ye have not the outward persecutors to war with in sufferings, with the spiritual weapons keep down that which would not be subject to Christ; that He, the Holy One, may reign in your hearts; that your lives, conversations, and words, may preach righteousness and truth; that ye may all show forth good ensamples of true believers in Christ, in virtue, and holiness, answering that which may be known of God in all people, that ye are the sons and daughters of God; standing fast in that righteous, holy liberty in Christ, the just and holy One, that has made you free, over the loose or false; shunning vain disputes, and foolish questions of men of corrupt minds; for the serpent was the first questioner of Eve, who drew her and Adam out of the truth. Therefore as ye have received Christ, live and walk in Him, who bruises the serpent's head, who is your safe sanctuary, in whom ye have election, reconciliation, and peace with God. Therefore live in the peace which ye have from Christ, which is not of this world; be at peace one with another, and seek the peace of all men in Christ Jesus; for blessed are the peacemakers. Labour to exercise a good conscience towards God, in obedience to him in what he requires; and in doing to all men the thing that is just and honest; in your conversations and words, giving no offence to Jew or Gentile, nor to the church of God. So ye may be as a city set on God's Sion-hill, which cannot be hid; and may be lights to the dark world, that they may see your good fruits and glorify your Father, which is in heaven; for he is glorified in your bringing forth good fruits, as ye abide in Christ, the vine, in this his day of life, power, and light, that shines over all. Therefore all you that believe in the light, walk in the light, as children of the light, and of Christ's everlasting day; that in the light ye may have fellowship with the Father and the Son, and one with another; keeping in the unity of his Holy Spirit, in the bond of his holy peace, in his church that he is head of. My desire is, that God's wisdom everywhere may be justified of her children, and that it may be showed forth in meekness, and in the fear of the Lord in this his day. Amen." G. F.

By that time the Yearly Meeting was over, I was very much wearied and spent; wherefore, about a week after the meeting, I got out of town to a Friend's house a little beyond EDMONTON, where, and at SOUTH STREET, I abode some time, and had meetings amongst Friends there; and at WINCHMORE-HILL and BERRY STREET. And having my mind continually exercised in the things of God, the sense of his infinite goodness and mercy to mankind in visiting them after they had transgressed and rebelled against him, and providing a way and means for their return to him again, was very much upon me, and in the opening of the Spirit of truth I wrote the following paper on that subject:—

"GOD, who made all mankind, though they have transgressed his commands and laws, rebelled against him, hated his light, grieved his Spirit, and walked despitefully against his Spirit of grace; God, who is merciful, would yet have all to be saved, and come to the knowledge of the truth. All that come to the knowledge of the truth must know it *in* their inward parts; I say, all that know and find the grace and truth which comes by Jesus, do know and find it *in* their hearts. And such find the hidden man of the heart, the pearl, the leaven, the lost piece of silver, and the kingdom of heaven *within*. For until they come to the light and truth *in* their hearts, all are strangers to these things,—are in Adam, in the fall from the image of God, and from his light, power, Spirit, and kingdom. But Christ that never fell, brings man and woman that follow him again to know these things, to know the truth, and Him the Saviour, and brings them into his image, and his everlasting kingdom.

"The devil, who is out of the truth, tempted man and woman to disobey God; and so drew them into the fall from the truth. It is the devil that hath stopped men's eyes, ears, and hearts from the truth, who is called the god of the world; who hath blinded the eyes of infidels, or heathen. But Christ, who bruises the serpent's head, and destroys the devil and his works, doth open men's hearts, eyes, and ears. He is their Saviour and Redeemer, and giveth life eternal to his people that obey him and his truth. Blessed be the Lord for ever through Jesus Christ, who hath tasted death for all men, to bring them out of the death of Adam; who is a propitiation for the sins of the whole world, and gave himself a ransom for all, to be testified of in due time. For as by Adam's transgression and disobedience death and condemnation came upon all, so by Christ's obedience unto death justification of life is come upon all; and he that believeth in Christ hath eternal life; but he that doth not is condemned already. But God would have all men to be saved, and come unto the knowledge of the truth as it is in Jesus, who is their Saviour; and in Him there is no condemnation."

G. F.

After I had been a while here, I went to a monthly meeting at ENFIELD, and thence with some Friends to HERTFORD; where I stayed three or four days, visiting Friends both at their public meetings on First-day, and at their quarterly meetings of men and women; and good service for the Lord I had amongst them. Then passing to WALTHAM ABBEY, I had a very good meeting with Friends there: and next day went thence to another place, to compose a difference, which, for want of a right understanding of each other, had happened between some Friends. I returned to Waltham that night; and next day went with some Friends to William Mead's house, in ESSEX.

Here I stayed some weeks, yet was not idle, but often visited the meetings thereabouts; as at WANSTEAD, BARKING, and at John Harding's. Between meeting and meeting I wrote many things for the spreading of truth, and for the opening of people's understandings to receive it. One was a paper proving, from the Scriptures, that people must repent before they can receive the gospel, and the Holy Spirit, and the kingdom of God, or be baptized; after this manner:—

"JOHN the Baptist came preaching in the wilderness of Judea, saying, 'Repent ye: for the kingdom of heaven is at hand,' Matt. iii. 2. And when John the Baptist was cast into prison, Mark says, 'That Jesus came into Galilee, preaching the gospel of the kingdom of God, and saying, The time is fulfilled, and the kingdom of God is at hand: Repent ye, and believe the gospel,' Mark i. 14, 15. Matthew also says, 'From that time Jesus began to preach, and to say, Repent, for the kingdom of heaven is at hand,' Matt. iv. 17. And when Christ sent forth his twelve disciples, two and two, they went out and preached that men should repent, Mark vi. 12. Christ said to the Jews, 'Except ye repent, ye shall all likewise perish,' Luke xiii. 3, 5. When the publicans and sinners came to hear Christ, and the Pharisees and Scribes murmured saying, 'This man receiveth sinners and eateth with them,' Luke xv. 1, 2, Christ reproved them by a parable, and then told them, 'Joy shall be in heaven over one sinner that repenteth, more than over ninety and nine just persons which need no repentance,' ver. 7, adding, 'There is joy in the presence of the angels of God over one sinner that repenteth,' ver. 10. Christ, after he was risen, said unto his disciples, 'That repentance and remission of sins should be preached in his name among all nations, beginning at Jerusalem,' Luke xxiv. 47. Peter said unto the Jews, 'Repent and be baptized, every one of you, in the name of Jesus Christ, for the remission of sins; and ye shall receive the gift of the Holy Ghost,' Acts ii. 38. And Paul said, 'The times of this ignorance God winked at; but now commandeth all men everywhere to repent,' Acts xvii. 30. Simon Magus was called to repentance, if he had regarded it, Acts viii. 22. And the apostle Paul preached at Damascus, and at Jerusalem, and throughout all the coasts of Judea, and then to the Gentiles (turning them from darkness to the light of Christ, and from the power of Satan to God), that they should 'repent and turn to God, and do works meet for repentance,' Acts xxvi. 20.

"Here ye may see that people must repent before they believe, and are baptized, and before they receive the Holy Ghost, and the kingdom of God. They must repent of their vain life and conversation before they receive the gospel, be turned from darkness to the light of Christ, and from the power of Satan unto God, before they receive his Holy Spirit, and his gospel of life and salvation. The Lord commands all men everywhere to repent, and do works meet for repentance. They must show forth that their lives and conversations are changed, and that they serve God in newness of life, with new tongues and new hearts." G. F.

Gooses, the 6th Month, 1687

Another short paper I wrote about the same time, showing wherein God's people should be like unto him. It was thus:—

"God is righteous; and he would have his people to be righteous, and to do righteously. God is holy; and he would have his people holy, and to do holily. God is just; and he would have his people to be just, and to do justly to all. God is light; and his children must walk in his light. God is an eternal, infinite Spirit; and his children must walk in the Spirit. God is merciful; and he would have his people to be merciful. God's sun shines upon the good and the bad, and he causes the rain to fall upon the evil and the good; so should his people do good unto all. God is love; and they that dwell in love dwell in God. Love worketh no ill to his neighbour: therefore 'love is the fulfilling of the law,' Rom. xiii. 10. The apostle says, 'All the law is fulfilled in one word, even in this, Thou shalt love thy neighbour as thyself,' Gal. v. 14. 'As the Father hath loved me, so I have loved you: continue ye in my love,' John xv. 9. This should be the practice of all God's people." G. F.

Gooses, the 6th Month, 1687.

And because most people would confess, that God's people should be thus, but few know how to come to this state; therefore in the openings of the Spirit of truth I wrote another short paper, directing to "the right way and means, whereby people might come unto Christ, and so be made like unto God." Thus:—

"Christ saith, 'I am the way, the truth, and the life; no man cometh unto the Father, but by me,' John xiv. 6. And again, 'No man can come to me, except the Father, which hath sent me, draw him,' John vi. 44. Now, what is the means by which God doth draw people to his Son, but by his Holy Spirit, who 'poureth out of his Spirit upon all flesh.' By this Holy Spirit, the holy and righteous God doth draw people from their unrighteousness and unholiness, to Christ, the righteous and holy One, the great Prophet in his New Covenant and New Testament, whom Moses in the Old Covenant and Testament said, God would raise up, like unto him, and whom people should 'hear in all things: and they that would not hear him, should be cut off.' They that do not hear the Son of God, the great Prophet, do not mind the drawing of the Father by his Holy Spirit to his Son; but to them that mind the drawings of the good Spirit of the Father to his Son, the Spirit giveth understanding to know God and Jesus Christ, which is eternal life. Then they know that Jesus Christ is the way, the truth, and the life, and that none can come unto God but by and through his Son, who is their Shepherd to feed them in his pastures and springs of life; and his sheep know his holy voice, in whom there was no sin, and in whose mouth there was no guile; and a hireling they will not hear, for he careth not for the sheep; for they are not the hireling's, but Christ's, who hath laid down his life for his sheep. He that robs and steals his neighbour's words, that climbeth up another way, and entereth not by the door, is a thief and a robber; but Christ is the door into his sheepfold, for his sheep to enter in by. They know that Christ is the Bishop of their souls, to see that they do not go astray from God, nor out of his pastures of life;

they know that Christ is their Mediator, and makes their peace with God; and they know that Christ is their High-priest, made higher than the heavens, and hath died for their sins, doth cleanse them with his blood, is risen for their justification; and is able to the utmost to save all that come to God by him." G. F.

Gooses, the 6th Month, 1687.

Before I left this place I wrote another paper, to show, by many instances from the Holy Scriptures, that the kingdom of God, which most people talk of at a distance, and refer altogether to another life, is in some measure to be known and entered into in this life; but that none can know an entrance thereinto, but such as are regenerated and born again. Of that paper the following is a copy:—

"Christ saith, 'Except a man be born again, he cannot see the kingdom of God,' John iii. 3. 'That which is born of the flesh, is flesh; and that which is born of the Spirit is spirit,' ver. 6. So, 'except a man be born of water and of the Spirit, he cannot enter into the kingdom of God,' ver. 5. And John, writing to the seven churches in Asia, calls himself their brother, and companion in tribulation, and in the kingdom and patience of Jesus Christ, Rev. i. 9. Here you may see, that John was in the kingdom; so he was born again: for he not only saw the kingdom, but was in it.

"And John saith, 'Behold, what manner of love the Father hath bestowed upon us, that we should be called the sons of God; therefore the world knoweth us not, because it knew him not,' 1 John iii. 1. 'Beloved, now are we the sons of God,' ver. 2. 'If ye know that he is righteous, ye know that every one that doeth righteousness is born of him,' chap. ii. 29. 'Whosoever is born of God, doth not commit sin; for his seed remaineth in him, and he cannot sin, because he is born of God,' chap. iii. 9. Again John saith, 'Let us love one another; for love is of God; and every one that loveth, is born of God, and knoweth God. He that loveth not, knoweth not God; for God is love,' chap. iv. 7, 8. 'Whosoever believeth that Jesus is the Christ, is born of God,' chap. v. 1. And, 'Whosoever is born of God, overcometh the world; and this is the victory that overcometh the world, even our faith,' ver. 4. Were not these, that were born of God, in the kingdom of God? And seeing, John says, every one that doeth righteousness, is born of God, do not such see the kingdom of God that stands in righteousness, and enter into it?

"Peter, in his first general epistle to the church of Christ, saith, 'As new-born babes desire the sincere milk of the Word, that ye may grow thereby,' 1 Pet. ii. 2. And he tells them they were a chosen generation, a royal priesthood, a holy nation, a peculiar people; that they should show forth the praises of Him who had called them out of darkness into his marvellous light, ver. 9. And that, as lively stones, they were built up a spiritual house, a holy priesthood, to offer up spiritual sacrifices, acceptable to God by Jesus Christ, ver. 5. Did not these new-born babes, these lively stones, spiritual household, royal priesthood, holy nation, and chosen generation, who were called out of darkness into Christ's marvellous light, see, and enter into his holy kingdom, being heirs of the same? who were born again, not of corruptible seed, but of incorruptible, by the Word of God, which liveth and abideth for ever, 1 Pet. i. 23. And had these not an entrance ministered to them into the everlasting kingdom of our Lord and Saviour Jesus Christ?

"James, in his general epistle to the church of Christ, says, 'Hath not God chosen the poor of this world, rich in faith, and heirs of the kingdom, which he hath promised to them that love him?' James ii. 5. The apostle Paul says, 'God sent forth his Son, made of a woman, &c., to redeem them that were under the law; that we might receive the adoption of sons; and because ye are sons, God hath sent forth the Spirit of his Son into your hearts, crying, Abba, Father. Wherefore thou art no more a servant, but a son; and if a son, then an heir of God through Christ,' Gal. iv. 4–7. The same apostle says, 'As many as are led by the Spirit of God, they are the sons of God;' and tells the saints at Rome, 'Ye have received the spirit of adoption, whereby we cry, Abba, Father. The Spirit itself beareth witness with our spirit, that we are the children of God; and if children, then heirs; heirs of God, and joint-heirs with Christ; if so be we suffer with him, that we may be also glorified together (namely, with Christ).' Rom. viii. 14–17. Now seeing they are the sons of God that are led by the Spirit of God, and the Spirit beareth witness unto their spirit, that they are the children of God, and heirs of God, and joint-heirs with Christ, are not all these children of God heirs of the righteous, glorious kingdom of God? and do they not see it, and enter into it?

"The Lord saith in Hosea i. 10, 'Where it was said unto them, Ye are not my people; there it shall be said unto them, Ye are the sons of the living God.' Did not this relate to the gospel-days of the new covenant? see Rom. ix. 26. And what the Lord said by the prophet Jeremiah, chap. xxxi. 1, the apostle applies to the gospel-days, and says, 'Be ye separate, saith the Lord, and touch not the unclean thing; and I will receive you, and will be a Father unto you, and ye shall be my sons and daughters, saith the Lord Almighty,' 2 Cor. vi. 18. Are not these the children that see, and enter into the righteous kingdom of God, that separate from that which is unclean, and touch it not?

"The Lord saith also by Isaiah, 'I will say to the north, Give up; and to the south, Keep not back; bring my sons from far, and my daughters from the ends of the earth?' Isa. xliii. 6. Then does not he bring them to his kingdom of glory, that stands in righteousness, and peace, and joy in the Holy Ghost?

"The Lord said to Job, 'When the morning stars sang together, and all the sons of God shouted for joy,' Job xxxviii. 7, where did these sons of God shout for joy? Was it not in his kingdom of glory?

"Christ saith, 'The least in the kingdom of God is greater than John,' Luke vii. 28. And in chap. xvi. 16, he says, 'The law and the prophets were until John: since that time (viz., since the law, and the prophets, and John) the kingdom of God is preached, and every man presseth into it.'

"'The good seed are the children of the kingdom,' Matt. xiii. 38.

And 'the righteous shall shine forth, as the sun, in the kingdom of their Father,' ver. 43. Christ said unto his disciples, 'Unto you it is given to know the mysteries of the kingdom of God,' Mark iv. 11. And Christ lifted up his eyes upon his disciples, and said, 'Blessed be ye poor: for yours is the kingdom of God,' Luke vi. 20. And the apostles preached the kingdom of God. These were born again; that saw and knew the kingdom of God, and preached it.

"Christ said to his disciples, 'Fear not, little flock, for it is your Father's good pleasure to give you the kingdom,' Luke xii. 32. And, 'I appoint unto you a kingdom,' said Christ, 'as my Father hath appointed unto me,' chap. xxii. 29. The Lord said, 'He that overcometh, shall inherit all things: and I will be his God, and he shall be my son,' Rev. xxi. 7. And John saith, 'I have written unto you, young men, because ye are strong, and the Word of God abideth in you, and ye have overcome the wicked one,' 1 John ii. 14. And Christ, by whom are all things, is said 'to bring many sons to glory,' Heb. ii. 10.

"Christ said, 'Woe unto you, scribes and Pharisees, hypocrites; for ye shut up the kingdom of heaven against men; for ye neither go in yourselves, neither suffer them that are entering, to go in,' Matt. xxiii. 13. He also said, 'Woe unto you, lawyers; for you have taken away the key of knowledge; ye enter not in yourselves; and them that were entering in ye hindered,' Luke xi. 52. Christ gives unto his children the key of the kingdom, his Spirit; but the scribes, and the Pharisees, and the lawyers, great professors, who were erred from the Spirit, like the great professors in our age that scoff at the Spirit, and draw people from the Spirit of God within, these shut up the kingdom from men, and draw people from the key of knowledge, and the key of the kingdom. 'For no man knows the things of God, but by the Spirit of God; for the things of God are spiritually discerned.' So the Spirit is the key, by which the kingdom of God, and the things of God, are revealed and discerned, and known, according to 1 Cor. ii. 10, 11, 13, 14. The apostle names some in his epistle to the Colossians, and says, 'These are my fellow-workers unto the kingdom of God,' Col. iv. 11. And he tells that church, that 'God hath delivered us from the power of darkness, and hath translated us into the kingdom of his dear Son,' chap. i. 13. So ye may see these were born again, that were translated into the kingdom of Christ, and were fellow-workers unto the kingdom of God.

"Christ exhorts his disciples to love and to do good, that they might be the children of their Father, which is in heaven, Matt. v. 45. He bids them be perfect, even as their Father which is in heaven, is perfect; ver. 48. The apostle saith to the church at Philippi, 'That ye may be blameless and harmless, the sons of God, without rebuke, in the midst of a crooked and perverse nation, amongst whom ye shine as lights in the world, holding forth the word of life,' &c. Phil. ii. 15, 16. And writing to the church of the Thessalonians, he puts them in mind how he had exhorted them that they would 'walk worthy of God, who had called them into his kingdom and glory,' 1 Thess. ii. 12.

"The Lord had promised by the prophet Joel, that he would 'pour out his Spirit upon all flesh,' and that 'sons and daughters should prophesy, old men should dream dreams, and young men see visions,' Joel ii. 28. Now the cause that sons and daughters, handmaids, servants, young men, and old men, have not these heavenly visions, dreams, and prophecies, is, because they are erred from the Spirit of God, which he poureth upon them: but as many as are led by the Spirit of God, are the sons of God.

"John saith, Christ was the 'true light, which lighteth every man that cometh into the world,' John i. 9; and that 'As many as received him, to them gave he power to become the sons of God;' ver 12, 'which were born, not of blood, nor of the will of the flesh, nor of the will of man, but of God,' ver. 13. Now, the reason why people do not become the sons of God, is because they do not receive Christ. The Jews, the great professors, who had the promises, prophecies, figures, and shadows of him, would not receive him when he came. And now the priests and high professors of Christ, are so far from receiving the light of Christ, and believing in it, that they hate the light, and scoff at it, calling it a natural conscience; and some, Jack-in-the-lantern. Such are not like to become the sons of God, nor to see the glorious kingdom of Christ, which stands in righteousness, peace, and joy in the Holy Ghost. For the light that shines in the heart, gives 'the light of the knowledge of the glory of God in the face of Christ Jesus.' They that do not receive Christ Jesus, but hate his light (which is the life in him) and yet profess him in words, neither know the children of the light, nor true fellowship in the light, nor the kingdom of God, that stands in righteousness, peace, and joy in the Holy Ghost; but by the light they are condemned. 'And this is the condemnation, that light is come into the world, and men love darkness rather than light, because their deeds are evil. For every one that doeth evil, hateth the light, neither cometh to the light, lest his deeds should be reproved,' John iii. 19, 20. But the children of the light, that walk in the light, come to heavenly Jerusalem, and to the city of the living God, to the innumerable company of angels, and to the general assembly and church of the firstborn, that are written in heaven, and can sing Hallelujah!" G. F.

Gooses, the 2nd of the 7th Month, 1687.

Having been more than a quarter of a year in the country, I returned to LONDON, somewhat better in health than formerly, having received much benefit by the country air. And it being now a time of general liberty, and great openness amongst the people, I had much service for the Lord in the city; being almost daily at public meetings, and frequently taken up in visiting Friends that were sick, and in other services of the church. I continued at London about three months; and then finding my strength much spent, with continual labouring in the work of the Lord, and my body much stopped for want of fresh air, I went down to my son Rous's, by KINGSTON, where I abode some time, and visited Friends at Kingston. While I was there, it came upon me to write a paper concerning the Jews, showing "how by their disobedience and rebellion, they lost the holy city and land." By which example the professed Christians may see what they are to expect, if they continue to disobey and provoke the Lord. The copy here follows:—

"THE Lord gave the Jews in the Old Testament the land of Canaan, and they built the temple at Jerusalem to worship in. It was called 'the holy temple;' and Jerusalem was called 'the holy city;' and Canaan 'the holy land.' But when the Jews rebelled against the good Spirit, which God gave to instruct them, rebelled against his law, set up idols and images, and defiled the land and the city, the Lord sent his prophets to cry against them, to bring them back again to his Spirit, and to his law, and so to God, to serve and worship him, that they might not worship images and idols, the works of their own hands. But instead of hearkening to God's prophets, they persecuted them, and at last killed his Son Christ Jesus, and persecuted his apostles. But Christ told the Jews, that both their city and temple should be laid waste, and they should be scattered over all nations: and it was so. Titus the Roman emperor came and took Jerusalem, and destroyed the city and temple; which was a day of vengeance upon the Jews for all their idolatries and their wickedness, and for the innocent blood they had shed, both in the city and country; and they were driven out of their own city and land, and scattered over all nations. The Jews have never had power to obtain the land since, nor to build Jerusalem, nor the temple; but the Turk hath both the land of Canaan, and that which is called 'the city of Jerusalem.' Now, the Turk neither makes images, nor worships images; and so it is a just hand of the Lord, that he should be over the persecuting, idolatrous Jews, so that they cannot defile the land of Canaan now with images and idols, for the Turk hath it, who neither makes images, nor idols, nor worships them. The Jews must never hope, believe, nor expect, that ever they shall go again into the land of Canaan, to set up an outward worship at Jerusalem, and there for their priests to offer outward sacrifices of rams, sheep, and heifers, &c., for burnt-offerings; for Christ, the one offering, hath offered himself once for all, and by this one offering he hath perfected for ever them that are sanctified. And Christ hath changed the priesthood of Aaron, that offered sacrifices, that was made after the power of a carnal commandment; but Christ was made after the power of an endless life, a Priest for ever, who is holy, harmless, separate from sinners, and made higher than the heavens. This is the Priest that gives power to all that receive him, to become the sons and daughters of God; and Jerusalem that is above, is the mother of all the sons and daughters of God, and is free; but Jerusalem that is below, is in bondage with her children. They that are the children of Jerusalem that is above, do not look down at Jerusalem that is below; but they look at Jerusalem that is above, which is their mother. Christ said, 'Neither at outward Jerusalem, nor in the mountain of Samaria, should God be worshipped; but God should be worshipped in Spirit and in truth; for he is a Spirit, and such he seeks to worship him,' John iv. This is the worship that Christ set up above sixteen hundred years ago; and therefore the idolatrous Jews must never think to offer their outward offerings and sacrifices, nor set up their outward worship at Jerusalem, in the holy land of Canaan more. For Christ, by the offering up of himself once for all, for the sins of the whole world, hath ended all the Jews' offerings, and changed the priesthood, and the law by which it was made; and hath blotted out the hand-writing of ordinances, which commanded both priests and offerings; and triumphed over them. So he is the offering and sacrifice of all the children of the New Testament, and New Covenant, and heavenly New Jerusalem, that is above. He is their Prophet that openeth to them; their Shepherd that feeds them; their Bishop that oversees them; and Priest that died for their sins, and is risen for their justification;—who sanctifies and presents them to God. He is the one Mediator between God and man, even the Man Christ Jesus." G. F.

Kingston, the 9th of the 10th Month, 1687.

After this I went to GUILDFORD to visit Friends there, and stayed three days with them; having a large and very good meeting there on First-day. After which I came back to KINGSTON again, and tarried about two weeks longer, visiting Friends, and having meetings amongst them, both at their public meeting-house and in their families. Many things I wrote while I was at Kingston; among which was the following:—

"'GOD so loved the world, that he gave his only begotten Son, that whosoever believeth in him, shall not perish (mark, not perish), but have everlasting life,' John iii. 16. Again, he saith, 'He that believeth on the Son of God, hath (mark, hath) everlasting life,' ver. 36. So these believers have everlasting life while they are upon the earth. And 'He that believeth on Christ is not condemned; but he that believeth not, is condemned already, and the wrath of God abideth on him.' And, 'He that heareth Christ's word, and believeth on God that sent him, hath (mark, hath) everlasting life, and shall not come into condemnation, but is passed from death,' the death in the first Adam, 'unto life,' the life in Christ, the second Adam, John v. 24. And that meat which Christ doth give, endureth unto everlasting life, as in John vi. 27. And the water that Christ doth give, shall be in him that drinks it, 'a well of water springing up into everlasting life,' John iv. 14. Christ said to the Jews, 'Search the Scriptures, for in them ye think ye have eternal life; and they are they which testify of me; and ye will not come to me, that ye might have life,' John v. 39, 40. Here ye may see eternal life is to be found in Christ, and not in the Scriptures, which testify of Him, the Life. Christ's sheep that hear his voice, know and follow him; he gives them eternal life, and they shall not perish, neither shall any pluck them out of his hand. They shall not pluck Christ's sheep, to whom he hath given eternal life, out of his hand. Christ said to Martha, 'I am the resurrection and the life; he that believeth in me, though he were dead (mark, though he were dead) yet shall he live; (mark, live, though he were dead); and whosoever liveth, and believeth in me, shall never die. Believest thou this? Martha said, Yea, Lord,' John xxv. 26. This is the true and substantial belief, which they that believe, shall not perish, but have everlasting life. John saith, 'This is the record, that God hath given to us eternal life; and this life is in his Son,' 1 John v. 11. 'The life was manifested, and we have seen it and bear witness, and show unto you that eternal life, which was with the

Father, and was manifested unto us,' 1 John i. 2. So these were the believers, that had eternal life in the Son of God, and showed it unto others. 'He that hath the Son hath life,' says John, 'and he that hath not the Son of God, hath not life,' 1 John v. 12. Christ says, 'Every one that hath forsaken houses, or brethren, or sisters, or father, or mother, or wife, or children, or lands, for my name's sake, shall receive an hundred fold, and shall inherit everlasting life,' Matt. xix. 29. The wicked that do not receive Christ, shall go into everlasting punishment; but the righteous into eternal life. The true servants of God have their fruits unto holiness, and their end is everlasting life; for 'the wages of sin is death; but the gift of God is eternal life, through Jesus Christ our Lord.' Such have a building of God, a house not made with hands, eternal in the heavens. Therefore I desire, that God's people may endure all things, that they may obtain this salvation, which is in Christ Jesus, with eternal glory. For Christ being made perfect, became the Author of eternal salvation to all them that obey him. This eternal salvation is above an external salvation; for they come to receive an eternal inheritance, and live in the possession of the everlasting gospel of joy, comfort, peace, and salvation, having everlasting life in Christ Jesus." G. F.

Kingston, the 6th of the 11th Month, 1687.

Another paper I wrote there, concerning the Stone spoken of by Daniel, chap. ii., which became a great mountain, and filled the whole earth; showing, "that thereby was set forth the kingdom and power of Christ:"—

"WHEN Christ, the Stone, that became a great mountain, and filled the whole earth, had broken to pieces the head of gold, and the breast of silver, and the belly of brass, and the legs of iron, and the feet part iron part clay (which were the four monarchies, to wit, the Babylonian and Mede, the Persian, the Grecian, and the Roman), and had ended the outward Jews' typical kingdom; Daniel saith, 'In the days of these kings shall the God of heaven set up a kingdom, which shall never be destroyed,' Dan. ii. 44. Christ saith, 'All power is given unto me in heaven and in earth,' Matt. xxviii. 18. And, 'My kingdom is not of this world,' John xviii. 36. 'Christ is the image of the invisible God, the Firstborn of every creature. For by him were all things created, that are in heaven, and that are in earth, visible and invisible, whether they be thrones, or dominions, or principalities, or powers; all things were created by him, and for him; and he is before all things, and by him all things consist,' Col. i. 15–17. Here ye may see, all things consist by Jesus Christ, and all things were created by Christ, and for him, whether they be things in heaven, or things in earth, visible or invisible, they were created by him and for him; yea, thrones, dominions, principalities, and powers, these were all created by him and for him. So Christ 'is King of kings and Lord of lords,' Rev. xix. 16. And the 'Prince of the kings of the earth,' chap. i. 5. Out of his mouth goeth a sharp sword, with which he shall smite the nations, and he shall rule them with a rod of iron; as the vessel of a potter, shall they be dashed in pieces, who do not obey Him, the King of kings and Lord of lords. This is Christ, who said, 'I am Alpha and Omega, the Beginning and the Ending, the First and the Last;' so he is over all nations, and above them all. We must understand this rod of iron, by which Christ rules the nations, is a figurative speech of Christ, who is ascended into heaven, and is at the right hand of God. All power in heaven and in earth is given unto him, and all things were created by him and for him; so then they are Christ's, and he hath power over all things, for all are his. So, as the Scripture saith, 'By me kings reign, and princes decree justice,' Prov. viii. 15. But if they abuse his power, and do not do justice, as is decreed by Christ, the King of kings and Lord of lords, the First and the Last, they must feel and know the weight of his rod of iron, by which he will rule such as abuse his power. That is decreed by Him, who hath all power in heaven and in earth given to him, and rules in the kingdoms of men." G. F.

Kingston, the 11th Month, 1687.

Several other things I wrote while at KINGSTON; for my spirit being continually exercised towards God, I had many precious openings of divine matters; and divers portions of Scripture, both in the Old Testament and in the New, relating to a state of regeneration, and sanctification, &c, were brought to my remembrance by the Holy Spirit; some of which I committed to writing, as follows:—

"THEY that touched the dead were unclean, and were to be cleansed by the water of purification, Num. xix. And they who touch the dead doctrines or faiths, and let them in, burden the pure, defile, and make themselves unclean, until the spring of the water of the Word do arise, and wash and cleanse them; for all the dead in Adam in the fall are unclean, and they must be washed by Christ, in his blood, and water of life, who quickens and makes alive."

"A dwarf might not come near to offer upon God's altar; but he might eat of the holy bread, that he might grow, Lev. xxi. 20, &c. So the new-born babes may eat of the milk of the Word, that they may grow thereby and increase. He that had any blemish might not come near to offer upon God's altar; neither might anything be offered upon God's altar that had any blemish, or was unclean, Lev. xxi. And it is said, 'The ungodly shall not stand in the judgment, nor sinners in the congregation of the righteous,' Psal. i. 5. But 'God standeth in the congregation of the mighty,'" Psal. lxxxii. 1.

"The camp of God was to be kept clean and holy. That which was unclean, or defiled, was to be kept out of God's camp in the Old Testament. And in the New Testament all that is defiled and unclean must be kept out of God's kingdom, the new and heavenly Jerusalem, that is from above. All was to pass through the fire (even of those things that would bear the fire), and to be purified by fire and water, before the people might come into God's camp, Num. xxxi. So all must be circumcised and baptized with the Holy Ghost and with fire, and be cleansed with the blood of Christ, and washed with the water of the Word, before they come into the kingdom of God, and into heavenly Jerusalem."

"The apostle Paul says, 'We know that if our earthly house of this tabernacle were dissolved, we have a building of God, a house not made with hands, eternal in the heavens. For in this we groan, earnestly desiring to be clothed upon with our house, which is from heaven, that mortality might be swallowed up of life,' 2 Cor. v. 1, 2, 4. Here is (WE in the earthly house of this tabernacle) which (WE) are they that have received Christ, and are become the sons of God, new creatures, and children of the light, that believe in Christ's light; who have an eternal house in the heavens, where mortality is swallowed up of life, in which house from heaven they will not groan."

"Peter said, 'I think it meet, as long as I am in this tabernacle, to stir you up by putting you in remembrance, knowing that shortly I must put off this my tabernacle, even as our Lord Jesus Christ hath showed me,' 2 Pet. i. 13, 14. So Peter knew he must put off this tabernacle shortly; but as long as he was in it he stirred up the saints to their duty in holiness, that they might remember it after he was deceased."

"The apostle Paul says, 'The first man is of the earth, earthly' (mark, earthly), 1 Cor. xv. 47. 'And as we have borne the image of the earthly, we shall also bear the image of the heavenly' (mark, the heavenly), ver. 69. And, 'We have this treasure in earthen vessels,' &c., 2 Cor. iv. 7. 'And I live,' said he, 'yet not I, but Christ liveth in me,' Gal. ii. 20, who is the life of all God's people."

"Christ said to the Jews, 'That the dead are raised, even Moses showed at the bush, when he calleth the Lord the God of Abraham, and the God of Isaac, and the God of Jacob: for he is not the God of the dead, but of the living; for all live unto him,' Luke xx. 37, 38. So, 'None of us liveth to himself, and no man dieth to himself; for whether we live, we live unto the Lord; and whether we die, we die unto the Lord. Whether we live, therefore, or die, we are the Lord's. For to this end Christ both died, and rose, and revived, that he might be Lord both of the dead and living,' Rom. xiv. 7–9. For all died in Adam; and Christ, by the grace of God, tasted death for every man, that they might come out of the death in Adam, to the eternal life in Jesus Christ. Who is also a quickening Spirit; for as in Adam all died, even so in Christ shall all be made alive. So Christ that died and rose again is Lord both of the living and of the dead: for the living live to the Lord, and die in him, and are blessed."

"All Christendom say they believe in God and in Christ, and that they believe Moses and the prophets, and preach Christ, Moses, and the prophets: so their words and writings are preached and printed; and ye say ye believe them. But what life do ye live? Are ye through the law dead to the law, that ye may live unto God? Are ye crucified with Christ? and doth Christ live in you? Is the life that ye now live in the flesh by the faith of the Son of God; and ye do not live, but Christ liveth in you, who gave himself for you? Is this your present life? for the just live by the faith which Christ is the author and finisher of: by which holy, divine, and precious faith they have victory over that which is vile, unholy, and not divine; and in this faith they please God, and have access to God and his Son, who fulfilleth the law and the prophets. For the law and the prophets were until John; and since that the kingdom of God hath been preached, and men press into it: and the least in the kingdom of God is greater than John, though he was the greatest prophet born of a woman. See whether ye are in the kingdom that stands in peace, and righteousness, and joy in the Holy Ghost, or not. Christ, 'who is the image of the invisible God, the firstborn of every creature, was before any creature; for by him were all things created that are in heaven and that are in earth, visible or invisible, whether they be thrones or dominions, principalities or powers, all things were created by him and for him; he was before all things, and by him all things consist: and he is the head of the body, the church, who is the beginning, the firstborn from the dead.' So here ye may see that all things were made by Christ Jesus, and created for him, and by him all things consist and have their being, who is the firstborn from the dead, and dieth no more. It pleased the Father that in him all fulness should dwell; and by Christ to reconcile all things unto himself, whether they be things in heaven, or things in the earth. 'In him are hid all the treasures of wisdom and knowledge,' who is the head of all principality and power; for 'all power in heaven and in earth is given to him,' the first-born of every creature, and the firstborn from the dead, who liveth for evermore in his power over all; the Lamb slain from the foundation of the world. While the world's spirit rules in men's hearts, they do not know Christ, nor the beginning nor ending of the work of God. Christ was outwardly crucified and slain without the gates of Jerusalem by the disobedient Jews; and they that hate the light of Christ, disobey his gospel, quench his Spirit, and are erred from his faith, crucify to themselves Christ afresh.' So Adam and Eve, and their children that disobeyed God, did slay the Lamb; and the blind Jews, that disobeyed God, crucified Christ Jesus; and the outward Christians, that live and walk not in Christ, but in sin and evil, though they make an outward profession of Christ, yet crucify to themselves Christ afresh. But as to Christ himself, he is 'ascended far above all principalities, thrones, powers, and dominions,' so that they cannot put him to death or crucify him any more as to himself: but what the killers, crucifiers, and persecutors do now upon the earth, is against Christ, as in themselves, and in his members; as Christ said to Saul, 'Why persecutest thou me,' Acts ix. 4. For what is done to his members Christ takes as done to himself, Matt. xxv. 40, 45. And they that did not visit Christ, but persecuted him in his members, persecuted Christ in themselves first."

"The serpent, that enemy to man and woman, the destroyer, the god of the world and prince of the air, that ruleth in the hearts of the disobedient, got in by disobedience. But Christ bruises his head, breaks his power to pieces, and destroys the devil and his works; and through death destroys death, and the devil, the power of death. So Christ, the light and life, hath all power in heaven and in earth, and openeth the prison-doors, and the eyes of the blind, and takes captive him that hath led into captivity, and gives gifts unto men. So Christ binds the strong man of sin, spoils his goods, and casts him out; hallelujah! For the strong man of sin is the god of the world, and his house is the whole world, that lieth in wickedness. And this god of the world hath kept his house, and his goods have been in peace, until a stronger than he comes and binds and casts him out; and then destroys him and his goods. So Christ, the Son of God, who is stronger than the devil, having destroyed the devil and his works, setteth up his own house. All the believers in the light are the children of light, are of the Son of God's spiritual house, and the Son of God is over his house for evermore: glory to God in the highest, through Jesus Christ. Amen."

"God spoke by the mouth of all his holy prophets concerning Christ Jesus, his Son, the Holy One: so they were holy men, and not unholy, that God spoke by. Therefore all that name the name of the Lord Jesus Christ are to depart from iniquity." G. F.

Kingston-upon-Thames, the 11th Month, 1687.

CHAPTER XIV.

1687–1690.—George Fox continues to have service in London and the neighbourhood—writes a paper respecting the gospel and the seed; being also an incentive to diligence—a general epistle to Friends, forewarning them of an approaching storm—Moses and Christ both faithful under their respective dispensations—Christ is on his throne—George Fox's health declining, he visits William Mead again for a few weeks—the world's teachers, and the emptiness of their teaching—those who turn people from the inward manifestation of Christ in the heart, remove them from the heavenly landmark, and bring a curse on themselves—the prophets, apostles, and holy men of old, were husbandmen and tradesmen, unlike the world's teachers—the vanity of being too much busied with, and spending the time in, hearing and telling news—though still declining, George Fox attends at the Parliament-house many days on behalf of his Friends—writes to Peter Hendricks, and to Friends at Dantzic, to strengthen and comfort them under their sufferings—to the magistrates and priests of Dantzic, showing the evil of persecution, and persuading to Christian moderation—an appendix to the Yearly Meeting's epistle—an epistle to the Northern Yearly Meeting, to be held at York—George Fox's health still impaired—writes an epistle to Friends in Barbadoes—to Friends in Pennsylvania and other parts of America—to all that profess the Truth of God; being a warning to the young against the world's fashions, and to the old against going into the earthly things—Christ is the "Ensign," prophesied of by Isaiah—an appendix to the Yearly Meeting's epistle—an epistle to Friends in the ministry—to Friends in the ministry gone to America—to suffering Friends in Ireland—death of George Fox in 1690—epistle written with his hand and found sealed up—some account of the interment.

I RETURNED to London towards the latter end of the 11th month, 1687, visiting Friends in the way at CHISWICK, and at HAMMERSMITH, where I had two meetings, one on a First-day, the other upon the occasion of a marriage there, at which were many people of other denominations, amongst whom I had a very seasonable opportunity of opening the way of truth.

Being come to LONDON, I visited Friends' meetings in and about the city, as the Lord led me, in whose service I continued labouring in the city until the middle of the first month, 1687–8. At which time I went down towards ENFIELD, and visited Friends there and thereabouts, and at BARNET, WALTHAM ABBEY, and other places, where I had many meetings, and very good service; in which I spent several weeks. I then returned to LONDON, where I continued labouring in the work of the gospel, till after the Yearly Meeting, which this year was about the beginning of the fourth month. A precious meeting it was; and a very refreshing season Friends had together, the Lord vouchsafing to honour our assemblies with his living and glorious presence in a very plentiful manner. At the conclusion of the meeting I felt a concern upon my spirit to give forth the following paper, to be dispersed amongst Friends:—

"ALL you believers in the light, that are become children of the light, walk as children of the light, and of the day of Christ; as a city set on a hill, that cannot be hid. Let your light shine, that people may see your good works, and glorify your Father, which is in heaven. For a good tree bringeth forth good fruit; therefore be ye trees of righteousness, the planting of the Lord, having fruits unto holiness; and then your end will be everlasting life. Such are the wells and cisterns, that hold the living water, which springs up in them to eternal life. Ye may all drink water out of your own cisterns, running water out of your own wells; and eat every one of his own fig-tree, and of his own vine: having salt every one in yourselves, to season every one's sacrifice, acceptable to God by Jesus Christ; and like unto the wise virgins, that have oil in their lamps, follow the Lamb, and enter in with the bridegroom. Now is the time to labour, while it is day (yea, the day of Christ), to stir up every one's pure mind, and the gift of God that is in them; and to improve your talents, that Christ hath bestowed upon you, that ye may profit; and to walk every one according to the measure that Christ hath given you; for 'the manifestation of the Spirit of God is given to every one to profit withal.'

"Consider what you have profited in spiritual and heavenly things, with the heavenly Spirit of God. Be not like the wicked and slothful, that hid his talent, from whom it was taken, and he cast into utter darkness. A dwarf, or one that had any blemish, was not to come nigh to offer upon God's altar; therefore mind the word of wisdom, to keep you out of that which will corrupt and blemish you; and that ye may grow in grace, and in faith, and in the knowledge of our Lord Jesus Christ: and feeding upon the milk of the word, may grow by it, that ye may not be dwarfs; and so offer your spiritual sacrifice upon God's holy altar. For the field or vineyard of the slothful grows over with thorns and nettles, and his walls go down. Such are they that are not diligent in the Spirit of God, and the power, which is the wall, a sure fence. The Spirit of God will weed all thorns, thistles, and nettles, out of the vineyard of the heart. And you, that are keepers of others' vineyards, see that you keep your own vineyard clean with the Spirit and power of Christ. Sanctify yourselves, and sanctify the Lord in your hearts, that ye may be a holy people to the Lord, who saith, 'Be ye holy, for I am holy:' that ye may be the holy members of the church of Christ, that is clothed with the sun, and hath the moon under her feet; the changeable world with all her changeable worships, religions, churches, and teachers. Be ye new and heavenly Jerusalem's children: for new and heavenly Jerusalem, that is above, is the mother of all the children of light, and that are born of the Spirit. These are they that have been persecuted, and have suffered by the false church, mystery Babylon, the mother of harlots.

"And now, all heavenly Jerusalem's and Sion's children, that are from above, labour in the gospel, the power of God, and the Seed, in which all nations, and all the families of the earth are blessed: which Seed, Christ, bruises the serpent's head, and destroys the devil and his works, and overcomes the whore, the false church, the beast, and the false prophet. He takes away the curse, and the veil that is spread over all nations, and over all the families of the earth; and brings the blessing upon all (if they will receive it) saying, 'In thy seed shall all nations and all the families of the earth be blessed.' This is the gospel of God preached to Abraham, before Moses wrote his five books, and was preached in the apostles' days, and is now preached again; which brings life and immortality to light; and is the gospel of peace, life, and salvation, to every one that believes it. So all nations, and all the families of the earth, must be in Christ, the Seed, if they be blessed, and be partakers of the blessing in the Seed.

"This gospel was revealed by Christ unto his apostles, who preached it; which is not of man, nor from man. Now, God and Christ hath revealed the same gospel unto me, and many others in this age (I say, the gospel and the Seed, in which all nations and families of the earth are blessed); in which gospel I have laboured, and do labour, that all may come into this blessed Seed, Christ, who bruises the head of the serpent, that in it they might have peace with God. This everlasting gospel is preached again to them, that dwell upon the earth; and they that believe it, and receive it, receive the blessing, the peace, joy, and comfort of it; and the stability in it, and the life and immortality, which it brings to light in them and to them. Such can praise the everlasting God in his everlasting gospel.

"And Friends, all seek the peace and good of all in Christ: for truth makes no Cains, Korahs, Balaams, nor Judases; for they come to be such that go out of the peaceable truth. Therefore walk in the peaceable truth, and speak the truth in the love of it, as it is in Jesus." G. F.

Some time after the Yearly Meeting, I went to my son Mead's house, in ESSEX, and abode there some weeks; often visiting Friends' meetings near, and sometimes at Barking. After I had been a while there, I went to visit Friends at WALTHAM ABBEY, HODDESDON, ENFIELD, SOUTH STREET, FORD GREEN, and WINCHMORE HILL; where I had several very serviceable meetings, the Lord opening many deep and weighty things through me, for informing the understandings of inquirers, building up those that were gathered into the truth, and establishing them therein.

In the 7th month I returned to London, having been near three months in the country for my health's sake, which was very much impaired; so that I was hardly able to stay in a meeting the whole time; and often after a meeting had to lie down on a bed. Yet did not my weakness of body take me off from the service of the Lord, but I continued to labour in and out of meetings, in his work, as he gave me opportunity and ability.

I had not been long in London before a great weight came upon me, and a sight the Lord gave me of the great bustles and troubles, revolution and change, which soon after came to pass. In the sense whereof, and in the movings of the Spirit of the Lord, I wrote "A general epistle to Friends, to forewarn them of the approaching storm, that they might all retire to the Lord, in whom safety is;" as follows:—

"My dear Friends and brethren everywhere, who have received the Lord Jesus Christ, and to whom he has given power to become his sons and daughters; in Him ye have life and peace, and in his everlasting kingdom, that is established and cannot be shaken, but is over all the world, and stands in his power, and in righteousness, and joy in the Holy Ghost, into which no unrighteousness, nor the foul, unclean spirit of the devil in his instruments can enter. Therefore, dear Friends and brethren, every one in the faith of Jesus, stand in His power, who has all power in heaven and in earth given to him, and will 'rule the nations with his rod of iron, and dash them to pieces, like a potter's vessel,' that are not subject and obedient to his power; whose voice will shake the heavens and the earth, that that which may be shaken may be removed, and that which cannot be shaken may appear. Stand in Him; and all things shall work together for good to them that love him.

"And now, dear Friends and brethren, though these waves, and storms, and tempests, be in the world, yet you may all appear the harmless and innocent lambs of Christ, walking in his peaceable truth, keeping in the Word of power, wisdom, and patience; and this Word will keep you in the day of trials and temptations, that will come upon the whole world, to try them that dwell upon the earth. For the Word of God was before the world, and all things were made by it; it is a tried Word, which gave all God's people in all ages wisdom, power, and patience. Therefore let your dwelling and walking be in Christ Jesus, who is called the Word of God; and in his power, which is over all. Set your affections on things that are above, where Christ sits at the right hand of God (mark), on those things which are above, where Christ sits; not on those things that are below, which will change, and pass away. Blessed be the Lord God, who by his eternal arm and power hath gathered a people to himself; and hath preserved his, faithful to himself through many troubles, trials, and temptations; his power and Seed, Christ, is over all, and in Him ye have life and peace with God. Therefore in Him all stand, and see your salvation, who is the First and Last, the Amen. God Almighty preserve and keep you all in Him, your ark and sanctuary; in Him you are safe over all floods, storms, and tempests; for He was before they were, and will be when they are all gone." G. F.

London, the 17th of the 8th Month, 1688.

About this time great exercise and weights came upon me (as had usually done before the great revolutions and changes of government), and my strength departed from me; so that I reeled, and was ready to fall, as I went along the streets. At length I could not go abroad at all, I was so weak, for some time, till I felt the power of the Lord to spring over all, and had received an assurance from him, that he would preserve his faithful people to himself through all.

In the time that I kept within, I wrote a paper, showing, how "Moses, as a servant, was faithful in all his house, in the Old Testament; and Christ, as a Son, is over his house, in the New Testament."

"The house of Israel was called God's Vineyard, in Isa. v. 7, and all the Israelites were called the house of Israel. Israel signifies 'a prince with God, and a prevailer with men,' Gen. xxxii. 28. When Peter preached Christ to the house of Israel, he said, 'Let all the house of Israel know assuredly, that God hath made the same Jesus, whom ye have crucified, both Lord and Christ,' Acts ii. 36. So they were all called the house of Israel. And it is said, 'Moses was faithful in all his house (to wit, this house of Israel), as a servant, for a testimony of those things which were to be spoken after; but Christ, as a son, over his own house, which house are we, if we hold fast the confidence, and the rejoicing of the hope firm unto the end,' Heb. iii. 5, 6. Here it is manifest, that Moses was faithful in all his house, as a servant, viz., in the house of Israel, in the Old Testament; but Christ Jesus, the Son of God, is over his house in his New Testament and Covenant; and all his true believers are of his house. The apostle tells the Ephesians (who were the church of Christ), 'They were fellow-citizens with the saints, and of the household of God,' Eph. ii. 19. And the saints are called 'the household of faith,' Gal. vi. 10. Peter in his general epistle tells the church of Christ, they were 'a chosen generation, a royal priesthood, a holy nation, a peculiar people,' 1 Pet. ii. 9. And that as lively stones, they were built up 'a spiritual house, an holy priesthood, to offer up spiritual sacrifices, acceptable to God by Jesus Christ,' ver. 5. The apostle says to the church of Christ at Corinth, 'If our earthly house of this tabernacle were dissolved, we have a building of God, a house not made with hands, eternal in the heavens,' 2 Cor. v. 1. And Christ said to his disciples, 'Let not your hearts be troubled; ye believe in God, believe also in me. In my Father's house are many mansions (a mansion is a dwelling, or abiding place); if it were not so, I would have told you; I go to prepare a place for you. And if I go and prepare a place for you, I will come again, and receive you unto myself, that where I am, there ye may be also,' John xiv. 1–3. The Psalmist saith, 'Those that be planted in the house of the Lord, shall flourish in the courts of our God; they shall bring forth fruit in old age; they shall be fat and flourishing,' Psal. xcii. 13, 14. Again, 'Holiness becomes thine house, O Lord, for ever,' Psal. xciii. 5. Isaiah also said by way of prophecy, 'It shall come to pass in the last days, that the mountain of the Lord's house shall be established in the top of the mountains, and shall be exalted above the hills, and all nations shall flow unto it,' Isa. ii. 2. Is not that a great house? Is not this mountain, Christ, who is over his house in the New Testament and New Covenant? To this mountain and house all the children of the New Testament and New Covenant flow in these latter days, so that it is come to pass, which was prophesied of by Isaiah; for he said, 'Many people shall go and say, Come ye, and let us go up to the mountain of the Lord, to the house of the God of Jacob, and he will teach us of his ways, and we will walk in his paths; for out of Zion shall go forth the law, and the word of the Lord from Jerusalem. And he shall judge among the nations, and shall rebuke many people; and they shall beat their swords into ploughshares, and their spears into pruning-hooks; nation shall not lift up sword against nation, neither shall they learn war any more. O house of Jacob, come ye, and let us walk in the light of the Lord, ver. 3–5. Here ye may see, they that come to the mountain of the house of God, and to God's teaching, must walk in the light of the Lord; yea, the house of Jacob. Jacob signifies a supplanter; he supplanted profane Esau, who is hated, and Jacob is loved. Now these two births must be known within; and they that walk in the light of the

Lord, and come to Christ, the mountain of the house of the Lord, established above all mountains and hills, break their swords into ploughshares, and their spears into pruning-hooks; and in Christ, this mountain and house of the Lord, there are no spears, nor swords to hurt one another withal. Christ, the Son of God, is over his house and great family, the children of the light, that believe in it, and walk in it, the children of the day of Christ, his holy and royal priesthood, that offer up spiritual sacrifice to God by him. All such are of Christ's (the spiritual man's) house, who are born of God, and led by his Spirit; they are of the Lord of lords, and King of kings' house and family, which he is over; and are of the household of the holy, divine, pure, and precious faith, which Christ is the author and finisher of. And they that are of the Son's house, are pure, righteous, and holy, and can do nothing against the truth, but for it, in their words, lives, and conversations; and so are a chosen generation, a holy nation, a peculiar people, that they should show forth the praise of Him, who hath called them out of darkness into his marvellous light. These are Christ's lively stones, that build up a spiritual house, which He (Christ, the spiritual man, the King of kings, and Lord of lords) is over." G. F.

London, the 10th Month, 1688.

Some time after this, my body continuing weak, I went down with my son Mead to his house in Essex, where I stayed some weeks. In which time I wrote many things relating to the service of truth, of which some were printed soon after, others were spread abroad in manuscript; and amongst other things, a few lines to this purpose:—

"That while men are contending for thrones here below, Christ is on his throne, and all his holy angels are about him; who is the Beginning and the Ending, the First and the Last, over all. And that the Lord will make way and room for himself, and for them that are born of his Spirit, who are heavenly Jerusalem's children, to come home to their free mother."

A few words also I wrote concerning the world's teachers, and the emptiness of their teaching. Which were thus:—

"Doth not all that, which is called Christendom, live in talking of Christ's, and of the apostles' and prophets' words, and the letter of the Scriptures? And do not their priests minister the letter, with their own conceptions thereupon, for money, though the Holy Scriptures were freely given forth from God and Christ, and his prophets and apostles? Yet the apostle says, 'The letter killeth; but the Spirit giveth life,' 2 Cor. iii. 6. The ministers of the New Testament are not ministers of the letter, but of the Spirit; and they sow to the Spirit, and of the Spirit reap life eternal. But people spending time about old authors, and talking of them, and of the outward letter, this doth not feed their souls. For talking of victuals and clothes, doth not clothe the body, nor feed it. No more are their souls and spirits fed and clothed, except they have the bread and water of life from heaven to feed them, and the righteousness of Christ to clothe them. Talking of outward things and spiritual things, and not having them, may starve both their bodies and their souls. Therefore, quench not the Spirit of God, which will lead to be diligent in all things."

With this I wrote another short paper, showing the hurt they did, and the danger they run into, who turned people from the inward manifestation of Christ in the heart:—

"The Jews were commanded by the law of God, 'Not to remove the outward land-mark,' Deut. xix. 14. They that did so, or that caused the blind to wander, were cursed in the Old Covenant, Deut. xxvii. 17. In the New Covenant the apostle saith, 'Let him be accursed, that preacheth any other gospel than that which he had preached,' Gal. i. 8. Now the gospel that he preached, was 'The power of God unto salvation, to every one that believeth,' Rom. i. 16. And the gospel that was preached to Abraham was, 'That in his seed all nations, and all the families of the earth should be blessed.' And in order to bring men to this blessed state, God poureth out of his Spirit upon all flesh; and Christ doth enlighten every one that cometh into the world; and the grace of God, which bringeth salvation, hath appeared unto all men, and teacheth Christians, the true believers in Christ; and God doth write his law in the true Christians' hearts, and putteth it in their minds, that they may 'all know the Lord, from the greatest to the least;' and he giveth his word in their hearts to obey and do, and the anointing within them; so that they need not any man to teach them, but as the anointing doth teach them. Now all such as turn people from the Light, Spirit, Grace, Word, and Anointing within, remove them from their heavenly landmark of their eternal inheritance, and make them blind; and cause the blind to wander from the living way to their eternal house in the heavens, and from the new and heavenly Jerusalem. So they are cursed, that cause the blind to wander out of their way, and to remove them from their heavenly landmark." G. F.

I wrote also a paper to show, by instances from the Scriptures, that "many of the holy men and prophets of God, and of the apostles of Christ, were husbandmen and tradesmen;" by which people might see how unlike to them the world's teachers now are:—

"Righteous Abel was a shepherd, 'a keeper of sheep,' Gen. iv. 2. Noah was a husbandman; and he was a 'just man, and perfect in his generation, and walked with God,' Gen. ix. 20; vi. 9. Abraham, the father of the faithful, was a husbandman, and had great flocks of cattle; and just Lot was a husbandman, and had great flocks and herds, Gen. xiii. Isaac also was a husbandman, and had great 'flocks and herds of cattle, and great store of corn,' Gen. xxvi. 12, 14. And the promise was with Isaac; for the Lord said to Abraham, 'In Isaac shall thy seed be called,' Gen. xxi. 12. Jacob was a husbandman, and his sons 'keepers of flocks of cattle,' Gen. lxvi. 32, 34, and God loved Jacob. Moses kept sheep, Exod. iii. 1, and the Lord spake to him when he was keeping sheep, ver. 4, and sent him to Pharaoh, to bring God's people, or sheep, out of Egypt. And by the hand and power of the Lord, he and Aaron his brother brought them out of Egypt, a land of anguish, bondage, darkness, and perplexity.

And Moses kept the Lord's people, or sheep, forty years in the wilderness; a meek shepherd of God he was, and kept his great flock of sheep; though some of them were scabbed with the leprosy of contention and murmuring, and were destroyed in the wilderness.

"David (though he afterwards came to be a king) was a keeper of his father's sheep in the wilderness, 1 Sam. xvii. 15, 28. And the Lord God called him from the sheepcotes to feed his sheep, the house of Israel, and to defend them from the spiritual wolves, bears, and lions; and he did it to purpose, who was a man after God's own heart.

"Elisha was a ploughman, 1 Kings xix. 19. He was called from the plough, to teach God's people, the children of Israel, to plough up the fallow ground of their hearts, that they might bring forth seed and fruits to God, their Creator.

"The word of the Lord came to Amos, when he was among the herdsmen of Tekoa, Amos i. 1. And Amaziah, the priest of Bethel, said to Amos, 'Prophesy not again any more at Bethel; for it is the king's chapel, and it is the king's court,' chap. vii. 13. Then answered Amos, and said to Amaziah, 'I was no prophet, neither was I a prophet's son; but I was a herdsman, and a gatherer of sycamore-fruit; and the Lord took me, as I followed the flock. And the Lord said unto me, Go, prophesy unto my people Israel,' ver. 14, 15. Here ye may see, how the Lord made use of a poor man, and how he called him from following the outward flock, and from gathering outward fruits, to gather his fruits, and to follow his people or flock, the children of Israel.

"Christ called Peter and Andrew his brother, when they were fishing, and casting their net into the sea (for they were fishers); 'and he said unto them, Follow me, and I will make you fishers of men,' Matt. iv. 18, 19. Christ likewise called James and John his brother, when they were 'in a ship, with Zebedee, their father, mending their nets; and they immediately left the ship, and their father, and followed him,' ver. 21, 22. He gave them power (a net that will hold, and not want mending), and made them fishers of men, to fish them out of the great sea, the world of wickedness. We read, that when Peter, Thomas, Nathanael, the sons of Zebedee, and other disciples, went a fishing together, and that night caught nothing, in the morning Jesus appeared to them and said, 'Cast the net on the right side of the ship, and ye shall find;' and they did so, and caught so great a multitude, that they were not able to draw them to shore. When thereupon one of the other disciples said unto Peter, 'It is the Lord,' Peter hearing that it was the Lord, 'girded his fisher's coat unto him,' John xxi. 2–7. This was after Christ was risen. So here ye may see, Peter had not laid aside his fisher's coat all the while that he had been preaching before Christ's death

"'Jesus saw Matthew sitting at the receipt of custom, and he said unto him, Follow me; and he arose and followed him,' Matt. ix. 9. And Christ employed Matthew to gather his people, that were scattered from God; another manner of treasure than the outward custom of the Romans. Luke was a physician, whom Christ made a physician spiritual; which was better than outward.

"Paul was a tent-maker; and being one of the same craft with Aquila and Priscilla, he abode with them at Corinth, and wrought (for by their occupation they were tent-makers), Acts xviii. 3." G. F.

Gooses, the 1st Month, 1688–9.

It was now a time of much talk; and people busied their minds and spent their time too much in hearing and telling news. To show them the vanity thereof, and to draw them from it, I wrote the following lines:—

"In the low region, in the airy life, all news is uncertain; there nothing is stable; but in the higher region, in the kingdom of Christ, there all things are stable and sure, and the news always good and certain. For Christ, who hath all power in heaven and in earth given unto him, ruleth in the kingdoms of men; and he, who doth inherit the heathen, and possess the utmost parts of the earth with his divine power and light, rules all nations with his rod of iron, and dashes them to pieces like a potter's vessel, the vessels of dishonour, and the leaky vessels, that will not hold his living water; and he doth preserve his elect vessels of mercy and honour. His power is certain, and changes not, by which he removes the mountains and hills, and shakes the heavens and the earth. Leaky, dishonourable vessels, the hills and mountains, and the old heavens and the earth, are all to be shaken, and removed, and broken to pieces, though they do not see it, nor him that doth it; but his elect and faithful both see it and know him, and his power, that cannot be shaken, and which changeth not."

The 5th of the 1st Month, 1688–9. G. F.

About the middle of the first month, 1688–9, I went to London, the parliament then sitting, and engaged about the bill for indulgence. Though I was weak in body, and not well able to stir about, yet so great a concern was upon my spirit on behalf of truth and Friends, that I attended con-continually for many days, with other Friends, at the parliament-house, labouring with the members, that the thing might be done comprehensively and effectually.

In this, and other services, I continued till towards the end of the second month, when, being much spent with continual labour, I got out of town for a little while as far Southgate and thereabouts. While I was there I wrote a letter to Peter Hendricks, a Friend at Amsterdam, in which I enclosed an epistle to the Friends at Dantzic, who at this time were under great persecution. And as I wrote to encourage and strengthen them in their testimony, and comfort them in their sufferings for the truth, so also I wrote a paper to their persecutors, the magistrates of Dantzic, laying before them the evil of persecution, and persuading them to Christian moderation, and "to do unto others in matters of religion as they would be done unto." Which papers were as follows:—

"To Peter Hendricks at Amsterdam, and to Friends at Dantzic who are under persecution.

"Dear Friend P. H.

"With my love to thee and thy wife, J. Claus, and J. Roeloffs, and all the rest of Friends everywhere in Christ Jesus, who reigns over all. I am glad to hear that Friends are well everywhere, except at Dantzic; and that you were so diligent in spreading my papers to the strengthening of Friends. I have lately printed the life of William Caton, but have not made a collection of his books. I think to send some of them to you, which you may translate and print, if you will; they may be serviceable among Friends, especially them that knew him.*

"Concerning the dear Friends at Dantzic, whom the Lord hath supported by his eternal arm and power to this day; I hope by the same arm and power he will support them, and in it they will feel his blessed presence with them in all their sufferings; who is over the cruelty of their persecutors, who will hardly let them breathe outwardly or inwardly in the common air of their native soil. Which shows both their immorality, inhumanity, and unchristianity, and that they want the counsel of a Gamaliel amongst them; whose actions are below the law of God, to 'do unto others as they would have others to do unto them:' God will not bless the doings of such. I desire, however, that Friends may mind the Lord's power, that is over all; be valiant for his truth, and keep upon their rock and foundation, Christ Jesus, that stands sure in this time of the heat of persecution, which is so hot upon you, that they will not suffer you to have so much as your houses to work and sleep in, nor to meet, nor serve God in. The Lord beholds all such actors and their actions. Therefore look over all to Him, who is able to deal with them and reward them according to their works. God Almighty preserve you all in Christ Jesus, in whom you have rest, life, and peace. Amen." G. F.

Southgate, the 28th of the 2nd Month, 1689.

"*To the Magistrates of Dantzic:—Christian Shroder, President of the Council, and Emanuel Dilger, N. Gadecken, and N. Fraterus, Deputies of the Council, and the rest of the Magistrates and Priests.*

"We have seen your order, and your breathing out persecution against that little flock, the lambs of Christ, that live under your jurisdiction in the city of Dantzic; and that you have imprisoned and banished two by the hangman out of the government of your city; and others you threatened to do the same to, with great punishment, if they return. Likewise

* William Caton, whose service was much in Holland, died at Amsterdam in 1665. He was one of the earliest associates of George Fox, being convinced by him in 1652, and is often mentioned in the earlier part of this Journal. He was not only a literary man, but zealous for religion; and being of a courteous and affable disposition, was in general esteem. When about fourteen years of age he went to reside in Judge Fell's family at Swarthmore Hall, as a companion for his son, sharing with him both in instruction and recreation. He was very early inclined to religion, and, as he grew in years, he advanced in godliness.

After joining Friends, he travelled considerably as a gospel minister, and underwent many sufferings for Christ's sake. At Maidstone, in 1654, he and another Friend were stripped, their necks and arms put in the stocks, and, in that condition, they were desperately whipped. At Yarmouth he was, with seven other Friends, taken from a religious meeting on the first day of the week, and confined six months in prison.

A valuable collection of letters of early Friends was met with at Swarthmore some

you threaten those with punishment they rent their houses of, if they let them have them either to live in, or meet in to serve and worship the Lord that made them. Truly I am heartily sorry for both your magistrates and priests, that go under the name of Christians, and show such immoral, inhuman, and unchristian actions, below the royal law of God, which is, to 'do to others as you would have them do unto you.' For would you think it was moral, human, or Christian, or according to the law of God, if the king of Poland, who is of another religion than you, should banish you out of your city by the hangman, and call you murderers of souls? Could you say, but this was according to the law of God, 'to do unto you as you have done unto others?' But if you say that you have the sword, the horn, and the power; blessed be the Lord that hath shortened your sword, your power, and your horn, that it reaches no further than your jurisdiction at Dantzic; and you do not know how long God may suffer you to have your horn, your power, and your sword. We are sure you have not the mind nor the Spirit of Christ; and the apostle saith, 'They that have not the Spirit of Christ are none of his,' Rom. viii. And Christ bids Peter 'put up his sword:' they that draw the sword concerning him, to defend him and his worship and faith, should perish with the sword. Peter and the apostles never drew the outward sword after; but said their weapons were spiritual, not carnal; and they did not wrestle with flesh and blood. Christ never gave any such command, that they should banish any by the hangmen that were not of their religion, and would not receive it. Are not you worse than the Turks, who let many religions be in their country, yea, Christians, and to meet peaceably? Yea, the Turkish patroons let our Friends that were captives meet together at Algiers, and said, 'it was good so to do.' You are worse than those barbarous people at Sallee who do not profess Christianity, for you profess Christ in words, but in works deny him. And did you ever find, either in Scripture or history, that any persecutors prospered long? You are worse than they are in the Mogul's country, who, they say, permits sixty religions in his dominions: and many others might be mentioned, all of whom you exceed in your cruelty and persecution of God's people, only for meeting together in the name of Jesus, and serving and worshipping God, their Creator. No, they must not breathe their natural air, neither natural nor spiritual, in your dominions. I pray, where had you these commands from? Neither from Christ nor his apostles. Do not you profess the Scriptures of the New Testament to be your rule? But, I pray you, what Scripture have you for this practice? It is good for you to be humble, to do justly, and love mercy; call home your banished ones, and love and cherish them: yea, though they were your enemies, you are to obey the command of Christ, and love them. I wonder how you and your wives and families can sleep quietly in your beds,

years ago, written nearly throughout by William Caton, and appears to have been intended by him for publication. It has a title page, dated Swarthmore, 23d of 6th Month, 1659; and a preface signed by himself, dated 7th of 2d Month, 1660. The life of Caton, George Fox mentions having been printed, was re-published in 1839, by John Barclay, forming one of the *Select Series*, to which the reader is referred for further particulars.

that do such cruel actions, without thinking the 'Lord may do to you the same!' You cannot be without sense and feeling, except you be given over to reprobation, and your consciences seared with a hot iron. But Christian charity hopes that you are not all in that state; but that there may be some relenting or consideration of your actions among some of you, either according to the law of God, or his gospel.

"From him that desires your temporal and eternal good and salvation, and not destruction. Amen." G. F.

Middlesex, the 28th of the 2nd Month, 1689.

"Peter, thou mayest translate this into high Dutch, and send them; and you may print it, if you will, and send it abroad; and translate that part of the letter that is to Friends into high Dutch, and send to them."

Having stayed in the country about three weeks, I returned to LONDON a little before the Yearly Meeting, which was in the third month this year, and was a very solemn, weighty meeting; the Lord, as formerly, visiting his people, and honouring the assembly with his glorious presence, to the great satisfaction and comfort of Friends. After the business was over, it was upon me to add a few lines to the Epistle which went from the meeting to Friends, after this manner:—

"DEAR FRIENDS AND BRETHREN,

"Who have known the Lord's eternal arm and power, that hath preserved you upon the heavenly rock and foundation, and hath built your house upon it; you have known many winds, tempests, and storms, that have risen out of that sea where the beast rose; and many raging storms that have risen by apostates of several sorts; but the Seed that bruises the serpent's head, and is the foundation of God's people, stands sure. Dear Friends and brethren, though there be great shakings in the world, the Lord's power is over all, and his kingdom cannot be shaken. Therefore all ye children of God, children of the light, and heirs of his kingdom, a joyful, peaceable habitation keep in; keeping out of all the contentions and disputes about things below. Lay hand on no man, nor nothing suddenly, lest they should be puffed up with that which fades, and so come to loss: but mind the Lord's power, that keeps open your heavenly eye, to see things present and to come; and in that ye will see and handle the word of life.

"Dear Friends everywhere, have power over your own spirits. As God hath blessed you with his outward things, have a care of trusting in them, or falling into difference one with another about these outward things that are below, which will pass away. But all live in the love of God, and in that live in peace with God, and one with another. Follow the works of charity, and overcome evil with good to all; for what good have all the tinklers done, with their cymbals and sounding brass? They always bred confusion, and never did good in any age; tinkling with their cymbals, and sounding with their brass, to draw out the simple to follow them. Therefore, it is good for all the children of God to keep in their possession of life, and in the love of God, that is everlasting.

"As for all the tumults of the world, and the apostates from the truth, the Lord's power is over them all, and Christ reigns; and the Lord saith, 'No weapon that is formed against thee shall prosper,' Isa. liv. 17. Now, Friends, you are not insensible how many weapons have been formed against us, who are the sons and daughters of God; and the Lord hath restrained them according to his promise; they have not prospered. The Lord said, 'Every tongue that shall rise up in judgment against thee, thou shalt condemn:' so God hath given such a power to his children, to condemn all the tongues that shall rise up in judgment against them, and this is the heritage of the servants of the Lord; 'their righteousness is of me, saith the Lord.' You are not insensible of the many tongues that have risen up against us in judgment, yea, of apostates and profane. But in and with the truth, the power of God, according to the promise of God, 'Every tongue that riseth against thee, thou shalt condemn.' It is not one tongue only thou shalt condemn, but 'every tongue that shall rise up in judgment against thee, thou shalt condemn.' The Lord giveth this power to his servants and children, to judge the evil tongues; and he doth restrain the weapons formed against them, so that they shall not prosper against his children that he hath begotten. Praises and honour be to his holy name for ever! Amen." G. F.

Soon after this, the Yearly Meeting began at York; which because of the largeness of that county, and for the conveniency of Friends in the northern parts, had for some years been held there. And inasmuch as there had been some hurt done in that place, by some that were gone out of the unity of Friends, it was upon me to write a few lines to that meeting, "to exhort them to keep in the pure, heavenly love, which brings into, and keeps in, the true unity." Which was thus:—

"Dear Friends and Brethren in Christ Jesus,

"Whom the Lord by his eternal arm and power hath preserved to this day, all walk in the power and Spirit of God, that is over all, in love and unity; for love overcomes, builds up, and unites all the members of Christ to him the Head. Love keeps out of all strife, and is of God. Love, or charity, never fails, but keeps the mind above all outward things, and strife about outward things. It overcomes evil, and casts out all false fears. It is of God, and unites all the hearts of his people together in the heavenly joy, concord, and unity. The God of love preserve you all, and establish you in Christ Jesus, your life and salvation, in whom ye have all peace with God. So walk in him, that ye may be ordered in his peaceable, heavenly wisdom, to the glory of God, and the comfort one of another. Amen." G. F.

London, the 27th of the 3rd Month, 1689.

Being much wearied and spent with many large meetings, and much business with Friends, during the time of the Yearly Meeting, and finding my health much impaired thereby, I went out of town with my daughter Rous, to their country-house near Kingston, and tarried there most of the remaining part of the summer. In which time I sometimes visited Friends at Kingston, and wrote divers things for the service of truth and Friends. One was an epistle to Friends in Barbadoes; as follows:—

"*To all Friends in Barbadoes, that are convinced of God's truth.*"

"My desires are that ye may live and walk in his peaceable truth, and show forth that ye are children of the light and of the truth; for the heavenly, gentle, and peaceable wisdom is justified of her children. But debate, strife, wilfulness, and laying open one another's nakedness and weakness, is not the practice of heavenly wisdom's children (but of Ham's), nor from the Spirit of Christ; neither such as bite and tear one another; that is from a devouring spirit, not from the Spirit of Jesus, which covers that which is uncomely, and can forgive. Now, my Friends, you profess that truth, which is beyond all the world's ways; therefore see that you excel them in the heavenly, gentle wisdom, that is easy to be entreated; for the wisdom of the world is not easy to be entreated; and sometimes will not be entreated at all. Pray see you excel the world in wisdom, in virtue, in kindness, in love that is over hatred, in meekness and humility, in sobriety, civility, and modesty, in temperance and patience, and in all morality and humanity, which will not act anything below men or unmanly. Show forth true Christianity, and that ye are the converted and translated believers in Christ, dwelling in the love of God, that beareth all things, endureth all things, is not puffed up, and envies not. For they that are out of this love of God and Christian charity, are nothing, but as a tinkling cymbal and as sounding brass, and are discontented, murmurers, and complainers, full of doubts, questions, and false jealousies. Keep that spirit out of the camp of God; for do not you read in the Scriptures, both of the New and Old Testament, that the end of such was misery? Therefore, in the love of God, build up one another; for love edifies the body of Christ, and he commands his believers to love enemies, and to love one another; by this they are known to be the disciples of Christ. But to live in envy, strife, and hatred, is a mark they are no disciples of Christ: 'For he that loveth not his brother, abides in death; and whosoever hates his brother, is a murderer: and ye know that no murderer hath eternal life abiding in him. But they that love the brethren, are passed from death to life,' 1 John iii. 14, 15. And, 'If a man say, I love God, and hateth his brother, he is a liar: for he that loveth not his brother whom he hath seen, how can he love God whom he hath not seen? And this commandment have we from God, that he who loveth God, love his brother also,' chap. iv. 20, 21. Therefore, 'love one another;' for love is of God, and hatred is of the devil; and every one that loveth is born of God, and knows God. All are children of God by creation; therefore in that state they are to love their neighbours as themselves; and to do unto all men as they would have them do unto them. Secondly, God poureth his Spirit upon all flesh (or all men and women); all that are led by the Spirit of God are the sons of God, heirs of God, and joint-heirs with Christ; and are in fellowship in the everlasting gospel; and in unity in the Spirit, the bond of peace. They that go out of this unity, out of the bond of peace, and do not keep it, break the King of kings' peace; but they that keep in the unity, and fellowship in the Spirit, and walk in the light, have fellowship one with another, and with the Father and the Son. It is not every one that talks of the light, of the word, of righteousness, of Christ, and of God, but he that 'doeth the will of God.' Therefore, my Friends, strive to excel one another in love, in virtue, in good life and conversation; and strive all to be of one mind, heart, and judgment in the Spirit of God; for in Christ all are one, and are in peace with him. The Lord God Almighty preserve you in him, your rock and foundation, that is heavenly and stands sure; that ye may be valiant for the truth upon earth, for the Lord and his glorious name; that ye may all serve him in your generation, and in his new creation in Christ Jesus. Amen.

"And now, that you are come into so much favour with the magistrates and powers, that they let you serve the office of constable, &c., without swearing or taking any oaths, hereby Christ's doctrine and command, and his apostle's is set up. Therefore, I desire, that you may double your diligence in your offices, in doing that which is just, and true, and righteous; so that ye may excel and exceed all, that are tied or bound by oaths to perform their offices; and you can do it upon your Yea and Nay; so say, and so do; according to Christ's doctrine and command. For Adam and Eve, by disobeying the command of God, fell under condemnation; and they that disobey the command of Christ, in taking oaths and swearing, go into evil and fall into condemnation, Matt. v.; James v. My love in the Lord is to you all." G. F.

Kingston-upon-Thames, the 10th of the 5th Month, 1689.

I stayed at Kingston till the beginning of the seventh month, where not only Friends came to visit me, but some considerable people of the world, with whom I discoursed about the things of God. Then leaving Kingston, I went to LONDON by water, visiting Friends as I went, and taking HAMMERSMITH meeting in my way. Having recovered some strength by being in the country, when I was come to LONDON, I went from meeting to meeting, labouring diligently in the work of the Lord, and opening the divine mysteries of the heavenly things, as God by his Spirit opened them in me. But I found my body would not long bear the city; wherefore, when I had travelled amongst Friends there about a month, I went to TOTTENHAM-HIGH-CROSS, and thence to Edward Man's country-house near WINCHMORE-HILL, and to ENFIELD, spending three weeks among Friends thereabouts; and had meetings at all those places. Then, being a little refreshed with being in the country, I went back to LONDON; where I tarried, labouring in the work of the ministry, till the middle of the ninth month; at which time I went down with my son Mead to his house in ESSEX, and abode there all the winter. During which I stirred not much abroad, unless it were sometimes to the meeting, to which that family belonged, which was about half a mile from thence; but I had meetings often in the house with the family, and those Friends that came thither. Many things also I wrote, while I was there; some of which follow. One was an epistle to the quarterly and yearly meetings of Friends in Pennsylvania, New-England, Virginia, Maryland, the Jerseys, Carolina, and other plantations in America. Which was thus:—

"MY DEAR FRIENDS AND BRETHREN IN THE LORD JESUS CHRIST,

"Who, by believing in his light, are become children of his light and of his day; my desires are, that you may all walk in the light and in the day, and keep the feast of Christ, our passover, who is sacrificed for us, not with old leaven, neither with the leaven of malice and wickedness; but let all that be purged out, that ye may be a new lump, keeping the feast of Christ our passover, with the unleavened bread of sincerity and truth. Let no leavened bread be found in your houses, nor in your meetings, nor in the camp of God, or household of faith, which are the household of Christ; but all that old leaven, which makes people's hearts sour, and burn one against another, must be purged out of the camp of God, and kept out. For the feast of Christ, our passover, must be kept in the New Covenant, with his heavenly, unleavened bread of life. The Jews' feast in the Old Testament was kept with outward, unleavened bread; and now, in the New Testament, in the gospel-day, our feast is to be kept with the heavenly, unleavened bread of sincerity and truth. Therefore, Friends, I desire you seriously to consider, and to keep this feast, which the apostle directed the church of Christ to keep. Do not you see Christendom, so called, keep their feasts with the leavened bread of malice and wickedness? which makes them so sour, and their hearts so burn one against another, that they have destroyed, and do destroy one another about religion. Therefore, all live in the love of God, which keeps above the love of the world; so that none of your hearts may be choked or surfeited with these outward things, or with the cares of the world, which will pass away; but mind ye the world and the life that is without end, that ye may be heirs of it. And Friends, you should strive to excel all, both professor and profane, in morality, humanity, and Christianity, modesty, sobriety, and moderation, and in a good, godly, righteous life and conversation, showing forth the fruits of the Spirit, and that you are the children of the living God, children of the light, and of the day, and not of the night. And serve God in newness of life; for it is the life, and a living and walking in the truth, that must answer the witness of God in all people; that 'they, seeing your good works, may glorify our Father, which is in heaven.' Therefore be valiant for God's holy, pure truth, and spread it abroad, among both professors and profane, and the Indians. And you should write over once a year, from all your yearly meetings to the yearly meeting here, concerning your diligence in the truth, and of its spreading, and of people's receiving it, both professors and profane, and the Indians; and concerning the peace of the church of Christ amongst yourselves. For, blessed be the Lord, truth gains ground in these parts, and many are made very loving to Friends, and the Lord's power and seed is over all; in which God Almighty keep all his people to his glory. Amen." G. F.

Gooses, the 28th of the 11th Month, 1689.

While I was in the city, I had a concern upon my spirit with respect to a twofold danger that attended some who professed truth: one was of young people's running into the fashions of the world; and the other was of old people's going into earthly things. And that concern coming now again weightily upon me, I was moved to give forth the following paper, as a reproof to such, and an exhortation and warning to all Friends to beware of, and keep out of those snares:—

"*To all that profess the Truth of God.*

"My desires are, that you may walk in humility in it. For when the Lord first called me forth, he let me see, that young people grew up together in vanity and the fashions of the world; and old people went downwards into the earth, raking it together; and to both these I was to be a stranger. And now, Friends, I see too many young people that profess the truth, grow up into the fashions of the world, and too many parents indulge them; and amongst the elder, some are going downwards, and raking after the earth. Therefore take heed, that you are not making your graves, while you are alive outwardly, and loading yourselves with thick clay (Hab. ii. 6). For if you have not power over the earthly spirit, and that which leadeth into a vain mind, and the fashions of the world, and into the earth, though you have often had the rain fall upon your fields, you will but bring forth thistles, briars, and thorns, which are for the fire. Such will become brittle, peevish, fretful spirits, that will not abide the heavenly doctrine, the admonitions, exhortations, and reproofs of the Holy Ghost, or heavenly Spirit of God; which would bring you to be conformable to the death of Christ, and to his image, that ye might have fellowship with him in his resurrection. Therefore it is good for all to bow to the name of Jesus, their Saviour, that all may confess him to the glory of God, the Father. For I have had a concern upon me, in a sense of the danger of young people's going into the fashions of the world, and old people's going into earthly things, and many going into a loose and false liberty, till at last they go quite out into the spirit of the world, as some have done. The house of such hath been built upon the sand on the sea-shore, not upon Christ, the Rock, that they are so soon in the world again, under a pretence of liberty of conscience. But it is not a pure conscience, nor in the Spirit of God, nor in Christ Jesus; for in the liberty in the Spirit there is the unity, which is the bond of peace; and all are one in Christ Jesus, in whom is the true liberty: and this is not of the world; for He is not of the world. Therefore all are to stand fast in Him, as they have received Him; for in Him there is peace, who is the Prince of Peace; but in the world there is trouble. For the spirit of the world is a troublesome spirit; but the Spirit of Christ is a peaceable Spirit; in which God Almighty preserve all the faithful. Amen." G. F.

Gooses, the 1st of the 2nd Month, 1690.

Another paper I wrote while I was here, "concerning the Ensign, which Isaiah prophesied the Lord should set up for the Gentiles, which I showed was Christ." Of which follows a copy:—

"The Lord saith, 'They shall not hurt nor destroy in all my holy mountain; for the earth shall be full of the knowledge of the Lord, as the waters cover the sea,' Isa. xi. 9. 'And in that day there shall be a root of Jesse, which shall stand for an Ensign of the people; to it shall the Gentiles seek, and his rest shall be glorious,' ver. 10. 'And he shall reign over the Gentiles, and in him shall the Gentiles trust,' Rom. xv. 12. This Ensign is Christ, who was prophesied of by the prophet; which prophecy the apostle, who was a minister to the Gentiles, showeth was fulfilled in the New Testament. And in this day of Christ, Isaiah saith, 'The Lord shall set his hand again the second time, to recover the remnant of his people, which shall be left, from Assyria and from Egypt,' &c. And he shall set up an Ensign for the nations, and shall assemble the outcasts of Israel, and gather together the dispersed of Judah from the four corners of the earth,' ver. 11, 12. This is in the day of Christ, and his gospel of life and salvation, which is preached to every creature under heaven; who 'enlighteneth every man that cometh into the world,' both Jews and Gentiles; that by his heavenly, divine light, they may see Christ, their Ensign, and Captain of their salvation; so Christ is one Ensign both to the Jews and Gentiles. Isaiah saith, 'The Redeemer shall come to Sion,' &c., Isa. lix. 20. And, 'This is my covenant with them, saith the Lord, my Spirit, that is upon thee (to wit, Christ), and my words, which I have put in thy mouth, shall not depart out of thy mouth, nor out of the mouth of thy seed, nor out of the mouth of thy seed's seed, saith the Lord, from henceforth and for ever,' ver. 21. 'Arise, shine, for thy light is come, and the glory of the Lord is risen upon thee,' chap. lx. 1. 'And the Gentiles shall come to thy light,' ver. 3. 'And the abundance of the sea shall be converted unto thee,' ver. 5 (the sea is the world). 'The Lord shall be thy everlasting light,' ver. 20. And, 'Thou shalt call thy walls, Salvation, and thy gates, Praise,' ver. 18. And the Lord saith, 'I will make the place of my feet glorious,' ver. 13. 'Heaven is his throne, and the earth is his footstool,' chap. lxvi. 1. 'And he that puts his trust in me, saith the Lord, shall possess the land, and shall inherit my holy mountain,' chap. lvii. 13. Which mountain is established above all the mountains and hills, Isa. ii. 2. The Lord saith (speaking of Christ), 'I have put my Spirit upon him, he shall bring forth judgment to the Gentiles,' Isa. xlii. 1. And he saith of him, 'I will give thee for a covenant of the people, for a light of the Gentiles; to open the blind eyes, to bring out the prisoners from the prison, and them that sit in darkness out of the prison-house. I am the Lord, that is my name, and my glory will I not give to another, neither my praise to graven images,' ver. 6–8. So Christ the Light is come, and the glory of the Lord is risen; and the Gentiles are come to the light of Christ. This prophecy of Isaiah concerning Christ, many of the Gentiles witness fulfilled, that 'Salvation is come to the Gentiles,' Rom. xi. 11. God gave his glory to his Son; and Christ saith, 'The glory, which thou gavest me, I have given them (namely, his believers and followers), that they may be one, even as we are one,' John xvii. 22. Now here you may see, the promises and prophecies are fulfilled in Christ Jesus, whom God hath given for an Ensign both to the Jews and Gentiles, and the Captain of their salvation; and he doth enlighten every one that cometh into the world; that with his heavenly, divine light, they might see Christ, the Lord from heaven, their Captain and Ensign, and trust in Him, their Conqueror, who bruises the serpent's head, and destroys the devil and his works; and Christ and his followers overcome the dragon, beast, and false prophet. Therefore all Jews, Gentiles, and Christians, that come to believe in Christ, are to stand to their Ensign, Christ; who is also the Captain of their salvation, above all ensigns and captains below; for he is from above; therefore all are to trust in him; for he is certain and able to save to the utmost, &c. He is the same Ensign and Captain to-day that he was yesterday, and so for ever, the First and the Last, the Beginning and the Ending, the Lord of all lords, and King of all kings upon the earth; and there is nothing certain to be trusted in below Christ Jesus, who is from above.

"You see in the Scriptures there were many ways and religions among the heathen, as there were many sects among the Jews when Christ came; and now there are many sects or religions among the Christians, who believe from the Scriptures that 'he is come,' as the Jews believed 'he was to come.' But they that close their eyes, and stop their ears to the Light of Christ, are not like to see Christ, who hath enlightened them, to be their Ensign and the Captain of their salvation, that see not with the heavenly eye, nor hear with the heavenly ear, to see and hear their heavenly Ensign and Captain of their salvation, to convert and heal them; that they might follow him, and be of his holy camp, his heavenly soldiers, to whom he gives spiritual arms and armour, the helmet of salvation, the breastplate of righteousness, the armour of light, and the shield of faith (which will quench all the fiery darts of Satan, and give victory), and the sword of the Spirit, the Word of God, which shall cut, hammer down, and burn up all the strongholds of Satan. Also he clothed his soldiers with fine linen, white and clean, his righteousness, and shoeth them with the everlasting gospel of peace, the power of God; which clothes and shoes will never wax old. And all that are shod with the everlasting gospel, the power of God, will never wax old, but will stand all storms and tempests in the world. They that are shod with the gospel, the power of God, can in it tread upon serpents, vipers, and scorpions, and all the venomous beasts upon the earth, and all the thorns, briars, brambles, thistles, and sharp rocks and mountains, and never be hurt, nor ever wear out their shoes; but their feet are always beautiful upon the mountains. Moses, a captain, the servant of the Lord, said unto the people of Israel, 'I have led you forty years in the wilderness; your clothes are not waxen old upon you, and thy shoe is not waxen old upon thy foot,' Deut. xxix. 5. Here ye may see the Jews in the Old Testament, their clothes and their shoes did not wax old; so they who are Christ's followers, whom he shoeth with his everlasting gospel of peace, clothes with his fine linen, his righteousness, and arms with his arms and armour, are clothed, shod, and armed, with that which will never decay, or wax old, never canker, or rust, corrupt, or grow blunt. Now, all (whether Christians, or Jews, or Gentiles) that hate the Light of Christ, and close their eyes and stop their ears to it, are not like to see Christ, their Ensign, and Captain of their salvation; but are blind. As no outward captain would enlist a company of blind and deaf men, and clothe and arm them with outward armour; so such as are blind and deaf, whose eyes are closed, and ears stopped to the heavenly Light of Christ, he is not likely to clothe them with his fine linen, and arm them with his heavenly and spiritual armour; neither are they like to be heavenly and spiritually disciplined, to see and know his holy, spiritual, living camp, nor to follow him, while they are deaf and blind, and hate his Light, which is the Life in Christ. For it is the Light that shines in the heart, which gives the knowledge of the glory of God in the face of Christ Jesus; who is the Ensign and Captain of men's salvation, and who hath brought, and doth bring many sons unto glory; praises, honour, and glory be unto the Lord over all, who liveth for ever. Amen." G. F.

Gooses, the 14th of the 2nd Month, 1690.

A week after this, I returned to LONDON; and after a little stay there went to visit Friends at KINGSTON, where I stayed not long; but came back to LONDON, and remained there in the Lord's work till after the Yearly Meeting, which was in the fourth month this year; in which the wonted goodness of the Lord was witnessed, his blessed presence enjoyed, and his heavenly power livingly felt, opening the hearts of his people unto him, and his divine treasures of life and wisdom in and unto them; whereby many useful and necessary things, relating to the safety of Friends and to the honour and prosperity of truth, were weightily treated of, and unanimously concluded.

After the meeting I wrote the following paper to Friends, to be added to the epistle which from the Yearly Meeting was sent into the several counties;—

"ALL Friends everywhere, that are alive to God through Jesus Christ, and are living members of Christ, the holy Head, be still; and stand still in the Lord's camp of holiness and righteousness; and therein see the salvation of God, and your eternal life, rest, and peace. In it you may feel and see the Lord's power is over all; and how the Lord is at work in his power, ruling the nations with his rod of iron, and breaking (in the nations) the old leaky vessels and cisterns to pieces, like the potter's vessels, that will not hold his living water; who are erred from his Spirit.

"But blessed be the Lord God of heaven and earth; who, by his eternal arm and power hath settled all his people upon the living, holy rock and foundation, that stands sure; whom he hath drawn by his Spirit to his Son, and gathered into the name of Jesus Christ, his only begotten Son, full of grace and truth; who hath all power in heaven and in earth given to him; whose name is above every name under the whole heaven; and all his living members know there is no salvation given by any other name than by the name of Jesus. He, their salvation and their living head, is felt in the midst of them in his light, life, Spirit, grace, and truth, and his word of patience, wisdom, and power; who is his people's prophet, that God hath raised up in his New Testament and Covenant, to open to them; and their living Shepherd, that hath purchased, redeemed, and bought them with his precious blood.

"Christ, the living One, feeds his living sheep in his pastures of life, and they know their living Shepherd's voice with his living bread and water, and follow him; and will not follow any of the world's hirelings, nor thieves, nor robbers, nor climbers, that are without Christ, the door. Christ's living children likewise know him, the bishop of their souls, to oversee them with his heavenly and spiritual eye, that they may be preserved in his fold of life, and go no more forth. They also know Christ, their holy priest, that by the grace of God tasted death for them, and for every man, and is a propitiation for their sins; and not for theirs only, but for the sins of the whole world: and by the one offering up of himself he hath perfected for ever them that are sanctified.

"Such a High-priest becomes Christ's sheep in his New Covenant and Testament, who is holy, harmless, and separate from sinners, and is made higher than the heavens; who is not made a priest after the order of Aaron, with his tithes, offerings, &c., but makes an end of all those things, having abolished them; and is made a High-priest after the power of an endless life, who ever liveth to make intercession for his people: and is able to save to the uttermost all that come to God through him. He is the one holy Mediator between God and man; who sanctifies his people, his church, that he is head of, and presents them to God without spot, or wrinkle, or blemish, or any such thing; and makes them a holy, royal priesthood, to offer up spiritual, holy sacrifices, acceptable to God by Jesus Christ, who is King of all kings, and Lord of all lords in the earth; so a holy, heavenly King, who hath all power in heaven and in earth given to him, and rules in all the hearts of his sheep and lambs, by his holy, divine, precious faith, that is held in all the pure consciences of his people: of which holy faith Christ, the holy One, is the author and finisher. By this holy faith all the just live; in which divine and precious faith all the just and holy ones have unity; by it they quench all the fiery darts of Satan, have access to the pure God, and in it please him.

"Christ, who is set on the right hand of the throne of the Majesty in heaven, in his New Testament and New Covenant, is the minister of the sanctuary and true tabernacle which the Lord hath pitched, and not man. Therefore all the lambs and sheep of Christ must feel this holy Minister in their temple and sanctuary, who ministers spiritual, holy, and heavenly things to them in their sanctuary and tabernacle. For all the tabernacles and sanctuaries that are built or pitched by man, men make ministers for them; and such ministers are of men and by men, with their worldly sanctuaries and tabernacles of men's pitching, by men's hands.

"And now, dear Friends and brethren everywhere that are of the flock of Christ; Christ our passover is sacrificed for us. Therefore let us all keep this heavenly feast of our passover in his New Testament and Covenant, not with old leaven, neither of malice nor wickedness; but let all that be purged out, with the sour, old leavened bread, that all may become a new lump; and so keep this heavenly feast of Christ, our heavenly Passover, with the unleavened bread (mark, with the unleavened bread) of sincerity and truth. My desires are, that all the flock of Christ everywhere may keep this heavenly feast of Christ, our heavenly passover, with his heavenly, unleavened bread of sincerity and truth. Amen." G. F.

I stayed in town three weeks or a month after the Yearly Meeting; and then went to TOTTENHAM-HIGH-CROSS, where was a meeting on First-day, which I was at; and then went to Edward Man's house, at FORD-GREEN, near Winchmore-Hill; and on the First-day following to the meeting at ENFIELD, where the Lord gave me many precious openings to declare to the people. Afterwards moving amongst Friends thereabouts, I visited the meetings at CHESTNUT, WALTHAM ABBEY, ENFIELD, TOTTENHAM, and WINCHMORE-HILL, frequently; the Lord being with me, and opening many deep and weighty truths, divine and heavenly mysteries to his people, through me, to their great refreshment, and my joy. After some time I went to HERTFORD, to visit Friends there; and was at their meeting on a First-day. And having something more particular upon me to the ancient Friends of that place, I had a meeting with some of them the next day, and imparted what the Lord had given me for them. Then passing to WARE, I made a little stay amongst Friends there, and was at their meeting. After which, returning, amongst Friends about EDMONTON side and TOTTENHAM, and taking meetings as I went, I came back to LONDON the end of the seventh month.

I remained at London till the beginning of the ninth month, being continually exercised in the work of the Lord, either in public meetings, opening the way of truth to people, and building up and establishing Friends therein, or in other services relating to the church of God. For the parliament now sitting, and having a bill before them concerning oaths, and another concerning clandestine marriages, several Friends attended the house, to get those bills so worded, that they might not be hurtful to Friends. In this service I also assisted, attending on the parliament, and discoursing the matter with several of the members.

Having stayed more than a month in London, and much spent myself in these services, I went to TOTTENHAM; and some time after to FORD-GREEN; at which places I continued several weeks, visiting Friends' meetings round about there, at TOTTENHAM, ENFIELD, and WINCHMORE-HILL. In this time several things came upon me to write; one was "an epistle to Friends in the ministry," as follows:—

"ALL Friends in the ministry everywhere, to whom God hath given a gift of the ministry, and who travel up and down in it, do not 'hide your talent, nor put your light under a bushel, nor cumber or entangle yourselves with the affairs of this world.' For the natural soldiers are not to cumber themselves with the world, much less the soldiers of Christ, who are not of this world; but are to mind the riches and glory of the world that is everlasting. Therefore, stir up the gift of God in you, and improve it; do not sit down, Demas-like, and embrace this present world, that will have an end; lest ye become idolaters. Be valiant for God's truth upon the earth, and spread it abroad in the day-light of Christ, you who have sought the kingdom of God, and the righteousness thereof, and have received it, and preached it; which 'stands in righteousness, and peace, and joy in the Holy Ghost.' As able ministers of the Spirit sow to the Spirit, that of the Spirit ye may reap life everlasting. Go on in the Spirit, ploughing with it in the purifying hope; and thrashing, with the power and Spirit of God, the wheat out of the chaff of corruption, in the same hope. For he that looks back from the spiritual plough into the world, is not fit for the spiritual and everlasting kingdom of God; and is not like to press into it, as the faithful do. Therefore you that are awakened to righteousness, and to the knowledge of the truth, keep yourselves awakened in it; then the enemy cannot sow his tares in your field; for truth and righteousness is over him, and before he was. My desires are, that all may fulfil their ministry, that the Lord Jesus Christ hath committed to them; and then by the blood (or life) and testimony of Jesus you will overcome the enemy that opposes it, within and without. All you that preach the truth, do it as it is in Jesus, in love: and all that are believers in Jesus, and receivers of him, he gives them power to become the sons of God, and joint-heirs with Christ; whom he calleth brethren; and he gives them the water of life, which shall be a well in them, springing up as a river to eternal life, that they may water the spiritual plants of the living God. So that all may be spiritual planters, and spiritual waterers; and may see with the spiritual eye the everlasting, eternal God, over all to give the increase, who is the infinite fountain. My desires are, that you may be kept out of all the beggarly elements of the world, which are below the spiritual region, to Christ the Head; and may hold Him, who bruiseth the head of enmity, and was before it was; that ye may all be united together in love, in your Head, Christ, and be ordered by his heavenly, gentle, peaceable wisdom, to the glory of God. For all that be in Christ, are in love, peace, and unity. In Him they are strong, and in a full persuasion: and in Him, who is the first and the last, they are in a heavenly resolution and confidence for God's everlasting honour and glory. Amen.

"From him, who is translated into the kingdom of his dear Son, with all his saints, a heavenly salutation. Salute one another with a holy kiss of charity, that never faileth." G. F.

Ford-Green, the 25th of the 9th Month, 1690.

Another epistle I wrote soon after, more particularly to the Friends in the ministry that were gone into America; after this manner:—

"Dear Friends and Brethren, Ministers, Exhorters, and Admonishers, that are gone into America and the islands thereaway. Stir up the gift of God in you, and the pure mind, and improve your talents, that ye may be the light of the world, a city set upon a hill, that cannot be hid. Let your light shine among the Indians, the Blacks, and the Whites, that ye may answer the truth in them, and bring them to the standard and ensign, that God hath set up, Christ Jesus. For from the rising of the sun to the going down of the same, God's name shall be great among the Gentiles; and in every temple, or sanctified heart, incense shall be offered up to God's name. And have salt in yourselves, that ye may be the salt of the earth, that ye may salt it; that it may be preserved from corruption and putrefaction; so that all sacrifices offered up to the Lord may be seasoned, and be a good savour to God. All grow in the faith and grace of Christ, that ye may not be like dwarfs, for a dwarf shall not come near to offer upon God's altar; though he may eat of God's bread, that he may grow by it.

And Friends, be not negligent, but keep up your negroes' meetings and your family meetings; and have meetings with the Indian kings, and their councils and subjects everywhere, and with others. Bring them all to the baptizing and circumcising Spirit, by which they may know God, and serve and worship Him. And all take heed of having your minds in earthly things, coveting and striving for them; for to be carnally minded brings death, and covetousness is idolatry. There is too much strife and contention about that idol, which makes too many go out of the sense and fear of God; so that some have lost morality, humanity, and true Christian charity. O therefore, be awakened to righteousness, and keep awakened: for the enemy soweth his tares, while men and women sleep in carelessness and security. Therefore so many slothful ones go in their filthy rags, and have not the fine linen, the righteousness of Christ; but are straggling, and ploughing with their ox and their ass, in their woollen and linen garments, mixed stuff, feeding upon torn food that dieth of itself, and drinking of the dregs of their old bottle, and eating the sour, leavened bread, which makes their hearts burn one against another. But all are to keep the feast of Christ, our passover, with the unleavened bread of sincerity and truth. This unleavened bread of life from heaven, makes all hearts and souls glad and joyful, lightsome and cheerful, to serve and love God, and to love and serve one another in the peaceable truth, and to keep in the unity of God's Spirit, which is the bond of peace. In this love and peace, God Almighty keep and preserve all his people, and make them valiant for his truth upon the earth, to spread it abroad in doctrine, good life, and conversation. Amen.

"All the members of Christ have need one of another. For the foot hath need of the hand, and the hand of the foot; the ear hath need of the eye, and the eye of the ear. So that all the members are serviceable in the body, which Christ is the head of; and the head sees their service. Therefore, let none despise the least member.

"Have a care to keep down that greedy, earthly mind, that raveneth and coveteth after the riches and things of this world, lest ye fall into the low region, like the Gentiles or heathen, and so lose the kingdom of God, that is everlasting: but seek that first, and God knows what things ye have need of; who takes care for all, both in heaven and in the earth: thanks be unto God for his unspeakable gifts, both temporal and spiritual."

Tottenham, the 11th of the 10th Month, 1690. G. F.

Not long after I returned to LONDON, and was almost daily with Friends at meetings. When I had been near two weeks in town, the sense of the great hardships and sore sufferings that Friends had been and were under in Ireland,* coming with great weight upon me, I was moved to write the following epistle, as a word of consolation unto them:—

* The sufferings of Friends in Ireland at this time were very great. The havoc and spoil they underwent were enormous, as related by the historians Sewell and Rutty, and more minutely by Besse, in his *Collection of Sufferings*, to which allusion has been made before, and to which the reader is now finally referred. The loss sus-

"DEAR Friends and Brethren in the Lord Jesus Christ, whom the Lord by his eternal arm and power hath upheld through your great sufferings, exercises, trials, and hardships (more, I believe, than can be uttered), up and down that nation, which I am very sensible of; and the rest of the faithful Friends, who have been partakers with you in your sufferings; and who cannot but suffer with the Lord's people that suffer. My confidence hath been in the Lord, that he would and will support you in all your sufferings; and that he would preserve all the faithful in his wisdom, that they might give no just occasion to one nor other to make them suffer; and if you did suffer wrongfully, or unjustly, that the righteous God would assist and uphold you; and reward them according to their works, that oppressed or wronged you. And now my desire is unto the Lord, that in the same holy and heavenly wisdom, ye may all be preserved to the end of your days, to the glory of God, minding His supporting hand and power, who is God All-sufficient, to strengthen, help, and refresh, in time of need. Let none forget the Lord's mercies and kindnesses, which endure for ever; but always live in the sense of them. And truly, Friends, when I consider the thing, it is the great mercy of the Lord, that ye have not been all swallowed up, seeing with what spirits ye have been compassed about. But the Lord carrieth his lambs in his arms, and they are as tender to him as the apple of his eye; and his power is his hedge about his vineyard of heavenly plants. Therefore it is good for all his children, to be given up to the Lord with their minds and souls, hearts and spirits, who is a faithful keeper, that never slumbers nor sleeps; but is able to preserve and keep you, and to save to the utmost; and none can hurt so much as a hair of your heads, except he suffer it, to try you; for he upholds all things, in heaven and in earth, by the Word of his power; all things were made by Christ, and by Him all things consist (mark, consist), whether they be visible, or invisible, &c. So he hath power over all; for all power in heaven and in earth is given to him; and to you that have received him, he hath given power to become the sons and daughters of God; so living members of Christ, the living head, grafted into Him, in whom ye have eternal life. Christ, the Seed, reigns, and his power is over all; who bruises the serpent's head, and destroys the devil and his works, and was before he was. So all of you live and walk in Christ Jesus; that nothing may be between you and God, but Christ, in whom ye have salvation, life, rest, and peace with God.

"As for the affairs of truth in this land and abroad, I hear that in Holland and Germany, and thereaway, Friends are in love, unity, and peace;

tained by Friends from persecution in a single year (1689) was estimated at £100,000, many being deprived of all their substance. Great numbers were immured years in prison, and many died there for Christ's sake. Others, when there was a prospect of their being released, because they could not satisfy the unjust demand of fees, as having done no wrong (thus bravely, though passively, asserting their Christian liberty), were either detained, or stripped of their clothes and turned out.

Surrounded as they were with perils on every hand, they placed their confidence in Divine protection; and, in the worst times of trial, when not in prison, they kept up their meetings for worship, as well as discipline; collected at the latter the accounts of the sufferings of their members, and took what care they could for their relief.

and in Jamaica, Barbadoes, Nevis, Antigua, Maryland, and New England, I hear nothing, but Friends are in unity and peace. The Lord preserve them all out of the world (in which there is trouble), in Christ Jesus, in whom there is peace, life, love, and unity. Amen. My love in the Lord Jesus Christ to all Friends everywhere in your land, as though I named them." G. F.

London, the 10th of the 11th Month, 1690.

Thus, reader, thou hast had some account of the life and travels, labours, sufferings, and manifold trials and exercises of this holy man of God, from his youth to almost the time of his death, of which himself kept a journal; out of which the foregoing sheets were transcribed. It remains that an account be added of the time, place, and manner of his death and burial, which were thus:—

The day after he had written the foregoing epistle to Friends in Ireland, he went to the meeting at Gracechurch Street, which was large, being the First-day of the week; and the Lord enabled him to preach the truth fully and effectually, opening many deep and weighty things with great power and clearness. After which having prayed, and the meeting being ended, he went to Henry Goldney's, in White-Hart-Court, near the meeting-house; and some Friends going with him there, he told them "he thought he felt the cold strike to his heart, as he came out of the meeting;" "yet," he added, "I am glad I was here: now I am clear, I am fully clear." As soon as the Friends withdrew, he lay down upon a bed (as he sometimes used to do, through weariness after meeting), but soon rose again; and in a little time lay down again, complaining still of cold. And his strength sensibly decaying, he was soon obliged to go into bed; where he lay in much contentment and peace, and very sensible to the last. And as, in the whole course of his life, his spirit, in the universal love of God, was bent upon the exalting of truth and righteousness, and the making known the way thereof to the nations and people afar of; so now, in the time of his outward weakness, his mind was intent upon, and (as it were) wholly taken up with that; and some particular Friends he sent for, to whom he expressed his mind and desire for the spreading of Friends' books, and truth thereby in the world. Divers Friends came to visit him in his illness; to some of whom he said, "All is well; the Seed of God reigns over all, and over death itself. And though," said he, "I am weak in body, yet the power of God is over all, and the Seed reigns over all disorderly spirits." Thus lying in a heavenly frame of mind, his spirit wholly exercised towards the Lord, he grew weaker and weaker in his natural strength; and on the third day of the week, between the hours of nine and ten in the evening, he quietly departed this life in peace, and sweetly fell asleep in the Lord, whose blessed truth he had livingly and powerfully preached in the meeting but two days before. Thus ended he his day in his faithful testimony, in perfect love and unity with his brethren, and in peace and good-will to all men, on the 13th of the 11th Month, 1690, being in the 67th year of his age.

After the death of George Fox, an epistle was found written with his own hand, and left sealed up, with this superscription; "Not to be opened before the time;" that is, not till after his decease. When it was opened, it was found to be addressed to "Friends, and to all the Children of God, in all places in the world." It was afterwards printed, and is inserted in the Appendix to this Journal.

On the day appointed for the interment of George Fox, a very great concourse of Friends, and others, assembled at the meeting-house in White-Hart-Court, near Gracechurch Street, about the middle of the day, to attend his body to the grave. The meeting held about two hours with great and heavenly solemnity, manifestly attended with the Lord's blessed presence and glorious power; in which divers living testimonies were given, from a lively remembrance and sense of the blessed ministry of this dear and ancient servant of the Lord, his early entering into the Lord's work at the breaking forth of this gospel-day, his innocent life, long and great travels, and unwearied labours of love in the everlasting gospel, for the turning and gathering of many thousands from darkness to the light of Christ Jesus, the foundation of true faith; the manifold sufferings, afflictions, and oppositions, which he met withal for his faithful testimony, both from his open adversaries, and from false brethren; and his preservations, deliverances, and dominion in, out of, and over them all, by the power of God; to whom the glory and honour always was by him, and is, and always ought to be by all, ascribed.

After the meeting was ended, his body was borne by Friends, and accompanied by very great numbers, to Friends' burying-ground, near Bunhill-Fields; where, after a solemn waiting upon the Lord, and several living testimonies borne, recommending the company to the guidance and protection of that Divine Spirit and power, by which this holy man of God had been raised up, furnished, supported, and preserved, to the end of his day, his body was committed to the earth; but his memorial shall remain, and be everlastingly blessed among the righteous.

APPENDIX;

CONTAINING

TESTIMONY OF MARGARET FOX RESPECTING HER HUSBAND GEORGE FOX.

TESTIMONY OF SOME OF THE AUTHOR'S RELATIONS.

TESTIMONY FROM THE MORNING MEETING IN LONDON.

TESTIMONY OF THOMAS ELLWOOD.

AN EPISTLE OF GEORGE FOX, FOUND AFTER HIS DEATH SEALED UP, ADDRESSED TO THE CHILDREN OF GOD EVERYWHERE.

THE APPEARANCE OF THE LORD'S EVERLASTING TRUTH, AND ITS BREAKING FORTH AGAIN IN HIS ETERNAL POWER, IN THIS OUR DAY AND AGE, IN ENGLAND.

A CHRONOLOGICAL REGISTER OF THE PLACES VISITED BY THE AUTHOR.

TEXTS OF SCRIPTURE OCCURRING IN THIS JOURNAL.

PARTICULARS OF THE VARIOUS EDITIONS OF GEORGE FOX'S JOURNAL, ETC.

TESTIMONY OF MARGARET FOX,

CONCERNING HER LATE HUSBAND

GEORGE FOX;

WITH A BRIEF ACCOUNT OF SOME OF HIS TRAVELS, SUFFERINGS, AND HARDSHIPS ENDURED FOR THE TRUTH'S SAKE.

It having pleased Almighty God to take away my dear husband out of this evil, troublesome world, who was not a man thereof, being chosen out of it; who had his life and being in another region, and whose testimony was against the world, that the deeds thereof were evil, and therefore the world hated him: so I am now to give in my account and testimony for him, whom the Lord hath taken unto his blessed kingdom and glory. And it is before me from the Lord, and in my view, to give a relation, and leave upon record the dealings of the Lord with us from the beginning.

He was the instrument in the hand of the Lord in this present age, which he made use of to send forth into the world, to preach the everlasting gospel, which had been hid from many ages and generations; the Lord revealed it unto him, and made him open that new and living way, that leads to life eternal, when he was but a youth, and a stripling. And when he declared it in his own country of Leicestershire, and in Derbyshire, Nottinghamshire, and Warwickshire, his declaration being against the hireling priests and their practices, it raised a great fury and opposition amongst the priests and people against him; yet there were always some that owned him in several places; but very few that stood firm to him when persecution came on him. He and one other were put in prison at Derby, but the other declined, and left him in prison there, where he continued almost a whole year; and when he was released out of prison, he went on with his testimony abroad, and was put in prison again at Nottingham; and there he continued a while, and after was released again.

He then travelled on into Yorkshire, and passed up and down that great county, and several received him, as William Dewsbury, Richard Farnsworth, Thomas Aldam, and others, who all came to be faithful ministers of the Spirit for the Lord. He continued in that country, and travelled through Holderness and the Wolds, and abundance were convinced: and several were brought to prison at York for their testimony to the truth, both men and women: so that we heard of such a people that were risen, and we did very much inquire after them. And after a while he travelled up farther towards the Dales in Yorkshire, as Wensleydale, and Sedbergh; and amongst the hills, dales, and mountains he came on, and convinced many of the eternal Truth.

In the year 1652 it pleased the Lord to draw him towards us; so he came on from Sedbergh, and so to Westmorland, as Firbank Chapel, where John Blakelin came with him; and so on to Preston, Grayrigg, Kendal, Underbarrow, Poolbank, Cartmell, and Stavely; and so on to Swarthmore, my dwelling-house, whither he brought the blessed tidings of the everlasting gospel, which I, and many hundreds in these parts, have cause to praise the Lord for. My then husband, Thomas Fell, was not at home at that time, but gone to the Welsh circuit, being one of the judges of assize; and our house being a place open to entertain ministers and religious people at, one of George Fox's friends brought him hither, where he stayed all night. The next day being a lecture, or a fast-day, he went to Ulverstone steeple-house, but came not in till people were gathered; I and my children had been a long time there before. And when they were singing before the sermon, he came in; and when they had done singing, he stood up upon a seat or form, and desired that he might have liberty to speak; and he that was in the pulpit said he might. And the first words that he spoke were as followeth: "He is not a Jew that is one outward; neither is that circumcision which is outward: but he is a Jew that is one inward; and that is circumcision which is of the heart." And so he went on, and said, how that Christ was the Light of the world, and lighteth every man that cometh into the world; and that by this Light they might be gathered to God, &c. I stood up in my pew and wondered at his doctrine; for I had never heard such before. And then he went on, and opened the Scriptures, and said, "the Scriptures were the prophets' words, and Christ's and the apostles' words, and what, as they spoke, they enjoyed and possessed, and had it from the Lord:" and said, "then what had any to do with the Scriptures, but as they came to the Spirit that gave them forth. You will say, Christ saith this, and the apostles say this; but what canst thou say? Art thou a child of Light, and hast thou walked in the Light, and what thou speakest, is it inwardly from God?" &c. This opened me so, that it cut me to the heart; and then I saw clearly we were all wrong. So I sat down in my pew again, and cried bitterly: and I cried in my spirit to the Lord, "We are all thieves; we are all thieves; we have taken the Scriptures in words, and know nothing of them in ourselves." So that served me, that I cannot well tell what he spoke afterwards; but he went on in declaring against the false prophets, and priests, and deceivers of the people. And there was one John Sawrey, a justice of peace, and a professor, that bid the churchwarden take him away; and he laid his hands on him several times, and took them off again, and let him alone; and then after a while he gave over, and came to our house again that night. And he spoke in the family amongst the servants, and they were all generally convinced; as William Caton, Thomas Salthouse, Mary Askew, Anne Clayton, and several other servants. And I was struck into such a sadness, I knew not what to do, my husband being from home. I saw it was the truth, and I could not deny it; and I did as the apostle saith, "I received the truth in the love of it:" and it was opened to me so clear, that I had never a tittle in my heart against it; but I desired the Lord that I might be kept in it; and then I desired no greater portion.

Then he went on to Dalton, Aldingham, Dendrum, and Ramside chapels and steeple-houses, and several places up and down, and the people followed him mightily; and abundance were convinced, and saw that what he spoke was truth; but the priests were all in a rage. About two weeks after, James Naylor and Richard Farnsworth followed him, and inquired him out, till they came to Swarthmore, and there stayed a while with me at our house, and did me much good, for I was under great heaviness and judgment. But the power of the Lord entered upon me within about two weeks that he came; and about three weeks' end my husband came home; and many were in a mighty rage. And a deal of the captains and great ones of the country went to meet my then husband as he was coming home, and informed him "that a great disaster was befallen amongst his family, and that they were witches; and that they had taken us out of our religion; and that he might either set them away, or all the country would be undone." But no weapon formed against the Lord shall prosper, as you may see hereafter.

So my husband came home greatly offended: and any may think what a condition I was like to be in, that either I must displease my husband, or offend God; for he was very much troubled with us all in the house and family, they had so prepossessed him against us. But James Naylor and Richard Farnsworth were both then at our house, and I desired them to come and speak to him, and so they did, very moderately and wisely; but he was at first displeased with them, till they told him they came in love and good-will to his house. And after that he had heard them speak a while, he was better satisfied; and they offered as if they would go away; but I desired them to stay, and not to go away yet, for George Fox will come this evening. And I would have had my husband to have heard them all, and satisfied himself farther about them; because they had so prepossessed him against them of such dangerous, fearful things, in his coming first home. And then was he pretty moderate and quiet; and his dinner being ready, he went to it; and I went in, and sat me down by him. And whilst I was sitting, the power of the Lord seized upon me; and he was struck with amazement, and knew not what to think; but was quiet and still. And the children were all quiet and still, and grown sober, and could not play on their music that they were learning: and all these things made him quiet and still.

At night George Fox came: and after supper my husband was sitting in the parlour, and I asked him, if George Fox might come in; and he said, Yes. So George came in without any compliment, and walked into the room, and began to speak presently; and the family, and James Naylor, and Richard Farnsworth came all in: and he spoke very excellently as ever I heard him, and opened Christ's and the apostles' practices, which they were in, in their day. And he opened the night of apostasy since the apostles' days, and laid open the priests and their practices in the apostasy; that if all in England had been there, I thought they could not have denied the truth of those things. And so my husband came to see clearly the truth of what he spoke, and was very quiet that night, said no more, and went to bed. The next morning came Lampitt, priest of Ulverstone, and got my husband into the garden, and spoke much to him there; but my husband had seen so much the night before, that the priest got little entrance upon him. And when the priest Lampitt was come into the house, George spoke sharply to him, and asked him "when God spoke to him, and called him to go and preach to the people?" but after a while the priest went away: this was on a sixth day of the week, about the fifth month, 1652. And at our house divers Friends were speaking one to another, how there were several convinced hereaways; and we could not tell where to get a meeting: my husband also being present, he overheard, and said of his own accord, "You may meet here, if you will:" and that was the first meeting we had that he offered of his own accord. And then notice was given that day and the next to Friends, and there was a good large meeting the first day, which was the first meeting that was at Swarthmore; and so continued there a meeting from 1652 till 1690. And my husband went that day to the steeple-house, and none with him but his clerk and his groom that rode with him; and the priest and people were all fearfully troubled: but praised be the Lord, they never got their wills upon us to this day.

After a few weeks George went to Ulverstone steeple-house again, and the said Justice Sawrey, with others, set the rude rabble upon him; and they beat him so that he fell down as in a swoon, and was sore bruised and blackened in his body, and on his head and arms. Then my husband was not at home; but when he came home he was displeased that they should do so; and spoke to Justice Sawrey, and said it was against law to make riots. And after that he was sore beat and stoned at Walney, till he fell down; and also at Dalton was he sore beat and abused; so that he had very hard usage in divers places in those parts. And then when a meeting was settled there, he went again into Westmorland, and settled meetings there; and there was a great convincement, and abundance of brave ministers came out thereaways, as John Camm, John Audland, Francis Howgill, Edward Burrough, Miles Halhead, and John Blakelin, with divers others. He also went over the sands to Lancaster, and Yealand, and Kellet, where Robert Widders, Richard Hubberthorn, and John Lawson, with many others, were convinced. And about that time he was in those parts, many priests and professors rose up, and falsely accused him of blasphemy, and did endeavour to take away his life; and got people to swear at a sessions at Lancaster that he had spoken blasphemy. But my then husband and Colonel West, having had some sight and knowledge of the truth, withstood the two persecuting justices, John Sawrey and Thompson, and brought him off, and cleared him; for indeed he was innocent. And after the sessions there was a great meeting in the town of Lancaster; and many of the town's-people came in, and many were convinced. And thus he was up and down about Lancaster, Yealand, Westmorland, and some parts of Yorkshire, and our parts above one year; in which time there were above twenty-four ministers brought forth, that were ready to go with their testimony of the Eternal Truth unto the world; and soon after Francis Howgill and John Camm went to speak to Oliver Cromwell.

In the year 1653, George's drawings were into Cumberland, by Millom, Lamplugh, Embleton, and Brigham, Pardshaw, and Cockermouth, where at or near Embleton he had a dispute with some priests, as Larkham and Benson; but chiefly with John Wilkinson, a preacher at Embleton and Brigham, who was afterwards convinced, and owned the Truth, and was a serviceable minister both in England, Ireland, and Scotland. Then he went to Coldbeck and several places, till he came to Carlisle, and went to their steeple-house; there they beat and abused him, and had him before the magistrates, who examined him, and put him in prison in the common jail among the thieves. At the assizes was one Anthony Pearson, who had been a justice of peace, and was convinced at Appleby (when he was upon the bench) by James Naylor and Francis Howgill, who were then prisoners there, and brought before him; so Anthony Pearson spoke to the justices at Carlisle, he being acquainted with them, having married his wife out of Cumberland; and after a while they released him. Afterwards he went into several parts of Cumberland, and many were convinced, and owned the Truth; and he gathered and settled meetings there amongst them, and up and down in several parts in the North.

In the year 1654, he went southward to his own country of Leicestershire, visiting Friends. And then Colonel Hacker sent him to Oliver Cromwell; and after having been kept prisoner a while, he was brought before Oliver, and released. He then stayed a while, visiting Friends in London, and the meetings therein; and so passed westward to Bristol, and visited Friends there. He afterwards went into Cornwall, where they put him in prison at Launceston, and one Edward Pyot with him, where he had a bad, long imprisonment. When he was released, he passed into many parts in that county of Cornwall, and settled meetings there. Then he travelled through many counties, visiting Friends and settling meetings all along; and so came into the North, and to Swarthmore, and to Cumberland.

And so for Scotland he passed in the year 1657, and there went with him Robert Widders, James Lancaster, John Grave, and others. He travelled through many places in that nation, as Douglas, Heads, Hamilton, Glasgow, and to Edinburgh, where they took him, and carried him before General Monk and the council, and examined him, and asked him his business into that nation; who answered, he came to visit the seed of God. And after they had threatened him, and charged him to depart their nation of Scotland, they let him go. Then he went to Linlithgow, and Stirling, and Johnstone, and many places, visiting the people; and several were convinced. And after he had stayed a pretty while, and settled some meetings, he returned into Northumberland, and into the bishopric of Durham, visiting Friends and settling meetings as he went; and then returned back again to Swarthmore, and stayed amongst Friends a while, and so returned south again. In 1658, Judge Fell died.

In 1660 he came out of the South into the North, and had a great general meeting about Balby in Yorkshire; and so came on, visiting Friends in many places, till he came to Swarthmore again. And King Charles then being come in, the justices sent out warrants, and took him at Swarthmore, charging him in their warrants, that he drew away the king's liege people, to the endangering the embruing the nation in blood; and sent him prisoner to Lancaster castle. And I having a great family, and he being taken in my house, I was moved of the Lord to go to the king at Whitehall; and took with me a declaration, and an information of our principles, and a long time, and much ado I had, to get to him. But at last, when I got to him, I told him if he was guilty of those things, I was guilty, for he was taken in my house; and I gave him the paper of our principles, and desired that he would set him at liberty, as he had promised that none should suffer for tender consciences; and we were of tender consciences, and desired nothing but the liberty of our consciences. Then with much ado, after he had been kept prisoner near half a year at Lancaster, we got a *habeas corpus*, and removed him to the king's bench, where he was released. And then would I gladly have come home to my great family, but was bound in my spirit, and could not have freedom to get away for a whole year. The king had promised me several times that we should have our liberty, but then the Monarchy-men rose; and then came the great and general imprisonment of Friends the nation through; and so could I not have freedom nor liberty to come home, till we had got a general proclamation for all our Friends' liberty. Then I had freedom and peace to come home.

In 1663 he came North again, and to Swarthmore. Then they sent out warrants, and took him again; and had him to Holcrof before the justices, who tendered him the oath of allegiance, and sent him prisoner to Lancaster castle. And about a month after, the justices sent for me also out of my house, and tendered me the oath, and sent me prisoner to Lancaster. And the next assizes they again tendered the oath of allegiance and supremacy to us both, and premunired me; but they had missed the date, and other things in the indictment, and so it was quashed; but they tendered him the oath again, and kept him prisoner a year and a half at Lancaster castle. And then they sent him to Scarbro' castle in Yorkshire, where they kept him prisoner close under the soldiers much of a year and a half, so that a Friend could scarcely have spoken to him; yet after that, it pleased the Lord that he was released; but I continued in prison, and a prisoner four years at that time; and an order was procured from the council, whereby I was set at liberty. And in that time I went down into Cornwall with my son and daughter Lower, and came back by London to the Yearly Meeting; and there I met with him again; and then he told me the time was drawing on towards our marriage, but he might first go into Ireland. And a little before this time was he prisoner in his own country at Leicester for a while, and then released. So into Ireland he went, and I went into Kent and Sussex, and came back to London again; and afterwards I went to the West, towards Bristol, in 1669, and there I stayed till he came over from Ireland, which was eleven years after my former husband's decease. In Ireland he had had a great service for the Lord and his eternal truth, amongst Friends and many people there, but escaped many dangers, and times of being taken prisoner, they having laid in wait aforehand for him in many places. And then he being returned, at Bristol he declared his intentions of marriage; and there also was our marriage solemnized. Within ten days after I came homewards, but my husband stayed up and down in the countries amongst Friends, visiting them.

Soon after I came home, there came another order from the council to cast me into prison again; and the sheriff of Lancashire sent his bailiff, and pulled me out of my own house, and had me prisoner to Lancaster castle (upon the old premunire), where I continued a whole year, and most part of that time was I sick and weakly; my husband also was weak and sickly at that time. After a while he recovered, and went about to get me out of prison, and a discharge at last was got under the great seal; and so I was set at liberty. Then I was to go up to London again, for my husband was intending for America. He was full two years away, before he came back again into England; and having arrived at Bristol, he came thence to London, intending to come to the middle of the nation with me; but when we came into some parts of Worcestershire, they got there information of him; and one Justice Parker, by his warrant, sent him and my son Lower to Worcester jail. The justices there tendered him the oath, and premunired him, but released my son Lower, who stayed with him most of the time he was prisoner there.

After some time he fell sick, in a long, lingering sickness, and many times was very ill; so they writ to me from London, that if I would see him alive, I might go to him; which accordingly I did. After I had tarried seventeen weeks with him at Worcester, and no discharge likely to be obtained for him, I went up to London, and wrote to the king an account of his long imprisonment, and how he was taken in his travel homewards, and that he was weak and sick, and not likely to live if they kept him long there. I went with it to Whitehall myself, where I met with the king and gave him the paper; and he said, I must go to the chancellor, he could do nothing in it. Then I wrote also to the lord chancellor, and went to his house, gave him my paper, and spoke to him, that the king had left it wholly to him; and if he did not take pity and release him out of that prison, I feared he would end his days there. The Lord Chancellor Finch was a very tender man, and spoke to the judge, who gave out an *habeas corpus* presently. When we got it we sent it down to Worcester, and they would not part with him at first, but said he was premunired, and was not to go out on that manner. Then we were forced to go to Judge North, and to the attorney-general, and we got another order, and sent down from them; and with much ado, and great labour and industry of William Mead and other friends, we got him up to

London, where he appeared in Westminster Hall at the king's bench, before Judge Hale, who was a very honest, tender man; and he knew they had imprisoned him but in envy. So that which they had against him was read, and our counsel pleaded that he was taken up in his travel and journey. And there was but a little said till he was acquitted. This was the last prison that he was in, being freed by the court of king's bench.

When he was at liberty he recovered again; and then I was very desirous to go home with him, which we did. This was the first time that he came to Swarthmore after we were married; and he stayed here much of two years, and then went to London again to the Yearly Meeting; and after a while went into Holland, and some parts of Germany, where he stayed a pretty while, and then returned to London again at the next Yearly Meeting. And after he had stayed a while in and about London, he came into the North to Swarthmore again, and stayed that time near two years; and then he grew weakly, being troubled with pains and aches, having had many sore and long travels, beatings, and hard imprisonments. But after some time he rode to York, and so passed on through Nottinghamshire and several counties, visiting Friends, till he came to London to the Yearly Meeting, and stayed there, and thereaways, till he finished his course, and laid down his head in peace.

And though the Lord had provided an outward habitation for him, yet he was not willing to stay at it, because it was so remote and far from London, where his service most lay. And my concern for God, and his holy eternal truth, was then in the North, where God had placed and sent me, and likewise for the ordering and governing of my children and family; so that we were very willing both of us, to live apart for some years upon God's account, and his truth's service, and to deny ourselves of that comfort which we might have had in being together, for the sake and service of the Lord and his truth. And if any took occasion, or judged hard of us because of that, the Lord will judge them; for we were innocent. And for my own part, I was willing to take many long journeys, for taking away all occasion of evil thoughts; and though I lived two hundred miles from London, yet have I been nine times there, upon the Lord and his truth's account; and of all the times that I was at London, this last time was most comfortable, that the Lord was pleased to give me strength and ability to travel that great journey, being seventy-six years of age, to see my dear husband, who was better in his health and strength than many times I had seen him before. I look upon it, that the Lord's special hand was in it, that I should go then, for he lived but about half a year after I left him; which makes me admire the wisdom and goodness of God, in ordering my journey at that time.

And now he hath finished his course, and his testimony, and is entered into his eternal rest and felicity. I trust in the same powerful God, that his holy arm and power will carry me through, whatever he hath yet for me to do; and that he will be my strength and support, and the bearer up of my head unto the end, and in the end. For I know his faithfulness and goodness, and I have experience of his love; to whom be glory and powerful dominion for ever. Amen. M. F.

TESTIMONY OF SOME OF THE AUTHOR'S RELATIONS.

Neither days nor length of time with us can wear out the memory of our dear and honoured father, George Fox, whom the Lord hath taken to himself. And though his earthly house of this tabernacle be dissolved, and mortality put off, yet we believe he has a "building with God eternally in the heavens, and is entered into rest," as a reward to those great labours, hard sufferings, and sore trials he patiently endured for God and his truth. Of which truth he was made an able minister, and one, if not the first promulgator of it in our age; who, though of no great literature, nor seeming much learned, as to the outward (being hid from the wisdom of this world), yet he had the tongue of the learned, and could speak a word in due season to the conditions and capacities of most, especially to them that were weary, and wanted soul's rest; being deep in the divine mysteries of the kingdom of God. And the word of life and salvation through him reached unto many souls, whereby many were convinced of their great duty of inward retiring to wait upon God; and as they became diligent in the performance of that service, were also raised up to be preachers of the same everlasting gospel of peace and glad tidings to others; who are as seals to his ministry both in this and other nations, and may possibly give a more full account thereof. Howbeit we knowing his unwearied diligence, not sparing, but spending himself in the work and service whereunto he was chosen and called of God, could not but give this short testimony of his faithfulness therein, and likewise of his tender love and care towards us; who, as a tender father to his children (in which capacity we stood, being so related unto him), never failed to give us his wholesome counsel and advice. And not only so, but, as a father in Christ, he took care of the whole family and household of faith, which the Lord had made him an eminent overseer of, and endued him with an excellent spirit of wisdom and understanding, to propose and direct such helps and advantages to the well-ordering and establishing of affairs and government in the church, as now are found very serviceable thereunto; and have greatly disappointed and prevented the false, loose, and libertine spirit of some who, to their own confusion, have endeavoured, by separation and division, to disturb the church's peace. And although many of that sort have at sundry times shot their poisonous darts at him, publicly in print, and privately other ways, yet he has been always preserved by the heavenly power of God, out of the reach of their envy, and all perils and difficulties that attended on their account; who, as a fixed star in the firmament of God's power, did constantly abide, and held his integrity to the last, being of a sweet, savoury life; and as to conversation, kept his garments clean: and though outwardly dead, yet he liveth, and his memory is right precious unto us; as it is and will be to all that abide in the love of truth, and have not declined the way of it. For he was one of the Lord's worthies, valiant for the truth upon earth, not turning his back in the day of battle; but his bow still abiding in its strength, he, through many hardships, brought gladness and refreshment to Israel's camp, being assisted by the might of that power that always put the armies of aliens and enemies to flight. And now having finished his course, he is removed from us into a glorious state of immortality and bliss, and is gathered unto the Lord as a shock of corn in its full season, and to that habitation of safety where the wicked cease from troubling and the weary are at rest.

JOHN ROUS,	MARGARET ROUS,
WILLIAM MEAD,	SARAH MEAD,
THOMAS LOWER,	MARY LOWER,
WILLIAM INGRAM,	SUSANNA INGRAM,
DANIEL ABRAHAM,	RACHEL ABRAHAM,
ABRAHAM MORRICE,	ISABEL MORRICE.

AN EPISTLE BY WAY OF TESTIMONY,

TO FRIENDS AND BRETHREN OF THE MONTHLY AND QUARTERLY MEETINGS IN ENGLAND, WALES, AND ELSEWHERE, CONCERNING THE DECEASE OF OUR FAITHFUL BROTHER, GEORGE FOX.

From our Second-day's Morning-Meeting in London, the 26th of the 11th Month, 1690.

DEAR and truly beloved friends, brethren and sisters in Christ Jesus, our blessed Lord and Saviour, we sincerely and tenderly salute you all in his free and tender love wherewith he hath graciously visited us, and largely shed it abroad in our hearts and souls, to our own unspeakable comfort and consolation, and towards his whole heritage and royal offspring; blessed be his pure and powerful name for evermore. And our souls do truly and fervently desire, and breathe unto the God of all our mercies, that you all may be preserved, and kept truly faithful and diligent in his work and service, according to your heavenly calling and endowments with his light, grace, and truth, unto the end of your days; as being livingly engaged thereby all your appointed time to serve him, and to wait till your change come; that none may neglect that true improvement of your times and talents, that God has afforded you here, for your eternal advantage hereafter, in that inheritance and life immortal that never fades away. And that the whole flock and heritage of Christ Jesus, which he has purchased and bought for himself with a price incorruptible, may always be so preserved in his own pure love and life, as to grow, increase, and prosper in the same; and thereby be kept in love, unity, and peace with one another, as becomes his faithful and true followers, is that which our very hearts and souls desire, being often truly comforted and enlarged in the living sense and feeling of the increase and aboundings thereof, among faithful friends and brethren.

And, dear brethren and sisters, unto this our tender salutation we are concerned, in brotherly love and true tender-heartedness, to add and impart unto you some account of the decease of our dear and elder brother in Christ, namely, His and His church's true and faithful servant and minister, George Fox; whom it hath pleased the Lord to take unto himself, as he hath divers others of his faithful servants and ministers of late time; who have faithfully served out their generation, and finished their testimony and course with joy and peace. Howbeit, O dear brethren and friends! that so many worthies in Israel, and serviceable instruments in the Lord's hand, are of late taken away and removed from us so soon one after another, appears a dispensation that deeply and sorrowfully affects us, and many more whose hearts are upright and tender towards God, and one to another in the truth. The consideration of the depth, weight, and meaning thereof is very weighty upon our spirits, though their precious life and testimony live with us, as being of that same body, united to one head, even Christ Jesus; in which we still, and hope ever shall, have secret comfort and union with them, whom the Lord has removed and taken to himself, out of their earthly tabernacles and houses into their heavenly and everlasting mansions.

This, our said dear brother, George Fox, was enabled, by the Lord's power, to preach the truth fully and effectually in our public meeting in White-Hart Court, by Gracechurch Street, London, on the 11th day of this instant 11th month, 1690: after which he said, "I am glad I was here; now I am clear, I am fully clear." Then he was the same day taken with some illness or indisposition of body more than usual; and continued weak in body for two days after, at our friend Henry Goldney's house, in the same court, close by the meeting-house, in much contentment and peace, and very sensible to the last. In which time he mentioned divers Friends, and sent for some in particular; to whom he expressed his mind for the spreading of Friends' books and truth in the world, and through the nations thereof; as his spirit in the Lord's love and power was universally set and bent for truth and righteousness, and the making known the way thereof to the nations and people afar off: signifying also to some Friends, "that all is well; and the Seed of God reigns over all, and over death itself: that though he was weak in body, yet that the power of God is over all, and the Seed reigns over all disorderly spirits;" which were his wonted sensible expressions, being in the living faith and sense thereof, which he kept to the end. And on the 13th instant, between the ninth and tenth hour in the night, he quietly departed this life in peace; being two days after the Lord enabled him to publish and preach the blessed truth in the meeting as aforesaid. So that he clearly and evidently ended his days in his faithful testimony, in perfect love and unity with his brethren, and peace and good-will to all men; being about sixty and six years of age (as we understand) when he departed this life.

And on the 16th of this instant, being the day appointed for his funeral, a very great concourse of Friends and people assembled at our meeting-house in White-Hart Court aforesaid, about the mid-day, in order to attend his body to our burying-place, near Bunhill-Fields, to be interred, as Friends' last office of love and respect due on that account. The meeting was held about two hours, with great and heavenly solemnity, manifestly attended with the Lord's blessed power and presence; and divers living testimonies given, from a lively remembrance and sense of this his dear ancient servant, his blessed ministry and testimony of the breaking forth of this gospel-day; his innocent life, long and great travels, and labours of love in the everlasting gospel, for the turning and gathering many thousands from darkness to the light of Christ Jesus, the foundation of true faith; also of his manifold sufferings, afflictions, and oppositions, which he met withal for his faithful testimony, both from his open adversaries and false brethren; and his preservations, dominion, and deliverances out of them all by the power of God; to whom the glory and honour was and is ascribed, in raising up and preserving this his faithful witness and minister to the end of his days; whose blessed memorial will everlastingly remain.

He loved truth and righteousness, and bore faithful testimony against deceit and falsehood, and the mystery of iniquity; and often, of late time especially, warned

Friends against covetousness, earthly-mindedness, against getting into the earth, and into a brittle spirit; and the younger sort, against looseness and pride of life, &c.

A few days before he died, he had a great concern upon his mind concerning some in whom the Lord's power was working, to lead them into a ministry and testimony to his truth; who, through their too much entangling themselves in the things of this world, did make themselves unready to answer the call and leadings of the power of God, and hurt the gift that was bestowed upon them, and did not take that regard to their service and ministry as they ought; and mentioned the apostle's exhortation to Timothy, to "take heed to his ministry, and to show himself approved," &c.: and expressed his grief concerning such as preferred their own business before the Lord's business, and sought the advancing worldly concerns before the concerns of truth: and concluded with a tender and fatherly exhortation to all to whom God had imparted of his heavenly treasure, that they would improve it faithfully, and be diligent in the Lord's work, that the earth might be sown with the Seed of the kingdom, and God's harvest might be minded by those whom he had called and enabled to labour therein: and that such would commit the care of their outward concerns to the Lord, who would care for them, and give a blessing to them. However, this is not mentioned to encourage any to run unsent, or without being called of God.

Many are living witnesses that the Lord raised him up by his power, to proclaim his mighty day to the nations, and made him an effectual instrument in our day to turn many from darkness to light, and from Satan's power to God; and freely to suffer and bear all reproaches, and the manifold persecutions, buffetings, halings, stonings, imprisonments, and cruelties, that were in the beginning, and for some time inflicted on him and others, for the name of Christ Jesus. He was in his testimony as a fixed star in the firmament of God's power, where all that be truly wise, and that turn many to righteousness, shall shine as the brightness of the firmament, and as the stars, for ever and ever. He knew and preached the mystery of Christ revealed, the life and substance, and the power of godliness, above all shadows and forms. The Lord endued him with a hidden wisdom and life. He loved peace, and earnestly laboured for universal love, unity, peace, and good order in the churches of Christ; and wherever he met with the contrary, it was his great grief and burthen. He was greatly for the encouragement of faithful labourers in the Lord's work; and it was a great offence and grief to him to have their testimony weakened, or labours slighted, through prejudice in any professing truth.

And inasmuch as the Lord suffered him not to be delivered up to the will of his enemies and persecutors, who often heretofore breathed out cruelty against him, and designed his destruction; but in his good pleasure so fairly and quietly took him away in his own time, when his testimony was so blessedly finished, and his work accomplished: this is all remarkable, and worthy of serious and due observation, as being by a special and Divine Providence and wisdom of God; to whom we ascribe the glory of all, and not unto man or creatures. Though we must needs allow, and own, that good report and due esteem, which faithful elders, ministers, and servants of God and Christ have by faith obtained, to the praise of that blessed Power that upheld them in every age in their day; many whereof are even of late taken away from the evil to come, and are at rest in the Lord, out of the reach of all envy and persecution, where the wicked cannot trouble them any more.

And we must patiently bear our parting with them, and our loss and sorrow on that account, with respect to their unspeakable gain; yet how can we avoid being deeply affected with sadness of spirit, and brokenness of heart, under the sense and consideration of such loss and revolutions, which we have cause to believe are ominous of calamities to the wicked world, though of good to the righteous? Did the death of plain upright Jacob, namely, Israel (who was as a prince of God), so deeply affect both his own children and kindred, as that they made a great and exceeding sore lamentation for him; and even the Egyptians also, that they bewailed him seventy days? and the death of Moses so deeply affect the children of Israel, as that they "did weep and mourn for him in the plain of Moab thirty days?" and the death of Stephen, that faithful martyr of Jesus, so deeply affect certain men, fearing God, as "that they made great lamentation for him?" and the apostle Paul, when taking his leave of the elders of the church of Ephesus, and telling them, "they should see his face no more?" If this did so deeply affect them, that they "wept all abundantly, sorrowing most of all for these words, that they should see his face no more;" with many more of this kind; how then can we otherwise choose, but be deeply affected with sorrow and sadness of heart, though not as those who have no hope, when so many of our ancient, dear, and faithful brethren, with whom we have had much sweet society, are removed from us one after another? (We pray God raise up and increase more such!) Yet must we all contentedly submit to the good pleasure and wisdom of the Lord our God in all these things; who taketh away, and none can hinder him, nor may any say unto him, What doest thou? Yet we have cause to bless the Lord that he hath of late raised, and is raising up, more to publish his name in the earth. And we that yet remain have but a short time to stay after them that are gone; but we shall be gone to them also. The Lord God of life keep us all faithful in his holy truth, love, unity, and life, to the end. He hath a great work still to bring forth in the earth, and great things to bring to pass, in order to make way for truth and righteousness to take place therein; and that his seed may come forth and be gathered, and the power and kingdom of our God and of his Christ made known and exalted in the earth unto the ends thereof.

Dear Friends and brethren, be faithful till death, that a crown of life you may obtain. All dwell in the love of God in Christ Jesus, in union and peace in him; to whom we tenderly commit you to keep and strengthen you, bless and preserve you, to the end of your days. In whose dear and tender love we remain,

Your dear friends and brethren,

STEPHEN CRISP,	NICHOLAS GATES,	DANIEL MONRO,
GEO. WHITEHEAD,	FRANCIS STAMPER,	JOHN HEYWOOD,
FRA. CAMFIELD,	JOHN VAUGHTON,	GEORGE BOWLES,
JAMES PARK,	GILBERT LATEY,	WILLIAM ROBINSON,
JOHN ELSON,	CHARLES MARSHALL,	WILLIAM BINGLEY,
PETER PRICE,	RICH. NEEDHAM,	JOHN BUTCHER,
JOHN FIELD,	JAMES MARTIN,	BENJAMIN ANTROBUS.
JOHN EDRIDGE,		

These names are since added, at the desire of the persons following:—

AMB. RIGG, SAM. GOODAKER, WILLIAM FALLOWFIELD.

P.S.—Before his death he wrote a little paper, desiring all Friends, everywhere, that used to write to him about the sufferings and affairs of Friends in their several countries, should henceforth write to their several correspondents in London, to be communicated to the Second-day's meeting, to take care that they be answered.

THOMAS ELLWOOD'S ACCOUNT OF THAT EMINENT AND HONOURABLE SERVANT OF THE LORD, GEORGE FOX.

(It was Thomas Ellwood who first transcribed this Journal for the press. See Note at p. 11, vol. ii.)

THIS holy man was raised up by God in an extraordinary manner, for an extraordinary work, even to awaken the sleeping world, by proclaiming the mighty day of the Lord to the nations, and publishing again the everlasting gospel to the inhabitants of the earth, after the long and dismal night of apostasy and darkness. For this work the Lord began to prepare him by many and various trials and exercises from his very childhood; and having fitted and furnished him for it, he called him into it very young, and made him instrumental, by the effectual working of the Holy Ghost, through his ministry, to call many others into the same work, and to turn many thousands from darkness to the light of Christ, and from the power of Satan unto God.

I knew him not till the year 1660; from that time to the time of his death I knew him well, conversed with him often, observed him much, loved him dearly, and honoured him truly; and upon good experience can say, he was indeed a heavenly-minded man, zealous for the name of the Lord, and preferred the honour of God before all things. He was valiant for the truth, bold in asserting it, patient in suffering for it, unwearied in labouring in it, steady in his testimony to it; immovable as a rock. Deep he was in divine knowledge, clear in opening heavenly mysteries, plain and powerful in preaching, fervent in prayer. He was richly endued with heavenly wisdom, quick in discerning, sound in judgment, able and ready in giving, discreet in keeping counsel; a lover of righteousness, an encourager of virtue, justice, temperance, meekness, purity, chastity, modesty, humility, charity, and self-denial in all, both by word and example. Graceful he was in countenance, manly in personage, grave in gesture, courteous in conversation, weighty in communication, instructive in discourse, free from affectation in speech or carriage; a severe reprover of hard and obstinate sinners; a mild and gentle admonisher of such as were tender, and sensible of their failings; not apt to resent personal wrongs; easy to forgive injuries; but zealously earnest, where the honour of God, the prosperity of truth, the peace of the church, were concerned; very tender, compassionate, and pitiful he was to all that were under any sort of affliction; full of brotherly love, full of fatherly care; for, indeed, the care of the churches of Christ was daily upon him, the prosperity and peace whereof he studiously sought. Beloved he was of God; beloved of God's people; and (which was not the least part of his honour) the common butt of all apostates' envy; whose good, notwithstanding, he earnestly sought.

He lived to see the desire of his soul, the spreading of that blessed principle of divine light, through many of the European nations, and not a few of the American islands and provinces, and the gathering many thousands into an establishment therein; which the Lord vouchsafed him the honour to be the first effectual publisher of, in this latter age of the world. And having fought a good fight, finished his course, and kept the faith, his righteous soul, freed from the earthly tabernacle, in which he had led an exemplary life of holiness, was translated into those heavenly mansions, where Christ our Lord went to prepare a place for his; there to possess that glorious crown of righteousness, which is laid up for, and shall be given by the Lord the righteous judge to all them that love his appearance.

Ages to come and people yet unborn shall call him blessed, and bless the Lord for raising him up. And blessed shall we also be, if we so walk, as we had him for an example; for whom this Testimony lives in my heart, "He lived and died the SERVANT of the LORD." T. E.

AN EPISTLE OF GEORGE FOX'S,

WRITTEN WITH HIS OWN HAND, AND LEFT SEALED UP WITH THIS SUPERSCRIPTION, VIZ., "NOT TO BE OPENED BEFORE THE TIME;" WHICH AFTER HIS DECEASE BEING OPENED, WAS THOUGHT MEET TO BE PRINTED, VIZ.:—

"*For the Yearly and Second-day's Meeting in London, and to all the Children of God in all places in the world. By and from G. F.*

"This for all the children of God everywhere, who are led by his Spirit, and walk in his Light, in which they have life, unity, and fellowship with the Father, and the Son, and one with another.

"KEEP all your meetings in the name of the Lord Jesus, that be gathered in his name by his Light, Grace, Truth, Power, and Spirit; by which you will feel his blessed and refreshing presence among you, and in you, to your comfort, and God's glory.

"And now, Friends, all your meetings, both men's and women's, monthly, quarterly, and yearly, &c., were set up by the power, and Spirit, and wisdom of God; and in them you know, that you have felt his power, and Spirit, and wisdom, and blessed refreshing presence among you, and in you, to his praise and glory, and your comfort; so that you have been 'a city set on a hill, that cannot be hid.'

"And although many loose and unruly spirits have risen betimes to oppose you and them, in print and other ways, you have seen how they have come to nought. The Lord hath blasted them, brought their deeds to light, and made them manifest to be trees without fruit, wells without water, wandering stars from the firmament of God's power, and raging waves of the sea, casting up their mire and dirt; and many of them are like the dog turned to his old vomit, and the sow that was washed, turned again to the mire. This hath been the condition of many, God knoweth, and his people!

"Therefore all stand steadfast in Christ Jesus, your Head, in whom you are all one, male and female, and know His government, of the increase of whose government and peace there shall be no end; but there will be an end of the devil's, and of all that are out of Christ, who oppose it and him, whose judgment doth not linger, and their damnation doth not slumber. Therefore in God and Christ's light, life, Spirit, and power, live and walk, that is over all (and the seed of it) in love, in innocency, and simplicity. In righteousness and holiness dwell, and in his power and Holy Ghost, in which God's kingdom doth stand. All children of New and Heavenly Jerusalem, that is from above, and is free, with all her holy, spiritual children, to her keep your eyes.

"As for this spirit of rebellion and opposition, that hath risen formerly and lately, it is out of the kingdom of God and Heavenly Jerusalem; and is for judgment and condemnation, with all its books, words, and works. Therefore Friends are to live and walk in the power and Spirit of God, that is over it, and in the Seed, that will bruise and break it to pieces. In which Seed you have joy and peace with God, and power and authority to judge it; and your unity is in the power and Spirit of God, that doth judge it: all God's witnesses in his tabernacle go out against it, and always have and will.

"Let no man live to self, but to the Lord, as they will die in him; and seek the peace of the church of Christ, and the peace of all men in him: for 'blessed are the peace-makers.' Dwell in the pure, peaceable, heavenly wisdom of God, that is gentle, and easy to be entreated, that is full of mercy; all striving to be of one mind, heart, soul, and judgment in Christ, having His mind and Spirit dwelling in you, building up one another in the love of God, which doth edify the body of Christ, his church, who is the holy Head thereof. Glory to God through Christ, in this age and all other ages, who is the Rock and Foundation, the Emmanuel, God with us, Amen, over all, the Beginning and the Ending. In Him live and walk, in whom you have life eternal; in whom you will feel me, and I you.

"All children of New Jerusalem, that descends from above, the holy city, which the Lord and the Lamb is the light of, and is the temple; in it they are born again of the Spirit; so Jerusalem that is above, is the mother of them that are born of the Spirit. They that come, and are come to heavenly Jerusalem, receive Christ; and he giveth them power to become the sons of God, and they are born again of the Spirit; so Jerusalem that is above is their mother. Such come to heavenly Mount Sion, and the innumerable company of angels, to the spirits of just men made perfect; and to the church of the Living God written in heaven, and have the name of God, and of the city of God, written upon them. So here is a new mother, that bringeth forth a heavenly and spiritual generation.

"There is no schism, no division, no contention, nor strife, in heavenly Jerusalem, nor in the body of Christ, which is made up of living stones, a spiritual house. Christ is not divided, for in Him there is peace. Christ saith, 'In me you have peace.' And He is from above, and not of this world; but in the world below, in the spirit of it, there is trouble: therefore keep in Christ, and walk in Him. Amen.

"Jerusalem was the mother of all true Christians before the apostasy; and since the outward Christians are broken into many sects, they have got many mothers: but all they that are come out of the apostasy by the power and Spirit of Christ, Jerusalem that is above, is their mother (and none below her), who doth nourish all her spiritual children." G. F.

[This epistle was read at the Yearly Meeting in London, 1691.]

THE APPEARANCE OF THE LORD'S EVERLASTING TRUTH,

AND ITS BREAKING FORTH AGAIN IN HIS ETERNAL POWER, IN THIS OUR DAY AND AGE IN ENGLAND—

WHEREIN the Lord's mighty power and word of life hath been richly and freely preached, to the gathering of many into reconciliation with God by it; to the exaltation and glory of the great God, through the bringing forth of the heavenly and spiritual fruits, from such as have been gathered by his eternal light, power, and Spirit, unto himself. And by the sowing to the Spirit in the hearts of people, life eternal hath been reaped; that the flocks have been gathered, which have the milk of the word plenteously; that the riches of the word have flourished, and mightily abounded; and God's heavenly plough with his spiritual men hath gone on cheerfully, to the overturning the fallow ground of the hearts, that had not borne heavenly fruit to God. And God's heavenly thrashers with his heavenly flail, have with joy and delight thrashed out the chaff, and the corruptions, that have been a-top of God's seed and wheat in man and woman. And thus have they thrashed in hope, and are made partakers of their hope, through which God's seed is come into his garner.

O! the unutterable glory, and the inexpressible excellency of the everlasting glorious truth, gospel, and word of life, that the infinite, invisible, and wise God (who is over all), hath revealed and manifested! And how have the professors, priests, and powers risen up in opposition against his children, that are born of the immortal Seed by the word of God! And, O! how great have the persecutions, and reproaches, and spoiling of goods been, that have been executed upon them! But notwithstanding these sufferings from such as have touched them, and do touch them, which are as dear to God as the apple of his eye, how hath the Lord manifested himself to stand by them, in overthrowing powers, priests, and states! What changes have there been since 1644, and 1650, and 1652! How have the jails been filled since then in this nation with the heirs of life, God's chosen ones, who had no helper in the earth but the Lord and his Christ! So that truth's faithful witnesses were scarcely to be found, but in jails and prisons, where the righteous were numbered among the transgressors; who had neither staff nor bag from man, but the staff, the bread of life, and the bag that holds the treasure, that waxes not old. But the Lord Jesus Christ, that sent them forth, was their exceeding great supporter and upholder by his eternal power and Spirit, both then and now.

G. F.

A CHRONOLOGICAL REGISTER OF THE PLACES VISITED BY THE AUTHOR.

1643.—[Vol. I.]
He leaves home and goes to
Lutterworth,
Northampton,
Newport-Pagnell.

1644.
Barnet,
London,
Returns home—goes to
Coventry,
Returns home—goes to
Mancetter.

1645 and 1646.
Tamworth,
Coventry, and other places.

1647.
Derbyshire,
Leicestershire,

Nottinghamshire,
Lancashire,
Duckingfield,
Manchester,
Broughton.

1648.

Nottingham,
Mansfield,
Derbyshire,
Leicestershire,
Warwickshire,
Leicester,
Nottinghamshire,
Vale of Beavor,
Nottinghamshire,
Mansfield,
Eaton, near Derby,
Mansfield,
Nottingham,
Clawson, in Vale of Beavor.

1649.

Nottingham, imprisoned,
Mansfield-Woodhouse,
Leicestershire,
Barrow,
Bagworth,
Coventry,
Atherstone,
Market-Bosworth,
Leicestershire,
Twy-Cross,
Derbyshire,
Chesterfield,
Kidsey-Park.

1650.

Derby, imprisoned a year.

1651.

Leicestershire,
Burton-on-Trent,
Bushel-House,
Lichfield,
Nottinghamshire,
Mansfield,
Derbyshire,
Yorkshire,
Doncaster,
Balby,
Wakefield,
Selby,
Beverley,
Crantsick,
York,
Burraby,
Cleveland,
Stath,
Whitby,
Scarbro',
Malton,
Pickering,
The Moors,
Crantsick,
Holderness,
Oram [suppose Ottringham],
Patrington,
Hull,
Balby,
Nottinghamshire,
Lincolnshire,
Gainsbro',
Yorkshire,
Warmsworth,
Balby,
Doncaster,
Tickhill,
Balby.

1652.

Wakefield,
Hightown,
Bradford,
Pendle-Hill,
Wensleydale,
Hawes,
Grisdale,
Dent,
Sedbergh,
Firbank Chapel,
Preston-Patrick,
Kendal,
Underbarrow,
Crook,
Newton-in-Cartmel,
Lyndale,
Ulverstone,
Swarthmore,
Aldenham,
Ramside,
Swarthmore,
Dalton,
Isle of Walney,
Swarthmore,
Becliffe,
Gleaston,
Swarthmore,
Westmorland,
Kendal,
Grisdale,
Swarthmore,
Underbarrow,
Kellet,
Lancaster,
Kendal,
Underbarrow,
Swarthmore,
Ulverstone,
Swarthmore,
Westmorland,
Crossland,
Lancashire,
Ulverstone,
Swarthmore,
Isle of Walney,
Cockan,
Swarthmore,
Yelland,
Lancaster,
Kellet,
Justice West's,
Swarthmore,
Westmorland,
Grayrig,
Cartmel.

1653.

Swarthmore,
Gleaston,
Lancashire,
Swarthmore,
Arn-Side,
Cumberland,
Col. West's,
Swarthmore,
Cumberland,
Bootle,
Near Cockermouth,
Millom-in-Bootle,
Cockermouth,
Brigham,
Coldbeck,
Carlisle, imprisoned
Coldbeck,
Westmorland,
Strickland-Head,
Swarthmore,
Coldbeck,
Wigton,
Bishoprick,
Northumberland,
Derwent-Water,
Hexham,
Gilsland,
Cumberland,
Langlands,
Brigham.

1654.

Swarthmore,
Lancaster,
Halifax,
T. Taylor's (Brighouse),
Synderhill-Green,
Yorkshire,
Holderness,
Thos. Taylor's (Brighouse),
Balby,
Lincolnshire,
Derbyshire,
Nottinghamshire,
Skegby,
Kidsey-Park,
Peak Country,

Derbyshire,
Swannington,
Twy-Cross,
Warwickshire,
Drayton,
Swannington,
Leicester,
Whetstone,
Harborough,
London,
Theobald's, near Waltham,
Whitehall,
Bedfordshire.

1655.

Luton (John Crook's),
London,
Kent,
Rochester,
Cranbrook,
Rye,
Romney,
Dover,
Canterbury,
Cranbrook,
Sussex,
Horsham,
Steyning,
Reading,
London,
Essex,
Coggeshall,
Colchester,
Ipswich,
Mendlesham,
Norfolk,
Norwich,
Yarmouth,
Lynn,
Sutton, near Isle of Ely,
Cambridge,
Bishop-Stortford,
Hertford,
London,
Bedfordshire,
Northamptonshire,
Wellingborough,
Leicestershire,
Whetstone,
Sileby,
Drayton,
Badgley,
Nottinghamshire,
Derbyshire,
Warwickshire,
Worcestershire,
Birmingham,
Chattan,
Evesham,
Worcester,
Tewkesbury,
Warwick,
Coventry,
Dun-Cow,
Leicestershire,
Badgley,
Swannington,
Higham,
Northamptonshire,
Bedfordshire,
Baldock,
Market Street,
Alban's,
London,
Ryegate,
Binscomb, in Godalming,
Horsham Park,
Arundel,
Chichester,
Portsmouth,
Ringwood,
Poole,
Southampton,
Dorchester,
Weymouth,
Honiton,
Topsham,
Totness,
Plymouth,
Cornwall,
Menheniot,
Penryn,
Helston,
Market-Jew,
Ives, where he and Edward Pyot are taken into custody and imprisoned in Launceston jail, about eight months.

1656.

Humphrey Lower's,
Loveday Hambley's,
Thos. Mounce's,
Launceston,
Oakhampton,
Exeter,
Collumpton,
Taunton,
Puddimoor,
J. Dander's,
Bristol (E. Pyot's),
Slattenford,
N. Crips's,
Marlbro',
Newbury,
Reading,
Kingston-on-Thames,
London,
Buckinghamshire,
Northamptonshire,
Nottinghamshire,
Lincolnshire,
Huntingdonshire,
Cambridgeshire,
Fen Country,
Crowland,
Boston (Lincolnshire),
Yorkshire,
Holderness,
Leicestershire,
Staffordshire,
Worcestershire,
Warwickshire,
Edge-Hill,
Warwick,
Badgley,
Gloucestershire,
Oxford,
Col. Grimes's,
Nat. Crips's,
Cirencester,
Evesham,
London,
Kent,
Sussex,
Surrey,
Farnham,
Basingstoke,
Bridport,
Portsmouth.

1657.

Poole,
Ringwood,
Weymouth,
Dorchester,
Lyme,
Exeter,
Bristol,
Wales,
The Slone,
Cardiff,
Swansea,
Brecknock,
Pontemoil,
Shrewsbury,
Wm. Gandy's (Cheshire),
Wales,
Montgomeryshire,
Radnorshire,
Leominster,
Tenby,
Pembrokeshire,
Pembroke,
Haverford-west,
Dolgelly,
Caernarvon,
Beaumaris,
Near Wrexham,
Flintshire,
Wrexham, and through every County in Wales,
West Chester,

Liverpool,
Richard Cubban's,
Malpas,
Manchester,
Preston,
Lancaster,
Kellet,
Sands-Side,
Swarthmore,
Westmorland,
John Audland's,
Kendal,
Strickland-Head,
Cumberland,
Gilsland,
Carlisle,
Abbey-Holme,
Langlands,
Pardsey-Crag,
Scotland,
Dumfries,
Douglas,
Heads,
Badcow,
Highlands,
Heads,
Badcow,
Garshore,
Linlithgow,
Edinburgh,
Leith,
Edinburgh,
Heads,
Glasgow,
Badcow,
Highlands,
Stirling,
Burnt Island,
Johnstons,
Leith,
Edinburgh,
Johnstons,
Edinburgh,
Dunbar,
Berwick,
Morpeth,
Newcastle,
Northumberland,
Bishoprick,
City of Durham,
A. Pearson's,
Cleveland,
Hull,
Pontefract,
G. Watkinson's,
Scale-House,
Swarthmore,
Yorkshire,
Cheshire,
Derbyshire.

1658.

Nottinghamshire,
Nottingham,
Warwickshire,
Northamptonshire,
Leicestershire,
Bedfordshire,
London,
Kingston,
Hampton-Court,
Kingston,
Isaac Penington's,
London,
Essex,
London,
Twickenham,
Reading.

1659.

London,
Essex,
Suffolk,
Norfolk,
Norwich,
Huntingdonshire,
Cambridgeshire,
London,
Surrey,
Sussex,
Hampshire,
Dorsetshire,
Ringwood,
Poole,
Dorchester,
Somersetshire,
Devonshire,
Plymouth,
Cornwall.

1660.

Land's End,
Horse-Bridge,
Devonshire,
Somersetshire,
Bristol,
Oldeston,
Nailsworth,
Nat. Crips's,
Gloucester,
Col. Grimes's,
Tewkesbury,
Worcester,
Badgley,
Drayton,
Twy-Cross,
Swannington,
Derbyshire,
Derby,
Nottinghamshire,
Synderhill-Green,
Yorkshire,
Balby,
Warmsworth,
Barton-Abbey,
Thos. Taylor's (Brighouse),
Skipton,
Lancaster,
R. Widder's (Kellet),
Arnside,
Kellet,
Swarthmore, apprehended and imprisoned in Lancaster jail—an Habeas Corpus is sent down and he is liberated on parole—he visits
Swarthmore,
Lancaster,
Preston,
Wm. Gandy's (Cheshire),
Staffordshire,
A. Bickley's (Warwickshire),
Non-Eaton,
London, appears to the writ, and is liberated by the King.

1661.—Visits

Essex,
Colchester,
Coggeshall,
London.

1662.

Bristol,
Wiltshire,
Berkshire,
London,
Leicestershire,
Skegby,
Barnet-Hills,
Swannington,
Leicester, imprisoned, but soon liberated.
Swannington,
Twy-Cross,
Warwickshire,
Northamptonshire,
Bedfordshire,
London,
Essex,
Norfolk,
Norwich,
Sutton,
Cambridgeshire,
Little-Port,
Isle of Ely,
Lincolnshire,
Huntingdonshire,
Fen Country,
Lynn.

1663.—[Vol. II.]
Norfolk,
Suffolk,
Essex,
Hertfordshire,
London,
Kent,
Ashford,
Cranbrook,
Tenterden,
Newick,
Hampshire,
Southampton,
Pulner,
Wiltshire,
Dorsetshire,
Topsham,
Totness,
Kingsbridge,
Plymouth,
Cornwall,
Falmouth,
Penryn,
Helston,
Land's End,
Redruth,
Truro,
Stoke,
Horse Bridge,
Devonshire,
Tiverton,
Collumpton,
Wellington,
Taunton,
Street,
Puddimoor,
Bristol,
Slattenford (Wilts),
Gloucestershire,
Herefordshire,
Hereford,
Radnorshire,
Wales,
Shropshire,
Warwickshire,
Derbyshire,
Staffordshire,
Whitehaugh,
Peak Country,
Synderhill-Green,
Holderness,
Scarbro'
Whitby,
Malton,
York,
Boroughbridge,
Bishoprick,
Stainmoor,
Yorkshire,
Sedbergh,
Westmorland,
Lancashire,
Swarthmore,
Arnside,
Kellet,
Underbarrow,
Grayrig,
Sedbergh,
Strickland-Head,
Northumberland,
Derwent-Water,
Cumberland,
Wigton,
Pardsey-Crag,
Westmorland,
Keswick,
Cartmel,
Swarthmore,
Kirby-Hall,
Swarthmore,
Holker-Hall,
Swarthmore,
Lancaster, imprisoned.

1664 and 1665.
Removed to Scarbro' castle.

1666.
Liberated by the King, after being incarcerated nearly three years —he then goes
To Whitby,
Burlington,
Oram,
Marmaduke Stor's,
Grace Barwick's,
Richard Shipton's,
Malton,
Hull,
Howden-Dyke,
York,
Geo. Watkinson's,
Thos. Taylor (Brighouse),
Synderhill-Green,
Derbyshire,
Nottinghamshire,
Skegby,
Mansfield,
Nottingham,
Leicester,
Sileby,
John Penford's,
Warwick,
Badgley,
Northamptonshire,
Bedfordshire,
Buckinghamshire,
Oxfordshire,
London,
Kingston,
Reading,
Wiltshire,
Bristol,
Nat. Crips's,
London,
Essex,
Suffolk,
Norfolk,
Huntingdonshire,
Bedfordshire,
Nottinghamshire,
Lincolnshire,
Nottinghamshire.

1667.
Leicestershire,
Warwickshire,
Derbyshire,
Peak-Hills
Staffordshire,
Cheshire,
Lancashire,
Sankey near Warrington,
Jane Milner's (Cheshire),
Shropshire,
Wales,
Denbighshire,
Montgomeryshire,
Merionethshire,
Shropshire,
Worcestershire,
Pashur,
Worcester,
Droitwich,
Shrewsbury,
Radnorshire,
Herefordshire,
Monmouthshire,
Ross,
Gloucestershire,
Bristol,
Wiltshire,
London,
Hertfordshire,
Baldock,
Waltham,
Shacklewell,
London,
Buckinghamshire,
Weston,
North-Newton, near Banbury,
Gloucestershire,
Monmouthshire.

1668.
Swansea,
Mumbles,
Cardiff,
Newport,
Shipton,
Forest of Dea
Oldstone,
Irb's Court, Somerset,

Portshead,
Minehead,
Barnstaple,
Appledon,
Stratton,
Truro,
Land's End,
Tregangeeves,
Devonshire,
Plymouth,
Kingsbridge,
Topsham,
Membury,
Ilchester,
Puddimoor,
Somersetshire,
Dorsetshire,
Southampton,
Hampshire,
Farnham,
Surrey,
Sussex,
Kent,
London.

1669.

Surrey,
Sussex,
Warwick,
Birmingham,
Badgley,
Nottingham,
Balby,
York,
Whitby,
Scarbro',
Through Yorkshire,
Wolds,
Holderness,
Thos. Taylor's, (Brighouse),
Eldreth,
Staffordshire,
Cheshire,
Wm. Barnes's (Sankey),
Liverpool,
Ireland,
Dublin,
New-Garden,
Bandon-Bridge,
Land's End,
Bandon,
Cork,
Dublin,
Liverpool,
Lancashire,
Cheshire,
Gloucestershire,
Nailsworth,
Bristol,
Oldstone,
Wiltshire,
Berkshire.
Oxfordshire,
Buckinghamshire,
London,
Essex,
Hertfordshire,
Cambridgeshire,
Huntingdonshire,
Leicestershire,
Derbyshire,
Warwickshire,
London.

1670.

Middlesex,
Buckinghamshire,
Oxfordshire,
Reading,
Baghurst (Hants),
Berkshire,
Surrey,
Guildford,
Sussex,
Kent,
Deal,
Canterbury,
Isle of Sheppy,
Rochester,
Gravesend,
Essex,
Hornchurch,
Stratford,
Gerrard Roberts's,
Enfield.

1671.

Gerrard Roberts's,
Shacklewell,
London,
Kingston,
Gravesend,
Downs,
Deal, sails for
Barbadoes,
Jamaica.

1672.

Maryland,
Long Island,
Rhode Island,
Providence,
Narraganset,
Shelter Island,
Long Island,
East Jersey,
Maryland,
Hatton's Island,
Virginia,
Carolina,
Virginia,
Maryland.

1673.

Old England,
Shirehampton,
Bristol,
Gloucestershire,
Wiltshire,
Slattenford,
Marlborough,
Ore,
Hampshire,
Oxfordshire,
Reading,
Buckinghamshire,
Kingston-on-Thames,
London,
Essex,
Middlesex,
London,
Kingston,
Surrey,
Kingston,
London,
Hendon,
Rickmansworth,
Aylesbury,
Adderbury,
Worcestershire,
Armscott,
Sent to Worcester jail, detained nearly fourteen months; at length liberated by proclamation.

1674.

London,
Kingston,
London,
Dunstable.

1675.

Newport-Pagnell,
Northampton,
Cossel,
Warrington,
Preston,
Lancashire,
Swarthmore.

1676.

This year he remained at Swarthmore.

1677.

Poolbank (Westmorland),
Carn's Gill,
Brigflatts,
Sedbergh,
Garsdale,
Wensleydale,
Counterside,
Scarr-House in Langstroth-Dale,
Bishopdale,

Middleham,
Barton,
Bedale,
Northallerton,
Burrowby
York,
Tadcaster,
Knottingley,
Doncaster,
Balby,
Ballowfield,
Stainsby,
Skegby,
Nottingham,
Wimeswould,
Sileby,
Leicester,
Knighton,
Swannington,
Hartshorn,
Badgley,
Whittington,
Hartshill,
Dingley,
Adingworth,
Northampton,
Olney,
Turvey,
Kempston,
Ampthill,
Bullock's-Hill,
Luton,
Market-Street,
Kensworth,
Alban's,
South-Mims,
Barnet,
Guttershedge,
Highgate,
London,
Sussex,
Surrey,
Worminghurst,
Warpledon,
Kingston,
London,
Colchester,
Harwich,—sails for
Holland,—lands at
Briel,—goes to
Rotterdam,
Delft,
Leyden,
Haarlem,
Amsterdam,
Buyckslote,
Purmerent,
Alkmaar,
Hoorn,
Enckhuysen,
Friesland,
Workum,
Harlingen,
Leeuwarden,
Dockum,
Strobus,
Groningen,
Appingdalem,
Delfziel,
Embden,
Leer,
Strikehuysen,
Deteren,
Apre,
Oldenburgh,
Delmenhurst,
Bremen,
Overdeland,
Fisherholder,
Closterseven,
Buxtehude,
Hamburg,
Elmshoorn,
Itzeho,
Hogenborn,
Frederickstadt,
Hamburg,
Bormer-Haven,
Bremen,
Keby,
Oldenburgh,
Leer,
Embden
Delfziel,
Groningen,
Strobus,
Dockum,
Leeuwarden,
Anderigo
Gardick,
Leeuwarden,
Franeker,
Harlingen,
Amsterdam,
Landameer,
Amsterdam,
Haarlem,
Amsterdam,
Leyden,
Hague,
Delft,
Rotterdam,
Briel, — sails for England, lands at
Harwich,—goes to
Colchester,
Halstead,
Braintree,
Felstead,
Saling,
Chelmsford,
London,
Kingston,
Buckinghamshire,
Amersham,
Hunger-Hill,
Jordans,
Hedgerly,
Wickham,
Turville-Heath,
Wickham,
Henley,
Corsham,
Reading,
Berkshire,
Wiltshire,
Bristol,
Winterbourne,
Sudbury,
Tedbury,
Nailsworth,
Finchcomb,
Nailsworth.

1678.

Cirencester,
Crown-Allins,
Cheltenham,
Stoke-Orchard,
Tewkesbury,
Worcester,
Pershore,
Evesham,
Ragley,
Stratford,
Lamcoat,
Armscott,
Oxfordshire,
Sibford,
North-Newton,
Banbury,
Adderbury,
Buckinghamshire,
Long-Crendon,
Ilmere,
Mendle,
Weston,
Cholsberry,
Chesham,
Isaac Penington's,
Hertfordshire,
Charlewood,
Watford,
Hempstead,
Market-Street,
Luton,
Alban's,
South-Mims,
Barnet,
Hendon,
London,
Hertford,
Rabley-Heath,
Stevenage,
Baldock,
Hitchin,
Ashwell,
Bedfordshire,
Huntingdon,
Ives,
Northamptonshire,
Great-Bowden,

Saddington,
Wigston,
Knighton,
Leicester,
Sileby,
Swannington,
Warwickshire,
Staffordshire,
Monyash,
Yorkshire,
Hill,
Kellet,
Arnside,
Swarthmore, where he remained about a year.

1680.

Westmorland,
Lancashire,
Yorkshire,
York,
Barton,
Nottinghamshire,
Derbyshire,
Leicestershire,
Warwickshire,
Warwick,
Southam,
Radway,
North-Newton,
Banbury,
Gloucestershire,
Northamptonshire,
Biddlesdon,
Lillingston,
Lovel,
Bugbrooke,
Stony-Stratford,
Bedfordshire,
Dunstable,
Market-Street,
Alban's,
Mims,
Barnet,
Guttershedge,
London,
Surrey,
Sussex,
Kingston,
Worplesdon,
Guildford,
Esher,
Capel,
Patchgate,
Worminghurst,
Bletchington,
Horsham,
Ifield,
Reigate,
Gatton, Kingston,
Hammersmith,
Battersea,
Wandsworth,
Kensington,
Hendon,
London,
Edmonton,
Hertford,
Waltham-Abbey,
Edmonton,
Shacklewell,
London.

1681.

Kingston-on-Thames,
London,
Waltham-Abbey,
Flamstead-Heath,
Edmonton,
Enfield,
Winchmore-Hill,
London,
Sussex,
London,
Edmonton,
Buckinghamshire,
Henley,
Reading,
Ore,
Oxfordshire,
Warborough,
Ilmore,
Mary Penington's,
Hunger-Hill,
Watford,
Uxbridge,
Longford,
Staines,
Sunbury,
Kingston,
Wandsworth,
Hammersmith,
London.

1682.

Dalston,
London,
Kingston,
London.

1683.

Kingston-on-Thames,
London,
Guildford,
Worminghurst,
Sussex,
Surrey,
Kingston,
London,
Kingston-on-Thames,
London,
Kingston,
London,
Essex,
Dalston,
London,
Kingston,
London,
Enfield,
London.

1684.

Colchester,
Harwich—sails for Briel in Holland,
Rotterdam,
Amsterdam,
Friesland,
Leeuwarden,
Franeker,
Harlingen,
Amsterdan
Osan-Over
Lansmeer,
Amsterdam,
Sardam,
Alkmaar,
Amsterdam,
Haarlem,
Rotterdam,
Briel—sails for Harwich,
Colchester,
Witham,
Hare Street,
William Mead's,
Enfield,
Dalston,
London.

1685.

South Street,
Ford-Green,
Enfield,
Waltham-Abbey,
Enfield,
Edmonton-Sid
London,
South Street,
Enfield,
London,
Epping Forest,
London,
Kingston,
Hammersmith,
London,
Bethnal-Green,
London,
Enfield.

1686.

London,
Bethnal-Green,
Enfield,
Chiswick,
London,
Kingston.

1687.
London,
Gooses (Essex),
London,
Edmonton,
South-Street,
Winchmore-Hill,
Berry-Street,
Enfield,
Hertford,
Waltham-Abbey,
Gooses (W. Mead's),
Wanstead
Barking,
John Harding's,
Gooses,
London,
Kingston,
Guildford,
Kingston,
Chiswick,
Hammersmith,
London.

1688.
Enfield,
Barnet,
Waltham-Abbey,
London,
Gooses,
Barking,
Waltham-Abbey,
Hoddesdon,
Enfield,
South-Street,
Ford-Green,
Winchmore-Hill,
London,
Gooses.

1689.
London,
Southgate,
London,
Kingston,
Hammersmith,
London,
Tottenham-High-Cross,
Winchmore-Hill,
Enfield,
London,
Gooses.

1690.
London,
Kingston,
Tottenham-High-Cross,
Ford-Green,
Enfield,
Cheshunt,
Waltham-Abbey,
Enfield,
Tottenham,
Winchmore-Hill,
Hertford,
Ware,
Edmonton,
Tottenham,
London,
Tottenham,
Ford-Green,
Tottenham,
Enfield,
Winchmore-Hill,
Ford-Green,
London, where he died 13th of 11th Month, 1690, in his 67th year.

TEXTS OF SCRIPTURE

OCCURRING IN THIS JOURNAL.

OLD TESTAMENT.

Genesis.

Ch. Ver.	Reference.
4 2,	ii. 334.
4 7,	i. 288.
6 9,	ii. 334.
9 20,	ii. 334.
13 —	ii. 334.
13 16,	ii. 308.
15 5,	ii. 308.
15 13, 14,	ii. 308.
21 12,	ii. 334.
22 17, 18,	ii. 308.
26 12, 14,	ii. 334.
32 28,	ii. 332.
66 32, 34,	ii. 334.

Exodus.

Ch. Ver.	Reference.
3 1, 4,	ii. 334.
11 29,	ii. 276.
14 13,	i. 288.
15 21,	ii. 276.
20 1,	ii. 102. 103.
20 25,	ii. 310.
22 20,	ii. 310.
23 18,	ii. 310.

Leviticus.

Ch. Ver.	Reference.
2 13,	ii. 285, 312.
21 —	ii. 324.

Numbers.

Ch. Ver.	Reference.
19 —	ii. 324.
31 —	ii. 324.

Deuteronomy.

Ch. Ver.	Reference.
19 14,	ii. 333.
27 17,	ii. 333.
29 5,	ii. 346.

Judges.

Ch. Ver.	Reference.
1-31,	ii. 276.

1 Samuel.

Ch. Ver.	Reference.
2 10,	ii. 276.
15 22,	ii. 312.
17 15, 28,	ii. 334.

1 Kings.

Ch. Ver.	Reference.
19 19,	ii. 335.

2 Kings.

Ch. Ver.	Reference.
23 14,	ii. 276.

2 Chronicles.

Ch. Ver.	Reference.
34 22,	ii. 276.

Ezra.

Ch. Ver.	Reference.
4 2, 3,	ii. 311.

Nehemiah.

Ch. Ver.	Reference.
9 —	ii. 147.

NEW TESTAMENT.

PARTICULARS OF THE VARIOUS EDITIONS

OF

GEORGE FOX'S JOURNAL, &c.

FIRST EDITION.—Printed for Thomas Northcott. Folio, . . . 1694.

SECOND EDITION.—(Generally so called, though not so stated on the title page). Printed by J. Sowle, in White-Hart Court, in Gracious Street. London, 2 vols. 8vo, ... 1709.

THIRD EDITION.—Corrected; printed by Richardson and Clarke for Luke Hinde. Folio, ... 1765.

FOURTH EDITION.—Not known. In a *History of Norfolk*, it is said Joseph Phipps was appointed by Friends to abridge the contents and superintend the *Journal of George Fox*. This may have been the fourth edition. . . ——

FIFTH EDITION.—Printed by William Phillips, George Yard, Lombard Street, London (from the first edition, printed for Northcott). 2 vols. 8vo, . . 1827.

SIXTH EDITION.—Leeds; printed by Anthony Pickard. 2 vols. royal 12mo, 1836.

SEVENTH EDITION.—The present; now for the first time divided into chapters and supplied with table of contents, and numerous notes, biographical and historical, &c., by Wilson Armistead. Printed and stereotyped by W. G. Blackie & Co., Glasgow. In 2 vols. 8vo, ... 1852.

In addition to the above editions of this standard work of the Society of Friends, several others have been issued at various times which are not enumerated in the count. Amongst these may be mentioned one called the fifth edition corrected, printed at Philadelphia in 1808, by Fry and Kammerer, for B. and T. Kite, 20, North Third Street. A stereotype edition has been subsequently printed in Philadelphia; and the first volume of the *Friends' Library*, edited by William and Thomas Evans of the same city, contains an excellent *Memoir of the Life, Travels, and Labours of George Fox*. This volume, a royal 8vo, printed at Philadelphia in 1837, was reprinted in London in 12mo, in 1839, and again in 1850. It was also printed in German in 1850. Both the "Memoir" in the *Friends' Library*, and the Philadelphia stereotype edition of the Journal, have had a wide circulation in North America.

Many abridged memoirs of George Fox have appeared at various times and in various forms. *The Life of George Fox* forms the first volume of Henry Tuke's *Biographical Notices of Members of the Society of Friends*, a 12mo, published in 1813, and a second edition in 1826. The second volume of the same work, called *A Supplement to the Life of George Fox*, containing a brief review of the doctrines and practices inculcated by him, appeared in 1815, and a second edition in 1826. The same, in French, was printed at Guernsey in 1824.

A brief Memoir of George Fox, 12mo (supposed by Edward Backhouse), was printed at Sunderland in 1842, and, with alterations, was reprinted there in the following year.

In 1847, appeared *A Popular Life of George Fox*, interspersed with remarks upon the imperfect reformation of the Anglican Church, and the consequent spread of dissent; by Josiah Marsh, 8vo, 400 pp., published by Gilpin, London. This "Popular Life" has been extensively circulated. Compiled as it is by one not of the Society of Friends, but a member of the Establishment, it may be recommended as a fair estimate of the character of George Fox, by an impartial hand. Though the work is not quite free from inaccuracies, the author's explanation of many of the most distinguishing views of Friends is clear and striking; and on many subjects the writer manifests a remarkable appreciation of the principles promulgated by George Fox, and believes them, illustrated as they were in his exemplary life, calculated to be serviceable to many in his own communion, in a day when the progress of opinions, tending to exalt outward forms, draws even the thoughtful and well concerned off from a due appreciation of the essential spirituality of the Christian religion.

A lengthy review of Marsh's *Popular Life of George Fox*, appeared in the *West-*

minster and Foreign Quarterly Review of July 1847. This was reprinted in a pamphlet of 72 pp. 12mo, and published by Gilpin, London, in 1848.

In addition to the foregoing, it may be stated, that a 12mo volume, entitled, *Selections from the Epistles of George Fox*, was printed at York in 1825, edited by Samuel Tuke. A second edition of this, with additions (above 300 pp. 8vo), was issued in London, in 1848. These Epistles are not from the Journal, but from a large folio, published in 1698, entitled, *A Collection of many Select and Christian Epistles*, &c.

The Introduction to the *Selection of Epistles*, by Samuel Tuke, is so excellent, I cannot forbear giving an extract from it in conclusion. In speaking of George Fox, he says, "The true knowledge of God, not as an intellectual speculation, but as that which gives rest to the awakened conscience, was the great object of his longing search from youth to manhood; and in this search his almost constant companion was the Bible. There he conversed with Patriarchs and Prophets, with the Lord Jesus and his Apostles, till he became most intimately imbued with the contents of the Holy Scriptures. But, though every word of Inspiration was precious to him, his great desire was to know the mind of the Spirit—the true harmony of the various parts of the divine records. He conversed extensively with esteemed religious teachers of various classes, but he found they were no physicians in his case. More and more, he was brought with child-like submissiveness to look to Christ as his only helper; and thus, after a course of deep spiritual discipline, his eye was opened more fully to see in the light of the Holy Spirit, the character of his Saviour, and to rejoice in Him exceedingly.

"Having partaken largely of the spiritual baptism of his Lord, many divine truths were opened upon his mind with great clearness. Unshackled from human ties, and from all the religious systems of men, the great elements and characteristics of the Christian dispensation, in its native simplicity and purity, rose gradually before him. As he travelled onward in his experience, he found that what was from time to time unfolded to his mind was in the fullest harmony with Holy Writ. Many things in the so-called religious world now appeared to him in a new light, and grieved in spirit with its multiplied corruptions, he felt himself required, by a divine impulse, to proclaim to others the Truth which he had found to the blessedness of his own soul. His great mission was not to found a sect, but to speak truth to all, and to call all out of every *untruth* to the knowledge for themselves, of Him who is the Truth. The acknowledgment of Christ with the lip as a divine person, and the talking about faith in Him, and of his various offices, were prevalent enough in many circles; but the true belief in Him with the heart unto righteousness—the acceptance of Him as the only Lord of the soul, and dependence upon Him for continual guidance by his Spirit —these were things which appeared to George Fox sadly deficient in his day.

"As the work of the Holy Spirit on the soul of man is the great means by which it is stimulated, and enabled to resist the world, the flesh, and the devil, so had all these powers combined to stultify its authority, and to give the name of Christianity to the dogmas or appointments of men, or too much to limit divine power to the agency of the inspired letter which the wisdom of man was so able to bend to its own purposes, but which his unassisted wisdom was wholly unable truly to unfold. He saw that the corruptions of the Christian Church had always been indicated by the increase of dependence upon man, in the work of religion—'the priests of old time ruled by their means, and the people loved to have it so.' These words appeared to him descriptive of a great human tendency, forming part of those lusts of the flesh, against which the Holy Spirit ever warreth, and he spake much of that divine light given to man, by which the inward working of these lusts was manifested, and of that inward warfare with the soul's enemies, in which every one must be a soldier for himself, under Christ his Captain—denouncing all those arts which he saw to be so prevalent, by which man was persuaded that he could gain the crown, without enlisting under the banner of the cross. Man's alienation by nature from God, and his reluctance to come to Him in truth, notwithstanding the drawings of his love, and the free offers of his mercy in Christ, the propitiation for the sins of the world, were the basis of his appeals. He was eminently a preacher of the free grace of God to all who repent, and who, in subjection to his Spirit, truly come unto Christ. The experimental work of the Spirit in bringing the soul in living faith to Christ as its Lord and Saviour, was indeed the great theme of his ministry; it was that which he felt himself called to urge upon all, that the foundation might be sound, and the superstructure solid."

INDEXES.

OF PERSONS, COUNTRIES, CITIES, TOWNS, AND PLACES MENTIONED IN THE FOREGOING JOURNAL.

OF THE PRINCIPAL SUBJECTS MENTIONED IN THE FOREGOING JOURNAL.

INDEX

OF PERSONS, COUNTRIES, CITIES, TOWNS, AND PLACES MENTIONED IN THE FOREGOING JOURNAL.

(*Those names with an * affixed have, in this Edition, some information accompanying them in foot-notes.*)

I.

J.

K.

T.

U.

INDEX

OF THE PRINCIPAL SUBJECTS MENTIONED IN THE FOREGOING JOURNAL.

NOTICE.

☞ This edition of *George Fox's Journal*, in two volumes, neatly bound in cloth, lettered, may be obtained through all Booksellers, at 5*s*. per copy; or at 5*s*. 9*d*. on extra paper.

Purchasers of quantities, for gratuitous distribution, may be supplied, with a liberal allowance, on application to the Editor.

Milton Keynes UK
Ingram Content Group UK Ltd.
UKHW022018310723
426115UK00005B/235

9 781019 173732